ARTIFICIAL INTELLIGENCE
and the Design of Expert Systems

The Benjamin/Cummings Series in Artificial Intelligence

Allen, *Natural Language Understanding*

Almasi/Gottlieb, *Highly Parallel Computing*

Kerschberg, editor, *Expert Database Systems: Proceedings from the First International Workshop*

Kerschberg, editor, *Expert Database Systems: Proceedings from the First International Conference*

Kerschberg, editor, *Expert Database Systems: Proceedings from the Second International Conference*

Luger/Stubblefield, *Artificial Intelligence and the Design of Expert Systems*

Maier/Warren, *Computing with Logic: Logic Programming with Prolog*

Negoita, *Expert Systems and Fuzzy Systems*

Touretzky, *LISP: A Gentle Introduction to Symbolic Computation* (forthcoming in 1990)

ARTIFICIAL INTELLIGENCE
and the Design of Expert Systems

George F. Luger

William A. Stubblefield

University of New Mexico, Albuquerque

The Benjamin/Cummings Publishing Company, Inc.

Redwood City, California • Fort Collins, Colorado
Menlo Park, California • Reading, Massachusetts • New York
Don Mills, Ontario • Wokingham, U.K. • Amsterdam • Bonn
Sydney • Singapore • Tokyo • Madrid • San Juan

Sponsoring Editor: Alan Apt
Associate Editor: Mark McCormick
Production Editor: Laura Kenney
Production Assistant: Eleanor Renner Brown
Copyeditor: Mary Prescott
Text and Cover Designer: Gary Head
Technical Artist: Merry Finley
Compositor: Graphic Typesetting Service

Cover and part-opener artwork by Thomas Barrow.

Library of Congress Cataloging-in-Publication Data
Luger, George F.
   Artificial intelligence and the design of expert systems / George F. Luger, William
A. Stubblefield.
      p.   cm. — (The Benjamin/Cummings series in computer science and
   engineering)
   Bibliography: p.
   Includes index.
   ISBN 0-8053-0139-9
   1. Artificial intelligence—Data processing.   2. Expert systems (Computer
   science)   3. LISP (Computer program language)   4. PROLOG (Computer program
   language)   I. Stubblefield, William A.   II. Title.   III. Series.
   Q336.L84 1989   88-26054
   006.3—dc19   CIP

ISBN 0-8053-0139-9

BCDEFGHIJ-DO-89

The Benjamin/Cummings Publishing Company, Inc.
390 Bridge Parkway
Redwood City, California 94065

For my wife, Kathleen Kelly Luger, and our children Sarah, David, and Peter,

and for my parents, George Fletcher Luger and Loretta Maloney Luger

> *Si quid est in me ingenii, judices . . .*
> Cicero, Pro Archia Poeta

GL

For my parents, William Frank Stubblefield and Maria Christina Stubblefield

WS

PREFACE

What we have to learn to do
we learn by doing . . .

—ARISTOTLE, Ethics

The Purpose of This Book

This book is a comprehensive introduction to the core concepts of artificial intelligence and the design of expert systems and other AI applications. In writing it, our goal has been to place AI within the larger context of engineering, science, and philosophy. This includes not only computer science but also the full range of scientific efforts to understand the nature of intelligent activity.

Four features of this text reflect our own attitudes toward teaching artificial intelligence and distinguish it from other introductory AI texts.

First, we base our treatment of applications and programming techniques on a detailed discussion of theoretical issues. Throughout its history, AI has exhibited two major methodological schools, often called the *neats* and the *scruffies*. The neats have emphasized formal treatment of the theory behind intelligent programs. The major emphasis of the neat school has been the analysis of search algorithms, establishment of a theory of knowledge representation using logic or other well-defined formalisms, and careful characterization of the soundness and completeness of inference strategies. The scruffies have taken a more application-oriented approach, beginning with a problem to be solved and finding, through intuition and experiment, the best techniques for solving that particular problem.

One of our major goals in writing this text has been to unify these two approaches; indeed, we believe that these schools have much more in common than the folklore admits. Theoretical work in AI has led to an increasing awareness that intelligent behavior relies on domain-specific knowledge, knowledge that must often be obtained by empirical methods. Conversely, the best implementations have always built on the knowledge-representation and problem-solving techniques developed in theoretical research.

In general, this text exhibits a well-marked separation between theory and practice, as when search is formally considered in Part II and later implemented using both PROLOG (Chapter 6) and LISP (Chapter 7). However, even the theory chapters use realistic examples to illustrate important issues. Much of our theoretical discussion of representation and search is illustrated through an extended example of an expert system for financial advice; our chapter on expert systems is anchored by a case study of the MYCIN expert system. The chapter on natural language concludes with a detailed discussion of the implementation of a natural language front end for a data base system.

Second, we build on the theory of representation and search in presenting the major application areas of artificial intelligence. The first of these is expert systems, which have emerged as the most successful and profitable area of AI problem solving. Based on their roots in representation and search, we discuss the techniques that knowledge engineers have developed for acquiring and representing expert-level problem-solving skills. We also implement expert system shells in both LISP and PROLOG; the student may use these tools to build expert systems or modify them to explore alternative representations and problem-solving strategies.

Natural language understanding is the second application area emphasized in this text. Natural language programs are important both for their intrinsic value and for the role they play in pushing the development of advanced representational and reasoning techniques. After discussing the knowledge representation techniques developed to represent meaning in natural language (Chapter 9), we discuss the integration of syntax and semantics and the implementation of natural language understanding programs.

Other application areas explored in the text include *automated reasoning* (Chapter 11), and *planning and learning* (Chapter 15). In addition to these traditional AI application areas, we briefly examine the role of AI in understanding human intelligence through a treatment of *cognitive science* and *neural networks* (Chapter 15).

The third feature of this text is the development, justification, and use of advanced representational formalisms. This begins with the classic approach to representation and problem solving using predicate calculus, recursion-based graph search, and heuristics. We then extend this model to the knowledge-intensive approaches used for modern intelligent systems.

Much of the emphasis of AI research is on the development of languages that directly support specific knowledge structures such as class hierarchies, schemata for objects and situations, and the semantics of natural language. We discuss the importance of structuring information and control with semantic nets, conceptual graphs, frames, inheritance systems, and other representational techniques. Chapter 14 introduces *object oriented programming* and its role in knowledge-based systems. We present two implementations of object-oriented representation (one LISP, one PROLOG), giving readers the opportunity to build and change them as they wish.

Finally, we show how the basic algorithms and data structures of AI programming can be built using both LISP and PROLOG. We have covered both languages because they represent two very different but equally important AI programming paradigms: logic programming in PROLOG and functional programming in LISP.

LISP, the major artificial intelligence language, is presented in two chapters: an introduction in Chapter 7 and an advanced discussion in Chapter 13. PROLOG, the newest general-purpose AI language, is introduced in Chapter 6; a number of advanced PROLOG programming techniques are discussed in Chapter 12. We feel that the skills of the programmer depend on a knowledge of the available tools, and each language has its representational strengths and search-based advantages. Indeed, in many modern programming environments the powers of both languages are often available.

The Contents of This Book

Chapter 1 introduces the science of artificial intelligence, beginning with a brief history of attempts to understand mind and intelligence in philosophy, psychology, and other traditional areas of research. In a very important sense, AI is an old science, its roots tracing back at least to Aristotle. An appreciation of these roots is essential to an understanding of the issues addressed in modern research. We build on this historical background with an overview of some of the important applications and research concerns in AI. Our goal in Chapter 1 is to provide background and motivation for the theory and applications that follow.

Chapters 2, 3, 4, and 5 (Part II) introduce the basic research tools for AI problem solving. These include the predicate calculus to describe the essential features of a domain (Chapter 2), search to reason about these descriptions (Chapter 3), and the algorithms and data structures used to implement search-based problem solvers (Chapter 4). In Chapter 5 we discuss the essential role of heuristics in focusing and constraining search-based problem solving.

Part III presents AI languages. In an introduction, these languages are compared to each other and to traditional programming languages to give appreciation of the AI approach to problem solving. Chapter 6 introduces PROLOG and Chapter 7, LISP. We demonstrate these languages as tools for AI problem solving by building the search and representation techniques of the earlier chapters, including breadth, depth, and best-first search algorithms. We implement these search techniques in a problem-independent fashion so they may later be extended to form shells for search in rule-based expert systems.

Chapters 8, 9, 10, and 11 make up Part IV of the test: representations for knowledge-based systems. In Chapter 8 we present the rule-based expert system. This model for problem solving is a natural evolution of the material in the first five chapters: using a production system of predicate calculus expressions to orchestrate a graph search. Both data- and goal-driven search are presented in this context, and the role of heuristics is demonstrated. We also discuss the unique problems encountered in applying expert systems in real domains. Examples are taken from the Stanford University research including presentations of MYCIN and Teiresias.

Chapters 9 and 10 present AI techniques for modeling semantic meaning, with a particular focus on natural language understanding. We begin with a discussion of semantic networks and extend this model to include conceptual dependency theory, conceptual graphs, frames, and scripts. Class hierarchies and inheritance are important representation tools; we discuss both the benefits and difficulties of implementing inheritance systems for realistic taxonomies. This material is strengthened by an in-depth examination of a particular formalism, conceptual graphs. This discussion emphasizes the epistemological issues involved in representing knowledge and shows how they have been addressed in a modern representation language. In Chapter 10 we show how conceptual graphs can be used to implement an English language data base front end.

Theorem proving, often referred to as automated reasoning, is one of the oldest and most important areas of AI research. In Chapter 11 we discuss some of the first programs in this area, including the Logic Theorist and the General Problem Solver. The primary focus of the chapter is resolution proof procedures, especially resolution refutations. More advanced inferencing with hyperresolution and paramodulation is also discussed.

Chapters 12 and 13 present advanced AI programming in PROLOG and LISP. Here, we discuss techniques for implementing the knowledge-representation and problem-solving algorithms of chapters 8, 9, and 10. A major feature of these chapters is the implementation of expert system shells in both LISP and PROLOG. These shells include certainty measures, user queries, and complete explanation facilities. They illustrate the major architectural features of expert system shells and provide a useful tool for building such systems. We also discuss the implementation of inheritance in frame and network representations. Both chapters discuss the formal underpinning of each language: resolution refutation systems for PROLOG and functional programming for LISP.

In Chapter 14 we discuss frame- or object-based expert systems, showing how object-oriented techniques are used both for organizing traditional programs and for developing knowledge-based systems. We then give examples of the techniques used to implement object-oriented programming in both LISP and PROLOG. Finally, the chapter discusses the integration of rule- and frame-based approaches in hybrid knowledge engineering environments.

Chapter 15 presents selected advanced topics including planning, machine learning, blackboard architectures, and cognitive science. We also introduce nonrepresentational approaches to AI with a discussion of neural networks and connectionism. Our goal in this chapter is to provide an introduction to these advanced topics and a set of references for further research.

The final chapter serves as an epilogue for the text, addressing contemporary challenges to AI, including the specific limitations of the representational approach and the more general philosophical limits of the scientific method itself. Chapter 16, "Artificial Intelligence as Empirical Inquiry," summarizes the important approaches of traditional AI as well as examines what we feel is its exciting future.

Using This Book

Artificial intelligence is a big field; consequently, this is a big book. Although it would require more than a single semester to cover all the material in the text, we have designed it so that a number of paths may be taken through the material. In teaching introductory artificial intelligence at the University of New Mexico, we have used a draft of this text for both one- and two-semester courses.

First we assume that most students will have had introductory courses in discrete mathematics, including predicate calculus and graph theory. If this is not true the instructor should spend more time on these concepts in the optional sections at the beginning of the text (2.1, 3.1). We also assume that students have had courses in data structures including trees, graphs, and recursion-based search using stacks and queues. If they have not, they should spend more time on the optional sections of chapters 3 and 4 (3.1, 4.1, and 4.2).

In presenting LISP and PROLOG, we do not have the space to discuss language syntax in full detail. Instead, we assume that the student is either familiar with the syntax of the languages or will take the time to pursue it in an appropriate language text. Our emphasis is on the use of these languages for building the algorithms and data structures discussed in the theoretical chapters of the book.

A number of different tracks may be taken through the text without destroying continuity. In a one-quarter course in AI and expert systems, we suggest that the instructor teach the theoretical material from chapters 1–5, 8, 9, and 16. In addition, the representation and search mechanisms of these chapters should be built in either LISP or PROLOG. Since there may not be time to teach both languages in a one-quarter course, we suggest that after going over the language issues in the introduction to Part III, the instructor present a single language, either Chapter 6 and topics from Chapter 12 (PROLOG) or Chapter 7 and topics from Chapter 13 (LISP). A final assignment could require students to build an expert system using the shell from either section 12.2 or 13.3.

A one-semester course could follow the same ordering with some time left over for selected topics from chapters 10, 11, 14, and 15. Alternatively, a one-semester course could attempt to cover both languages along with the basic theoretical material.

Ideally, this text would serve as the core of a full-year course, which would allow time for a full treatment of all the theoretical material. Such a course could focus on one language for advanced AI data structures, but we recommend covering the introductory chapters of both languages. Chapter 14 can also be covered from the focus of either language, omitting 14.2 if you are doing LISP exclusively or 14.3 if you are using PROLOG. A full year would also allow instructors to lengthen their treatment of important topics, supplementing the text with selected papers from the AI literature. The epilogues to each chapter suggest a variety of supplementary material.

Regardless of the combination of chapters chosen, we feel the power of our text is to constructively blend the theoretical insights offered by AI formalisms with good programming practice. Only then can the reader get a proper focus on the strengths (and inherent limitations) of the AI approach to problem solving.

The Pseudocode

The algorithms are described using a Pascal-based pseudocode. This notation uses the control structures of Pascal along with English descriptions of the tests and operations. However, we have added two useful constructs to the Pascal control structures. The first is a modified **case** statement. Rather than comparing the value of a variable with constant case labels, as in standard Pascal, it lets each item be labeled with an arbitrary Boolean test. It evaluates these tests in order until one of them evaluates to **true** and then performs the associated action; all other actions are ignored. Those of you who are familiar with LISP will note that this has the same semantics as the LISP **cond** statement.

The other addition to the language is a **return** statement, which takes one argument and can appear anywhere within a procedure or function. When the **return** statement is encountered, it causes the program to immediately exit the function, returning its argument as a result. Other than these modifications, we have tried to stick to basic Pascal structure, with a reliance on the English descriptions to make the algorithms clear.

Acknowledgments

First we would like to thank our reviewers, whose comments often suggested important additions of material and focus. Our reviewers included Rachel Adar, James Allen, Alan D. Christiansen, Sarah A. Douglas, Stefan Feyock, Aki Fleshler, Michael Lebowitz, Lynn Peterson, Robert F. Simmons, George C. Stockman, and Bob Veroff. We are grateful to our editors, especially Alan Apt, Mary Ann Telatnik, Mark McCormick, Mary Prescott, and Laura Kenney. Their support and patience were crucial for delivering an intellectually mature as well as good-looking final product. We also thank Merry Finley for her work on the figures used in this text.

Aki Fleshler and Carl Stern, colleagues at the University of New Mexico, and Brendon McGonigle at the University of Edinburgh, have been especially helpful in the technical editing of this book. Steve Verzi and Mark McLaughlin assisted in preparing the code. We thank two years of students who used this text in its preliminary stages and helped remove its typos and bugs. We would like to thank the University of Edinburgh and Herriot Watt University in Scotland and the University of New Mexico for computing and other resources that supported our writing.

We wish to thank Thomas Barrow, internationally recognized artist and University of New Mexico professor of art, who created the six photograms especially for this book after reading an early draft of the manuscript.

In a number of places, we have used figures or quotations from the work of other authors. We would like to thank the authors and publishers for their permission to use this material. These contributions are listed at the end of the text.

We have enjoyed writing this material; may you enjoy it also as you come to see the power and challenges of AI problem solving.

George F. Luger

William A. Stubblefield

I would like to further thank my wife Kathleen for both emotional and intellectual support during the creation of this manuscript. Without her dedicated understanding, demands for intellectual purity, and research and proofreading skills, this text would be just another good idea. I especially dedicate this book to her. I also thank my coauthor for the most important gifts of patience, friendship, and intellectual companionship.

G.F.L.

I share George's gratitude to all of the people who have helped us during the three years of this book's development. They have taught me that individuals can only achieve their full growth with the support and challenge of friends and colleagues. I would also like to thank George Luger for overseeing my apprenticeship in the craft of AI and having faith in my ability to assume the responsibilities of a journeyman.

W.A.S.

1 July 1988

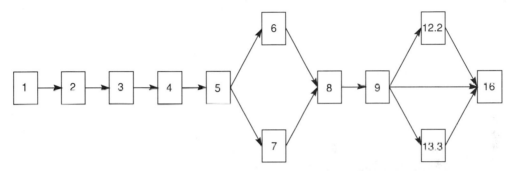

Partial ordering of chapters for a one-quarter or a minimal one-semester course.

CONTENTS

PART II

ARTIFICIAL INTELLIGENCE AS REPRESENTATION AND SEARCH 27

2 THE PREDICATE CALCULUS 41

3 STRUCTURES AND STRATEGIES FOR STATE SPACE SEARCH 77

PART III
LANGUAGES FOR AI PROBLEM SOLVING 187

6   AN INTRODUCTION TO PROLOG 203

PART IV
REPRESENTATIONS FOR KNOWLEDGE-BASED SYSTEMS 285

10   NATURAL LANGUAGE   377

13 ADVANCED LISP PROGRAMMING TECHNIQUES FOR ARTIFICIAL INTELLIGENCE 487

14 OBJECTS, MESSAGES, AND HYBRID EXPERT SYSTEM DESIGN 515

PART VI
EPILOGUE 591

APPENDIX 1
PROLOG PROGRAMS 603

APPENDIX 2
LISP PROGRAMS 619

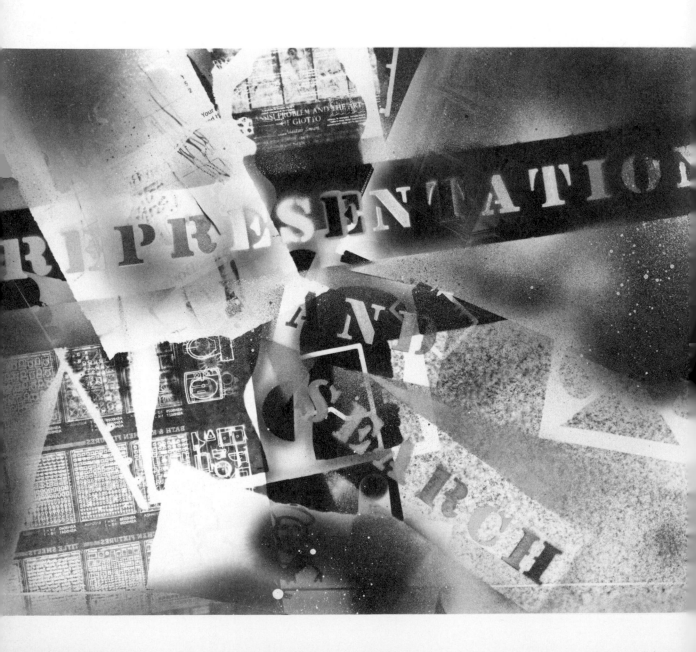

PART I

ARTIFICIAL INTELLIGENCE, ITS ROOTS AND SCOPE

Everything must have a beginning, to speak in Sanchean phrase; and that beginning must be linked to something that went before. The Hindus give the world an elephant to support it, but they make the elephant stand upon a tortoise. Invention, it must be humbly admitted, does not consist in creating out of void, but out of chaos; the materials must, in the first place, be afforded....

—MARY SHELLEY, *Frankenstein*

Artificial Intelligence—An Attempted Definition

Artificial intelligence may be defined as the branch of computer science that is concerned with the automation of intelligent behavior. This definition is particularly appropriate to this text in that it emphasizes our conviction that AI is a part of computer science and, as such, must be based on sound theoretical and applied principles of that field. These principles include the data structures used in knowledge representation, the algorithms needed to apply that knowledge, and the languages and programming techniques used in their implementation.

However, this definition suffers from the fact that intelligence itself is not very well defined or understood. Although most of us are certain that we know intelligent behavior when we see it, it is doubtful that anyone could come close to defining intelligence in a way that would be specific enough to help in the evaluation of a supposedly intelligent computer program, while still capturing the vitality and complexity of the human mind.

Thus the problem of defining artificial intelligence becomes one of defining intelligence itself: Is intelligence a single faculty, or is it just a name for a collection of distinct and unrelated abilities? To what extent is intelligence learned as opposed to having an a priori existence? Exactly what does happen when learning occurs? What is creativity? Intuition? Can intelligence be inferred from observable behavior, or does it require evidence of a particular internal mechanism? How is knowledge represented in the nerve tissue of a living being, and what lessons does this have for the design of intelligent machines? What is self-awareness, and what role does it play in intelligence? Is it necessary to pattern an intelligent computer program after what is known about human intelligence, or is a strict "engineering" approach to the problem sufficient? Is it even possible to achieve intelligence on a computer, or does an intelligent entity require the richness of sensation and experience that might be found only in a biological existence?

These are all unanswered questions, and all of them have helped to shape both the problems and solution methodologies that constitute the core of modern AI. In fact, part of the tremendous appeal of artificial intelligence is that it offers a unique and powerful tool for exploring exactly these questions. AI offers both a medium and a test-bed for theories of intelligence: such theories may be stated in the language of computer programs and consequently verified through their execution on an actual computer.

For these reasons, our initial definition of artificial intelligence seems to fall short of unambiguously defining the field. If anything, it has only led to further questions and the paradoxical notion of a field of study whose major goals include its own definition. But this difficulty in arriving at a precise definition of AI is entirely appropriate. Artificial intelligence is still a young discipline, and its structure, concerns, and methods are less clearly defined than those of a more mature science such as physics.

Artificial intelligence has always been more concerned with expanding the boundaries of computer science than with clearly defining those borders. Keeping this exploration grounded in sound theoretical principles is one of the challenges facing AI researchers in general and this text in particular.

We need to summarize the major questions and assumptions that dominate the field of artificial intelligence to provide background and motivation for the methodologies presented in this text. This goal is better met with the following recursive definition: Artificial intelligence is the collection of problems and methodologies studied by artificial intelligence researchers. This definition may seem silly and meaningless, but it makes an important point: artificial intelligence, like every science, is a human endeavor and may best be understood in that context.

There are reasons why any science, AI included, concerns itself with a certain set of problems and develops a particular body of techniques for approaching these problems. A short history of artificial intelligence and the people and assumptions that have shaped it will explain why a certain set of questions have come to dominate the field and why the methods discussed in this text have been taken for their solution.

AI: HISTORY AND APPLICATIONS

*Hear the rest, and you will marvel even more at the
crafts and resources I have contrived. Greatest was this: in
the former times if a man fell sick he had no defense
against the sickness, neither healing food nor drink,
nor unguent; but through the lack of drugs men
wasted away, until I showed them the blending of
mild simples wherewith they drive out all manner of
diseases. . . .*

*It was I who made visible to men's eyes
the flaming signs of the sky that were before
dim. So much for these. Beneath the earth, man's
hidden blessing, copper, iron, silver, and gold—will
anyone claim to have discovered these before I did?
No one, I am very sure, who wants to speak truly and
to the purpose. One brief word will tell the whole
story: all arts that mortals have come from Prometheus.*

—AESCHYLUS, *Prometheus Bound*

1.1 From Eden to ENIAC: Attitudes Toward Intelligence, Knowledge, and Human Artifice

Prometheus speaks of the fruits of his transgression against the gods of Olympus: his purpose was not merely to steal fire for the human race but also to enlighten humanity through the gift of intelligence or *nous*: the "rational mind." This intelligence forms the foundation for all of human technology and ultimately all human civilization. The work of the classical Greek dramatist illustrates a deep and ancient awareness of the extraordinary power of knowledge. Artificial intelligence, in its very direct concern for

3

Prometheus's gift, has been applied to all the areas of his legacy—medicine, psychology, biology, astronomy, geology—and many areas of scientific endeavor that Aeschylus could not have imagined.

While Prometheus's action freed humanity from the sickness of ignorance, it also earned him the wrath of Zeus. Outraged over this theft of the knowledge that previously belonged only to the gods of Olympus, Zeus commanded that Prometheus be chained to a barren rock to suffer the ravages of the elements for eternity. The notion that human efforts to gain knowledge constitute a transgression against the laws of God or nature is deeply ingrained in Western thought. It is the basis of the story of Eden and appears in the work of Dante and Milton. Both Shakespeare and the ancient Greek tragedians portrayed intellectual ambition as the cause of disaster. The belief that the desire for knowledge must ultimately lead to disaster has persisted throughout history, enduring the Renaissance, the age of Enlightenment, and even the scientific and philosophical advances of the nineteenth and twentieth centuries. Thus, we should not be surprised that artificial intelligence inspires so much controversy in both academic and popular circles.

Indeed, rather than dispelling this ancient fear of the consequences of intellectual ambition, modern technology has only made those consequences seem likely, even imminent. The legends of Prometheus, Eve, and Faustus have been retold in the language of technological society. In her introduction to *Frankenstein* (subtitled, interestingly enough, *The Modern Prometheus*), Mary Shelley writes:

> Many and long were the conversations between Lord Byron and Shelley to which I was a devout and silent listener. During one of these, various philosophical doctrines were discussed, and among others the nature of the principle of life, and whether there was any probability of its ever being discovered and communicated. They talked of the experiments of Dr. Darwin (I speak not of what the doctor really did or said that he did, but, as more to my purpose, of what was then spoken of as having been done by him), who preserved a piece of vermicelli in a glass case till by some extraordinary means it began to move with a voluntary motion. Not thus, after all, would life be given. Perhaps a corpse would be reanimated; galvanism had given token of such things: perhaps the component parts of a creature might be manufactured, brought together, and endued with vital warmth.

Shelley shows us the extent to which scientific advances such as the work of Darwin and the discovery of electricity had convinced even nonscientists that the workings of nature were not divine secrets, but could be broken down and understood systematically. Frankenstein's monster is not the product of shamanistic incantations or unspeakable transactions with the underworld: it is assembled from separately "manufactured" components and infused with the vital force of electricity. Although nineteenth-century science was inadequate to realize the goal of understanding and creating a fully intelligent agent, it affirmed the notion that the mysteries of life and intellect might be brought into the light of scientific analysis.

By the time Mary Shelley finally and perhaps irrevocably joined modern science with the Promethean myth, the philosophical foundations of modern work in artificial intelligence had been developing for several thousand years. Although the moral and cultural issues raised by artificial intelligence are both interesting and important, our introduction is more properly concerned with its intellectual technical heritage. The logical starting point for such a history is the genius of Aristotle, or as Dante refers to him, "the master of those who know." Aristotle wove together the insights, wonders, and fears of the early Greek tradition with the careful analysis and disciplined thought that were to become the standard for more modern science.

For Aristotle, the most fascinating aspect of nature was change (Aristotle 1941). In his *Physics*, he defined his "philosophy of nature" as the "study of things that change." He distinguished between the "matter" and "form" of things: a sculpture is fashioned from the "material" bronze and has the "form" of a human. Change occurs when the bronze is molded to a new form. The matter/form distinction provides a philosophical basis for modern notions such as "symbolic" computing and data "abstraction." In computing (even with "numbers") we are manipulating patterns that are the forms of electromagnetic material, with the changes of form of this material representing aspects of the solution process. Abstracting the form from the medium of its representation not only allows these forms to be manipulated computationally but also provides the promise of a "theory" of data structures, the heart of modern computer science.

In his *Metaphysics* (located just after, *meta*, the *Physics* in his writing), Aristotle developed a science of things that never change, including his cosmology and theology. More relevant to artificial intelligence, however, was Aristotle's epistemology or science of knowing, discussed in his *Logic*. Aristotle referred to his logic as the "instrument" (*organon*), because he felt that the study of thought itself was at the basis of all knowledge. In his *Logic*, he investigated whether certain propositions can be said to be "true" because they are related to other things that are known to be true. Thus if we know that "all men are mortal" and that "Socrates is a man," then we can conclude that "Socrates is mortal." This argument is an example of what Aristotle referred to as a syllogism using the deductive form modus ponens.

Although the formal axiomatization of reasoning needed another two thousand years for its full flowering in the works of Gottlob Frege, Bertrand Russell, Kurt Godel, Alan Turing, Alfred Tarski, and others, its roots may be traced to Aristotle.

Renaissance thought, building on the Greek tradition, initiated the evolution of a different and powerful way of thinking about humanity and its relation to the natural world. Empiricism began to replace mysticism as a means of understanding nature. Clocks and, eventually, factory schedules superseded the rhythms of nature for thousands of city dwellers. Most of the modern social and physical sciences found their origin in the notion that processes, whether natural or artificial, could be mathematically analyzed and understood. In particular, scientists and philosophers realized that thought itself, the way that knowledge was represented and manipulated in the human mind, was a difficult but essential subject for scientific study. Efforts to understand the nature of intelligent thought go back much farther than the digital computer, and even so modern a science as AI has much to gain from these centuries of philosophical activity.

Perhaps the major event in the development of the modern world view was the Copernican revolution, the replacement of the ancient earth-centered model of the universe with the idea that the earth and other planets actually rotate around the sun. After centuries of an "obvious" order, in which the scientific explanation of the nature of the cosmos was consistent with the teachings of religion and common sense, a drastically different and not at all obvious model was proposed to explain the motions of heavenly bodies. For perhaps the first time, *our ideas about the world were seen as fun-*

damentally distinct from its appearance. This split between the human mind and its surrounding reality, between ideas about things and things themselves, is essential to the modern study of the mind and its organization. This breach was widened by the writings of Galileo, whose scientific observations further contradicted the ''obvious'' truths about the natural world and whose development of mathematics as a tool for describing that world emphasized the distinction between the world and our ideas about it. It is out of this breach that the modern notion of the mind evolved: introspection became a common motif in literature, philosophers began to study epistemology and mathematics, and the systematic application of the scientific method rivaled the senses as tools for understanding the world.

Although the seventeenth and eighteenth centuries saw a great deal of work in epistemology and related fields, here we have space only to discuss the work of René Descartes. Descartes is a central figure in the development of the modern notion of thought and the mind. In his famous *Meditations*, Descartes attempted to find a basis for reality purely through cognitive introspection. Systematically rejecting the input of his senses as untrustworthy, Descartes was forced to doubt even the existence of the physical world and was left with only the reality of thought; even his own existence had to be justified in terms of thought: ''Cogito ergo sum'' (I think, therefore I am). After he established his own existence purely as a thinking entity, Descartes inferred the existence of God as an essential creator and ultimately reasserted the reality of the physical universe as the necessary creation of a benign God. We can make two interesting observations here: first, the schism between the mind and the physical world had become so complete that the process of thinking could be discussed in complete isolation from any specific sensory input or worldly subject matter; and second, the connection between mind and the physical world was so tenuous that it required the intervention of a benign God to allow reliable knowledge of the physical world. This view of the duality between the mind and the physical world underlies all of Descartes's thought, including his development of analytic geometry. How else could he have unified such a seemingly worldly branch of mathematics as geometry with such an abstract mathematical framework as algebra?

Why have we included this philosophical discussion in a text on artificial intelligence? There are two consequences of this analysis that are essential to the enterprise of AI:

1. By finally separating the mind and the physical world, Descartes and related thinkers established that the structure of ideas about the world was not necessarily the same as the structure of their subject matter. This underlies the subject matter and basic methodology of the field of AI (along with the fields of epistemology, psychology, much of higher mathematics, and most of modern literature): mental processes had an existence of their own, obeyed their own laws, and could be studied in and of themselves.

2. Once the mind and the body were separated, philosophers found it necessary to find a way to reconnect the two, since some kind of interaction between the mental and the physical is essential for human existence. Although millions of words have been written on the *mind-body problem*, and numerous solutions proposed, no one has successfully explained the obvious interactions between

mental states and physical actions while affirming a fundamental difference between them. The most widely accepted response to this problem, and the one that provides an essential foundation for the study of AI, holds that the mind and the body are not fundamentally different entities at all. In this view, mental processes are indeed achieved by physical systems such as brains (or computers). Consequently, mental processes, like physical processes, can ultimately be characterized through formal mathematics. Or, as stated by the Scots philosopher David Hume, "Cognition is computation."

Once thinking had come to be regarded as a form of computation, its formalization and eventual mechanization were logical next steps. In the seventeenth century, Gottfried Wilhelm von Leibniz introduced the first system of formal logic and constructed machines for automating calculation (Leibniz 1887). Euler, in the eighteenth century, with his analysis of the "connectedness" of the bridges joining the riverbanks and islands of the city of Konigsburg (see the introduction to Chapter 3), introduced the study of representations that abstractly capture the structure of relationships in the world (Euler 1735).

The formalization of graph theory also afforded the possibility of *state space search*, a major conceptual tool of artificial intelligence. This modern model of problem solving, based on Euler's graphs, looks for a solution by systematically searching through the various situations (states) of a problem. These situations are "connected" by the "legal moves" of a game or "inference rules" of an expert reasoning system. In either case they form a graph of interconnected stages in a solution process. Searching this graph can construct the succession of steps that lead to a solution (Section 1.3 and Chapter 3).

It is this philosophical heritage that Charles Babbage, Ada Lovelace, Gottlob Frege, George Boole, Bertrand Russell, and other Victorian and modern thinkers built into the science of computation.

As one of the originators of the science of operations research, as well as the designer of the first programmable mechanical computing machines, Charles Babbage is arguably the earliest practitioner of artificial intelligence (Morrison and Morrison 1961). Babbage's "difference engine" was a special-purpose machine for computing the values of certain polynomial functions and was the forerunner of his "analytical engine." The analytical engine, designed but not successfully constructed during Babbage's lifetime, was a general-purpose programmable computing machine that presaged many of the architectural assumptions underlying the modern computer.

In describing the analytical engine, Ada Lovelace, Babbage's friend, supporter, and collaborator, said:

> We may say most aptly that the Analytical Engine weaves algebraical patterns just as the Jacquard loom weaves flowers and leaves. Here, it seems to us, resides much more of originality than the difference engine can be fairly entitled to claim.

Babbage's inspiration was his desire to apply the technology of his day to liberate humans from the drudgery of arithmetic calculation. In this sentiment, as well as his conception of his computers as mechanical devices, Babbage was thinking in purely nineteenth-century terms. His analytical engine, however, included many modern notions, such as the separation of memory and processor (the "store" and the "mill" in Babbage's terms), the concept of a digital rather than analog machine, and programmability based on the execution of a series of operations encoded on punched pasteboard cards. The most striking feature of Ada Lovelace's description, and of Babbage's work in general, is its treatment of the "pattern" of an intellectual activity as an entity that may be studied, characterized, and finally implemented mechanically without concern for the particular values that are finally passed through the "mill" of the calculating machine: an implementation of the "abstraction and manipulation of form" first described by Aristotle.

The goal of creating a formal language for thought also appears in the work of George Boole, another nineteenth-century mathematician whose work must be included in any discussion of the roots of artificial intelligence (Boole 1847, 1854). Although he made contributions to a number of areas of mathematics, his best known work was in the mathematical formalization of the laws of logic, an accomplishment that forms the very heart of modern computer science. While the role of Boolean algebra in the design of logic circuitry is well known, Boole's own goals in developing his system seem closer to those of contemporary AI researchers than they do to more traditional branches of computer science. In the first chapter of *An Investigation of the Laws of Thought, on which are founded the Mathematical Theories of Logic and Probabilities*, Boole described his goals as

> to investigate the fundamental laws of those operations of the mind by which reasoning is performed: to give expression to them in the symbolical language of a Calculus, and upon this foundation to establish the science of logic and instruct its method; ... and finally to collect from the various elements of truth brought to view in the course of these inquiries some probable intimations concerning the nature and constitution of the human mind.

The greatness of Boole's accomplishment is in the extraordinary power and simplicity of the system he devised: three operations, "AND" (denoted by $*$ or $\wedge$), "OR" (denoted by $+$ or $\vee$), and not (denoted by $\neg$), formed the heart of his logical calculus. These operations have remained the basis for all subsequent developments in formal logic, including the design of modern computers. While keeping the meaning of these symbols nearly identical to the corresponding algebraic operations, Boole noted that "the Symbols of logic are further subject to a special law, to which the symbols of quantity, as such, are not subject." This law states that for any X, an element in the algebra, $X*X=X$ (or that once something is known to be true, repetition cannot augment that knowledge). This led to the characteristic restriction of Boolean values to the only two numbers that may satisfy this equation: 1 and 0. The standard definitions of Boolean multiplication (AND) and addition (OR) follow from this insight. Boole's system not only provided the basis of binary arithmetic but also demonstrated that an extremely simple formal system was adequate to capture the full power of logic. This assumption and the system Boole developed to demonstrate it form the basis of all modern efforts to formalize logic, from Russell and Whitehead's *Principia Mathematica* (Whitehead and Russell 1950), through the work of Turing and Godel, up to the most modern automated reasoning systems.

Gottlob Frege, in his *Foundations of Arithmetic* (Frege 1879, 1884), created a mathematical specification language for describing this calculation process in a clear and precise fashion. With this language Frege formalized many of the issues first addressed by Aristotle's *Logic*. Frege's language, now called the *first-order predicate calculus*, offers a tool for describing the propositions and truth value assignments that make up the philosophical basis of mathematical reasoning and describes the axiomatic basis of "meaning" for these expressions. The formal system of the predicate calculus, which includes predicate symbols, a theory of functions, and quantified variables, was intended to be a language for describing mathematics and its philosophical foundations. It also plays a fundamental role in creating a theory of representation for artificial intelligence (Chapter 2). The first-order predicate calculus offers the tools necessary for automating a theory of reasoning: a language for expressions, a theory for assumptions related to the meaning of expressions, and a logically sound calculus for inferring new true expressions.

Russell and Whitehead's work is particularly important to the foundations of AI, in that their stated goal was to derive the whole of mathematics through purely formal operations on a collection of axioms. Although many mathematical systems have been constructed from basic axioms, what is interesting is Russell and Whitehead's commitment to mathematics as a purely formal system. This meant that axioms and theorems would be treated solely as strings of characters; no "meaning" would be attributed to those character strings. Proofs would proceed solely through the application of well-defined rules for manipulating these strings: there would be no reliance on intuition or the meaning of theorems as a basis for proofs. Every step of a proof followed from the strict application of formal (syntactic) rules to either axioms or previously proven theorems, even where traditional proofs might regard such a step as "obvious." What "meaning" the theorems and axioms of the system might have in relation to the world would be independent of their logical derivations. This treatment of mathematical reasoning in purely formal (and hence mechanical) terms provided an essential basis for its automation on physical computers. The logical syntax and formal rules of inference developed by Russell and Whitehead are still a basis for automatic theorem-proving systems as well as the theoretical foundations of artificial intelligence.

Alfred Tarski is another mathematician whose work is essential to the foundations of AI. Tarski created a *theory of reference* wherein the *well-formed formulae* of Frege or Russell and Whitehead can be said to refer, in a precise fashion, to the "physical world" (Tarski 1944, 1956). This insight underlies most theories of formal semantics. In his paper "The semantic conception of truth and the foundation of semantics," Tarski describes his theory of reference and truth value relationships. Modern computer scientists, especially Scott, Strachey, Burstall (Burstall and Darlington 1977), and Plotkin have related this theory of "semantics" to programming languages and other specifications for computing.

Although in the eighteenth, nineteenth, and early twentieth centuries the formalization of science and mathematics created the intellectual prerequisite for the study of artificial intelligence, it was not until the twentieth century and the introduction of the digital computer that AI became a viable scientific discipline. By the end of the 1940s electronic digital computers had demonstrated their potential to provide the amounts of memory and processing power required by intelligent programs. It was now possible to implement formal reasoning systems on a computer and empirically test their sufficiency for exhibiting intelligence. An essential component of the science of artificial intelligence is this commitment to digital computers as the vehicle of choice for creating and testing theories of intelligence.

Digital computers are not merely a vehicle for testing theories of intelligence. Their architecture also suggests a specific paradigm for such theories: intelligence is a form of information processing. The notion of search as a problem-solving methodology, for example, owes more to the sequential nature of computer operation than it does to any biological model of intelligence. Most AI programs represent knowledge in some formal language that is then manipulated by algorithms, honoring the separation of data and program fundamental to the von Neumann style of computing. Formal logic has emerged as the lingua franca of AI research, while graph theory plays an indispensable role in the analysis of problem spaces as well as providing a basis for semantic networks and similar models of semantic meaning. These techniques and formalisms are discussed in detail throughout the body of this text; we mention them here to emphasize the symbiotic relationship between the modern digital computer and the theoretical underpinnings of artificial intelligence.

We often forget that the tools we create for our own purposes tend to shape our conception of the world through their structure and limitations. Although seemingly restrictive, this interaction is an essential aspect of the evolution of human knowledge: a tool (and scientific theories are ultimately only tools) is developed to solve a particular problem. As it is used and refined, the tool itself seems to suggest other applications, leading to new questions and, ultimately, the development of new tools.

One of the earliest papers to address the question of machine intelligence specifically in relation to the modern digital computer was written in 1950 by the British mathematician Alan Turing. "Computing machinery and intelligence" (Turing 1950) is still timely in both its assessment of the arguments against the possibility of creating an intelligent computing machine and its answers to those arguments. Turing, known mainly for his contributions to the theory of computability, considered the question of whether or not a machine could actually be made to think. Noting that the fundamental ambiguities in the question itself (what is thinking? what is a machine?) precluded any rational answer, he proposed that the question of intelligence be replaced by a more clearly defined empirical test.

The Turing test measures the performance of an allegedly intelligent machine against that of a human being, arguably the best and only standard for intelligent behavior. The test, which Turing called the "imitation game," places the machine and a human counterpart in rooms apart from a second human being, referred to as the interrogator (Figure 1.1). The interrogator is not able to see or speak directly to either of them, does not know which entity is actually the machine, and may communicate with them solely by use of a textual device such as a terminal. The interrogator is asked to distinguish the computer from the human being solely on the basis of their answers to questions asked over this device. If the interrogator is unable to reliably distinguish the machine from the human, then, Turing argues, the machine may be assumed to be intelligent.

By isolating the interrogator from both the machine and the other human participant, the test ensures that the interrogator will not be biased by the appearance of the machine or any mechanical property of its voice. The interrogator is free, however, to

Figure 1.1   The Turing test.

ask any questions, no matter how devious or indirect, in an effort to uncover the computer's identity. For example, the interrogator may ask both subjects to perform a rather involved arithmetic calculation, assuming that the computer will be more likely to get it correct than the human; to counter this strategy, the computer will need to know when it should fail to get a correct answer to such problems in order to seem like a human. To discover the human's identity on the basis of emotional nature, the interrogator may ask both subjects to respond to a poem or work of art; this strategy will require that the computer have knowledge concerning the emotional makeup of human beings.

The important features of this test are:

1. It gives us an objective notion of intelligence, i.e., the behavior of a known intelligent being in response to a particular set of questions. This provides a standard for determining intelligence that avoids the inevitable debates over the ''true'' nature of intelligence.

2. It prevents us from being sidetracked by such confusing and currently unanswerable questions as whether or not the computer uses the appropriate internal processes, or whether or not the machine is actually conscious of its actions.

3. It eliminates any bias in favor of living organisms over machine intelligence by forcing the interrogator to focus solely on the content of the answers to questions.

Because of these advantages, the Turing test provides a basis for many of the schemes actually used to evaluate modern AI programs. Given a program that has potentially achieved intelligence in some area of expertise, it may be evaluated by comparing its performance on a given set of problems to that of a human expert. This evaluation technique is just a variation of the Turing test: a group of humans are asked to blindly compare the performance of a computer and a human being on a particular set of problems. As we will see, this methodology has become an essential tool in both the development and verification of modern expert systems.

The Turing test, in spite of its intuitive appeal, is vulnerable to a number of justifiable criticisms. One of the most important of these is aimed at its bias toward purely symbolic problem-solving tasks. It does not test abilities requiring perceptual skill or manual dexterity, even though these are important components of human intelligence. Conversely, it is sometimes suggested that the Turing test needlessly constrains machine intelligence to fit a human mold. Perhaps machine intelligence is simply different from human intelligence and trying to render it in human terms is a fundamental mistake. Do we really wish the machine to do mathematics as slowly and inaccurately as the human does it? Shouldn't an intelligent machine capitalize on its own assets, such as an infallible memory, rather than trying to emulate human cognition?

Turing also addressed the feasibility of constructing such a program on a digital computer. By thinking in terms of a specific model of computation (an electronic discrete state computing machine), Turing made some well-founded conjectures concerning the storage capacity, program complexity, and basic design philosophy required for such a system. Finally, he addressed a number of moral, philosophical, and scientific objections to the possibility of constructing such a program in terms of an actual technology. The reader is referred to Turing's article for a perceptive and still relevant summary of the debate over the possibility of intelligent machines.

Two of the objections cited by Turing are worth considering further. "Lady Lovelace's Objection," first stated by Ada Lovelace, argues that computers can only do as they are told and consequently cannot perform original (hence, intelligent) actions. This objection has become a reassuring if somewhat dubious part of contemporary technological folklore. Expert systems, for example, have reached conclusions unanticipated by their designers. Indeed, a number of researchers now feel that human creativity can be expressed in a computer program.

The other related objection, the "Argument from Informality of Behavior," asserts the impossibility of creating a set of rules that will tell an individual exactly what to do under every possible set of circumstances. Certainly, the flexibility that enables a biological intelligence to respond to an infinite range of situations in a reasonable if not necessarily optimal fashion is a hallmark of intelligent behavior. While it is true that the control structure used in most traditional computer programs does not demonstrate great flexibility or originality, it is not true that all programs must be written in this fashion. Indeed, much of the work done in AI over the past 25 years has been in the development of programming languages and philosophies such as production systems, object-based systems, network representations, and others discussed in this text that attempt to overcome this deficiency.

Modern AI programs generally consist of a collection of extremely modular components, rules of behavior, that do not execute in a rigid order, but rather are invoked as needed in response to the structure of a particular problem instance. Pattern matchers allow general rules to apply over a range of instances. These systems have an extreme flexibility that enables relatively small programs to exhibit a vast range of possible behaviors in response to differing problems and situations.

Whether these systems can ultimately be made to exhibit the flexibility shown by a living organism is still the subject of much debate. Nobel laureate Herbert Simon has argued that much of the originality and variability of behavior shown by living creatures is due to the richness of their environment rather than the complexity of their own internal programs. In *The Sciences of the Artificial* (Simon 1981), Simon describes an ant progressing circuitously along an uneven and cluttered stretch of ground. Although the ant's path seems quite complex, Simon argues that the ant's goal is very simple: to return to its colony as quickly as possible. The twists and turns in its path are caused by the obstacles it encounters on its way. Simon concludes that

> An ant, viewed as a behaving system, is quite simple. The apparent complexity of its behavior over time is largely a reflection of the complexity of the environment in which it finds itself.

This idea, if ultimately proved to apply to organisms of higher intelligence as well as such simple creatures as insects, constitutes a powerful argument that such systems are relatively simple and, consequently, comprehensible. It is interesting to note that if one applies this idea to humans, it becomes a strong argument for the importance of culture in the forming of intelligence. Rather than growing in the dark like mushrooms, intelligence seems to depend on an interaction with a suitably rich environment. Culture is just as important in creating humans as human beings are in creating culture. Rather than denigrating our intellects, this idea emphasizes the miraculous richness and coherence of the cultures that have formed out of the lives of separate human beings.

Our preliminary discussion of the possibility of a theory of automated intelligence is in no way intended to overstate the progress made to date or minimize the work that lies ahead. As we emphasize throughout this text, it is important to be aware of our limitations and to be honest about our successes. For example, there have been only limited results with programs that in any interesting sense can be said to ''learn.'' Our accomplishments in modeling the semantic complexities of a natural language such as English have also been very modest. Even fundamental issues such as organizing knowledge or fully managing the complexity and correctness of very large computer programs (such as large knowledge bases) require considerable further research. Expert systems, while they have achieved marketable engineering successes, still have many limitations in the quality and generality of their reasoning. These include their inability to perform *common-sense reasoning* or to exhibit knowledge of rudimentary physical reality, such as how things change over time.

But we must maintain a reasonable perspective. It is easy to overlook the accomplishments of artificial intelligence when honestly facing the work that remains. In the next section, we establish this perspective through an overview of several areas of artificial intelligence research and development.

1.2 Overview of AI Application Areas

The Analytical Engine has no pretensions whatever to originate anything. It can do whatever we know how to order it to perform.

—ADA BYRON, *Countess of Lovelace*

I'm sorry Dave; I can't let you do that.

—HAL 9000 in *2001: A Space Odyssey* by Arthur C. Clarke

We now return to our stated goal of defining artificial intelligence through an examination of the ambitions and accomplishments of workers in the field. The two most fundamental concerns of AI researchers are *knowledge representation* and *search*. The first of these addresses the problem of capturing the full range of knowledge required for intelligent behavior in a formal language, i.e., one suitable for computer manipulation. Chapter 2 introduces predicate calculus as a language for describing the properties and relationships among objects in problem domains that require qualitative reasoning rather than arithmetic calculations for their solutions. Later chapters (9, 10, 11, and 14) discuss other languages that artificial intelligence has developed for better capturing the ambiguities and complexities of areas such as commonsense reasoning and natural language understanding.

Search is a problem-solving technique that systematically explores a space of *problem states*, i.e., successive and alternative stages in the problem-solving process. Examples of problem states might include the different board configurations in a game or intermediate steps in a reasoning process. This space of alternative solutions is then searched to find a final answer. Newell and Simon (1976) have argued that this is the essential basis of human problem solving. Indeed, when a chess player examines the effects of different moves or a doctor considers a number of alternative diagnoses, they are searching among alternatives. The implications of this model and techniques for its implementation are discussed in chapters 3, 4, and 5.

Like most sciences, AI is decomposed into a number of subdisciplines that, while sharing an essential approach to problem solving, have concerned themselves with different applications. In this section we outline several of these major application areas and their contributions to artificial intelligence as a whole.

1.2.1 Game Playing

Much of the early research in state space search was done using common board games such as checkers, chess, and the 16-puzzle. In addition to their inherent intellectual appeal, board games have certain properties that made them ideal subjects for this early work. Most games are played using a well-defined set of rules: this makes it easy to generate the search space and frees the researcher from many of the ambiguities and complexities inherent in less structured problems. The board configurations used in playing these games are easily represented on a computer, requiring none of the complex formalisms needed to capture the semantic subtleties of real-world problem domains. Since games can be easily played, testing a game-playing program presents no financial or ethical burden. State space search, the paradigm underlying most game-playing research, is presented in chapters 3 and 4.

Games can generate extremely large search spaces. These are large and complex enough to require powerful techniques for determining what alternatives to explore in the problem space. These techniques are called *heuristics* and constitute a major area of AI research. A heuristic is a useful but potentially fallible problem-solving strategy, such as checking to make sure that an unresponsive appliance is plugged in before assuming that it is broken, or trying to protect your queen from capture in a chess game. Much of what we call intelligence resides in the heuristics used by humans to solve problems.

Because most of us have some experience with these simple games, it is possible to devise and test the effectiveness of our own heuristics. We do not need to find and consult an expert in some esoteric problem area such as medicine or mathematics (chess is an obvious exception to this rule). For these reasons, games provide a rich domain for the study of heuristic search. Chapter 5 introduces heuristics using these simple games; Chapter 8 extends their application to expert systems.

Game-playing programs, in spite of their simplicity, offer their own challenges, including an opponent whose moves may not be reliably anticipated. This presence of the opponent further complicates program design by adding an element of unpredictability and the need to consider psychological as well as tactical factors in game strategy.

1.2.2   Automated Reasoning and Theorem Proving

We could argue that automatic theorem proving is the oldest branch of artificial intelligence, tracing its roots back through Newell and Simon's Logic Theorist (Newell and Simon 1963a) and General Problem Solver (Newell and Simon 1963b) to its origins in Russell and Whitehead's efforts to treat all of mathematics as the purely formal derivation of theorems from basic axioms. In any case, it has certainly been one of the most fruitful branches of the field. Theorem-proving research was responsible for much of the early work in formalizing search algorithms and developing formal representation languages such as predicate calculus (Chapter 2) and the logic programming language PROLOG (Chapter 12).

Most of the appeal of automated theorem proving lies in the rigor and generality of logic. Because it is a formal system, logic lends itself to automation. A wide variety of problems can be attacked by representing the problem description and relevant background information as logical axioms and treating problem instances as theorems to be proved. This insight is the basis of work in automatic theorem proving and mathematical reasoning systems (Chapter 11).

Unfortunately, early efforts at writing theorem provers failed to develop a system that could consistently solve complicated problems. This was due to the ability of any reasonably complex logical system to generate an infinite number of provable theorems: without powerful techniques (heuristics) to guide their search, automated theorem provers proved large numbers of irrelevant theorems before stumbling onto the correct one. In response to this inefficiency, many argue that purely formal, syntactic methods of guiding search are inherently incapable of handling such a huge space and that the only alternative is to rely on the informal, ad hoc strategies that humans seem to use in solving problems. This is the approach underlying the development of expert systems, and it has proved to be a fruitful one.

Still, the appeal of reasoning based in formal mathematical logic is too strong to ignore. Many important problems such as the design and verification of logic circuits, verification of the correctness of computer programs, and control of complex systems seem to respond to such an approach. In addition, the theorem-proving community has enjoyed increasing success in devising powerful heuristics that rely solely on an evaluation of the syntactic form of a logical expression, reducing the complexity of the search space without resorting to the ad hoc techniques used by human problem solvers.

Another reason for the continued interest in automatic theorem provers is the realization that such a system does not have to be capable of independently solving extremely complex problems without human assistance. Many modern theorem provers function as intelligent assistants, letting humans perform the more demanding tasks of decomposing a large problem into subproblems and devising heuristics for searching the space of possible proofs. The theorem prover then performs the simpler but still demanding task of proving lemmas, verifying smaller conjectures, and completing the formal aspects of a proof outlined by its human associate (Boyer and Moore 1979).

1.2.3 Expert Systems

One major insight gained from early work in problem-solving was the importance of domain-specific knowledge. A doctor, for example, is not effective at diagnosing illness solely because she possesses some innate general problem-solving skill; she is effective because she knows a lot about medicine. Similarly, a geologist is effective at discovering mineral deposits because he is able to apply a good deal of theoretical and empirical knowledge about geology to the problem at hand. Expert knowledge is a combination of a theoretical understanding of the problem and a collection of heuristic problem-solving rules that experience has shown to be effective in the domain. Expert systems are constructed by obtaining this knowledge from a human expert and coding it into a form that a computer may apply to similar problems.

This reliance on the knowledge of a human domain expert for the system's problem-solving strategies is a major feature of expert systems. Although some programs are written in which the designer is also the source of the domain knowledge, it is far more typical to see such programs growing out of a collaboration between a domain expert such as a doctor, chemist, geologist, or engineer and a separate artificial intelligence specialist. The domain expert provides the necessary knowledge of the problem domain through a general discussion of her problem-solving methods and by demonstrating those skills on a carefully chosen set of sample problems. The AI specialist, or *knowledge engineer*, as expert systems designers are often known, is responsible for implementing this knowledge in a program that is both effective and seemingly intelligent in its behavior. Once such a program has been written, it is necessary to refine its expertise through a process of giving it example problems to solve, letting the domain expert criticize its behavior, and making any required changes or modifications to the program's knowledge. This process is repeated until the program has achieved the desired level of performance.

One of the earliest systems to exploit domain-specific knowledge in problem solving was DENDRAL, developed at Stanford in the late 1960s (Lindsay et al. 1980). DENDRAL was designed to infer the structure of organic molecules from their chemical formulas and mass spectrographic information about the chemical bonds present in the molecules. Because organic molecules tend to be very large, the number of possible structures for these molecules tends to be huge. DENDRAL addresses the problem of this large search space by applying the heuristic knowledge of expert chemists to the structure elucidation problem. DENDRAL's methods proved remarkably effective, routinely finding the correct structure out of millions of possibilities after only a few trials.

The approach has proved so successful that descendants of the system are used in chemical laboratories throughout the country.

While DENDRAL was one of the first programs to effectively use domain-specific knowledge to achieve expert level problem-solving performance, MYCIN established the methodology of contemporary expert systems (Buchanan 1984). MYCIN uses expert medical knowledge to diagnose and prescribe treatment for spinal meningitis and bacterial infections of the blood.

MYCIN, developed at Stanford in the mid-1970s, was one of the first programs to address the problems of reasoning with uncertain or incomplete information. MYCIN provided clear and logical explanations of the reasoning, used a control structure appropriate to the specific problem domain, and identified criteria to reliably evaluate its performance. Many of the expert system development techniques currently in use were first developed in the MYCIN project (Chapter 8).

Other classic expert systems include the PROSPECTOR program for determining the probable location and type of ore deposits based on geological information about a site (Duda et al. 1979a, 1979b), the INTERNIST program for performing diagnosis in the area of internal medicine, the Dipmeter Advisor developed to interpret the results of oil well drilling logs (Smith and Baker 1983), and XCON for configuring VAX computers. XCON has been in use since 1981; every VAX sold by Digital Equipment Corporation is now configured by XCON. Numerous other expert systems are currently solving problems in areas such as medicine, education, business, design, and science (Waterman 1986).

It is interesting to note that most expert systems have been written for relatively specialized, expert level domains. These domains are generally well studied and have clearly defined problem-solving strategies. Problems that depend on a more loosely defined notion of "common sense" are much more difficult to solve by these means (Part IV).

In spite of the promise of expert systems, it would be a mistake to overestimate the ability of this technology. Current deficiencies include:

1. Difficulty in capturing "deep" knowledge of the problem domain. MYCIN, for example, lacks any real knowledge of human physiology. It does not know what blood does or the function of the spinal cord. Folklore has it that once, when selecting a drug for treatment of meningitis, MYCIN asked if the patient was pregnant, even though it had been told that the patient was male. Whether this actually occurred or not, it does illustrate the narrowness of current expert systems.

2. Lack of robustness and flexibility. If humans are presented with a problem instance that they cannot solve immediately, they can generally return to an examination of first principles and come up with some strategy for attacking the problem. Expert systems generally lack this ability.

3. Inability to provide deep explanations. Because expert systems lack deep knowledge of their problem domains, their explanations are generally restricted to a description of the steps they took in finding a solution. They cannot tell "why" a certain approach was taken.

4. Difficulties in verification. While the correctness of any large computer system is difficult to prove, expert systems are particularly difficult to verify. This is a serious problem, as expert systems technology is being applied to critical applications such as air traffic control, nuclear reactor operations, and weapons systems.

5. Little learning from experience. Current expert systems are handcrafted; once the system is completed, its performance will not improve without further attention from its programmers. This leads to severe doubts about the intelligence of such systems.

In spite of these limitations, expert systems are proving their value in a number of important applications. It is hoped that these limitations will only encourage the student to pursue study and research in this important new branch of computer science. Expert systems are a major topic in this text and are discussed in chapters 4, 8, 12, 13, and 14.

1.2.4 Natural Language Understanding and Semantic Modeling

One of the long-standing goals of artificial intelligence is the creation of programs that are capable of understanding human language. Not only does the ability to understand natural language seem to be one of the most fundamental aspects of human intelligence, but also its successful automation would have an incredible impact on the usability and effectiveness of computers themselves. Much effort has been put into writing programs that understand natural language; although these programs have achieved success within certain restricted contexts, systems that can use natural language with the flexibility and generality that characterize human speech are beyond current methodologies.

Understanding natural language involves much more than parsing sentences into their individual parts of speech and looking those words up in a dictionary. Real understanding depends on extensive background knowledge about the domain of discourse and the idioms used in that domain and an ability to apply general contextual knowledge to resolve the omissions and ambiguities that are a normal part of human speech.

Consider, for example, the difficulties in carrying on a conversation about baseball with an individual who understands English but knows nothing about the rules, players, or history of the game. Could this person possibly understand the meaning of the sentence: "With none down in the top of the ninth and the go-ahead run at second, the manager called his relief from the bull pen"? Even though all of the words in the sentence may be individually understood, this sentence would be gibberish to even the most intelligent non-baseball fan.

The task of collecting and organizing this background knowledge in such a way that it may be applied to language comprehension forms the major problem in automating natural language understanding. Responding to this need, researchers have developed many of the techniques for structuring semantic meaning used throughout artificial intelligence (chapters 9 and 10).

Because of the tremendous amounts of knowledge required for understanding natural language, most work is done in well-understood, specialized problem areas. One of the earliest programs to exploit this "micro world" methodology was Winograd's

SHRDLU, a natural language system that could "converse" about a simple configuration of blocks of different shapes and colors (Winograd 1973). SHRDLU could answer queries such as "what color block is on the blue cube?" and plan actions such as "move the red pyramid onto the green brick." Problems of this sort, involving the description and manipulation of simple arrangements of blocks, have appeared with surprising frequency in AI research and are known as "blocks world" problems.

In spite of SHRDLU's success in conversing about arrangements of blocks, its methods did not generalize from the blocks world. The representational techniques used in the program were too simple to capture the semantic organization of much richer real-world domains in a useful way. Much of the current work in natural language understanding is devoted to finding representational formalisms that are general enough to be used in a wide range of applications, yet adapt themselves well to the specific structure of a given domain. A number of different techniques (most of which are extensions or modifications of *semantic networks*) are explored for this purpose and used in the development of programs that can understand natural language in constrained but interesting knowledge domains. General natural language understanding, however, remains beyond the current state of the art.

1.2.5   Modeling Human Performance

Although much of the above discussion uses human intelligence as a reference point in considering artificial intelligence, it does not follow that programs should pattern themselves after the organization of the human mind. Indeed, many AI programs are engineered to solve some useful problem without regard for their similarities to human mental architecture. Even expert systems, while deriving much of their knowledge from human experts, do not really attempt to simulate human internal mental processes. If performance is the only criterion by which a system will be judged, there may be little reason to attempt to simulate human problem-solving methods; in fact, programs that take nonhuman approaches to solving problems are often more successful than their human counterparts. Still, the design of systems that explicitly model some aspect of human problem solving has been a fertile area of research in both artificial intelligence and psychology.

Human performance modeling, in addition to providing AI with much of its basic methodology, has proved to be a very powerful tool for formulating and testing theories of human cognition. The problem-solving methodologies developed by computer scientists have given psychologists a new metaphor for exploring the human mind. Rather than casting theories of cognition in the vague language used in early research, or abandoning the problem of describing the inner workings of the human mind entirely (as suggested by the behaviorists), many psychologists have adopted the language and theory of computer science to formulate models of human intelligence. Not only do these techniques provide a new vocabulary for describing human intelligence, but also computer implementations of these theories offer psychologists an opportunity to empirically test, critique, and refine their ideas. Further discussion of the relationship between artificial intelligence and efforts to understand human intelligence is found throughout the text and summarized in Chapter 15.

1.2.6 Planning and Robotics

Planning is an important aspect of the effort to design robots that perform their task with some degree of flexibility and responsiveness to the outside world. Briefly, planning assumes a robot that is capable of performing certain atomic actions. It attempts to find a sequence of those actions that will accomplish some higher-level task such as moving across an obstacle-filled room.

Planning is a difficult problem for a number of reasons, not the least of which is the size of the space of possible sequences of moves. Even an extremely simple robot is capable of generating a vast number of potential move sequences. Imagine, for example, a robot that can move forward, backward, right, or left, and consider how many different ways that robot can possibly move around a room. Assume also that there are obstacles in the room and that the robot must select a path that moves around them in some efficient fashion. Writing a program that can intelligently discover the best path under these circumstances, without being overwhelmed by the huge number of possibilities, requires sophisticated techniques for representing spatial knowledge and controlling search.

One method that human beings use in planning is *hierarchical problem decomposition*. If you are planning a trip to London, you will generally treat the problems of arranging a flight, getting to the airport, making airline connections, and finding ground transportation in London separately, even though they are all part of a bigger overall plan. Each of these may be further decomposed into smaller subproblems such as finding a map of the city, negotiating the subway system, and finding a decent pub. Not only does this approach effectively restrict the size of the space that must be searched, but also you can save frequently used subplans for future use.

While humans plan effortlessly, creating a computer program that can do the same is a difficult challenge. A seemingly simple task such as breaking a problem into independent subproblems actually requires sophisticated heuristics and extensive knowledge about the planning domain. Determining what subplans should be saved and how they may be generalized for future use is an even harder problem, which is currently explored in research situations (Chapter 15).

A robot that blindly performs a sequence of actions without responding to changes in its environment or being able to detect and correct errors in its own plan could hardly be considered intelligent. Often, a robot will have to formulate a plan based on incomplete information and correct its behavior as it executes the plan. A robot may not have adequate sensors to locate all obstacles in the way of a projected path. Such a robot must begin moving through the room based on what it has ''perceived'' and correct its path as other obstacles are detected. Organizing plans in a fashion that allows response to environmental conditions is another major problem for planning.

1.2.7 Languages and Environments for AI

Some of the most important by-products of artificial intelligence research are advances in programming languages and software development environments. For a number of reasons, including the sheer size of most AI application programs, the tendency of search algorithms to generate huge spaces, and the difficulty of predicting the behavior of heuristically driven programs, AI programmers have been forced to develop a powerful set of programming methodologies.

Programming environments include knowledge-structuring techniques such as object-oriented programming and expert systems frameworks (these are discussed in Part IV). High-level languages, such as LISP and PROLOG, which strongly support modular development, help manage program size and complexity. Trace packages allow a programmer to reconstruct the execution of a complex algorithm and make it possible to unravel the complexities of heuristically guided search. Without such tools and techniques, it is doubtful that many significant AI systems could have been built.

Many of these techniques are now standard tools for software engineering and have little relationship to the core of AI theory. Others, such as object-oriented programming, are of significant theoretical and practical interest (Chapters 9, 12, 13, and 14).

The languages developed for artificial intelligence programming are intimately bound to the theoretical structure of the field. We cover both LISP and PROLOG in this text and prefer to remain apart from religious debates over the relative merits of these languages. Rather, we adhere to the adage "a good workman knows all of his (or her) tools." The language chapters (6, 7, 12, and 13) discuss the advantages of each language for specific programming tasks.

1.2.8   Machine Learning

Learning has remained a difficult problem for AI programs, in spite of their success as problem solvers. This shortcoming seems severe, particularly since the ability to learn is one of the most important components of intelligent behavior. An expert system may perform extensive and costly computations to solve a problem. Unlike a human being, however, if it is given the same or a similar problem a second time, it will not remember the solution. It performs the same sequence of computations again. This is true the second, third, fourth, and every time it solves that problem—hardly the behavior of an intelligent problem solver.

Most expert systems are hindered by the inflexibility of their problem-solving strategies and the difficulty of modifying large amounts of code. The obvious solution to these problems is for programs to learn on their own, either from experience, analogy, and examples or by being "told" what to do.

Learning is a difficult area of research. Several programs have been written that suggest that this is not an impossible goal. Perhaps the most striking such program is AM, the Automatic Mathematician, designed to discover mathematical laws (Lenat 1977, 1982). Initially given the concepts and axioms of set theory, AM was able to induce such important mathematical concepts as cardinality and integer arithmetic and many of the results of number theory. AM conjectured new theorems by modifying its current knowledge base and used heuristics to pursue the most "interesting" of a number of possible alternatives.

Other influential work includes Patrick Winston's research on the induction of structural concepts such as "arch" from a set of examples in the blocks world (Winston 1975a). Meta-DENDRAL learns rules for interpreting mass spectrographic data in organic chemistry from examples of data on known compounds of known structure.

Teiresias, an intelligent "front end" for expert systems, converts high-level advice into new rules for its knowledge base (Davis 1982). Hacker devises plans for performing blocks world manipulations through an iterative process of devising a plan, testing it, and correcting any flaws discovered in the candidate plan (Sussman 1975).

The success of these and other machine learning programs suggests the existence of a set of general learning principles that will allow the construction of programs with the ability to learn in realistic domains. We discuss machine learning in more detail in Chapter 15.

1.3 Artificial Intelligence—A Summary

We have attempted to define artificial intelligence through a discussion of the major areas of research and application in the field. This survey reveals a young and promising field of study whose primary concern is finding an effective way to understand and apply intelligent problem-solving, planning, and communication skills to a wide range of practical problems. In spite of the variety of problems addressed in artificial intelligence research, a number of important features emerge that seem common to all divisions of the field; these include:

1. The use of computers to do symbolic reasoning.
2. A focus on problems that do not respond to algorithmic solutions. This underlies the reliance on heuristic search as an AI problem-solving technique.
3. A concern with problem solving using inexact, missing, or poorly defined information and the use of representational formalisms that enable the programmer to compensate for these problems.
4. An effort to capture and manipulate the significant qualitative features of a situation rather than relying on numeric methods.
5. An attempt to deal with issues of semantic meaning as well as syntactic form.
6. Answers that are neither exact nor optimal, but are in some sense "sufficient." This is a result of the essential reliance on heuristic problem-solving methods in situations where optimal or exact results are either too expensive or not possible.
7. The use of large amounts of domain-specific knowledge in solving problems. This is the basis of expert systems.
8. The use of meta-level knowledge to effect more sophisticated control of problem-solving strategies. Although this is a very difficult problem, addressed in relatively few current systems, it is emerging as an essential area of research.

We hope that this introduction provides some feel for the overall structure and significance of the field of artificial intelligence. We also hope that the brief discussions of such technical issues as search and representation were not excessively cryptic and obscure; they are developed in proper detail throughout the remainder of the text. They were included here to demonstrate their significance in the more general organization of the field.

As we mentioned in the discussion of knowledge representation, objects take on meaning through their relationships with other objects. This is equally true of the facts, theories, and techniques that constitute a field of scientific study. We have intended to give a sense of those interrelationships, so that when the separate technical themes of artificial intelligence are presented, they will find their place in a developing understanding of the overall substance and directions of the field. In writing this text we were guided by an observation made by Gregory Bateson, the psychologist and systems theorist (Bateson 1979):

> Break the pattern which connects the items of learning and you necessarily destroy all quality.

1.4   Epilogue and References

The challenging field of AI reflects some of the oldest concerns of Western civilization in the light of the modern computational model. The notions of rationality, representation, and reason are now under scrutiny as perhaps never before, since we computer scientists demand to understand them operationally, even algorithmically! At the same time, the political, economic, and ethical situation of our species forces us to confront our responsibility for the effects of our artifices. The interplay between applications and the more humanistic inspirations for much of AI continues to inspire hosts of rich, challenging questions. We hope you will glean from the following chapters both a familiarity with the contemporary concepts and techniques of AI and an appreciation for the timelessness of the problems they address.

Several excellent sources available on the topics raised in this chapter are *Mind Design* (Haugheland 1981), *Artificial Intelligence: The Very Idea* (Haugheland 1985), *Brainstorms* (Dennett 1978), and *Elbow Room* (Dennett 1984). Several of the primary sources are also readily available, including Aristotle's *Physics, Metaphysics,* and *Logic,* papers by Frege, and the writings of Babbage, Boole, and Russell and Whitehead. Turing's papers are also very interesting, especially his discussions of the nature of intelligence and the possibility of designing intelligent programs (Turing, 1950). Turing's biography, *Alan Turing: The Enigma* (Hodges 1983), also makes excellent reading.

Computer Power and Human Reason (Weizenbaum 1976) and *Understanding Computers and Cognition* (Winograd and Flores 1986) offer some sobering comments on the limitations of and ethical issues in AI. *The Sciences of the Artificial* (Simon 1981) is a positive statement on the possibility of artificial intelligence and its role in society.

The AI applications mentioned in Section 1.2 are intended to introduce the reader to the broad interests of AI researchers and outline many of the important questions under investigation. The *Handbook of Artificial Intelligence* (Barr and Feigenbaum 1981) offers an introduction to each of these areas. Besides the *Handbook* we recommend, for extended treatment of game playing, *Principles of Artificial Intelligence* (Nilsson 1980) and *Heuristics* (Pearl 1984); this is also an important topic in our chapters 2 through 5. We discuss automated reasoning in chapters 2, 3, and 11; some of the highlights in the literature of automated reasoning are *Automated Reasoning* (Wos et al. 1984), ''Non-resolution theorem proving'' (Bledsoe 1977), and *A Computational Logic* (Boyer and Moore 1979).

After reading our chapters 8 and 14, the reader can get a good feel of the area for expert systems in *Expert Systems: Artificial Intelligence in Business* (Harmon and King 1985), *Building Expert Systems* (Hayes-Roth et al. 1983), and *A Guide to Expert Systems* (Waterman 1986). Natural language understanding is a dynamic field of study; some important points of view are expressed in *Natural Language Understanding* (Allen 1987), *Language as a Cognitive Process* (Winograd 1983), *Inside Computer Understanding* (Schank and Riesbeck 1981), *Computer Models of Thought and Language* (Schank and Colby 1973), and *Grammar, Meaning and the Machine Analysis of Language* (Wilks 1972); an introduction to the field is presented in our chapters 9 and 10.

Using computers to model human performance, which we present in Chapter 15, is discussed in some depth in *Human Problem Solving* (Newell and Simon 1972), *Computation and Cognition* (Pylyshyn 1984), and ''Arguments concerning representations for mental imagery'' (Anderson 1978). Planning and robotics (see our Chapter 15) are well surveyed in Volume 3 of the *Handbook of Artificial Intelligence*.

The subject of AI-oriented languages and environments is explored in chapters 6, 12, 13, and 14 of this text; see also *Principles of Programming Languages* (MacLennan 1987) and *Smalltalk/V* (Anon. Digitalk 1986). Machine learning is discussed in some detail in Chapter 15; volumes I & II of *Machine Learning* (Michalski et al. 1983, 1986) and the *Journal of Machine Learning* are important sources.

1.5   Exercises

1. Create and justify your own definition of artificial intelligence.

2. Give several other examples of Aristotle's distinction between ''matter'' and ''form.'' Can you show how your examples might fit into a theory of abstraction?

3. Much traditional Western thought has dwelt on the mind-body relationship. Are the mind and body:

   a. distinct entities somehow interacting, or
   b. is mind an expression of ''physical processes,'' or
   c. is body just an illusion of the rational mind?

   Discuss your thoughts on the mind-body problem and its importance for a theory of artificial intelligence.

4. Criticize Turing's criteria for computer software being ''intelligent.''

5. Describe your own criteria for computer software to be considered ''intelligent.''

6. Although computing is a relatively new discipline, philosophers and mathematicians have been thinking about the issues involved in automating problem solving for thousands of years. What is your opinion of the relevance of these philosophical issues to the design of a device for intelligent problem solving? Justify your answer.

7. Given the differences between the architectures of modern computers and that of the human brain, what relevance does research into the physiological structure and function of biological systems have for the engineering of AI programs? Justify your answer.

8. Pick one problem area that you feel would justify the energy required to design an expert system solution. Spell the problem out in some detail. Based on your own intuition, which aspects of this solution would be most difficult to automate?

9. Add two more benefits for expert systems to those already listed in the text. Discuss these in terms of intellectual, social, or financial results.

10. List and discuss two potentially negative effects on society of the development of artificial intelligence techniques.

PART II

ARTIFICIAL INTELLIGENCE AS REPRESENTATION AND SEARCH

All sciences characterize the essential nature of the systems they study. These characterizations are invariably qualitative in nature, for they set the terms with which more detailed knowledge can be developed. . . .

The study of logic and computers has revealed to us that intelligence resides in physical-symbol systems. This is computer science's most basic law of qualitative structure. Symbol systems are collections of patterns and processes, the latter being capable of producing, destroying and modifying the former. The most important property of patterns is that they can designate objects, processes or other patterns, and that when they designate processes they can be interpreted. . . .

A second law of qualitative structure for artificial intelligence is that symbol-systems solve problems by generating potential solutions and testing them—that is by searching. Solutions are usually sought by creating symbolic expressions and modifying them sequentially until they satisfy the conditions for a solution.

—NEWELL AND SIMON, ACM *Turing Award Lecture, 1976 (Newell and Simon 1976)*

In their Turing Award Lecture, Newell and Simon argue that intelligent activity, in either human or machine, is achieved through the use of:

1. Symbol patterns to represent significant aspects of a problem domain.
2. Operations on these patterns to generate potential solutions to problems.
3. Search to select a solution from among these possibilities.

These assumptions form the basis for what is known as the *physical symbol system hypothesis* (Section 16.1). This hypothesis justifies our efforts to build intelligent machines and makes explicit the underlying assumptions of artificial intelligence research.

The physical symbol system hypothesis implicitly distinguishes between the *patterns* formed by an arrangement of symbols and the *medium* used to implement them. If intelligence derives only from the structure of a symbol system, then any medium that successfully implements the correct patterns and processes will achieve intelligence, regardless of whether it is composed of neurons, logic circuits, or Tinkertoys. The possibility of building a machine that will pass the Turing test depends on this distinction. According to the Church-Turing thesis (Machtey and Young 1979), computers are capable of implementing *any* effectively described symbolic process. It follows that a properly programmed digital computer will achieve intelligence.

The physical symbol system hypothesis also outlines the major foci of AI research and application development: defining the symbol structures and operations necessary for intelligent problem solving and developing strategies to efficiently and correctly search the potential solutions generated by these structures and operations. These are the interrelated issues of *knowledge representation* and *search*; together, they are at the heart of modern research in artificial intelligence.

The physical symbol system hypothesis is disputed by critics who argue that intelligence is inherently biological and existential and cannot be captured symbolically (Searle 1980; Winograd and Flores 1986). These arguments provide a well-considered challenge to the dominant direction of AI research, and we examine them in Chapter 16. In spite of these challenges, the assumptions of the physical symbol system hypothesis underlie nearly all practical and theoretical work in expert systems, planning, and natural language understanding.

Knowledge Representation

The function of any representation scheme is to capture the essential features of a problem domain and make that information accessible to a problem-solving procedure. It is obvious that a representation language must allow the programmer to express the knowledge needed for a problem solution. It is also important that the resulting programs be computationally efficient. *Expressiveness* and *efficiency* are major dimensions for evaluating knowledge representation languages. As we will see (chapters 9 and 10), many highly expressive representations are too inefficient for use in certain classes of problems. Sometimes, expressiveness must be sacrificed to improve efficiency. This must be done without limiting the representation's ability to capture essential problem-solving knowledge. Optimizing this trade-off is a major task for designers of intelligent systems.

Knowledge representation languages are also tools for helping humans solve problems. As such, a representation should provide a *natural* framework for expressing problem-solving knowledge; it should make that knowledge available to the computer and assist the programmer in its organization.

The computer representation of floating-point numbers illustrates these trade-offs (see Figure II.1). In general, real numbers require an infinite string of digits to be fully described; this cannot be accomplished on a finite device, indeed a finite-state machine. The best answer to this dilemma is to represent the number in two pieces: its *significant*

The real number: π

The decimal equivalent: 3.1415927 . . .

The floating point representation: 31416 │ 1

                                              ↑   ↑
                                              │   └── Exponent
                                              └───────── Mantissa

The representation in computer memory: 11100010

Figure II.1   Different representations of the real number π.

digits and the location within those digits of the decimal point. Thus, while it is not possible to actually store a real number in a computer, it is possible to create a representation that captures its important features.

Floating-point representation thus sacrifices full expressive power in order to make the representation efficient, in this case to make it possible. The representation allows algorithms for multiple-precision arithmetic, giving effectively infinite precision by limiting round-off error to any prespecified tolerance. It also guarantees well-behaved round-off errors. Like all representations, it is only an abstraction, a symbol pattern that designates a desired entity and not the entity itself.

The array is another representation common in computer science. For many problems, it is more natural and efficient than the memory architecture implemented in computer hardware. This gain in naturalness and efficiency involves compromises in expressiveness, as illustrated by the following example from image processing. Figure II.2 is a digitized image of human chromosomes in a stage called metaphase. The image is processed to determine the number and structure of the chromosomes, looking for breaks, missing pieces, and other abnormalities.

The visual scene is made up of a number of picture points. Each picture point, or *pixel*, has both a location and a number value representing its gray level. It is natural, then, to collect the entire scene into a two-dimensional array where the row and column address gives the location of a pixel (X and Y coordinates) and the content of the array element is the gray level at that point. Algorithms are designed to perform operations like looking for isolated points to remove noise from the image, finding threshold levels for discerning objects and edges, summing contiguous elements to determine size or density, and in various other ways transforming the picture point data. Implementing these algorithms is straightforward, given the array representation and the FORTRAN language. This task would be quite cumbersome using other representations such as the predicate calculus, records, or assembly code, because these do not have a natural fit with the material being represented.

When we represent the picture as an array of pixel points, we sacrifice fineness of resolution (compare a photo in a newspaper to the original print of the same picture). In addition, pixel arrays cannot express the deeper semantic organization of the image. For example, a pixel array cannot represent the organization of chromosomes in a single cell nucleus, their genetic function, or the role of metaphase in cell division. This knowledge is more easily captured using a representation like predicate calculus (Chapter 2) or semantic networks (Chapter 9).

Figure II.2 Digitized image of chromosomes in metaphase.

A representational scheme should:

1. Be adequate to express all of the necessary information.
2. Support efficient execution of the resulting code.
3. Provide a natural scheme for expressing the required knowledge.

McDermott and others have stated that the key to writing a successful knowledge-based program is the selection of appropriate representational tools. Often, lower-level language (BASIC, FORTRAN, etc.) programmers fail in building expert systems simply because these languages do not provide the representational power and modularity required for knowledge-based programming (McDermott 1981).

In general, the problems AI attempts to solve do not lend themselves to the representations offered by more traditional formalisms such as arrays. Artificial intelligence is concerned with qualitative rather than quantitative problem solving, with reasoning rather than calculation, with organizing large and varied amounts of knowledge rather than implementing a single, well-defined algorithm. In order to support these needs, an AI representation language must:

A. Handle qualitative knowledge.
B. Allow new knowledge to be inferred from a basic set of facts.
C. Allow representation of general principles as well as specific situations.
D. Capture complex semantic meaning.
E. Allow for meta-level reasoning.

These topics make up the remainder of our discussion of knowledge representation.

A. Handle qualitative knowledge.

Artificial intelligence programming requires a means of capturing and reasoning about the *qualitative* aspects of a problem. As a simple example, consider Figure II.3, the arrangement of blocks on a table:

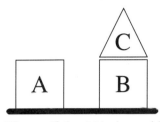

Figure II.3 A blocks world.

One way to represent this blocks arrangement would be to use a Cartesian coordinate system, giving the X and Y coordinates of each vertex of a block. While this approach certainly describes the blocks world and is the correct representation for many tasks, it fails to capture directly the properties and relations required for qualitative reasoning. These include determining which blocks are stacked on other blocks and which blocks have clear tops so that they can be picked up. *Predicate calculus*, a subset of formal logic, directly captures this descriptive information. Using predicate calculus, the blocks world could be described by the logical assertions:

```
clear(c).
clear(a).
ontable(a).
ontable(b).
on(c, b).
cube(b).
cube(a).
pyramid(c).
```

The first word of each expression (**on, ontable**, etc.) is a *predicate* denoting some property or relationship among its arguments (appearing within parentheses). The arguments are symbols denoting objects (blocks) in the domain. The collection of logical clauses describes the important properties and relationships of the blocks world. Predicate calculus provides artificial intelligence programmers with a well-defined language for describing and reasoning about qualitative aspects of a system. While it is not the only approach to representation, it is probably the best understood. In addition, it is sufficiently general to provide a foundation for other formal models of knowledge representation. Predicate calculus is discussed in detail in Chapter 2.

B.   Allow new knowledge to be inferred from a basic set of facts.

The ability to infer additional knowledge from a basic world description is essential to any intelligent entity. Humans, for example, do not store an inflexible description of every situation encountered; this would be impossible. Rather, we are able to formulate and reason from abstract descriptions of classes of objects and situations. A knowledge representation language must provide this capability.

In the blocks world example, we might like to define a test to determine whether a block is *clear*, that is, has nothing stacked on top of it. This is important if a robot hand is to pick it up or stack another block on top of it. It is not necessary to explicitly add this to our description for all such blocks. Instead, we define a general rule that allows the system to infer this information from the given facts. In predicate calculus, the rule can be written

$$\forall\, X \,\neg\, \exists\, Y \; on(Y,X) \Rightarrow clear(X)$$

or, "for all X, X is clear if there does not exist a Y such that Y is on X." This rule can be applied to a variety of situations by substituting different values for X and Y. By letting the programmer form general rules of inference, predicate calculus allows much greater economy of representation, as well as the possibility of designing systems that are flexible and general enough to respond intelligently to a range of situations.

C.   Allow representation of general principles as well as specific situations.

In addition to demonstrating the use of logical rules to infer additional knowledge from basic facts, the blocks example introduced the use of variables in the predicate calculus. Because an intelligent system must be as general as possible, any useful representation language needs variables. The requirements of qualitative reasoning make the use and implementation of variables subtly different from their treatment in traditional programming languages. The assignment, type, and scope rules we find in calculation-oriented languages are too restrictive for reasoning systems. Good knowledge representation languages handle the bindings of variable names, objects, and values in a highly dynamic fashion (chapters 2, 6, 7, and 14).

D.   Capture complex semantic meaning.

Many artificial intelligence problem domains require large amounts of highly structured interrelated knowledge. It is not sufficient to describe a car by listing its component parts; a valid description must also describe the ways in which those parts are combined and the interactions between them. This view of structure is essential to a range of situations including taxonomic information, such as the classification of plants by genus and species, or a description of complex objects such as a diesel engine or a human body in terms of their component parts. In our blocks example, the interactions among predicates were the basis of a complete description of the arrangement.

Semantic relationships are also important in describing the causal relationships between events occurring over time. These are necessary to understand simple narratives such as a child's story or to represent a robot's plan of action as a sequence of atomic actions that must be executed in order.

While all of these situations can ultimately be represented as collections of predicates or similar formalisms, some higher-level notion of structure is desirable to help both program and programmer deal with complex concepts in a coherent fashion. For example, a simple description of a bluebird might be ''a bluebird is a small blue-colored bird and a bird is a feathered flying vertebrate.'' This may be represented as a set of logical predicates:

```
size(bluebird,small).
hascovering(bird,feathers).
hascolor(bluebird,blue).
hasproperty(bird,flies).
isa(bluebird,bird).
isa(bird,vertebrate).
```

This description could also be represented graphically by using the *arcs* (or *links*) in a graph instead of predicates to indicate relations (Fig. II.4). This description, called a *semantic network*, is a fundamental technique for representing semantic meaning.

Because relationships are explicitly denoted by the links of the graph, an algorithm for reasoning about the domain could make relevant associations simply by following links. In the bluebird illustration, a system need only follow two links in order to determine that a bluebird is a vertebrate. This is more efficient than exhaustively searching a data base of predicate calculus descriptions of the form isa(X,Y).

In addition, knowledge may be organized to reflect the natural class-instance structure of the domain. Certain links in a semantic network (the *ISA* links in Fig. II.4) indicate class membership and allow properties attached to a class description to be *inherited* by all members of the class. This inheritance mechanism is built into the language itself and allows knowledge to be stored at the highest possible level of abstraction. Inheritance is a natural tool for representing taxonomically structured information and

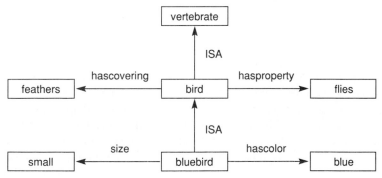

Figure II.4 Semantic network description of a bluebird.

ensures that all members of a class share common properties. Because of these gains in efficiency and naturalness of expression and because they make the power of graph theory available for reasoning about the structural organization of a knowledge base, semantic nets are an important alternative to predicate calculus. Semantic networks are discussed in detail in Chapter 9.

We have just seen an example of a single problem description having two or more representations. Selecting the proper representation is a critical task for AI programmers. The benefits of a higher-level representation such as a semantic network are not unlike the advantages of a higher-level programming language such as Pascal over low-level machine code: although every Pascal program is ultimately compiled down to machine code, a higher-level language is almost essential for the creation of well-designed, coherent programs. Continuing this simile, predicate calculus or LISP s-expressions may be thought of as machine languages for AI representation. AI knowledge-structuring techniques such as frames, semantic networks, scripts, and plans provide more powerful constructs for organizing knowledge (chapters 9 and 14).

E.   Allow for meta-level reasoning.

An intelligent system not only should know things but also should know what it knows. It should be able not only to solve problems but also to explain how it solved the problems and why it made certain decisions. It should be able to describe its knowledge in both specific and general terms, recognize the limitations of its knowledge, and learn from its interactions with the world. This "knowing about what you know" constitutes a higher level of knowledge called *meta-knowledge*, and its automation is essential to the design and development of truly intelligent systems.

The problem of formalizing meta-knowledge was first explored by Bertrand Russell in his theory of logical types. Briefly, if sets are allowed to be members of other sets (a situation analogous to having knowledge about knowledge), it is possible to have sets that are members of themselves. As Russell discovered, this leads to irresolvable paradoxes. Russell disallowed these paradoxes by classifying sets as being of different types depending on whether they were sets of individuals, sets of sets of individuals, etc. Sets could not be members of sets of a smaller or equal type number. This corresponds to the distinctions between knowledge and meta-knowledge. As Russell discovered, there are numerous difficulties in attempting to formally describe this reasoning (Whitehead and Russell 1950).

The ability to learn from examples, from experience, or even from high-level instructions (as opposed to being programmed) depends on the application of meta-knowledge. The representational techniques developed for AI programming offer the flexibility and modifiability required of learning systems and form a basis for this research (chapters 14 and 15).

In order to meet the needs of symbolic computing, artificial intelligence has developed representation languages such as the predicate calculus, semantic networks, frames (Chapter 9), and objects (Chapter 14). LISP and PROLOG are languages for implementing these and other representations. All of these tools are examined in detail throughout the text.

Problem Solving as Search

The second aspect of Newell and Simon's symbol system hypothesis, that problems are solved by searching among alternative choices, is supported by a commonsense view of human problem solving. Humans generally consider a number of alternative strategies on their way to solving a problem. A chess player typically considers a number of possible next moves, selecting the best according to such criteria as the opponent's possible responses or the degree to which various moves support some global game strategy. A player also considers short-term gain (such as taking the opponent's queen), opportunities to sacrifice a piece for positional advantage, or conjectures concerning the opponent's psychological makeup and level of skill. A mathematician will choose from a different but no less complex set of strategies to find a proof for a difficult theorem, a physician may systematically evaluate a number of possible diagnoses, and so on. This aspect of intelligent behavior underlies the problem-solving technique of *state space search*.

Consider, as a simple example, the game of tic-tac-toe. Given any board situation, there is only a finite number of moves that a player can make. Starting with an empty board, the first player may place an **X** in any one of nine places. Each of these moves yields a different board that will allow the opponent eight possible responses, and so on. We can represent this collection of possible moves and responses by regarding each board configuration as a *node* in a graph. The *links* of the graph represent legal moves from one board configuration to another. These nodes thus correspond to different *states* of the game board. The resulting structure is called a *state space graph*.

If we begin with an empty board (indicating the start of a game) and construct a graph through the process of drawing links from the board to all board states that may be reached through a legal move, we will construct the state space graph for the game of tic-tac-toe (Fig. II.5). The significance of this construction is that by starting at the node representing a new board and moving along arcs until we get to a state representing either a win or a tie, it is possible to trace the sequence of moves in any potential game. The state space representation thus enables us to treat all possible games of tic-tac-toe as different paths through this state space graph. Given this representation, an effective game strategy will search through the graph for the paths that lead to the most wins and fewest losses and play in a way that always tries to force the game along one of these optimal paths. Not only is this strategy an effective one but also because of the regularity and precision of the state space representation, it is straightforward to implement on a computer.

As an example of how search is used to solve a more complicated problem, consider the task of diagnosing a mechanical fault in an automobile. Although this problem does not initially seem to lend itself to state space search as easily as tic-tac-toe or chess, it actually fits this strategy quite well. Instead of letting each node of the state space graph represent a "board state," we let it represent a state of partial knowledge about the automobile's mechanical problems. The process of examining the symptoms of the fault and inducing its cause may be thought of as searching through states of increasing knowledge. The starting node of the graph is empty, indicating that nothing is known about the cause of the problem. The first thing a mechanic might do is ask the customer

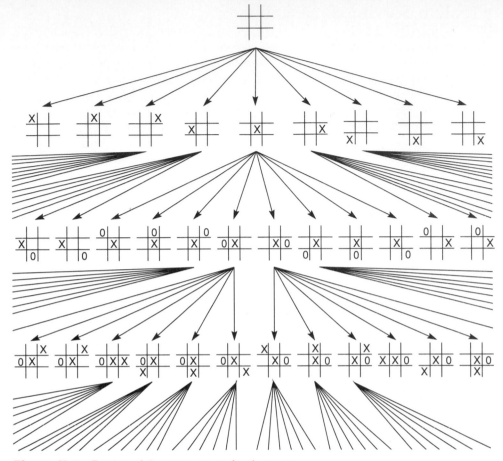

Figure II.5 Portion of the state space for tic-tac-toe.

which major system (engine, transmission, steering, brakes, etc.) seems to be causing the trouble. This is represented by a collection of arcs from the start states to states that indicate a focus on a single subsystem of the automobile (Fig. II.6).

Each of the states in the graph has arcs (corresponding to basic diagnostic checks) that lead to states representing further accumulation of knowledge in the diagnostic process. For example, the engine trouble node has arcs to nodes labeled engine starts and engine won't start. From the won't start node we may move to nodes labeled turns over and won't turn over. The won't turn over node has arcs to nodes labeled battery dead and battery ok (Fig. II.7).

We can construct a graph that includes all possible diagnostic checks and leads to a set of nodes that represent final diagnostic conclusions. A problem solver can diagnose car trouble by searching for a path through this graph that is consistent with the symptoms of a particular defective car. Note that the diagnostic checks performed in a given instance are determined by the path through the graph, with each decision eliminating certain tests from consideration. Although this problem is very different from that of

Figure II.6 State space description of the first step in diagnosing an automotive problem.

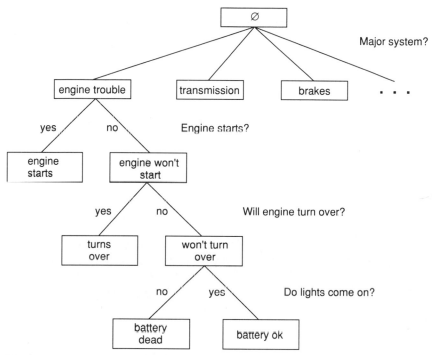

Figure II.7 State space description of the automotive diagnosis problem.

finding an optimal way to play tic-tac-toe, it is equally amenable to solution by state space search.

In spite of this apparent universality, state space search is not, by itself, sufficient for automating intelligent problem-solving behavior; if it were, intelligent machines would already be a reality. It would be fairly simple, for example, to write a program that plays chess by searching through the entire state space for the sequence of moves most likely to bring a victory. This problem-solving method is known as *exhaustive search*. While exhaustive search can be applied to any state space, the overwhelming size of the state space for interesting problems makes this approach a practical impossibility. The game of chess, for example, has approximately 10^{120} different board states. This is a number larger than the number of molecules in the universe or the number of nanoseconds that have passed since the "big bang". Search of a space that large is well beyond the capabilities of any computing device whose dimensions must be confined to the known universe and whose execution must be completed before that universe succumbs to the ravages of entropy.

Throughout the text we show how state space search may be used to approach practically any problem. Search provides a framework for automating problem solving, but it is a framework devoid of intelligence. It enables us to give a problem a formal description that can be implemented in a computer program, but simple exhaustive search of a large space is generally impractical and intuitively fails to capture the substance of intelligent activity.

Humans use search: a chess player considers a number of possible moves, a doctor examines several possible diagnoses, a computer scientist entertains different designs before beginning to write code. Human beings do not use exhaustive search: the chess player examines only moves that experience has shown to be effective, the doctor does not require tests that are not somehow indicated by the symptoms at hand, software design is guided by experience and theoretical sophistication. Human problem solving seems to be based on judgmental rules that guide our search to those portions of the state space that seem somehow "promising".

These rules are known as *heuristics*, and they constitute one of the central topics of AI research. A heuristic, (the name is taken from the Greek word "to discover") is a strategy for selectively searching a problem space. It guides our search along lines that have a high probability of success while avoiding wasted or apparently stupid efforts. Human beings use a large number of heuristics in problem solving. If you ask a mechanic why your car is overheating, she may say something like "Usually that means the thermostat is bad." If you ask a doctor what could cause nausea and stomach pains, he might say it is "probably either stomach flu or food poisoning."

Heuristics are not foolproof: even the best game strategy can be defeated, diagnostic tools developed by expert physicians sometimes fail, experienced mathematicians sometimes fail to prove a difficult theorem. But while it does not always guarantee an optimal solution to a problem, a good heuristic can and should come close most of the time. Most important, it employs knowledge about the nature of a problem to find a solution efficiently.

If state space search gives us a means of formalizing the problem-solving process, then heuristics allow us to infuse that formalism with intelligence. These techniques are discussed in detail in the early chapters of this text and remain at the heart of most modern work in AI, including expert systems, natural language understanding, theorem provers and learning.

Throughout the text we explore the theoretical aspects of knowledge representation and search and the use of this theory in building effective programs. The treatment of knowledge representation begins with the predicate calculus (Chapter 2). Although the predicate calculus is only one of the schemes used in knowledge representation, it has the advantage of a well-defined semantics and provably correct *inference rules*. Using logic, we introduce the issues of knowledge representation and its relationship to search. Once the reader has gained experience in these issues, we demonstrate limitations of the predicate calculus and introduce alternative representation schemes (chapters 9 and 14).

Chapter 3 introduces search in the context of simple games. By beginning with games, we can study the issues involved in state space search without the problems involved in representing real-world problems. This methodology is then applied to the more complex state spaces defined by logic problem solvers and expert systems (chapters 4, 5 and 8).

In Chapter 4, we discuss the implementation of search algorithms, with particular attention to production systems, a general and powerful model of search-based problem solving. Chapter 5 looks at the use of heuristics to guide search, again beginning with games and then generalizing these observations to more complex problems.

THE PREDICATE CALCULUS

A science is more exact than, and prior to, another when it studies the fact and the reason, not just the fact apart from the reason.

A science that studies properties not as contained in a subject is prior to one that treats them in that relationship. Arithmetic is prior to harmonics.

A science that works with fewer principles is prior to one that requires additional principles· arithmetic is prior to geometry.

—ARISTOTLE, *Posterior Analytics, Book 1*

2.0 Introduction

In this chapter we introduce the predicate calculus as a representation language for artificial intelligence. The importance of the predicate calculus was discussed in the introduction to Part II; these advantages include a well-defined *formal semantics* and *sound* and *complete* inference rules. This chapter begins with a brief review of the propositional calculus (Section 2.1). Section 2.2 defines the syntax and semantics of the predicate calculus. In Section 2.3 we discuss predicate calculus inference rules and their use in problem solving. Finally, the chapter demonstrates the use of the predicate calculus to implement a knowledge base of financial investment advice.

2.1 The Propositional Calculus (Optional Review)

2.1.1 Symbols and Sentences

The propositional calculus and, in the next subsection, the predicate calculus are first of all languages. Using their words, phrases, and sentences, we can represent and reason about properties and relationships in the world. The first step in describing a language is to introduce the pieces that make it up: its set of symbols.

DEFINITION

PROPOSITIONAL CALCULUS SYMBOLS

The *symbols* of propositional calculus are the propositional symbols:

P, Q, R, S, T, ...

truth symbols:

true, false

and connectives:

$\land, \lor, \neg, \Rightarrow, =$

Propositional symbols denote *propositions*, or statements about the world that may be either true or false, such as "the car is red" or "water is wet." Propositions are denoted by uppercase letters near the end of the English alphabet.

Sentences in the propositional calculus are formed from these atomic symbols according to the following rules:

DEFINITION

PROPOSITIONAL CALCULUS SENTENCES

Every propositional symbol and truth symbol is a sentence.

For example: true, P, Q, and R are four sentences.

The *negation* of a sentence is a sentence.

For example: $\neg$P and $\neg$false are sentences.

The *conjunction* or *and* of two sentences is a sentence.

For example: P$\land\neg$P is a sentence.

The *disjunction* or *or* of two sentences is a sentence.

For example: P$\lor\neg$P is a sentence.

The *implication* of one sentence for another is a sentence.

For example: P$\Rightarrow$Q is a sentence.

The *equivalence* of two sentences is a sentence.

For example: P$\lor$Q=R is a sentence.

Legal sentences are also called *well-formed formulas* or *WFFs*.

In expressions of the form P∧Q, P and Q are called the *conjuncts*. In P∨Q, P and Q are referred to as *disjuncts*. In an implication, P⇒Q, P is the *premise* or *antecedent* and Q the *conclusion* or *consequent*.

In propositional calculus sentences, the symbols (and) and [and] are used to group symbols into subexpressions and so control their order of evaluation and meaning. For example, (P∨Q)=R is quite different from P∨(Q=R), as can be demonstrated using truth tables (Section 2.1.2).

We can determine whether an expression is a sentence in the propositional calculus by using this inductive definition: ''here are the basic units, here is how the basic units are composed. . . .'' Only expressions that are formed of legal symbols through some sequence of these rules are well-formed formulas. For example,

$$((P∧Q)⇒R)=¬P∨¬Q∨R$$

is a well-formed sentence in the propositional calculus since:

P, Q, and R are propositions and thus sentences.

P∧Q, the conjunction of two sentences, is a sentence.

(P∧Q)⇒R, the implication of a sentence for another, is a sentence.

¬P and ¬Q, the negations of sentences, are sentences.

¬P∨¬Q, the disjunction of two sentences, is a sentence.

¬P∨¬Q∨R, the disjunction of two sentences, is a sentence.

((P∧Q)⇒R)=¬P∨¬Q∨R, the equivalence of two sentences, is a sentence.

This is our original sentence, which has been constructed through a series of applications of legal rules and is therefore well formed.

2.1.2   The Semantics of the Propositional Calculus

Section 2.1.1 presented the syntax of the propositional calculus by defining a set of rules for producing legal sentences. In this section we formally define the *semantics* or ''meaning'' of these sentences. Since AI programs must reason with their representational structures, it is important to demonstrate that the truth of their conclusions depends only on the truth of their initial knowledge, i.e., that logical errors are not introduced by the inference procedures. A precise treatment of semantics is essential to this goal.

A proposition symbol corresponds to a statement about the world. For example, P may denote the statement ''it is raining'' or Q the statement ''I live in a brown house.'' A proposition may be either true or false, given some state of the world. The truth value assignment to propositional sentences is called an *interpretation*, an assertion about their truth in some *possible world*.

Formally, an interpretation is a mapping from the propositional symbols into the set {T, F}. As mentioned in the previous section, the symbols true and false are part of the set of well-formed sentences of the propositional calculus; i.e., they are distinct from the truth value assigned to a sentence. To enforce this distinction, the symbols T and F are used for truth value assignment.

Each possible mapping corresponds to a possible world of interpretation. For example, if P denotes the proposition "it is raining" and Q denotes "I am at work," then the set of propositions {P, Q} has four different functional mappings into the truth values {T, F}. These correspond to four different possible worlds.

Given an interpretation of a set of propositions, it is necessary to define the truth values for compound expressions. These values depend on the operator used to form the expression and the truth values assigned to the operands. The semantics of propositional calculus, like its syntax, is defined inductively.

DEFINITION

PROPOSITIONAL CALCULUS SEMANTICS

An *interpretation* of a set of propositions is the assignment of a truth value, either T or F, to each propositional symbol.

The symbol true is always assigned T, and the symbol false is assigned F.

The interpretation or truth value for sentences is determined by:

The truth assignment of *negation*, ¬P, where P is any propositional symbol, is F if the assignment to P is T and T if the assignment to P is F.

The truth assignment of *conjunction*, ∧, is T only when both conjuncts have truth value T; otherwise it is F.

The truth assignment of *disjunction*, ∨, is F only when both disjuncts have truth value F; otherwise it is T.

The truth assignment of *implication*, ⇒, is F only when the premise or symbol before the implication is T and the truth value of the consequent or symbol after the implication is F; otherwise it is always T.

The truth assignment of *equivalence*, =, is T only when both expressions have the same truth assignment for all possible interpretations; otherwise it is F.

The truth assignments of compound propositions are often described in *truth tables*. A truth table lists all possible truth value assignments to the atomic propositions of an expression and gives the truth value of the expression for each assignment. In a sense, a truth table enumerates all possible worlds of interpretation that may be given to an expression.

The semantics of a connective may be defined using truth tables. For example, the truth table for P∧Q lists its truth value for each possible truth assignment to the operands. There are four possible truth assignments for a conjunctive expression:

1. Both P and Q are T, in which case P∧Q is T.
2. P is T in the world and Q is F, in which case P∧Q is F.

P	Q	P∧Q
T	T	T
T	F	F
F	T	F
F	F	F

Figure 2.1   Truth table for the operator ∧.

P	Q	¬P	¬P∨Q	P⇒Q	(¬P∨Q)=(P⇒Q)
T	T	F	T	T	T
T	F	F	F	F	T
F	T	T	T	T	T
F	F	T	T	T	T

Figure 2.2   Truth table demonstrating the equivalence of
P ⇒ Q and ¬ P ⋁ Q.

3. P is F and Q is T in the world, in which case P∧Q is F.

4. Both P and Q are F; P∧Q is also F.

The truth table for ∧ is given in Figure 2.1.

Or (∨), not (¬) implies (⇒), and equivalence (=) are defined in a similar fashion. The construction of these truth tables is left as an exercise.

Two expressions in the propositional calculus are equivalent if they have the same value under all truth value assignments. This may be proved using truth tables. For example, a proof of the equivalence of P⇒Q and ¬P∨Q is given by the truth table of Figúre 2.2.

By demonstrating that they have identical truth tables, we can prove the following propositional calculus equivalences. These expressions represent commonly used identities in the propositional calculus. The reader should confirm the truth of at least a few of them through the truth table method.

For propositional expressions P, Q, and R:

¬(¬P)=P

(P∨Q)=(¬P⇒Q)

de Morgan's law: ¬(P∨Q)=(¬P∧¬Q)

de Morgan's law: ¬(P∧Q)=(¬P∨¬Q)

distributive law: P∨(Q∧R)=(P∨Q)∧(P∨R)

distributive law: P∧(Q∨R)=(P∧Q)∨(P∧R)

commutative law: $(P \land Q)=(Q \land P)$

commutative law: $(P \lor Q)=(Q \lor P)$

associative law: $((P \land Q) \land R)=(P \land (Q \land R))$

associative law: $((P \lor Q) \lor R)=(P \lor (Q \lor R))$

contrapositive law: $(P \Rightarrow Q)=(\neg Q \Rightarrow \neg P)$

Identities such as these can be used to change predicate calculus expressions into a syntactically different but logically equivalent form. These identities may be used instead of truth tables to prove that two expressions are equivalent: find a series of identities that transform one expression into the other. An early AI program, the Logic Theorist (Newell and Simon 1956), designed by Newell, Simon, and Shaw, used transformations between equivalent forms of expressions to prove many of the theorems in Russell and Whitehead's *Principia Mathematica*. The ability to change a logical expression into a different form with equivalent truth values is also important when using inference rules (modus ponens, Section 2.4, and resolution, Chapter 11) that require expressions to be in a specific form.

2.2 The Predicate Calculus

In propositional calculus, each atomic symbol (P, Q, etc.) denotes a proposition of some complexity. There is no way to access the components of an individual assertion. Predicate calculus provides this ability. For example, instead of letting a single propositional symbol, P, denote the entire sentence "it rained on Tuesday," we can create a predicate weather that describes a relationship between a date and the weather: weather(tuesday, rain). Through inference rules we can manipulate predicate calculus expressions, accessing their individual components and inferring new sentences.

Predicate calculus also allows expressions to contain variables. Variables let us create general assertions about classes of entities. For example, we could state that for all values of X, where X is a day of the week, the statement weather(X, rain) is true; i.e., it rains every day. As with propositional calculus, we will first define the syntax of the language and then discuss its semantics.

2.2.1 The Syntax of Predicates and Sentences

Before defining the syntax of correct expressions in the predicate calculus, we define an alphabet and grammar for creating the *symbols* of the language. This corresponds to the lexical aspect of a programming language definition. Predicate calculus symbols, like the *tokens* in a programming language, are irreducible syntactic elements: they cannot be broken into their component parts by the operations of the language.

Predicate calculus symbols are strings of letters and digits beginning with a letter. Blanks and nonalphanumeric characters cannot appear within the string, although the underscore, "_," may be used to improve readability.

PREDICATE CALCULUS SYMBOLS

The alphabet that makes up the symbols of the predicate calculus consists of:

1. The set of letters, both upper- and lowercase, of the English alphabet.
2. The set of digits, 0, 1, ..., 9.
3. The underscore, "_."

Symbols in the predicate calculus begin with a letter and are followed by any sequence of these legal characters.

Legitimate characters in the alphabet of predicate calculus symbols include

a R 6 9 p _ z

Examples of characters not in the alphabet include

\# % @ / & " "

Legitimate predicate calculus symbols include

George   fire3   tom_and_jerry   bill   XXXX   friends_of

Examples of strings that are not legal symbols are

3jack   "no blanks allowed"   ab%cd   ***71   duck!!!

Symbols, as we see in Section 2.2.2, are used to denote objects, properties, or relations in a world of discourse. As with most programming languages, the use of "words" that suggest the symbol's intended meaning assists us in understanding program code. Thus, even though l(g,k) and likes(george, kate) are formally equivalent (i.e., they have the same structure), the second can be of great help (for human readers) in indicating what relationship the expression represents. It must be stressed that these descriptive names are intended solely to improve the readability of expressions. The only meaning that predicate calculus expressions may be said to have is through their formal semantics.

Parentheses "()", commas ",", and periods "." are used solely to construct well-formed expressions and do not denote objects or relations in the world. These are called *improper symbols*.

Predicate calculus symbols may represent either *variables*, *constants*, *functions*, or *predicates*.

Constants name specific objects or properties in the world. Constant symbols must begin with a lowercase letter. Thus george, tree, tall, and blue are examples of well-formed constant symbols. The constants true and false are reserved as *truth symbols*.

Variable symbols are used to designate general classes of objects or properties in the world. Variables are represented by symbols beginning with an uppercase letter. Thus George, BILL, and KAte are legal variables, whereas, geORGE and bill are not.

Predicate calculus also allows functions on objects in the world of discourse. Function symbols (like constants) begin with a lowercase letter. Functions denote a mapping of one or more elements in a set (called the *domain* of the function) into a unique element of another set (the *range* of the function). Elements of the domain and range are objects in the world of discourse. In addition to common arithmetic functions such as addition and multiplication, functions may define mappings between nonnumeric domains.

Note that our definition of predicate calculus symbols does not include numbers or arithmetic operators. The number system is not included in the predicate calculus primitives; instead it is defined axiomatically using ''pure'' predicate calculus as a basis (Manna 1985). While the particulars of this derivation are of theoretical interest, they are less important to the use of predicate calculus as an AI representation language. For convenience, we assume this derivation and include arithmetic in the language.

Every function symbol has an associated *arity*, indicating the number of elements in the domain mapped onto each element of the range. Thus father could denote a function of arity 1 that maps people onto their (unique) male parent. plus could be a function of arity 2 that maps two numbers onto their arithmetic sum.

A *function expression* is a function symbol followed by its arguments. The arguments are elements from the domain of the function; the number of arguments is equal to the arity of the function. The arguments are enclosed in parentheses and separated by commas. For example,

```
f(X,Y)
father(david)
price(bananas)
```

are all well-formed function expressions.

Each function expression denotes the mapping of the arguments onto a single object in the range, called the *value* of the function. For example, if father is a unary function, then

```
father(david)
```

is a function expression whose value (in the authors' world of discourse) is george. If plus is a function of arity 2, with domain the integers, then

```
plus(2,3)
```

is a function expression whose value is the integer 5. The act of replacing a function with its value is called *evaluation*.

A predicate calculus *term* is either a constant, variable, or function expression. Terms denote objects and properties in a problem domain. Examples of terms are

```
cat
times(2,3)
blue
X
mother(jane)
kate
```

These concepts are formalized in the following definition.

DEFINITION

SYMBOLS AND TERMS

Predicate calculus symbols include:

1. *Truth symbols* true and false (these are reserved symbols).
2. *Constant symbols*, which are symbol expressions having the first character lowercase.
3. *Variable symbols*, which are symbol expressions beginning with an upper-case character.
4. *Function symbols*, which are symbol expressions having the first character lowercase. Functions have an attached arity indicating the number of elements of the domain mapped onto each element of the range.

A *term* is either a constant, variable, or function expression.

A *function expression* consists of a function constant of arity n, followed by n terms, $t_1, t_2, \cdots, t_n$, enclosed in parentheses and separated by commas.

Symbols in predicate calculus may also represent predicates. Predicate symbols, like constants and function names, begin with a lowercase letter. A predicate names a relationship between zero or more objects in the world. The number of objects so related is the arity of the predicate. Examples of predicates are

likes   equals   on   near   part_of

An *atomic sentence* in predicate calculus is a predicate of arity n followed by n terms enclosed in parentheses and separated by commas. Predicate calculus sentences are delimited by a period. Examples of atomic sentences are

```
likes(george,kate).                 likes(X,george)
likes(george, susie).               likes(X,X).
likes(george,sarah,tuesday).        friends(bill,richard).
friends(bill,george).               friends(father(david),father(andrew)).
helps(bill,george).                 helps(richard,bill).
```

The predicate symbols in these expressions are likes, friends, and helps. Note that a predicate symbol may be used with different numbers of arguments. In this example there are two different likes, one with two and the other with three arguments. When a predicate symbol is used in sentences with different arities, it is considered to represent two different relations. Thus, a predicate relation is defined by its name and its arity. There is no reason why the two different likes cannot make up part of the same description of the world; however, good coding practice encourages us to avoid this whenever possible.

In the predicates above, bill, george, kate, etc., are constant symbols and represent objects in the problem domain. The arguments to a predicate are terms and may also include variables or function expressions. For example,

friends(father(david),father(andrew)).

is a predicate describing a relationship between two objects in a domain of discourse. These arguments are represented as function expressions whose mappings (given that the father of david is george and the father of andrew is allen) form the parameters of the predicate. After the function expressions are evaluated, the expression becomes

friends(george,allen).

These ideas are formalized in the following definition.

DEFINITION

PREDICATES AND ATOMIC SENTENCES

Predicate symbols are symbols beginning with a lowercase letter.

Predicates have an associated positive integer referred to as the *arity* or ''argument number'' for the predicate. Predicates with the same name but different arities are considered distinct.

An atomic sentence is a predicate constant of arity n, followed by n terms, $t_1, t_2, \cdots, t_n$, enclosed in parentheses and separated by commas.

The truth values, true and false, are also atomic sentences.

Atomic sentences are also called *atomic expressions*, *atoms,* or *propositions*.

We may combine atomic sentences using logical operators to form *sentences* in the predicate calculus. These are the same logical connectives used in propositional calculus: $\wedge$, $\vee$, $\neg$, $\Rightarrow$, and $=$.

When a variable appears as an argument in a sentence, it refers to unspecified objects in the domain. Predicate calculus includes two symbols, the *variable quantifiers*

∀ and ∃, that constrain the meaning of a sentence containing a variable. A quantifier is followed by a variable and a sentence, for example,

∀ X likes(X, ice_cream). ∃ Y friends(Y, peter).

The *universal quantifier*, ∀, indicates that the sentence is true for all values of its variable. In the example above, likes(X, ice_cream) is true for all values in the domain of the definition of X. The *existential quantifier*, ∃, indicates that the sentence is true for some value(s) in the domain. friends(Y, peter) is true for some objects, indicated by the variable Y. Quantifiers are discussed in more detail in Section 2.2.2.

Sentences in the predicate calculus are defined inductively.

DEFINITION

PREDICATE CALCULUS SENTENCES

Every atomic sentence is a sentence.

1. If s is a sentence, then so is its negation, ¬s.
2. If s_1 and s_2 are sentences, then so is their conjunction, $s_1 \wedge s_2$.
3. If s_1 and s_2 are sentences, then so is their disjunction, $s_1 \vee s_2$.
4. If s_1 and s_2 are sentences, then so is their implication, $s_1 \Rightarrow s_2$.
5. If s_1 and s_2 are sentences, then so is their equivalence, $s_1 = s_2$.
6. If X is a variable and s a sentence, then ∀ X s is a sentence.
7. If X is a variable and s a sentence, then ∃ X s is a sentence.

Examples of well-formed predicate calculus sentences follow. Let times and plus be function symbols of arity 2 and let equal and foo be predicate symbols with arity 2 and 3, respectively.

plus(two, three) is a sentence since it is an atomic sentence.

equal(plus(two, three), five) is an atomic sentence.

equal(plus(2,3), seven) is an atomic sentence. Note that this sentence, given the standard interpretation of plus and equal, is false. Well-formedness and truth value are independent issues.

∃ X foo(X, two, plus(two, three)) ∧ equal(plus(two, three), five) is a sentence since both conjuncts are sentences.

(foo(two, two, plus(two, three))) ⇒ (equal(plus(three, two), five))=true) is a sentence since all its components are sentences, appropriately connected by logical operators.

The definition of predicate calculus sentences and the examples just presented suggest a method for verifying that an expression is a sentence. This is written as a recursive algorithm, verify_sentence. verify_sentence takes as argument a candidate expression and returns success if the expression is a sentence.

```
procedure verify_sentence(expression);

begin

  case

    expression is an atomic sentence: return(success);

    expression is of the form Q X s, where Q is either ∀ or ∃, X is a variable,
    and s is a sentence:
      if verify_sentence(s) returns success
      then return(success);

    expression is of the form ¬s:
      if verify_sentence(s) returns success
      then return(success);

    expression is of the form s₁ op s₂, where op is a binary logical operator:
      if verify_sentence(s₁) returns success  and
        verify_sentence(s₂) returns success
      then return(success);

    otherwise: return(fail)

  end
end.
```

We conclude this section with an example of the use of predicate calculus to describe a simple world. The domain of discourse is a set of family relationships in a biblical genealogy:

```
mother(eve,abel).
mother(eve,cain).
father(adam,abel).
father(adam,cain).

∀ X ∀ Y father(X, Y) ∨ mother(X, Y) ⇒ parent(X, Y).
∀ X ∀ Y ∀ Z parent(X, Y) ∧ parent(X, Z) ⇒ sibling(Y, Z).
```

In this example we use the predicates mother and father to define a set of parent-child relationships. The implications give general definitions of other relationships, such as parent and sibling, in terms of these predicates. Intuitively, it is clear that these implications can be used to infer facts such as sibling(cain,abel). To formalize this process so that it can be performed on a computer, care must be taken to define inference algorithms and to ensure that such algorithms indeed draw correct conclusions from a set of predi-

---

cate calculus assertions. In order to do so, we define the semantics of the predicate calculus (Section 2.2.2) and then address the issue of inference rules (Section 2.3).

2.2.2 A Semantics for the Predicate Calculus

Having defined well-formed expressions in the predicate calculus, it is important to determine their meaning in terms of objects, properties, and relations in the world. Predicate calculus semantics provide a formal basis for determining the truth value of well-formed expressions. The truth of expressions depends on the mapping of constants, variables, predicates, and functions into objects and relations in the domain of discourse. The truth of relationships in the domain determines the truth of the corresponding expressions.

For example, information about a person, George, and his friends Kate and Susie may be expressed by

> friends(george,susie).
> friends(george,kate).

If it is indeed true that George is a friend of Susie and George is a friend of Kate then these expressions would each have the truth value (assignment) T. If George is a friend of Susie but not of Kate, then the first expression would have truth value T and the second would have truth value F.

To use the predicate calculus as a representation for problem solving, we describe objects and relations in the domain of interpretation with a set of well-formed expressions. The terms and predicates of these expressions denote objects and relations in the domain. This data base of predicate calculus expressions, each having truth value T, describes the "state of the world." The description of George and his friends is a simple example of such a data base. Another example is the *blocks world* in the introduction to Part II.

Based on these intuitions, we formally define the semantics of predicate calculus. First, we define an *interpretation* over a domain D. Then we use this interpretation to determine the *truth value assignment* of sentences in the language.

D E F I N I T I O N

INTERPRETATION

Let the domain D be a nonempty set.

An *interpretation* over D is an assignment of the entities of D to each of the constant, variable, predicate, and function symbols of a predicate calculus expression, such that:

1. Each constant is assigned an element of D.

2. Each variable is assigned to a nonempty subset of D; these are the allowable substitutions for that variable.

3. Each predicate p of arity n is defined on n arguments from D and defines a mapping from D^n into {T, F}.

4. Each function f of arity m is defined on m arguments of D and defines a mapping from D^m into D.

Given an interpretation, the meaning of an expression is a truth value assignment over the interpretation.

DEFINITION

TRUTH VALUE OF PREDICATE CALCULUS EXPRESSIONS

Assume an expression E and an interpretation I for E over a nonempty domain D. The truth value for E is determined by:

1. The value of a constant is the element of D it is assigned to by I.

2. The value of a variable is the set of elements of D it is assigned to by I.

3. The value of a function expression is that element of D obtained by evaluating the function for the parameter values assigned by the interpretation.

4. The value of truth symbol "true" is T and "false" is F.

5. The value of an atomic sentence is either T or F, as determined by the interpretation I.

6. The value of the negation of a sentence is T if the value of the sentence is F, and F if the value of the sentence is T.

7. The value of the conjunction of two sentences is T if the value of both sentences is T, and F otherwise.

8.–10. The truth value of expressions using $\lor$, $\Rightarrow$, and = is determined from the value of their operands as defined in Section 2.1.2.

Finally, for a variable X and a sentence S containing X:

11. The value of $\forall$ X S is T if S is T for all assignments to X under I, and F otherwise.

12. The value of $\exists$ X S is T if there is an assignment to X in the interpretation under which S is T; otherwise it is F.

Quantification of variables is an important part of predicate calculus semantics. When a variable appears in a sentence, such as X in likes(george,X) in the first example of Section 2.2.2, the variable functions as a placeholder. Any constant allowed under the interpretation can be substituted for it in the expression. By substituting for X in likes(george,X) we can form the statements likes(george, kate) and likes(george, susie).

The variable X stands for all constants that might appear as the second parameter of the sentence. This variable name might be replaced by any other variable name, say Y or PEOPLE, without changing the meaning of the expression. In this sense the variable is said to be a dummy.

In predicate calculus, there are two ways variables may be used or *quantified*. In the first, the sentence is true for all constants that can be substituted for the variable under the intended interpretation. The variable is said to be *universally* quantified.

The symbol indicating universal quantification is ∀. Parentheses are often used to indicate the *scope* of quantification, that is, the instances of a variable name over which a quantification holds. Thus

$$\forall\, X\, (p(X) \wedge q(Y) \Rightarrow r(X)).$$

indicates that X is universally quantified in both p(X) and r(X).

Universal quantification introduces problems in computing the truth value of a sentence, since all the possible values of a variable symbol must be tested to see if the expression remains true. For example, to test the truth value of ∀ X likes(george,X), where X ranges over the set of all humans, all possible values for X must be tested. If the domain of an interpretation is infinite, exhaustive testing of all substitutions to a universally quantified variable is computationally impossible: the algorithm will never halt. Because of this problem, the predicate calculus is said to be *undecidable*.

Since the propositional calculus does not use variables, sentences have only a finite number of possible truth assignments, and we can exhaustively test all possible assignments. This is what is done in a truth table.

Variables may also be quantified *existentially*. In this case the expression containing the variable is said to be true for at least one substitution from the domain of definition. The existential quantifier is indicated by an ∃. The scope of an existentially quantified variable is also indicated by enclosing the quantified occurrences of the variable in parentheses.

Evaluating the truth of an expression containing an existentially quantified variable may be no easier than evaluating the truth of expressions containing universally quantified variables. Suppose we attempt to determine the truth of the expression by trying substitutions until one is found that makes the expression true. If the domain of the variable is infinite and the expression is false under all substitutions, the algorithm will never halt.

Several relationships between negation and the universal and existential quantifiers are given below. These relationships are used in resolution refutation systems described in Chapter 11. The notion of a variable name as a dummy symbol that stands for a set of constants is also noted. For predicates p and q and variables X and Y:

$$\neg\, \exists\, X\, p(X) = \forall\, X\, \neg\, p(X)$$

$$\neg\, \forall\, X\, p(X) = \exists\, X\, \neg\, p(X)$$

$$\exists\, X\, p(X) = \exists\, Y\, p(Y)$$

$$\forall\, X\, q(X) = \forall\, Y\, q(Y)$$

$$\forall\, X\, (p(X) \wedge q(X)) = \forall\, X\, p(X) \wedge \forall\, Y\, q(Y)$$

$$\exists\, X\, (p(X) \vee q(X)) = \exists\, X\, p(X) \vee \exists\, Y\, q(Y)$$

In the language we have defined, universal and existential quantified variables may refer only to objects (constants) in the domain of discourse. Predicate and function names may not be replaced by quantified variables. This language is called the first-order predicate calculus.

DEFINITION

FIRST-ORDER PREDICATE CALCULUS

First-order predicate calculus allows quantified variables to refer to objects in the domain of discourse, and not to predicates or functions.

For example,

∀ (Likes) Likes(george, kate).

is not a well-formed expression in the first-order predicate calculus. There are *higher-order* predicate calculi where such expressions are meaningful. Some researchers (McCarthy 1968; Appelt 1985) have used higher-order languages to represent knowledge in natural language understanding programs.

Almost any grammatically correct English sentence may be represented in first-order predicate calculus using the symbols, connectives, and variable symbols defined in this section. It is important to note that there is no unique mapping of sentences into predicate calculus expressions; in fact, an English sentence may have a number of different predicate calculus representations. A major challenge for AI programmers is to find a scheme for using these predicates that optimizes the expressiveness and efficiency of the resulting representation. Examples of English sentences represented in predicate calculus are:

If it doesn't rain tomorrow, Tom will go to the mountains.
¬ weather(rain,tomorrow) ⇒ go(tom,mountains)

Emma is a Doberman pinscher and a good dog.
gooddog(emma) ∧ isa(emma,doberman)

All basketball players are tall.
∀ X (basketball_player(X) ⇒ tall(X))

Some people like anchovies.
∃ X (person(X) ∧ likes(X,anchovies)).

If wishes were horses, beggars would ride.
equal(wishes,horses) ⇒ ride(beggars).

Nobody likes taxes.
¬∃ X likes(X,taxes).

We conclude this section by giving an extended example of a truth value assignment to a set of predicate calculus expressions. Suppose we want to model the blocks world of Figure 2.3 to design a control algorithm for a robot arm. We can use predicate

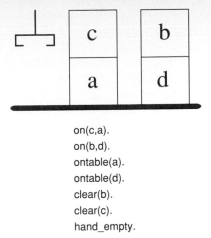

on(c,a).
on(b,d).
ontable(a).
ontable(d).
clear(b).
clear(c).
hand_empty.

Figure 2.3 A blocks world with its predicate calculus
description.

calculus sentences to represent the qualitative relationships in the world: does a given block have a clear top surface? can we pick up block A? etc. Assume that the computer has knowledge of the location of each block and the arm itself and is able to keep track of these locations (perhaps in the form of three-dimensional coordinates) as the hand moves blocks about the table.

In order to pick up a block and stack it on another block, both blocks must be clear. In Figure 2.3, block a is not clear. Since the arm can move blocks, it can change the state of the world and clear a block. Suppose it removes block c from block a and updates the knowledge base to reflect this by deleting the assertion on(c,a). The program needs to be able to infer that block a has become clear.

The following rule describes when a block is clear:

$$\forall X (\neg \exists Y \ on(Y, X) \Rightarrow clear(X)).$$

That is, for all X, X is clear if there does not exist a Y such that Y is on X.

This rule not only defines what it means for a block to be clear but also provides a basis for determining how to clear blocks that are not. For example, block d is not clear, since if variable X is given value d, substituting b for Y will make the statement false. Therefore, to make this definition true, block b must be removed from block d. This is easily done since the computer has a record of all the blocks and their locations.

Besides using implications to define when a block is clear, other rules may be added that describe operations such as stacking one block on top of another. For example: To stack X on Y first empty the hand, then clear X, then clear Y, then pick_up X and put_down X on Y.

$$\forall X \ \forall Y \ (hand\_empty \wedge clear(X) \wedge clear(Y) \wedge pick\_up(X) \wedge put\_down(X, Y)$$
$$\Rightarrow stack(X, Y)).$$

Note that in implementing the above description it is necessary to "attach" an action of the robot arm to each predicate such as pick_up(X). It is also necessary for such an implementation to augment the semantics of predicate calculus by requiring that the actions be performed in the order in which they appear in a rule premise. However, much is gained by separating these issues from the use of predicate calculus to define the relationships and operations in the domain.

Figure 2.3 gives a semantic interpretation of these predicate calculus expressions. This interpretation maps the constants and predicates in the set of expressions into a domain D, here the blocks and relations between them. The interpretation gives truth value T to each expression in the description. Another interpretation could be offered by a different set of blocks in another location, or perhaps by some obscure religious custom for congregations that have exactly four members. The important question is not the uniqueness of interpretations, but whether the interpretation provides a truth value for all expressions in the set and whether the expressions describe the world in sufficient detail that all necessary inferences may be carried out by manipulating the symbolic expressions. The next section uses these ideas to provide a formal basis for predicate calculus inference rules.

2.3   Using Inference Rules to Produce Predicate Calculus Expressions

2.3.1   Inference Rules

The semantics of predicate calculus provide a basis for a formal theory of *logical inference*. The ability to infer new correct expressions from a set of true assertions is an important feature of the predicate calculus. These new expressions are correct in that they are *consistent* with all previous interpretations of the original set of expressions. First we will discuss these ideas informally and then create a set of definitions to make them precise.

An interpretation that makes a sentence true is said to *satisfy* that sentence. An interpretation that satisfies every member of a set of expressions is said to satisfy the set. An expression X *logically follows* from a set of predicate calculus expressions S if every interpretation that satisfies S also satisfies X. The function of logical inference is to produce new sentences that logically follow a given set of predicate calculus sentences.

It is important that the precise meaning of "logically follow" be understood: the expression X is true for every interpretation that satisfies S (Figure 2.4).

The term itself, "logically follows," may be a bit confusing. It does not mean that X is deduced from or even that it is deducible from S. It simply means that X is true for every (potentially infinite) interpretation that satisfies S. However, because systems of predicates can have a potentially infinite number of possible interpretations, it is seldom practical to try all interpretations. Instead, *inference rules* provide a computationally feasible way to determine when an expression logically follows from another. The concept "logically follows" provides a formal basis for proofs of the soundness and correctness of inference rules.

S: ∀ X human(X) ⇒ mortal(X).   human(socrates).

Socrates
the Human

I:

Here Lies
Everyman

Here Lies
Socrates

X: mortal(socrates).

Figure 2.4 S, a set of predicate calculus sentences; I, an
interpretation; and X, an expression logically
following from S (also satisfied by I).

An inference rule is essentially a mechanical means of producing new predicate calculus sentences from other sentences.   That is, inference rules produce new sentences based on the syntactic form of given logical assertions. When every sentence X produced by an inference rule operating on a set S of logical expressions logically follows from S, the inference rule is said to be *sound*.

If the inference rule is able to produce every expression that logically follows from S, then it is said to be *complete*. *Modus ponens*, to be introduced below, and *resolution*, introduced in Chapter 11, are examples of inference rules that are sound and, when used with certain appropriate strategies, complete. Logical inference systems generally use sound rules of inference, although later chapters (5, 9, 10, and 14) examine heuristic reasoning and commonsense reasoning, which relax this requirement. It is less important, although often desirable, that inference procedures be complete.

We formalize these ideas through the following definitions:

D E F I N I T I O N

SATISFY, MODEL, VALID, INCONSISTENT

For a predicate calculus expression S and an interpretation I:

If S has a value of T under I and a particular variable assignment, then S is said to be *satisfied*.

If I satisfies S for all variable assignments, then I is a *model* of S.

S is *satisfiable* if and only if there exist an interpretation and variable assignment that satisfy it; otherwise, it is *unsatisfiable*.

A set of expressions is *satisfiable* if and only if there exist an interpretation and variable assignment that satisfy every element.

If a set of expressions is not satisfiable, it is said to be *inconsistent*.

If S has a value T for all possible interpretations, it is said to be *valid*.

In the blocks world example of Figure 2.3, the blocks world was a model for logical description. All of the sentences in the example were true under this interpretation. When a knowledge base is implemented as a set of true assertions about a problem domain, that domain is a model for the knowledge base.

The expression $\exists X (p(X) \land \neg p(X))$ is inconsistent, since it may not be satisfied under any interpretation or variable assignment. On the other hand, the expression $\forall X (p(X) \lor \neg p(X))$ is valid.

The truth table method can be used to test validity for any expression not containing variables. Because it is not always possible to decide the validity of expressions containing variables (as mentioned above, the process may not terminate), the full predicate calculus is "undecidable." There are *proof procedures*, however, that can produce any expression that logically follows from a set of expressions. These are called *complete* proof procedures.

DEFINITION

PROOF PROCEDURE

A *proof procedure* is a combination of an inference rule and an algorithm for applying it to a set of logical expressions to generate new sentences. We present proof procedures for the *resolution* inference rule in Chapter 11.

Using these definitions, we may formally define "logically follows."

DEFINITION

LOGICALLY FOLLOWS, SOUND, AND COMPLETE

A predicate calculus expression X *logically follows* from a set S of predicate calculus expressions if every interpretation and variable assignment that satisfies S also satisfies X.

An inference rule is *sound* if every predicate calculus expression produced by the rule from a set S of predicate calculus expressions also logically follows from S.

An inference rule is *complete* if, given a set S of predicate calculus expressions, it can infer every expression that logically follows from S.

Modus ponens is a sound inference rule. If we are given an expression of the form $p \Rightarrow q$ and another expression of the form p such that both are true under an interpretation I, then modus ponens allows us to infer that q is also true for that interpretation.

Indeed, because modus ponens is sound, q will be true for *all* interpretations for which p and p $\Rightarrow$ q are true.

Modus ponens and a number of other useful inference rules are defined below.

DEFINITION

MODUS PONENS, MODUS TOLENS, AND ELIMINATION, AND
INTRODUCTION, AND UNIVERSAL INSTANTIATION

If the sentences P and P $\Rightarrow$ Q are known to be true, then *modus ponens* lets us infer Q.

Under the inference rule *modus tolens*, if P $\Rightarrow$ Q is known to be true and Q is known to be false, we can infer ¬P.

And elimination allows us to infer the truth of either of the conjuncts from the truth of a conjunctive sentence. For instance, P $\wedge$ Q lets us conclude P and Q are true.

And introduction lets us infer the truth of a conjunction from the truth of its conjuncts. For instance, if P and Q are true, then P $\wedge$ Q are true.

Universal instantiation states that if any universally quantified variable in a true sentence is replaced by any appropriate term from the domain, the result is a true sentence. Thus, if a is from the domain of X, the $\forall$ X p(X) lets us infer p(a).

As a simple example of the use of modus ponens in the propositional calculus, assume the following observations: "if it is raining then the ground will be wet" and "it is raining." If P denotes "it is raining" and Q is "the ground is wet" then the first expression becomes P $\rightarrow$ Q. Since it is indeed now raining (P is true), our set of axioms becomes

P $\Rightarrow$ Q
P

Through an application of modus ponens, the fact that the ground is wet (Q) may be added to the set of true expressions.

Modus ponens can also be applied to expressions containing variables. Consider as an example the common syllogism "all men are mortal and Socrates is a man; therefore Socrates is mortal." "All men are mortal" may be represented in predicate calculus by

$\forall$ X (man(X) $\Rightarrow$ mortal(X)).

"Socrates is a man" is

man(socrates).

Because the X in the implication is universally quantified, we may substitute any value in the domain for X and still have a true statement under the inference rule of universal instantiation. By substituting socrates for X in the implication, we infer the expression

man(socrates) $\Rightarrow$ mortal(socrates).

We can now apply modus ponens and infer the conclusion mortal(socrates). This is added to the set of expressions that logically follow from the original assertions. An algorithm called *unification* can be used by an automated problem solver to determine that socrates may be substituted for X in order to apply modus ponens. Unification is discussed in Section 2.3.2.

Chapter 11 discusses a more powerful rule of inference called resolution, which is the basis of many automated reasoning systems.

2.3.2   Unification

In order to apply inference rules such as modus ponens, an inference system must be able to determine when two expressions are the same or *match*. In propositional calculus, this is trivial: two expressions match if and only if they are syntactically identical. In predicate calculus, the process of matching two sentences is complicated by the existence of variables in the expressions. Universal instantiation allows universally quantified variables to be replaced by terms from the domain. This requires a decision process for determining the variable substitutions under which two or more expressions can be made identical (usually for the purpose of applying inference rules).

Unification is an algorithm for determining the substitutions needed to make two predicate calculus expressions match. We already saw this done in the previous subsection, where socrates in man(socrates) was substituted for X in $\forall$ X(man(X) $\Rightarrow$ mortal(X)). This allowed the application of modus ponens and the conclusion mortal(socrates). Another example of unification was seen previously when dummy variables were discussed. Since p(X) and p(Y) are equivalent, Y may be substituted for X to make the sentences match.

Unification and inference rules such as modus ponens allow us to make inferences on a set of logical assertions. In order to do this, the logical data base must be expressed in an appropriate form.

An essential aspect of this form is the requirement that all variables be universally quantified. This allows full freedom in computing substitutions. Existentially quantified variables may be eliminated from sentences in the data base by replacing them with the constants that make the sentence true. For example, $\exists$ X parent(X,tom) could be replaced by the expression parent(bob,tom) or parent(mary,tom), assuming that bob and mary are tom's parents under the interpretation.

The process of eliminating existentially quantified variables is complicated by the fact that the value of these substitutions may depend on the value of other variables in the expression. For example, in the expression $\forall$ X $\exists$ Y mother(Y,X), the value of the existentially quantified variable Y depends on the value of X. *Skolemization* replaces each existentially quantified variable with a function that returns the appropriate constant as a function of other variables in the sentence. In the above example, since the value of Y depends on X, Y could be replaced by a *skolem function*, f, of X. This yields the predicate $\forall$ X mother(X,f(X)). Skolemization is discussed in more detail in Chapter 11.

Once the existentially quantified variables have been removed from a logical data base, unification may be used to match sentences in order to apply inference rules such as modus ponens.

Unification is complicated by the fact that a variable may be replaced by any term, including other variables and function expressions of arbitrary complexity. These expressions may themselves contain variables. For example, father(jack) may be substituted for X in man(X) to infer that jack's father is mortal.

Some instances of the expression

foo(X, a, goo(Y)).

generated by legal substitutions are given below:

1) foo(fred,a,goo(Z))
2) foo(W,a,goo(jack))
3) foo(Z,a,goo(moo(Z)))

In this example, the substitution instances or *unifications* that would make the initial expression identical to each of the other three are written as

1) {fred/X, Z/Y}
2) {W/X, jack/Y}
3) {Z/X, moo(Z)/Y}

The notation X/Y,... indicates that X is substituted for the variable Y in the original expression. Substitutions are also referred to as *bindings*. A variable is said to be *bound* to the value substituted for it.

In defining the unification algorithm that computes the substitutions required to match two expressions, a number of issues must be taken into account.

Although a constant may be systematically substituted for a variable, any constant is considered a ''ground instance'' and may not be replaced. Neither can two different ground instances be substituted for one variable.

A variable cannot be unified with a term containing that variable. X cannot be replaced by p(X) as this creates an infinite expression: p(p(p(p(...X)...). The test for this situation is called the *occurs check*.

Generally, a problem-solving process will require multiple inferences and, consequently, multiple successive unifications. Logic problem solvers must maintain consistency of variable substitutions. It is important that any unifying substitution be made consistently across all occurrences of the variable in both expressions being matched. This was seen before when socrates was substituted not only for the variable X in man(X) but also for the variable X in mortal(X).

Once a variable has been bound, future unifications and inferences must take the value of this binding into account. If a variable is bound to a constant, it may not be given a new binding in a future unification. If a variable X_1 is substituted for another variable X_2 and at a later time X_1 is replaced by a constant, then X_2 must also reflect this binding. The complete set of substitutions used in a sequence of inferences is important, because it may contain the answer to the original query (Chapter 11).

For example, $p(a, X)$ unifies with the premise of $p(Y, Z) \Rightarrow q(Y, Z)$ under the substitution $\{a/Y, X/Z\}$. Modus ponens lets us infer $q(Y, Z)$ under the same substitution, i.e., $q(a, X)$. If we then match this result with the premise of $q(W, b) \Rightarrow r(W)$, we may infer $r(W)$ under the substitution set $\{a/W, b/X\}$.

This requires that the results of successive unifications be *composed* into a single consistent substitution set. The set $\{a/W, b/X\}$ in the above example was derived by composing $\{a/Y, X/Z\}$ from the first unification with $\{Y/W, b/Z\}$ from the second.

If S and S′ are two substitution sets, then the *composition* of S and S′ (written S′S) is obtained by applying S to the elements of S′ and adding the result to S.

Consider the example of composing the sequence of substitutions

$\{X/Y, W/Z\}, \{V/X\}, \{a/V, f(b)/W\}.$

These are equivalent to the single substitution

$\{a/Y, f(b)/Z\}.$

This was produced by composing $\{X/Y, W/Z\}$ with $\{V/X\}$ to yield $\{V/Y, W/Z\}$, and composing this with $\{a/V, f(b)/W\}$ to produce $\{a/Y, f(b)/Z\}$.

Composition can be shown to be associative but not commutative. The exercises will present these issues in more detail.

A final requirement of the unification algorithm is that the unifier be as general as possible, that the *most general unifier* be found for the two expressions. This is important, as will be seen in the next example, because, if generality is lost in the solution process, it will lessen the scope of the eventual solution or even eliminate the possibility of a solution entirely.

For example, in unifying $p(X)$ and $p(Y)$ any constant expression such as $\{fred/X, fred/Y\}$ will do the trick. However, fred is not the most general unifier; any variable would work and produce a more general expression: $\{Z/X, Z/Y\}$. The solutions obtained from the first substitution instance would always be restricted by having the constant fred limit the resulting inferences; i.e., fred would be a unifier, but it would lessen the generality of the result.

DEFINITION

MOST GENERAL UNIFIER (mgu)

If s is any unifier of expressions E and g is the most general unifier of that set of expressions, then for s applied to E there exists another unifier s′ such that Es = Egs′ (where gs′ is the composition of unifiers as seen above).

The most general unifier for a set of expressions is unique except for alphabetic variations; i.e., whether a variable is eventually called X or Y really doesn't make any difference to the generality of the resulting unifications.

Unification is critically important for any artificial intelligence problem solver that uses the predicate calculus as a representation language. Unification specifies the conditions under which two (or more) predicate calculus expressions may be said to be equivalent. This underlies the possibility of using inference rules such as modus ponens or resolution with logical representations such as PROLOG or the LISP-based logic programming language described in Chapter 13.

We conclude by presenting the pseudocode for a function, unify, that computes the unifying substitutions (when this is possible) between two predicate calculus expressions. Unify takes as arguments two expressions in the predicate calculus and returns either the most general unifying substitutions or the constant FAIL if no unification is possible. It is defined as a recursive function: first, it recursively attempts to unify the initial components of the expressions. If this succeeds, any substitutions returned by this unification are applied to the remainder of both expressions. These are then passed in a second recursive call to unify, which attempts to complete the unification. The recursion stops when either argument is a symbol (a predicate, function name, constant, or variable) or the elements of the expression have all been matched.

In order to simplify the manipulation of predicate calculus expressions, the algorithm assumes a slightly modified expression syntax. Since unify simply performs syntactic pattern matching, it can effectively ignore the predicate calculus distinction between predicates, functions, and arguments. By representing a sentence as a *list* (an ordered sequence of elements) with the predicate or function name as the first element followed by its arguments, we simplify the manipulation of expressions. Expressions in which an argument is itself a predicate or function expression are represented as lists within the list, thus preserving the structure of the expression. Lists are delimited by parentheses, ( ), and list elements are separated by spaces. Examples of expressions in both predicate calculus and list syntax are:

PC SYNTAX	LIST SYNTAX
p(a,b)	(p a b)
p(f(a),g(X,Y))	(p (f a) (g X Y))
equal(eve,mother(cain))	(equal eve (mother cain))
$p(X) \land q(Y)$	$((p\ X) \land (q\ Y))$

It should be stressed again that this modification of the syntax is done purely to simplify the definition of unify and implies no alteration of predicate calculus semantics. Alternative versions of the algorithm could be written that parse expressions in their original syntax, although this would complicate its definition. It is interesting to note that this form is based on the syntax of the LISP programming language. For reasons that are discussed later in the text, LISP is the most commonly used AI programming language, with many LISP implementations of predicate calculus using this syntax.

```
function unify(E1, E2);

begin
case

    both E1 and E2 are either constants or the empty list:    %recursion stops

        if E1 = E2 then return {}
                else return FAIL;
```

```
E1 is a variable: if E1 occurs in E2
            then return FAIL
            else return {E2/E1};

E2 is a variable: if E2 occurs in E1
            then return FAIL
            else return {E1/E2}

otherwise:     % both E1 and E2 are lists
   begin
     HE1 := first element of E1;
     HE2 := first element of E2;
     SUBS1 := unify(HE1,HE2);

     if SUBS1 = FAIL
       then return fail;

     TE1 := apply(SUBS1, rest of E1)
     TE2 := apply(SUBS1, rest of E2)

     SUBS2 := unify(TE1,TE2);

     if SUBS2 = FAIL
       then return FAIL;
       else return the composition of SUBS1 and SUBS2.
   end

end    %end case
end
```

2.3.3   A Unification Example

The behavior of the preceding algorithm may be clarified by tracing the call

unify((parents X (father X) (mother bill)), (parents bill (father bill) Y))

When unify is first called, since neither argument is an atomic symbol, i.e., a variable or constant, it will attempt to recursively unify the first elements of each expression, calling

unify(parents, parents).

This succeeds, returning the empty substitution, { }. Applying this to the remainder of the expressions creates no change; the algorithm then calls

unify((X (father X) (mother bill)), (bill (father bill) Y)).

A tree depiction of the execution at this stage appears in Figure 2.5.

1. unify((parents X (father X) (mother bill)), (parents bill (father bill) Y))

Unify first elements
and apply
substitutions to rest

return { }

2. unify(parents,parents)

3. unify((X(father X) (mother bill)),(bill(father bill) Y))

Figure 2.5   Initial steps in the unification of (parents X
(father X)(mother bill)) and (parents bill
(father bill) Y).

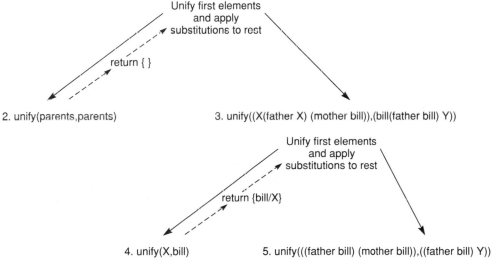

1. unify((parents X (father X) (mother bill)), (parents bill (father bill) Y))

Unify first elements
and apply
substitutions to rest

return { }

2. unify(parents,parents)

3. unify((X(father X) (mother bill)),(bill(father bill) Y))

Unify first elements
and apply
substitutions to rest

return {bill/X}

4. unify(X,bill)

5. unify(((father bill) (mother bill)),((father bill) Y))

Figure 2.6   Further steps in the unification of (parents X
(father X)(mother bill)) and (parents bill
(father bill) Y).

In the second call to unify, neither expression is atomic, so the algorithm separates
each expression into its first component and the remainder of the expression. This leads
to the call

unify(X, bill).

This call succeeds, since both expressions are atomic and one of them is a variable. It
returns the substitution {bill/X}. This substitution is applied to the remainder of each
expression and unify is called on the results (Figure 2.6):

unify(((father bill) (mother bill)), ((father bill),Y))).

The first action of this call is to unify (father bill) with (father bill). This leads to the calls

unify(father,father)

unify(bill, bill)

unify((), ())

All of these succeed, returning the empty set of substitutions (Figure 2.7).
Unify is then called on the remainder of the expressions:

unify(((mother bill)), (Y)).

This, in turn, leads to calls

unify((mother bill), Y)

unify((),()).

In the first of these, (mother bill) unifies with Y. Notice that unification substitutes the whole *structure* (mother bill) for the variable Y. Thus, unification succeeds and returns the substitution {(mother bill)/Y}. The call

unify((),())

returns { }. These are composed, along with the earlier substitution {bill/X}, to return the answer {bill/X (mother bill)/Y}. A trace of the entire execution appears in Figure 2.7. Each call is numbered to indicate the order in which it was made; the substitutions returned by each call are noted on the arcs of the tree.

2.4   Application: A Logic-Based Financial Advisor

As a final example of the use of predicate calculus to represent and reason about problem domains, we design a simple financial advisor using predicate calculus. Although a simple example, it illustrates many of the issues involved in realistic applications.

The function of the advisor is to help a user decide whether to invest in a savings account or the stock market. Some investors may want to split their money between the two. The investment that will be recommended for individual investors depends on their income and the current amount they have saved according to the following criteria:

1. Individuals with inadequate savings should always make increasing the amount saved their first priority, regardless of their income.
2. Individuals with adequate savings and an adequate income should consider a riskier but potentially more profitable investment in the stock market.

1. unify((parents X (father X) (mother bill)), (parents bill (father bill) Y))

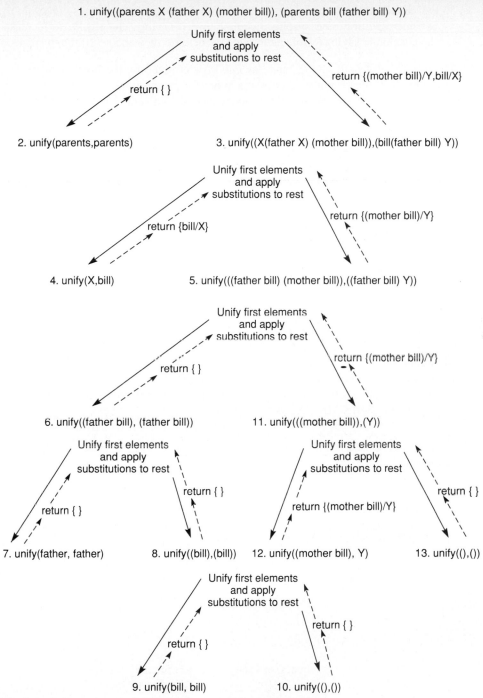

Figure 2.7 Full trace of the unification of (parents X (father X)(mother bill)) and (parents bill (father bill) Y).

3. Individuals with a lower income who already have adequate savings may want to consider splitting their surplus income between savings and stocks, to increase the cushion in savings while attempting to increase their income through stocks.

The adequacy of both savings and income is determined by the number of dependents an individual must support. Our rule is to have at least $5000 in the bank for each dependent. An adequate income must be a steady income and supply at least $15,000 per year plus an additional $4000 for each dependent.

To automate this advice, we translate these guidelines into sentences in the predicate calculus. The first task is to determine the major features that must be considered. Here, they are the adequacy of the savings and the income. These are represented by the predicates savings and income, respectively. Both of these are unary predicates, and their argument could be either adequate or inadequate. Thus,

```
savings(adequate).
savings(inadequate).
income(adequate).
income(inadequate).
```

are their possible values.

Conclusions are represented by the unary predicate investment, with possible values of its argument being stocks, savings, or combination (implying that the investment should be split).

Using these predicates, the different investment strategies are represented by implications. The first rule, that individuals with inadequate savings should make increased savings their main priority, is represented by

```
savings(inadequate) ⇒ investment(savings).
```

Similarly, the remaining two possible alternatives are represented by

```
savings(adequate) ∧ income(adequate) ⇒ investment(stocks).

savings(adequate) ∧ income(inadequate) ⇒
investment(combination).
```

Next, the advisor must determine when savings and income are adequate or inadequate. This will also be done using implication. The need to do arithmetic calculations requires the use of functions. To determine the minimum adequate savings, the function minsavings is defined. minsavings takes one argument, the number of dependents, and returns 5000 times that argument.

Using minsavings, the adequacy of savings is determined by the rules

```
∀ X amountsaved(X) ∧ ∃ Y (dependents(Y) ∧ greater(X, minsavings(Y))) ⇒
savings(adequate).
```

$\forall$ X amountsaved(X) $\wedge$ $\exists$ Y (dependents(Y) $\wedge$ $\neg$ greater(X, minsavings(Y))) $\Rightarrow$
savings(inadequate).

where minsavings(X) = 5000 $\times$ X.

In these definitions, amountsaved(X) and dependents(Y) assert the current amount in savings and the number of dependents of an investor; greater(X,Y) is the standard arithmetic test for one number being greater than another and is not formally defined in this example.

Similarly, a function minincome is defined as

minincome(X)=15000+(4000*X).

minincome is used to compute the minimum adequate income when given the number of dependents. The investor's current income is represented by a predicate, earnings. Since an adequate income must be both steady and above the minimum, earnings takes two arguments: the first is the amount earned, and the second must be equal to either steady or unsteady. The remaining rules needed for the advisor are

$\forall$ X earnings(X, steady) $\wedge$ $\exists$ Y (dependents(Y) $\wedge$ greater(X, minincome(Y))) $\Rightarrow$
income(adequate).

$\forall$ X earnings(X, steady) $\wedge$ $\exists$ Y (dependents(Y) $\wedge$ $\neg$ greater(X, minincome(Y))) $\Rightarrow$
income(inadequate).

$\forall$ X earnings(X, unsteady) $\Rightarrow$ income(inadequate).

In order to perform a consultation, a description of a particular investor is added to this set of predicate calculus sentences using the predicates amountsaved, earnings, and dependents. Thus, an individual with three dependents, $22,000 in savings, and a steady income of $25,000 would be described by

amountsaved(22000).
earnings(25000, steady).
dependents(3).

This yields a logical system consisting of the following sentences:

1. savings(inadequate)$\Rightarrow$investment(savings).
2. savings(adequate)$\wedge$income(adequate)$\Rightarrow$ investment(stocks).
3. savings(adequate) $\wedge$ income(inadequate)$\Rightarrow$ investment(combination).
4. $\forall$Xamountsaved(X) $\wedge$ $\exists$Y(dependents(Y) $\wedge$
   greater(X, minsavings(Y))) $\Rightarrow$ savings(adequate).
5. $\forall$ X amountsaved(X) $\wedge$ $\exists$ Y (dependents(Y) $\wedge$
   $\neg$ greater(X, minsavings(Y))) $\Rightarrow$savings(inadequate).

6. $\forall$ X earnings(X, steady) $\wedge \exists$ Y (dependents (Y) $\wedge$
   greater(X, minincome(Y))) $\Rightarrow$income(adequate).
7. $\forall$ X earnings(X, steady) $\wedge \exists$ Y (dependents(Y) $\wedge$
   $\neg$ greater(X, minincome(Y))) $\Rightarrow$income(inadequate).
8. $\forall$ X earnings(X, unsteady) $\Rightarrow$ income(inadequate).
9. amountsaved(22000) .
10. earnings(25000, steady) .
11. dependents(3) .

where minsavings(X) = $5000 \times$ X and minincome(X) = 15000 + (4000*X).

This set of logical sentences describes the problem domain. The assertions are numbered so that they may be referenced in the following trace.

Using unification and modus ponens, a correct investment strategy for this individual may be inferred as a logical consequence of these descriptions. A first step would be to unify the conjunction of 10 and 11 with the first two components of the premise of 7; i.e.,

earnings(25000, steady) $\wedge$ dependents(3)

unifies with

earnings(X, steady) $\wedge$ dependents(Y)

under the substitution {25000/X, 3/Y}. Performing this substitution yields the new implication

earnings(25000, steady) $\wedge$ dependents(3) $\wedge \neg$ greater(25000, minincome(3)) $\Rightarrow$
income(inadequate).

Evaluating the function minincome yields the expression

earnings(25000, steady) $\wedge$ dependents(3) $\wedge \neg$ greater(25000, 27000) $\Rightarrow$
income(inadequate).

Because all three components of the premise are individually true, by 10, 3, and the mathematical definition of greater, their conjunction is true and the entire premise is true. Modus ponens may therefore be applied, yielding the conclusion income(inadequate). This is added as assertion 12.

12. income(inadequate).

Similarly,

amountsaved(22000) $\wedge$ dependents(3)

unifies with the first two elements of the premise of assertion 4 under the substitution {22000/X, 3/Y}, yielding the implication

amountsaved(22000) ∧ dependents(3) ∧ greater(22000, minsavings(3)) ⇒
savings(adequate).

Here, evaluating the function minsavings(3) yields the expression

amountsaved(22000) ∧ dependents(3) ∧ greater(22000, 15000) ⇒
savings(adequate).

Again, because all of the components of the premise of this implication are true, the entire premise evaluates to true and modus ponens may again be applied, yielding the conclusion savings(adequate), which is added as expression 13.

13. savings(adequate).

As an examination of expressions 3, 12, and 13 indicates, the premise of implication 3 is also true. When we apply modus ponens a third time, the conclusion is investment(combination). This is the suggested investment for this individual.

This example illustrates how predicate calculus may be used to reason about a realistic problem, drawing correct conclusions by applying inference rules to the initial problem description. We have not discussed exactly how an algorithm can determine the correct inferences to make to solve a given problem or the way in which this can be implemented on a computer. These topics are discussed in chapters 3 and 4.

2.5   Epilogue and References

In this chapter we introduced predicate calculus as a representation language for AI problem solving. The symbols, terms, expressions, and semantics of the language were described and defined. Based on the semantics of predicate calculus, we defined inference rules that allow us to derive sentences that logically follow a given set of expressions. We defined a unification algorithm that determines the variable substitutions that make two expressions match. Matching is essential to the application of inference rules. We concluded the chapter with the example of a financial advisor that represents financial knowledge in predicate calculus and demonstrates logical inference as a problem-solving technique.

Predicate calculus is discussed in detail in a number of computer science books, including *The Logical Basis for Computer Programming* by Zohar Manna and Richard Waldinger (1985), *Logic for Computer Science* by Jean H. Gallier (1986), *Symbolic Logic and Mechanical Theorem Proving* by Chin-liang Chang and Richard Char-tung Lee (1973), and *An Introduction to Mathematical Logic and Type Theory* by Peter B. Andrews (1986).

Books that describe the use of predicate calculus as an artificial intelligence representation language include *Logical Foundations of Artificial Intelligence* by

Michael Genesereth and Nils Nilsson (1987), *Principles of Artificial Intelligence* by Nils Nilsson (1980), *Automated Reasoning* by Larry Wos et al. (1984), and *Computer Modelling of Mathematical Reasoning* by Alan Bundy (1983). *Readings in Knowledge Representation* by Ronald Brachman and Hector Levesque (1985) includes a number of articles on the use of predicate calculus for knowledge representation.

2.6 Exercises

1. Using truth tables, prove the identities of Section 2.1.2.

2. A new operator, ⊕, or *exclusive-or* may be defined by the following truth table:

p	q	p ⊕ q
T	T	F
T	F	T
F	T	T
F	F	F

   Create a propositional calculus expression using only ∧, ∨ and ¬ that is equivalent to p ⊕ q. Prove their equivalence using truth tables.

3. The logical operator ⇔ is read if and only if p ⇔ q is defined as being equivalent to (p ⇒ q) ∧ (q ⇒ p). Based on this definition, show that p ⇔ q is logically equivalent to (p ∨ q) ⇒ (p ∧ q):

   a. By using truth tables.

   b. By a series of substitutions using the identities in Figure 2.2.

4. Prove that implication is transitive in the propositional calculus, that is, that ((P ⇒ Q) ∧ (Q ⇒ R)) ⇒ (P ⇒ R).

5. a. Prove that modus ponens is sound for propositional calculus. Hint: use truth tables to enumerate all possible interpretations.

   b. *Abduction* is an inference rule that infers P from P ⇒ Q and Q. Show that abduction is not sound.

6. Assume that we have chosen to represent "Maria is Bill's mother" by mother(bill,maria) and "Amanda is one of Bill's ancestors" by ancestor(bill,amanda). Write a predicate calculus expression stating that every one of Bill's ancestors is either his mother, father, or one of their ancestors.

7. Attempt to unify the following pairs of expressions. Either show their most general unifiers or explain why they will not unify.

   a. p(X, Y). and p(a, Z).

   b. p(X, X). and p(a, b).

   c. ancestor(X, Y). and ancestor(bill, father(bill)).

   d. ancestor(X, father(X)). and ancestor(david, george).

   e. q(X). and ¬ q(a).

   f. p(X, a, Y). and p(Z, Z, b).

8. a. Compose the substitution sets {a/X, Y/Z} and {X/W, b/Y}.

   b. Prove that composition of substitution sets is associative.

   c. Construct an example to show that composition is not commutative.

9. Implement the unification algorithm of Section 2.3.2 in the computer language of your choice.

10. Give two alternative interpretations for the blocks world description of Figure 2.3.

11. Jane Doe has four dependents, a steady income of $30,000.00, and $15,000.00 in her savings account. Add the appropriate predicates describing her situation to the general investment advisor of the example in Section 2.4 and perform the unifications and inferences needed to determine her suggested investment.

12. Write a set of logical predicates that will perform simple automobile diagnostics (e.g., if the engine won't turn over and the lights won't come on, then the battery is bad). Don't try to be too elaborate, but cover the cases of bad battery, out of gas, bad spark plugs and bad starter motor.

13. The following story is quoted from N. Wirth's "Algorithms + data structures = programs" (Wirth 1976).

> I married a widow (let's call her W) who has a grown-up daughter (call her D). My father (F), who visited us quite often, fell in love with my step-daughter and married her. Hence my father became my son-in-law and my step-daughter became my mother. Some months later, my wife gave birth to a son (S_1), who became the brother-in-law of my father, as well as my uncle. The wife of my father, that is, my step-daughter, also had a son (S_2).

Using predicate calculus, create a set of expressions that represent the situation in the above story. Add expressions defining basic family relationships such as the definition of father-in-law and use modus ponens on this system to prove the conclusion that "I am my own grandfather."

STRUCTURES AND STRATEGIES
FOR STATE SPACE SEARCH

Two roads diverged in a yellow wood,
And sorry I could not travel both
And be one traveler, long I stood
And looked down one as far as I could
To where it bent in the undergrowth;

Then took the other . . .

—Robert Frost ''The Road Not Taken''

3.0   Introduction

Chapter 2 introduced predicate calculus as an example of an artificial intelligence representation language. Well-formed predicate calculus expressions provide a means of describing objects and relations in a problem domain, while inference rules such as modus ponens allow us to infer new knowledge from these descriptions. These inferences define a space that is searched to find a problem solution. Chapter 3 introduces the theory of state space search.

To successfully design and implement search algorithms, a programmer must be able to analyze and predict their behavior. Questions that need to be answered include:

Is the problem solver guaranteed to find a solution?

Will the problem solver always terminate, or can it become caught in an infinite loop?

When a solution is found, is it guaranteed to be optimal?

What is the complexity of the search process in terms of time usage? Space usage?

How can the interpreter most effectively reduce search complexity?

How can an interpreter be designed to most effectively utilize a representation language?

The theory of *state space search* is our primary tool for answering these questions. By representing a problem as a *state space graph*, we can use *graph theory* to analyze the structure and complexity of both the problem and the procedures used to solve it.

A graph consists of a set of *nodes* and a set of *arcs* or *links* connecting pairs of nodes. In the state space model of problem solving, the nodes of a graph are taken to represent discrete *states* in a problem-solving process, such as the results of logical inferences or configurations of a game board. The arcs of the graph represent transitions between states. These transitions correspond to logical inferences or legal moves of a game. In expert systems, for example, states describe our knowledge of a problem instance at some stage of a reasoning process. Expert knowledge, in the form of *if ... then rules*, allows us to generate new information; the act of applying a rule is represented as an arc between states.

Graph theory is our best tool for reasoning about the structure of objects and relations; indeed, this is precisely the need that led to its creation in the early eighteenth century. The Austrian mathematician Leonhard Euler invented graph theory to solve the ''bridges of Königsberg problem.'' The city of Königsberg occupied both banks and two islands of a river. The islands and the riverbanks were connected by seven bridges, as indicated in Figure 3.1.

The bridges of Königsberg problem asks if there is a walk around the city that crosses each bridge exactly once. Although the residents had failed to find such a walk and doubted that it was possible, no one had proved its impossibility. Devising a form of graph theory, Euler created an alternative representation for the map, presented in Figure 3.2. The riverbanks (rb1 and rb2) and islands (i1 and i2) are described by the nodes of a graph; the bridges are represented by labeled arcs between nodes (b1, b2, ..., b7). The graph representation preserves the essential structure of the bridge system, while ignoring extraneous features such as distance and direction.

Alternatively, we may represent the Königsberg bridge system using predicate calculus. The connect predicate corresponds to an arc of the graph, asserting that two land

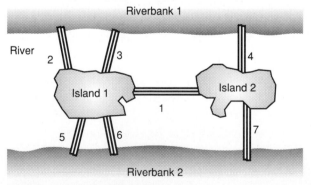

Figure 3.1   The city of Königsberg.

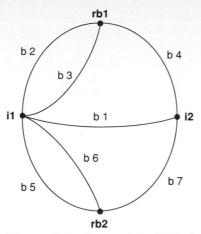

Figure 3.2 Graph of the Königsberg bridge system.

masses are connected by a particular bridge. Each bridge requires two **connect** predicates, one for each direction in which the bridge may be crossed:

connect(i1,i2,b1).   connect(i2,i1,b1).
connect(rb1,i1,b2).   connect(i1,rb1,b2).
connect(rb1,i1,b3).   connect(i1,rb1,b3).
connect(rb1,i2,b4).   connect(i2,rb1,b4).
connect(rb2,i1,b5).   connect(i1,rb2,b5).
connect(rb2,i1,b6).   connect(i1,rb2,b6).
connect(rb2,i2,b7).   connect(i2,rb2,b7).

This is equivalent to the graph representation in that the connectedness is preserved. Indeed, an algorithm could translate between the two representations with no loss of information. However, the structure is made explicit in the graph representation, while it is left implicit in the predicate calculus version. Euler's proof illustrates this distinction.

In proving that the walk was impossible, Euler focused on the *degree* of the nodes of the graph, observing that a node could be of either *even* or *odd* degree. An *even* degree node has an even number of arcs joining it to neighboring nodes. An *odd* degree node has an odd number of arcs.

With the exception of its beginning and ending nodes, the desired walk would have to leave each node exactly as often as it entered it. Nodes of odd degree could be used only as the beginning or ending of the walk, since such nodes could be crossed only a certain number of times before they proved to be a dead end. The traveler could not exit the node without using a previously traveled arc.

Euler noted that unless a graph contained either exactly zero or two nodes of odd degree, the walk was impossible. If there were two odd-degree nodes, the walk could start at the first and end at the second; if there were no nodes of odd degree, the walk could begin and end at the same node. The walk is not possible for graphs containing any other number of nodes of odd degree, as is the case with the city of Königsberg. This problem is now called finding an *Euler path* through a graph.

Note that the predicate calculus representation, while capturing the relationships between bridges and land in the city, does not suggest the concept of the degree of a node. In the graph representation there is a single instance of each node with arcs between the nodes, rather than multiple occurrences of constants as arguments in a set of predicates. For this reason, the representation suggests the concept of node degree and the focus of Euler's proof. This illustrates graph theory's power for analyzing the structure of objects, properties, and relationships. In Chapter 9 we examine the advantages of graph theory for knowledge representation (semantic networks); this chapter uses it to construct a computational theory of problem solving.

After reviewing basic graph theory, we present the state space description of problems, along with graph search as a problem-solving methodology. Depth- and breadth-first search are two strategies for searching a state space. We compare these and make the added distinction between goal-driven and data-driven search. Section 3.3 demonstrates how state space search is used to characterize logical reasoning. Throughout the chapter, we use graph theory to analyze the structure and complexity of a variety of problems.

3.1 Graph Theory (Optional Review)

3.1.1 Structures for State Space Search

A graph is a set of nodes and arcs that connect them. A *labeled* graph has one or more descriptors (labels) attached to each node that distinguish it from any other node in the graph. In a state space graph, these descriptors identify states in a problem-solving process. If there are no descriptive differences between two nodes, they are considered the same. The arc between two nodes is indicated by the labels of the connected nodes.

The arcs of a graph may also be labeled. Arc labels are used to indicate that an arc represents a named relationship (as in a semantic network) or to attach weights to arcs (as in the traveling salesperson problem). If there are different arcs between the same two nodes (as in Figure 3.2), these can also be distinguished through labeling.

A graph is *directed* if arcs have an associated directionality. The arcs in a directed graph are usually drawn as arrows or have an arrow attached to indicate direction. Arcs that can be crossed in either direction may have two arrows attached but more often have no direction indicators at all. Figure 3.3 is a labeled, directed graph: arc ab may only be crossed from node a to node b but arc bc is crossable in either direction.

A *path* through a graph connects a sequence of nodes through successive arcs. The path is represented by an ordered list that records the nodes in the order they occur in the path. In Figure 3.3, [a, b, c, d] represents the path through nodes a, b, c, d in that order.

A *rooted* graph has a unique node, called the *root*, such that there is a path from the root to all nodes within the graph. In drawing a rooted graph, the root is usually drawn at the top of the page, above the other nodes. The state space graphs for games are usually rooted graphs with the start of the game as the root. The initial moves of the tic-tac-toe

Nodes = {a,b,c,d,e}

Arcs = {(a,b),(a,d),(b,c),(c,b),(c,d),(d,a),(d,e),(e,c),(e,d)}

Figure 3.3 A labeled directed graph.

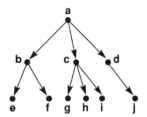

Figure 3.4 A rooted tree, exemplifying family relationships.

game graph are represented by the rooted graph of Figure II.5. This is a directed graph with all arcs having a single direction. Note that this graph contains no cycles; players cannot (as much as they might sometimes wish!) undo a move.

A *tree* is a graph in which two nodes have at most one path between them. Trees often have roots, in which case they are usually drawn with the root at the top, like a rooted graph. Since each node in a tree has only one path of access from any other node, it is impossible for a path to *loop* or *cycle* continuously through a sequence of nodes.

Terms used to describe relationships between nodes include *parent*, *child*, and *sibling*. These are used in the usual familial fashion with the parent preceding its child along a directed arc. The children of a node are called *siblings*. Similarly, an *ancestor* comes before a *descendant* in some path of a directed graph. In Figure 3.4, b is a *parent* of nodes e and f (which are, therefore, *children* of b and *siblings* of each other). Nodes a and c are *ancestors* of states g, h, and i, and g, h, and i are *descendants* of a and c.

Before introducing the state space representation of problems we formally define these concepts.

DEFINITION

GRAPH

A graph consists of:

A set of *nodes* N_1, N_2, N_3, ... N_n..., which need not be finite.

A set of *arcs* that connect pairs of nodes.

(Arcs are often described as an ordered pair of nodes; i.e., the arc (N_3, N_4) connects node N_3 to node N_4.)

A *directed* graph has an indicated direction for traversing each arc. For example, a directed graph might have (N_3, N_4) as an arc but not (N_4, N_3). This would indicate that a path through the graph could go from node N_3 to N_4 but not from N_4 to N_3.

If a directed arc connects N_j and N_k, then N_j is called the *parent* of N_k and N_k the *child* of N_j. If the graph also contains an arc (N_j, N_l), then N_k and N_l are called *siblings*.

A *rooted* graph has a unique node N_S from which all paths in the graph originate. That is, the root has no parent in the graph.

A *tip* or *leaf* node is a node that has no children.

An ordered sequence of nodes $[N_1, N_2, N_3, ..., N_n]$, where each N_i, N_{i+1} in the sequence represents an arc (N_i, N_{i+1}), is called a *path* of length n in the graph.

On a path in a rooted graph, a state is said to be an *ancestor* of all states positioned after it (to its right) and a *descendant* of all states before it (to its left).

A path that contains any state more than once (some N_j in the definition of path above is repeated) is said to contain a *cycle* or *loop*.

A *tree* is a graph in which there is a unique path between every pair of nodes. (The paths in a tree, therefore, contain no cycles.)

The edges in a rooted tree are directed away from the root. Each node in a rooted tree has a unique parent.

Two states in a graph are said to be *connected* if a path exists that includes them both.

3.1.2   State Space Representation of Problems

In the *state space representation* of a problem, nodes of a graph correspond to partial problem solution *states* and the arcs to steps in a problem-solving process. An *initial state*, corresponding to the given information in a problem instance, forms the root of the graph. The graph also defines a *goal* condition, which is the solution to a problem instance. *State space search* characterizes problem solving as the process of finding a *solution path* from the start state to a goal.

A goal may describe a state, such as a winning board in tic-tac-toe (Fig. II.5) or a goal configuration in the 8-puzzle (Fig. 3.6). Alternatively, a goal can describe some property of the solution path itself. In the traveling salesperson problem (Figs. 3.7 and 3.8), search terminates when the ''shortest'' path is found through all nodes of the graph. In the parsing problem (Section 3.3), the path of successful analysis of a sentence indicates termination.

Arcs of the state space correspond to steps in a solution process and paths through the space represent solutions in various stages of completion. Paths are searched, beginning at the start state and continuing through the graph until either the goal description is satisfied or they are abandoned. The actual generation of new states along the path is done by applying operators, such as ''legal moves'' in a game or inference rules in a logic problem or expert system, to existing states on a path.

We now formally define the state space representation of problems.

D E F I N I T I O N

STATE SPACE SEARCH

A *state space* is represented by a four-tuple [N,A,S,GD], where:

N is the set of nodes or states of the graph. These correspond to the states in a problem-solving process.

A is the set of arcs (or links) between nodes. These correspond to the steps in a problem-solving process.

S, a nonempty subset of N, contains the start state(s) of the problem.

GD, a nonempty subset of N, contains the goal state(s) of the problem. The states in GD are described using either:

1. A measurable property of the states encountered in the search.

2. A property of the path developed in the search.

A *solution path* is a path through this graph from a node in S to a node in GD.

The task of a search algorithm is to find a solution path through such a problem space. Search algorithms must keep track of the paths from a start to a goal node, because these paths contain the series of operations that lead to the problem solution.

One of the general features of a graph, and one of the problems that arise in the design of a graph search algorithm, is that states can sometimes be reached through different paths. For example, in Figure 3.3 a path can be made from state a to state d either through b and c or directly from a to d. This makes it important to choose the *best* path according to the needs of a problem. In addition, multiple paths to a state can lead to loops or cycles in a solution path that prevent the algorithm from reaching a goal. A (blind) search for goal state e in the graph of Figure 3.3 might search the sequence of states abcdabcdabcd... forever!

If the space to be searched is a tree (as in Fig. 3.4), the problem of cycles does not occur. It is, therefore, important to distinguish between problems whose state space is a tree and those that may contain loops. General graph search algorithms must detect and eliminate loops from potential solution paths, while tree searches may gain efficiency by eliminating this test and its overhead.

Tic-tac-toe and the 8-puzzle exemplify the state spaces of simple games. Both of these examples demonstrate termination conditions of type 1 in the above definition. Example 3.1.3, the traveling salesperson problem, has a goal description of type 2.

EXAMPLE 3.1.1 TIC-TAC-TOE

The state space representation of tic-tac-toe appears in Figure II.5. The start state is an empty board, and the termination or goal description is a board state having three Xs in a row, column, or diagonal (assuming that the goal is a win for X). The path from the start state to a goal state gives the series of moves in a winning game.

The states in the space are all the different configurations of Xs and Os that the game can have. Of course, while there are 3^9 ways to arrange {blank, X, O} in nine spaces, most of them could never occur in an actual game. Arcs are generated by legal moves of the game, alternating between placing an X and an O in an unused location. The state space is a graph rather than a tree, since some states on the third and deeper levels can be reached by different paths. However, there are no cycles in the state space, because the directed arcs of the graph do not allow a move to be undone. It is impossible to "go back up" the structure once a state has been reached. No checking for cycles in path generation is necessary. A graph structure with this property is called a *directed acyclic graph*, or *DAG*, and is common in state space search.

The state space representation provides a means of determining the complexity of the problem. In tic-tac-toe, there are nine first moves with eight possible responses to each of them, followed by seven possible responses to each of these, and so on. It follows that $9 \times 8 \times 7 \times \ldots$ or 9! different paths can be generated. While it is not impossible for a computer to search this number of paths (362,880) exhaustively, many important problems also exhibit factorial or exponential complexity, although on a much larger scale. Chess has 10^{120} possible game paths; checkers has 10^{40}. These spaces are difficult or impossible to search exhaustively. Strategies for searching such large spaces rely on heuristics to reduce the complexity of the search (Chapter 5).

EXAMPLE 3.1.2: THE 8-PUZZLE

In the *15-puzzle* of Figure 3.5, 15 differently numbered tiles are fitted into 16 spaces on a grid. One space is left blank so that tiles can be moved around to form different patterns. The goal is to find a series of moves of tiles into the blank space that places the board in a goal configuration. This is a common game that most of us played as children. (The version we remember was about 3 inches square and had red and white tiles in a black frame.)

A number of interesting aspects of this game have made it useful to researchers in problem solving. The state space is large enough to be interesting but is not completely

15-puzzle   8-puzzle

Figure 3.5 The 15-puzzle and the 8-puzzle.

intractable (16! if symmetric states are treated as distinct). Game states are easy to represent. The game is rich enough to provide a number of interesting heuristics (see Chapter 5).

The *8-puzzle* is a 3 × 3 version of the 15-puzzle in which eight tiles can be moved around in nine spaces. Because it generates a smaller state space than the full 15-puzzle, it is used for many of the examples in this text.

Although in the physical puzzle moves are made by moving tiles (''move the 7 tile right, provided the blank is to the right of the tile'' or ''move the 3 tile down''), it is much simpler to think in terms of ''moving the blank space'' instead. This simplifies the definition of move rules since there are eight tiles but only a single blank. The legal moves are:

move the blank up   ↑
move the blank right   →
move the blank down   ↓
move the blank left   ←

In order to apply a move, we must make sure that it does not move the blank off the board. Therefore, all four moves are not applicable at all times; for example, when the blank is in one of the corners only two moves are possible.

If we specify a beginning state and a goal state for the 8-puzzle, it is possible to give a state space accounting of the problem-solving process (Figure 3.6). States could

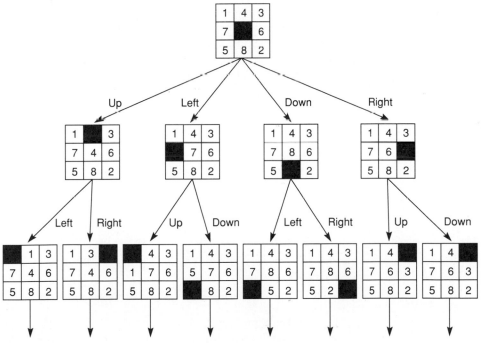

Figure 3.6 State space of the 8-puzzle generated by "move blank" operations.

be represented using a simple 3×3 array. A predicate calculus representation could use a "state" predicate with nine parameters (for the locations of numbers in the grid). Four procedures, describing each of the possible moves of the blank, define the arcs in the state space.

As with tic-tac-toe, the state space for the 8-puzzle is a graph (with most states having multiple parents), but unlike tic-tac-toe, cycles are possible. The GD or goal description of the state space is a particular state or board configuration. When this state is found on a path, the search terminates. The path from the start to the goal is the desired series of moves.

It is interesting to note that the complete state space of the 15-puzzle consists of two disconnected (and in this case equal-sized) subgraphs. This makes half the possible states in the search space impossible to reach from any given start state. If we exchange (by prying loose!) two immediately adjacent tiles, states in the other component of the space become reachable.

EXAMPLE 3.1.3: THE TRAVELING SALESPERSON

Suppose a salesperson has five cities to visit and then must return home. The goal of the problem is to find the shortest path for the salesperson to travel, visiting each city, and then return to the starting city. Figure 3.7 gives an instance of this problem. The nodes of the graph represent cities, and each arc is labeled with a weight indicating the cost of traveling that arc. Let us assume the salesperson lives in city A and will return there.

The path [A,D,C,B,E,A], with associated cost of 450 miles, is an example of a possible circuit. The goal description requires a complete circuit with minimum cost. Note that the goal description is a property of the entire path, rather than of a single state. This is a goal description of type 2 from the definition of state space search.

Figure 3.8 shows one way in which possible solution paths may be generated and compared. Beginning with node A, possible next states are added until all cities are included and the path returns home. The goal is the lowest-cost path.

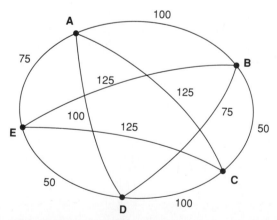

Figure 3.7   An instance of the traveling salesperson problem.

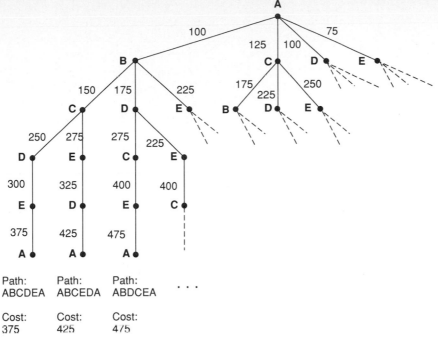

Figure 3.8 Search of the traveling salesperson problem. Each arc is marked with the total weight of all paths from the start node (A) to its endpoint.

As Figure 3.8 suggests, the complexity of exhaustive search in the traveling salesperson problem is $(N - 1)!$, where N is the number of cities in the graph. For 9 cities we may exhaustively try all paths, but for any problem instance of interesting size, 50 cities for example, simple exhaustive search cannot be performed within a practical length of time.

There are several techniques that reduce the search complexity. One is called *branch and bound* (Horowitz and Sabni 1978). Branch and bound generates paths one at a time, keeping track of the best circuit found so far. This value is used as a *bound* on future candidates. As paths are constructed a city at a time, the algorithm examines each partially completed path. If it determines that the best possible extension to a path will have greater cost than the bound, it eliminates that partial path and *all* of its possible extensions. This reduces search considerably but still leaves an exponential number of paths (1.26^N rather than $N!$).

Another strategy for controlling search constructs the path according to the rule "go to the closest unvisited city." The "nearest neighbor" path through the graph of Figure 3.8 is [A,E,D,B,C,A], at a cost of 375 miles. This method is highly efficient, since there is only one path to be tried! The nearest neighbor heuristic is fallible, as graphs exist for which it does not find the shortest path (Figure 3.9), but it is a possible compromise when the time required makes exhaustive search impractical.

Section 3.2 examines strategies for state space search.

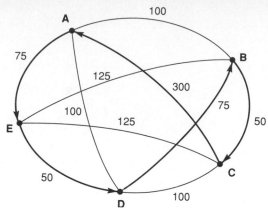

Figure 3.9 An instance of the traveling salesperson problem with the nearest neighbor path in bold. Note that this path (A, E, D, B, C, A), at a cost of 550, is not the shortest path. The comparatively high cost of arc (C, A) defeated the heuristic.

3.2 Strategies for State Space Search

3.2.1 Data-Driven and Goal-Driven Search

A state space may be searched in two directions: from the given data of a problem instance toward a goal or from a goal back to the data.

In *data-driven search*, sometimes called *forward chaining*, the problem solver begins with the given facts of the problem and a set of legal moves or rules for changing state. Search proceeds by applying rules to facts to produce new facts, which are in turn used by the rules to generate more new facts. This process continues until (we hope!) it generates a path that satisfies the goal condition.

An alternative approach is possible: Take the goal that we want to solve. See what rules or legal moves could be used to generate this goal and determine what conditions must be true to use them. These conditions become the new goals, or *subgoals*, for the search. Search continues, working backward through successive subgoals until (we hope!) it works back to the facts of the problem. This finds the chain of moves or rules leading from data to a goal, although it does so in backward order. This approach is called *goal-driven* reasoning, or *backward chaining*, and is like the simple childhood trick of trying to solve a maze by working back from the finish to the start.

To summarize: data-driven reasoning takes the facts of the problem and applies the rules and legal moves to produce new facts that lead to a goal; goal-driven reasoning focuses on the goal, finds the rules that could produce the goal, and chains backward through successive rules and subgoals to the given facts of the problem.

In the final analysis, both data-driven and goal-driven problem solvers search the same state space graph; however, the order and actual number of states searched can differ. The preferred strategy is determined by the properties of the problem itself. These include the complexity of the rules, the "shape" of the state space, and the nature and availability of the problem data. All of these vary for different problems.

As an example of the effect a search strategy can have on the complexity of search, consider the problem of confirming or denying the statement "I am a descendant of Thomas Jefferson." A solution is a path of direct lineage between the "I" and Thomas Jefferson. This space may be searched in two directions, startingwith the "I" and working along ancestor lines to Thomas Jefferson or starting with Thomas Jefferson and working through his descendants.

Some simple assumptions let us estimate the size of the space searched in each direction. Thomas Jefferson was born about 250 years ago; if we assume 25 years per generation, the required path will be about length 10. Since each person has exactly two parents, search back from the "I" would examine on the order of of 2^{10} ancestors. A search that worked forward from Thomas Jefferson would examine more states since people tend to have more than two children (particularly in the eighteenth and nineteenth centuries). If we assume an average of only three children per family, the search would examine on the order of 3^{10} nodes of the family tree. Thus, a search back from the "I" would examine fewer nodes. Note, however, that both directions yield exponential complexity.

Expert systems have been written using each of the data- and goal-driven approaches; the decision is based on the structure of the problem to be solved. Goal-driven search is suggested if:

1. A goal or hypothesis is given in the problem statement or can easily be formulated. In a mathematics theorem prover, for example, the goal is the theorem to be proved. Many diagnostic systems, such as MYCIN, consider potential diagnoses in a systematic fashion, confirming or eliminating them using goal-driven reasoning.

2. There are a large number of rules that match the facts of the problem and thus produce an increasing number of conclusions or goals. Early selection of a goal can eliminate most of these branches, making goal-driven search more effective in pruning the space (Figure 3.10). In a mathematics theorem prover, for example, the number of rules that conclude a given theorem is much smaller than the number of rules that may be applied to the entire set of axioms.

3. Problem data are not given but must be acquired by the problem solver. In this case, goal-driven search can help guide data acquisition. In a medical diagnosis program, for example, a wide range of diagnostic tests can be applied. Doctors order only those that are necessary to confirm or deny a particular set of hypotheses.

Goal-driven search thus uses knowledge of the desired goal to guide the search through relevant rules and eliminate branches of the space.

Data-driven search is appropriate to problems in which:

1. All or most of the data are given in the initial problem statement. Interpretation problems often fit this mold by presenting a collection of data and asking the system to provide a high-level interpretation. Systems that analyze particular

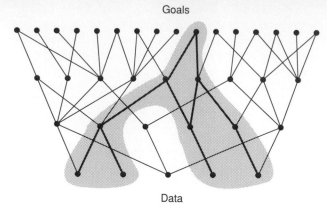

Goals

Data

Figure 3.10 State space in which goal-directed search effectively prunes extraneous goals and their antecedents.

data (such as the PROSPECTOR or Dipmeter programs, which interpret geological data or attempt to find what minerals are likely to be found at a site) fit the data-driven approach.

2. There are a large number of potential goals, but there are only a few ways to use the facts and given information of a particular problem instance (Figure 3.11). The DENDRAL program, an expert system that finds the molecular structure of organic compounds based on their formula, mass spectrographic data, and knowledge of chemistry, is an example of this. For any organic compound, there are an enormous number of possible structures. However, the mass spectrographic data on a compound allow DENDRAL to eliminate all but a few of these.

3. It is difficult to form a goal or hypothesis. In a DENDRAL consultation, for example, little is initially known about the possible structure of a compound.

Data-driven search uses the knowledge and constraints found in the given data of a problem to guide search along lines known to be true.

To summarize, there is no substitute for careful analysis of the particular problem, considering such issues as the *branching factor* of rule applications (see Chapter 5; on average, how many new states are generated by rule applications in both directions?), availability of data, and ease of determining potential goals.

3.2.2 Implementing Graph Search

In solving a problem using either goal- or data-driven search, a problem solver must find a path from a start state to a goal through the state space graph. The sequence of arcs in this path corresponds to the ordered steps of the solution. If a problem solver were given an oracle or other infallible mechanism for choosing a solution path, search would not be

Goals

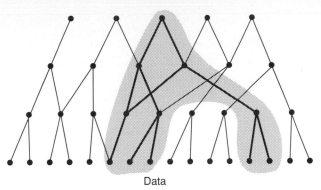

Figure 3.11   State space in which data-directed search effectively prunes irrelevant data and their consequents.

Data

required. It would move unerringly through the space to the desired goal, constructing the path as it went. Since oracles do not exist for interesting problems, a problem solver must consider different paths through the space until it finds a goal. *Backtracking* is a technique for systematically trying all different paths through a state space.

Backtracking search begins at the start state and pursues a path until it reaches either a goal or a "dead end." If it finds a goal, it quits and returns the solution path. If it reaches a dead end, it "backtracks" to the most recent node on the path having unexamined siblings and continues down one of these branches. The algorithm's behavior at each node is described in the following recursive rule:

> If the present state S does not meet the requirements of the goal description, then generate its first descendant S_{child_1} and apply the backtrack procedure recursively to this node. If backtrack does not find a goal node in the subgraph rooted at S_{child_1}, repeat the procedure for its sibling S_{child_2}. This continues until either some descendant of a child is a goal node or all of the children have been so searched. If none of the children of S leads to a goal, then backtrack "fails back" to the parent of S, where it is applied to the siblings of S, and so on.

The algorithm continues in this fashion until it finds a goal or exhausts the state space. Figure 3.12 shows the backtrack algorithm applied to a hypothetical state space. The direction of the dashed arrows on the tree indicates the progress of search up and down the space. The number beside each node indicates the order in which it is visited.

Below, we define an algorithm that performs a backtracking search. It uses three lists to keep track of nodes in the state space:

> SL, for state list, lists the states in the current path being tried. If a goal is found, SL contains the ordered list of states on the solution path.

> NSL, for new state list, contains nodes awaiting evaluation, i.e., nodes whose descendants have not yet been generated and searched.

Figure 3.12 Depth-first backtracking search of a hypothetical state space.

DE, for dead ends, lists states whose descendants have failed to contain a goal node. If these states are encountered again, they will be detected as elements of DE and eliminated from consideration immediately.

In defining the backtrack algorithm for the general case (a graph rather than a tree), it is necessary to detect multiple occurrences of any state so that it will not be reentered and cause (infinite) loops in the path. This is accomplished by testing each newly generated state for membership in any of these three lists. If a new state belongs to any of these lists, then it has already been visited and may be ignored.

The state currently under consideration is called CS for current state. CS is always equal to the state most recently added to SL and represents the "frontier" of the solution path currently being explored. Inference rules, moves in the game, or other appropriate problem-solving operators are ordered and applied to CS. The result is an ordered set of new states, the children of CS. The first of these children is made the new current state and the rest are placed in order on NSL for future examination. The new current state is added to SL and search continues. If CS has no children, it is removed from SL (this is where the algorithm "backtracks") and any remaining children of its predecessor on SL are examined.

```
function backtrack;

begin

    SL := [Start];  NSL := [Start];  DE := [ ];  CS := Start;     % initialize:

    while NSL ≠ [ ]                  %while there are states to be tried
        do begin

        if CS = goal (or meets goal description)
            then return(SL);          % on success, return list of states in path.
```

```
          if CS has no children (excluding nodes already on DE, SL, and NSL)
            then begin
                while SL is not empty and CS = the first element of SL
                  do begin
                    add CS to DE;              % record state as dead end
                    remove first element from SL;    %backtrack
                    remove first element from NSL;
                    CS := first element of NSL;
                  end;
                  add CS to SL;
            end
            else begin
                place children of CS (except nodes already on DE, SL, or NSL) on NSL;
                CS := first element of NSL;
                add CS to SL
            end
      end;

      return FAIL;       % state space is exhausted.

   end.
```

A trace of **backtrack** on the graph of Figure 3.12 is given by:

Initialize: SL = [A];   NSL = [A];   DE = [ ];   CS = A;

AFTER ITERATION	CS	SL	NSL	DE
0	A	[A]	[A]	[ ]
1	B	[B A]	[B C D A]	[ ]
2	E	[E B A]	[E F B C D A]	[ ]
3	H	[H E B A]	[H I E F B C DA]	[ ]
4	I	[I E B A]	[I E F B C D A]	[H]
5	F	[F B A]	[F B C D A]	[E I H]
6	J	[J F B A]	[J F B C D A]	[E I H]
7	C	[C A]	[C D A]	[B F J E I H]
8	G	[G C A]	[G C D A]	[B F J E I H]

As presented here, **backtrack** implements data-driven search, taking the root as a start state and evaluating its children to search for the goal. The algorithm can be restructured into a goal-driven search by letting the goal be the root of the graph and evaluating descendants back in an attempt to find a start state. Also, if the goal description is of type 2, the algorithm must determine a goal state by examining the path on SL.

backtrack is a basic algorithm for searching state space graphs. The graph search algorithms in the remainder of the text, including depth first, breadth first, and best first search, exploit the ideas used in backtrack, including:

1. The use of a list of unprocessed states (NSL) to allow the algorithm to return (backtrack) to any of these states.

---

2. A list of ''bad'' states (DE) to prevent the algorithm from retrying useless paths.

3. A list of nodes (SL) on the current solution path that is returned if a goal is found.

4. Explicit checks for membership of new states in these lists to prevent looping.

The next section introduces search algorithms that, like backtrack, use lists to keep track of states in a search space. These algorithms, including *depth-first*, *breadth-first* and *best-first* (Chapter 5) search, differ from backtrack in providing a more flexible basis for implementing alternative graph search strategies.

3.2.3 Depth- and Breadth-First Search

In addition to specifying a search direction (data- or goal-driven), a search algorithm determines the order in which states are examined in the tree or graph. This section considers two possibilities: *depth-first* and *breadth-first* search.

Consider the graph represented in Figure 3.13. States are labeled (A, B, C, . . .) so that they can be referred to in the discussion that follows. In depth-first search, when a state is examined, all of its children and their descendants are examined before any of its siblings. Depth-first search goes deeper into the search space whenever this is possible. Only when no further descendants of a state can be found are its siblings considered. Depth-first search examines the states in the graph of Figure 3.13 in the order A,B,E,K,S,L,T,F,M,C,G,N,H,O,P,U,D,I,Q,J,R. The backtrack algorithm of Section 3.2.2 implemented depth-first search.

Breadth-first search, in contrast, explores the space in a level-by-level fashion. Only when there are no more states to be explored at a given level does the algorithm move on to the next. A breadth-first search of the graph of Figure 3.13 considers the states in the order A,B,C,D,E,F,G,H,I,J,K,L,M,N,O,P,Q,R,S,T,U.

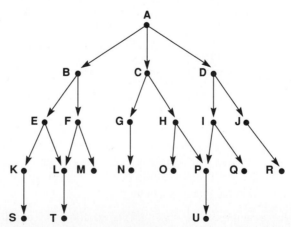

Figure 3.13 Graph for breadth- and depth-first search examples.

We implement breadth-first search using lists, open and closed, to keep track of progress through the state space. open, like NSL in backtrack, lists states that have been generated but whose children have not been examined. The order in which states are removed from open determines the order of the search. closed records states that have already been examined. closed is the union of the DE and SL lists of the backtrack algorithm.

procedure breadth_first_search

Initialize: open = [Start]; closed = [ ]

while open ≠ [ ] do
begin
  remove the leftmost state from open, call it X;

  if X is a goal then return(success);

  generate all children of X;

  put X on closed;

  eliminate any children of X already on either open or closed, as these will cause
    loops in the search;

  put the remaining descendants, in order of discovery, on the right end of open

end.

Child states are generated by inference rules, legal moves of a game, or other state transition operators. Each iteration produces all children of the state X and adds them to open. Note that open is maintained as a queue, or first in first out (FIFO) data structure. States are added to the right of the list and removed from the left. This biases search toward the states that have been on open the longest, causing the search to be breadth first.

Child states that have already been discovered (already appear on either open or closed) are eliminated.

If the algorithm terminates because the condition of the "while" loop is no longer satisfied (open = [ ]) then it has searched the entire graph without finding the desired goal; i.e., the search has failed.

A trace of breadth_first_search on the graph of Figure 3.13 appears below. Each successive number, 2,3,4, . . . , represents an iteration of the "while" loop. U is the desired goal state.

1. open = [A]; closed = [ ]
2. open = [B,C,D]; closed = [A]
3. open = [C,D,E,F]; closed = [B,A]
4. open = [D,E,F,G,H]; closed = [C,B,A]

5. open = [E,F,G,H,I,J]; closed = [D,C,B,A]
6. open = [F,G,H,I,J,K,L]; closed = [E,D,C,B,A]
7. open = [G,H,I,J,K,L,M] (since L is already on open); closed = [F,E,D,C,B,A]
8. open = [H,I,J,K,L,M,N]; closed = [G,F,E,D,C,B,A]
9. and so on until either U is found or open = [ ]

Figure 3.14 illustrates the graph of Figure 3.13 after six iterations of breadth_first_search. The states on open and closed are highlighted. States not shaded have not been discovered by the algorithm. Note that open records the states on the ''frontier'' of the search at any stage and closed records states already visited.

Since breadth-first search considers every node at each level of the graph before going deeper into the space, all states are first reached along the shortest path from the start state. Breadth-first search is therefore guaranteed to find the shortest path from the start state to the goal. Furthermore, since all states are first found along the shortest path, any states encountered a second time are found along a path of equal or greater length. Since there is no chance that duplicate states were found along a better path, the algorithm simply discards them.

It is often useful to keep other information on open and closed besides the names of the states. For example, note that breadth_first_search does not maintain a list of states on the current path to a goal as backtrack did on the list SL; all visited states are kept on closed. If the path is required for a solution, it can be returned by the algorithm.

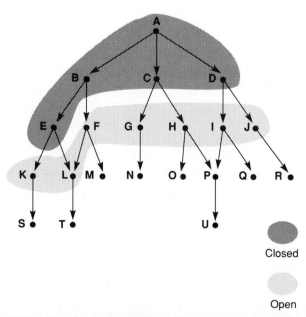

Closed

Open

Figure 3.14 Graph of Figure 3.13 at iteration 6 of breadth-first search. States on open and closed are highlighted.

Figure 3.15 Breadth-first search of the 8-puzzle, showing order in which states were removed from open.

This can be done by storing ancestor information along with each state. A state may be saved along with a record of its parent state, i.e., as an ordered pair (state, parent). If this is done in the search of the algorithm of Figure 3.13, the contents of open and closed at the fourth iteration would be:

open = [(D,A), (E,B), (F,B), (G,C), (H,C)]; closed = [(C,A), (B,A), (A,nil)]

The path (A, B, F) that led from A to F could easily be constructed from this information. When a goal is found, the algorithm may construct the solution path by tracing back along parents from the goal to the start state. Note that state A has a parent of nil, indicating that it is a start state; this stops reconstruction of the path. Because breadth-first search finds each state along the shortest path and retains the first version of each state, this is the shortest path from a start to a goal.

Figure 3.15 shows the states removed from open and examined in a breadth-first search of the graph of the 8-puzzle. As before, arcs correspond to moves of the blank up, to the right, down, and to the left. The number next to each state indicates the order in which it was removed from open. States left on open when the algorithm halted are not shown.

Depth-first search is implemented by modifying the algorithm for breadth-first search:

procedure depth_first_search

Initialize: open = [Start], closed = [ ]

while open ≠ [ ] do
  begin
    remove the next state from the left of open, call it X;

    if X is a goal then return(success);

    generate all possible children of X;

    put X on closed;

    eliminate any children of X already on either open or closed, as these will cause
      loops in the search;

    put the remaining children of X, in order of discovery, on the left of open

end.

In examining the algorithm, note that the descendant states are both added and removed from the *left* end of open: open is maintained as a *stack*, or last in first out (LIFO) structure. The organization of open as a stack biases search toward the most recently generated states, giving search a depth-first order.

A trace of depth_first_search on the graph of Figure 3.13 appears below. Each successive iteration of the "while" loop is indicated by a single line (2, 3, 4, ...). The initial states of open and closed are given on line 1. Assume U is the goal state.

1. open = [A]; closed = [ ]
2. open = [B,C,D]; closed = [A]
3. open = [E,F,C,D]; closed = [B,A]
4. open = [K,L,F,C,D]; closed = [E,B,A]
5. open = [S,L,F,C,D]; closed = [K,E,B,A]
6. open = [L,F,C,D]; closed = [S,K,E,B,A]
7. open = [T,F,C,D]; closed = [L,S,K,E,B,A]
8. open = [F,C,D]; closed = [T,L,S,K,E,B,A]
9. open = [M,C,D], since L is already on closed; closed = [F,T,L,S,K,E,B,A]
10. open = [C,D]; closed = [M,F,T,L,S,K,E,B,A]
11. open = [G,H,D]; closed = [C,M,F,T,L,S,K,E,B,A]

and so on until either U is discovered or open = [ ]

As with breadth_first_search, open lists all states discovered but not yet evaluated (the current "frontier" of the search), while closed records states already

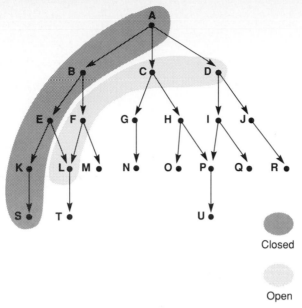

Closed

Open

Figure 3.16 Graph of Figure 3.13 at iteration 6 of depth-first search. States on open and closed are highlighted.

considered. Figure 3.16 shows the graph of Figure 3.13 at the sixth iteration of the **depth_first_search**. The contents of **open** and **closed** are highlighted. As with **breadth_first_search**, the algorithm could store a record of the parent along with each state, allowing it to reconstruct the path that led from the start state to a goal.

Unlike breadth-first search, a depth-first search is not guaranteed to find the shortest path to a state the first time it is encountered. Later in the search, a different path may be found to any state. If path length matters in a problem solver, when the algorithm encounters a duplicate state, it should save the version reached along the shortest path. This could be done be storing each state as a triple: (**state, parent, length_of_path**). When children are generated, the value of the path length is simply incremented by one and saved with the child. If a child is reached along multiple paths, this information can be used to retain the best version. This is treated in more detail in the discussion of *algorithm A* in Chapter 5. Note that retaining the best version of a state in a simple depth-first search does not guarantee that a goal will be reached along the shortest path.

Figure 3.17 gives a depth-first search of the 8-puzzle. As noted previously, the space is generated by the four ''move blank'' rules (up, down, left, and right). The numbers next to the states indicate the order in which they were considered, i.e., removed from **open**. States left on **open** when the goal is found are not shown. A depth bound of five was imposed on this search to keep it from getting lost deep in the space.

As with choosing between data- and goal-driven search for evaluating a graph, the choice of depth-first or breadth-first search depends on the specific problem being solved. Important features include the importance of finding the shortest path to a goal,

Figure 3.17 Depth-first search of the 8-puzzle with a depth bound of 5.

the branching of the state space, the available time and space resources, and the average length of paths to a goal node. In making these decisions, there are advantages and disadvantages for each approach.

Breadth First   Since it always examines all the nodes at level n before proceeding to level n + 1, breadth-first search always finds the shortest path to a goal node. In a problem where it is known that a simple solution exists, this solution will be found. Unfortunately, if there is a bad branching factor, i.e., states have a high average number of descendants, the combinatorial explosion may prevent the algorithm from finding a solution using the available space. This is due to the fact that all unexpanded nodes for each level of the search must be kept on **open**. For deep searches, or state spaces with a high branching factor, this can become quite cumbersome.

The space utilization of breadth-first search, measured in terms of the number of states on **open**, is an exponential function of the length of the path at any time. If each state has an average of B children, the number of states on a given level is B times the number of states on the previous level. This gives B^n states on level n. Breadth-first search will have placed all of these on **open** when it begins examining level n. This can be prohibitive if solution paths are long.

Depth First Depth-first search gets quickly into a deep search space. If it is known that the solution path will be long, depth-first search won't waste time searching a large number of "shallow" states in the graph. On the other hand, depth-first search can get "lost" deep in a graph, missing shorter paths to a goal or even becoming stuck in an infinitely long path that does not lead to a goal.

Depth-first search is much more efficient for search spaces with many branches since it does not have to keep all the nodes at a given level on the open list. The space usage of depth-first search is a linear function of the length of the path. At each level, open retains only the children of a single state. If a graph has an average of B children per state, this requires a total space usage of B × n states to go n levels deep into the space.

The best answer to the "depth-first versus breadth-first" issue is to examine the problem space carefully and consult experts in the area. In chess, for example, breadth-first search is simply not possible. In simpler games, breadth-first search not only may be possible but also may be the only way to avoid losing.

3.2.4   Depth-First Search with Iterative Deepening

A nice compromise on these trade-offs is to use a depth bound on depth-first search. The depth bound forces a failure on a search path once it gets below a certain level. This causes a breadthlike sweep of the search space at that depth level. When it is known that a solution lies within a certain depth or when time constraints, such as occur in an extremely large space like chess, limit the number of states that can be considered, then a depth-first search with a depth bound may be most appropriate. Figure 3.17 showed a depth-first search of the 8-puzzle in which a depth bound of five caused the sweep across the space at that depth.

This insight leads to a search algorithm that remedies many of the drawbacks of both depth-first and breadth-first search. *Depth-first iterative deepening* (Korf 1987) performs a depth-first search of the space with a depth bound of one. If it fails to find a goal, it performs another depth-first search with a depth bound of two. This continues, increasing the depth bound by one at each iteration. At each iteration, the algorithm performs a complete depth-first search to the current depth bound. No information about the state space is retained between iterations.

Since the algorithm searches the space in a level-by-level fashion, it is guaranteed to find a shortest path to a goal. Since it does only depth-first search at each iteration, the space usage at any level n is B × n, where B is the average number of children of a node.

Interestingly, although it seems as if depth-first iterative deepening would be much less time efficient than either depth-first or breadth-first search, its time complexity is actually of the same order of magnitude as either of these: $O(B^n)$. An intuitive explanation for this seeming paradox is given by Korf (1987):

> Since the number of nodes in a given level of the tree grows exponentially with depth, almost all the time is spent in the deepest level, even though shallower levels are generated an arithmetically increasing number of times.

Unfortunately, all the search strategies discussed in this chapter—bidirectional, depth first, breadth first, and depth-first iterative deepening—may be shown to have worst-case exponential time complexity. This is true for all *uninformed* search algorithms. The only approaches to search that reduce this complexity employ heuristics to guide search. *Best-first search* is a search algorithm that is similar to the algorithms for depth- and breadth-first search just presented. However, best-first search orders the states on the open list, the current fringe of the search, according to some measure of their heuristic merit. At each iteration, it considers neither the deepest nor the shallowest but the "best" state. Best-first search is the main topic of Chapter 5.

3.3 Using the State Space to Represent Reasoning with the Predicate Calculus

3.3.1 State Space Description of a Logical System

When we defined state space graphs in Section 3.1, we noted that nodes must be distinguishable from one another, with each node representing some state of the solution process. Predicate calculus can be used as the formal specification language for making these distinctions and for mapping the nodes of a graph onto the states of a problem-solving process. Furthermore, inference rules can be used to create and describe the arcs between states. In this fashion, problems in the predicate calculus, such as determining whether a particular expression is a logical consequence of a given set of assertions, may be solved using search.

The soundness and completeness of predicate calculus inference rules guarantee the correctness of conclusions derived through this form of graph-based reasoning. This ability to produce a formal proof of the integrity of a solution through the same algorithm that produces the solution is a unique attribute of much artificial intelligence and theorem proving–based problem solving.

Although many problems (such as tic-tac-toe) may be more naturally described by other data structures (such as arrays), the power and generality of logical representation allow most AI problem solving to use predicate calculus descriptions and inference rules as just described. Other representations such as rules (Chapter 9), semantic networks, or frames (chapters 11 and 14) employ similar search strategies and may also be understood using the structures introduced in this chapter. Solution strategies in all of these instances can be quite conveniently represented as graph search algorithms.

EXAMPLE 3.3.1.

The first example of how a set of logical assertions may be viewed as defining a graph is from the propositional calculus. Assume the following set of assertions:

$q \Rightarrow p$
$r \Rightarrow p$
$v \Rightarrow q$
$s \Rightarrow r$

$$t \Rightarrow r$$
$$s \Rightarrow u$$
$$s$$
$$t$$

From this set of assertions and the inference rule modus ponens, certain propositions (p, r, and u) may be inferred; others (such as v and q) may not be so inferred and indeed do not logically follow from these assertions. The relationship between the initial assertions and these inferences is expressed in the directed graph in Figure 3.18.

In Figure 3.18 the arcs correspond to logical implications ($\Rightarrow$). Propositions that are given as true (s and t) correspond to the given data of the problem. Propositions that are logical consequences of this set of assertions correspond to the nodes that may be reached along a directed path from a state representing a true proposition; such a path corresponds to a sequence of applications of modus ponens. For example, the path [s, r, p] corresponds to the sequence of inferences:

s and $s \Rightarrow r$ yields r.

r and $r \Rightarrow p$ yields p.

Given this representation, determining whether a given proposition is a logical consequence of a set of propositions becomes a problem of finding a path from a boxed node (the start node) to the proposition (the goal node). It has been cast as a graph search problem. The search strategy used here is data driven, since it proceeds from what is known (the true propositions) toward the goal. Alternatively, a goal-directed strategy could be applied to the same state space by starting with the proposition to be proved (the goal) and searching back along arcs to find support for it among the true propositions. In addition, we can search this space of inferences in either a depth-first or breadth-first fashion.

3.3.2   And/Or Graphs

In Example 3.3.1, all of the assertions were simple implications of the form "$p \Rightarrow q$." We did not discuss the way in which the logical operators and and or could be

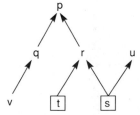

Figure 3.18   State space graph of a set of implications in the propositional calculus.

Figure 3.19 And/or graph of the expression q ∧ r ⇒ p.

Figure 3.20 And/or graph of the expression q ∨ r ⇒ p.

represented in such a graph. Expressing the logical relationships defined by these operators requires an extension to the basic graph model known as an *and/or graph*. And/or graphs are an important tool for describing the search spaces generated by many AI problems, including those solved by logical theorem provers and expert systems.

In expressions of the form q ∧ r ⇒ p, both q and r must be true in order for p to be true. In expressions of the form q ∨ r ⇒ p, the truth of either q or r is sufficient to prove p. (Since implications containing disjunctive premises may be written as separate implications, this expression is often written as q ⇒ p, r ⇒ p.) In order to represent these different relationships graphically, and/or graphs distinguish between and nodes and or nodes. If the premises of an implication are connected by an and operator, they are called and nodes in the graph and the arcs from this node are joined by a curved link. The expression q ∧ r ⇒ p is represented by the and/or graph of Figure 3.19.

The link connecting the arcs in Figure 3.19 captures the idea that both q and r must be true in order to prove p. If the premises are connected by an or operator, they are regarded as or nodes in the graph. Arcs from or nodes to their parent node are not so connected (Figure 3.20). This captures the notion that the truth of any one of the premises is independently sufficient to determine the truth of the conclusion.

An and/or graph is actually a specialization of a type of graph known as a *hypergraph*, which connects nodes by sets of arcs rather than by single arcs. A hypergraph is defined as follows:

D E F I N I T I O N

DEFINITION: HYPERGRAPH

A *hypergraph* consists of:

N, a set of nodes.

H, a set of hyperarcs defined by ordered pairs in which the first element of the pair is a single node from N and the second element is a subset of N.

An ordinary graph is a special case of hypergraph in which all the sets of descendant nodes have a cardinality of 1.

Hyperarcs are also known as *k-connectors*, where k is the cardinality of the set of descendant nodes. If k = 1, the descendant may be thought of as an or node. If k > 1, the elements of the set of descendants may be thought of as and nodes. In this case, the connector is drawn with individual edges from the parent node to each of the descendant nodes; these individual edges are then joined with a curved link as in the example above.

EXAMPLE 3.3.2.

The second example is also from the propositional calculus but generates a graph that contains both and and or descendants. Assume a situation in the world where the following propositions are true:

a
b
c
$a \wedge b \Rightarrow d$
$a \wedge c \Rightarrow e$
$b \wedge d \Rightarrow f$
$f \Rightarrow g$
$a \wedge e \Rightarrow h$

This set of assertions generates the and/or graph in Figure 3.21.

Questions that might be asked (answers deduced by the search of this graph) are:

1. Is h true?

2. Is h true if b is no longer true?

3. What is the shortest path (i.e., the shortest sequence of inferences) to show that X (some proposition) is true?

4. Show that the proposition p (note that p is not supported) is false. What does this mean? What would be necessary to achieve this conclusion?

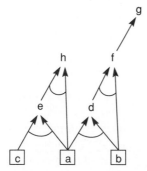

Figure 3.21   And/or graph of a set of propositional calculus expressions.

And/or graph search requires only slightly more record keeping than search in regular graphs, an example of which was the backtracking algorithm, previously discussed. The or descendants are checked as they were in backtrack: once a path is found connecting a goal to a start node along or nodes, the problem will be solved. If a path leads to a failure, the algorithm may backtrack and try another branch. In searching and nodes, however, all of the and descendants of a node must be solved (or proved true) in order to solve the parent node.

In the example of Figure 3.21, a goal-directed strategy for determining the truth of h first attempts to prove both a and e. The truth of a is immediate, but the truth of e requires the truth of both c and a; these are given as true. Once the problem solver has traced all these arcs down to true propositions, the true values are recombined at the and nodes to verify the truth of h.

A data-directed strategy for determining the truth of h, on the other hand, would begin with the known facts (c, a, and b) and begin adding new propositions to this set of known facts according to the constraints of the and/or graph. e or d might be the first proposition added to the set of facts. These additions make it possible to infer new facts. This process continues until the desired goal, h, has been proved.

One way of looking at and/or graph search is that the and operator (hence the and nodes of the graph) indicates a problem decomposition in which the problem is broken into (simpler) subproblems such that all of the subproblems must be solved to solve the original problem. An or operator in the predicate calculus representation of the problem indicates a selection, a point at which a choice may be made between alternative problem-solving strategies, any of which, if successful, is sufficient to solve the problem.

3.3.3 Further Examples and Applications

EXAMPLE 3.3.3

One natural example of an and/or graph is a program for symbolically integrating mathematical functions. MACSYMA is a well-known program that is used extensively by mathematicians. The reasoning of MACSYMA can be represented as an and/or graph. In performing integrations, one important class of strategies involves breaking an expression into sub-expressions that may be integrated independently of one another, with the result being combined algebraically into a solution expression. Examples of this strategy include the rule for integration by parts and the rule for decomposing the integral of a sum into the sum of the integrals of the individual terms. These strategies, representing the decomposition of a problem into independent subproblems, can be represented by and nodes in the graph.

Another class of strategies involves the simplification of an expression through various algebraic substitutions. Since any given expression may allow a number of different substitutions, each representing an independent solution strategy, these strategies are represented by or nodes of the graph. Figure 3.22 illustrates the space searched by such a problem solver. The search of this graph is goal directed, in that it begins with the query "find the integral of ???" and searches back to the algebraic expressions that define that integral. Note that this is an example in which goal-directed search is the

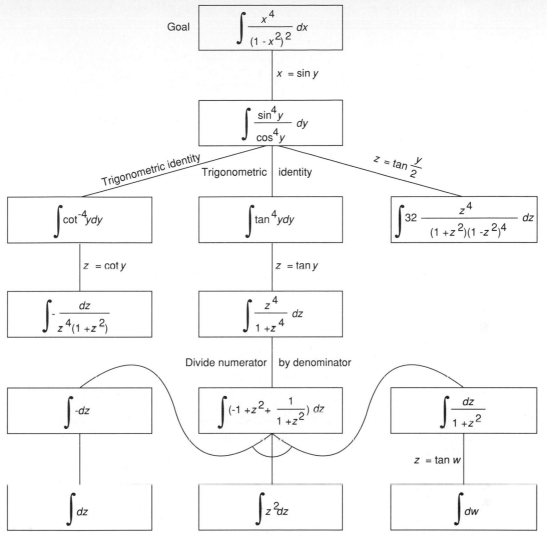

Figure 3.22 And/or graph representing part of the state space for integrating a function.

obvious strategy. It would be practically impossible for a problem solver to determine the algebraic expressions that formed the desired integral without working back from the query.

EXAMPLE 3.3.4

This example is taken from the predicate calculus and represents a goal-driven graph search where the goal to be proved true is a predicate calculus expression, often containing variables. The axioms are the logical descriptions of a relationship between a dog, Fred, and his master, Sam.

The facts and rules of this example are given as English sentences followed by their predicate calculus equivalents:

1. Fred is a collie.
   collie(fred).

2. Sam is Fred's master.
   master(fred,sam).

3. It is Saturday.
   day(saturday).

4. It is cold on Saturday.
   ¬ (warm(saturday)).

5. Fred is a trained dog.
   trained(fred).

6. Spaniels or collies that are trained are good dogs.
   ∀ X[spaniel(X) ∨ (collie(X) ∧ trained(X)) ⇒ gooddog(X)]

7. If a dog is a good dog and has a master then he will be with his master.
   ∀ (X,Y,Z) [gooddog(X) ∧ master(X,Y) ∧ location(Y,Z) ⇒ location(X,Z)]

8. If it is Saturday and warm, then Sam is at the park.
   day(sat) ∧ warm(sat) ⇒ location(sam, park).

9. If it is Saturday and not warm, then Sam is at the museum.
   day(sat) ∧ ¬(warm(sat)) ⇒ location(sam,museum).

The goal is the expression ∃Xlocation(fred,X), meaning "where is fred?" A backward search algorithm examines alternative means of establishing this goal: "if fred is a good dog and fred has a master and fred's master is at a location then fred is at that location also." The premises of this rule are then examined: what does it mean to be a "good dog," etc.? This process continues, constructing the and/or graph of Figure 3.23.

Let us examine the search of Example 3.3.4 in more detail, particularly since it is the first example of goal-driven search using the predicate calculus and it illustrates the role of unification in the generation of the search space. The problem to be solved is "where is fred?" More formally, it may be seen as determining a substitution for the variable X, if such a substitution exists, under which location(fred,X) is a logical consequence of the initial assertions.

When it is desired to determine Fred's location, clauses are examined that have location as their conclusion. The first of these is clause 7. This conclusion, location(P,Q), is then unified with location(fred, X) by the substitutions {fred/P, X/Q}. The premises of this rule, under the same substitution, form the "and" descendants of the top goal in the graph:

gooddog(fred) ∧ master(fred, Y) ∧ location(Y,Z).

This expression may be interpreted as meaning that one way to find Fred is to see if Fred is a good dog, find out who Fred's master is, and find out where the master is. The initial goal has thus been replaced by three subgoals. These are and nodes and all of them must be solved.

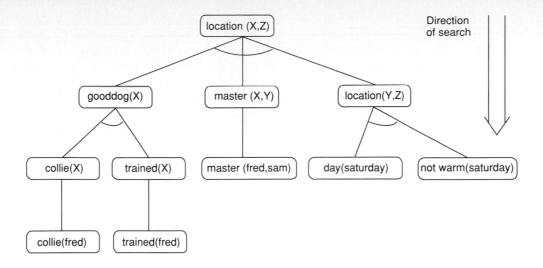

Substitutions = {fred/X, sam/Y, museum/Z}

Figure 3.23 And/or graph showing fred is at the museum.

To solve these subgoals, the problem solver first determines if Fred is a good dog. This matches the conclusion of clause 6. The premise of clause 6 is the **or** of two expressions:

$\forall X$ spaniel(X) $\lor$ (collie(X) $\land$ trained(X))

The first of these **or** nodes is spaniel(X). The data base doesn't contain this assertion, so the problem solver must assume it is false. The other **or** node is (collie(X) $\land$ trained(X)), i.e., is Fred a collie and is Fred trained. Both of these need to be true, which they are by clauses 1 and 5.

This proves that gooddog(fred) is true. The problem solver then examines the second of the premises of clause 7: master(X, Y). Under the substitution {fred/X}, this becomes master(fred, Y), which unifies with the fact (clause 2) of master(fred, sam). This produces the unifying substitution of {sam/Y}, which also gives the value of sam to the third subgoal of clause 7, creating the new goal location(sam, Z).

In solving this, assuming the problem solver tries rules in order, the goal location(sam, Z) will first unify with the conclusion of clause 7. Note that the same rule is being tried with different bindings for X. Recall (Chapter 2) that X is a "dummy" variable and could have any name (any string beginning with an uppercase letter). Since the extent of the meaning of any variable name is contained within the clause in which it appears, the predicate calculus has no global variables. Another way of saying this is that values of variables are passed to other clauses as parameters and have no fixed (memory) locations. Thus, the multiple occurrences of X in different rules in this example indicate *different* formal parameters (Section 12.3).

In attempting to solve the premises of rule 7 with these new bindings, the problem solver will fail since sam is not a good dog. Here, the search will backtrack to the goal location(sam, Z) and try the next match, the conclusion of rule 8. This will also fail, causing another backtrack and a unification with the conclusion of clause 9, at(sam, museum).

Since the premises of clause 9 are supported in the set of assertions (clauses 3 and 4), it follows that the conclusion of clause 9 may be taken as true. This final unification goes all the way back up the tree to finally answer location(fred, X)? with location(fred, museum).

It is important to examine carefully the nature of the goal-driven search of a graph and compare it with the data-driven search of Example 3.3.2. Further discussion of this issue, including a more rigorous comparison of these two methods of searching a graph, will continue in the next example but will be seen in full detail only in the discussion of production systems in the next chapter and in the application to expert systems in Part IV. Another point implicit in this example is that the order of clauses affects the order of search. In the example above, the multiple location clauses were tried in order, with backtracking search eliminating those that failed to be proved true.

EXAMPLE 3.3.5

In the last example of Chapter 2 we used predicate calculus to represent a set of rules for giving investment advice. In that example, modus ponens was used to infer a proper investment for a particular individual. We did not discuss the way in which a program might determine the appropriate inferences. This is, of course, a search problem; the present example illustrates one approach to implementing the logic-based financial advisor, using goal-directed, depth-first search with backtracking. The discussion uses the predicates found in Section 2.4; these predicates are not duplicated here.

Assume that the individual has two dependents, $20,000 in savings, and a steady income of $30,000. As discussed in Chapter 2, we can add predicate calculus expressions describing these facts to the set of predicate calculus expressions. Alternatively, the program may begin the search without this information and ask the user to add it as needed. This has the advantage of not requiring data that may not prove necessary for a solution. This approach is often taken in expert systems and is illustrated in this example.

In performing a consultation, the goal is to find an investment; this is represented as the predicate calculus expression investment(X). Note the use of the unbound variable X in the goal. This goal is also referred to as a query. There are three rules (1, 2, and 3) that conclude about investments, since the query will unify with the conclusion of these rules. If we select rule 1 for initial exploration, its premise savings(inadequate) becomes the subgoal, i.e., the child node that will be expanded next.

In generating the children of savings(inadequate), the only rule that may be applied is rule 5. This produces the and node:

amountsaved(X) ∧ dependents(Y) ∧ ¬greater(X, minsavings(Y))

If we attempt to satisfy these in left-to-right order, amountsaved(X) is taken as the first subgoal. Since the system contains no rules that conclude this subgoal, it will query the user. When amountsaved(20000) is added the first subgoal will succeed, with unification substituting 20000 for X. Note that since an and node is being searched, a failure here would eliminate the need to examine the remainder of the expression.

Similarly, the subgoal dependents(Y) leads to a user query, and the response, dependents(2), is added to the logical description. The subgoal matches this expression with the substitution {2/Y}. The search will then evaluate the truth of

$\neg$ greater(X, minsavings(Y)).

This evaluates to false, causing failure of the entire and node. The search then backtracks to the parent node, savings(inadequate), and attempts to find an alternative way to prove it true. This corresponds to the generation of the next child in the search. Since no other rules conclude this subgoal, search fails back to the top-level goal, investment(X). The next rule whose conclusions unify with this goal is rule 2, producing the new subgoals

savings(adequate) $\wedge$ income(adequate).

Continuing the search, savings(adequate) is proved true as the conclusion of rule 4, and income(adequate) follows as the conclusion of rule 6. Although the details of the remainder of the search will be left to the reader, the and/or graph that is ultimately searched appears in Figure 3.24.

EXAMPLE 3.3.6

The final example is not from the predicate calculus but consists of a set of rewrite rules for parsing sentences in a subset of English grammar. Rewrite rules take an expression and transform it into another by replacing the pattern on one side of the arrow ($\leftarrow$) with the pattern on the other side. For example, a set of rewrite rules could be defined to change an expression in one language (English, say) into another language (perhaps French or a predicate calculus clause). The rewrite rules given here transform a subset of English sentences into higher level grammatical constructs such as noun phrase, verb phrase, and sentence. These rules are used to *parse* sequences of words, i.e., to determine whether they are well-formed sentences (are grammatically correct or not) and to model the linguistic structure of the sentences.

Five rules for a simple subset of English grammar are:

1. A sentence is a noun phrase followed by a verb phrase.
   sentence $\leftarrow$ np vp
2. A noun phrase is a noun.
   np $\leftarrow$ n
3. A noun phrase is an article followed by a noun.
   np $\leftarrow$ art n
4. A verb phrase is a verb.
   vp $\leftarrow$ v
5. A verb phrase is a verb followed by a noun phrase.
   vp $\leftarrow$ v np

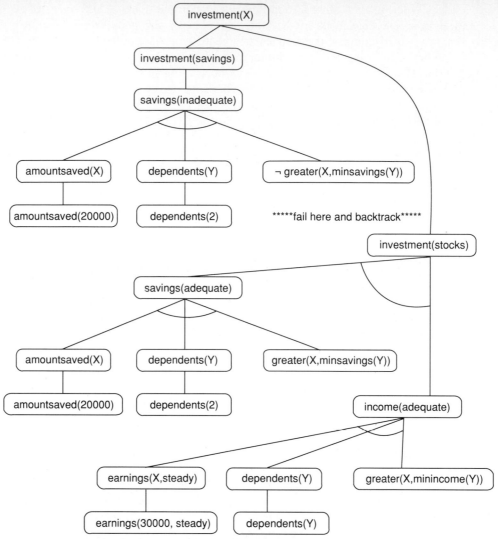

Figure 3.24 And/or graph searched by the financial advisor.

In addition to these grammar rules, a parser needs a dictionary of words in the language. These words are called the *terminals* of the grammar. They are defined by their parts of speech using rewrite rules. In the following "dictionary," "a," "the," "man," "dog," "likes," and "bites" are the terminals of our simple grammar:

   6. art ← a
   7. art ← the
("a" and "the" are articles)
   8. n ← man

9. n ← dog

("man" and "dog" are nouns)

10. v ← likes

11. v ← bites

("likes" and "bites" are verbs)

These rewrite rules define the and/or graph of Figure 3.25. Sentence is the root. The elements on the left of a rewrite rule correspond to and nodes in the graph. Multiple rules with the same conclusion form the or nodes. Notice that the leaf or terminal nodes of this graph are the English words in the grammar (hence, they are called *terminals*).

An expression is well formed in a grammar if it consists entirely of terminal symbols and there is a series of substitutions in the expression using rewrite rules that reduce it to the sentence symbol. Alternatively, this may be seen as constructing a *parse tree* that has the words of the expression as its leaves and the sentence symbol as its root.

For example, we may parse the sentence the dog bites the man, constructing the parse tree of Figure 3.26. This tree is a subtree of the and/or graph of Figure 3.25 and is constructed by searching this graph. A *data-driven parsing* algorithm would implement this by matching right-hand sides of rewrite rules with patterns in the sentence, trying these matches in the order in which the rules are written. Once a match is found, the part of the expression matching the right-hand side of the rule is replaced by the pattern on the left-hand side. This continues until the sentence is reduced to the symbol sentence

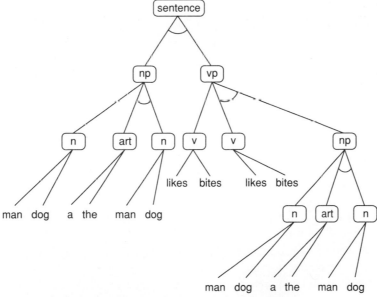

Figure 3.25 And/or graph for the grammar of Example 3.3.6. Some of the nodes (np, art, etc.) have been written more than once to simplify drawing the graph.

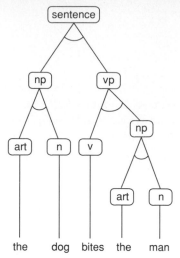

Figure 3.26 Parse tree for the sentence "The dog bites the man." Note that this is a subtree of the graph of Figure 3.25.

(indicating a successful parse) or no more rules can be applied (indicating failure). A trace of the parse of the dog bites the man is:

1. The first rule that will match is 7, rewriting the as art. This yields: art dog bites the man.

2. The next iteration would find a match for 7, yielding art dog bites art man.

3. Rule 8 will fire, producing art dog bites art n

4. Rule 3 will fire to yield art dog bites np.

5. Rule 9 produces art n bites np.

6. Rule 3 may be applied, giving np bites np.

7. Rule 11 yields np v np.

8. Rule 5 yields np vp.

9. Rule 1 reduces this to sentence, accepting the expression as correct.

The above example implements a data-directed depth-first parse, since it always applies the highest-level rule to the expression; e.g., art n reduces to np before bites reduces to v. Parsing could also be done in a goal-directed fashion, taking sentence as the starting string and finding a series of replacements of patterns that match left-hand sides of rules leading to a series of terminals that match the target sentence.

Parsing is important, not only for natural language (Chapter 10) but also for constructing compilers and interpreters for computer languages (Aho 1977). The literature is full of parsing algorithms for all classes of languages. These use various techniques to manage the combinatorics of complex grammars. For example, many goal-directed parsing algorithms will look ahead to the actual input stream to determine which rule to apply next.

In this example we have taken a very simple approach of searching the and/or graph in an uninformed fashion. One thing that is interesting in this example is the implementation of the search. This approach of keeping a record of the current expression and trying to match the rules in order is an example of the use of the *production system* to implement search. This is the major topic of the next chapter.

Another way in which rewrite rules are used is to generate legal sentences according to the rules of the grammar. Legal sentences may be generated by a goal-driven search, beginning with sentence as the top level goal and ending when no more rules can be applied. This produces a string of terminal symbols that is a legal sentence in the grammar. For example:

A sentence is an np followed by a vp (rule 1).

np is replaced by n (rule 2).

man is the first n available (rule 8).

At this point, np is satisfied and vp is attempted. Rule 3 replaces vp with v.

Rule 10 replaces v with likes.

man likes is found as the first acceptable sentence.

If it is desired to create all acceptable sentences, this may be systematically repeated until all possibilities are tried and the entire state space has been searched exhaustively. This generates sentences including a man likes, the man likes, and so on. There are 84 correct sentences that are produced by an exhaustive search. These include such anomalies as the man bites the dog.

Parsing and generating rules can be used together in a variety of ways to handle different problems. For instance, if it is desired to find all sentences to complete the string the man, then the problem solver may be given an incomplete string the man .... It can work upward in a data-driven fashion to produce the goal of completing the sentence rule (rule 1) where np is replaced by the man, and then work in a goal-driven fashion to determine all possible vps that will complete the sentence. This would create sentences such as the man likes, the man bites the man, and so on. Again, this example deals only with syntactic correctness. The issue of semantics (whether the string has a mapping into some "world" with "truth") is entirely different. Chapter 2 examined the issue of constructing a semantics for expressions in formal logic; for expressions in natural language, the issue is much more difficult and is discussed in Chapters 9 and 10.

This last example illustrates the extreme flexibility with which state spaces may be searched. The next chapter discusses the production system, a formalism for controlling the application of problem-solving rules and other techniques for implementing search in a variety of problems and representation languages. In Chapter 5 we discuss the use of heuristics to focus search on the smallest possible portion of the state space.

3.4   Epilogue and References

Chapter 3 introduced the theoretical foundations of state space search, using graph theory to analyze the structure and complexity of problem-solving strategies. In reviewing the basics of graph theory, we showed how it may be used to model problem solving as search through a graph of problem states. The chapter compared data- and goal-driven reasoning and depth-first and breadth-first search.

And/or graphs allow us to apply state space search to the implementation of logical reasoning. The search strategies of Chapter 3 were demonstrated on a number of examples, including the financial advisor introduced in Chapter 2.

Basic graph search is discussed in a number of textbooks on computer algorithms. These include *Walls and Mirrors* by Paul Helman and Robert Veroff (1986), *Algorithms* by Robert Sedgewick (1983), and *Fundamentals of Computer Algorithms* by Ellis Horowitz and Sartaj Sahni (1978).

The use of graph search to model intelligent problem solving is presented in *Human Problem Solving* by Alan Newell and Herbert Simon (1972). Artificial intelligence texts that discuss search strategies include Nils Nilsson's *Principles of Artificial Intelligence* (1980), Patrick Winston's *Artificial Intelligence* (1984), and *Artificial Intelligence* by Eugene Charniak and Drew McDermott (1985). *Hueristics* by Judea Pearl (1984) presents search algorithms and lays a groundwork for the material we present in Chapter 5.

3.5   Exercises

1. Define a hamiltonian path as a path that uses every node of the graph exactly once. What conditions are necessary for such a path to exist? Is there such a path in the Königsberg map?

2. Give the graph representation for the farmer, wolf, goat, and cabbage problem of Figure 6.2. Let the nodes represent states of the world; e.g., the farmer and the goat are on the west bank and the wolf and cabbage on the east. Discuss the advantages of each alternative for searching this space.

3. Write a graph representation for the relationships in Exercise 13 of Chapter 2. Let the nodes correspond to the people and the arcs to the relationships. Informally discuss what it might mean to perform inferences on such a graph and how a system might make the conclusion ''I am my own grandfather'' from this representation. Contrast the logical and the graph-based representations.

4. Give an instance of the traveling salesperson problem for which the nearest-neighbor strategy fails to find an optimal path. Suggest another heuristic for this problem.

5. ''Hand run'' the backtrack algorithm on the graph in Figure 3.27. Begin from state A. Keep track of the successive values of NSL, SL, CS, etc.

6. Implement a backtrack algorithm in
   a. Pascal or C.
   b. FORTRAN.

7. Determine whether goal- or data-driven search would be preferable for solving each of the following problems. Justify your answer.
   a. Diagnosing mechanical problems in an automobile.
   b. You have met a person who claims to be your distant cousin, with a common ancestor named John Doe. You would like to verify her claim.
   c. Another person claims to be your distant cousin. He does not know the common ancestor's name but knows that it was no more than eight generations back. You would like to either find this ancestor or determine that she did not exist.

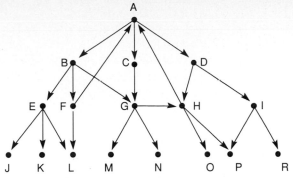

Figure 3.27 A graph to be searched.

d. A theorem prover for plane geometry.

e. A program for examining sonar readings and interpreting them, e.g., telling a large submarine from a small submarine from a whale from a school of fish.

f. An expert system that will help a human classify plants by species, genus, etc.

8. Extend the graphs of Figures 3.15 and 3.17 to show the states left on **open** when the algorithms halt.

9. In depth-first search, the children of each node are generated and expanded in some order. What criteria should be considered in determining the best order in which to generate the child nodes?

10. Would you use breadth-first or depth-first search for each of the following problems? What would you base your choice on?

   a. A chess playing program.

   b. A medical diagnostic program.

   c. A planner to find a path to get a robot from A to B.

   d. A program to determine the best sequence of manufacturing steps to go from raw materials to a finished product.

   e. A program that attempts to determine if two expressions in the propositional calculus are equivalent.

11. Produce a graph representing a goal-driven search of the problem of Figure 3.19.

12. Answer questions 1 through 4 from Example 3.3.2.

13. Write a backtrack algorithm for and/or graphs.

14. Trace the good-dog problem of Example 3.3.4 in a data-driven fashion.

15. Give another example of an and/or graph search problem. Develop part of the search space.

16. Trace a data-driven execution of the financial advisor of Example 3.3.5 for the case of an individual with four dependents, $18,000 in the bank, and a steady income of $25,000 per year. Based on a comparison of this problem and the example in the text, suggest a generally ''best'' strategy for solving the problem.

17. Add rules defining adjectives and adverbs to the grammar of Example 3.3.6.

18. Add rules for (multiple) prepositional phrases to Example 3.3.6.

CONTROL AND IMPLEMENTATION OF STATE SPACE SEARCH

What we call the beginning is often the end
And to make an end is to make a beginning.
The end is where we start from . . .

—T.S. Eliot, *Four Quartets*

function define-recursion;
  begin
    if you understand then stop
                    else define-recursion
  end;

4.0   Introduction

Chapter 3 introduced problem solving as search through a graph of problem states. The state space model of problem solving allows graph theory to be used as a tool for designing and analyzing intelligent programs. The chapter then defined a general backtracking graph search algorithm as well as algorithms for both depth-first and breadth-first search. These definitions characterized the fundamental data and control structures used to implement state space search:

1. Representation of a problem solution as a path from a start state to a goal.

2. Search to test systematically alternative paths to a goal.

3. Backtracking to allow an algorithm to "recover" from paths that fail to lead to a goal.

4. Lists to keep explicit records of states under consideration.
   a. The *open* list allows the algorithm to backtrack to untried states if necessary.
   b. The *closed* list of visited states allows the algorithm to implement loop detection and avoid repeating fruitless paths.

5. Use of a *stack* to implement depth-first search and a *queue* to implement breadth-first search.

Chapter 4 introduces higher-level techniques for implementing search algorithms. The first of these, *recursive search*, implements depth-first search with backtracking in a more concise, natural fashion than the algorithms of Chapter 3 and forms the basis for many of the algorithms in this text. Recursive search is augmented through the use of unification to search the state space generated by predicate calculus assertions. This *pattern-directed search* algorithm is the basis of PROLOG (Chapter 6) and many of the expert system shells discussed in chapters 8 and 14. Finally, we introduce *production systems*, a general architecture for pattern-directed problem solving that has been used extensively both to model human problem solving and to build expert systems and other AI applications. The use of heuristics to further focus and control search within these frameworks is introduced in Chapter 5.

4.1 Recursion-Based Search

4.1.1 Recursion (Optional Review)

In mathematics, a recursive definition uses the term being defined as part of its own definition. In computer science, recursion is used to define and analyze both data structures and procedures. A recursive procedure consists of:

1. A recursive step in which the procedure calls itself to repeat a sequence of actions.

2. A terminating condition that stops the procedure from recurring endlessly (the recursive version of an endless loop).

Both of these components are essential and appear in all recursive definitions and algorithms. Recursion is a natural control construct for data structures that have no definite size, such as lists, trees, and graphs. This makes it particularly appropriate for state space search.

A simple example of recursion is an algorithm for determining if an item is a member of a list. Lists are ordered sequences of elements and fundamental building blocks for computer science data structures. Lists have already been used as an alternative syntax for predicate calculus expressions (Chapter 2) and to implement the open and closed lists in the search algorithms of Chapter 3. A procedure for testing whether an element is a member of a list is defined recursively by:

```
procedure member(item, list);

begin
  if list is empty
    then return(fail)              % terminating condition #1
```

```
         else if item = first element of list
            then return(success)              % terminating condition #2
         else begin
                  tail := list with its first item removed;
                  member(item, tail)     % recursive call
         end
end
```

This procedure first tests whether list is empty; if so, the algorithm returns fail. Otherwise, it compares item to the first element of list; if these are equal, the procedure halts with success. These are the terminating conditions of the procedure. If neither terminating condition is met, member removes the first element from list and calls itself on the shortened list. In this fashion, member examines each element of the list in turn. Note that since list is finite and each step reduces its size by one element, the algorithm always halts.

This algorithm uses two fundamental list operations: one that returns the first element (the *head*) of a list and a *tail* operation, which returns the list with its first element removed. When coupled with recursion, these operations are the basis for higher-level list operations such as member. These operations are supported by both LISP and PRO-LOG and are described in detail in the chapters on each language.

When supported by a programming language, recursion offers all the power of more traditional control constructs such as loops and conditional branching. In other words, *anything* that can be done using explicit iteration can be done recursively. The benefit of recursive formulations is greater clarity and compactness of expression. Mathematical notations such as logic or functions do not support such concepts as sequencing, branching, and iteration; instead, they use recursion to indicate repetition. Since recursion is easier to describe mathematically than explicit iteration, it is easier to analyze formally the correctness and complexity of recursive algorithms. Recursive formulations are also used frequently by systems that automatically generate or verify programs, and they play an important role in implementing compilers and interpreters. More important, however, is the power and naturalness of recursion as a tool for implementing AI problem-solving strategies such as graph search.

4.1.2   Recursive Search

A direct translation of the depth-first search algorithm of Chapter 3 into recursive form illustrates the equivalence of recursion and iteration. This algorithm uses global variables closed and open to maintain lists of states:

```
function depthsearch;

  begin

    if open is empty then return(fail);
    current_state := the first element of open;
```

```
        if current_state is a goal state
          then return(success)
          else begin
                  open := the tail of open;
                  closed := closed with current_state added
                  for each child of current_state not in open or closed
                    add the child to the front of open
          end;
          depthsearch                    % recursive call
        end.
```

Breadth-first search can be implemented with the same algorithm, simply by implementing **open** as a queue rather than a stack.

The implementation of depth-first search just presented does not utilize the full power of recursion. It is possible to simplify the procedure further by using recursion itself (rather than an explicit open list) to organize states and paths through the state space. In this version of the algorithm, **closed** is still maintained as a global variable and used to detect duplicate states and prevent loops.

```
    function depthsearch(current_state);

    begin
      if current_state is a goal
        then return(success)
        else begin
                add current_state to closed;
                while current_state has unexamined children
                  do begin
                      child := next unexamined child of current_state;
                      if child is not a member of closed    % check for loops
                          then if depthsearch(child) = success
                                      then return(success)
                  end
        end;
      return(fail)
    end.
```

Rather than generating all children of a state and placing them on an open list, this algorithm produces the child states one at a time and recursively searches the descendants of each child before generating its sibling. Note that the algorithm assumes an order to the state generation operators. In recursively searching a child state, if some descendant of that state is a goal, the recursive call returns success and the algorithm ignores the siblings. If the recursive call on the child state fails to find a goal, the next sibling is generated and all of its descendants are searched. In this fashion, the algorithm searches the entire graph in a depth-first order. The reader should verify that it actually searches the graph in the same order as the depth-first search algorithm of Section 3.2.3.

The omission of an explicit open list is made possible through recursion. The mechanisms by which a programming language implements recursion include a separate *activation record* (Aho 1977) of each recursive call. These record the local variables and state of execution of each procedure call. When the procedure is called recursively with a new state, a new activation record stores its parameters (the state), any local variables, and the current state of execution. In a recursive search algorithm, the series of states on the current path are recorded in the sequence of activation records of the recursive calls. The record of each call also indicates the last operation used to generate a child state; this allows the next sibling to be generated when needed.

Backtracking is effected when all descendants of a state fail to include a goal, causing the recursive call to fail. This returns fail to the procedure expanding the parent state, which generates and recurs on the next sibling. The internal mechanisms of recursion thus do the work of the open list used in the iterative version. The recursive implementation allows the programmer to restrict his or her point of view to a single state and its children rather than having to explicitly maintain an open list of states. The ability of recursion to express global concepts in a closed form is a major source of its power.

State space search is an inherently recursive process. To find a path from a current state to a goal, move to a child state and recur. If that child state does not lead to a goal, try its siblings in order. Recursion breaks a large and difficult problem (searching the whole space) into smaller, simpler pieces (generate the children of a single state) and applies this strategy (recursively) to each of them. This process continues until a goal state is discovered or the space is exhausted.

Symbolic integration, discussed in Section 3.3.3, is an excellent example of the power of a recursive approach to search problems. When attempting to integrate an expression, it applies either a substitution or a decomposition to the expression, replacing it with one (in the case of a substitution) or more (in the case of a decomposition) simpler subproblems. These subproblems are then solved recursively, with the separate solutions being recombined into a final answer. For example, after applying the rule that the integral of a sum equals the sum of the integrals of the terms, it recursively attempts to integrate each term. This may lead to further decompositions or substitutions, until each term has been integrated. These results are then combined (summed) to produce the final result. Recursion is a natural tool for systematically decomposing a problem and recombining partial solutions into a final answer.

In the next section, this recursive approach to problem solving is extended into a controller for a logic-based problem solver that uses unification and inference to generate and search a space of logical relations.

4.2 Pattern-Directed Search

The recursive search algorithm of Section 4.1 does not specify the representation of states or the operations that produce new states. Chapter 2 discussed the advantages of predicate calculus as an AI representation; Chapter 3 showed how inferences on predicate calculus assertions define a state space that may be searched. This section applies recursive search to a space of logical inferences; the result is a general search procedure for predicate calculus.

Suppose, for example, we want to write an algorithm that determines if a predicate calculus expression is a logical consequence of some set of assertions. The algorithm must find a sequence of inferences that produce the goal expression. This suggests a goal-directed search with the initial query forming the goal and modus ponens the transitions between states. Given a goal (such as p(a)), the algorithm uses unification to select the implications whose conclusions match the goal (e.g., q(X) → p(X)). Since the algorithm treats implications as potential rules for solving the query, they are often simply called *rules*. After unifying the goal with the conclusion of the implication (or rule) and applying the resulting substitutions throughout the rule, the rule premise becomes a new goal (q(a)). This is called a *subgoal*. The algorithm then recurs on the subgoal. If a subgoal matches a fact in the knowledge base, search terminates. The series of inferences that led from the initial goal to the given facts prove the truth of the original goal.

Search is performed by a modified version of the recursive search algorithm that uses unification to determine when two expressions match and modus ponens to generate the children of states. The current focus of the search is represented by the variable current_goal. If current_goal matches with a fact, the algorithm returns success. Otherwise it attempts to match it with the conclusion of some rule, recursively attempting to solve the premise. If current_goal does not match any of the given assertions, it returns fail. This algorithm also handles conjunctive goals such as are often found in the premise of a rule:

```
function pattern_search(current_goal);

begin
if current_goal is a member of closed     % Test for loops
    then return fail
    else add current_goal to closed;

while data base contains untried facts or rules which unify with current_goal
    do begin
      case
        current_goal unifies with a fact:
            return (success);

        current_goal is a conjunctive query (p ∧ ...):
          begin
            call pattern_search on each element of the conjunction;
            if all of these return success
              then return (success)
              else return (fail)
          end

        current_goal unifies with a rule conclusion (p in p ⇐ q):
            begin
                apply the substitutions needed to unify query with the rule conclusion
                    to the rule premise;
                pattern_search(premise)
            end
        end;
    return  fail
end.
```

Figure 4.1 Legal moves of a chess knight.

For simplicity, this algorithm does not address the problem of maintaining consistency among the variable substitutions produced by unification. This is important when solving conjunctive queries with shared variables (as in $p(X) \land q(X)$). Not only must both conjuncts succeed, but they must succeed with unifiable bindings for X. This problem is addressed at the end of this section.

The major advantage of using general methods such as unification and modus ponens to generate states is that the resulting algorithm may search *any* space of logical inferences. The specifics of a problem are described using predicate calculus assertions. Thus, we have a means of separating problem-solving knowledge from its control and implementation on the computer. Pattern_search provides our first implementation of the separation of knowledge and control.

The use of predicate calculus with a general search controller to solve search problems is illustrated through an example: a reduced version of the *knight's tour problem*. In the game of chess, a knight can move two squares either horizontally or vertically followed by one square in an orthogonal direction (as long as it does not move off the board). There are thus eight possible moves that the knight may make (Figure 4.1).

As traditionally defined, the knight's tour problem attempts to find a series of legal moves in which the knight lands on each square of the chessboard exactly once. This problem has been a mainstay in the development and presentation of search algorithms. The example given in this chapter is a simplified version of the knight's tour problem: Is there a series of legal moves that will take the knight from one square to another on a reduced-size (3×3) chessboard? (The details of the full knight's tour problem on an 8×8 chessboard are discussed in examples 4.3.2 and 4.3.3.)

Figure 4.2 shows a 3×3 chessboard with each square labeled with a positive integer (1 to 9). This labeling scheme is used instead of the more general approach of giving each space a row and column number in order to further simplify the example.

move(1,8).	move(6,1).
move(1,6).	move(6,7).
move(2,9).	move(7,2).
move(2,7).	move(7,6).
move(3,4).	move(8,3).
move(3,8).	move(8,1).
move(4,9).	move(9,2).
move(4,3).	move(9,4).

Figure 4.2   A 3 × 3 chessboard with move rules.

Because of the reduced size of the problem, we simply enumerate the alternative moves rather than developing a general move operator. The legal moves on the board are then described in predicate calculus using a predicate called move, whose parameters are the starting and ending squares of a legal move. For example, move(1,8) takes the knight from the upper left-hand corner to the middle of the bottom row. The predicates of Figure 4.2 enumerate all possible moves for the 3 × 3 chessboard.

These predicates form the knowledge base for the knight's tour problem. As an example of how unification is used to access this knowledge base, we test for the existence of various moves on the board. To determine whether there is a move from 1 to 8, call pattern_search(move(1,8)). Since this goal unifies with move(1,8) in the knowledge base, the result is success, with no variable substitutions required.

Another request might be to find where the knight can move from a particular location, such as square 2. The goal move(2,X) unifies with two different predicates in the knowledge base, with the substitutions of {7/X} and {9/X}. Given the goal move(2,3), the response is fail, since there is no move(2,3) in the knowledge base. The goal query move(5,Y) also fails since there are no assertions that define a move from square 5.

The next task in constructing a search algorithm is to devise a general definition for a path of successive moves around the board. This is done through the use of predicate calculus implications. These are added to the knowledge base as *rules* for creating paths of successive moves. To emphasize the goal-directed use of these rules, we have reversed the direction of the implication arrow; i.e., the rules are written as Conclusion ← Premise.

For example, a two-move path could be formulated as:

$$\forall\ X,Y\ [path2(X,Y) \leftarrow \exists\ Z\ [move(X,Z) \wedge move(Z,Y)]]$$

This rule says that for all locations X and Y, there is a two-move path between them if there exists a location Z such that the knight can move from X to Z and in turn move from Z to Y.

The general path2 rule can be applied in a number of ways. First, it may be used to determine if there is a two-move path from one location to another. If pattern_search is called with the goal path2(1,3), it matches the goal with the consequence of the rule path2(X,Y), and the substitutions are made in the rule's premise; the result is a specific rule that defines the conditions required for the path:

$$path2(1,3) \leftarrow \exists \, Z \, [move(1,Z) \wedge move(Z,3)]$$

Pattern_search then calls itself on this premise. Since this is a conjunction of two expressions, pattern_search will attempt to solve each of these subgoals separately. This requires not only that both subgoals succeed but also that any variable bindings be consistent across subgoals. Substituting 8 for Z allows both subgoals to succeed.

Another request might be to find all locations that can be reached in two moves from location 2. This is accomplished by giving pattern_search the goal path2(2,Y). Through a similar process, a number of such substitutions may be found, including {6/Y} and {2/Y} (with intermediate Z being 7) and {2/Y} and {4/Y} (with intermediate location 9). Further requests could be to find a two-move path from a number to itself, or from any number to 5, and so on. Notice here one of the advantages of pattern-driven control: a variety of queries may be taken as the initial goal.

Similarly, a three-move path is defined as including two intermediate locations that are part of the path from the initial location to the goal. This is defined by:

$$\forall \, X,Y \, [path3(X,Y) \leftarrow \exists \, Z,W \, [move(X,Z) \wedge move(Z,W) \wedge move(W,Y)]]$$

This clause can solve such goals as path3(1,2), path3(1,X), or even path3(X,Y). Tracing the results of these queries is left as an exercise.

Similar path rules can be constructed for four or more move paths. It soon becomes evident that the path moves are the same for a path of any length, simply requiring the proper number of intermediate places to "land." It is also evident that the path moves could be stated in terms of each other, such as:

$$\forall \, X,Y \, [path3(X,Y) \leftarrow \exists \, Z \, [move(X,Z) \wedge path2(Z,Y)]]$$

This suggests the single, general recursive rule:

$$\forall \, X,Y \, [path(X,Y) \leftarrow \exists \, Z[move(X,Z) \wedge path(Z,Y)]]$$

The last path rule can be used to determine whether a path of any length exists. The rule may be stated as "to find a path from one square to another, first make a move from the starting square to an intermediate location and then find a path from the intermediate to the final square."

This recursive "path" rule is incomplete in that it includes no terminating condition. Any attempt to solve a goal involving the path predicate would fail to halt since each attempt to solve the rule premise would lead to another recursive call on path(Z,Y). There is no test in the rule to determine whether the desired goal state is ever reached. This can be remedied by adding the clause path(X,X) to the knowledge base. Since path(X,X) will unify only with predicates such as path(3,3) or path(5,5), it defines the desired terminating condition. The general recursive path definition is then given by two predicate calculus formulas:

$\forall$ X path(X,X)

$\forall$ X,Y [path(X,Y) $\leftarrow$ $\exists$ Z [move(X,Z) $\wedge$ path(Z,Y)]]

Note once again the elegance and simplicity of the recursive formulation. When combined with the recursive control provided by pattern_search, these rules will search the space of possible paths in the knight's tour problem. Combined with the move rules, this yields the complete problem description (or knowledge base):

move(1,8).   move(1,6).   move(2,9).   move(2,7).
move(3,4).   move(3,8).   move(4,9).   move(4,3).
move(6,1).   move(6,7).   move(7,2).   move(7,6).
move(8,3).   move(8,1).   move(9,2).   move(9,4).

$\forall$ X path(X,X)
$\forall$ X,Y [path(X,Y) $\leftarrow$ $\exists$ Z [move(X,Z) $\wedge$ path(Z,Y)]]

It is important to note that the solution to the problem is implemented through *both* the logical descriptions that define the state space and the use of pattern_search to control search of that space. Although the path rule is a satisfactory definition of a path, it does not tell us how to find that path. Indeed, many undesirable or meaningless paths around the chessboard also fit this definition. For example, without some way to prevent loops, the goal path(1,3) could lead to a path that simply goes back and forth between 1 and 8, instead of finding the correct path from 1 to 8 to 3. Both the loop and the correct path are logical consequences of the knowledge base. Similarly, if the recursive rule is tried before the terminating condition, the fact that path(3,3) should terminate the search could be overlooked, allowing the search to continue meaninglessly.

Although the initial version of pattern_search defined the basic behavior of a search algorithm for predicate calculus expressions, there are several subtleties that must still be addressed. One of these is the order with which it tries alternative matches; the other is proper handling of the full set of logical operators ($\wedge$, $\vee$, and $\neg$). The final version of pattern_search is a general inference engine for logical expressions (chapters 8, 12, and 13).

Logic is nondeterministic: it defines a space of possible inferences but does not tell a problem solver how to make the useful ones. To use this, we need a control regime that systematically searches the space, avoiding meaningless paths, loops, etc. A control algorithm such as pattern_search must try alternative matches in some sequential order. Knowing this order allows the program designer (the knowledge engineer) to control search by properly ordering rules in the knowledge base. The simplest way to define such an order is to require that the algorithm try rules and facts in the order in which they appear in the knowledge base. In the knight's tour, this ensures that the terminating condition (path(X,X)) is tried before the recursive step.

A second issue is the existence of logical connectives in the rule premises; e.g., implications of the form "p $\leftarrow$ q $\wedge$ r" or "p $\leftarrow$ q $\vee$ (r $\wedge$ s)." As will be recalled from the discussion of and/or graphs, an **and** operator indicates that both expressions must be shown to be true in order for the entire premise to be true. In addition, the conjuncts of the expression must be solved with consistent variable bindings. Thus, to solve $p(X) \land q(X)$, it is not sufficient to solve $p(X)$ with the substitution $\{a/X\}$ and $q(X)$ with the substitution $\{b/X\}$. Both must be solved with the same or unifiable bindings for X. An **or** operator, on the other hand, indicates that either expression must be found to be true. The search algorithm must take this into account.

The last addition to the algorithm is the ability to solve goals involving logical negation ($\neg$). **Pattern_search** handles negated goals by first solving the operand of the $\neg$. If this subgoal succeeds, then **pattern_search** returns **fail**. If the operand fails, then **pattern_search** returns an empty substitution set, indicating success. Note that even though a subgoal may contain variables, the result of solving its negation may not contain any substitutions. This is because $\neg$ can succeed only if its operand *fails*; hence it cannot return any bindings for the operand. This exemplifies the problems encountered in implementing logical negation in a reasoning system.

Finally, the algorithm should not return **success** but should return the bindings involved in the solution. Consider the goal $move(1,X)$; the substitutions $\{6/X\}$ and $\{8/X\}$ are an essential part of the solution.

The complete version of **pattern_search**, which takes these into account, is given by:

```
function pattern_search(current_goal);
begin

    if current_goal is a member of closed    % Test for loops in the search

      then return fail
      else add current_goal to closed;
  while data base contains untried facts or rules which unify with current_goal
      do begin
        case
          current_goal unifies with a fact:
              return the substitutions produced by this unification;

          current_goal is a negated subgoal (¬ p):
              call pattern_search on the operand of the ¬ ( p);
              If pattern_search returns fail
                then return the empty set of substitutions {}    % success of
                  the negated goal
                else return fail;
```

```
current_goal is a conjunction (p ∧ ...):
    begin
    call pattern_search on the first element of the conjunction;
    if pattern_search returns fail
        then return fail
        else begin
            apply the substitutions returned by pattern_search to the rest of the
                conjunctive goal;
            call pattern_search on the rest of the goal;
            if pattern_search succeeds
                then return the composition of both sets of substitutions
                    else return fail
        end
    end

current_goal is a disjunctive query (p ∨ ...):
    begin
    call pattern_search on the first element of the disjunction;
    if pattern_search succeeds
        then return the substitutions returned by pattern_search
        else call pattern_search on the remainder of the goal and return the result
    end
current_goal unifies with a rule conclusion (p in p ⇐ q):
    begin
        apply the substitutions needed to unify current_goal with the rule
            conclusion to the premise of the rule;
        call pattern_search(premise);
        return the composition of the substitutions returned by pattern_search and
            those produced by matching current_goal with the premise;
    end
    end;
    return fail
end.
```

This algorithm for searching a space of predicate calculus rules and facts is the basis of PROLOG and many goal-directed expert system shells. Its behavior is further illustrated in chapters 6, 8, and 12, as well as in a LISP implementation of it in Chapter 13. An alternative control structure for pattern-directed search is provided by the *production system*, discussed in the next section.

4.3   Production Systems

4.3.1   Definition and History

The *production system* is a model of computation that has proved particularly important in AI, both for implementing search algorithms and for modeling human problem solving. A production system provides pattern-directed control of a problem-solving process and consists of a set of *production rules*, a *working memory*, and a *recognize-act* control cycle (Brownston et al. 1985).

DEFINITION

PRODUCTION SYSTEM

A *production system* is defined by:

1. *The set of production rules.* These are often simply called *productions*. A production is a *condition-action* pair and defines a single chunk of problem-solving knowledge. The *condition part* of the rule is a pattern that determines when that rule may be applied to a problem instance. The *action part* defines the associated problem-solving step.

2. *Working memory* contains a description of the *current state of the world* in a reasoning process. This description is a pattern that is matched against the condition part of a production to select appropriate problem-solving actions. When the condition element of a rule is matched by the contents of working memory, the action associated with that condition may then be performed. The actions of production rules are specifically designed to alter the contents of working memory.

3. *The recognize-act cycle.* The control structure for a production system is straightforward: The current state of the problem-solving process is maintained as a set of patterns in *working memory*. Working memory is initialized with the beginning problem description. The patterns in working memory are matched against the conditions of the production rules; this produces a subset of the productions, called the *conflict set*, whose conditions match the patterns in working memory. The productions in the conflict set are said to be *enabled*. One of the productions in the conflict set is then selected (*conflict resolution*) and the production is *fired*. That is, the action of the rule is performed, changing the contents of working memory. After the selected production rule is fired, the control cycle repeats with the modified working memory. The process terminates when no rule conditions are matched by the contents of working memory.

Conflict resolution chooses a rule from the conflict set for firing. Conflict resolution strategies may be simple, such as selecting the first rule whose condition matches the state of the world, or may involve complex rule selection heuristics. This is an important way in which a production system allows the addition of heuristic control to a search algorithm.

The *pure* production system model has no mechanism for recovering from dead ends in the search; it simply continues until no more productions are enabled and halts. Many practical implementations of production systems allow backtracking to a previous state of working memory in such situations.

A schematic drawing of a production system is presented in Figure 4.3.

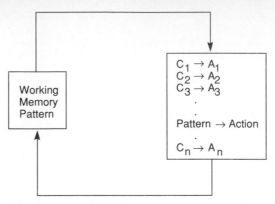

Figure 4.3 A production system. Control loops until working memory pattern no longer matches the conditions of any productions.

A very simple example of production system execution appears in Figure 4.4. This is a production system program for sorting a string composed of the letters a, b, and c. In this example, a production is enabled if its condition matches a portion of the string in working memory. When a rule is fired, the substring that matched the rule condition is replaced by the string on the right-hand side of the rule. As this example suggests, production systems are a general model of computation that can be programmed to do anything that can be done on a computer. Their real strength, however, is as an architecture for knowledge-based systems.

The idea for the "production"-based design for computing came originally from writings of Post (1943), who proposed a production rule model as a formal theory of computation. The main construct of this theory was a set of rewrite rules for strings (in many ways similar to the parsing rules in the example in Chapter 3). It is also closely related to the approach taken by markov algorithms (Markov 1954).

An interesting application of production rules to modeling human cognition is found in the work of Newell and Simon at the Carnegie Institute of Technology (now Carnegie Mellon University) in the 1960s and 1970s. The programs they developed, including the *General Problem Solver*, are largely responsible for the importance of production systems in AI. In this research, human subjects were monitored in various problem-solving activities such as solving problems in predicate logic and playing games like chess. The *protocol* (behavior patterns, including verbal descriptions of the problem-solving process, eye movements, etc.) of problem-solving subjects was recorded and broken down to its elementary components. These components were regarded as the basic bits of problem-solving knowledge in the human subjects and were composed as a search through a graph (called the *problem behavior graph*). A production system was then used to implement search of this graph.

The production rules represented the set of problem-solving skills of the human subject. The present focus of attention was represented as the current state of the world.

Production set:

1. ba → ab
2. ca → ac
3. cb → bc

Iteration #	Working memory	Conflict set	Rule fired
0	cbaca	1, 2, 3	1
1	cabca	2	2
2	acbca	3, 2	2
3	acbac	1, 3	1
4	acabc	2	2
5	aacbc	3	3
6	aabcc	Ø	Halt

Figure 4.4   Trace of a simple production system.

In executing the production system, the "attention" or "current focus" of the problem solver would match a production rule, which would change the state of "attention" to match another production-encoded skill, and so on.

It is important to note that in this work Newell and Simon used the production system not only as a vehicle for implementing graph search but also as an actual model of human problem-solving behavior. The productions corresponded to the problem-solving skills in the human's *long-term memory*. Like the skills in long-term memory, these productions are not changed by the execution of the system; they are invoked by the "pattern" of a particular problem instance, and new skills may be added without requiring "recoding" of the previously existing knowledge. The production system's working memory corresponds to *short-term memory* (or current focus of attention) in the human and describes the current stage of solving a problem instance. The contents of working memory are generally not retained after a problem has been solved.

This research is described in *Human Problem Solving* by Newell and Simon (1972) and in Luger (1978). Newell, Simon, and others have continued to use production rules to model the difference between novices and experts (Larkin et al. 1980; Simon and Simon 1978) in areas such as solving algebra word problems and physics problems. Production systems also form a basis for studying learning in both humans and computers (Klahr et al. 1987).

Production systems provide a model for encoding human expertise in the form of rules and designing pattern-driven search algorithms, tasks that are central to the design of the rule-based expert system. In expert systems, the production system is not necessarily assumed to actually model human problem-solving behavior; however, the aspects of production systems that make them useful as a potential model of human problem solving (modularity of rules, separation of knowledge and control, separation of working memory and problem-solving knowledge) make them an ideal tool for building expert systems.

An important family of AI languages comes directly out of the production system language research at Carnegie Mellon. These are the OPS languages; OPS stands for Official Production System. Although their origins are in modeling human problem solving, these languages have proved highly effective for programming expert systems and other AI applications. OPS5, the newest dialect, is the major implementation language for the VAX configurer (XCON) and other expert systems developed at Digital Equipment Corporation (McDermott 1981, 1982).

In the next section we give examples of how the production system may be used to solve a variety of search problems.

4.3.2 Examples of Production Systems

EXAMPLE 4.3.1: THE 8-PUZZLE

The search space generated by the 8-puzzle, introduced in Chapter 3, is both complex enough to be interesting and small enough to be tractable, so it is frequently used to explore different search strategies, such as depth- and breadth-first search, as well as the heuristic strategies discussed in Chapter 5. It also lends itself to solution using a production system.

Recall that we gain generality by thinking of "moving the blank space" rather than moving a numbered tile. Legal moves are defined by the productions in Figure 4.5. Of course, all four of these moves are applicable only when the blank is in the center; when it is in one of the corners only two moves are possible. If a beginning state and a goal state for the 8-puzzle are now specified, it is possible to make a production system accounting of the problem's search space.

An actual implementation of this problem might represent each board configuration with a "state" predicate with nine parameters (for nine possible locations of the eight tiles and the blank); rules could be written as implications whose premise performs the required condition check. Alternatively, arrays or list structures could be used for board states.

An example of the space searched in finding a solution for the problem given in Figure 4.5 follows in Figure 4.6. Because this solution path can go very deep if unconstrained, a depth bound has been added to the search. (A simple means for adding a depth bound is to keep track of the length of the current path and to force backtracking if this bound is exceeded.) A depth bound of five is used in the solution of Figure 4.6. Note that the number of possible states of working memory grows exponentially with the depth of the search.

EXAMPLE 4.3.2: THE KNIGHT'S TOUR PROBLEM

The 3×3 knight's tour problem presented in Section 4.2 may be solved using a production system approach. Here each move would be represented as a production whose con-

Start state:

2	8	3
1	6	4
7	■	5

Goal state:

1	2	3
8	■	4
7	6	5

Production set:

Condition		Action
goal state in working memory	→	halt
blank is not on the top edge	→	move the blank up
blank is not on the right edge	→	move the blank right
blank is not on the bottom edge	→	move the blank down
blank is not on the left edge	→	move the blank left

Working memory is the present board state and goal state.

Control regime:

1. Try each production in order.
2. Do not allow loops.
3. Stop when goal is found.

Figure 4.5 The 8-puzzle as a production system.

dition is the location of the knight on a particular square and whose action moves the knight to another square. Sixteen productions represent all possible moves of the knight:

RULE #	CONDITION		ACTION
1	knight on square 1	→	move knight to square 8
2	knight on square 1	→	move knight to square 6
3	knight on square 2	→	move knight to square 9
4	knight on square 2	→	move knight to square 7
5	knight on square 3	→	move knight to square 4
6	knight on square 3	→	move knight to square 8
7	knight on square 4	→	move knight to square 9
8	knight on square 4	→	move knight to square 3
9	knight on square 6	→	move knight to square 1
10	knight on square 6	→	move knight to square 7
11	knight on square 7	→	move knight to square 2
12	knight on square 7	→	move knight to square 6
13	knight on square 8	→	move knight to square 3
14	knight on square 8	→	move knight to square 1
15	knight on square 9	→	move knight to square 2
16	knight on square 9	→	move knight to square 4

Figure 4.6 State space of the 8-puzzle searched by a production system with loop detection and a depth bound of 5.

Working memory contains both the current board state and the goal state. The control regime applies rules until the current state equals the goal state and then halts. A simple conflict resolution scheme would fire the first rule that did not cause the search to loop. Because the search may lead to dead ends (from which every possible move leads to a previously visited state and, consequently, a loop), the control regime should also allow backtracking. An execution of this production system that determines if there is a path from square 1 to square 2 is charted in Figure 4.7.

It is interesting to note that in implementing the **path** predicate in the knight's tour example of Section 4.2, we have actually implemented this production system solution! From this point of view, **pattern_search** is simply an interpreter, with the actual search implemented by the **path** definition. The productions are the **move** facts, with the first parameter specifying the condition (the square the piece must be on to make the move) and the second parameter the action (the square to which it can move). The recognize-act cycle is implemented by the recursive **path** predicate. Working memory contains the current state and the desired goal state and is represented as the parameters of the **path** predicate. On a given iteration, the conflict set is all of the move expressions that will unify with the goal **move(X,Z)**. This program uses the simple conflict resolution strategy of selecting and firing the first move predicate encountered in the knowledge base that

Iteration #	Working memory		Conflict set (rule #'s)	Fire rule
	Current square	Goal square		
0	1	2	1, 2	1
1	8	2	13, 14	13
2	3	2	5, 6	5
3	4	2	7, 8	7
4	9	2	15, 16	15
5	2	2		Halt

Figure 4.7 Production system solution to the 3 × 3 knight's tour problem.

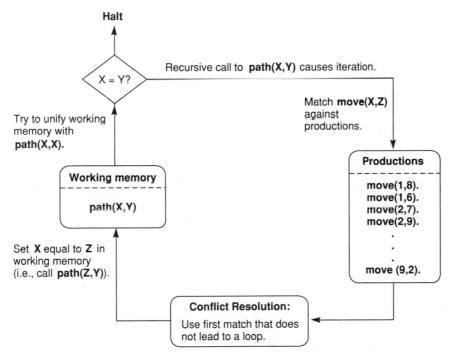

Figure 4.8 Recursive path algorithm as a production system.

does not lead to a repeated state. The controller also backtracks from dead-end states. This characterization of the path definition as a production system is given in Figure 4.8.

Production systems are capable of generating infinite loops when searching a state space graph. These loops are particularly difficult to spot in a production system since the rules can fire in any order. That is, looping may appear in the execution of the system but it cannot easily be found from a syntactic inspection of the rule set. For example, with the "move" rules of the knight's tour problem ordered as in Section 4.2 and a conflict resolution strategy of selecting the first match, the pattern move(2,X) would match with move(2,9), indicating a move to square 9. On the next iteration, the pattern move(9,X) would match with move(9,2), taking the search back to square 2, causing a loop.

To prevent looping, pattern_search checked a global list (closed) of visited states. The actual conflict resolution strategy was therefore: select the first matching move *that leads to an unvisited state.*

In a production system, the proper place for recording such case-specific data as a list of previously visited states is not a global closed list but the working memory itself. We can alter the path predicate to use working memory for loop detection.

Assume that pattern_search does not maintain a global closed list or otherwise perform loop detection. Assume that our predicate calculus language is augmented by the addition of a special construct, assert(X), which causes its argument X to be entered into the working memory. assert is not an ordinary predicate but an action that is performed; hence, it always succeeds.

assert is used to place a "marker" in working memory to indicate when a state has been visited. This marker is represented as a unary predicate, been(X), which takes as its argument a square on the board. been(X) is added to working memory when a new state X is visited. Conflict resolution may then require that been(Z) must not be in working memory before move(X,Z) can fire. For a specific value of Z this can be tested by matching a pattern against working memory.

The modified recursive path definition is written:

$$\forall\ X\ \text{path}(X,X).$$
$$\forall\ X,Y\ \text{path}(X,Y) \Leftarrow \exists\ Z\ \text{move}(X,Z) \land \neg(\text{been}(Z)) \land \text{assert}(\text{been}(Z)) \land \text{path}(Z,Y)$$

In this definition, move(X,Z) succeeds on the first match with a move predicate. This binds a value to Z. If been(Z) matches with an entry in working memory, $\neg$(been(Z)) will cause a failure (i.e., it will be false). pattern_search will then backtrack and try another match for move(X,Z). If square Z is a new state, the search will continue, with been(Z) asserted to the working memory to prevent future loops. The actual firing of the production takes place when the path algorithm recurs. Thus, the presence of been predicates in working memory implements loop detection in this production system.

Note that although predicate calculus is used as the language for both productions and working memory entries, the procedural nature of production systems requires that the goals be tested in left-to-right order in the path definition. This order of interpretation is provided by pattern_search.

EXAMPLE 4.3.3: THE FULL KNIGHT'S TOUR

We may generalize the knight's tour solution to the full 8×8 chessboard. Because it makes little sense to enumerate moves for such a complex problem, we replace the 16 move facts with a set of 8 rules to generate legal knight moves. These moves (productions) correspond to the 8 possible ways a knight can move (Figure 4.1).

If we index the chessboard by row and column numbers, we can define a production rule for moving the knight down two squares and right one square:

CONDITION: current row <= 6 ∧ current column number <= 7

ACTION: new row = current row + 2 ∧ new column = current column + 1

If we use predicate calculus to represent productions, then a board square could be defined by the predicate square(R,C), representing the Rth row and Cth column of the board. The above rule could be rewritten in predicate calculus as:

move(square(Row,Column),square(Newrow,Newcolumn))⇐
    less_than_or_equals(Row,6) ∧
    equals(Newrow,plus(Row,2)) ∧
    less_than_or_equals(Column,7) ∧
    equals(Newcolumn,plus(Column,1))

plus is a function for arithmetic addition; less_than_or_equals and equals have the obvious arithmetic interpretations. Seven addition rules can be designed that similarly compute the remaining possible moves. These eight rules replace the move facts in the 3 × 3 version of the problem.

The path definition from the 3 × 3 example defines the control loop for this problem. As we have seen, when predicate calculus descriptions are interpreted procedurally (such as through the pattern_search algorithm), subtle changes are made to the semantics of predicate calculus. One such change is the sequential fashion in which goals are solved. This imposes an ordering, or *procedural semantics*, on predicate calculus expressions. Another change is the introduction of *meta-logical* predicates such as assert, which indicate actions beyond the truth value interpretation of predicate calculus expressions. These issues are discussed in more detail in the PROLOG chapters (6 and 12) and in the LISP implementation of a logic programming engine (Chapter 13).

EXAMPLE 4.3.4:   THE FINANCIAL ADVISOR AS A PRODUCTION SYSTEM

In the previous two chapters, we developed a small financial advisor, using predicate calculus to represent the financial knowledge and graph search to make the appropriate inferences in a consultation. The production system provides a natural vehicle for its implementation. The implications of the logical description form the productions. The case-specific information (an individual's salary, dependents, etc.) is loaded into working memory. Rules are enabled when their premises are satisfied. A rule is chosen from this conflict set and fired, adding its conclusion to working memory. This continues until all possible top-level conclusions have been added to the working memory. Indeed, many expert system "shells" are production systems with added features for supporting the user interface, handling uncertainty in the reasoning, editing the knowledge base, tracing execution, etc. (Sections 12.2.1 and 13.4).

4.3.3 Control of Search in Production Systems

The production system model offers a range of opportunities for adding heuristic control to a search algorithm. These include the choice of data- or goal-driven strategies, the structure of the rules themselves, and the choice of strategies for conflict resolution.

Control Through Choice of Data- or Goal-Driven Search Strategy. Data-driven search begins with a problem description (such as a set of logical axioms, symptoms of an illness, or a body of data that needs interpretation) and infers new knowledge from the data. This is done by applying rules of inference, legal moves in a game, or other state-generating operations to the current description of the world and adding the results to that problem description. This process continues until a goal is reached.

This description of data-driven reasoning emphasizes its close fit with the production system model of computation. The "current state of the world" (data that have either been assumed to be true or deduced as true with previous use of production rules) is placed in working memory. The recognize-act cycle then passes it in front of the (ordered) set of productions. When these data match (are unified with) the condition(s) of one of the production rules, the action of the production adds (by modifying working memory) a new piece of information to the current state of the world.

All productions have the form CONDITION $\Rightarrow$ ACTION. When the CONDITION matches some elements of working memory, its ACTION is performed. If the production rules are formulated as logical implications and the ACTION adds assertions to working memory, then the act of firing a rule corresponds to an application of modus ponens. This creates a new state of the graph.

Figure 4.9 presents a simple data-driven search on a set of productions expressed as propositional calculus implications. The conflict resolution strategy is a simple one of choosing the enabled rule that has fired least recently (or not at all); in the event of ties, the first rule is chosen. Execution halts when a goal is reached. The figure also presents the sequence of rule firings and the stages of working memory in the execution, along with a graph of the space searched.

Although we have treated production systems in a data-driven fashion, they may also be used to characterize goal-driven search. As defined in Chapter 3, goal-driven search begins with a goal and works backward to establish its truth. To implement this in a production system, the goal is placed in working memory and matched against the ACTIONS of the production rules. These ACTIONS are matched (by unification, for example) just as the CONDITIONS of the productions were matched in the data-driven reasoning. All production rules whose conclusions (ACTIONS) match the goal form the conflict set.

When the ACTION of a rule is matched, the CONDITIONS are added to working memory and become the new subgoals (states) of the search. The new states are then matched to the ACTIONS of other production rules. The process continues until a fact is found, usually in the problem's initial description or, as is often the case in expert systems, by directly asking the user for specific information. The search stops when the CONDITIONS of all the productions fired in this backward fashion are found to be true. These CONDITIONS and the chain of rule firings leading to the original goal form a proof of its truth through successive inferences such as modus ponens. See Figure 4.10

Production set:

1. $p \land q \rightarrow$ goal
2. $r \land s \rightarrow p$
3. $w \land r \rightarrow q$
4. $t \land u \rightarrow q$
5. $v \rightarrow s$
6. start $\rightarrow v \land r \land q$

Trace of execution:

Iteration #	Working memory	Conflict set	Rule fired
0	start	6	6
1	start, v, r, q	6, 5	5
2	start, v, r, q, s	6, 5, 2	2
3	start, v, r, q, s, p	6, 5, 2, 1	1
4	start, v, r, q, s, p, goal	6, 5, 2, 1	halt

Space searched by execution:

Figure 4.9 Data-driven search in a production system.

for an instance of goal-driven reasoning on the same set of productions used in Figure 4.9. Note that the goal-driven search fires a different series of productions and searches a different space than the data-driven version.

As this discussion illustrates, the production system offers a natural characterization of both goal- and data-driven search. The production rules are the encoded set of inferences (the "knowledge" in a rule-based expert system) for changing state within the graph. When the current state of the world (the set of true statements describing the world) matches the CONDITIONS of the production rules and this match causes the ACTION part of the rule to create another (true) descriptor for the world, it is referred to as data-driven search.

Alternatively, when the goal is matched against the ACTION part of the rules in the production rule set and their CONDITIONS are then set up as subgoals to be shown to be "true" (by matching the ACTIONS of the rules on the next cycle of the production system), the result is goal-driven problem solving.

Since a set of rules may be executed in either a data- or goal-driven fashion, we can compare and contrast the efficiency of each approach in controlling search. The complexity of search for either strategy is measured by such notions as *branching factor* or *penetrance* (Chapter 5). These measures of search complexity can provide a cost estimate for both the data- and goal-driven versions of a problem solver and therefore help in selecting the most effective strategy.

Production set:

1. $p \wedge q \rightarrow$ goal
2. $r \wedge s \rightarrow p$
3. $w \wedge r \rightarrow p$
4. $t \wedge u \rightarrow q$
5. $v \quad \rightarrow s$
6. start $\rightarrow v \wedge r \wedge q$

Trace of execution:

Iteration #	Working memory	Conflict set	Rule fired
0	goal	1	1
1	goal, p, q	1, 2, 3, 4	2
2	goal, p, q, r, s	1, 2, 3, 4, 5	3
3	goal, p, q, r, s, w	1, 2, 3, 4, 5	4
4	goal, p, q, r, s, w, t, u	1, 2, 3, 4, 5	5
5	goal, p, q, r, s, w, t, u, v	1, 2, 3, 4, 5, 6	6
6	goal p, q, r, s, w, t, u, v, start	1, 2, 3, 4, 5, 6	halt

Space searched by execution:

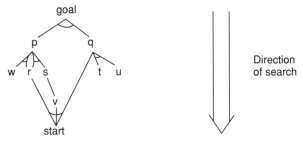

Direction of search

Figure 4.10   Goal-driven search in a production system.

We can also employ combinations of strategies. For example, we can search in a forward direction until the number of states becomes large and then switch to a goal-directed search to use possible subgoals to select among alternative states. The danger in this situation is that, when heuristic or best-first search (Chapter 5) is used, the parts of the graphs actually searched may ''miss'' each other and ultimately require more search than a simpler approach (Fig. 4.11). However, when the branching of a space is constant and exhaustive search is used, a combined search strategy can cut back drastically the amount of space searched. (See Figure 4.12.)

Control of Search Through Rule Structure.   The structure of rules in a production system, including the distinction between the condition and the action and the order in which conditions are tried, determines the fashion in which the space is searched. In introducing predicate calculus as a representation language, we emphasised the *declarative* nature of its semantics. That is, predicate calculus expressions simply define true relationships in a problem domain and make no assertion about the order in which their components are interpreted. Thus, an individual rule might be $\forall$ X (foo(X) $\wedge$ goo(X) $\Rightarrow$ moo(X)). Under the rules of predicate calculus, an alternative form of the same rule is $\forall$ X (foo(X) $\Rightarrow$ moo(X) $\vee \neg$ goo(X)). The equivalence relationship between these two clauses can be demonstrated by the truth table method of Section 2.1.

Start

States examined by
forward search

States examined by
backward search

Goal

Figure 4.11 Bidirectional search missing in both
directions, resulting in excessive search.

Start

States examined by
forward search only

States examined by
combination of
forward and
backward search

Goal

Figure 4.12 Bidirectional search meeting in the middle,
eliminating much of the space examined by
unidirectional search.

Although these formulations are logically equivalent, they do not lead to the same results when interpreted as productions since the production system implementation imposes an order on the matching and firing of rules. For this reason, the specific form of the rules determines the ease (or possibility) of matching a rule against a problem instance. This is a result of differences in the way in which the production system *interprets* the rules. The production system imposes a *procedural semantics* on the declarative language used to form the rules.

Because the production system tries rules in a specific order, the programmer may control search through the structure and order of rules in the production set. Although logically equivalent, $\forall$ X (foo(X) $\land$ goo(X) $\Rightarrow$ moo(X)) and $\forall$ X (foo(X) $\Rightarrow$ moo(X) $\lor \neg$ goo(X)) do not have the same behavior in a search implementation.

Human experts encode crucial heuristics within their rules of expertise. The order of premises encodes important procedural information for solving the problem. It is important that this form be preserved in building a program that "solves problems like the expert." When a mechanic says "if the engine won't turn over and the lights don't come on then check the battery," he or she is suggesting a specific sequence of things to try. This information is not captured by the logically equivalent statement: "the engine turns over or the lights come on or check the battery." This form of the rules is critical in controlling search, making the system behave logically, making traces of rule firings more understandable, etc.

Control of Search Through Conflict Resolution. While production systems (like all architectures for knowledge-based systems) allow heuristics to be encoded in the knowledge content of rules themselves, they offer other opportunities for heuristic control through conflict resolution. Although the simplest such strategy is to choose the first rule that matches the contents of working memory, any strategy may potentially be applied to conflict resolution. For example, conflict resolution strategies supported by OPS5 (Brownston et al. 1985) include:

1. *Refraction.* Refraction specifies that once a rule has fired, it may not fire again until the working memory elements that match its conditions have been modified. This discourages looping.

2. *Recency.* The recency strategy prefers rules whose conditions match with the patterns most recently added to working memory. This focuses the search on a single line of reasoning.

3. *Specificity.* This strategy assumes that a more specific problem-solving rule is preferable to a general rule. A rule is more specific than another if it has more conditions. This implies that it will match fewer potential working memory patterns.

These are representative of the general strategies that may be used in conflict resolution.

4.3.4 Advantages of Production Systems for AI

As illustrated by the preceding examples, the production system offers a general framework for implementing search. Because of its simplicity, modifiability, and flexibility in applying problem-solving knowledge, the production system has proved to be an important tool for the construction of expert systems and other AI applications. The major advantages of production systems for artificial intelligence include:

Separation of Knowledge and Control. The production system is an elegant model of separation of knowledge and control in a computer program. Control is provided by the recognize-act cycle of the production system loop, and the problem-solving knowledge is encoded in the rules themselves. The advantages of this separation include ease of modifying the knowledge base without requiring a change in the code for program control and, conversely, the ability to alter the code for program control without changing the set of production rules.

A Natural Mapping onto State Space Search. The components of a production system map naturally into the constructs of state space search. The successive states of working memory form the nodes of a state space graph. The production rules are the set of possible transitions between states, with conflict resolution implementing the selection of a branch in the state space. These rules simplify the implementation, debugging, and documentation of search algorithms.

Modularity of Production Rules. An important aspect of the production system model is the lack of any syntactic interactions between production rules. Rules may only effect the firing of other rules by changing the pattern in working memory; they may not "call" another rule directly as if it were a subroutine, nor may they set the value of variables in other production rules. The scope of the variables of these rules is confined to the individual rule. This syntactic independence supports the incremental development of expert systems by successively adding, deleting, or changing the knowledge (rules) of the system.

Pattern-Directed Control. The problems addressed by AI programs require particular flexibility in program execution. This goal is served by the fact that the rules in a production system may fire in any sequence. The descriptions of a problem that make up the current state of the world determine the conflict set and, consequently, the particular search path and solution.

Opportunities for Heuristic Control of Search. These were described in the preceding section.

Tracing and Explanation. The modularity of rules and the iterative nature of their execution make it easier to trace execution of a production system. At each stage of the recognize-act cycle, the selected rule may be displayed. Since each rule corresponds to a single "chunk" of problem-solving knowledge, the rule content should provide a meaningful explanation of the system's current state and action (Chapter 8). In contrast, a single line of code in a traditional language such as Pascal or FORTRAN is virtually meaningless.

Language Independence. The production system control model is independent of the representation chosen for rules and working memory, as long as that representation supports pattern matching. We described production rules as predicate calculus implications of the form $A \Rightarrow B$, where the truth of A and the inference rule modus ponens allow us to conclude B. Although there are many advantages to using logic as both the basis for representation of knowledge and the source of sound inference rules, the production system model may be used with other representations.

Although predicate calculus offers the advantage of logically sound inference, much ''real-world'' reasoning is not sound in the logical sense. Instead, it involves probabilistic reasoning, use of uncertain evidence, and default assumptions. Later chapters (8, 9, and 11) discuss alternative inference rules that provide these capabilities. Regardless of the type of inference rules employed, however, the production system provides a vehicle for searching the state space.

A Plausible Model of Human Problem Solving.   Modeling human problem solving was among the first uses of production systems; they continue to be used as a model for human performance in much cognitive science research (Chapter 15).

4.4   Epilogue and References

Chapter 4 discussed the implementation of the search strategies of Chapter 3. It presented recursion as an important tool for programming graph search, implementing the backtrack algorithm of Chapter 3 in recursive form. Pattern-directed search using unification and inference rules (Chapter 2) simplifies the implementation of search through a space of logical inferences.

The production system was shown as a natural architecture for modeling problem solving and implementing search algorithms. The chapter concluded with examples of production system implementations of data- and goal-driven search.

The references listed in the epilogue to Chapter 3 are also appropriate to this chapter. For references on recursion see Chapter 4.

The production system has always been an important paradigm for AI programming, beginning with work by Newell and Simon and their colleagues at Carnegie Mellon University (Newell and Simon 1972; Klahr et al. 1987). Two references on current implementations of production systems are *Programming Expert Systems in OPS5* by Lee Brownston et al. (1985) and *Pattern Directed Inference Systems* by Donald Waterman and Frederick Hayes-Roth (1978).

4.5   Exercises

1. The member algorithm of Section 4.1.1 recursively determines whether a given element is a member of a list.

    a. Write an algorithm to count the number of *elements* in a list.
    b. Write an algorithm to count the number of *atoms* in a list.
    (The distinction between atoms and elements is that an element may itself be a list.)

2. Write a recursive algorithm (using open and closed lists) to implement breadth-first search. Does recursion allow the omission of the open list when implementing breadth-first search? Explain.

3. Trace the execution of the recursive depth-first search algorithm (the version that does not use an open list) on the state space of Figure 3.10.

4. In an ancient Hindu tea ceremony, there are three participants, an elder, a servant, and a child. The four tasks they perform are feeding the fire, serving cakes, pouring tea, and reading poetry; this order reflects the decreasing importance of the tasks. At the beginning of the ceremony, the child performs all four tasks. They are passed one at a time to the servant and the elder until, at the end of the ceremony, the elder is performing all four tasks. No one can take on a less important task than those they already perform. Generate a sequence of moves to transfer all the tasks from the child to the elder. Write a recursive algorithm to perform the move sequence.

5. Using the move and path definitions for the knight's tour of Section 4.2, trace the execution of pattern_search on the goals:
   a. path(1,9).
   b. path(1,5).
   c. path(7,6).
   When the move predicates are attempted in order, c leads to looping in the search. Discuss loop detection and backtracking in this situation.

6. Write the pseudocode definition for a breadth-first version of pattern_search (Section 4.2). Discuss the time and space efficiency of this algorithm.

7. Using the rule in Example 4.3.3 as a model, write the eight move rules needed for the full 8 × 8 version of the knight's tour.

8. Using the goal and start states of Figure 4.5, hand run the production system solution to the 8-puzzle:
   a. In goal-driven fashion.
   b. In data-driven fashion.

9. Consider the financial advisor problem discussed in chapters 2, 3, and 4. Using predicate calculus as a representation language:
   a. Write the problem explicitly as a production system.
   b. Generate the state space and stages of working memory for the data-driven solution to the example in Chapter 3.
   c. Repeat b for a goal-driven solution.

10. Section 4.3.2 presented the general conflict resolution strategies of refraction, recency, and specificity. Propose and justify two more such strategies.

5

HEURISTIC SEARCH

The task that a symbol system is faced with, then, when it is presented with a problem and a problem space, is to use its limited processing resources to generate possible solutions, one after another, until it finds one that satisfies the problem defining test. If the symbol system had some control over the order in which potential solutions were generated, then it would be desirable to arrange this order of generation so that actual solutions would have a high likelihood of appearing early. A symbol system would exhibit intelligence to the extent that it succeeded in doing this. Intelligence for a system with limited processing resources consists in making wise choices of what to do next. . . .

—NEWELL AND SIMON, 1976 Turing Award Lecture

I been searchin'
Searchin' . . . Oh yeah
Searchin' every which-a-way . . .

—LIEBER AND STOLLER

5.0   Introduction

George Polya defines *heuristic* as "the study of the methods and rules of discovery and invention" (Polya 1945). This meaning can be traced to the term's Greek root, the verb *eurisco*, which means "I discover." When Archimedes emerged from his famous bath clutching the golden crown, he shouted "Eureka!" meaning "I have found it!" In state space search, *heuristics* are formalized as rules for choosing those branches in a state space that are most likely to lead to an acceptable problem solution.

AI problem solvers employ heuristics in two basic situations:

1. A problem may not have an exact solution because of inherent ambiguities in the problem statement or available data. Medical diagnosis is an example of this. A

given set of symptoms may have several possible causes; doctors use heuristics to choose the most likely diagnosis and formulate a plan of treatment. Vision is another example of an inherently inexact problem. Visual scenes are often ambiguous, allowing multiple interpretations of the connectedness, extent, and orientation of objects. Optical illusions exemplify these ambiguities. Vision systems use heuristics to select the most likely of several possible interpretations of a given scene.

2. A problem may have an exact solution, but the computational cost of finding it may be prohibitive. In many problems (like chess), state space growth is combinatorially explosive, with the number of possible states increasing exponentially or factorially with the depth of the search. In these cases, exhaustive, *brute-force* search techniques such as depth-first or breadth-first search may fail to find a solution within any practical length of time. Heuristics attack this complexity by guiding the search along the most ''promising'' path through the space. By eliminating states and their descendants from consideration, a heuristic algorithm can (its designer hopes) defeat this combinatorial explosion and find an acceptable solution.

Unfortunately, like all rules of discovery and invention, heuristics are fallible. A heuristic is only an informed guess of the next step to be taken in solving a problem. It is often based on experience or intuition. Since heuristics use limited information, such as the descriptions of the states currently on the open list, they are seldom able to predict the exact behavior of the state space farther along in the search. A heuristic can lead a search algorithm to a suboptimal solution or fail to find any solution at all. This is an inherent limitation of heuristic search. It cannot be eliminated by ''better'' heuristics or more efficient search algorithms (Garey and Johnson 1979).

Heuristics and the design of algorithms to implement heuristic search have long been a core concern of artificial intelligence research. Game playing and theorem proving are two of the oldest applications in artificial intelligence; both of these require heuristics to prune spaces of possible solutions. It is not feasible to examine every inference that can be made in a mathematics domain or every possible move that can be made on a chessboard. Heuristic search is often the only practical answer.

More recently, expert systems research has affirmed the importance of heuristics as an essential component of problem solving. When a human expert solves a problem, he or she examines the available information and makes a decision. The ''rules of thumb'' that a human expert uses to solve problems efficiently are largely heuristic in nature. These heuristics are extracted and formalized by expert systems designers.

It is useful to think of heuristic algorithms as consisting of two parts: the heuristic measure and an algorithm that uses it to search the state space. In Section 5.1.1 we present an algorithm for heuristic or ''best-first'' search. The design and evaluation of effective heuristics are covered in the remainder of the chapter.

Consider the game of tic-tac-toe (Fig. II.5). The combinatorics for exhaustive search are high, but not insurmountable. Each of the nine first moves has eight possible responses, which in turn have seven continuing moves, and so on. A simple counting principle puts the total number of states that need to be considered in an exhaustive search at $9 \times 8 \times 7 \times 6 \cdots$ or 9!.

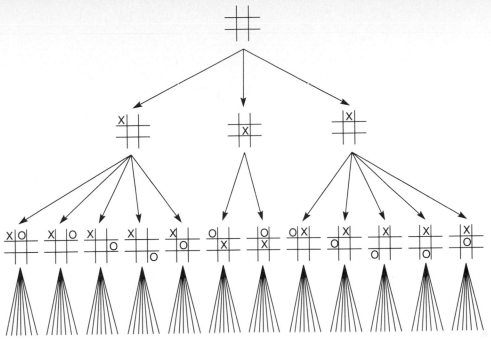

Figure 5.1   First three levels of the tic-tac-toe state
space reduced by symmetry.

Symmetry reduction can decrease the search space a little. Many configurations are actually equivalent under symmetric operations on the game board. For example, there are really only three initial moves: to a corner, to the center of a side, and to the center of the grid. Symmetry reductions on the second level of states further reduce the number of possible paths through the space to a total of $12 \times 7!$. This reduced space is seen in Figure 5.1. It is smaller than the original space but is still factorial in its growth.

A simple heuristic, however, can almost eliminate search entirely: We may move to the board in which X has the most winning lines. (The first three states in the tic-tac-toe game are so measured in Figure 5.2.) In case of states with equal numbers of potential wins, take the first such state found. The algorithm (which actually implements the heuristic search) then selects and moves to the state with the highest heuristic value. In this case X takes the center of the grid. Note that not only are the other alternatives eliminated, but so are all their descendants. Two-thirds of the space is pruned away with the first move (Fig. 5.3).

After the first move, the opponent can choose either of two alternatives (as seen in Figure 5.3). Whichever is chosen, the heuristic can be applied to the resulting board, selecting among the possible moves. As search continues, each move evaluates the children of a single node; brute-force search is not required. (Figure 5.3 shows the reduced search after three steps in the game. States are marked with their heuristic values.)

Although it is difficult to compute the exact number of states that must be so examined, a crude upper bound can be computed by assuming a maximum of nine moves in a

Three wins through a corner square

Four wins through the center square

Two wins through a side square

Figure 5.2 The "most wins" heuristic applied to the first children in tic-tac-toe.

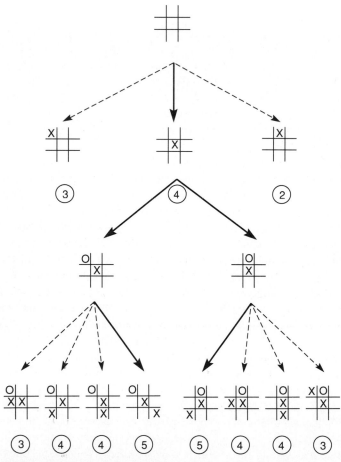

Figure 5.3 Heuristically reduced state space for tic-tac-toe.

game and an average of eight possible children per move. This yields an upper bound of 4.5×9 or about 40 states, a considerable improvement over 9!.

The next section (5.1) presents an algorithm for implementing heuristic search and demonstrates its performance using various heuristics to solve the 8-puzzle. In Section 5.2 we discuss some theoretical issues related to heuristic search, such as *admissibility* and *monotonicity*. Section 5.3 examines the use of *minimax* and *alpha-beta pruning* to apply heuristics to multiple-person games. The final section examines the complexity of heuristic search and reemphasizes its essential role in intelligent problem solving.

5.1 An Algorithm for Heuristic Search

5.1.1 Implementing ''Best-First'' Search

The simplest way to implement heuristic search is through a procedure called *hill climbing* (Pearl 1984). Hill-climbing strategies expand the current node in the search and evaluate its children. The best child is selected for further expansion; neither its siblings nor its parent are retained. Search halts when it reaches a state that is better than any of its children. Hill climbing is named for the strategy that might be used by an eager, but blind mountain climber: go uphill along the steepest possible path until you can go no farther. The problem with hill-climbing strategies is that an erroneous heuristic can lead along deep or even infinite paths that fail. Because it keeps no history, the algorithm cannot recover from these failures.

Hill-climbing strategies can also become stuck at local maxima. If they reach a state that has a better evaluation than any of its children, the algorithm halts. If this state is not a goal, but just a local maximum, the algorithm fails to find a solution. That is, performance might well improve in a limited setting, but because of the shape of the entire space, it may never reach the overall best. An example of local maxima in games occurs in the 8-puzzle. Very often, in order to move a particular tile to its destination, other tiles that are already in goal position have to be moved. This is necessary to solve the puzzle but temporarily worsens the board state. Since ''better'' need not be ''best'' in an absolute sense, hill-climbing methods are unable to distinguish between local and global maxima. There are various approaches to getting around this problem, such as randomly perturbing the evaluation function to break out of local maxima, but in general there is no way of guaranteeing optimal performance with hill-climbing techniques. We give an example of hill climbing with Samuel's checker-playing program in Section 5.3.2.

In spite of its limitations, hill climbing can be used effectively if the evaluation function is sufficiently informative to avoid local maxima and infinite paths. In general, however, heuristic search requires a more informed algorithm; this is provided by *best-first search*.

Like the depth-first and breadth-first search algorithms of Chapter 3, best-first search uses lists to maintain states: **open** to keep track of the current fringe of the search and **closed** to record states already visited. An added step in the algorithm orders the states on open according to some heuristic estimate of their "closeness" to a goal. Thus, each iteration of the loop considers the most "promising" state on the open list. The pseudocode for best-first search appears below.

```
procedure best_first_search

Initialize: open = [Start]; closed = [ ];
while open ≠ [ ] do
begin
  remove the next state from open, call it X;
  If X is a goal then return the solution path that led to X;
  process X, generating all its children;
  for each child of X
    do case

        the child is not already on open or closed:
          begin
            assign a heuristic value to the child state;
            add the child state to open;
          end;

        the child is already on open:
          if the child was reached along a shorter path than the state currently
            on open
          then give the state on open this shorter path value

        the child is already on closed:
          if the child was reached along a shorter path than the state currently
            on closed
          then
            begin
              give the state on closed this shorter path value;
              move this state from closed to open
            end

      end;
  put X on closed;
  re-order states on open according to heuristic merit (best values first)
end;
return (failure);          % open is exhausted
end.
```

At each iteration, best_first_search removes the first element from the open list. If it meets the goal conditions, the algorithm returns the solution path that led to the goal. Note that this assumes each state retains ancestor information to allow the algorithm to return the final solution path. (See Section 3.2.3.)

If the first element on open is not a goal, the algorithm applies all matching production rules or operators to generate its descendants. If a child state is already on open or closed, the algorithm checks to make sure that the state records the shorter of the two partial solution paths. Duplicate states are not retained. By updating the ancestor history

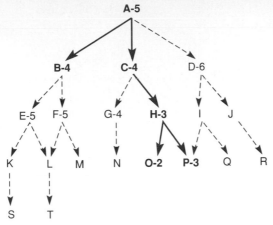

Figure 5.4 Heuristic search of a hypothetical state space.

of nodes on **open** and **closed** when they are rediscovered, the algorithm is more likely to find a shorter path to a goal.

best_first_search then applies a heuristic evaluation to the states on **open**, and the list is sorted according to the heuristic values. This brings the "best" state to the front of **open**. Note that since these estimates are heuristic in nature, the next state to be examined may be from any level of the state space.

Figure 5.4 shows a hypothetical state space with heuristic evaluations attached to some of its states. The states with attached evaluations are those actually generated in best-first search. The states expanded by the heuristic search algorithm are indicated in **this typeface**; note that it does not search all of the space. The goal of best-first search is to find the goal state by looking at as few states as possible, the more *informed* (Section 5.2.3) the heuristic, the fewer states are processed in finding the goal.

A trace of the execution of best_first_search on this graph appears below. Suppose P is the goal state in the graph of Figure 5.4. Since P is the goal, states along the path to P tend to have low heuristic values. The heuristic is fallible: the state O has a lower value than the goal itself and is examined first. Unlike hill climbing, the algorithm recovers from this error and finds the correct goal.

1. open = [A5]; closed = [ ]
2. evaluate A5; open = [B4,C4,D6]; closed = [A5]
3. evaluate B4; open = [C4,E5,F5,D6]; closed = [B4,A5]
4. evaluate C4; open = [H3,G4,E5,F5,D6]; closed = [C4,B4,A5]
5. evaluate H3; open = [O2,P3,G4,E5,F5,D6]; closed = [H3,C4,B4,A5]
6. evaluate O2; open = [P3,G4,E5,F5,D6]; closed = [O2,H3,C4,B4,A5]
7. evaluate P3; the solution is found!

States on open   States on closed

Figure 5.5 Heuristic search of a hypothetical state space
with open and closed states highlighted.

Figure 5.5 shows the space as it appears after the fifth iteration of the while loop. The states contained in open and closed are indicated. open records the current frontier of the search and closed records states already considered. Note that the frontier of the search is highly uneven, reflecting the opportunistic nature of best-first search.

The best-first search algorithm always selects the most promising state on open for further expansion. However, since it is using a heuristic that may prove erroneous, it does not abandon all the other states but maintains them on open. In the event a heuristic leads the search down a path that proves incorrect, the algorithm may retrieve some previously generated ''next best'' state from open, and shift its focus to another part of the space. In the example of Figure 5.4, after the children of state B were found to have poor heuristic evaluations, the search shifted its focus to state C. The children of B were kept on open in case the algorithm needed to return to them later. In best_first_search, as in the algorithms of Chapter 3, the open list allows backtracking from paths that fail to produce a goal.

5.1.2   Implementing Heuristic Evaluation Functions

We now evaluate the performance of several different heuristics for solving the 8-puzzle. Figure 5.6 shows a start and goal state for the 8-puzzle, along with the first three states generated in the search.

The simplest heuristic is to count the tiles out of place in each state when it is compared with the goal. This is intuitively appealing, since it would seem that, all else being

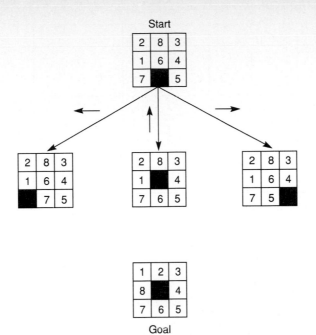

Figure 5.6 The start state, first set of moves, and goal state for an 8-puzzle instance.

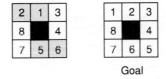

Goal

Figure 5.7 An 8-puzzle state with a goal and two reversals: 1 and 2, 5 and 6.

equal, the state that had fewest tiles out of place is probably closer to the desired goal and would be the best to examine next.

However, this heuristic does not use all of the information available in a board configuration, since it does not take into account the distance the tiles must be moved. A ''better'' heuristic would sum all the distances by which the tiles are out of place, one for each square a tile must be moved to reach its position in the goal state.

Both of these heuristics can be criticized for failing to acknowledge the difficulty of tile reversals. That is, if two tiles are next to each other and the goal requires their being in opposite locations, it takes (many) more than two moves to put them back in place, as the tiles must ''go around'' each other (Fig. 5.7).

A heuristic that takes this into account multiplies a small number (2, for example) times each direct tile reversal (where two adjacent tiles must be exchanged to be in the

State	Tiles out of place	Sum of distances out of place	2 x the number of direct tile reversals
2 8 3 / 1 6 4 / _ 7 5	5	6	0
2 8 3 / 1 _ 4 / 7 6 5	3	4	0
2 8 3 / 1 6 4 / 7 5 _	5	6	0

Goal:

| 1 2 3 |
| 8 _ 4 |
| 7 6 5 |

Figure 5.8   Three heuristics applied to states in the 8-puzzle.

order of the goal). Figure 5.8 shows the result of applying each of these three heuristics to the three child states of Figure 5.6.

In the example of Figure 5.8, the ''sum of distances'' heuristic does indeed seem to provide a more accurate estimate of the work to be done than the simple count of the number of tiles out of place. Also, note that the tile reversal heuristic fails to distinguish between these states, giving each an evaluation of 0. Although it is an intuitively appealing heuristic, it breaks down since none of these states have any direct reversals. A fourth heuristic, which may overcome the limitations of the tile reversal heuristic, adds the sum of the distances out of place and 2 times the number of direct reversals.

This example illustrates the difficulty of devising good heuristics. Our goal is to use the limited information available in a single state descriptor to make intelligent choices. Each of the heuristics proposed above ignores some critical bit of information and is subject to improvement. The design of good heuristics is an empirical problem; judgment and intuition help, but the final measure of a heuristic must be its actual performance on problem instances.

Since heuristics are fallible, it is possible that a search algorithm can be misled down some path that fails to lead to a goal. This problem arose in depth-first search, where a depth count was used to detect fruitless paths. This idea may also be applied to heuristic search. If two states have the same or nearly the same heuristic evaluations, it is generally preferable to examine the state that is nearest to the root state of the graph. This state will have a greater probability of being on the *shortest* path to the goal. The distance from the starting state to its descendants can be measured by maintaining a depth count for each state. This count is 0 for the beginning state and is incremented by

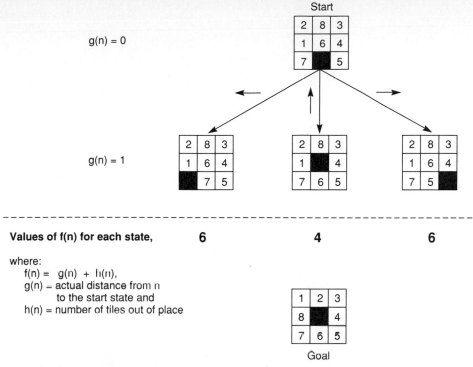

Values of f(n) for each state, 6 4 6

where:
  f(n) = g(n) + h(n),
  g(n) – actual distance from n
       to the start state and
  h(n) = number of tiles out of place

Goal

Figure 5.9 The heuristic **f** applied to states in the 8-puzzle.

1 for each level of the search. It records the actual number of moves that have been used to go from the starting state in the search to each descendant. This can be added to the heuristic evaluation of each state to bias search in favor of states found shallower in the graph.

This makes our evaluation function, f, the sum of two components:

$$f(n) = g(n) + h(n)$$

where $g(n)$ measures the actual length of the path from any state n to the start state and $h(n)$ is a heuristic estimate of the distance from state n to a goal.

In the 8-puzzle, for example, we can let $h(n)$ be the number of tiles out of place. When this evaluation is applied to each of the child states in Figure 5.6, their f values are 6, 4, and 6, respectively (Fig. 5.9).

The full best-first search of the 8-puzzle graph, using f as defined above, appears in Figure 5.10. Each state is labeled with a letter and its heuristic weight, $f(n) = g(n) + h(n)$. The number at the top of each state indicates the order in which it was taken off the **open** list. Some states (h, g, b, d, n, k, and i) are not so numbered, since they were still on **open** when the algorithm terminated.

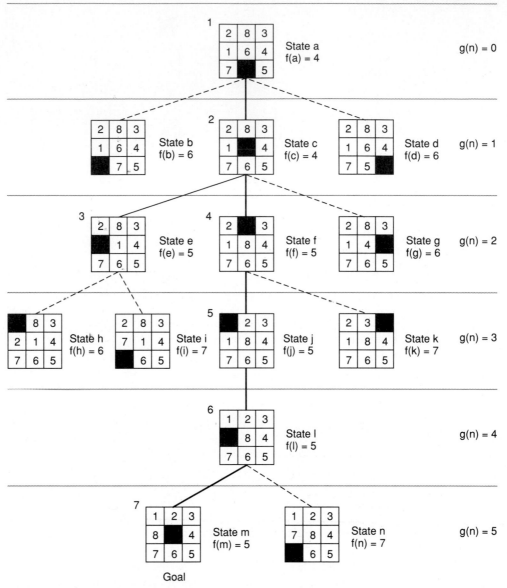

Figure 5.10 State space generated in heuristic search
of the 8-puzzle graph.

The successive stages of open and closed that generate this graph are:

1. open = [a4];
   closed = [ ]

2. open = [c4, b6, d6];
   closed = [a4]

3. open = [e5, f5, g6, b6, d6];
   closed = [a4, c4]

4. open = [f5, h6, g6, b6, d6, l7];
   closed = [a4, c4, e5]

5. open = [j5, h6, g6, b6, d6, k7, l7];
   closed = [a4, c4, e5, f5]

6. open = [l5, h6, g6, b6, d6, k7, l7];
   closed = [a4, c4, e5, f5, j5]

7. open = [m5, h6, g6, b6, d6, n7, k7, l7];
   closed = [a4, c4, e5, f5, j5, l5]

8. success, m = goal!

In step 3 of the execution, both e and f have a heuristic evaluation of 5. State e is examined first, producing its children, h and i. Although state h, the immediate child of e, has the same number of tiles out of place as f, it is one level deeper in the state space. The depth measure, g(n), therefore causes the algorithm to select f for evaluation in step 4. The algorithm backtracks to the shallower state and continues to the goal. The state space graph at this stage of the search, with open and closed highlighted, appears in Figure 5.11. Notice the opportunistic nature of best-first search.

In effect, the g(n) component of the evaluation function gives the search more of a breadth-first flavor. This prevents it from being misled by an erroneous evaluation: if a heuristic continuously returns "good" evaluations for states along a path that fails to reach a goal, the g value will grow to dominate h and force search back to a shorter solution path. This guarantees that the algorithm will not become permanently lost, descending an infinite branch. Section 5.2 examines the conditions under which best-first search using this evaluation function can actually be guaranteed to produce the shortest path to a goal.

When used in conjunction with the procedure best_first_search, the evaluation function f provides a general formulation of heuristic search. To summarize:

1. Production rules or other operations on states generate the children of the state currently under examination.

2. Each state is checked to see if it has occurred before (is on either open or closed), thereby preventing loops.

3. Each state n is given an f value equal to the sum of its depth in the search space g(n) and a heuristic estimate of its distance to a goal h(n). The h value guides search toward heuristically promising states while the g value prevents search from persisting indefinitely on a fruitless path.

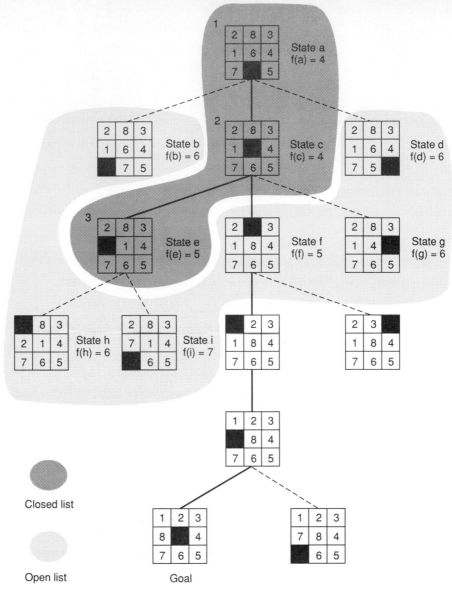

Figure 5.11 **open** and **closed** as they appear after the third iteration of heuristic search.

4. States on **open** are sorted by their f values. By keeping all states on **open** until they are examined or a goal is found, the algorithm can backtrack from fruitless paths. At any one time, **open** may contain states at different levels of the state space graph, allowing full flexibility in changing the focus of the search.

5. The efficiency of the algorithm can be improved by careful maintenance of the

open and closed lists. For example, implementing open as a *heap* or *leftist tree* (Helman and Veroff 1986) can reduce sorting time.

Best-first search is a general algorithm for heuristically searching any state space graph (as were the breadth- and depth-first algorithms presented earlier). It is equally applicable to data- and goal-driven searches and supports a variety of heuristic evaluation functions. It will continue (Section 5.2) to provide a basis for examining the behavior of heuristic search. Because of its generality, best-first search can be used with a variety of heuristics, ranging from subjective estimates of a state's ''goodness'' to sophisticated measures based on the probability of a state leading to a goal. Bayesian statistical measures (Chapter 8) offer an important example of this approach.

Another interesting approach to implementing heuristics is the use of confidence measures by expert systems to weigh the results of a rule. When human experts employ a heuristic, they are usually able to give some estimate of their confidence in its conclusions. Expert systems employ *confidence measures* to select the conclusions with the highest likelihood of success. States with extremely low confidences can be eliminated entirely. This approach to heuristic search is examined in the next section and again in Chapter 8.

5.1.3 Heuristic Search and Expert Systems

Simple games such as the 8-puzzle are ideal vehicles for exploring the design and behavior of heuristic search algorithms for a number of reasons:

1. The search spaces are large enough to require heuristic pruning.

2. Most games are complex enough to suggest a rich variety of heuristic evaluations for comparison and analysis.

3. Games generally do not involve complex representational issues. A single node of the state space is just a board description and usually can be captured in a straightforward fashion. This allows researchers to focus on the behavior of the heuristic, rather than the problems of knowledge representation (see chapters 9 and 14).

4. Because each node of the state space has a common representation (e.g., a board description), a single heuristic may be applied throughout the search space. This contrasts with systems such as the financial advisor, where each node represents a different subgoal with its own distinct description.

More realistic problems greatly complicate the implementation and analysis of heuristic search. However, the insights gained from simple games generalize to more realistic problems such as those found in expert systems applications. Unlike the 8-puzzle, a single heuristic may not apply to each state in these spaces. Instead, the problem-solving heuristics are in the content of the production rules themselves. Each rule is a heuristic that may be applied in a particular case; the pattern matcher of the production system matches the appropriate rule (heuristic) with the relevant state in the space.

Reconsider the financial advisor presented in chapters 2 through 4. So far, the knowledge base has been treated as a set of logical implications, whose conclusions are either true or false, depending on the truth value of the premises. In actuality, these rules are highly heuristic in nature. For example, one rule states that an individual with adequate savings and income should invest in stocks:

savings(adequate) ∧ income(adequate) ⇒ investment(stocks).

In reality, it is possible that such an individual may prefer the added security of a combination strategy or even that of placing all investment money in savings. Thus, the rule is a heuristic, and the problem solver should try to account for this uncertainty. We could take additional factors, such as the age of the investor and the long-term prospects for security and advancement in the investor's profession, into account to make the rules more informed and capable of finer distinctions. However, this does not change the fundamentally heuristic nature of financial advice.

One way in which expert systems have addressed this issue is to attach a numeric weight (called a *confidence measure* or *certainty factor*) to the conclusion of each rule. This measures the confidence that may be placed in their conclusions.

Each rule conclusion is given a confidence measure, a real number between −1 and 1, with 1 corresponding to certainty (true) and −1 to a definite value of false. Values in between reflect varying confidence in the conclusion. For example, the preceding rule may be given a confidence of, say, 0.8, reflecting a small possibility that it may not be correct. Other conclusions may be drawn with different confidence weights:

savings(adequate) ∧ income(adequate) ⇒ investment(stocks)
  with confidence = 0.8.

savings(adequate) ∧ income(adequate) ⇒ investment(combination)
  with confidence = 0.5.

savings(adequate) ∧ income(adequate) ⇒ investment(savings)
  with confidence = 0.1.

These rules now reflect the judgment that while an individual with adequate savings and income would be most strongly advised to invest in stocks, there is some possibility that a combination strategy should be pursued and a very slight chance that they may want to continue investing in savings.

Heuristic search algorithms can use these certainty factors in a number of ways. For example, the results of all applicable rules could be produced along with their associated confidences. This is an exhaustive search, with varying certainties placed on multiple conclusions. Alternatively, the program might return only the result with the strongest confidence value. This would allow the program to ignore other rules, radically pruning the search space. A more conservative pruning strategy could ignore rules that draw a conclusion with a confidence less than a certain value (0.2 for example).

A number of important issues must be addressed in using confidence measures to weight rule conclusions. What does it really mean to have a "numeric confidence measure''? For example, how are the confidences handled if the conclusion of one rule is used as the premise of others? How are confidences combined in the event that more than one rule draws the same conclusion? How are the proper confidence measures assigned to rules in the first place? These issues are discussed in detail in Chapter 8.

5.2   Admissibility, Monotonicity, and Informedness

We may evaluate the behavior of heuristics along a number of dimensions. For instance, we may not only desire a solution, but may require the algorithm to find the shortest path to the goal. This could be important when an application might have an excessive cost for extra solution steps, such as planning a path for an autonomous robot through a dangerous environment. Heuristics that find the shortest path to a goal whenever it exists are said to be *admissible*. In other applications a minimal solution path might not be as important as overall problem-solving efficiency.

We may want to ask whether any better heuristics are available. In what sense is one heuristic ''better'' than another? This is the *informedness* of a heuristic.

When a state is discovered by using heuristic search, is there any guarantee that the same state won't be found later in the search at a cheaper cost (with a shorter path from the start state)? This is the property of monotonicity. The answers to these and other questions related to the effectiveness of heuristics make up the content of this section.

5.2.1   Admissibility Measures

A search algorithm is *admissible* if it is guaranteed to find a minimal path to a solution whenever such a path exists. Breadth-first search is an admissible search strategy. Since it looks at every state at level n of the graph before considering any state at the level n + 1, any goal nodes are found along the shortest possible path. Unfortunately, breadth-first search is often too inefficient for practical use.

Using the evaluation function $f(n) = g(n) + h(n)$ that was introduced in the last section, we may characterize a class of admissible heuristic search strategies. Before doing so, we formalize some definitions from the first part of this chapter:

D E F I N I T I O N

ALGORITHM A, ADMISSIBILITY

Consider the evaluation function $f(n) = g(n) + h(n)$,

where

n is any state encountered in the search.

$g(n)$ is the cost of n from the start state.

$h(n)$ is the heuristic estimate of the cost of going from n to a goal.

If this evaluation function is used with the best_first_search algorithm of Section 5.1, the result is called *algorithm A*.

A search algorithm is *admissible* if, for any graph, it always terminates in the optimal solution path whenever a path from the start to a goal state exists.

If n is a node in the state space graph, g(n) measures the depth at which that state has been found in the graph, and h(n) is the heuristic estimate of the distance from n to a goal. In this sense f(n) estimates the total cost of the path from the start state through n to the goal state.

In determining the properties of admissible heuristics, it is useful to define first an evaluation function f^*:

$$f^*(n) = g^*(n) + h^*(n)$$

where $g^*(n)$ is the cost of the *shortest* path from the start node to node n and h^* returns the *actual* cost of the shortest path from n to the goal. It follows that $f^*(n)$ is the actual cost of the optimal path from a start node to a goal node that passes through node n.

If we employ best_first_search with the evaluation function f^*, the resulting search strategy is admissible. (Proof is left to the reader.)

Although *oracles* such as f^* do not exist for most real problems, we would like the evaluation function f to be a close estimate of f^*. In algorithm A, g(n), the cost of the current path to state n, is a reasonable estimate of g^*, but they may not be equal: $g(n) \geq g^*(n)$. These are equal only if the graph search has discovered the optimal path to state n.

Similarly, we replace $h^*(n)$ with h(n), a heuristic estimate of the minimal cost to a goal state. Although we usually may not compute h^*, it is often possible to determine whether or not the heuristic estimate, h(n), is bounded from above by the actual cost of a minimal path, $h^*(n)$. If algorithm A uses an evaluation function f in which $h(n) \leq h^*(n)$, it is called algorithm A^*.

DEFINITION

ALGORITHM A^*

If algorithm A is used with an evaluation function in which h(n) is less than or equal to the cost of the minimal path from n to the goal, the resulting search algorithm is called algorithm A^* (pronounced "A STAR").

It is now possible to state a property of A^* algorithms:

All A^* algorithms are admissible.

This property is a theorem and the exercises at the end of the chapter give hints for its proof. The theorem says that any A^* algorithm, i.e., one that uses a heuristic h(n) such that $h(n) \leq h^*(n)$ for all n, is guaranteed to find the minimal path from n to the goal, if such a path exists.

Note that breadth-first search may be characterized as an A^* algorithm in which $f(n) = g(n) + 0$. The decision for considering a state is based solely on its distance from the start state. We will show (Section 5.2.3) that the set of nodes considered by an A^* algorithm is a subset of the states examined in breadth-first search.

Several heuristics from the 8-puzzle provide examples of A^* algorithms. Although we may not be able to compute the value of $h^*(n)$ for the 8-puzzle, we may determine when a heuristic is bounded from above by the actual cost of the shortest path to a goal.

For instance, the heuristic of counting the number of tiles not in the goal position is certainly less than or equal to the number of moves required to move them to their goal position. Thus, this heuristic is admissible and guarantees an optimal (or shortest) solution path. The sum of the direct distances of tiles out of place is also less than or equal to the minimum actual path. Even using small multipliers for direct tile reversals gives an admissible heuristic.

This approach to proving admissibility of 8-puzzle heuristics may be applied to any heuristic search problem. Even though the actual cost of the shortest path to a goal may not always be computed, we can often prove that a heuristic is bounded from above by this value. When this can be done, the resulting search will terminate in the discovery of the shortest path when such a path exists.

5.2.2   Monotonicity

Recall that the definition of A^* algorithms did not require that $g(n) = g^*(n)$. This means that admissible heuristics may initially reach nongoal states along a suboptimal path, as long as the algorithm eventually finds an optimal path to all states on the path to a goal. It is natural to ask if there are heuristics that are "locally admissible," i.e., that consistently find the minimal path to each state they encounter in the search. This property is called monotonicity.

DEFINITION

MONOTONICITY

A heuristic function h is monotone if

1. For all states n_i and n_j, where n_j is a descendant of n_i,

$$h(n_i) - h(n_j) \leq cost(n_i, n_j),$$

where $cost(n_i, n_j)$ is the actual cost (in number of moves) of going from state n_i to n_j.

2. The heuristic evaluation of the goal state is zero, or $h(\text{Goal}) = 0$.

One way of describing the monotone property is that the search space is everywhere locally consistent with the heuristic employed. The difference between the heuristic measure for a state and any one of its successors is bound by the actual cost of going between that state and its successor. This is to say that the heuristic is everywhere admissible, reaching each state along the shortest path from its ancestors.

If the graph search algorithm for best-first search is used with a monotonic heuristic, a important step may be omitted. Since the heuristic finds the shortest path to any state the first time that state is discovered, when a state is rediscovered, it is not necessary to check if the new path is shorter. It won't be! This allows any state that is rediscovered in the space to be dropped immediately without updating the path information retained on open or closed.

When using a monotonic heuristic, as the search moves through the space the heuristic measure for each state n is replaced by the actual cost for generating that piece of the path to n. Since the actual cost is equal to or larger than the heuristic in each instance, f will not decrease; i.e., f is monotonically nondecreasing (hence the name).

A simple argument can show that any monotonic heuristic is admissible. This argument considers any path in the space as a sequence of states $s_1, s_2, \ldots, s_g$, where s_1 is the start state and s_g the goal. For the sequence of moves in this arbitrarily selected path:

$$s_1 \text{ to } s_2 \qquad h(s_1) - h(s_2) \leq cost(s_1, s_2) \text{ by monotone property}$$
$$s_2 \text{ to } s_3 \qquad h(s_2) - h(s_3) \leq cost(s_2, s_3)$$
$$s_3 \text{ to } s_4 \qquad h(s_3) - h(s_4) \leq cost(s_3, s_4)$$

$$\cdot \qquad \cdot \qquad \cdot \qquad \cdot$$
$$\cdot \qquad \cdot \qquad \cdot$$

$$s_{g-1} \text{ to } s_g \qquad h(s_{g-1}) - h(s_g) \leq cost(s_{g-1}, s_g)$$

Summing each column and using the monotone property of $h(s_g) = 0$:

$$\text{path } s_1 \text{ to } s_g \qquad h(s_1) \leq cost(s_1, s_g)$$

This means that monotone heuristic h is A^* and admissible.

It is left as an exercise whether the admissibility property of a heuristic implies monotonicity.

5.2.3 When One Heuristic Is Better: More Informed Heuristics

The final issue of this subsection is the notion of one heuristic being somehow better than another for finding the minimal path. An interesting case occurs when both heuristics are A^*.

D E F I N I T I O N

INFORMEDNESS

For two A^* heuristics h_1 and h_2, if $h_1(n) \leq h_2(n)$, for all states n in the search space, heuristic h_2 is said to be *more informed* than h_1.

We can use this definition to compare the heuristics proposed for solving the 8-puzzle. As pointed out previously, breadth-first search is equivalent to the A^* algorithm

Figure 5.12 Comparison of state space searched using heuristic search with space searched by breadth-first search. The portion of the graph searched heuristically is shaded. The optimal solution path is in bold. Heuristic used is **f(n) = g(n) + h(n)** where **h(n)** is tiles out of place.

with heuristic h_1 such that $h_1(x) = 0$ for all states x. This is, trivially, less than h^*. We have also shown that h_2, the number of tiles out of place with respect to the goal state, is a lower bound for h^*. In this case $h_1 \leq h_2 \leq h^*$. It follows that the "number of tiles out of place" heuristic is more informed than breadth-first search. Figure 5.12 compares the spaces searched by these two heuristics. Both h_1 and h_2 find the optimal path, but h_2 evaluates many fewer states in the process.

Similarly, we can argue that the heuristic that calculates the sum of the direct distances by which all the tiles are out of place is again more informed than the calculation of the number of tiles that are out of place with respect to the goal state, and indeed this is the case. One can visualize a sequence of search spaces, each smaller than the previous one, converging on the direct optimal path solution.

If a heuristic h_2 is more informed than h_1, then the set of states examined by h_2 is a subset of those expanded by h_1. This can be verified by assuming the opposite (that there is one state expanded by h_2 and not by h_1). However, since h_2 is more informed than h_1, for all n, $h_2(n) < h_1(n)$, which is contradicted by our assumption.

In general, then, the more informed an A^* algorithm, the less of the space it needs to expand to get the optimal solution. We must be careful, however, that the computations necessary to employ the more informed heuristic are not so inefficient as to offset the gains from reducing the number of states searched. (See Figure 5.22 and related comments.)

5.3   Using Heuristics in Games

5.3.1   The Minimax Procedure on Exhaustively Searchable Graphs

Games have always been an important application area for heuristic algorithms. Two-person games are more complicated than simple puzzles because of the existence of a "hostile" and essentially unpredictable opponent. Thus, they provide some interesting opportunities for developing heuristics, as well as greater difficulties in developing search algorithms.

First we consider games whose state space is small enough to be exhaustively searched to find winning states; here the problem is systematically searching the space of possible moves and countermoves by the opponent. Then we look at games in which it is either impossible or undesirable to exhaustively represent and search the game graph. Since only a portion of the state space can be generated and searched; the game player must use heuristics to guide play along a path to a winning state.

Consider *nim*, a game whose state space may be exhaustively searched. To play nim, a number of matches are placed on a table between the two opponents; at each move, the player must divide a pile of matches into two nonempty piles with different numbers of matches in each pile. Thus, 6 matches may be divided into piles of 5 and 1 or 4 and 2, but not 3 and 3. The first player who can no longer make a move loses the game. For a reasonable number of matches, the state space can be exhaustively searched. Figure 5.13 illustrates the space for a game with 7 matches.

In playing games whose state space may be exhaustively delineated, the primary difficulty is in accounting for the actions of the opponent. A simple way to handle this is to assume that your opponent uses the same knowledge of the state space as you use and applies that knowledge in a consistent effort to win the game. While this assumption has its limitations (which are discussed in Section 5.3.2), it provides a reasonable basis for predicting their behavior. *Minimax* implements game search under this assumption.

The opponents in a game are referred to as MIN and MAX. Although this is partly for historical reasons, the significance of these names is straightforward: MAX represents the player trying to win, or to MAXimize her advantage. MIN is the opponent who attempts to MINimize MAX's score. We assume that MIN uses the same information and always attempts to move to a state that is worst for MAX.

In implementing minimax, we label each level in the search space according to whose move it is at that point in the game, MIN or MAX. In the example of Figure 5.14,

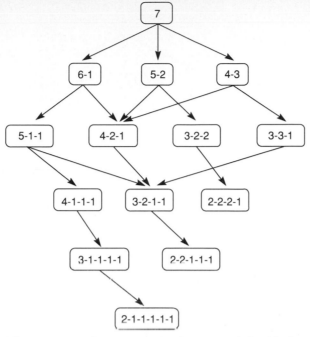

Figure 5.13 State space for the game of nim. Each state partitions the seven matches into one or more piles.

MIN is allowed to move first. Each leaf node is given a value of 1 or 0, depending on whether it is a win for MAX or for MIN. Minimax propagates these values up the graph through successive parent nodes according to the rule:

If the parent state is a MAX node, give it the maximum value among its children

If the parent is a MIN node, give it the minimum value of its children.

The value that is thus assigned to each state indicates the value of the best state that this player can hope to achieve (assuming the opponent plays as predicted by the minimax algorithm). These derived values are used to choose among possible moves. The result of applying minimax to the state space graph for nim appears in Figure 5.14.

The values of the leaf nodes are propagated up the graph using minimax. Since all of MIN's possible first moves lead to nodes with a derived value of 1, the second player, MAX, always can force the game to a win, regardless of MIN's first move. MIN could win only if MAX played foolishly. In Figure 5.14, MIN may choose any of the first move alternatives, with the resulting win paths for MAX in bold arrows.

Although there are many games where it is also possible to enumerate and exhaustively search the state space (as was done in Figure 5.14), the most interesting cases do not allow exhaustive search. We examine the heuristic application of minimax in the next section.

Figure 5.14 Exhaustive minimax for the game of nim.
Bold lines indicate forced win for MAX.
Each node is marked with its derived value
(0 or 1) under minimax.

5.3.2 Minimaxing to Fixed Ply Depth

In applying minimax to more complicated games, it is seldom possible to expand the state space graph out to the leaf nodes. Instead, the state space is searched to a predefined number of levels, as determined by available resources of time and memory. This strategy is called an n-*move look-ahead*, where n is the number of levels explored. Since the leaves of this subgraph are not final states of the game, it is not possible to give them values that reflect a win or a loss. Instead, each node is given a value according to some heuristic evaluation function. The value that is propagated back to the root node is not an indication of whether or not a win can be achieved (as in the previous example) but is simply the heuristic value of the best state that can be reached in n moves from this start node. Look-ahead increases the power of a heuristic by allowing it to be applied over a greater area of the state space. Minimax consolidates these separate evaluations into a single value of an ancestor state.

In a game of conflict, each player attempts to overcome the other, so many game heuristics directly measure the advantage of one player over another. In checkers or chess, piece advantage is important, so a simple heuristic might take the difference in the number of pieces belonging to MAX and MIN and try to maximize the difference between these piece measures. A more sophisticated strategy might assign different

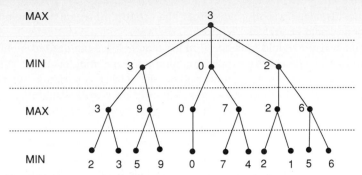

Figure 5.15 Minimax applied to a hypothetical state space. Leaf states show heuristic values; internal states show backed-up values.

values to the pieces, depending on their value (e.g., queen vs. pawn or king vs. ordinary checker) or location on the board. Most games provide limitless opportunities for designing heuristics.

Game graphs are searched by level or *ply*. As we saw in Figure 5.14, MAX and MIN alternately select moves. Each move by a player defines a new ply of the graph. Game-playing programs typically look ahead a fixed ply depth, often determined by the space/time limitations of the computer. The states on that ply are measured heuristically and the values are propagated back up the graph using minimax. The search algorithm then uses these *derived values* to select among possible next moves.

After assigning an evaluation to each state on the selected ply, the program propagates a value up to each parent state. If the parent is on a MIN level, the minimum value of the children is backed up. If the parent is a MAX node, minimax assigns it the maximum value of its children.

Maximizing for MAX parents and minimizing for MIN, the values go back up the graph to the children of the current state. These values are then used by the current state to select among its children. Figure 5.15 shows minimax on a hypothetical state space with a four-ply look-ahead.

The earliest AI work in this area was Samuel's checker-playing program (1959). This program was exceptional for its time and the limitations of the 1950s computers and is still a classic. Not only did Samuel's checker player apply heuristic search to checker playing, it also implemented a simple form of learning.

Samuel's program evaluated board states with a weighted sum of several different heuristic measures:

$$\sum_i a_i x_i$$

The x_i in this sum was a feature of the game board such as piece advantage, piece location, control of center position, opportunities to sacrifice players in order to jump more of the opponent's pieces, and even a calculation of moments of inertia of one player's pieces about an axis of the board. The coefficients of these x_i were specially tuned weights that tried to model the importance of that factor in the overall board evaluation.

Thus, if piece advantage was more important than control of the center, the piece advantage coefficient would be greater.

Samuel's program would look ahead in the search space the desired number of plies (usually imposed by space and/or time limitations of the computer) and evaluate all the states at that level with the evaluation polynomial. Using a variation on minimax, it propagated these values back up the graph. The checker player would then move to the best state; after the opponent's move, the process would be repeated for the new board state.

If the evaluation polynomial led to a losing series of moves, the program adjusted its coefficients in an attempt to improve performance. Evaluations with large coefficients were given most of the blame for losses and had their weights decreased, while smaller weights were increased to give these evaluations more influence. If the program won, the opposite was done. The program trained by playing either against a human partner or against another version of itself.

Samuel's program thus took a hill-climbing approach to learning, attempting to improve performance through local improvements on the evaluation polynomial. Samuel's checker player was able to improve its performance until it played a very good game of checkers. However, because it relied on hill climbing, it retained certain interesting limitations. For example, since it had no notion of a global strategy, it was vulnerable to strategies that used the evaluation function to lead the program into traps. The learning component of the program was vulnerable to inconsistencies in the opponent's play; for example, if the opponent used widely varying strategies, or simply played foolishly, the weights on the evaluation polynomial might begin to take on "random" values, leading to an overall degradation of performance.

We can make several final points about the minimax procedure. First, and most important, evaluations to any (previously decided) fixed ply depth may be seriously misleading. When a heuristic is applied with a limited look-ahead, it is possible that the depth of the look-ahead may not detect that a heuristically promising path leads to a bad situation later in the game. For example, if your opponent in chess offers a rook as a lure to take your queen, and the evaluation only looks ahead to the ply where the rook is offered, the evaluation is going to be biased toward this state. Unfortunately, selection of the state may cause the entire game to be lost! This is referred to as the *horizon effect*. It is usually countered by searching several plies deeper from states that look exceptionally good. This selective deepening of search in important areas will not make the horizon effect go away, however. The search must stop somewhere and therefore will be blind to states beyond that point.

There is another effect that occurs in minimaxing backups. The evaluations that take place very deep in the space can be biased by their very depth (Pearl 1984). In the same way that the average of a product differs from the product of averages, the estimate of minimax (which is what we desire) is different from the minimax of estimates (which is what we are doing). In this sense, deeper search with evaluation and minimax need not always mean better search. Further discussion of these issues and possible remedies is found in Pearl (1984).

In concluding the discussion of minimax, we present its application to tic-tac-toe (Section 5.1) (Nilsson 1980). We use a slightly more complex heuristic, one that

X has 6 possible win paths;
O has 5 possible wins

$E(n) = 6 - 5 = 1$

X has 4 possible win paths;
O has 6 possible wins

$E(n) = 4 - 6 = -2$

X has 5 possible win paths;
O has 4 possible wins

$E(n) = 5 - 4 = 1$

Heuristic is $E(n) = M(n) - O(n)$

where $M(n)$ is the total of My possible winning lines

$O(n)$ is total of Opponent's possible winning lines

$E(n)$ is the total Evaluation for state n

Figure 5.16   Heuristic measuring conflict applied to
states of tic-tac-toe.

attempts to measure the conflict in the game. The heuristic takes a state to be measured, counts all winning lines open to MAX, and then subtracts the total number of winning lines open to MIN. The search attempts to maximize this difference. If a state is a forced win for MAX, it is evaluated as $+\infty$, a forced win for MIN as $-\infty$. Figure 5.16 shows this heuristic applied to several sample states.

The figures that follow show the heuristic of Figure 5.16 with a two-ply minimax. MAX (X) has the first move in the game. The next three figures show the heuristic evaluation, the minimax backup, and MAX's choice of move.

5.3.3   The Alpha-Beta Procedure

Straight minimax requires a two-pass analysis of the search space (the first to descend to the ply depth and there apply the heuristic, the second to propagate values back up the tree). Minimax pursues all branches in the space, including many that could be ignored (pruned) by a more intelligent algorithm. Researchers in game playing have developed a class of search techniques called *alpha-beta* pruning to improve the efficiency of search in two-person games (Pearl 1984).

The idea for alpha-beta search is simple: rather than searching the entire space to the ply depth, alpha-beta search proceeds in a depth-first fashion. Two values, called *alpha* and *beta*, are created during the search. The alpha value, associated with MAX

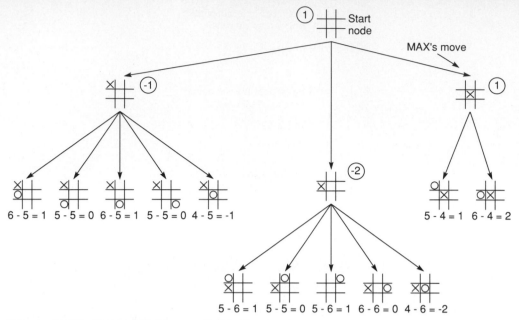

Figure 5.17 Two-ply minimax applied to the opening move of tic-tac-toe.

nodes, can never decrease, and the beta value, associated with MIN nodes, can never increase. Suppose a MAX node's alpha value is 6. Then MAX need not consider any backed-up value less than or equal to 6 that is associated with any MIN node below it. Alpha is the worst that MAX can "score" given that MIN will also do its "best." Similarly, if MIN has a beta value of 6, it need not consider further any MAX node below it that has a value of 6 or more.

To begin alpha-beta search, we descend to full ply depth in a depth-first fashion and apply our heuristic evaluation to a state and all its siblings. Let's say these are MIN nodes. The maximum of these MIN values is then backed up to the parent (a MAX node, just as in minimax). This value is then offered to the grandparent of these MINs as a potential beta cutoff.

Next, the algorithm descends to other grandchildren and terminates exploration of their parent if any of their values is equal to or larger than this beta value. Similar procedures can be described for alpha pruning over the grandchildren of a MAX node.

Two rules for terminating search, based on alpha and beta values, are:

1. Search can be stopped below any MIN node having a beta value less than or equal to the alpha value of any of its MAX ancestors.

2. Search can be stopped below any MAX node having an alpha value greater than or equal to the beta value of any of its MIN node ancestors.

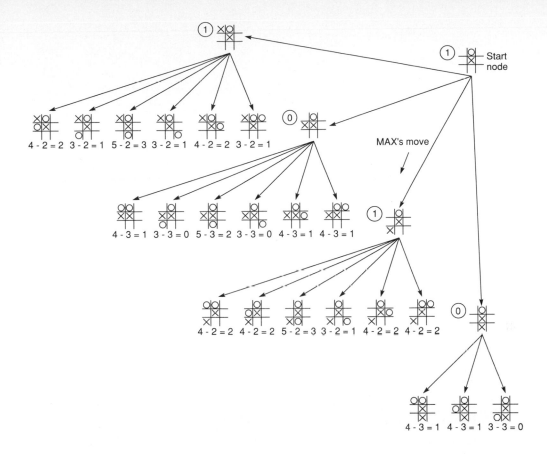

4 - 2 = 2   3 - 2 = 1   5 - 2 = 3   3 - 2 = 1   4 - 2 = 2   3 - 2 = 1

4 - 3 = 1   3 - 3 = 0   5 - 3 = 2   3 - 3 = 0   4 - 3 = 1   4 - 3 = 1

4 - 2 = 2   4 - 2 = 2   5 - 2 = 3   3 - 2 = 1   4 - 2 = 2   4 - 2 = 2

4 - 3 = 1   4 - 3 = 1   3 - 3 = 0

MAX's move

Start node

Figure 5.18   Two-ply minimax applied to **X**'s second
move of tic-tac-toe.

Alpha-beta pruning thus expresses a relation between nodes at ply n and nodes at ply $n + 2$ under which entire subtrees rooted at level $n + 1$ can be eliminated from consideration.

As an example, Figure 5.20 takes the space of Figure 5.15 and applies alpha-beta pruning. Note that the resulting backed-up value is identical to the minimax result and the search saving is considerable.

With a fortuitous ordering of states in the search space, alpha-beta can effectively double the depth of the search space considered with a fixed space/time computer commitment (Nilsson 1980). If there is a particular unfortunate ordering, alpha-beta searches no more of the space than normal minimax; however, the search is done in only one pass.

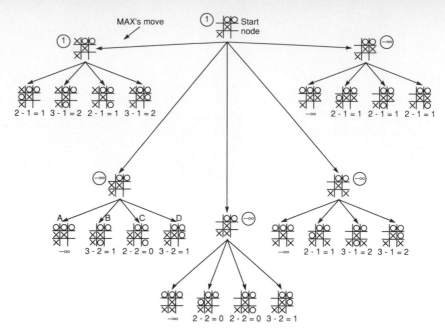

Figure 5.19 Two-ply minimax applied to **X**'s move near end game.

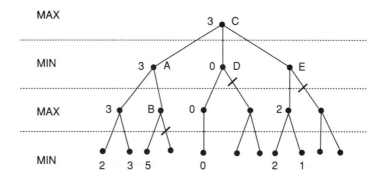

A has $\beta = 3$ (A will be no larger than 3)

B is β pruned, since $5 > 3$

C has $\alpha = 3$ (C will be no smaller than 3)

D is α pruned, since $0 < 3$

E is α pruned, since $2 < 3$

C is 3

Figure 5.20 Alpha-beta prune applied to state space of Figure 5.15. States without numbers are not evaluated.

5.4 Complexity Issues

The most difficult aspect of combinatorial problems is that the "explosion" often takes place without program designers realizing that it is happening. Since most activity, computing and otherwise, takes place in a world of linear algorithms and processing, we have difficulty appreciating the full meaning of exponential growth. The complaint is too often heard, "If only I had a larger (or faster or highly parallel . . .) computer my problem would be solved." Such claims, often made in the aftermath of the explosion, are usually rubbish. The problem wasn't understood properly and/or the proper steps were not taken to address the combinatorics of the situation.

The full extent of combinatorial growth staggers the imagination. It has been estimated that the number of states produced by a full search of the space of possible chess moves is about 10^{120}. If this seems "just another large number," it is comparable to the number of molecules in the universe or the number of nanoseconds since the "big bang." It is simply not going to be computed!!

Several measures have been developed to help calculate complexity. One of these is the *branching factor* of a space. This is defined as the average number of descendants that emerge from any state in the space. The number of states at depth n of the search is equal to the branching factor raised to the nth power. Once the branching factor is computed for a space it is possible to estimate the search cost to generate a path of any particular length. Figure 5.21 gives the relationship between B (branching), L (path length),

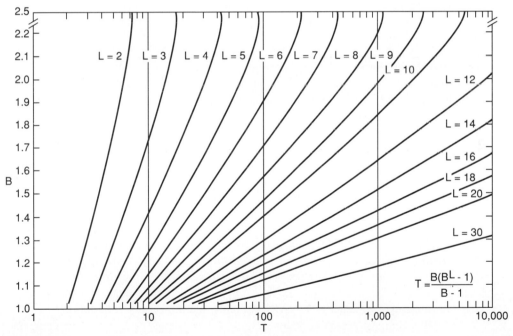

Figure 5.21 Number of nodes generated as a function of branching factor for various lengths of solution paths.

and T (total states in the search) for small values. The figure is logarithmic in T, so L is not the straight line it looks in the graph.

Several examples using this figure show how bad things can get. If the branching factor is 2 (in a binary tree, for example), it takes a search of about 100 states to examine all paths that extend six levels deep into the search space. It takes a search of about 10,000 states to consider paths 12 moves deep. If the branching can be cut down to 1.5 (by some heuristic or reformulation of the problem), then a path twice as long can be considered for the same amount of states searched.

The mathematical formula that produced the relationships of Figure 5.21 is straight-forward:

$$T = B + B^2 + B^3 + \cdots + B^L$$

where T is total states, L is path length, and B is branching factor. This equation reduces to:

$$T = B(B^L - 1)/(B - 1)$$

Determining measurement aspects for a search space is by and large empirical and done by considerable playing about with and testing of a problem. Suppose, for example, we wish to establish the branching factor of the 8-puzzle. We calculate the total number of possible moves: 2 from each corner for a total of 8 corner moves, 3 from the center of each side for a total of 12, and 4 from the center of the grid for a grand total of 24. This divided by 9, the different number of possible locations of the blank, gives an average branching factor of 2.67. As can be seen in Figure 5.21, this is not very good for a deep search. If we eliminate moves directly back to a parent state (already built into the search algorithms of this chapter) there is one less move from each state. This gives a branching factor of 1.67, a considerable improvement, which might (in some state spaces) make exhaustive search possible.

In the attempt to bring down the branching of a search or otherwise constrain the search space, we presented the notion of **more informed** heuristics. The more informed the search, the less the space must be searched to get the minimal path solution. As we pointed out in Section 5.3, the computational costs of the additional information needed to further cut down the search space may not always be acceptable. In solving problems on a computer, it is not enough to find a minimum path. We must also minimize total cpu costs.

Figure 5.22, taken from an analysis by Nilsson (1980), is an informal attempt to get at these issues. The "informedness" coordinate marks the amount of information that is included in the evaluation heuristic to improve its performance. The cpu coordinate marks the cpu costs for implementing aspects of the search. As the information included in the heuristic increases, the cpu cost of the heuristic increases. Similarly, as the heuristic gets more informed, the cpu cost of evaluating states gets smaller, since fewer states are considered. The critical cost, however, is the total cost of computing the heuristic PLUS evaluating states, and it is usually desirable that this cost be minimized.

Finally, heuristic search of and/or graphs is also an important area of concern, since the state spaces for expert systems are often of this form. The fully general search of these structures is made up entirely of the components already discussed in this and the preceding chapter. Since all **and** children must be searched to find a goal, the heuristic

Figure 5.22 Informal plot of cost of searching and cost
of computing heuristic evaluation against
informedness of heuristic.

estimate of the cost of searching an *and* node is the sum of the estimates of searching the children.

More comments are made on heuristic-based and/or search in Section 8.3, where we present the design of expert systems and the implementation of appropriate search strategies.

5.5   Epilogue and References

The search spaces for interesting problems tend to grow exponentially; heuristic search is a primary tool for managing this combinatorial explosion. After presenting an algorithm for implementing best-first search, the chapter analyzed the behavior of heuristic algorithms, considering properties such as admissibility, monotonicity, and informedness.

Heuristic search was introduced using simple games such as the 8-puzzle and extended to the more complex problem spaces generated by rule-based expert systems (Chapter 8). The chapter also applied heuristic search to two-person games, using minimax and alpha-beta pruning to implement look-ahead and predict the behavior of the opponent.

A thorough understanding of complexity theory is essential to any analysis of state space growth and heuristic pruning. We especially recommend *Computers and Intractability* by Michael R. Garey and David S. Johnson (1979) for this material.

Heuristics by Judea Pearl (1984) provides a comprehensive treatment of the design and analysis of heuristics for computer problem solving. We are also indebted to Nils Nilsson (1980) for the general approach and many of the particular examples presented in this chapter.

5.6 Exercises

1. Give a heuristic that a block-stacking program might use to solve problems of the form "stack block X on block Y." Is it admissible? Monotonic?

2. The sliding-tile puzzle consists of three black tiles, three white tiles, and an empty space in the configuration shown in Figure 5.23.

Figure 5.23   The sliding block puzzle.

The puzzle has two legal moves with associated costs:

> A tile may move into an adjacent empty location. This has a cost of 1. A tile can hop over one or two other tiles into the empty position. This has a cost equal to the number of tiles jumped over.

The goal is to have all the white tiles to the left of all the black tiles. The position of the blank is not important.

a. Compare the use of predicate calculus and other representations to describe this problem.

b. Analyze the state space with respect to complexity and looping.

c. Propose a heuristic for solving this problem and analyze it with respect to admissibility, monotonicity, and informedness.

3. Compare the three 8-puzzle heuristics of Figure 5.8 and the fourth heuristic of adding the sum of distances out of place to 2 times the number of direct reversals. Compare them in terms of:

a. Accuracy in estimating distance to a goal. This requires that you first derive the shortest path solution and use it as a standard.

b. Informedness. Which heuristic most effectively prunes the state space?

c. Admissibility. Which of these heuristics are bounded from above by the actual cost of a path to the goal? Either prove your conclusions for the general case or give a counterexample.

4. a. As presented in the text, best-first search uses the **closed** list to implement loop detection. What would be the effect of eliminating this test and relying on the depth test, $g(n)$, to detect loops? Compare the efficiencies of the two approaches.

b. **best_first_search** does not test a state to see if it is a goal until it is removed from the **open** list. This test could be performed when new states are generated. What effect would doing so have on the efficiency of the algorithm? Admissibility?

5. Prove A* is admissible. Hint: the proof should show that:

    a. During its execution there is always a node on open that lies on an optimal path to the goal.

    b. If there is a path to a goal, A* will terminate by finding the optimal path.

6. Does (or when does) admissibility imply monotonicity of a heuristic?

7. Prove that the set of states expanded by algorithm A* is a subset of those examined by breadth-first search.

8. Prove that more informed heuristics develop the same or less of the search space. Hint: formalize the argument presented in Section 5.2.3.

9. A Caesar cipher is a simple encryption scheme based on cyclic permutations of the alphabet, with the ith letter of the alphabet replaced by the (i + n)th letter of the alphabet. For example, in a Caesar cipher with a shift of 4, "Caesar" would be encrypted as "Giewev."

    a. Give four heuristics that might be used for solving Caesar ciphers.

    b. In a simple substitution cipher, each letter is replaced by another letter under some arbitrary one-to-one mapping. Which of the heuristics proposed for the Caesar cipher may be used to solve substitution ciphers? Explain. (Thanks to Don Morrison for this problem.)

10. Perform minimax and alpha-beta pruning on the tree shown in Figure 5.24.

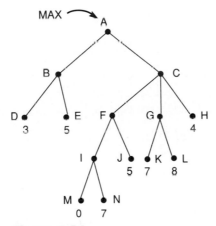

Figure 5.24

11. Perform a left-to-right alpha-beta prune on the tree of Exercise 10. Perform a right-to-left prune on the same tree. Discuss why different pruning occurs.

12. Another way in which Samuel's checker player learned was to maintain a data base of previously encountered board states along with their derived evaluation under minimax. When a board was to be evaluated, the program first looked in the data base of board states. Discuss the effect this would have on the effectiveness of minimax. Give some "ballpark" estimates of the growth of this data base as a function of games played. Discuss ways in which this implementation may be made more efficient and more effective.

13. Why do game-playing programs work from a current state to a goal, rather than backward from a goal? What properties of a game might suggest using a backward strategy?

14. It was mentioned in the text that extending a heuristic minimax to extreme depths of the state space could degrade the effectiveness of the algorithm. Formalize this argument. Hint: see Chapter 10 of Pearl (1984).

15. Samuel's checker-playing program employed up to 16 different parameters in its evaluation polynomial. Suggest three evaluation functions for checkers that were not mentioned in the text.

16. Consider three-dimensional tic-tac-toe. Discuss representational issues; analyze the complexity of the state space. Propose a heuristic for playing this game.

17. Perform the alpha-beta pruning on the tic-tac-toe search of Figures 5.17–5.19. How many leaf nodes can be eliminated in each case?

18. a. Define an algorithm for heuristically searching and/or graphs. Note that all descendants of an and node must be solved in order to solve the parent. Thus, in computing heuristic estimates of costs to a goal, the estimate of the cost to solve an and node must be at least the sum of the estimates to solve the different branches.

    b. Use this algorithm to search the graph in Figure 5.25.

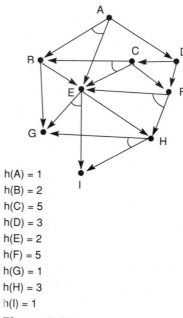

h(A) = 1
h(B) = 2
h(C) = 5
h(D) = 3
h(E) = 2
h(F) = 5
h(G) = 1
h(H) = 3
h(I) = 1

Figure 5.25

LANGUAGES FOR AI PROBLEM SOLVING

---

looking through a glass onion . . .

—Lennon and McCartney

for now we see as through a glass darkly . . .

—Paul to the Corinthians

The map is not the territory; the name is not the thing named.

—Gregory Bateson

In Part III we discuss the major issues in selecting a language for artificial intelligence programming. The primary function of an AI language is to implement the representation and control structures needed for symbolic computing. The nature of these structures to a great extent determines the features that an implementation language should provide. In this introduction, we enumerate the programming language features desired for symbolic programming and give an overview of LISP and PROLOG, two of the major languages currently used in AI.

Chapters 6 and 7 treat LISP and PROLOG in detail; later in the text (chapters 9 and 15), we introduce *object-oriented programming*, which structures programs in terms of messages passed between objects in a class hierarchy. Object-oriented programming, the underlying model for Smalltalk, Flavors, Common Objects, and a number of other languages, has emerged as an important programming methodology. It is also the basis of a number of expert system development environments currently available on the commercial market. The evolution of the object-oriented paradigm is presented in Chapter 9, and the design of object-oriented programming languages is discussed in Chapter 15.

Languages, Understanding, and Levels of Abstraction

The ability to form higher-level abstractions from the particulars of experience is one of the most powerful and fundamental abilities of the human mind. Abstraction allows us to consolidate the details of a complicated domain into a general characterization of its organization and behavior; these abstractions allow us to understand the full range of instances in that domain. If we enter a strange house, for example, we will be able to find our way around; the organization of the living room, bedrooms, kitchen, and bathrooms generally conforms to a standard model of a house. The abstraction lets us manage the particulars of different houses. A picture may be worth a thousand words, but an abstraction can define the important features of an entire class of pictures.

When we form theories to describe classes of phenomena, the significant qualitative and quantitative features of the class are abstracted out from the details that characterize its individual members. This loss of detail is compensated for by the descriptive and predictive power of a valid theory. Abstraction is an essential tool for understanding and managing the complexity of the world around us, as well as that of our own mental structures. Indeed, this process of abstraction occurs continuously and recursively in the act of knowing: knowledge is built in layers of abstraction, from the mechanisms that extract structure from the chaos of raw sensory stimuli all the way up to the most subtle of scientific theories. Ultimately, most of our ideas are about other ideas.

Hierarchical abstraction, the organization of experience into increasingly abstract classes and descriptions, is an essential tool for understanding the behavior and organization of complex systems, including computer programs. Just as the behavior of an animal may be studied without concern for the underlying physiology of its nervous system, an algorithm has a characterization of its own, quite separate from the program that implements it.

Consider, for example, two different implementations of binary search, one written in FORTRAN using arrays and calculations on array indices and the other written in Pascal using pointers to implement binary search trees; in a very deep sense, these programs are the same. This separation of an algorithm from the code used to implement it is only one example of hierarchical abstraction in computer science.

Allen Newell has distinguished between the *knowledge level* and the *symbol-level* of describing an intelligent system (Newell 1982). The symbol level is concerned with the particular formalisms used to represent problem-solving knowledge; the discussion of predicate logic as a representation language in Chapter 2 is an example of such a symbol-level consideration. Above the symbol level is the knowledge level, which is concerned with the knowledge content of the program and the way in which that knowledge is used.

This analysis is particularly appropriate to knowledge-based systems. Because the knowledge base is separate from the control aspects of the program, it is natural to separate the knowledge level of the program from its other aspects. Similarly, the symbol level is manifested through the choice of a representation language, such as logic or production rules, for the knowledge base. The implementation of the symbol-level representation constitutes a still lower level.

The capabilities of a knowledge-based system are largely determined at the knowledge level. The knowledge content is independent of the formalisms used to represent it, as long as the representation language is sufficiently expressive. Knowledge-level concerns include such questions as: What objects and relations are important in the domain? What queries will be made of the system? How is new knowledge added to the system? Will the facts change over time? Will the system need to reason about its own knowledge? Does the domain of discourse have a well-understood taxonomy? Does the domain involve uncertain or missing knowledge? Careful analysis at this level is an important step in designing the overall architecture of the program and in choosing the particular method of representation used at the symbol level.

At the symbol level, decisions are made about the structures used to represent and organize knowledge. The selection of a representation language is a symbol-level concern. As we shall see in chapters 8, 9, and 15, logic is only one of many formalisms currently available for knowledge representation; others include network representations such as frames or semantic networks, procedural representations that capture knowledge as a body of instructions describing how to perform a certain task, and numerous extensions and variations on standard logic such as multivalued and temporal logics.

Each of these formalisms has its strengths and weaknesses. Not only must a representation language be able to express the knowledge required for an application, it also must be concise, modifiable, and computationally efficient, and must assist the programmer in acquiring and organizing the knowledge base. These goals often conflict and necessitate trade-offs in the design of representation languages.

Just as we have distinguished between the knowledge and symbol levels of a program, we can also distinguish between the symbol level and the algorithms and data structures used to implement it. For example, with the exception of efficiency, the behavior of a logic-based problem solver should be unaffected by the choice between a hash table and a binary tree to implement a table of its symbols. These are implementation decisions and should be invisible at the symbol level. Many of the algorithms and data structures used in implementing representation languages for AI are common computer science techniques such as binary trees and tables. Others are more specific to AI and are presented in pseudocode throughout the text and in the chapters on LISP and PROLOG programming techniques.

Below the algorithm/data structure level is the language level. It is here that the implementation language for the program becomes significant. Other levels exist below this one, including the assembly language level, possible microcode extensions to the machine architecture, and others leading to the underlying hardware.

These levels (Fig. III.1) are relatively independent. In consulting a knowledge base, users generally ignore the representation used at the symbol level and are concerned only with the system's knowledge and its ability to solve their problem. Similarly, in building the knowledge base, the programmer is very conscious of the representations used at the symbol level but usually ignores the lower levels of the system. The importance of these distinctions cannot be overemphasized: they allow a user or programmer to ignore the complexity hidden at lower levels and focus on issues appropriate to the current level of abstraction. They allow the theoretical foundations of artificial intelligence to be kept free of the nuances of a particular implementation or programming language. They allow us to modify an implementation, improving its efficiency or porting it to another machine, without affecting its behavior at higher levels.

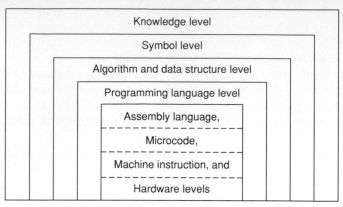

Figure III.1 Levels of a knowledge-based system.

Some thought about the nature of these higher levels and the demands they place on an implementation language is useful in understanding why certain languages and language features have proved important in AI programming. In the remainder of this section, we present requirements for AI languages based on the needs of AI problem solving. We then introduce the major AI programming languages: LISP and PROLOG.

Requirements for AI Languages

An important feature of these levels of abstraction is a degree of insensitivity of higher levels to the underlying implementation language. This observation has been verified in practice, with successful knowledge-based systems implemented in languages as diverse as LISP, PROLOG, C, Pascal, or even FORTRAN. Similarly, several systems have originally been implemented in LISP (ART, from Inference Corporation) or PROLOG (M1 from Teknowledge) and later ported to C to improve their efficiency and portability. In both cases, behavior at the symbol level was largely unaffected.

However, these levels are not completely independent: the nature of the higher-level structures does influence the commitments we make at lower levels. In particular, the demands that AI programming places on the symbol level are repeated at the language level. For example, the data structures for symbolic computation do not lend themselves to such highly regular formalisms as arrays; lists are a much more flexible and natural implementation tool. In addition, AI is still a very new science, and many projects are started without a full understanding of the final form the program will assume. For this reason, much AI development is necessarily experimental and exploratory in nature. This requirement also places demands on a language and the tools it must provide. A language not only should be adequate to implement higher-level structures, it also should provide a natural and efficient tool for program development.

In the cases of ART and M1, mentioned above, LISP and PROLOG were used to implement the original versions of the programs; only when these versions had been tested and reached a final form were they translated to C. In other cases where a traditional language such as Pascal, C, or FORTRAN was used to implement an AI system, the particular symbol-level structures being implemented were well understood. For these reasons, most AI programming is done in LISP and PROLOG, and these languages remain essential tools for work in artificial intelligence.

In the next five subsections, we discuss the requirements that the symbol-level structures of AI programs place on an implementation language:

Support of symbolic computation.

Flexibility of control.

Support of exploratory programming methodologies.

Late binding and constraint propagation.

A clear and well-defined semantics.

Support of Symbolic Computation Although there are numerous ways of organizing knowledge at the symbol level, all of them are ultimately implemented as actions on patterns of symbols. This methodological commitment is summarized in Newell and Simon's physical symbol system hypothesis, discussed in the introduction to Part II. The physical symbol system hypothesis not only characterizes the dominant direction of AI research but underscores the need for a programming language that simplifies the implementation of a range of operations on symbolic rather than numeric data. The numeric data types and operations emphasized by traditional programming languages are not well suited for implementing search algorithms or AI representation languages. Instead, an AI programming language should simplify the creation of arbitrary symbol structures and operations on these structures. This is the most fundamental requirement for an AI programming language.

Predicate calculus, described in Chapter 2, is a powerful and general tool for constructing qualitative descriptions of a domain. The significant features of a domain may be represented as sets of logical assertions: Through the use of variables, it is possible to create general assertions about classes of entities; logical implications allow the representation of dependencies and other relationships between objects in a domain. PROLOG, discussed in Chapter 6, is a general programming language based on the first-order predicate calculus.

PROLOG programs are collections of descriptive facts about a domain and rules for deriving conclusions from those facts. Because PROLOG is based on concise mathematical notation, the programs tend to be compact, capturing problem-solving knowledge in a few statements. As an implementation of formal logic, PROLOG is sometimes used directly as a representation language at the symbol level. However, its real power is as a language for implementing more specialized and complex representations such as frames and networks in a concise and systematic fashion. Many symbol-level structures are easily built using the higher-level constructs of PROLOG. In chapters 6, 12, and 14, we show how PROLOG may be used to implement various search algorithms, an expert system shell, and a simple semantic network.

Another important tool for building symbol structures is the list. A list is a sequence of elements in which each element may be either another list or an atomic symbol. Several examples of lists, using the syntax of the LISP programming language, are:

(this is a list)

((this is) (a list) (of lists))

(times (plus 1 3) (plus 2 3))

((1 2 3) (4 5 6) (7 8 9))

Note that several of these examples include lists nested within lists; this allows us to represent structural relations. The power of lists is largely a result of their ability to represent any symbol structure, regardless of its complexity, dimensionality, or the operations it must support. This includes trees, arbitrary graphs, collections of logical predicates, arrays, data bases allowing keyword retrieval—in short, any conceivable structure may be captured in an appropriate arrangement of lists and lists within lists. Lists are such important representational building blocks that both LISP and PROLOG provide the user with the data elements and operations for manipulating and composing them into more complicated structured types. The exact way in which these structures may be built up from the list is discussed in the chapters on the individual languages.

While PROLOG is based directly in the predicate calculus and includes lists as an additional representational tool, LISP uses the list as the basis of both data types and programs. All LISP structures are built from lists, and the language provides a rich set of tools for manipulating these structures and defining new functions for creating, accessing, and changing them. LISP's syntactic uniformity and extensibility make it easy to construct interpreters for any representation language. By taking an abstract data type approach, the LISP programmer can define the symbol structures and operations needed for any higher-level formalism, including search controllers, logic theorem provers, and other high-level representations.

Flexibility of Control   One of the hallmarks of intelligent behavior is its flexibility. Indeed, critics of AI have argued that intelligence cannot be achieved by the step-by-step execution of fixed instruction sequences exhibited by traditional computer programs. Fortunately, this is not the only way of organizing computation.

One of the oldest and most important paradigms for building an AI program is the production system, described in Chapter 4. In a production system, the program is a set of rules; these rules are executed in an order determined by the pattern of the data in a given problem instance. Production rules can fire in virtually any order in response to a given situation. In this fashion, a production system can provide both the flexibility and the coherency required for intelligent behavior.

While AI uses a number of different control structures, many of them are related to production systems, and virtually all of them involve pattern matching. Pattern-directed control allows knowledge to be applied opportunistically in response to the features of a particular problem instance. Pattern matchers, such as unification, determine when the features of a problem instance match a particular chunk of program knowledge, selecting that knowledge for application to the problem. It is important that an AI language either provide this directly or simplify the development of pattern-directed control.

In PROLOG, unification (Chapter 2) and search algorithms are built into the language itself, forming the heart of the PROLOG interpreter. Using this built-in unification algorithm, it is simple to construct any pattern-driven control regime: depth-first search is given as a default, and other regimes such as breadth-first or best-first search may be constructed with a few lines of code (Chapter 6).

LISP does not provide a pattern-matching algorithm directly, but the sophistication of its symbolic computing facilities and the easy extensibility of the language make it simple to write pattern matchers and interpreters of arbitrary complexity and organization (Chapter 7). One advantage of this approach is that the pattern matcher and associated control structures may easily be tailored to fit the demands of a particular problem or representation.

Support of Exploratory Programming Methodologies   The problems that AI addresses do not always respond to such standard software engineering approaches as top-down design, successive refinement, and program development from detailed formal specifications. Because of the very nature of AI problems, it is seldom possible to give a correct and complete specification of the final form of an AI program before building at least a prototype. Often, our understanding of the problem the program is intended to solve changes through the course of program development. Reasons for this include:

1. Most AI problems are initially poorly specified. Because of the extreme youth of the field, it is seldom possible to examine a problem and determine conclusively the exact approach that should be taken to its solution. By contrast, in more familiar domains we have developed methods for creating complete and accurate problem specifications and generating code that meets these specifications.

    A complex reasoning task is inherently more difficult to characterize formally than something like sorting a list or maintaining a file system. Exactly what does it mean, for example, to design a circuit or diagnose an illness? How does a human expert perform these tasks? What is a satisfactory level of performance for a given problem domain? What knowledge is required to solve the problem? The role and importance of such things as common sense, for example, are difficult to define or delineate in most domains. For these reasons, most AI problems are initially stated in very general terms and made more specific as code development illuminates the nature of the problem.

2. The approaches taken to solving problems tend to be very domain specific. While there are general frameworks for AI problem solving such as production systems, search, and representation languages, each problem domain tends to require unique strategies. This means that successful solutions to problems seldom generalize fully to new domains: each application is, to some extent, a new ballgame.

3. Heuristic methods are inherently empirical. Even the techniques used by human experts have been developed through trial and error. This means that heuristic

strategies, unlike algorithms, must be implemented and tested before their value can be fully known.

4. Knowledge-based programming seems to be fundamentally incremental in nature. This is really just a different way of stating the previous point, but it stresses the fact that intelligent systems use knowledge to solve problems, and knowledge is acquired by degree.

5. The structures and formalisms for AI representations are new and not completely understood. Although experience helps greatly in choosing and applying a representation, there is currently no substitute for trying an idea and seeing how it works.

For these reasons, AI programming is inherently exploratory; the program is often the vehicle through which we explore the problem domain and discover solution strategies. The challenge for AI programming is one of finding ways to do exploratory programming that are efficient, systematic, and well structured. Among the features that an exploratory programming language should provide are:

1. Modularity.
2. Extensibility.
3. Useful high-level constructs.
4. Support of early prototyping.
5. Program "readability."
6. Interpreted and compiled modes.
7. Software support for exploratory programming.

We discuss these topics in the following paragraphs:

1. Modularity and modifiability of code. It is important that a language for exploratory programming support frequent modifications of its code. This implies that programs should consist of small, well-bounded chunks rather than large bodies of complex code. The interactions between program components should be limited and clearly defined. This includes avoiding side effects and global variables and ensuring that the role of any single chunk in the program execution is easily determined.

LISP programs are written as collections of individual functions; in a well-written LISP program, each function is small and performs a single, well-defined task. Thus, it is usually simple to locate and correct the cause of any deficiencies. The parameter passing (a variation of "pass by value") and variable scoping rules of LISP also serve to reduce function side effects. Global variables, while supported by the language, are avoided in good LISP code.

In PROLOG the basic unit of the program is the rule. PROLOG rules, like LISP functions, tend to be small and specialized. Since the scope of variables in PROLOG is always restricted to a single rule and the language does not allow global variables, modifiability is simplified. Both LISP and PROLOG include trace facilities, which, when combined with a clear program structure, simplify the assignment of blame and credit in debugging.

2. Extensibility and embedded languages. Exploratory programming usually proceeds in a bottom-up fashion, with the higher-level structures of the program emerging as the code is developed. An important technique for doing this in a systematic and well-structured fashion is the development of an *embedded language*.

Often, while it is not possible to specify the final form of an AI program, it is possible to determine the higher-level structures useful for exploring the domain. These structures can include pattern matchers, search controllers, and functions for defining a representation language. Essentially, this approach says "if you can't determine the final structure a program will take, attempt to define the language constructs that help develop that structure."

To support this methodology, a programming language should be easily extensible and should simplify the development of interpreters. By extensibility, we mean the ability to define new language constructs with maximum freedom and flexibility. LISP, PROLOG, and the object-oriented languages all allow easy definition of new functions, predicates, and objects, respectively. Once defined, these user-created constructs behave exactly like the built-in components of the language. One programs these languages by extending their basic capabilities from the bottom up until a solution is achieved. In a sense, traditional programs are "constructed" but AI programs are "grown."

This contrasts with the sharp distinction that traditional languages make between built-in features and user-developed programs. In Pascal, for example, we may define new functions or procedures, but their syntax is more restricted than the syntax of the built-in constructs of the language; this limits the flexibility and utility of these extensions. Consider, for example, the difficulty of writing a new control structure, such as a production system, in Pascal.

LISP and PROLOG also simplify the writing of interpreters. In LISP, both programs and data are syntactically represented as lists. This makes it very easy to write programs that manipulate LISP code as if they were data, greatly simplifying the development of interpreters. Many historically and commercially important AI languages such as PLANNER, ROSIE, KEE, and OPS were built on these capabilities of LISP. (We design a meta-interpreter in LISP in Chapter 13.) PROLOG provides this capability through a number of "meta-predicates," predicates for manipulating other PROLOG predicates, again simplifying the writing of arbitrary interpreters. As with LISP, a number of higher-level AI languages have been built on PROLOG using this methodology. (We present several meta-interpreters for PROLOG in Chapter 12.)

3. Existence of useful high-level constructs. Exploratory programming is aided by the existence of powerful high-level constructs in the language. These powerful but general abstractive constructs allow the programmer to quickly develop specialized structures for knowledge representation and program control.

In LISP, these include the basic list data type, which allows the construction of arbitrarily complex data structures, as well as powerful functions for defining operations on these structures. Because LISP is extensible and has been used for several decades, the most general and powerful of these user-defined functions have become standard features of the language. Most modern LISPs have evolved in this fashion to include literally hundreds of functions for creating data structures, building user interfaces, tracing program execution, and editing LISP structures.

PROLOG has remained a comparatively small language, partly because of its new-ness and partly out of a commitment to simplicity and compactness. However, PROLOG allows users to create their own library of specialized predicates, and the most useful of these have found their way into standard implementations.

4. Support for early prototyping. Another important exploratory programming methodology is early prototyping. Here, the programmer builds a "quick and dirty" solution to the problem and uses it to explore the problem space. Once we have explored the problem and outlined a viable solution strategy, we throw the prototype away and build a final program that emphasizes correctness and efficiency of implementation. While it is generally difficult to throw away something that has required as much work to build as a computer program, doing so often saves time in the long run and improves the quality of the final program. The structures and methods provided by AI languages greatly speed up the development of prototypes.

5. Program readability and documentation. Since most AI programs are modified extensively through their lifetime, it is important that the code be readable and well documented. While there is no substitute for clear natural language comments in the code, AI languages, by yielding highly modular code composed of high-level constructs, greatly simplify this goal.

6. Interpretation versus compilation. Most AI languages are interpreted rather than compiled during program development. This means that the programmer does not have to wait for lengthy recompilations every time the code is changed. In addition, the interactive interpreters provided for AI languages include extensive trace and debug facilities (discussed next). Since interpreted code runs slowly, modern AI languages usually allow the compilation of final versions of programs.

7. Software support for exploratory programming. Modern AI languages include rich programming environments, providing tools for tracing the execution of either whole programs or sections of programs. Debuggers allow the programmer to step through program execution incrementally, to temporarily change the value of program variables or even the code itself, to insert break points that halt program execution at prespecified points, and to freeze the execution environment at the point where an error is detected so that the program state may be examined. In addition, many language implementations include intelligent editors that spot syntax errors as code is being writ-ten. Because of the complexity of AI programs and the difficulty of predicting the behavior of such flexible control regimes as production systems, the importance of these support facilities cannot be overestimated.

Late Binding and Constraint Propagation   Constraint propagation is an important AI programming methodology that should be supported by an implementation language. Often, the problems addressed by an AI program require that the values of certain enti-ties remain unknown until sufficient information has been gathered to determine an assignment. This information may be seen as a series of constraints on the values that a variable may assume; as constraints are accumulated, the set of possible values is reduced, ultimately converging on a solution that satisfies all the constraints.

A simple example of this approach may be seen in a medical diagnostic system that gathers information about a patient's symptoms until the possible explanations have been reduced to a single diagnosis. The programming language analog of this methodology is late variable binding, or the ability to maintain a variable as explicitly unbound while manipulating it in the program code. Both LISP and PROLOG allow variables to be defined and manipulated as explicitly unbound, while defining the relationships and dependences between those variables and other program units. This enables the easy and natural implementation of constraint propagation.

A Clear and Well-Defined Semantics   This is a need that AI languages share with any programming language intended for the development of large, complicated, yet reliable systems. Unfortunately, traditional programming languages such as FORTRAN and Pascal tend to have complex and difficult semantic definitions. This shortcoming can be traced to the fact that such languages are essentially higher-level characterizations of the architecture of the underlying von Neumann computer and inherit many of the complexities of that physical system. Since AI languages have often been based on mathematical formalisms such as logic (PROLOG) or recursive function theory (LISP), they tend to have simpler semantics, inheriting much of the notational power and elegance of formal mathematics. This makes these languages particularly useful for researchers in areas such as implementing knowledge representation languages, formalizing the process of code development, proving programs correct, and automating the generation of efficient code from formal specifications. These research areas require that the semantics of the programming languages be clearly and formally specified.

It should also be noted that although the *function* of most AI programs is highly complex, the code that *implements* that function should strive for simplicity and clarity. Large blocks of complex opaque code do not imply good AI. A well-defined language semantics is an important tool for achieving these ends.

The Primary AI Languages: LISP and PROLOG

By meeting the needs outlined in the previous section, LISP, PROLOG, and to a lesser extent object-oriented programming have emerged as the dominant languages for AI research and development. When learning these languages, the student should keep these needs in mind and think about the ways in which they are supported by the specific features of each language.

These languages exemplify three of the most important alternative approaches to programming language design. Traditional languages are procedural in nature and treat programming in terms of a separation of data and executable code. The code is a body of sequentially executed statements acting on a store of passive data. Because of a number of limitations that seem to be inherent in this model of programming (Backus 1978), researchers are continuing to explore alternative ways of designing programming languages. AI, because of the demands it places on an implementation language, has always played an important role in this research. Currently, three of the most important alternative approaches to programming are functional programming, logic programming, and object-oriented programming; these approaches are exemplified by LISP, PROLOG, and Smalltalk or Flavors, respectively.

Table III.1   COMPARISON OF FEATURES OF MAJOR LANGUAGE PARADIGMS

	PASCAL	LISP	PROLOG	OBJECT-ORIENTED LANGUAGES
Language model	Procedural programming	Functional programming	Logic programming	Object-oriented programming
Data types	Scalars, arrays, and records	Symbolic and numeric atoms, lists and list structures, property and association lists	Symbolic and numeric atoms, predicates, lists and list structures	Symbolic and numeric atoms, slots and values, classes and instances
Data manipulation	Assignment, parameter passing by value and reference, function returns	Function returns, parameter passing by value, binding of local and global variables	Variable binding through unifications	Message passing, instantiating slot values in objects
Program control	Sequencing, branching, looping, recursion	Function evaluation, conditional evaluation, recursion, looping	Pattern-directed search, recursion	Method invocation through message passing
Program structure	Block structure, nested procedure definitions	Functions in a global environment, let blocks	Rules and facts in a data base	Objects in a class hierarchy, inheritance
Variable scoping	Global and nested local scopes	Bound variables, lexical or dynamic scoping of free variables, local variables using let blocks	Variable scope confined to a single rule or fact	Values bound to slots in an object, slot values visible to subclasses and instances through inheritance
Mode of interaction	Interpreted or compiled in batch mode	Interactive interpreter, compiler	Interactive interpreter, compiler	Interactive interpreter, compiler

To support the study and comparison of these languages, we summarize their features in Table III.1. We include Pascal to provide a comparison with a more "traditional" programming language. Although many of the entries in the table will not be completely clear until you learn the languages, the table provides an overview of their major features to keep in mind while you study them.

PROLOG

The first PROLOG program was written in Marseille, France, in the early 1970s as part of a project in natural language understanding (Colmerauer et al. 1973; Roussel 1975;

Kowalski 1979*a*). The theoretical background for the language PROLOG has even earlier roots, especially in the work of Kowalski, Hayes, and others (Kowalski 1979*a*, 1979*b*; Hayes 1977; Lloyd 1984).

PROLOG is the best-known example of a *logic programming language*. A logic program is a set of specifications in formal logic; PROLOG uses the first-order predicate calculus. An interpreter executes the program by systematically making inferences from these specifications. Indeed, the name itself comes from PROgramming in LOGic. The idea of using the representational power of the first-order predicate calculus to express specifications for problem solving is one of the central contributions of PROLOG to computer science in general and to artificial intelligence in particular. The benefits of using first-order predicate calculus for a programming language include a clean and elegant syntax and well-defined semantics.

The implementation of PROLOG has its roots in research on theorem proving by J. A. Robinson (1965). Robinson designed a proof procedure called *resolution*, which is the primary method for computing with PROLOG. The chapter on automated theorem proving demonstrates this implementation as a *resolution refutation system* (sections 11.2 and 12.3).

Because of these features, PROLOG has proved to be a useful vehicle for investigating such experimental programming issues as automatic code generation, program verification, and design of high-level specification languages. PROLOG and other logic-based languages support a declarative programming style, that is, constructing a program in terms of high-level descriptions of a problem's constraints rather than as a sequence of instructions for performing an algorithm. This mode of programming essentially tells the computer ''what is true'' and ''what needs to be done'' rather than ''how to do it.'' This allows programmers to focus their energies on problem-solving specifications rather than the details of writing low-level control code.

The major development of the PROLOG language was carried out from 1975 to 1979 at the department of artificial intelligence of the University of Edinburgh. The group in Edinburgh responsible for the implementation of PROLOG were David H. D. Warren and Fernando Pereira. They produced the first PROLOG interpreter robust enough for delivery to the general computing community. This product was built on the DEC-system 10 and could operate in both interpretive and compiled modes (Warren et al. 1979). Further descriptions of this early code and comparisons of PROLOG with LISP may be found in Warren et al. (1977). This ''Warren and Pereira'' PROLOG became the early standard, and the book *Programming in PROLOG* (Clocksin and Mellish 1984) was the chief vehicle for delivering this PROLOG to the computing community. This text uses this standard, which has come to be known as the Edinburgh syntax.

During the period of development of the Warren-Pereira interpreter, a number of other projects at Edinburgh investigated the expressive power of this new language. These were:

1. A plan formation program (see Chapter 15) called WARPLAN, also developed by Warren (1976).

2. A program to solve algebraic equations and to prove theorems in geometry (Welham 1976; Bundy and Welham 1981).

3. A ''compiler writing'' program (Warren 1980).

4. A program to solve "mechanics" problems from their English language specifications (Bundy et al. 1979).

Originally developed in Europe, PROLOG attracted considerable interest in the United States as a result of its adoption as the language for the Japanese Fifth Generation Computing Project. The advantages of the language have been further demonstrated by a number of research projects designed to evaluate and extend the expressive power of logic programming. The Alvey program in Britain is a primary contributor to this research. PROLOG has also enjoyed increasing success in the development of artificial intelligence applications, as can be found in the Proceedings of the International Joint Conference on Artificial Intelligence and the Symposium on Logic Programming.

LISP

LISP was first proposed by John McCarthy in the late 1950s. The language was originally intended as an alternative model of computation, one based on the theory of recursive functions. In an early paper, McCarthy (1960) outlined his goals: to create a language for symbolic rather than numeric computation, to implement a model of computation based on the theory of recursive functions (Church 1941), to provide a clear definition of the language's syntax and semantics, and to demonstrate formally the completeness of this computational model. Although LISP is one of the oldest computing languages still in existence (along with FORTRAN and COBOL), the careful thought given to its original design and the extensions made to the language through its history have kept it in the vanguard of programming languages. In fact, this programming model has proved so effective that a number of other languages have been based on functional programming (e.g., SCHEME, ML, FP).

The list is the basis of both programs and data structures in LISP: LISP is an acronym for LISt Processing. The power of lists for symbolic computing had been demonstrated in earlier work such as the Logic Theorist of Newell and Simon (1956). LISP provides a powerful set of list-handling functions implemented internally as linked pointer structures. LISP gives programmers the full power and generality of linked data structures while freeing them from the responsibility for explicitly managing pointers and pointer operations.

Originally, LISP was a very small and simple language, consisting of functions for constructing and accessing lists, defining new functions, a few predicates for detecting equality, and functions for evaluating function calls. The only means of program control were recursion and a single conditional. More complicated functions, when needed, were defined in terms of these primitives. Through time, the best of these new functions became part of the language itself. This process of extending the language by adding new functions has led to the development of numerous dialects of LISP, often including hundreds of specialized functions for data structuring, program control, real and integer arithmetic, I/O, editing LISP functions, and tracing program execution. These dialects are the vehicle by which LISP has evolved from a simple and elegant theoretical model of computing into a rich, powerful, and practical environment for building large software systems.

Among the most important LISP dialects are INTERLISP, a rich, "user-sensitive" dialect, chiefly supported be Xerox LISP machines; MACLISP, a more efficient dialect developed at MIT; FRANZ LISP, a descendant of MACLISP designed for use under the UNIX operating systems; ZETA LISP, designed for the Symbolics LISP machine; and numerous other extensions of the basic LISP kernel developed by industry and academia. Because of this proliferation of dialects, the Defense Advanced Research Projects Agency in 1983 proposed a standard dialect of the language, known as Common LISP.

Although Common LISP has emerged as the lingua franca of LISP dialects, it is unlikely that all of the other dialects will disappear. Indeed, Common LISP has been criticized as excessively complicated and unwieldy, sacrificing elegance and clarity in an attempt to be "all things to all people." A number of simpler dialects continue to be widely used. These dialects include SCHEME, an elegant rethinking of the language that has been used both for AI development and for teaching the fundamental concepts of computer science, and XLISP, a compact dialect that also supports object-oriented programming. The dialect we use throughout the remainder of our text is Common LISP (Steele 1984).

Selecting an Implementation Language

LISP and PROLOG are both capable of implementing any representation and control structures required by a given program. Each of them is based on a different model of computation. Currently, there is some debate over the relative merits of the different languages used for AI programming. We feel that both languages are an essential part of the AI programmer's skills and deserve treatment in an artificial intelligence text. However, this debate does call for some comment:

1. The important issue is to be familiar with the trade-offs involved in selecting an AI language, not to take a stand on which language is best.
2. Good programmers should be familiar with all the available tools; different jobs will often require the features of one language over another.
3. Different languages are used in the literature, and programmers must be familiar with them to keep up with the field.
4. Each of the languages discussed in the text exemplifies one or more very important high-level language concepts such as functional programming, list-based data structures, formal logic, pattern-directed control, and object-oriented programming. These concepts not only are important tools for writing correct, understandable code in any language but also exemplify some of the major directions currently being explored in the design of future languages.

Given the current state of the art, it is certain that AI professionals will find themselves programming in one or more of the languages discussed in this text. It is also certain that given limitations of all currently available programming languages and the challenges and the vitality found in the field of AI language design, students will be programming in a very different and much improved language by the end of their careers. The treatment of languages in this text will prepare students for both of these eventualities.

More detailed analysis of the languages of this chapter and full references are presented in chapters 6, 7, 12, 13, and 14.

AN INTRODUCTION
TO PROLOG

A syllogism is discourse in which, certain things being stated, something other than what is stated follows of necessity from their being true....

—ARISTOTLE, *Prior Analytics*

The only way to rectify our reasonings is to make them as tangible as those of the mathematicians, so that we can find our error at a glance, and when there are disputes among persons we can simply say, "Let us calculate ... to see who is right."

—LEIBNIZ, *The Art of Discovery*

6.0　Introduction

PROLOG has only recently reached a place of importance in the tool kit of the artificial intelligence community. Nonetheless, as a practical implementation of logic as a programming language, it has made many interesting contributions to AI problem solving. These include its *declarative semantics*, a means of directly expressing problem relationships in AI, as well as, with built-in unification, some high-powered techniques for pattern matching and search. We address many of the important issues of *logic programming* in this chapter and in Chapter 12.

In Section 6.1 we present the basic PROLOG syntax and several simple programs. These programs implement several of the algorithms introduced in Part II and demonstrate the use of the predicate calculus as a representation language.

Section 6.2 introduces the design of control in PROLOG problem solving. We show how to use the *cut* with PROLOG's implicit depth-first control to improve efficiency. Then we design breadth-first and best-first search algorithms.

In Section 6.3 we examine PROLOG as a nonprocedural problem-solving representation and give several small examples to emphasize this important concept. The chapter ends with the discussion of the general issues of programming in logic and procedural versus declarative problem solving.

6.1 Syntax for Predicate Calculus Programming

6.1.1 Representing Facts and Rules

Although there are numerous dialects of PROLOG, the syntax used throughout this text is the original Warren and Periera C-PROLOG (Clocksin and Mellish 1984). To simplify our presentation of PROLOG, our version of predicate calculus syntax in Chapter 2 used many PROLOG conventions. There are, however, a number of differences between PROLOG and predicate calculus syntax. In C-PROLOG, for example, the symbol :- replaces the ← of first-order predicate calculus. Several other symbols differ from those used in Chapter 2:

ENGLISH	PREDICATE CALCULUS	PROLOG
and	∧	,
or	∨	;
implies	←	:-
not	¬	not

As in Chapter 2, predicate names and bound variables are expressed as a sequence of alphanumeric characters beginning with an alphabetic. Variables are represented as a string of alphanumeric characters beginning (at least) with an uppercase alphabetic. Thus:

    likes(X, susie).

could represent the fact that "everyone likes Susie." Or

    likes(george,Y), likes(susie,Y).

could represent the set of things (or people) that are liked by both George and Susie.

Suppose, for example, it was desired to represent in PROLOG the following relationships: "George likes Kate and George likes Susie." This could be stated as:

    likes(george, kate), likes(george, susie).

Similarly, "George likes Kate or George likes Susie" is:

    likes(george, kate); likes(george, susie).

Also, "George likes Susie if George likes Kate" is:

    likes(george, susie) :- likes(george, kate).

Finally, "Kate does not like Susie" is:

    not(likes(kate, susie)).

These examples show how the predicate calculus connectives ∧, ∨, ¬, and ← are expressed in PROLOG. The predicate names (likes), the number or order of parameters, and even whether one predicate always has the same number of parameters are determined by the design requirements (the implicit "semantics") of the problem. There are no expressive limitations other than the syntax of well-formed formulas in the language.

A PROLOG program is a set of specifications in the first-order predicate calculus describing the objects and relations in a problem domain. The set of specifications, or what is true about a particular problem situation, is referred to as the *data base* for that problem. The PROLOG interpreter responds to questions about this set of specifications. Queries to the data base are patterns in the same logical syntax as the data base entries. The PROLOG interpreter uses pattern-directed search to find if these queries logically follow from the contents of the data base.

The interpreter processes user queries, searching the data base to find out if the query is a logical consequence of the data base of specifications. PROLOG is primarily an interpreted language. Some versions of PROLOG run in interpretive mode only, while others (including the original DEC-10 PROLOG) allow compilation of part or all of the set of data base specifications for faster execution.

PROLOG is an interactive language; the user enters queries in response to the PROLOG prompt: ?-. This prompt appears in all PROLOG examples in the chapter. For the reader's convenience, we indicate the user's query and the PROLOG response by placing U: and P: before the appropriate query or response strings.

Suppose that we would like to describe a "world" consisting of George, Kate, and Susie's likes and dislikes in a PROLOG data base. The data base would contain the following set of predicates:

```
likes(george, kate).
likes(george, susie).
likes(george, wine).
likes(susie, wine).
likes(kate, gin).
likes(kate, susie).
```

This set of specifications has the obvious interpretation, or mapping into the world of George and his friends. This world is a model for the data base (Section 2.3). The interpreter may then be asked questions:

```
U: ?- likes(george, kate).
P: yes
U: ?- likes(kate, susie).
P: yes
U: ?- likes(george, X).
P: X = kate
U: ;
P: X = susie
U: ;
P: X = wine
U: ;
P: no
```

U: ?- likes(george, beer).
P: no

Note several things in these examples. First, in the request likes(george, X), the interpreter returns all the terms in the data base specification that may be substituted for the X in unifying the query with likes(george, X). Note that they are returned in the order in which they are found in the data base: kate before susie before wine. It is important to understand this bias of the order of predicates in the data base. While it goes against the philosophy of nonprocedural specifications (Sections 4.2 and 6.3), a determined order of evaluation is a property of most interpreters implemented on sequential machines. The PROLOG programmer must be aware of the order in which PROLOG searches entries in the data base.

Also note that further responses to queries are produced when the user prompts with the ; (or). This forces a backtrack on the most recent result. Continued ;s will force PROLOG to find all possible solutions to the query. When there are no further solutions, the interpreter responds no.

The above example also illustrates the *closed world assumption* or *negation as failure*. PROLOG assumes that "anything is false whose opposite is not provably true." In the query likes(george, beer), the interpreter looks for the predicate likes(george, beer) or some rule that could establish that likes(george, beer) is true. Failing in this task, it asserts that the request is false. Thus, PROLOG assumes that all knowledge of the world is present in the data base.

The closed world assumption introduces a number of practical and philosophical difficulties in the language (presented in detail in Section 12.3). For example, failure to include a fact in the data base often means that its truth is unknown; the closed world assumption treats it as false. If a predicate was omitted or there was a misspelling (e.g., likes(george, beeer)), the response remains no. The negation-as-failure issue is currently a very important topic in AI research, where both its advantages (how it can be used to represent aspects of the world) and disadvantages (what role does not have in the theory of logic specifications?) are under investigation. Several of these issues are addressed again in the chapters on advanced representations.

The PROLOG expressions used above were examples of *fact* specifications. PROLOG also lets us define *rules* to describe relationships between facts using logical implication, :-. In creating a PROLOG rule, only one not negative predicate is permitted on the left-hand side of the if symbol, :-. All predicate calculus expressions that contain implication or equivalence relationships ($\leftarrow$, $\rightarrow$, and $\leftrightarrow$) must be reduced to this form. This form for predicate calculus statements is referred to as *Horn clause* logic. In Horn clause form, the left-hand side (conclusion) of an implication must be a single positive literal. The *Horn clause calculus* is equivalent to the full first-order predicate calculus for proofs by refutation. (See chapters 11 and 12.)

Suppose we add a rule for determining whether two people are friends to the set of specifications of the previous example. This may be defined:

friends(X, Y) :- likes(X, Z), likes(Y, Z).

This expression might be interpreted as "X and Y are friends if there exists a Z such that X likes Z and Y likes Z." Two issues are important here: first, since neither the predicate calculus nor PROLOG has global variables, the scope (extent of definition) of X, Y, and Z is limited to the friends rule. Second, values bound to (unified with, Chapter 2) X, Y, and Z are consistent across the entire expression. The treatment of the friends rule by the PROLOG interpreter is seen in the following example.

With the friends rule added to the set of specifications of the preceding example, query the interpreter:

U: ?- friends(george, susie).
P: yes

In solving the query, the PROLOG interpreter searches the data base using the backtrack algorithm presented in chapters 3 and 4. The query friends(george, susie) is matched (unified) with the conclusion of the rule friends(X, Y) :- likes(X, Z), likes(Y, Z), where X is george and Y is susie. The interpreter then tries to find a Z such that likes(george, Z) is true. This is found with the first fact in the data base, where Z is kate.

The interpreter then tries to find out if likes(susie, kate) is true. When it is found to be false (using the closed world assumption), the value for Z (kate) is rejected. The interpreter then goes back to the data base (backtracks) to find a second value for the Z in likes(george, Z).

likes(george, Z) then matches the second clause in the data base, with Z binding to susie. The interpreter then tries to match likes(susie, susie). When this also fails (there is nothing in the data base that says that people like themselves!), the interpreter goes back to the data base (backtracks) for yet another value for Z. This time wine is found in the third predicate, and the interpreter goes on to show that likes(susie, wine) is true. In this case "wine is the binding that ties" (sorry!).

Note that PROLOG tries to match goals with patterns in the specification in the order in which they are entered in the data base.

It is important to state at this point the relationship between universal and existential quantification in the predicate calculus and the treatment of variables in a PROLOG program. When a variable is placed in the specifications of a PROLOG data base, it is assumed to be universally quantified. For example, likes(susie, Y) means, according to the semantics of the previous examples, "Susie likes everyone." In the course of interpreting some query, any term (or list or predicate!) may be bound to Y. Similarly, in the rule friends(X, Y) :- likes(X, Z), likes(Y, Z), any X, Y, and Z that meet the specifications of the expression are acceptable variable bindings.

If we desire to represent an existentially quantified variable in PROLOG, two approaches may be taken. First, if the existential value of a variable is known, it may be entered directly into the data base. Thus, likes(george, wine) is an instance of likes(george, Z) and may be thus entered into the data base, as it was in the previous examples.

Second, to find an instance of a variable that makes an expression true, we may make a query to the interpreter. For example, to find whether there exists a Z such that likes(george, Z) is true, we put this query directly to the interpreter. It will find any value of Z under which the expression is true. Some PROLOG interpreters find all such existentially quantified values; C-PROLOG requires repeated use of ; to get all values.

6.1.2 Recursion-Based Search in PROLOG

The previous subsection presented PROLOG syntax in several simple examples. These examples introduced PROLOG as an engine for computing with predicate calculus expressions (in Horn clause form). This is consistent with all the principles of predicate calculus inference presented in Chapter 2. PROLOG uses unification for pattern matching and returns the bindings that make an expression true. These values are unified with the variables in a particular expression and are not bound in the global environment.

Recursion is the primary control mechanism for PROLOG programming. We demonstrate this with the knight's tour problem by designing a PROLOG-based production system to search its graph. But first we consider some simple list-processing examples. These examples are based on the ideas introduced in Section 4.1 and Chapter 5.

The list is a data structure consisting of ordered sets of elements (or indeed lists). Recursion is the "natural" way to process the list structure. Unification and recursion come together in list processing in PROLOG.

In PROLOG, list elements are enclosed by brackets [ ] and separated by commas. Examples of PROLOG lists are:

```
[1, 2, 3, 4]
[[george, kate], [allen, amy], [don, pat]]
[tom, dick, harry, fred]
```

The first elements of a list may be separated from the tail of the list by the bar operator: |. The tail of a list is the list with its first element(s) removed. For instance, when the list is [tom,dick,harry,fred], the first element is tom and the tail is the list: [dick, harry, fred]. Using the vertical bar operator and unification, we can break a list into its components:

If [tom,dick,harry,fred] is matched to [X|Y] then X = tom and Y = [dick,harry,fred].

If [tom,dick,harry,fred] is matched to [X,Y|Z] then X = tom and Y = dick and Z = [harry,fred].

If [tom,dick,harry,fred] is matched to [X,Y,Z|W] then X = tom and Y = dick and Z = harry and W = [fred].

If [tom,dick,harry,fred] is matched to [W,X,Y,Z|V] then W = tom and X = dick and Y = harry and Z = fred and V = [].

[tom,dick,harry,fred] will not match (unify with) [V,W,X,Y,Z|U].

[tom,dick,harry,fred] will unify with [tom,X|[harry,fred]] to give X = dick.

and so on.

The last example demonstrates that besides "tearing lists apart" to get at particular elements, unification can be used to "build" the list structure. For example, if X = tom, Y = [dick], and L unifies with [X|Y], then L will be bound to [tom,dick]. To summarize, the terms separated by commas before the | are all elements of the list, while the structure after the | is always a list, often referred to as the tail of the list.

Let's take a simple example of recursive processing of lists: the member check. We define a predicate to determine whether an item, represented by X, is in a list. This predicate, member, takes two arguments, an element and a list, and is true if the element is a member of the list. For example:

```
U: ?- member(a, [a, b, c, d, e]).
P: yes

U: ?- member(a, [1, 2, 3, 4]).
P: no

U: member(X, [a, b, c]).
P: X = a
U: ;
P: X = b
U: ;
P: X = c
U: ;
P: no
```

To define member, we first test whether the element is the first item in the list. We define this check in the following manner:

```
member(X,[X|T]).
```

This tests whether X and the first element of the list are identical. If they are not, then it is natural to check whether X is an element of the rest (T) of the list. This is defined by:

```
member(X,[Y|T]) :- member(X,T).
```

The two lines of PROLOG for checking set membership are then:

```
member(X,[X|T]).
member(X,[Y|T]) :- member(X,T).
```

The first line asks if X and the head of the list are identical. If this fails (X isn't the head of the list), member checks if X is a member of the tail of the list.

This example illustrates the importance of PROLOG's built-in order of search to programming in the language. The terminating condition is placed in the data base before the recursive call; this guarantees that it will be tested before the algorithm recurs. If the order of the predicates is reversed, the terminating condition will not be checked. The trace of the call, member(c,[a,b,c]), follows:

For this example,

    1. is member(X,[X|T]).
    2. is member(X,[Y|T]) :- member(X,T).

  U: ?- member(c,[a,b,c]).
      call 1. fail, since c ≠ a
      call 2. X = c, Y = a, T = [b,c], member(c,[b,c])?

        call 1. fail, since c ≠ b
        call 2. X = c, Y = b, T = [c], member(c,[c])?

          call 1. success, c = c

        yes (to second call 2.)

      yes (to first call 2.)

  P: yes

In Section 4.2 we represented the 3×3 knight's tour problem in the predicate calculus. We numbered the board squares like this:

  1   2   3

  4   5   6

  7   8   9

The legal moves are represented in PROLOG using a move predicate. The path predicate defines an algorithm for finding a path of zero or more moves between its arguments. Note that path is defined recursively:

move(1,6).	move(3,4).	move(6,7).	move(8,3).
move(1,8).	move(3,8).	move(6,1).	move(8,1).
move(2,7).	move(4,3).	move(7,6).	move(9,4).
move(2,9).	move(4,9).	move(7,2).	move(9,2).

path(Z,Z).
path(X,Y) :- move(X,W), not(been(W)), assert(been(W)), path(W,Y).

This definition of path is a PROLOG implementation of the algorithm defined in Chapter 3. assert is a built-in PROLOG predicate that always succeeds and has the side effect of placing its argument in the data base of specifications. The been predicate is used to record previously visited states and avoid loops.

As mentioned previously, this use of the **been** predicate violates the program designer's goal of creating predicate calculus specifications that do not use global variables. Thus **been(3)**, when asserted into the data base, is indeed a fact available to any other procedure in the data base, and, as such, has global extension. Even more important, creating global structures to alter program control violates the basic tenet of the production system model, where the logic (of problem specifications) is kept separate from the control of the program. Here **been** structures were created as global specifications to modify the program execution.

As we proposed in Chapter 3, a list may be used to keep track of visited states and so keep the **path** call from looping. The **member** predicate is used to detect duplicate states (loops). This approach remedies the problems of using global **been(w)** assertions. The PROLOG-based specification of the following clauses exactly implements the depth-first graph search with backtracking algorithm of chapters 3 and 4:

```
path(Z,Z,L).
path(X,Y,L) :- move(X,Z), not(member(Z,L)), path(Z,Y,[Z|L]).
```

where:

```
member(X,[X|T]).
member(X,[Y|T]) :- member(X,T).
```

The third parameter of **path** is the local variable representing the list of states that have already been visited. When a new state is generated (using the **move** predicate) and this state is not already on the list of visited states, **not(member(Z,L))**, it is placed on the front of the state list [Z|L] for the next **path** call.

It should be noted that all the parameters of **path** are local and get their current values depending on where they are called in the graph search. Each recursive call adds a state to this list. If all continuations from a certain state fail, then that particular **path** call fails. When the interpreter backs up to the parent call, the third parameter, representing the list of states visited, has its previous value. Thus, states are added to and deleted from this list as the backtracking search moves through the graph.

When the **path** call finally succeeds, the first two parameters are identical. The third parameter is the list of states visited on the path from the start state to the goal state (in reverse order). Thus we can print out the solution path. The PROLOG specification for the knight's tour problem using lists and a depth-first search employing backtrack may be obtained by using this definition of **path** with the **move** specifications and **member** predicates just presented.

The call to the PROLOG interpreter **path(X,Y,[X])**, where X and Y are replaced by numbers between 1 and 9, finds a path from state X to state Y, if the path exists. The third parameter initializes the path list with the starting state X. Note that there is no typing distinction in PROLOG: the first two parameters are any representation of states in the problem space and the third is a list of states. Unification makes this generalization of pattern matching across data types possible. Thus, **path** is a general depth-first search algorithm that may be used with any graph. In Section 6.1.3 we use this to implement a production system solution to the farmer, wolf, goat, and cabbage problem, with state specifications replacing square numbers in the call to path.

We now present the trace of a solution for the 3 × 3 knight's tour. It is left as an exercise for the reader to design the set of specifications for the full 8 × 8 knight's tour problem in PROLOG. (See exercises in chapters 4 and 6.)

For this example:

    1. is path(Z,Z,L).
    2. is path(X,Y,L) :– move(X,Z), not(member(Z,L)), path(Z,Y,[Z|L]).

    U: ?- path(1,3,[1]).

        path(1,3,[1]) attempts to match 1. fail 1 ≠ 3.
        path(1,3,[1]) matches 2. X is 1, Y is 3, L is [1]
          move(1,Z) matches Z as 6, not(member(6,[1])) is true, call path(6,3,[6,1])

            path(6,3,[6,1]) attempts to match 1. fail 6 ≠m, 3.
            path(6,3,[6,1]) matches 2. X is 6, Y is 3, L is [6,1].
              move(6,Z) matches Z as 7, not(member(7,[6,1]) is true, path(7,3,[7,6,1])

                path(7,3,[7,6,1]) attempts to match 1. fail 7 ≠ 3.
                path(7,3,[7,6,1]) matches 2. X is 7, Y is 3, L is [7,6,1].
                  move(7,Z) is Z = 6, not(member(6,[7,6,1])) fails, backtrack!
                  move(7,Z) is Z = 2, not(member(2,[7,6,1])) true, path(2,3,[2,7,6,1]))

                    path call attempts 1, fail, 2 ≠ 3.
                    path matches 2, X is 2, Y is 3, L is [2,7,6,1]
                      move matches Z as 7, not(member(…)) fails, backtrack!
                      move matches Z as 9, not(member(…)) true, path(9,3,[9,2,7,6,1])

                        path fails 1, 9 ≠ 3.
                        path matches 2, X is 9, Y is 3, L is [9,2,7,6,1]
                          move is Z = 4, not(member(…)) true, path(4,3,[4,9,2,7,6,1])

                          path fails 1. 4 ≠ 3.
                          path matches 2, X is 4, Y is 3, L is [4,9,2,7,6,1]
                            move Z = 3, not(member(…)) true, path(3,3,[3,4,9,2,7,6,1])

                          path attempts 1, true, 3 = 3, yes

                      yes

                  yes

              yes

            yes

        yes
      P: yes

In summary, the recursive path call is a *shell* or general control structure for search in a graph. All the checks are made for a graph search algorithm: in path(X, Y, L), X is the present state, Y is the goal state. When X and Y are identical, the recursion terminates. L is the list of states on the current path to state Y, and as each new state Z is found with the call move(X, Z) it is placed on the list: [Z | L]. The state list is checked, using not (member(Z,L)), to be sure the path does not loop.

The difference between the state list L in the path call above and closed in Chapter 4 is that closed records all states visited, while the state list L keeps track of only the present path. It is quite straightforward to expand the record keeping in the path call along the lines presented in Chapter 4, and we do this in Section 6.2.

6.1.3 A Production System Example in PROLOG

In this section we write a production system solution to the farmer, wolf, goat, and cabbage problem. This problem is stated as follows:

> A farmer with his wolf, goat, and cabbage come to the edge of a river they wish to cross. There is a boat at the river's edge, but, of course, only the farmer can row. The boat also can carry only two things (including the rower) at a time. If the wolf is ever left alone with the goat, the wolf will eat the goat; similarly, if the goat is left alone with the cabbage, the goat will eat the cabbage. Devise a sequence of crossings of the river so that all four characters arrive safely on the other side of the river.

In the next several paragraphs we present a production system solution to this problem. First, we observe that the problem may be represented as a search through a graph. To do this we consider the possible moves that might be available at any time in the solution process. Some of these moves are eventually ruled out because they produce states that are unsafe (something will be eaten).

For the moment, suppose that all states are safe, and simply consider the graph of possible states. The boat can be used in four ways: to carry the farmer and wolf, the farmer and goat, the farmer and cabbage, and the farmer by himself. A state of the world is some combination of the characters on the two banks. Several states of the search are represented as in Figure 6.1. States of the world are represented using a predicate, state(F, W, G, C), with the location of the farmer as first parameter, location of the wolf as second parameter, the goat as third, and the cabbage as fourth. We assume that the river runs "north to south" and the characters are on either the east, e, or west, w, bank. Thus, state(w, w, w, w) has all characters on the west bank to start the problem.

It must be pointed out that these choices are conventions that have been arbitrarily chosen by the authors. Indeed, as researchers in AI continually point out, the selection of an appropriate representation is often the most critical aspect of problem solving. These conventions are selected to fit the predicate calculus representation in PROLOG. Different states of the world are created by different crossings of the river, represented by changes in the values of the parameters of the state predicate (Figure 6.1). Other representations are certainly possible.

We now describe a general graph for this river-crossing problem. For the time being, we ignore the fact that some states are unsafe. In Figure 6.2 we see the beginning of the graph of possible moves back and forth across the river. Note that in this graph it

Figure 6.1 Sample crossings for the farmer, wolf, goat, and cabbage problem.

is not necessary to have a separate representation for the location of the boat (why?). Figure 6.2 represents part of the graph that is to be searched for a solution path.

The recursive path call previously described provides the control mechanism for the production system search. The production rules are the rules for changing state in the search. We define these as move rules in PROLOG form.

Since PROLOG uses Horn clauses, a production system designed in PROLOG must either represent production rules directly in Horn clause form or translate rules to this format. We take the former option here, the latter in Section 12.2. Horn clauses require that the pattern for the present state and the pattern for the next state both be placed in the head of the Horn clause (or to the left of :−). These are the arguments to the move predicate. The conditions that the production rule requires to fire (and return the next state) are placed to the right of :−. As is seen in the following example, these conditions are also expressed as unification constraints.

The first rule we define is for the farmer to take the wolf across the river. This rule must account for both the transfer from east to west and the transfer from west to east, and it must not be applicable when the farmer and wolf are on opposite sides of the river. Thus it must transform state(e,e,G,C) to state(w,w,G,C) and state(w,w,G,C) to state(e,e,G,C). It must also fail for state(e,w,G,C) and state(w,e,G,C). The variables G and C represent the fact that the third and fourth parameters can be bound to

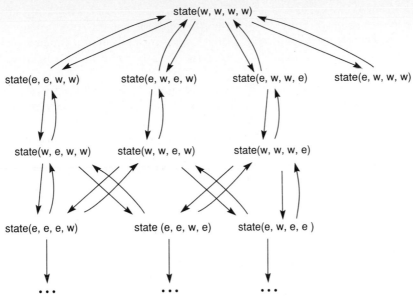

Figure 6.2 Portion of the state space graph of the farmer, wolf, goat, and cabbage problem (including unsafe states).

either **e** or **w**. Whatever their values, they remain the same after the move o f the farmer and wolf. Some of the states produced may indeed be ''unsafe.''

The following move rule operates only when the farmer and wolf are in the same location and takes them to the opposite side of the river. Note that the goat and cabbage do not change their present location (whatever it might be).

    move(state(X,X,G,C), state(Y,Y,G,C)) :- opp(X,Y).

    opp(e,w).
    opp(w,e).

This rule fires when a state (the present location in the graph) is presented to the first parameter of move in which the farmer and wolf are at the same location. When the rule fires, a new state, the second parameter of move, is produced with the value of X opposite, opp, the value of Y. Two conditions are satisfied to produce the new state: first, that the values of the first two parameters are the same, and second, that their new location is opposite the old.

The first condition was checked implicitly in the unification process, in that move is not even called unless the first two parameters are the same. This test may be done explicitly by using the following rule:

    move(state(F,W,G,C), state(Z,Z,G,C)) :- F = W, opp(F,Z).

This equivalent move rule first tests whether F and W are the same and, only if they are, assigns the opposite value of F to Z. Note that the closest that PROLOG comes to "assignment" is through the binding of variable values in unification. Bindings are shared by all occurrences of a variable in a clause and the scope of a variable is limited to the clause in which it occurs.

Pattern matching, a powerful tool in AI programming, is especially important in pruning search. States that do not fit the patterns in the rule are automatically pruned. In this sense, the first version of the move rule presented is a more efficient representation, since unification doesn't even consider the clause if the first two parameters aren't identical.

Next, we create a predicate to test whether each new state is safe, so that nothing is eaten in the process of getting across the river. Again, unification plays an important role in this definition. Any state where the second and third parameters are the same and opposite the first parameter is unsafe; the wolf eats the goat. Alternatively, if the third and fourth parameters are the same and opposite the first parameter, the state is unsafe: the goat eats the cabbage.

These unsafe situations may be represented with the following rules.

```
unsafe(state(X,Y,Y,C)) :- opp(X,Y).
unsafe(state(X,W,Y,Y)) :- opp(X,Y).
```

Several points should be mentioned here: First, if a state is to be not unsafe (i.e., safe), according to the definition of not in PROLOG, neither of these unsafe predicates can be true. Thus both of these predicates must not unify with the current state or, if they do unify, their conditions must not be satisfied. Second, not in PROLOG isn't exactly equivalent to the logical not of the first-order predicate calculus; not is rather "negation by failure of its opposite." The reader should test a number of states to verify that unsafe does what it is intended to do.

Now, a not unsafe test may be added to the previous production rule:

```
move(state(X,X,G,C), state(Y,Y,G,C))
              :- opp(X,Y), not(unsafe(state(Y,Y,G,C))).
```

The not unsafe test calls unsafe, as mentioned above, to see if the generated state is an acceptable new state in the search. When all criteria are met, including the check in the path algorithm that the new state is not a member of the visited-state list, path is (recursively) called on this state to go deeper into the graph. When path is called, the new state is added to the visited-state list.

In a similar fashion, we can create the three other production rules to represent the farmer taking the goat, cabbage, and himself across the river. We have added a writelist command to each production rule to print a trace of the rule being tried.

The rpt (reverse print) command is used in the terminating condition of path to print out the final solution path. Finally, we add a fifth "pseudorule" that always fires (since no conditions are placed on it). This rule fires when all previous rules have failed; it indicates that the path call is backtracking from the current state, and then it itself fails. This "pseudorule" is added only to assist the user in seeing what is going on as the production system is running.

We now present the full production system program in PROLOG to solve the farmer, wolf, goat, and cabbage problem.

```
move(state(X,X,G,C), state(Y,Y,G,C))
          :- opp(X,Y), not(unsafe(state(Y,Y,G,C))),
             writelist(['try farmer takes wolf',Y,Y,G,C]).

move(state(X,W,X,C), state(Y,W,Y,C))
          :- opp(X,Y), not(unsafe(state(Y,W,Y,C))),
             writelist(['try farmer takes goat',Y,W,Y,C]).

move(state(X,W,G,X), state(Y,W,G,Y))
          :- opp(X,Y), not(unsafe(state(Y,W,G,Y))),
             writelist(['try farmer takes cabbage',Y,W,G,Y]).

move(state(X,W,G,C), state(Y,W,G,C))
          :- opp(X,Y), not(unsafe(state(Y,W,G,C))),
             writelist(['try farmer takes self',Y,W,G,C]).

move(state(F,W,G,C), state(F,W,G,C))
          :- writelist(['     BACKTRACK from:',F,W,G,C]), fail.


path(Z,Z,L) :- write('Solution Path Is: ' ), rpt(L).
path(X,Y,L) :- move(X,Z), not(member(Z,L) ), path(Z,Y,[Z|L]).

member(X,[X|T ]).
member(X,[Y|T ]) :- member(X,T).

writelist([]) :- nl.   %"nl" produces a newline
writelist([H|T ]):- print(H), tab(1), writelist(T).   %"tab(n)" skips n spaces.

rpt([]).
rpt([H|T ]) :- rpt(T), write(H), nl.

opp(e,w).
opp(w,e).
```

We now present a trace of program execution. The code is called by requesting:

U: ?- path(state(w,w,w,w), state(e,e,e,e), [state(w,w,w,w)]).

Note the backtracks from states that allow no further progress. Also trace the various variables local to each call of path. It should be noted that this program is a general program for moving the four creatures from any (legal) position on the banks to any other (legal) position. Thus:

U: ?- path(state(e,e,e,e), state(w,w,w,w), [state(e,e,e,e)]).
U: ?- path(state(w,e,w,e), state(e,w,e,w), [state(w,e,w,e)]).

are both legal queries to the data base.

The code may also be asked to find a path from the goal back to the start state:

U: ?- path(state(w,w,w,w), state(e,e,e,e), [state(e,e,e,e)]).

if the first two parameters in path are exchanged, i.e., path(Y,X,[X]). Several other interesting features of production systems, including the fact that different orderings of the rules can produce different searches through the graph, are presented in the exercises. A trace of the execution of the program is:

U: ?- path(state(w,w,w,w), state(e,e,e,e), [state(w,w,w,w)]).

P: try farmer takes goat e w e w
   try farmer takes self w w e w
   try farmer takes wolf e e e w
   try farmer takes goat w e w w
   try farmer takes cabbage e e w e
   try farmer takes wolf w w w e
   try farmer takes goat e w e e
       BACKTRACK from e,w,e,e
       BACKTRACK from w,w,w,e
   try farmer takes self w e w e
   try farmer takes goat e e e e
   Solution Path Is:
   state(w,w,w,w)
   state(e,w,e,w)
   state(w,w,e,w)
   state(e,e,e,w)
   state(w,e,w,w)
   state(e,e,w,e)
   state(w,e,w,e)
   state(e,e,e,e)

In summary, this PROLOG program implements a production system solution to the farmer, wolf, goat, and cabbage problem. The move rules make up the content of the production memory. The working memory is represented by the arguments of the path call. The production system control mechanism is defined by the recursive path call. We show how this control may be altered in the next subsections. Finally, the ordering of generation of children from each state (conflict resolution) is determined by the order in which the rules are placed in the production memory.

6.2 Designing Alternative Search Strategies in PROLOG

As the previous subsection demonstrated, PROLOG itself uses depth-first search with backtracking. Thus the PROLOG interpreter is an implementation of this search strategy as originally presented in Chapter 3. This strategy is a result of PROLOG's implementation (a resolution theorem prover, chapters 11 and 12). We now show how the alternative search strategies of chapters 4 and 5 can be implemented in PROLOG. The *cut* is an important predicate for controlling backtracking. In this section, we demonstrate the effect of the cut and show how it can be used to control PROLOG's built-in search mechanism. Then we implement the breadth-first and best-first search algorithms.

6.2.1 Use of the Cut to Control Search in PROLOG

The *cut* is represented by an exclamation point: !. The syntax for cut is that of a goal with no arguments. It has several side effects: first, it always succeeds, and second, if it is "failed back to" in the normal course of backtracking, it causes the entire clause in which it is contained to fail.

For a simple example of the effect of the cut, recall the two-move path call from the knight's tour example (Section 4.2). There the predicate path2 could be created:

path2(X,Y) :- move(X,Z), move(Z,Y).

(There is a two-move path between X and Y if there exists an intermediate stop Z between them.) For this example, assume part of the knight's data base:

move(1,6).
move(1,8).
move(6,7).
move(6,1).
move(8,3).
move(8,1).

When the interpreter is asked to find all the two-move paths from 1, there are four answers:

U: ?- path2(1,W).
P: W = 7
U: ;
P: W = 1
U: ;
P: W = 3
U: ;
P: W = 1
U: ;
P: no

When path2 is altered to contain the cut:

```
path2(X,Y) :- move(X,Z), !, move(Z,Y).
```

and the same goal is presented:

```
P: ?- path2(1,W).
```

Only two answers result:

```
P: W = 7
U: ;
P: W = 1
U: ;
P: no
```

This occurs because variable Z takes on only one value (the first value it is bound to), namely 6. Once the first subgoal succeeds, Z is bound to 6 and the cut is encountered. This prohibits further backtracking to the first subgoal; no further bindings for the Z parameter are tried.

There are several uses for the cut in programming: First, as this example demonstrated, it allows the programmer to explicitly control the shape of the search tree. When further (exhaustive) search is not required, the tree can be explicitly pruned at that point. This allows PROLOG code to have the flavor of function calling: when one set of values (bindings) is ''returned'' by a PROLOG predicate (or set of predicates) and the cut is encountered, the interpreter does not search for other unifications. If that set of values does not lead on to a solution then no further values are attempted.

A second use of cut is to control recursive calls. In the recursive **path** call seen above, cut may be added after the recursive call:

```
path(Z,Z,L).
path(X,Z,L) :- move(X,Y), not(member(Y,L)), path(Y,Z,[Y|L]), !.
```

This addition of cut means that (at most) one solution to the graph search is produced. Only one solution is produced because further solutions occur after the clause path(Z,Z,L) is satisfied. If the user asks for more solutions, path(Z,Z,L) is then failed, and the second **path** call is reinvoked to continue the (exhaustive) search of the graph. When the cut is placed after the recursive **path** call, the call can't be reentered (backed into) for further search.

An important side effect of the cut is to make the program run faster and conserve memory locations. When cut is used within a predicate, the pointers in memory needed for backtracking to predicates to the left of the cut are not created. This is, of course, because they will never be needed. Thus, cut produces the desired solution, and only the desired solution, with more efficient use of memory.

The cut can also be used with recursion to reinitialize the **path** call for further search within the graph. When searching through a series of rules, PROLOG stores an activation record of each unification on an internal stack. This stack keeps track of the successive calls to a recursive predicate. Sometimes in a recursive predicate we need to retain only the most recent bindings of the parameters. The cut is then placed after the recursive call to keep the interpreter from recording all parent calls on the stack. This prevents the stack from getting too cumbersome and makes the program more efficient.

In particular, our implementations of breadth- and best-first search (Section 6.2.3) use open and closed lists to record states in the search; the records of local variables on the stack are not used for this purpose. When search fails at any point we do not go back to the preceding values of open and closed (as found on the stack). Instead, open and closed are updated within the path call and the search continues with these new values. The cut is used in these implementations to keep PROLOG from storing old versions of open and closed.

6.2.2 Backtracking with a Global Record of Dead States

Because the values of variables are restored when recursion backtracks, the list of visited states in the depth-first path algorithm records states only on the current path to the goal. Although the test for membership in this list prevents loops, it still allows branches of the space to be reexamined if they are reached along different paths. A more efficient implementation would keep track of all the states that have ever been encountered. This more complete collection of states made up the list called closed in Chapter 3.

closed holds all states on the current path plus the states that were rejected when we backtracked out of them. A simple method for creating closed, without relinquishing a current ordered list of states on the path to the present state, is to record rejected states in the data base. This record must be global since these states have been exhaustively examined and rejected, and the search should not consider them again. (If a ''dead'' state were local to a particular path call, it would be lost to us on backtrack from that call.)

This global structure can be created by adding assert(dead(S)) to the algorithm. All the states on the present path list L plus the dead states make up closed. (An even better method for handling closed is presented later, where closed is again a local variable but backtracking is controlled by the cut.)

The proper time for recording a state as dead is after all the production rules have failed and before the recursive path call fails back to its preceding success. This situation was captured in the fifth move rule of the farmer, wolf, goat, and cabbage example, when the four true rules for moving had all failed. At that time the current state, having no further successors, is dead. Whenever a new state is discovered in the search, we must check whether it was ever seen, not just whether it is a member of the current path.

We now present a shell structure for depth-first search in PROLOG, keeping track of closed and checking each new state to be sure it was not previously visited. path, as before, has three arguments and is called:

U: path(Start, Goal, [Start]).

Start and Goal are variables having the values of the start and goal states. The third parameter represents the path list. The move predicates are as before, but the final move rule records the present state as dead before failing.

```
path(G,G,L) :- write('Solution Found. The path is:' ), rpt(L), nl.

path(S,G,L) :- move(S,N), not(member(N,L) ), not(dead(N)),
                   path(N,G,[N|L]).


move(Present, New) :- ... %test first rule.
move(Present, New) :- ... %test second rule.
 ....
 ....

move(Present, New) :- assert(dead(Present)), write('Backtrack here'), nl, fail.

rpt([]).
rpt([H|T ]) :- rpi(T), write(H), nl.
```

An alternative program for depth-first search keeps track of states in **open** and **closed** lists, like breadth- and best-first search. To implement depth-first search, we maintain **open** as a stack. This implementation collects all used states in a list **closed**, which would be a local variable to **path**, not global like the **dead** predicate used above. This choice makes creating the solution path list more difficult.

6.2.3   Breadth-First Search in PROLOG

We now present the *shell* of an algorithm for breadth-first search using explicit open and closed lists. This shell can be used with the move rule for any search problem. This algorithm is called by:

```
U: ?- path([Start], [], Goal).
```

Start and **Goal** have their obvious values. The first parameter of **path** is the open list and the second is the closed list. *Don't care* variables, those whose values are not used in a clause, are written as _.

```
path([], _ , _) :- write('graph searched, no solution found ').
path([G|T],_,G) :- write('solution found ').
path([S|T ],C,G) :- write('open: '), printlist([S|T]),
                    write('closed: '), printlist(C),
                    bagof(X, moves(S,T,C,X), List),  % see comment below
                    append(T,List,O),
                    !,
                    path(O,[S|C],G).

moves(S,T,C,X) :- move(S,X), X /= S,
                  not(member(X,T)), not(member(X,C) ).
```

```
member(X,[X|_]).
member(X,[_|T]) :- member(X,T).

append([],L,L).
append([H|T],L,[H|NT]) :- append(T,L,NT).

printlist([]).
printlist([H|T]) :- write(H), nl, printlist(T).
```

The algorithm is a shell in that no **move** rules are given. These must be supplied to fit the specific problem domain.

Note that a new termination condition is defined for the case that **path** is called with its first argument, the open list, empty. This will happen only when there are no more states in the graph remaining to be searched, and the solution has not been found. A successful solution is found in the second termination condition when the head of **open** and the goal state are identical. **open** and **closed** may be printed after each call to **path** to watch the progress of the search.

The algorithm uses **bagof**, a PROLOG predicate standard to most interpreters. **bagof** lets us gather all the unifications of a pattern into a single list. The second parameter to **bagof** is the pattern to be matched in the data base. The first parameter specifies the components of the second parameter that we wish to collect. For example, we may be interested in the values bound to a single variable of a predicate. All bindings of the first parameter resulting from these matches are collected in a list and bound to the third parameter.

In this program, **bagof** collects the states reached by firing ALL of the enabled production rules. Of course, this is necessary to gather all descendants of a particular state so that we can add them, in proper order, to **open**. **bagof** has three arguments; the second argument, a new predicate named **moves**, calls the **move** predicates to generate all the states that may be reached using the production rules. The arguments to **moves** are the present state, the open list, the closed list, and a variable that is the state reached by a good move. Before returning this state, **moves** checks that it is not a member of either **open** or **closed**. **bagof** calls **moves** and collects all the states that meet these conditions.

(In some implementations, **bagof** fails when there are no matches for the second argument and thus the third argument is empty. This can be remedied by substituting (bagof(X, moves(S,T,C,X), List); List = []) for the current calls to **bagof** in the code.)

The third argument of **bagof** represents the new states that are placed in their proper position on **open**. This is done using the **append** predicate to join two lists together and add the new states to the end of the open list (**append** is discussed in more detail in Section 6.3). The list passed back from **bagof** is the second argument of **append** and thus is placed on the right end of **open**, forming a queue, according to the breadth-first search algorithm.

The open list then becomes the first argument of **path**, where its head is taken as the next state for evaluation. The head of **open**, once it has been used by **bagof** for generation of descendants, is added to **closed**. **path** is then called again, with the modified open and closed lists.

6.2.4 Best-First Search in PROLOG

Our shell for best-first search is a modification of the breadth-first algorithm in which open is ordered by heuristic merit before each new call to path.

In our algorithm, we attach a heuristic measure permanently to each new state on open and use these measures for ordering states on open. This saves recalculating the heuristics each time open is sorted. Other versions of the algorithm could also retain the parent of the state. This information can be used to build the solution path once the goal is found, as discussed in Chapter 4.

Each state is represented as a list of four elements: the state description, an integer giving the depth in the graph of its discovery, an integer giving the heuristic measure of the state, and the integer sum of the second and third elements. The first element is found in the usual way; the second is determined by adding one to the depth of its parent; the third is determined by the heuristic measure of the particular problem. The fourth element, eventually used for ordering the states on open, is $f(n)=g(n)+h(n)$, as presented in Chapter 5.

As before, the move rules are not specified; this will be defined to fit the specific problem. printlist, append, and member are as in the preceding example. calculate is a measure applied to each state to determine its heuristic weight, the value of the third parameter in its descriptive list. calculate also depends, of course, on the problem domain. The predicates to sort the list of new states returned by bagof and to merge the sorted result with open must also be supplied (see exercises for hints).

This algorithm, as breadth-first search above, also has two termination conditions for failure and success. The algorithm is called by:

U: ?- path([[Start,0,H,H]|[]], [], [Goal,_,_,_]).

H is the heuristic evaluation of the start state and we "don't care" about the second, third, and fourth parameters of the goal. The code for best-first search is:

```
path([], _, _) :- write('Search over, no solution found. ').
path([[Goal, _, _, _]| _], _, [Goal, _, _, _]) :- write('Solution found. ').
path([S, D, H, T]| R], C, [Goal, _, _, _]) :-
            write('present state: '), write(S),
            write('open: '), printlist(R),
            write('closed: '), printlist(C),
            bagof(X, moves([S, D, H, T], R, C, X), NL),
            sort(NL, SNL), merge(R, SNL, NR),
            !,
                 path(NR, [[S, D, H, T]| C], [Goal, _, _, _]).

moves([S, D, H, T], R, C, [A, B, E, F]) :-
            move(S, A), S /= A,
            not(member([A, _, _, _], R)), not(member([A, _, _, _], C)),
            B is D + 1,
            calculate(A, E),
            F is E + B.
```

```
member([X, _, _, _], [[X, _, _, _]| _]).
member([X, _, _, _], [[ _, _, _, _]|T]) :- member([X, _, _, _], T).
```

```
move(S, NS)   to be added by the reader
calculate(NS, V) to be added by the reader
sort(O, NO) to be added by the reader
merge(NO, NNO) to be added by the reader
```

6.3   PROLOG: Toward a Nonprocedural Computing Language

In traditional computer languages such as FORTRAN and C, the logic for the problem's specification and the control for executing the solution algorithm are inextricably mixed together. A program in these languages is simply a sequence of things to be done to get an answer. This is the accepted notion of a *procedural* language.

One of the goals of the designers of PROLOG has been to separate the logic or specification for a problem from the execution of that specification. There are several reasons for this separation, not the least of which is the ability to determine after the specifications are created what might be the best control for executing them.

Another goal of this separation of logic from control is that each aspect of the problem may be analyzed separately. The specifications may themselves be translated to other specifications before execution. Specifications may be checked for correctness or otherwise evaluated independently of their execution.

In the future, it might even be possible to send a specification to a number of processors, where the number of processors and the partition and assignment of the specification set to processors are seen as a deterministic aspect of the specifications themselves.

Needless to say, PROLOG has not yet achieved this state of computing nirvana! It is still possible, however, to show how logic programming, as represented by the PROLOG language, exhibits some of the benefits of a nonprocedural semantics. How the interpreter achieves these features can be clearly understood only after the subsection on Horn clause resolution in chapters 11 and 12.

For the first example consider the predicate **append**. This predicate is defined:

```
append([], L, L).
append([X|T], L, [X|NL]) :- append(T, L, NL).
```

We can understand **append** by tracing its execution in joining two lists together. If the following call is made:

```
U: ?- append([a,b,c], [d,e], Y).
```

the response is:

P: Y = [a,b,c,d,e]

The execution of append is not tail recursive, in that the local variable values are accessed after the recursive call has succeeded. In this case, X is placed on the head of the list ([X | NL]) after the recursive call has finished. This requires that a record of each call be kept on the PROLOG stack. Here is the trace of append on the above query:

For purposes of reference in this trace:
    1 is append([], L, L).
    2 is append([X | T], L, [X | NL]) :– append(T, L, NL).

U: ?- append([a,b,c], [d,e], Y).

    try match 1, fail [a, b, c] ≠ []
    match 2, X is a, T is [b, c], L is [d, e], call append([b, c], [d, e], NL)

        try match 1, fail [b, c] ≠ []
        match 2, X is b, T is [c], L is [d, e], call append([c], [d, e], NL)

            try match 1, fail [c] ≠ []
            match 2, X is c, T is [], L is [d, e], call append([], [d, e], NL)

                match 1, L is [d, e] (for BOTH parameters), yes

            yes, NL is [d, e], [X | NL] is [c, d, e]

        yes, NL is [c, d, e], [X | NL] is [b, c, d, e]

    yes, NL is [b, c, d, e], [X | NL] is [a, b, c, d, e]

P: Y = [a,b,c,d,e], yes

In the PROLOG algorithms shown this chapter, the parameters of the predicates seem to be intended as either "input" or "output" parameters; most definitions assume that certain parameters would be bound in the call and others would be unbound. This need not be so. In fact, there is no commitment at all to parameters being input or output in PROLOG!

PROLOG code is intended to be simply a set of specifications of what is true, a statement of the logic of the situation. Thus, append specifies the relationship between three lists, such that the third list is the catenation of the first onto the front of the second.

To demonstrate this fact we can give append a different set of goals:

U: ?- append([a,b], [c], [a,b,c]).
P: yes
U: ?- append([a], [c], [a,b,c]).
P: no

We can also use an unbound variable for different parameters of the call to **append**:

```
U: ?- append(X, [b,c], [a,b,c]).
P: X = [a]
U: ?- append(X, Y, [a,b,c]).
P: X = []
   Y = [a, b, c]
U: ;
P: X = [a]
   Y = [b, c]
U: ;
P: X = [a, b]
   Y = [c]
U: ;
P: X = [a, b, c]
   Y = []
U: ;
P: no
```

In the last query, PROLOG returns all the lists X and Y that appended together give [a,b,c], four pairs of lists in all. As mentioned above, **append** is a statement of the logic of a relationship between three lists. What the interpreter produces depends on the specific query it is given.

Our second example of the nonprocedural nature of logic programming is a simple program that is both a parser and a generator of sentences. We selected this example both to demonstrate nonprocedurality and to show a common method of parsing and generating sentences using PROLOG. (This is also a direct implementation of the ''parser'' in the applications section of Chapter 3 and a precursor of parsing and grammars in Chapter 10.)

Consider the subset of English grammar rules below. With this subset of rules a large number of simple sentences can be judged as well formed or not.

```
Sentence ⇔ NounPhrase VerbPhrase
NounPhrase ⇔ Noun
NounPhrase ⇔ Article Noun
VerbPhrase ⇔ Verb
VerbPhrase ⇔ Verb NounPhrase
```

Adding some vocabulary to the grammar rules:

```
Article(a)
Article(the)
Noun(man)
Noun(dog)
Verb(likes)
Verb(bites)
```

The parse tree of a simple sentence (the man bites the dog) is shown in Figure 6.3.

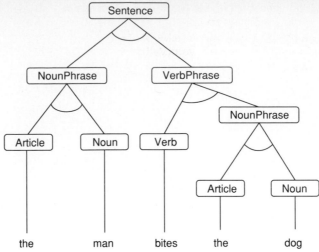

Figure 6.3 Parse tree for the sentence "The man bites the dog."

The specification rules of the grammar are transcribed into PROLOG rules in a natural fashion. For example, a **sentence** is a **nounphrase** and a **verbphrase**. This is represented as the PROLOG rule:

sentence(Start, End) :- nounphrase(Start, Rest), verbphrase(Rest, End).

Each PROLOG rule takes two parameters. The first is a sequence of words in list form. The rule attempts to determine whether some initial part of the list is a legal part of speech. Any remaining suffix of the list not parsed will match the second parameter. Thus, we are implementing a left-to-right parse of the sentence. If the sentence rule succeeds, the second parameter of **sentence** will have the value of what remains after the **nounphrase** and **verbphrase** parse; if the list is a correct sentence, this is []. The two alternative forms of noun phrases and verb phrases are similarly defined.

The sentence itself, for simplicity, is cast as a list: [the, man, likes, the, dog]. The list is now broken up and passed to the various grammar rules to be examined for syntactic correctness. Note how the ''pattern matching'' works on the list in question: pulling off the head, or the head and second element, passing on what is left over, and so on.

The complete grammar is defined below. The **utterance** predicate takes the list to be parsed as its argument and calls the sentence rule. It initializes the second parameter of **sentence** to [], indicating that nothing should remain in the list after a successful parse.

utterance(X) :- sentence(X,[]).

sentence(Start, End) :- nounphrase(Start, Rest), verbphrase(Rest, End).

```
nounphrase([Noun|End], End) :- noun(Noun).
nounphrase([Article, Noun|End], End) :- article(Article), noun(Noun).

verbphrase([Verb|End], End) :- verb(Verb).
verbphrase([Verb|Rest], End) :- verb(Verb), nounphrase(Rest, End).

article(a).
article(the).
noun(man).
noun(dog).
verb(likes).
verb(bites).
```

Example sentences may be tested for well-formedness:

```
U: ?- utterance([the,man,bites,the,dog]).
P: yes
U: ?- utterance([the,man,bites,the]).
P: no
```

New, partial sentences may be proposed and the interpreter asked to fill in potential remaining words so that the sentence is syntactically correct:

```
U: ?- utterance([the,man,likes,X]).
P: X = man
U: ;
P: X = dog
U: ;
P: no
```

PROLOG finds all legitimate ways in which the sentence may be concluded!

Finally, the same code may be used to generate the set of all well-formed sentences using this limited dictionary and set of grammar rules:

```
U: ?- utterance(X).
P: [man, likes]
U: ;
P: [man, bites]
U: ;
P: [man, likes, man]
U: ;
P: [man, likes, dog]
etc.
```

If the user continues asking for more solutions, eventually all possible well-formed sentences that can be generated from the grammar rules and our vocabulary are returned as values for X.

The grammar rules are the specification set for well-formedness of expressions in this subset of legitimate sentences of English. The PROLOG code represents this set of logic specifications. The interpreter is asked questions about this set of specifications. Thus the answer is a function of the specifications and the question asked. This is a major difference in computing with a language that is itself a theorem prover operating on specifications! There will be further details on PROLOG as a theorem prover in Chapter 12.

The previous example can be extended in a rather straightforward fashion. Suppose we desire to have proper noun-verb agreement in sentences. In the dictionary entry for each word its singular or plural form can be noted as such. Then in the grammar specifications for nounphrase and verbphrase a further parameter can be entered to signify the number of each phrase. Thus a singular noun has to be associated with a singular verb.

This modification increases the power of the grammar considerably. While the first version implemented a context-free grammar, this version implements a context-sensitive grammar (Chapter 10). It retains the contextual information needed to check number agreement. These additions are made to the previous code:

```
utterance(X) :- sentence(X, []).


sentence(Start, End) :- nounphrase(Start, Rest, Number),
    verbphrase(Rest, End, Number).

nounphrase([Noun|End], End, Number) :- noun(Noun, Number).
nounphrase([Article, Noun|End], End, Number) :- noun(Noun, Number),
                                article(Article, Number).

verbphrase([Verb|End], End, Number) :- verb(Verb, Number).
verbphrase([Verb|Rest], End, Number) :- verb(Verb, Number),
                                nounphrase(Rest, End, _).

article(a, singular).
article(these, plural).
article(the, singular).
article(the, plural).
noun(man, singular).
noun(men, plural).
noun(dog, singular).
noun(dogs, plural).
verb(likes, singular).
verb(like, plural).
verb(bites, singular).
verb(bite, plural).
```

New sentences may now be tested:

```
U: ?- utterance([the,men,like,the,dog]).
P: yes
U: ?- utterance([the,men,likes,the,dog]).
P: no
```

The answer to the second query is no, since the subject (men) and the verb (likes) do not agree in number. If we enter the goal:

U: ?- utterance([the,men|X]).

X will return all well-formed verb phrases for completing the sentence "the men...." with noun-verb number agreement! As before, we may request all legitimate sentences, according to the grammar and dictionary:

U: ?- utterance(X).

The present example uses the parameters on dictionary entries to introduce more information on the meanings in the sentence. This approach may be generalized to a powerful parser for natural language. More and more information may be included in the dictionary about the items described in the sentences, implementing a knowledge base of the meaning of English words. For example, men are animate and human. Similarly, dogs may be described as animate and nonhuman. With these descriptions new rules may be added for parsing, such as "humans do not bite animate nonhumans" to eliminate sentences such as [the,man,bites,the,dog]. If the nonhuman is no longer animate, of course, it might be eaten in a restaurant!

Semantic networks and other representational formalisms of this sort have played an important role in artificial intelligence research. These topics are seen again in some detail in chapters 9 and 10.

6.4   Epilogue and References

PROLOG is a general-purpose language, and we ignored a great number of its important concepts because of the space limitations of our book. We recommend that the interested reader pursue some of the many excellent texts available, such as *Programming in PROLOG* (Clocksin and Mellish 1984), *Computing with Logic* (Maier and Warren 1988), or *The Art of PROLOG* (Sterling and Shapiro 1986).

We focused our introduction to PROLOG on developing the representation and search topics introduced in chapters 2, 3, 4, and 5 of this text. The reader should do many of the exercises presented at the end of the chapter for exactly this reason.

The most important topic of this chapter, however, is the introduction of the language itself. The notion of solving a problem based on a set of specifications for correct relationships in a domain area coupled with the action of a theorem prover is exciting and important. Some say this way of casting a problem and its solution influenced the Japanese adoption of the concepts of logic programming, seen in PROLOG, as the core of their Fifth Generation project.

Of course, PROLOG is not a pure "nonprocedural" language. This will probably not be created using computing architectures as they are currently known. However, the move that PROLOG offers toward a fully declarative specification language is important.

Indeed, a strength of PROLOG interpreters is that they are open to a procedural as well as a declarative conceptualization (Kowalski 1979*b*). Thus a clause such as:

A :- B, C, D.

might in one instance be a specification logic:

A is true if B and C and D are true

and in another instance be a procedure for doing something:

To accomplish A go out and first do B and then do C and finally do D.

This procedural interpretation lends representational flexibility to the PROLOG language.

How the PROLOG interpreter works cannot be properly understood without the concepts of resolution theorem proving, especially the Horn clause refutation process. This is presented in detail in chapters 11 and 12.

The intellectual roots of PROLOG reside in the theoretical concepts of using logic for problem specification and solution. The main commentator on these issues is Robert Kowalski. Especially recommended are *Logic for Problem Solving* (Kowalski 1979*b*) and ''Algorithm = logic + control'' (Kowalski 1979*a*). Further references may be found in the introduction to Part III.

6.5. Exercises

1. Create a relational data base in PROLOG. Represent the data tuples as facts and the constraints on the data tuples as rules. Suitable examples might be from stock in a department store or records in a personnel office. For example, the facts may include the cost, supplier, part number, and amount in stock for each product sold. Constraints might include rules for when to reorder items, the ability to calculate the total value of the inventory, and optimal reorder amounts for best price.

2. Write a PROLOG program to answer Wirth's ''I am my own grandfather'' problem (Chapter 2, Exercise 13).

3. Write the ''member check'' program in PROLOG. What happens when an item is not in the list? Form a query to the ''member'' specification that would cause it to break a list into all its component elements.

4. Lists may be used as the basis for representing sets. This use requires the definition of the set operations of union, intersection, and difference. member, as defined above, may be thought of as performing a set membership check. Implement PROLOG definitions of these operations. Note that when lists are used to represent sets, duplicate elements should not appear in the lists. For example, union should be defined so that it behaves as follows:

union([a,b,c],[b,d,a,e],X).

X = [a,b,c,d,e]

5. Design a PROLOG program unique(Bag, Set) that takes a Bag (a list that may contain duplicate elements) and returns a Set (no elements are repeated).

6. Write a PROLOG program to count the elements in a list (a list within the list counts as one element). Write a program to count the atoms in a list (count the elements within any sublist). (Hint: there are several meta-predicates such as atom() that can be helpful.)

7. Write the PROLOG code for the farmer, wolf, goat, and cabbage problem.

   a. Execute this code and draw a graph of the search space.
   b. Alter the rule ordering to produce alternative solution paths.
   c. Use the shell in the text to produce a breadth-first solution.
   d. Describe a heuristic that might be appropriate for this problem.
   e. Build the heuristic search solution.

8. Do a to e as in Exercise 7 for the missionary and cannibal problem:

   Three missionaries and three cannibals come to the bank of a river they wish to cross. There is a boat that will hold only two, and any of the group is able to row it. If there are ever more missionaries than cannibals on any side of the river the cannibals will get converted. (Some consider this a fate worse than death!) Devise a series of moves to get all the people across the river with no conversions.

9. Use your code to check alternative forms of the missionary and cannibal problem—for example, when there are four missionaries and four cannibals and the boat holds only two. What if the boat can hold three? Try to generalize solutions for the whole class of missionary and cannibal problems.

10. Write PROLOG code to solve the full 8 × 8 knight's tour problem. Use the production system architecture proposed in this chapter and Chapter 4. Create the code so that you can get the program to solve a number of different tasks, such as getting from any one square to another. Do tasks a to e described with Exercise 7 above.

11. Do a to e as in Exercise 7 for the water jugs problem:

   There are two jugs, one holding 3 and the other 5 gallons of water. There are a number of things that can be done with the jugs: they can be filled, emptied, and dumped one into the other either until the poured-into jug is full, or until the poured-out-of jug is empty. Devise a sequence of actions that will produce 4 gallons of water in the larger jug. (Hint: only integer values of water will be used.)

12. Use your explorations of Exercise 11 to create the full graph of the water jugs problem. Discuss this graph: which nodes can be reached from where, which are impossible states, and when can breadth-first search be an advantage?

13. Take the path algorithm presented for the knight's tour problem in the text. Rewrite the path call in the recursive code to the following form:

   path(X,Y) :- path(X,W), move(W,Y).

   Examine the trace of this execution and describe what is happening. Can you generalize these results to the missionary and cannibal and water jugs problems?

14. Write the PROLOG code for a subset of English grammar rules, as in Section 6.3. Add:

   a. Adjectives and adverbs that can modify verbs and nouns, respectively.
   b. Prepositional phrases. (Can you do this with a recursive call?)
   c. Compound sentences (two sentences joined by a conjunction).

15. The simple natural language parser presented in this chapter will accept grammatically correct sentences that may not have a commonsense meaning, such as "the man bites the dog." These sentences may be eliminated from the grammar by augmenting the parser to include some notion of what is semantically plausible. Design a small "semantic network" in PROLOG (see comments in text) to allow you to reason about some aspect of the possible interpretations of the English grammar rules, such as when it is reasonable for "the man to bite the dog."

16. Write a program to pass values up to the top level of a game tree or graph:
    a. Using MIN-MAX.
    b. Using alpha-beta pruning of the tree.
    c. Using both of these on the game of tic-tac-toe.

17. Write a PROLOG program to build the search process for the financial advisor program that was used in chapters 2–5. Use the production system architecture. Add several more advisory rules to make the program more interesting.

18. Write merge sort in PROLOG.

7

LISP

". . . The name of the song is called 'Haddocks' Eyes.' *"*

"Oh, that's the name of the song, is it?" Alice said, trying to feel interested.

"No, you don't understand," the Knight said, looking a little vexed. "That's what the name is called. *The name really is* 'The Aged Aged Man.' *"*

"Then I ought to have said 'That's what the song is called'?" Alice corrected herself.

"No, you oughtn't: that's quite another thing! The song *is called* 'Ways and Means': *but that's only what it's* called *you know!"*

"Well, what is the song, then?" said Alice, who was by this time completely bewildered.

"I was coming to that," the Knight said.

—Lewis Carroll, *Through the Looking Glass*

7.0 Introduction

For the 30 years of its existence, LISP has been the dominant language for artificial intelligence programming. Originally designed for symbolic computing, LISP has been extended and refined over its lifetime in direct response to the needs of AI programming. Like most traditional programming languages, LISP is *procedural*; LISP programs describe *how* to perform an algorithm. This contrasts with declarative languages like PROLOG, whose programs are *declarative* assertions about a problem domain. However, unlike traditional procedural languages (FORTRAN, Pascal, etc.), LISP is *functional*: its syntax and semantics are derived from the mathematical theory of recursive functions. The power of functional programming, illustrated in the examples of this chapter, combined with a powerful set of high-level tools for building symbolic data structures, is largely responsible for LISP's popularity in the AI community.

In the early days of artificial intelligence, many programs were implemented directly in LISP, taking advantage of its built-in facilities for manipulating symbolic data structures. Later, as higher-level formalisms such as production systems, logic theorem provers, and rule-based expert systems were developed, LISP emerged as a primary language for their implementation. Many modern environments for expert systems are implemented in LISP. Even when using these tools, programmers frequently find it necessary to access the underlying LISP environment to augment the functionality of the higher-level language. In a very real sense, LISP has become the ''assembly language'' of artificial intelligence.

In this chapter we introduce the basic syntactic and semantic aspects of LISP, with particular emphasis on the features of the language that make it useful for AI programming: the use of lists to create symbolic data structures and the implementation of interpreters and search algorithms to manipulate these structures. In chapters 13 and 14 we use LISP to implement high-level tools including theorem provers, rule-based expert system shells, frames, semantic networks, and object-oriented programming languages. It is not our goal to provide a complete introduction to LISP; there are a number of excellent texts (see the epilogue to this chapter) that do this in far greater detail than our space allows. Instead, we have focused on the use of LISP to implement the representation languages and algorithms of artificial intelligence programming, especially those presented in chapters 1–5.

Common LISP is the dialect used in this text; however, most of our examples can easily be ported to other dialects. Where we use some feature that is unique to Common LISP, we have attempted to label it as such.

7.1 LISP: A Brief Overview (Optional)

7.1.1 Symbolic Expressions, the Syntactic Basis of LISP

This section briefly introduces the syntax and semantics of LISP. LISP is a large and complex language; consequently, this introduction is far from complete. It is included as a review for those who have programmed in LISP some time ago or as a supplement to a LISP text for those who are learning the language for the first time. The remainder of this chapter will then focus on specific AI programming techniques in LISP.

The syntactic elements of the LISP programming language are *symbolic expressions*, also known as *s-expressions*. Both programs and data are represented as s-expressions. An s-expression may be either an *atom* or a *list*. LISP atoms are the basic syntactic units of the language and include both numbers and symbols. Symbolic atoms are composed of letters, numbers, and certain nonalphanumeric characters:

    * - + / @ $ % ^ & _ < > ˜ .

Examples of LISP atoms include:

```
3.1416
100
x
hyphenated-name
?some-predicate
nil
```

A list is a sequence of either atoms or other lists separated by blanks and enclosed in parentheses. Examples of lists include:

```
(1 2 3 4)
(tom mary john joyce)
()
(on block-1 table)
(likes bill ?X)
(( 2467 (lovelace ada) programmer) ( 3592 (babbage charles) computer-designer))
((key-1 value-1) (key-2 value-2) (key-3 value-3))
(* 7 9)
(- (+ 3 4) 7)
```

Note that lists may be elements of lists. This nesting may be arbitrarily deep and allows us to create symbol structures of any desired form and complexity. The empty list, "()", plays a special role in the construction and manipulation of LISP data structures and is given the special name nil. nil is the only s-expression that is considered to be both an atom and a list. Two of the examples, (on block-1 table) and (likes bill ?X), may be interpreted as trivial syntactic variants on expressions in the predicate calculus. This syntax is used for predicate calculus expressions in the unification algorithm of this chapter. The next two examples suggest ways in which lists may be used to implement the data structures needed in a data base application. Thus lists may be used to implement a variety of representational formalisms.

The last two of the above examples are of particular interest in that they may be interpreted as arithmetic expressions in a prefix notation. This is exactly how LISP treats these expressions, with (* 7 9) representing the product of 7 and 9, etc. LISP is an *interpreted* language: when it is invoked on the computer, the user enters an interactive dialogue with the LISP interpreter. The interpreter prints a prompt (in the examples in this text, a >), reads the user input, attempts to evaluate that input, and, if successful, prints the result. For example:

```
> (* 7 9)
63
>
```

Here, the user enters (* 7 9) and LISP responds with 63, i.e., the *value* associated with that expression. LISP then prints another prompt and waits for more user input. This cycle is known as the *read-eval-print loop* and is the heart of the LISP interpreter.

When given a list, the LISP evaluator attempts to interpret the first element of the list as the name of a function and the remaining elements of the list as its arguments. Thus, the s-expression (f x y) is equivalent to the more traditional mathematical function notation f(x,y). The value printed by LISP is the result of *applying* the function to its arguments. LISP expressions that may be meaningfully evaluated are called *forms*. If the user enters an expression that may not be correctly evaluated, LISP will print an error message and allow the user to trace and correct the problem (the tools that LISP provides for tracing/debugging vary among implementations and are not discussed in this chapter). A sample LISP session appears below:

```
> (+ 14 5)
19
> (+ 1 2 3 4)
10
> (- (+ 3 4) 7)
0
> (* (+ 2 5) (- 7 (/ 21 7)))
28
> (= (+ 2 3) 5)
t
> (> (* 5 6) (+ 4 5))
t
```

These examples illustrate the behavior of LISP when evaluating simple arithmetic expressions. All modern LISP implementations provide a rich collection of such arithmetic functions, including operators for both real and integer arithmetic.

Several of the examples have arguments that are themselves lists, such as (- (+ 3 4) 7). This indicates the composition of functions, in this case "subtract 7 from the *result* of adding 3 to 4." The word "result" is emphasized here to indicate that the function - is not passed the s-expression "(+ 3 4)" as an argument but rather the result of *evaluating* that expression.

In evaluating a function, LISP first evaluates its arguments and then applies the function indicated by the first element of the expression to the results of these evaluations. If the arguments are themselves function expressions, LISP applies this rule recursively to their evaluation. Since this rule is applied recursively when the arguments are evaluated, LISP allows nested function calls of arbitrary depth. It is important to remember that by default, LISP evaluates everything. LISP uses the convention that numbers always evaluate to themselves. If, for example, 5 is typed into the LISP interpreter, LISP will respond with 5. Symbols, such as x, may have a value *bound* to them. If a symbol is bound, the binding is returned when the symbol is evaluated (one way in which symbols become bound is in a function call; see Section 7.1.2). If it is unbound, it is an error to evaluate the symbol.

For example, in evaluating the expression (+ (* 2 3) (* 3 5)), LISP first evaluates the arguments, (* 2 3) and (* 3 5). In evaluating (* 2 3), LISP evaluates the arguments 2 and 3, which return their respective arithmetic values; these values are multiplied to yield 6. Similarly, (* 3 5) evaluates to 15. These results are then passed to the top-level

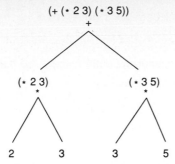

Figure 7.1 Tree diagram of the evaluation of a simple LISP function.

addition, which is then evaluated, returning 21. A diagram of this evaluation appears in Figure 7.1.

The concepts of this section are summarized in the following definition:

DEFINITION

An s-expression is defined recursively:

1. An atom is an s-expression.
2. If $s_1, s_2, \ldots, s_n$ are s-expressions, then so is (s_1 s_2 ... s_n).

A list is a nonatomic s-expression.

A form is an s-expression that is intended to be evaluated. If it is a list, the first element is treated as the function name and the subsequent elements are evaluated to obtain the function arguments.

In evaluating an s-expression:

If the s-expression is a number, return the value of the number.

If the s-expression is an atomic symbol, return the value bound to that symbol; if it is not bound it is an error.

If the s-expression is a list, evaluate the second through the last arguments and apply the function indicated by the first argument to the results.

It is important to note that both programs and data in LISP are represented as s-expressions. Not only does this make the syntax of the language very simple but also, when combined with the ability to to control the evaluation of s-expressions, it makes it easy to write programs that treat other LISP programs as data. This simplifies the implementation of interpreters in LISP.

7.1.2   Programming in LISP: Creating New Functions

All modern LISP dialects support a large number of built-in functions, including:

A full range of arithmetic functions, supporting both integers and real numbers.

A variety of looping and program control functions.

List manipulation and other data structuring functions.

Input/output functions.

Forms for the control of function evaluation.

Functions for the control of the LISP environment and operating system.

LISP includes too many functions to list in this chapter; for a more detailed discussion of LISP functions, consult a specialized LISP text or the manual for your particular LISP implementation.

In LISP, we program by defining new functions in the LISP environment; we build up application programs from this already rich repertoire of built-in functions. These new functions are defined in terms of existing functions using the LISP form **defun**, which is short for **define function**. Once a function is defined using **defun**, it may be used in the same fashion as functions that are built into the language.

Suppose, for example, the user would like to define a function called **square** that takes a single argument and returns the square of that argument. **square** may be created by having LISP evaluate the following expression:

```
(defun square (x)
    (* x x))
```

The first argument to a **defun** is the name of the function being defined; the second is a list of the formal parameters for that function, which must all be symbolic atoms; the remaining arguments are s-expressions, which constitute the body of the new function, the LISP code that actually defines its behavior. Unlike most LISP functions, **defun** does not evaluate its arguments; instead, it uses them as specifications to create a new function. As with all LISP functions, however, **defun** returns a value, although the value returned is simply the name of the new function.

The important result of evaluating a **defun** is the side effect of creating a new function and adding it to the LISP environment. In the above example, **square** is defined as a function that takes one argument and returns the result of multiplying that argument by itself. Once a function is defined, it must be called with the same number of arguments, or "actual parameters," as there are formal parameters specified in the **defun**. When a function is called, the actual parameters are bound to the formal parameters. The body of the function is then evaluated with these bindings. For example, the call **(square 5)** causes **5** to be bound to the formal parameter **x** in the body of the definition. When the body **(* x x)** is evaluated, LISP first evaluates the arguments to the function. Since **x** is bound to **5** by the call, this leads to the evaluation of **(* 5 5)**.

More concisely, the syntax of a **defun** expression is:

```
(defun <function name> (<formal parameters>) <function body>)
```

(This notational convention will be used throughout the text to define LISP forms, with descriptions of the elements of a form being enclosed in angle brackets, <>.) Note that the formal parameters in a **defun** are enclosed in a list.

A newly defined function may be used just like any built-in function. Suppose, for example, that a function is needed to compute the length of the hypotenuse of a right triangle given the lengths of the other two sides. This function may be defined according to the Pythagorean theorem, using the previously defined **square** function along with the built-in function **sqrt**. Comments are included in the example. LISP supports "end of line comments"; it ignores all text from the first ";" to the end of the same line.

```
(defun hypotenuse (x y)    ; the length of the hypotenuse is
   (sqrt  (+ (square x)    ; the square root of the sum of
            (square y))))  ; the squares of the other sides.
```

This example is typical in that most LISP programs are built up of relatively small functions, each performing a single well-defined task. Once defined, these functions are used to implement higher-level functions until the desired "top-level" function has been defined.

7.1.3   Program Control in LISP: Conditionals and Predicates

LISP branching is based on function evaluation. Consider, for example, the following definition of the absolute value function using the LISP form, **cond**:

```
(defun abs (x)
     (cond ((< x 0) (* x -1))  ; if x is negative, multiply it by -1
           ((>= x 0) x)))   ; otherwise return x unchanged.
```

cond takes as arguments a number of *condition-action pairs*:

```
( cond ( <condition₁> <action₁> )
       ( <condition₂> <action₂> )
       . . .
       ( <conditionₙ> <actionₙ> ))
```

These pairs may be arbitrary s-expressions, and each pair is enclosed in parentheses. Like **defun**, **cond** does not evaluate all of its arguments according to the LISP default. Instead, it first evaluates the conditions in order until one of them returns a non-nil value. When this occurs, the associated action is evaluated and this result is returned as the value of the **cond** expression. None of the other actions and none of the subsequent conditions are evaluated. If all of the conditions evaluate to nil, the **cond** returns nil.

An alternative definition of the absolute value function, **abs**, is:

```
(defun abs (x)
     (cond ((< x 0) (* -1 x))   ; if x is less than 0, return -x
           (t x)))              ; otherwise, return x
```

This version notes that the second condition, (>= x 0), is always true if the first is false. The "t" atom in the final condition of the cond statement is a built-in LISP atom that roughly corresponds to "true." By convention, t always evaluates to itself; this causes the last action to be evaluated if "(< x 0)" returns nil. This construct is extremely useful, as it provides a way of giving a cond statement a default action that is evaluated if and only if t he preceding conditions all return nil. It is used frequently in LISP code as a way of giving a conditional a final "else" action.

Although any evaluable s-expressions may be used as the conditions of a cond, generally these are a particular kind of LISP function called a *predicate*. A predicate is simply a function that returns a value of either true or false depending on whether or not its arguments possess some property. The most obvious examples of predicates are the relational operators typically used in arithmetic such as =, >, and >=. Here are some examples of arithmetic predicates in LISP:

```
> (= 9 (+ 4 5))
t
> (>= 17 4)
t
> (< 8 (+ 4 2))
nil
> (oddp 3)          ; oddp tests whether its argument is odd or not
t
> (minusp 6)        ; minusp tests whether its argument is less than 0
nil
> (numberp 17)   ; numberp tests whether its argument is numeric
t
> (numberp nil)
nil
> (zerop 0)
t
```

One interesting thing about the above examples is that the predicates do not return "true" or "false" but rather t or nil. Actually, LISP is defined so that a predicate may return nil to indicate "false" and anything other than nil (not necessarily t) to indicate "true." An example of this is the member predicate, which is defined later in the chapter. member takes two arguments, the second of which must be a list, and determines whether the first s-expression is a member of the second. If it is not, member returns nil; if it is, member returns the suffix of the second argument, which contains the first argument as its initial element. For example:

```
> (member 3 '(1 2 3 4 5))
(3 4 5)
```

One rationale for this convention is that it allows a predicate to return a value that, in the "true" case, may be of use in further processing. It also allows any LISP function to be used as a condition in a cond form. (This particular aspect of the language is actually the source of some controversy, since allowing predicates to return values other than "true" and "false" does cloud the semantics of the language. While this debate will doubtless continue, it is a small issue and of little importance to the utility of the language.)

In addition to cond, LISP offers a wide selection of alternative branching constructs, including an if form, which provides a simpler syntax for two-way branches, and a number of iterative constructs such as do and while loops. Although these functions provide LISP programmers with a wide range of control structures that fit almost any situation and programming style, we will not discuss them in this section; the reader is again referred to a more specialized LISP text for this information.

However, one of the more interesting program control techniques in LISP involves the use of the logical connectives and, or, and not. not takes one argument and returns t if its argument is nil and nil otherwise. Both and and or may take any number of arguments and behave as you would expect from the definitions of the corresponding logical operators. It is important to note, however, that and and or are based on *conditional evaluation.*

In evaluating an and form, LISP evaluates its arguments in left-to-right sequence, stopping when any one of the arguments evaluates to nil or the last argument has been evaluated. Upon completion, the and form returns the value of the last argument evaluated. It therefore returns non-nil only if all its arguments return non-nil. Similarly, the or form evaluates its arguments only until a non-nil value is encountered, returning this value as a result. Both functions may leave some of their arguments unevaluated, as may be seen by the behavior of the print statements in the following example. (Note that in addition to printing its argument, print returns a value of nil on completion.)

```
> (and (oddp 2) (print "second statement was evaluated "))
nil
> (and (oddp 3) (print "second statement was evaluated "))
second statement was evaluated nil

> (or (oddp 3) (print "second statement was evaluated "))
nil
> (or (oddp 2) (print "second statement was evaluated "))
second statement was evaluated nil
```

Since (oddp 2) evaluates to nil in the first of the above expressions, the and simply returns nil without evaluating the print form. In the second expression, however, (oddp 3) evaluates to t and the and form then evaluates the print. A similar analysis may be applied to the or examples. It is important to be aware of this behavior, particularly if some of the arguments are forms whose evaluations have side affects. (Sources of possible side effects, in addition to the print function, may include changes in a global variable, as discussed in Section 7.1.8.)

The conditional evaluation of logical connectives makes them useful in controlling the flow of execution of LISP programs. For example, an or form may be used to try several alternative solutions to a problem, evaluating them in order until one of them returns a non-nil result. An example of this may be found in the implementation of the farmer, wolf, goat, and cabbage problem at the end of this chapter.

7.1.4 Functions, Lists, and Symbolic Computing

Although the preceding sections have introduced LISP syntax and demonstrated a few useful LISP functions, they have done so in the context of simple arithmetic examples. The real power of LISP, however, is in symbolic computing and is based on the use of lists to construct arbitrarily complex data structures of symbolic and numeric atoms, along with the forms needed for manipulating them. We illustrate the ease with which LISP handles symbolic data structures, as well as the naturalness of data abstraction techniques in LISP with a simple data base example. Our data base application requires the manipulation of employee records containing name, salary, and employee number fields.

These records are represented as lists, with the name, salary, and number fields as the first, second, and third elements of a list. The individual fields of the record are accessed through a built-in LISP form called nth. nth takes two arguments, a number and a list, and returns the ''numberth'' element of that list. For example:

```
> (nth 0 '(a b c d))  ; note that nth begins numbering with 0.
a
> (nth 2 '(a b c d))
c
```

The single quote, ', that appears in the above examples is used to prevent evaluation of s-expressions that represent data rather than programs. It will be discussed in greater detail shortly.

Using nth, it is possible to define access functions for the various fields of a data record. For example:

```
(defun name-field (record)
    (nth 0 record))
```

will have the behavior:

```
> (name-field '((Ada Lovelace) 45000.00 38519))
(Ada Lovelace)
```

Similarly, the functions salary-field and number-field may be defined to access the appropriate fields of a data record. Also, since a name is itself a list containing two elements, a first name and a last name, it is useful to define functions that take a name as argument and return either the first or last name as a result.

```
(defun first-name (name)
    (nth 0 name))
```

will have the behavior:

```
> (first-name (name-field '((Ada Lovelace) 45000.00 338519)))
Ada
```

In addition to accessing individual fields of a data record, it is also necessary to implement functions to create and modify data records. These are defined using the built-in LISP function list. List takes any number of arguments, evaluates them, and returns a list containing those values as its elements. For example:

```
> (list 1 2 3 4)
(1 2 3 4)
> (list '(Ada Lovelace) 45000.00 338519)
((Ada Lovelace) 45000.00 338519)
```

As the second of these examples suggests, list may be used to define a basic record constructor for the data base, that is, a function that takes a name, salary, and employee number as arguments and returns an employee record as a result:

```
(defun build-record (name salary emp-number)
    (list name salary emp-number))
```

will have the behavior:

```
> (build-record '(Alan Turing) 50000.00 135772)
((Alan Turing) 50000.00 135772)
```

Now, using build-record and the access functions, we may construct functions that return a modified copy of a record. For example:

```
(defun replace-salary-field (record new-salary)
    ( build-record (name-field record)
                   new-salary
                   (number-field record)))
```

will behave:

```
> (replace-salary-field '((Ada Lovelace) 45000.00 338519) 50000.00)
((Ada Lovelace) 50000.00 338519)
```

Notice that this function does not actually update the record itself, but produces a modified copy of the record, sort of a ''copy-update.'' This updated version may be saved by binding it to a global variable using a setq (Section 7.1.7). Although LISP provides forms that allow a particular element in a list to be modified ''in place,'' these operations are somewhat tricky and are not covered in this text. For LISP applications involving all but extremely large structures, modifications are generally done by creating a new copy of the structure.

In the above examples, we have created an abstract data type for employee records. Later sections of this chapter introduce the functions and techniques needed to write code for searching and maintaining large collections of such records. By using the various access and update functions defined in this section, this code may be implemented using a specialized language appropriate to the meaning of the records, without requiring that the programmer be constantly aware of the actual list structures being used to implement the records. This simplifies the later development of higher-level code, as well as making that code much easier to maintain and understand.

Generally, AI programs use large amounts of varied knowledge about ''real-world'' domains. The data structures used to represent this knowledge, such as frames and semantic networks, are complex, and humans generally find it easier to relate to this knowledge in terms of its meaning rather than the particular syntax of its internal representation. Therefore, data abstraction techniques, always good computer science, are essential tools for the AI programmer. Because of the ease with which LISP supports the definition of new functions, it is an ideal language for data abstraction.

7.1.5 Control of LISP Evaluation: quote and eval

In the previous section, several of the examples included arguments that were lists preceded by a single quotation mark, '. The purpose of the quote is to prevent evaluation of an s-expression that should be treated as data rather than an evaluable form. As mentioned in Section 7.1.1, in evaluating an s-expression, LISP will first try to evaluate all of its arguments. If the LISP interpreter was given the expression (nth 0 (a b c d)), it would first try to evaluate the argument (a b c d). This attempted evaluation would result in an error, since a, the first element of this s-expression, does not represent any known LISP function.

To prevent this erroneous evaluation, LISP provides the user with the built-in function quote. quote is a LISP form that simply takes one argument and returns that argument without evaluating it. For example:

```
> (quote (a b c))
(a b c)
> (quote (+ 1 3))
(+ 1 3)
```

Because quote is used so often, LISP allows it to be abbreviated by a single quotation mark, '. Thus, the preceding example could be written:

```
> '(a b c)
(a b c)
> '(+ 1 3)
(+ 1 3)
```

In general, quote is used to prevent the evaluation of arguments to a function when these arguments are intended to be treated as data rather than evaluable forms. In the earlier examples of simple LISP arithmetic, quote was not needed, since numbers always evaluate to themselves. Consider the effect of quote in the following two calls to the list function:

```
> (list (+ 1 2) (+ 3 4))
(3 7)
```

```
> (list '(+ 1 2) '(+ 3 4))
((+ 1 2) (+ 3 4))
```

In the first example, the arguments are not quoted; they are therefore evaluated and passed to list according to the default LISP evaluation scheme. In the second example, quote prevents this evaluation, with the s-expressions themselves being passed on to list. Even though (+ 1 2) is a meaningful LISP form, quote prevents its evaluation. The ability to prevent evaluation of programs and manipulate them as data is an important feature of LISP.

As a complement to quote, LISP also provides a function, eval, that allows the programmer to evaluate an s-expression at will. eval takes one s-expression as an argument: this argument is evaluated as is usual for arguments to functions; however, the result is then evaluated *again* and this final result is returned as the value of the eval expression. Examples of the behavior of eval and quote include:

```
> (quote (+ 2 3))
(+ 2 3)
> (eval (quote (+ 2 3)))  ; eval undoes the effect of quote
5
> (list '* 2 5)          ; this constructs an evaluable s-expression
(* 2 5)
> (eval (list '* 2 5))  ; this constructs and evaluates it
10
```

The eval function is precisely what is used by LISP in the ordinary evaluation of s-expressions. By making this function available to the programmer, LISP greatly simplifies the development of *meta-interpreters*. This important programming methodology is illustrated in the ''infix-interpreter'' of Section 7.6 and the design of an expert system shell in Chapter 13.

7.1.6 Lists as Recursive Structures

In the previous section, we used the list manipulation functions nth and list to implement access functions for records in a simple "employee" data base. Since all employee records were of a determinate length (three elements), these two functions were sufficient to access the fields of records. However, they are not adequate for performing operations on lists of unknown length, such as searching through an unknown number of employee records. To manipulate lists of indeterminate length, we must be able to scan down a list iteratively or recursively, terminating when certain conditions are met (e.g., the desired record is found) or the list is exhausted. In this section we introduce list operations, along with the use of recursion to create list processing functions. Although LISP includes a number of constructs for doing explicit iteration, the fundamentally recursive structure of lists makes recursion a natural vehicle for list manipulation, and it is the primary technique of this text.

The basic functions for accessing the components of lists are car and cdr. car takes a single argument, which must be a list, and returns the first element of that list. cdr also takes a single argument, which must be a list, and returns that list with its first argument removed. For example:

```
> (car '(a b c))    ; note that the list is quoted
a
> (cdr '(a b c))
(b c)
> (car '((a b) (c d)))    ; the first element of a list may be a list
(a b)
> (cdr '((a b) (c d)))
((c d))
> (car (cdr '(a b c d)))
b
```

The way in which car and cdr operate suggests a recursive approach to manipulating list structures:

To perform an operation on each of the elements of a list:

1. *If the list is empty, quit.*

2. *Perform the operation on the first element of the list, and recur on the remainder of the list.*

Using this scheme, we can define a member function that takes two arguments, an arbitrary s-expression and a list. It returns nil if the s-expression is not a member of the list; otherwise it returns the portion of the list containing the s-expression as its first element:

```
(defun member (element list)
   (cond ((null list) nil)                   ; element not in list
         ((equal element (car list)) list)   ; element found
         (t (member element (cdr list)))))   ; recursive step
```

member has the behavior

```
> (member 4 '(1 2 3 4 5 6))
(4 5 6)
> (member 5 '(a b c d))
nil
```

Additional examples of functions that may be defined using this recursive scheme include length, a function for taking the length of a list and nth. Although both of these functions are already built into Common LISP, they may easily be defined in the language.

```
(defun length (list)
   (cond ((null list) 0)
         (t (+ (length (cdr list) 1)))))
```

```
(defun nth (n list)
   (cond ((zerop n) (car list))        ; zerop tests if its argument is zero.

         (t (nth (- n 1) (cdr list))))))
```

In addition to the functions car and cdr, LISP provides a number of functions for constructing lists. One of these, list, which takes as arguments any number of s-expressions, evaluates them, and returns a list of the results, was introduced in Section 7.1.3. A more primitive list constructor is the function cons. cons takes two s-expressions as arguments and returns a list whose car is the first argument and whose cdr is the second:

```
> (cons 1 '(2 3 4))
(1 2 3 4)
> (cons '(a b) '(c d e))
((a b) c d e)
```

cons bears an inverse relationship to car and cdr in that the car of the value returned by a cons form is always the first argument to the cons, and the cdr of the value returned by a cons form is always the second argument to that form:

```
> (car (cons 1 '(2 3 4)))
1
> (cdr (cons 1 '(2 3 4)))
(2 3 4)
```

An example of the use of cons is seen in the definition of the function filter-negatives, which takes a list of numbers as an argument and returns that list with any negative numbers removed. filter-negatives recursively examines each element of the list; if the first element is negative, it is discarded and the function returns the result of filtering the negative numbers from the cdr of the list. If the first element of the list is positive, it is consed onto the result of filtering negatives from the rest of the list:

```
(defun filter-negatives (number-list)
   (cond ((null number-list) nil)        ; termination condition
         ((plusp (car number-list)) (cons (car number-list)
                                    (filter-negatives (cdr number-list))))
         (t (filter-negatives (cdr number-list)))))
```

which behaves:

```
> (filter-negatives '(1 -1 2 -2 3 -4))
(1 2 3)
```

This example is typical of the way cons is often used in recursive functions on lists. car and cdr tear lists apart and "drive" the recursion; cons selectively constructs the result as the recursion "unwinds." Another example of this use of cons is:

```
(defun append (list1 list2)
  (cond ((null list1) list2)
        (t (cons (car list1) (append (cdr list1) list2)))))
```

which yields the behavior:

```
> (append '(1 2 3) '(4 5 6))
(1 2 3 4 5 6)
```

Note that the same recursive scheme is used in the definitions of append, length, and member. In each definition, the cdr function is used to remove an element from the list, allowing a recursive call on the shortened list, with the recursion "bottoming out" on the empty list. Recursion is used to go down the list, element by element; as the recursion is unwound, the answer is formed, with the cons function used to reassemble the appended lists in append, just as the + function is used to assemble a total in the length function. This particular recursive scheme is known as *cdr recursion*, since it uses the cdr function to move across the elements of a list, and is an important tool for operations that linearly scan the elements of a list.

7.1.7 Nested Lists, Structure, and car / cdr Recursion

Although both cons and append may be used to combine smaller lists into a single list, it is important to note the difference between these two functions. If cons is called with two lists as arguments, it makes the first of these a new first element of the second, whereas append returns a list whose elements are the elements of the two arguments:

```
> (cons '(1 2) '(3 4))
((1 2) 3 4)
> (append '(1 2) '(3 4))
(1 2 3 4)
```

It is important to distinguish between the lists (1 2 3 4) and ((1 2) 3 4), which have fundamentally different structures.

This difference may be noted graphically by exploiting the isomorphism between lists and trees. The simplest way to map lists onto trees is to create an unlabeled node for each list, with descendants equal to the elements of that list. This rule is applied recursively to the elements of the list that are themselves lists; elements that are atoms are mapped onto leaf nodes of the tree. Thus, the two lists mentioned above generate the different tree structures illustrated in Figure 7.2.

This example illustrates the representational power of lists, particularly as a means of representing any tree structure such as a search tree or a parse tree (Fig. 7.1). In addition, nested lists provide a way of hierarchically structuring complex data. In the

Figure 7.2 Mapping lists onto trees, showing structural differences.

employee records example of Section 7.1.4, the name field was itself a list consisting of a first name and a last name. This list could be treated as a single entity or its individual components could be accessed.

The simple cdr-recursive scheme discussed in the previous section is not sufficient to implement all manipulations on nested lists, since it does not distinguish between items that are lists and those that are simple atoms. Suppose, for example, that the length function defined in Section 7.1.6 is applied to a nested list structure:

```
> (length '((1 2) 3 (1 (4 (5)))))
3
```

In the above example, length returns 3 since the list has 3 elements, (1 2), 3, and (1 (4 (5))). This is, of course, the correct and desired behavior for a length function. If we had wanted the function to count the number of *atoms* in the list, however, we would have needed a different recursive scheme, one that, in addition to scanning along the elements of the list, "opens up" nonatomic list elements and recursively applies itself to the task of counting their atoms. This function, which will be called count-atoms, is defined:

```
(defun count-atoms (list)
  (cond ((null list) 0)
        ((atom list) 1)
        (t (+ (count-atoms ( car list))   ; open up an element
              (count-atoms (cdr list))))))  ; scan down the list
```

which behaves:

```
> (count-atoms '((1 2) 3 (((4 5 (6))))))
6
```

The above definition is an example of car-cdr *recursion*. Instead of just recurring on the cdr of the list, count-atoms also recurs on the car of its argument, with the + function combining the two components into an answer. Recursion halts when it encounters an atom or empty list. One way of thinking of this scheme is that it adds a second dimension to simple cdr-recursion, that of "going down into" each of the list elements. Compare the diagrams of calls to length and count-atoms in Figure 7.3.

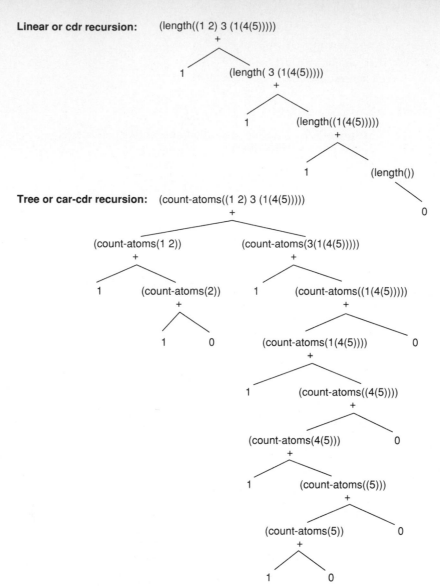

Linear or cdr recursion: (length((1 2) 3 (1(4(5)))))

Tree or car-cdr recursion: (count-atoms((1 2) 3 (1(4(5)))))

Figure 7.3 Diagrams of linear and tree recursive executions.

Note the similarity between the structure of car-cdr recursion and the recursive definition of s-expressions given in Section 7.1.1.

Another example of the use of car-cdr recursion is in the definition of the function flatten. flatten takes as argument a list of arbitrary structure and returns a list that consists of the same atoms in the same order but with all the atoms at the same level. Note the similarity between the definition of flatten and that of count-atoms; both use car-cdr recursion to tear apart lists and drive the recursion, both terminate when the argument is either null or atomic, and both use a second function (append or +) to construct an answer from the results of the recursive calls.

```
(defun flatten (lst)
  (cond ((null lst) nil)
        ((atom lst) (list lst))
        (t (append (flatten (car lst))(flatten (cdr lst))))))
```

Examples of calls to flatten include:

```
> (flatten '(a (b c) (((d) e f))))
(a b c d e f)
> (flatten '(a b c))   ; this list is already flattened
(a b c)
> (flatten '(1 (2 3) (4 (5 6) 7)))
(1 2 3 4 5 6 7)
```

car-cdr recursion is the basis of our implementation of unification in Section 7.6.

7.1.8 Functional Programming, Side Effects, setq, and let

It has been stated that LISP is based on the theory of recursive functions; early LISP was the first example of a functional or *applicative* programming language. An important aspect of purely functional languages is the lack of any side effects as a result of function execution. This means that the value returned by a function call depends only on the function definition and the value of the parameters in the call. While LISP is based on mathematical functions, it is possible to define LISP forms that violate this important property. Consider the following LISP interaction:

```
> (f 4)
5
> (f 4)
6
> (f 4)
7
```

Note that f does not behave as a true function in that its output is not determined solely by the calling parameter; each time it is called with 4, it returns a different value. Execution of the function creates a side effect that influences the behavior of future calls. f is implemented using a LISP built-in function called setq:

```
(defun f (x)
  (setq inc (+ inc 1))
  (+ x inc))
```

setq takes two arguments, a symbol and an arbitrary s-expression. setq evaluates the second argument and binds this value to the first parameter. This binding is in the global LISP environment; it remains after the function has terminated. In the above example, if inc is first set to 0 (by the call (setq inc 0)), each subsequent evaluation will increment its parameter by one more than the previous evaluation.

Although this makes it possible to create LISP objects that are not pure functions in the mathematical sense, the ability to bind a value to a variable in the global environment is a useful feature. Many programming tasks are most naturally implemented using this ability to define objects whose state persists across function calls. The classic example of this is the "seed" in a random number generator: each call to the function changes and saves the value of the seed. Similarly, it would be natural for a data base program (such as was described in Section 7.1.3) to store the data base by binding it to a variable in the global environment.

So far, we have seen two ways of binding a value to a symbol: explicitly using setq, or implicitly when a function call binds the calling parameters to the formal parameters in the definition. In the examples seen so far, all variables in a function body were either *bound* or *free*. A bound variable is one that appears as a formal parameter in the definition of the function, while a free variable is one that appears in the body of the function but is not a formal parameter. When a function is called, any bindings that a bound variable may have in the global environment are saved and the variable is rebound to the calling parameter. After the function has completed execution, the original bindings are restored. Thus, setting the value of a bound variable inside a function body has no effect on the global bindings of that variable, as illustrated by the following LISP interaction:

```
> (defun foo (x)
   (setq x (+ x 1))   ; increment bound variable x
    x)    ; return its value
foo
> (setq y 1)
1
> (foo y)
2
> y     ; note that value of y is unchanged
1
```

In the earlier example, x was bound in the function f, while inc was free in that function. As we demonstrated in the example, free variables in a function definition are the primary source of side effects in functions.

Another useful function for explicitly controlling the binding of variables is the let function. let allows the creation of local variables. As an example of the use of let, consider a function to compute the roots of a quadratic equation. This function takes as arguments the three parameters (a, b, and c) of the equation

$$ax^2+bx+c=0$$

and returns a list of the two roots of the equation. For example:

```
> (quad-roots 1 2 1)
(-1.0 -1.0)
> (quad-roots 1 6 8)
(-2.0 -4.0)
```

These roots would be calculated from the formula

$$x = \frac{-b \pm \sqrt{b^2 - 4ac}}{2a}$$

In computing the two roots, the value of

$$\sqrt{b^2 - 4ac}$$

is used twice. For reasons of efficiency, as well as elegance, we should compute this value only once, saving it in a variable for use in computing the two roots. Based on this idea, an initial implementation of quad-roots might be:

```
(defun quad-roots-1 (a b c)
  (setq temp (sqrt (- (* b b) (* 4 a c))))
  (list (/ (+ (- b) temp) (* 2 a))
        (/ (- (- b) temp) (* 2 a)))))
```

Note that the above implementation assumes that the equation does not have imaginary roots, since attempting to take the square root of a negative number would cause the sqrt function to halt with an error condition. Modifying the code to handle this case is straightforward and not relevant to this discussion. Although, with this exception, the code is correct, evaluation of the function body will have the side effect of setting the value of temp in the global environment:

```
> (quad-roots-1 1 2 1)
(-1.0 -1.0)
> temp
0.0
```

It is much more desirable to make temp local to the function quad-roots, thereby eliminating this side effect. This can be done through the use of a let block. A let expression has the syntax:

(let (<local-variables>) <expressions>)

where the elements of (<local-variables>) are either symbolic atoms or pairs of the form:

(<symbol> <expression>)

When a let form (or block) is evaluated, it establishes a local environment consisting of all of the symbols in (<local-variables>). If a symbol is the first element of a pair, the second element is evaluated and the symbol is bound to this result; symbols that are not included in pairs are bound to nil. If any of these symbols are already bound in the global environment, these global bindings are saved and restored when the let block terminates.

After these local bindings are established, the <expressions> are evaluated in order within this environment. When the let statement terminates, it returns the value of the last expression evaluated within the block.

The behavior of the let block is illustrated by the following example:

```
> (setq a 0)
0
> (let ((a 3) b)
    (setq b 4)
    (+ a b))
7
> a
0
> b
ERROR - b is not bound at top level.
```

In this example, before the let block is executed, a is bound to 0 and b is unbound at the top-level environment. When the let is evaluated, a is bound to 3 and b is bound to nil. The setq binds b to 4, and the sum of a and b is returned by the let statement. Upon termination of the let, a and b are restored to their previous values, including the unbound status of b.

Using the let statement, quad-roots is implemented with no global side effects:

```
(defun quad-roots-2 (a b c)
  (let (temp)
      (setq temp (sqrt (- (* b b) (* 4 a c))))
      (list (/ (+ (- b) temp) (* 2 a))
          (quotient (- (- b) temp) (* 2 a)))))
```

Alternatively, temp may be bound when it is declared in the let statement, giving a somewhat more concise implementation of quad-roots. In this final version, the denominator of the formula, 2a, is also computed once and saved in a local variable, denom:

```
(defun quad-roots-3 (a b c)
  (let ((temp (sqrt (- (* b b) (* 4 a c))))
        (denom (* 2 a)))
      (list (/ (+ (- b) temp) denom)
          (/ (- (- b) temp) denom))))
```

In addition to avoiding side effects, quad-roots-3 is the most efficient of the three versions, since it does not recompute values unnecessarily.

The preceding few pages are not a complete description of LISP. Instead, they supplement the reader's knowledge of LISP with a discussion of interesting features of the language that will be of use in implementing AI data structures and algorithms. These features include:

1. The naturalness with which LISP supports a data abstraction approach to programming.
2. The use of lists to create symbolic data structures.
3. The use of cond and recursion to control program flow.
4. The recursive nature of list structures and the recursive schemes involved in their manipulation.
5. The use of quote and eval to control function evaluation.
6. The use of setq and let to control variable bindings and side effects.

The remainder of this chapter builds on these ideas to demonstrate the use of LISP for typical AI programming tasks such as pattern matchers and search algorithms.

7.2 Search Algorithms in LISP: A Functional Approach to the Farmer, Wolf, Goat, and Cabbage Problem

As an introduction to AI programming in LISP, we solve the farmer, wolf, goat, and cabbage problem:

A farmer with his wolf, goat, and cabbage come to the edge of a river they wish to cross. There is a boat at the river's edge, but, of course, only the farmer can row it. The boat also can carry only two things (including the rower) at a time. If the wolf is ever left alone with the goat, the wolf will eat the goat, similarly, if the goat is left alone with the cabbage, the goat will eat the cabbage. Devise a sequence of crossings of the river so that all four characters arrive safely on the other side of the river.

This problem was first presented and solved in PROLOG in Chapter 6. The LISP version searches the same space and has structural similarities to the PROLOG solution; however, it differs in ways that reflect the procedural orientation of LISP.

The heart of the program is a set of functions that define states of the world as an abstract data type. These functions hide the internals of state representation from higher-level components of the program. Allowing the programmer to ignore the internals of state representation is, of course, just good software engineering; while such abstraction is not really necessary for this simple example, most AI programs involve complex representations that require this approach.

Internally, states are represented as lists of four elements, where each element denotes the location of the farmer, wolf, goat, or cabbage, respectively. Thus, (e w e w) represents the problem state in which the farmer (the first element) and the goat (the third element) are on the east bank and the wolf and cabbage are on the west bank. The basic functions defining the state data type will be a constructor, make-state, which takes as arguments the locations of the farmer, wolf, goat, and cabbage and returns a state, and four access functions, farmer-side, wolf-side, goat-side, and cabbage-side, which take a state and return the location of an individual. These functions are defined:

```
(defun make-state (f w g c) (list f w g c))

(defun farmer-side (state)
  (nth 0 state))

(defun wolf-side (state)
  (nth 1 state))

(defun goat-side (state)
  (nth 2 state))

(defun cabbage-side (state)
  (nth 3 state))
```

The rest of the program is built on these state access and construction functions. In particular, they are used to implement the four possible actions the farmer may take: rowing across the river either alone or with either the wolf, goat, or cabbage.

These functions use the access functions to tear a state apart into its components. A function called opposite (to be defined shortly) determines the new location of the individuals that cross the river, and make-state reassembles these into the new state. For example, the function farmer-takes-self may be defined:

```
(defun farmer-takes-self (state)
  (make-state (opposite (farmer-side state))
              (wolf-side state)
              (goat-side state)
              (cabbage-side state)))
```

Note that this function returns the new state, regardless of whether it is safe or not. A state is unsafe if the farmer has left the goat alone with the cabbage or left the wolf alone with the goat. The program must find a solution path that does not contain any unsafe states. Although this "safe" check may be done at a number of different stages of the program, our approach is to perform it in the move functions. This is implemented by using a function called safe; safe, which is also defined shortly, has the following behavior:

```
> (safe '(w w w w))      ; safe state, return unchanged.
(w w w w)
> (safe '(e w w e))      ; wolf eats goat, return nil.
nil
> (safe '(w w e e))      ; goat eats cabbage, return nil.
nil
```

safe is used in each move function to filter out the unsafe states. Thus, any move that moves to an unsafe state will return nil instead of that state. The recursive path algorithm can check for this nil and use it to prune that state. Using safe, a final definition of farmer-takes-self is:

```
(defun farmer-takes-self (state)
  (safe (make-state (opposite (farmer-side state))
        (wolf-side state)
        (goat-side state)
        (cabbage-side state))))
```

The remaining move functions are defined similarly but include a conditional test to determine whether the farmer and the prospective passenger are on the same side of the river. If a move cannot be made because the farmer and the passenger are not on the same bank, these functions return nil:

```
(defun farmer-takes-wolf (state)
  (cond ((equal (farmer-side state) (wolf-side state))
    (safe (make-state (opposite (farmer-side state))
      (opposite (wolf-side state))
      (goat-side state)
      (cabbage-side state))))
   (t nil)))

(defun farmer-takes-goat (state)
  (cond ((equal (farmer-side state) (goat-side state))
    (safe (make-state (opposite (farmer-side state))
      (wolf-side state)
      (opposite (goat-side state))
      (cabbage-side state))))
   (t nil)))

(defun farmer-takes-cabbage (state)
  (cond ((equal (farmer-side state) (cabbage-side state))
    (safe (make-state (opposite (farmer-side state))
      (wolf-side state)
      (goat-side state)
      (opposite (cabbage-side state)))))
   (t nil)))
```

These definitions use the state manipulation functions from above and a function opposite, which returns the opposite of a given side:

```
(defun opposite (side)
  (cond ((equal side 'e) 'w)
        ((equal side 'w) 'e)))
```

safe is defined using a cond to check for the two unsafe conditions: the farmer on the opposite bank from the wolf and the goat and the farmer on the opposite bank from the goat and the cabbage. If the state is safe, it is returned unchanged:

```
(defun safe (state)
  (cond ((and (equal (goat-side state) (wolf-side state))      ; wolf eats goat
              (not (equal (farmer-side state) (wolf-side state)))) nil)
        ((and (equal (goat-side state) (cabbage-side state))   ; goat eats cabbage
              (not (equal (farmer-side state) (goat-side state)))) nil)
    (t state)))
```

path implements the backtracking search of the state space. It takes as arguments a state and a goal and first checks to see if they are equal, indicating a successful termination of the search. If they are not equal, path generates all four of the neighboring states in the state space graph, calling itself recursively on each of these neighboring states in turn to try and find a path from them to a goal. Translating this simple definition directly into LISP will yield something like:

```
(defun path (state goal)
  (cond ((equal state goal) 'success)
        (t (or (path (farmer-takes-self state) goal)
               (path (farmer-takes-wolf state) goal)
               (path (farmer-takes-goat state) goal)
               (path (farmer-takes-cabbage state) goal)))))
```

This version of the path function is a simple translation of the recursive path algorithm from English into LISP and has several ''bugs'' that need to be corrected. It does, however, capture the essential structure of the algorithm and should be examined before continuing. The first test in the cond statement is for a successful completion. If this occurs, the recursion stops and the atom success is returned. Otherwise, path generates the four descendant nodes of the graph and calls itself on each of them in turn.

In particular, note the use of the or form to control evaluation of its arguments. Recall that an or evaluates its arguments in turn until one of them returns a non-nil value. When this occurs, the or terminates without evaluating the other arguments and returns this non-nil value as a result. Thus, the or not only is used as a logical operator but also provides a way of controlling branching. It is used here instead of a cond because the value that is being tested and the value that should be returned if the test is non-nil are the same.

One problem with this definition is that a move function may return a value of nil if the move may not be made or if it leads to an unsafe state. To prevent path from attempting to generate the children of a nil state, it must first check whether the current state is nil. If it is, path should return nil.

The other issue that needs to be addressed in the implementation of path is that of loops in the search space. If the above implementation of path is run, the farmer will soon find himself going back and forth alone between the two banks; i.e., the algorithm will be stuck in an infinite loop between identical states. To prevent this from happening, path is given a third parameter, been-list, a list of all the states that have already been visited. Each time that path is called recursively on a new state of the world, the parent state will be added to been-list. On entry to path the member predicate is used to make sure that the current state is not a member of been-list, i.e., that it has not already been visited. This is accomplished by checking the current state for membership in been-list before generating its descendants. path is now defined:

```
(defun path (state goal been-list)
  (cond ((null state) nil)
        ((equal state goal) (reverse (cons state been-list)))
        ((not (member state been-list :test #'equal))
          (or (path (farmer-takes-self state) goal (cons state been-list))
          (path (farmer-takes-wolf state) goal (cons state been-list))
          (path (farmer-takes-goat state) goal (cons state been-list))
          (path (farmer-takes-cabbage state) goal (cons state been-list))))))
```

In the above implementation, member is a Common LISP built-in function that behaves in essentially the same way as the member function defined in this chapter. The only difference is the inclusion of :test #'equal in the argument list. Unlike our "home-grown" member function, the Common LISP built-in form allows the programmer to specify the function that is used in testing for membership. This wrinkle increases the flexibility of the function and should not cause too much concern in this discussion.

Rather than having the function return just the atom success, it is better to have it return the actual solution path. Since the series of states on the solution path is already contained in the been-list, this list is returned instead. Because the goal is not already on been-list, it is consed onto the list; also, because the list is constructed in reverse order (with the start state as the last element), the list is reversed (constructed in reverse order using another LISP built-in function, reverse) prior to returning it.

Finally, because the been-list parameter should be kept "hidden" from the user, a top-level calling function may be written that takes as arguments a start and a goal state and calls path with a nil value of been-list:

```
(defun solve-fwgc (state goal) (path state goal nil))
```

Let us compare the LISP version of the farmer, wolf, goat, and cabbage problem with the PROLOG solution presented in Chapter 6. Not only does the LISP program solve the same problem, it also searches exactly the same state space as the PROLOG version. This underscores the point that the state space conceptualization of a problem is independent of the implementation of a program for searching that space. Because both programs search the same space, the two implementations have strong similarities; the differences tend to be subtle but provide an interesting contrast between declarative and procedural programming styles.

States in the PROLOG version are represented using a predicate, state(e,e,e,e), and the LISP implementation uses a list. These two representations are more than syntactic variations on one another. The LISP representation of state is defined not only by its list syntax but also by the access and move functions that constitute the abstract data type "state." In general, the extensibility of LISP, combined with the representational flexibility of lists, makes data abstraction natural in LISP programs. In the PRO-LOG version, states are patterns; their meaning is determined by the way in which they match other patterns in PROLOG rules, which indeed, could also be lists.

The LISP version of path is slightly longer than the PROLOG version. One reason for this is that the LISP version must explicitly implement a search strategy while the PROLOG version takes advantage of PROLOG's built-in search algorithm. The control algorithm is explicit in the LISP version but is implicit in the PROLOG version.

In conclusion, a comparison of LISP and PROLOG is more a matter of understanding the trade-offs made in each language than of selecting one language as "better" than the other. Because PROLOG is built on declarative representation and theorem-proving techniques, the PROLOG program is more concise and has a flavor of describing the problem domain, without directly implementing the search algorithm. The price paid for this conciseness is that much of the program's behavior is hidden, determined by PROLOG's built-in inference strategies. Programmers may also feel more pressure to make the problem solution conform to PROLOG's representational formalism and search strategies. LISP, on the other hand, allows greater flexibility for the programmer. The price paid here is that the programmer cannot draw on a built-in representation or search strategy and must implement this explicitly in the algorithm.

7.3   Search Strategies in LISP

7.3.1   Breadth-First Search

In the previous example, a depth-first search solution to the farmer, wolf, goat, and cabbage problem, we presented a recursive backtrack algorithm. Now we implement the search algorithms from Chapter 4, using open and closed lists to manage search through the state space.

The LISP implementation of breadth-first search follows the algorithm of Chapter 4, maintaining the *open* list as a first in first out structure. We maintain *open* and *closed* as global variables. This is done for reasons of efficiency, avoiding the overhead of passing large *open* and *closed* lists as parameters to each call to breadth-first-search. By convention, global variables in Common LISP are written to begin and end with *. Breadth-first-search is defined:

```
(defun breadth-first-search (goal)
  (cond ((null *open*) nil)
        ((equal (car *open*)goal) 'success)
        (t (setq *closed* (cons (car *open*) *closed*))
           (setq *open* (append (cdr *open*)
                                (eliminate-duplicates
                                  (generate-descendants
                                    (car *open*)))))
           (breadth-first-search goal))))
```

In this algorithm, the *open* list is tested: if it is nil, the algorithm returns nil, indicating failure; otherwise it examines the first element of *open*. If this is equal to the goal, the algorithm halts and returns success; otherwise, it produces the children of the current state, adds them to the *open* list and recurs. The function eliminate-duplicates removes any children which already appear on *open* or *closed*. This prevents wasted effort, since any duplicate states will have already been reached along a shorter path from the start state.

generate-descendants takes a state and returns its descendants; the particulars of generate-descendants depend on the particular problem being solved; an example of its implementation for the farmer, wolf, goat, and cabbage problem is:

```
(defun generate-descendants (state)
    (delete nil (list (farmer-takes-self state)
                (farmer-takes-wolf state)
                (farmer-takes-goat state)
                (farmer-takes-cabbage state))))
```

This function constructs a list of all descendants of the parameter state. Because some of these may equal nil, the LISP built-in delete is used to remove occurrences of nil from the list.

eliminate-duplicates takes a list of children and returns this list, minus any states that already appear on either *open* or *closed*. It does this through a cdr-recursive search down the list of children, retaining only those states that are not members of *open* or *closed*. eliminate-duplicates is defined:

```
(defun eliminate-duplicates (children)
    (cond ((null children) nil)
            ((member (car children) *open*)
                    (eliminate-duplicates (cdr children)))
            ((member (car children) *closed*)
                    (eliminate-duplicates (cdr children)))
            (t (cons (car children)
                    (eliminate-duplicates (cdr children))))))
```

By appropriately defining generate-descendants, this search algorithm may be used to search any state space in a breadth-first fashion. It is called with *open* initialized to contain the start state, *closed* bound to nil and goal set to the goal state. A top level calling function that performs these initializations may be defined:

```
(defun solve (start goal)
    (setq *open* (list (make-tuple start nil)))
    (setq *closed* nil)
    (breadth-first-search goal))
```

One difficulty that remains with this algorithm is its inability to print the list of states along the path from a start to a goal. Although all the states that lead to the goal are present in the closed list when the algorithm halts, these are mixed with all other states from earlier levels of the search space. The algorithm can be modified to save a list containing the state and its parent. For example, if the state (e e e e) generates the state (w e w e), the list containing both states, ((w e w e) (e e e e)), is placed on closed. Other functions that access these states (such as generate-descendants, eliminate-duplicates, and the test for successful completion of the search) must be changed to accommodate this representation.

When the current state is found to equal the goal, this ancestor information can be used to reconstruct the path from the goal back to the start state by tracing back along successive parents. This augmented version of breadth-first-search along with an example of generate-descendants for the farmer, wolf, goat, and cabbage problem is:

```
(defun breadth-first-search (goal)
  (cond ((null *open*) nil)
        ((equal (get-state (car *open*)) goal)
                (cons goal (build-solution (get-parent (car *open*)))))
        (t (setq *closed* (cons (car *open*) *closed*))
           (setq *open* (append (cdr *open*)
                  (eliminate-duplicates
                      (generate-descendants (get-state (car *open*)))
                                            (get-state (car *open*)))))
           (breadth-first-search goal))))

(defun generate-descendants (state)
  (delete nil (list (make-pair (farmer-takes-self state) state)
                    (make-pair (farmer-takes-wolf state) state)
                    (make-pair (farmer-takes-goat state) state)
                    (make-pair (farmer-takes-cabbage state) state))))

(defun make-pair (state parent) (list state parent))

(defun get-state (state-pair) (nth 0 state-pair))
```

make-pair and get-state handle state-parent pairs. The implementation of build-solution and the revised eliminate-descendants is left as an exercise.

7.3.2 Depth-First and Best-First Search

Depth-first search may be implemented by modifying breadth-first-search to maintain *open* as a stack:

```
(defun depth-first-search (goal)
  (cond ((null *open*) nil)
        ((equal (get-state (car *open*)) goal)
                (cons goal (build-solution (get-parent (car *open*)))))
        (t (setq *closed* (cons (car *open*) *closed))
           (setq *open* append
                          (eliminate-duplicates (generate-descendants (get-state (car *op⊷
                                  (get-state (car *open*))
                                  (plus 1 (get-depth (car *open*))))

                          (cdr *open*)))
           (depth-first-search goal))))
```

Since a state may be reached along different paths in depth-first search, eliminate-duplicates must keep track of the length of the path that led to the state and retain the version of duplicate states reached along the shortest path from the start state. Thus, states on open are stored as 3-tuples:

(current-state   parent-state   length-of-path-to-goal)

eliminate-duplicates is passed the list of child states, the parent state and the incre-mented depth of search. Implementation of eliminate-duplicates is left as an exercise.

Best-first-search may be implemented through similar modifications. Specifically, the heuristic evaluation is saved along with each state. The tuples on *open* are then sorted accoring to this evaluation. best-first-search is defined

```
(defun best-first-search (goal)
  (cond ((null *open*) nil)
        ((equal (get-state (car *open*)) goal)
              (cons goal (build-solution (get-parent (car *open*)))))
        (t (setq *closed* (cons (car *open*) *closed*))
           (setq *open* (cdr *open*))
           (insert-into-open
                (eliminate-duplicates (generate-descendants (get-state (car *closed*)))
                                      (get-state (car *closed*))
                                      (plus 1 (get-depth (car *closed*)))
                                goal))
           (best-first-search goal))))
```

insert-into-open adds the new states to *open* in order determined by their heuristic weights. As with depth-first search, eliminate-duplicates should retain the version of duplicate states reached along the shortest path. In order to provide the infor-mation needed by sort-on-evaluations, eliminate-duplicates, and build-solution, states on open are stored as 4-tuples:

(current-state   parent-state   length-of-path-to-goal   heuristic-weight)

Completion of best-first-search is left to the reader.

As mentioned in Chapter 4, these three search algorithms are essentially the same, differing chiefly in the maintenance of the open list. This suggests the possibility of creating a general search algorithm that allows the user to specify the organization of open and, consequently, the specific search strategy employed. We do this in the next section.

7.3.3   A General Graph Search Algorithm

We now define a general graph search function that varies its search depending on the definition of functions for maintaining open. Thus, the open list is maintained as an abstract data type and search disciplines are changed solely by changing its definition. Depending on these definitions, graph-search performs either a depth-first, breadth-first, or best-first search. States are added to open using a function add-to-open. In order to generalize control, we assume appropriate functions for maintaining *open*.

```
(defun graph-search (goal)
  (cond ((null *open*) nil)
        ((equal (get-state (car *open*)) goal)
            (cons goal (build-solution (get-parent (car *open*)))))
        (t (setq *closed* (cons (car *open*) *closed*))
          (setq *open* (cdr *open*))
            (add-to-open
                (eliminate-duplicates (generate-descendants (get-state (car *closed*)))
                                      (get-state (car *closed*))
                                      (plus 1 (get-depth (car *closed*)))
                                      goal))
          (graph-search goal))))
```

In using this general graph search function, we define the appropriate functions for maintaining states on open. For example, to implement best-first search, we define:

add-to-open so that it adds the list of child states to open and then sorts the result.

get-state and get-parent so that they return the current state and the parent state from an entry on the open list.

generate-descendants so that it returns a list of 4-tuples consisting of a descendant state, a parent state, the heuristic evaluation, and the length of the path from the state to the start state.

Similarly, we may implement breadth-first search by defining add-to-open so that it maintains open as a queue; depth-first search requires maintaining open as a stack. To do this, we change only the definition of add-to-open; since the particulars of maintaining open have been abstracted out, the same definition of graph-search is used for all three searches. Implementation of these functions is left as an exercise.

By varying the definition of add-to-open and related functions for maintaining states on open, we have defined an abstract control procedure for different search strategies. Procedural abstraction is further supported in LISP through the use of *higher-order functions*, the ability to define functions that take other functions as arguments and/or return functions as results. This would let us define graph-search so that the functions for generating and maintaining states on open would be passed in as arguments to path, rather than being defined in the global environment. Higher-order functions are discussed in the next section.

7.4 Higher-Order Functions and Procedural Abstraction

7.4.1 Maps and Filters

A *filter* is a function that applies a test to the elements of a list, eliminating those that fail the test. filter-negatives, presented earlier in this chapter, was an example of a filter. *Maps* take a list of data objects and apply a function to each one, returning a list of the results. This idea may be further generalized through the development of general maps and filters that take as arguments both lists and the functions or tests that are to be applied to their elements. Functions that take other functions as parameters or return them as results are called *higher-order functions* and constitute an important tool for procedural abstraction.

To begin with an example, recall the function filter-negatives from Section 7.1.6. This function took as its argument a list of numbers and returned that list with all negative values deleted. For example, a function to filter out all the even numbers in a list may be defined:

```
(defun filter-evens (number-list)
  (cond ((null number-list) nil)   ; termination condition
        ((oddp (car number-list))
            (cons (car number-list) (filter-evens (cdr number-list))))
        (t (filter-evens (cdr number-list)))))
```

Because these two functions differ *only* in the name of the predicate used to filter elements from the list, it is natural to think of generalizing them into a single function that takes the filtering predicate as a second parameter.

This may be defined using a LISP form called funcall, which takes as arguments a function and a series of arguments and applies that function to those arguments:

```
(defun filter (list-of-elements test)
  (cond ((null list-of-elements) nil)
        ((funcall test (car list-of-elements))
            (cons (car list-of-elements) (filter (cdr list-of-elements) test)))
        (t (filter (cdr list-of-elements) test))))
```

The function, filter, applies the test to the first element of the list. If the test returns non-nil it conses the element onto the result of filtering the cdr of the list; otherwise, it just returns the filtered cdr. This function may be used with different predicates passed in as parameters to perform a variety of filtering tasks:

```
> (filter '(1 3 -9 5 -2 -7 6) #'plusp)
(1 3 5 6)
> (filter '(1 2 3 4 5 6 7 8 9) #'evenp)
(2 4 6 8)
> (filter '(1 a b 3 c 4 7 d) #'numberp)
(1 3 4 7)
```

When a function is passed as a parameter, as in the above examples, it should be preceded by a #' instead of just a '. The purpose of this convention is to flag arguments that are functions so that they may be given appropriate treatment by the LISP interpreter. In particular, when a function is passed as an argument in Common LISP, the bindings of free variables (if any) must be included with that function. This combination of function definition and bindings of free variables is called a *lexical closure*; the #' informs LISP that the lexical closure must be constructed and passed with the function.

More formally, funcall is defined as having the syntax:

(funcall <function> <arg$_1$> <arg$_2$> ... <arg$_n$>)

In this definition, <function> is a LISP function and <arg$_1$> ... <arg$_n$> are zero or more arguments to the function. The result of evaluating a funcall is the same as the result of evaluating <function> with the specified arguments as actual parameters.

A similar function is apply, which performs the same task as funcall but requires that the arguments be in a list. Except for this syntactic difference, apply and funcall behave the same; the programmer can choose the function that seems more convenient for a given application. These two functions are similar to eval in that all three of these functions allow the user to specify that function evaluation should take place. The difference is that eval requires its argument to be an s-expression that is evaluated, while funcall and apply take a function and its arguments as separate parameters. Examples of the behavior of these functions are:

```
> (funcall #'plus 2 3)
5
> (apply #'plus '(2 3))
5
> (eval '(plus 2 3))
5
> (funcall #'car '(a b c))
a
> (apply #'car '((a b c)))
a
```

Another important class of higher-order functions consists of *mapping functions*, functions that will apply a given function to all the elements of a list. Using funcall, a simple mapping function, map-simple, which returns a list of the results of applying a functional argument to all the elements of a list, is defined:

```
(defun map-simple (func list)
  (cond ((null list) nil)
    (t (cons (funcall func (car list))
        (map-simple func (cdr list))))))
```

For example, map-simple has the behavior:

```
> (map-simple 'add1 '(1 2 3 4 5 6))
(2 3 4 5 6 7)
> (map-simple 'listp '(1 2 (3 4) 5 (6 7 8)))
(nil nil t nil t)
```

map-simple is actually a simplified version of a LISP built-in function called map-car. mapcar extends map-simple by allowing more than one argument list. This enables functions of more than one argument to be applied to corresponding elements of several lists:

```
> (mapcar 'add1 '(1 2 3 4 5 6))        ; this is the same as map-simple
(2 3 4 5 6 7)
> (mapcar 'plus '(1 2 3 4) '(5 6 7 8))
(6 8 10 12)
> (mapcar 'max '(3 9 1 7) '(2 5 6 8))
(3 9 6 8)
```

mapcar is only one of many mapping functions provided by LISP, as well as only one of many higher-order functions built in to the language.

7.4.2 Functional Arguments and Lambda Expressions

In the preceding examples, function arguments were passed in by their name and applied to a series of arguments. This requires that the functions be previously defined in the global environment. Frequently, however, it is desirable to pass a simple function definition directly, without first defining it globally. This is made possible through the lambda expression.

Essentially, the lambda expression allows us to separate a function definition from the function name. The origin of lambda expressions is in the *lambda calculus*, a mathematical model of computation that provides (among other things) a particularly thoughtful treatment of this distinction between an object and its name. The syntax of a lambda expression is similar to the function definition in a defun, except that the function name is replaced by the term lambda. That is,

```
(lambda (<formal-parameters>) <body>)
```

Lambda expressions may be used in place of a function name in a funcall. The funcall will execute the body of the lambda expression with the arguments bound to the parameters of the funcall. As with named functions, the number of formal parameters and the number of actual parameters must be the same. For example:

```
> (funcall #'(lambda (x) (* x x)) 4)
16
```

Here, x is bound to 4 and the body of the lambda expression is then evaluated. The result, the square of 4, is returned by funcall. Other examples of the use of lambda expressions with funcall and apply are:

```
> (apply #'(lambda (x y) (+ (* x x) y)) (2 3))
7
> (funcall #'(lambda (x) (append x x)) '(a b c))
(a b c a b c)
> (funcall #'(lambda (x1 x2) (append (reverse x1) x2)) '(a b c) '(d e f))
(c b a d e f)
```

Lambda expressions may be used in a higher-order function such as mapcar in place of the names of globally defined functions. For example:

```
> (mapcar #'(lambda (x) (* x x)) '(1 2 3 4 5))
(1 4 9 16 25)
> (mapcar #'(lambda (x) (* x 2)) '(1 2 3 4 5))
(2 4 6 8 10)
> (mapcar #'(lambda (x) (and (> x 0) (< x 10))) '(1 24 5 -9 8 23))
(t nil t nil t nil)
```

Without lambda expressions the programmer must define every function in the global environment using a defun, even though that function may be used only once. Lambda expressions free the programmer: if it is desired to square each element in a list, the lambda form is passed to mapcar as the first of the above examples illustrates. It is not necessary to define a squaring function first.

The lambda expression, combined with higher-order functions, is another tool for abstraction that LISP makes available to the programmer.

7.5 Pattern Matching in LISP

Pattern matching is an important AI methodology that has already been discussed in the PROLOG chapters and the discussion of production systems. In this section we implement a recursive pattern matcher and use it to build a pattern-directed retrieval function for a simple data base.

The heart of this retrieval system is a function called match, which takes as arguments two s-expressions and returns t if the expressions match. Matching requires that both expressions have the same *structure*, as well as having identical atoms in corresponding positions. In addition, match allows the inclusion of variables, denoted by ? in an s-expression. Variables are allowed to match with any s-expression, either a list or an atom. Examples of the desired behavior for match appear below. If the examples seem reminiscent of the PROLOG examples in Chapter 6, this is because match is actually a simplified version of the unification algorithm that forms the heart of PRO-

LOG, as well as many other pattern-directed AI systems. In Section 7.6 we expand match into the full unification algorithm by allowing named variables and returning a list of bindings required for a match.

```
> ( match '(likes bill wine) '(likes bill wine))
t
> (match '(likes bill wine) '(likes bill milk))
nil
> (match '(likes bill ?) '(likes bill wine)) ; example with a variable
t
> (match '(likes ? wine) '(likes bill ?)) ; note variables in both expressions
t
> (match '(likes bill ?) '(likes bill (prolog lisp smalltalk)))
t
> (match '(likes ?) '(likes bill wine))
nil
```

match is used to define a function called get-matches, which takes as arguments two s-expressions. The first argument is a pattern to be matched against elements of the second s-expression, which must be a list. get-matches returns a list of the elements of the list that match the first argument. In effect, the second argument is a data base of s-expressions, with get-matches implementing pattern-directed retrieval from that data base. In the example below, get-matches is used to retrieve records from an employee data base as described earlier in this chapter.

In the following example, note the use of the setq function. It is used here to simplify the example; since the data base is a large and relatively complex s-expression, it is clearer and simpler to assign it to a global variable and use that variable as an argument to get-matches than to recopy the entire data base as an argument for each call.

```
> (setq database '(((lovelace ada) 50000.00 1234)
            ((turing alan) 45000.00 3927)
            ((shelley mary) 35000.00 2850)
            ((vonNeumann john) 40000.00 7955)
            ((simon herbert) 50000.00 1374)
            ((mccarthy john) 48000.00 2864)
            ((russell bertrand) 35000.00 2950))
database
> (get-matches '((turing alan) 45000.00 3927) database)
((turing alan) 45000.00 3927)
> (get-matches '(? 50000.00 ?) database)      ; all people who make 50000.
(((lovelace ada) 50000.00 1234) ((simon herbert) 50000.00 1374))
> (get-matches '((? john) ? ?) database)  ; all people named john
(((vonNeumann john) 40000.00 7955) ((mccarthy john) 48000.00 2864))
```

We implement get-matches through a straightforward use of cdr-recursion to scan down the data base looking for elements that match with the first argument (the pattern).

All elements of the data base that match the pattern are consed together to form the answer. get-matches is defined:

```
(defun get-matches (pattern database)
  (cond ((null data-base) ())
        ((match pattern (car data-base))          ; match found, add to result
          (cons (car data-base) (get-matches pattern (cdr data-base))))
        ( t (get-matches pattern (cdr data-base)))))  ; no match,
```

The heart of the system is the match function, a predicate that determines whether or not two s-expressions containing variables actually match. match is based on the idea that two lists match if and only if their respective cars and cdrs match. This suggests a car-cdr recursive scheme for the algorithm, with a successful match requiring that both the car and the cdr match. The recursion terminates when either of the arguments is atomic (this includes the empty list, nil, which is both an atom and a list). If both patterns are the same atom or if one of the patterns is a variable atom, ?, which can match with anything, then termination is with a successful match; otherwise, the match will fail. Notice that if either of the patterns is a variable, the other pattern may or may not be atomic; variables may match with s-expressions of arbitrary complexity.

Because the handling of the terminating conditions is complex, the implementation of match uses a function called match-atom that takes two arguments, one or both of which is an atom, and checks to see if the patterns match. Also, by hiding this complexity in match-atom the car-cdr recursive structure of match is more apparent:

```
(defun match (pattern1 pattern2)
  (cond (or ( atom pattern1) (atom pattern2))       ; one of the patterns is atomic
           (match-atom pattern1 pattern2))            ; call match-atom, otherwise
        (t      (and (match (car pattern1) (car pattern2))  ; match both car and cdr
                     (match (cdr pattern1) (cdr pattern2))))))
```

The implementation of match-atom makes use of the fact that when it is called, at least one of the arguments is an atom. Because of this assumption, a simple test for equality of patterns is all that is needed to test that both patterns are the same atom (including both being a variable); it will fail either if the two patterns are different atoms or if one of them is nonatomic. If the first test fails, the only way a match can succeed is if one of the patterns is a variable. This check constitutes the remainder of the function definition. Finally, a function variable is defined to test whether or not a pattern is a variable. Treating variables as an abstract data type now will simplify later extensions to the function (e.g., named variables as in PROLOG). The following definitions complete the pattern-matching retrieval system:

```
(defun match-atom (pattern1 pattern2)
  (or (equal pattern1 pattern2)  ; both patterns are the same, or
      (variable pattern1)        ; one of them is a variable.
      (variable pattern2)))
```

```
(defun variable (x) (equal x '?))
```

7.6 A Recursive Unification Function

In Section 7.5 we implemented a recursive pattern-matching algorithm that allowed the inclusion of unnamed variables (denoted by ?) in patterns. Now we extend this simple pattern matcher into the full unification algorithm presented in Chapter 2. The function, unify, allows named variables in both of the patterns to be matched and returns a list of the variable bindings required for the match. This unification function is the basis of the inference systems developed in Chapter 13.

7.6.1 Implementing the Unification Algorithm

As in Section 7.5, patterns are either constants, variables, or list structures. In a full unifier, variables may be distinguished from one another by their names. Named variables are represented as lists of the form (var <name>), where <name> is usually an atomic symbol. (var x), (var y), and (var newstate) are all examples of legal variables.

The function unify takes as arguments two patterns to be matched and a set of variable substitutions (bindings) to be employed in the match. Generally, this set will be empty (nil) when the function is first called. On a successful match, unify returns a (possibly empty) set of substitutions required for a successful match. If no match was possible, unify returns the symbol failed; nil is used to indicate an empty substitution set, i.e., a match in which no substitutions were required. The representation of substitution sets is discussed in Section 7.6.2.

An example of the behavior of unify, with comments, appears below.

```
> (unify '(p a (var x)) '(p a b) ())   ; returns substitution of b for (var x)
(((var x) . b))
> (unify '(p (var y) b) '(p a (var x)) ())  ; variables appear in both patterns
(((var x) . b) ((var y) . a))
> (unify '(p (var x)) '(p (q a (var y))) ()) ; variable bound to more complex pattern
(((var x) q a (var y)))
> (unify '(p a) '(p a) ())  , nil indicates no substitution required
nil
> (unify '(p a) '(q a) ())  ; returns the atom failed to indicate failure
failed
```

unify, like the pattern matcher of Section 7.5, uses a car-cdr recursive scheme and is defined by:

```
(defun unify (pattern1 pattern2 substitution-list)
  (cond ((equal substitution-list 'failed) 'failed)
        ((varp pattern1) (match-var pattern1 pattern2 substitution-list))
        ((varp pattern2) (match-var pattern2 pattern1 substitution-list))
        ((is-constant-p pattern1)
          (cond ((equal pattern1 pattern2) substitution-list)
                (t 'failed)))
        ((is-constant-p pattern2) 'failed)
        (t (unify (cdr pattern1) (cdr pattern2)
          (unify (car pattern1) (car pattern2) substitution-list)))))
```

On entering unify, the algorithm first checks whether the substitution list is equal to failed. (This could occur if a prior attempt to unify the cars of two patterns had failed.) If this condition is met, the function returns failed.

Next, if either of the patterns is a variable, the function match-var is called to perform further checking and possibly add a new binding to the substitution list. If neither of the patterns is a variable, unify tests whether either is a constant, returning the unchanged substitution list if they are the same constant, failed otherwise.

The last item in the cond statement implements the tree-recursive decomposition of the problem: first the cars of the patterns are unified using the bindings in substitution-list. The result is passed as the third argument to the call of unify on the cdrs of both patterns. This allows the variable substitutions made in matching the cars to be applied to other occurrences of those variables in the cdrs of both patterns.

match-var, which handles the case of matching a variable and a pattern, is defined by:

```
(defun match-var (var pattern substitution-list)
  (cond ((equal var pattern) substitution-list)
    (t (let ((binding (get-binding var substitution-list)))
        (cond (binding (unify (get-binding-value binding) pattern substitution-list))
              ((occursp var pattern) 'failed)
              (t (add-substitution var pattern  substitution-list))))))))
```

match-var first checks whether the variable and the pattern are the same; unifying a variable with itself requires no added substitutions, so substitution-list is returned unchanged.

If var and pattern are not the same, match-var checks whether the variable is already bound. If a binding exists, unify is called recursively to match the *value* of the binding with pattern. Note that this binding value may be a constant, a variable, or a pattern of arbitrary complexity; this requires a call to the full unification algorithm to complete the match.

If no binding currently exists for var, the function calls occursp to test whether var appears in pattern. The *occurs check* is needed to prevent attempts to unify a variable with a pattern containing that variable, leading to a circular structure. For example, if (var x) was bound to (p (var x)), any attempt to apply those substitutions to a pattern would result in an infinite loop. If var appears in pattern, match-var returns failed; otherwise, it adds the new substitution pair to substitution-list using add-substitution.

unify and match-var are the heart of the unification algorithm. occursp (which performs a tree walk on a pattern to find any occurrences of the variable in that pattern), varp, and is-constant-p (which test if their argument is a variable or a constant, respectively) appear below. Functions for handling substitution sets are discussed in the next section.

```
(defun occursp (var pattern)
  (cond ((equal var pattern) t)
    ((or (varp pattern) (is-constant-p pattern)) nil)
    (t (or (occursp var (car pattern))
        (occursp var (cdr pattern))))))
```

```
(defun is-constant-p (item)
  (atom item))


(defun varp (item)
  (and (listp item)
       (equal (length item) 2)
       (equal (car item) 'var)))
```

7.6.2 Implementing Substitution Sets Using Association Lists

Sets of substitutions are represented using a built-in LISP data type called the *association list* or *a-list*. This is the basis for the functions add-substitutions, get-binding, and binding-value. An association list is a list of data records, or *key/data* pairs. The car of each record is a *key* for its retrieval; the cdr of each record is called the *datum*. The datum may be a list of values or a single atom. Retrieval is implemented by the function assoc, which takes as arguments a key and an association list and returns the first member of the association list that has the key as its car. An optional third argument to assoc specifies the test to be used in comparing keys. The default test is the Common LISP function eql, a form of equality test that requires that two arguments be exactly the same object (i.e., either the same memory location or the same numeric value). In implementing substitution sets, we will specify a less strict test, equal, which requires only that they match syntactically (i.e., are designated by identical names). An example of assoc's behavior appears below:

```
> (assoc 3 '((1 a) (2 b) (3 c) (4 d)))
(3 c)
> (assoc 'd '((a b c) (b c d e) (d e f) (c d e)) :test #'equal)
(d e f)
> (assoc 'c '((a . 1) (b . 2) (c . 3) (d . 4)) :test #'equal)
(c . 3)
> (assoc 'jimmy '((ron . nancy) (jimmy . ros) (jerry . betty) (dick . pat)) :test #'equal)
(jimmy . ros)
```

Note that assoc returns the entire record matched on the key; the datum may be retrieved from this list by the cdr function. Also, notice that in the last two calls the members of the a-list are not lists, but a structure called *dotted pairs* (e.g., (a . 1), (ron . nancy)):

The dotted pair, or *cons pair*, is actually the fundamental constructor in LISP. It is the result of consing one s-expression onto another; the list notation that we have used throughout the chapter is just a notational variant of dotted pairs. For example, the value returned by (cons 1 nil) is actually (1 . nil); this is equivalent to (1). Similarly, the list (1 2 3) may be written in dotted pair notation as (1 . (2 . (3 . nil))). Although the actual effect of a cons is to create a dotted pair, the list notation is cleaner and is generally preferred. It is important to realize that a list is really just a series of dotted pairs.

If two atoms are consed together, the result is always written using dotted pair notation. The cdr of a dotted pair is the second element in the pair, rather than a list containing the second atom. For example:

```
> (cons 'a 'b)
(a . b)
> (car '(a . b))
a
> (cdr '(a . b))
b
```

Dotted pairs occur naturally in association lists when one atom is used as a key for retrieving another atom, as well as in other applications that require the formation and manipulation of pairs of atomic symbols. Because unifications often substitute a single atom for a variable, dotted pairs appear often in the association list returned by the unification function.

Along with assoc, Common LISP defines the function acons, which takes as arguments a key, a datum, and an a-list and returns a new association list whose first element is the result of consing the key onto the datum. For example:

```
> (acons 'a 1 nil)
((a . 1))
```

Note that when acons is given two atoms, it adds a dotted pair to the association list:

```
> (acons 'ron 'nancy '((jimmy . ros) (jerry . betty) (dick . pat)))
((ron . nancy) (jimmy . ros) (jerry . betty) (dick . pat))
> (acons 'pets
    '(emma jack clyde)
    '((name . bill) (hobbies music skiing movies) (job . programmer)))
((pets emma jack clyde) (name . bill) (hobbies music skiing movies)
  (job . programmer))
```

Members on an association list may be either dotted pairs or lists.

Association lists provide a convenient way to implement a variety of tables and other simple data retrieval schemes. In implementing the unification algorithm, association lists are used to represent sets of substitutions: the keys are the variables, and the data are the values of their bindings. The datum may be a simple variable or constant or a more complicated structure.

Using association lists, the substitution set functions are defined:

```
(defun get-binding (var substitution-list)
    (assoc var substitution-list :test #'equal))

(defun get-binding-value (binding) (cdr binding))
```

```
(defun add-substitution (var pattern substitution-list)
  (acons var pattern substitution-list))
```

This completes the implementation of the unification algorithm.

7.7   Interpreters and Embedded Languages

The top level of the LISP interpreter is known as the *read-eval-print* loop. This describes the interpreter's behavior in reading, evaluating, and printing the value of s-expressions entered by the user. The eval function, defined in Section 7.1.4, is the heart of the LISP interpreter; using eval, it is possible to write the top-level read-eval-print loop in LISP itself. In the next example, we develop a simplified version of this loop. This version is simplified chiefly in that it does not have the error-handling abilities of the built-in loop, although LISP does provide the functionality needed to implement such capabilities.

To write the read-eval-print loop, we use two more LISP functions, read and print. read is a function that takes no parameters; when it is evaluated, it simply returns the next s-expression entered at the keyboard. print is a function that takes a single argument, evaluates it, and then prints that result to standard output. On completion, print returns a value of nil. Another function that will prove useful is terpri, a function of no arguments that causes a newline character to be sent to standard output. terpri also returns a value of nil on completion.

Using these functions, the read-eval-print loop is based on a simple nested s-expression:

```
(print (eval (read)))
```

When this is evaluated, the innermost s-expression, read, is evaluated first. The value returned by the read, the next s-expression entered by the user, is passed to eval, where it is evaluated. The result of this evaluation is passed to print, where it is sent to the display screen. To complete the loop we add a print expression to output the prompt, a newline after the result has been printed, and a recursive call to repeat the cycle. Thus, the final read-eval-print loop is defined:

```
(defun my-read-eval-print ()      ; this function takes no arguments
  (print ':)                      ; output a prompt, ours is a ":"
  (print (eval (read)))           ; read-eval-print
  (terpri)                        ; output a newline
  (my-read-eval-print) )          ; do it all again
```

This may be used ''on top of'' the built-in interpreter:

```
> (my-read-eval-print)
:(+ 1 2)              ; note the new prompt
3
:                     ; etc.
```

As this example illustrates, by making functions like quote and eval available to the user, LISP gives the programmer a high degree of control over the handling of functions. Since LISP programs and data are both represented as s-expressions, we may write programs that perform any desired manipulations of LISP expressions prior to evaluating them. This underlies much of LISP's power as a procedural representation language, since it allows arbitrary LISP code to be stored, modified, and evaluated when needed. It also makes it simple to write specialized interpreters that may extend or modify the behavior of the built-in LISP interpreter in some desired fashion. This capability is at the heart of many LISP-based expert systems, where the system is basically a loop that reads user queries and responds to them according to the expertise contained in its knowledge base.

As an example of the way in which such a specialized interpreter may be implemented in LISP, we may modify my-read-eval-print so that it evaluates arithmetic expressions in an infix rather than a prefix notation. That is, the loop should function as an interpreter for arithmetic expressions in an infix notation, as in the following example (note the modified prompt, infix->):

```
infix-> (1 + 2)
3
infix-> (7 - 2)
5
infix-> ((5 + 2) * (3 - 1))   ; the loop should allow nesting of expressions
14
```

In order to simplify the example, the infix interpreter handles only arithmetic expressions. A further simplification restricts the interpreter to binary operations and requires that all expressions be fully parenthesized, eliminating the need for more sophisticated parsing techniques or worries about operator precedence. However, it does allow expressions to be nested to arbitrary depth and handles all the binary arithmetic operators supported by LISP.

Our approach is to modify the previously developed read-eval-print loop by adding a function that translates infix expressions into prefix expressions prior to passing them on to eval. A first attempt at writing this function, might look like:

```
(defun simple-in-to-pre (exp)
   (list (nth 1 exp)     ; middle element (operator) becomes first element.
      (nth 0 exp)        ; first operand
      (nth 2 exp)))      ; second operand
```

simple-in-to-pre is effective in translating simple expressions; however, it is not able to correctly translate nested expressions, that is, expressions in which the operands are themselves infix expressions. To handle this situation properly, the operands must also be translated into prefix notation. Recursion is halted by testing the argument to determine whether it is a number, returning it unchanged if it is. The completed version of the infix-to-prefix translator is:

```
(defun in-to-pre (exp)
  (cond ((numberp exp) exp)
        (t (list (nth 1 exp)
                 (in-to-pre (nth 0 exp))
                 (in-to-pre (nth 2 exp))))))
```

Using this translator, the read-eval-print loop may be modified to interpret infix expressions, as defined below:

```
(defun in-eval ()
  (print 'infix->)
  (print (eval (in-to-pre (read))))
  (terpri)
  (in-eval))
```

This will allow the interpretation of binary expressions in infix form:

```
> (in-eval)
infix->(2 + 2)
4
infix->((3 * 4) - 5)
7
```

In the above example, we have implemented a new language, the language of infix arithmetic, in LISP. Because of the powerful facilities LISP provides for symbolic computing (lists and functions for their manipulation) along with the ability to control evaluation, this was much easier to do than in most programming languages. This example is important in that it illustrates an important AI programming methodology, that of *embedded languages*. Very often in AI programming, a problem is not completely understood, or the program required to solve a problem is extremely complex. So it becomes desirable to place another conceptual layer between LISP and the final solution to the problem. This layer is either a collection of functions or a higher-level language that, while not directly solving the problem, provides a more powerful tool for exploring the problem and eventually implementing a full solution to it. In effect, rather than being used to code a problem solution, LISP is used to implement a language that seems more directly applicable to the development of such a program. Features that typically appear in embedded languages in AI include pattern matchers, production system controllers, and access functions for data structures such as frames and semantic networks (Chapter 13).

7.8   Epilogue and References

While this chapter has given some examples of the use of LISP in solving a number of AI problems, it has discussed only a few of the rich ideas included in the language. A number of texts provide further discussion of the language. *Common LISP: The*

Language by Guy L. Steele, Jr. (1984), is the standard reference on the syntax and semantics of the language. Other books, which give a more tutorial treatment of the language and its use, include: *Lisp* by Patrick Winston and Berthold K. P. Horn (1984), *Common Lispcraft* by Robert Wilensky (1986), and *Introduction to Common LISP* by Taiichi Yuasa and Masami Hagiya (1986).

A comprehensive book on AI programming techniques using LISP is *Artificial Intelligence Programming* by Charniak, Riesbeck, and McDermott (1987).

The Structure and Interpretation of Computer Programs by Abelson and Sussman (1985) is a particularly interesting book based on the LISP dialect SCHEME. This is much more than a book on a programming language: it is a rethinking of computer science based on techniques suggested by the SCHEME dialect.

Finally, for an interesting theoretical discussion of functional programming, including the implementation issues involved in LISP-like languages, *Functional Programming* by Henderson (1980) is recommended.

7.9   Exercises

1. Newton's method for solving roots takes an estimate of the value of the root and tests it for accuracy. If the guess does not meet the required tolerance, it computes a new estimate and repeats. Pseudocode for using Newton's method to take the square root of a number is:

   function root-by-newtons-method (x, tolerance)

   begin
     guess := 1;
     repeat
       guess := 1/2(guess + x/guess)
     until x - guess*guess < tolerance.

   Write a recursive LISP function to compute square roots by Newton's method.

2. a. Write a LISP function that will reverse the elements of a list.
   b. Write a LISP function that will take a list nested to any depth and print the mirror image of that list. For instance, the function should have the behavior:

   > (mirror '((a b) (c (d e))))
   (((e d) c) (b a))

3. Write a random number generator in LISP. This function must maintain a global variable, **seed**, and return a different random number each time it is called. For a description of a reasonable random number algorithm, consult any basic algorithms text.

4. Write the functions initialize, push, top, pop, and list-stack to maintain a global stack. These functions should behave:

```
> (initialize)
nil
> (push 'foo)
foo
> (push 'bar)
bar
> (top)
bar
> (list-stack)
(bar foo)
> (pop)
bar
> (list-stack)
(foo)
```

5. Sets may be represented using lists. Note that these lists should not contain any duplicate elements. Write LISP implementations of the set operations union, intersection, and difference.

6. The tower of Hanoi problem is based on the following legend:

In a Far Eastern monastery, there is a puzzle consisting of three diamond needles and 64 gold disks. The disks are of graduated sizes. Initially, the disks are all stacked on a single needle in decreasing order of size. The monks are attempting to move all the disks to another needle under the following rules:

a. Only one disk may be moved at a time.
b. No disk can ever rest on a smaller disk.

Legend has it that when the task has been completed, the universe will end.

Write a LISP program to solve this problem. For safety's sake (and in order to write a program that will finish in your lifetime) do not attempt the full 64-disk problem. Three or four disks is more reasonable.

7. Write a compiler for arithmetic expressions of the form:

```
(op operand1 operand2)
```

Where op is either +, −, *, or / and the operands are either numbers or nested expressions. An example of a legal expression is (* (+ 3 6) (- 7 9)). Assume that the target machine has instructions:

```
(move value register)
(add register-1 register-2)
(subtract register-1 register-2)
(times register-1 register-2)
(divide register-1 register-2)
```

All the arithmetic operations will leave the result in the first register argument. To simplify, assume an unlimited number of registers. Your compiler should take an arithmetic expression and return a list of these machine operations.

8. Implement a depth-first backtracking solution (such as was used to solve the farmer, wolf, goat, and cabbage problem in Section 7.2) to the missionary and cannibal problem:

> Three missionaries and three cannibals come to the bank of a river they wish to cross. There is a boat that will hold only two, and any of the group is able to row it. If there are ever more missionaries than cannibals on any side of the river the cannibals will get converted. (Some consider this a fate worth than death!) Devise a series of moves to get all the people across the river with no conversions.

9. Implement a depth-first solution to the water jugs problem:

> There are two jugs, one holding 3 and the other 5 gallons of water. There are a number of things that can be done with the jugs: they can be filled, emptied, and dumped one into the other either until the poured-into jug is full, or until the poured-out-of jug is empty. Devise a sequence of actions that will produce 4 gallons of water in the larger jug. (Hint: only integer values of water will be used.)

10. Implement build-solution and eliminate-duplicates for the breadth-first search algorithm of Section 7.3.

11. Use the breadth-first search algorithm of Exercise 10 to solve:
   a. The farmer, wolf, goat, and cabbage problem (see Section 7.2).
   b. The missionary and cannibal problem (see Exercise 8).
   c. The water jugs problem (see Exercise 8).

   Compare the breadth-first results to the depth-first results. (The differences will probably be the most telling for the water jugs problem. Why?)

12. Finish implementing best-first search using the general path algorithm described in Section 7.3.3. Use this along with appropriate heuristics to solve each of the three problems mentioned in Exercise 11.

13. Write a LISP program to solve the full 8×8 version of the knight's tour problem.

14. Write a LISP program to solve the 8-queens problem. (This problem is to find a way to place eight queens on a chessboard so that no queen may capture any other through a single move.)

15. Modify the general search algorithms of Section 7.3 to eliminate the overhead of passing open and closed as parameters; i.e., implement these lists as global variables.

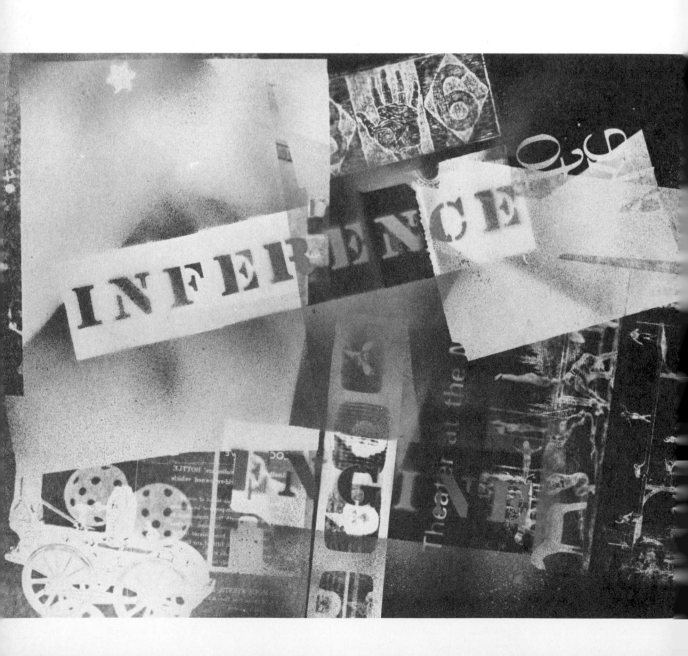

PART IV

REPRESENTATIONS FOR KNOWLEDGE-BASED SYSTEMS

Nam et ipsa scientia potestas est (Knowledge is power).

—FRANCIS BACON

Horatio: O day and night but this is wondrous strange!

Hamlet: And therefore as a stranger give it welcome.
    There are more things in heaven and earth, Horatio,
    Then are dreamt of in your philosophy.
    But come . . .

—WILLIAM SHAKESPEARE, *Hamlet*

In the late 1950s and early 1960s, Alan Newell and Herbert Simon wrote several computer programs to test the hypothesis that intelligent behavior resulted from heuristic search. Their first major program, the Logic Theorist, developed in conjunction with J. C. Shaw (Newell and Simon 1963*a*), proved theorems in elementary logic using the notation and axioms provided by Russell and Whitehead's *Principia Mathematica*. The authors describe their research as being

> aimed at understanding the complex processes (heuristics) that are effective in problem solving. Hence, we are not interested in methods that guarantee solutions, but which require vast amounts of computation. Rather we wish to understand how a mathematician, for example, is able to prove a theorem even though he does not know when he starts how, or if, he is going to succeed.

A later program, Newell and Simon's General Problem Solver (GPS) (Newell and Simon 1963*b*; 1972), continued this effort to find general principles of intelligent problem solving. The GPS solved problems formulated as a start state and a goal state; legal problem-solving steps were a set of operations for modifying these state representations. The General Problem Solver searched for a sequence of operations that would transform

Current state Goal

Figure IV.1 A state that must temporarily be moved farther from the goal in order to find a solution path.

the start state into the goal state, searching a space of possible state transformations in the same fashion as the search algorithms discussed in earlier chapters of this text.

GPS used *means-ends analysis*, a general heuristic for selecting among alternative state transformation operations, to guide search through the problem space. Means-ends analysis examines the *syntactic* differences between the current state and the goal state and selects an operator that reduces these differences. Suppose, for example, that GPS is attempting to prove the equivalence of two logical expressions. If the current state contains an ∧ operator and the goal does not contain an ∧, then means-ends analysis would select a transformation, such as de Morgan's law, to remove ∧ from expressions.

Like all heuristics, means-ends analysis is not foolproof; it fails, for example, when given expressions that must first have their differences temporarily increased in order to find a solution path. Consider, for example, the 8-puzzle board of Figure IV.1. Although only one tile, **3**, is out of place, the only possible next step is to move either tile **2** or **4**. Since either of these moves increases the difference between the board and the goal, a strictly applied difference reduction heuristic cannot select either of them.

A deeper problem with the GPS is its restriction to a heuristic based solely on the syntactic form of state descriptors. By using a heuristic that examines only the syntactic form of states, it was hoped that GPS would indeed prove to be a *general* architecture for intelligent problem solving, no matter what the domain. Programs like the GPS, which restrict themselves to strategies that can be applied across a wide variety of applications, are known as *weak problem solvers*. Because they attempt to implement general strategies, such as those described in chapters 2 through 5, weak problem solvers may only examine the syntactic form of state descriptions. They may not use theoretical or empirical knowledge about a specific problem domain.

Weak methods are an important class of problem-solving techniques that are used where general search strategies are required or where it is difficult to extract a suitable body of strong heuristics. Besides the problem solving described in chapters 2 through 5, automatic theorem proving (Chapter 11) depends heavily on weak methods, as does much research in machine learning (Chapter 15).

Unfortunately, there does not seem to be a single heuristic that can successfully be applied to all problem domains. In general, the methods we use to solve problems employ a great deal of knowledge about the domain. Doctors are able to diagnose illness because they have extensive knowledge of medicine, in addition to their general problem-solving abilities. Architects are able to design houses because they know about architecture. The heuristics used in medical diagnosis would be useless in designing an office building.

Weak methods stand in sharp contrast to *strong methods*, which use knowledge of a particular problem domain. For example, a strong heuristic for diagnosing automotive problems might be:

if
the engine does not turn over, and
the lights do not come on
then
the problem is battery or cables

This heuristic, phrased as an *if . . . then* rule, focuses search on the battery/cable subsystem of the automobile, eliminating other components and pruning the search space. Notice that this particular heuristic, unlike means-ends analysis, uses empirical knowledge of how automobiles function, for instance, knowledge of the relationships between the battery, lights, and starter. It is useless in any problem domain except auto repair.

Many important problems depend on domain-specific knowledge for their solution. These include most of the problem areas that we associate with expert level performance in humans, such as medicine, engineering, science, and business. This knowledge-intensive approach contrasts sharply with GPS's goal of finding a single general heuristic for solving all problems.

Not only do strong problem solvers use domain-specific heuristics, they generally require large amounts of such knowledge to be effective. The bad-battery heuristic, for example, would not be of much use in diagnosing a bad carburetor; an automotive diagnostic program must have a number of such specific rules to handle a range of possible diagnoses. The major challenge in designing a knowledge-based program is the acquisition and organization of large amounts of specific problem-solving knowledge.

Most of the techniques that AI has developed for solving these problems depend on the separation of the knowledge and control aspects of the program. Levesque (Levesque and Brackman 1985) has given a simple illustration of the benefits of this separation in the form of two PROLOG programs:

```
% Version 1

print_color(rose) :- write(red), nl,!.
print_color(sky) :- write(yellow), nl,!.
print_color(grass) :- write(green), nl,!.
print_color(_) :- write('color not known'),nl,!.


% Version 2

print_color(X) :- color(X,Y),write(Y), nl,!.
print_color(_) :- write('color not known'),nl,!.


color(rose,red).
color(sky,yellow).
color(grass,green).
```

Although both of these programs have identical behavior, the second has represented the relationship between an object and its color explicitly using the color predicate. These color predicates constitute a *knowledge base* that is distinct from the control and implementation details found in the definition of print_color. A *knowledge-based system* is one that uses a separate base of explicitly represented problem-solving knowledge.

Because it is separate from the control aspects of the program, the knowledge base is highly modular and modifiable. The programmer does not have to worry about the implementation of the control aspects of the program but may focus on the acquisition and organization of the knowledge itself. Another benefit of this separation is that it allows knowledge to be represented in a concise and intuitively appealing form, e.g., the color predicate.

Note, however, that both versions of the program allow incorrect knowledge (the sky is yellow) to be included. Although this approach assists the programmer by making the contents of the knowledge base explicit, it does not guarantee correctness of the knowledge.

The separation of knowledge and control is so intuitively appealing and so common in AI that it is often taken for granted as the best way to design an intelligent program. Before proceeding with Part IV, we would like to emphasize that in following this approach, we are making certain assumptions about the nature of intelligent systems. In addition to its benefits, the knowledge-based approach has subtle implications for the questions proposed in AI research and the paths taken toward their solution.

These assumptions have been formalized by Brian Smith (1985) as the *knowledge representation hypothesis*. This hypothesis states that

> any mechanically embodied intelligent process will be comprised of structural ingredients that (a) we as external observers naturally take to represent a propositional account of the knowledge that the overall process exhibits, and (b) independent of such external semantic attribution, play a formal role in engendering the behavior that manifests that knowledge.

The important aspects of this hypothesis include the assumption that knowledge will be represented *propositionally*, i.e., in a form that explicitly represents the knowledge in question and may be seen by an outside observer as a ''natural'' description of that knowledge. The second major assumption is that the behavior of the system should be directly caused by the propositions in the knowledge base and that this behavior should be consistent with our perceived meaning of those propositions. Note that this assumption does not require a particular syntax for the representation, such as expressions in formal logic; it only requires that we be able to understand their intended meaning by examining the contents of the knowledge base. This eliminates programs that represent knowledge implicitly in a formalism such as arrays of numbers or circuits. For examples of the nonpropositional approach to AI, the reader is referred to work in neural networks or connectionist models of intelligence (Chapter 15).

The knowledge representation hypothesis makes explicit the assumptions underlying the majority of work in artificial intelligence.

One of the major benefits of the separation of knowledge and control is greater freedom in the design of knowledge representation languages. In Part II, we introduced the predicate calculus as a representation language for AI. Another important representation is found in the *rule-based expert system*. Much of the pioneering work in knowledge-based programming was done using rule-based representations, and this approach continues to be used in numerous applications. In Chapter 8 we discuss this work and examine the problems involved in the acquisition, formalization, and debugging of a knowledge base.

In spite of the benefits of logical and rule-based representations, the demands of knowledge-based problem solving have continued to stimulate work in the design of knowledge representation languages. In Chapter 9 we examine the major alternatives to rules and logic, including *semantic networks*, *frames*, and *objects*.

Because enormous amounts of knowledge are needed to unravel the complexity and ambiguity of human language, *natural language understanding* has remained one of the most difficult areas of AI research and motivated much of this research in knowledge representation. Using a knowledge-based approach, researchers have successfully developed programs that understand natural language in specific domains. In Chapter 10 we introduce some of the techniques for writing natural language understanding programs.

In spite of the successes of expert systems and similar strong problem solvers, there are many domains that require general methods. In fact, the control strategies of expert systems themselves depend on good weak problem-solving methods. Much promising work on weak problem solvers has been done in the automatic theorem proving community. These techniques have found application in a number of important areas including integrated circuit design and proofs of program correctness. In Chapter 11 we examine work in automated reasoning and continue the presentation of formal reasoning we started in Chapter 2.

RULE-BASED EXPERT SYSTEMS

The first principle of knowledge engineering is that the problem solving power exhibited by an intelligent agent's performance is primarily the consequence of its knowledge base, and only secondarily a consequence of the inference method employed. Expert systems must be knowledge-rich even if they are methods-poor. This is an important result and one that has only recently become well understood in AI. For a long time AI has focused its attentions almost exclusively on the development of clever inference methods; almost any inference method will do. The power resides in the knowledge.

—EDWARD FEIGENBAUM, Stanford University

I hate to criticize, Dr Davis, but did you know that
most rules about what the category of
an organism might be
that mention:
> *the site of a culture and*
> *the infection*
also mention:
> *the portal of entry of the organism?*
Shall I try to write a clause to account for this?

—The program Teiresias helping a Stanford physician improve the MYCIN knowledge base

8.0   Introduction

An *expert system* is a knowledge-based program that provides ''expert quality'' solutions to problems in a specific domain. Generally, its knowledge is extracted from human experts in the domain and it attempts to emulate their methodology and performance. As with skilled humans, expert systems tend to be specialists, focusing on a narrow set of problems. Also, like humans, their knowledge is both theoretical and practical, having been perfected through experience in the domain. Unlike a human being, however, current programs cannot learn from their own experience; their knowledge must be extracted from humans and encoded in a formal language. This is the major task facing expert system builders.

Expert systems should not be confused with cognitive modeling programs, which attempt to simulate human mental architecture in detail. These are discussed in Chapter 15. Expert systems neither copy the structure of the human mind nor are mechanisms for general intelligence. They are practical programs that use heuristic strategies developed by humans to solve specific classes of problems.

Because of the heuristic, knowledge-intensive nature of expert level problem solving, expert systems are generally:

1. Open to inspection, both in presenting intermediate steps and in answering questions about the solution process.
2. Easily modified, both in adding and in deleting skills from the knowledge base.
3. Heuristic, in using (often imperfect) knowledge to obtain solutions.

An expert system is "open to inspection" in that the user may, at any time during program execution, inspect the state of its reasoning and determine the specific choices and decisions that the program is making. There are several reasons why this is desirable: first, if a human expert such as a doctor or an engineer is to accept a recommendation from the computer, they must be satisfied the solution is correct. "The computer did it" is not sufficient reason to follow its advice. Indeed, few human experts will accept advice from another human without understanding the reasons for that advice. This need to have answers explained is more than mistrust on the part of users; explanations help people relate the advice to their existing understanding of the domain and apply it in a more confident and flexible manner.

Second, when a solution is open to inspection, we can evaluate every aspect and decision taken during the solution process, allowing for partial agreement and the addition of new information or rules to improve performance. This plays an essential role in the refinement of a knowledge base.

The exploratory nature of AI and expert system programming requires that programs be easily prototyped, tested, and changed. These abilities are supported by AI programming languages and environments and the use of good programming techniques by the designer. In a pure production system, for example, the modification of a single rule has no global syntactic side effects. Rules may be added or removed without requiring further changes to the larger program. Expert system designers have commented that easy modification of the knowledge base is a major factor in producing a successful program (McDermott 1981).

The third feature of expert systems is their use of heuristic problem-solving methods. As expert system designers have discovered, informal "tricks of the trade" and "rules of thumb" are often more important than the standard theory presented in textbooks and classes. Sometimes these rules augment theoretical knowledge; occasionally they are simply shortcuts that seem unrelated to the theory but have been shown to work.

The heuristic nature of expert problem-solving knowledge creates problems in the evaluation of program performance. Although we know that heuristic methods will occasionally fail, it is not clear exactly how often a program must be correct in order to be accepted: 98% of the time? 90%? 80%? Perhaps the best way to evaluate a program is to compare its results to those obtained by human experts in the same area. This suggests a variation of the Turing test (Chapter 1) for evaluating the performance of expert systems: a program has achieved expert level performance if people working in the area could not differentiate, in a blind evaluation, between the best human efforts and those of the program. In evaluating the MYCIN program for diagnosing meningitis infections, Stanford researchers had a number of infectious-disease experts blindly evaluate the performance of both MYCIN and human specialists in infectious diseases. Similarly, Digital Equipment Corporation decided that XCON, a program for configuring VAX computers, was ready for commercial use when its performance was comparable to that of human engineers.

Expert systems have been built to solve a range of problems in domains such as medicine, mathematics, engineering, chemistry, geology, computer science, business, law, defense, and education. These programs have addressed a wide range of problem types; the following list, adapted from Waterman (1986), is a useful summary of general expert system problem categories. Another excellent survey of expert system applications is Smart and Langeland-Knudsen (1986).

1. *Interpretation*—forming high-level conclusions or descriptions from collections of raw data.

2. *Prediction*—projecting probable consequences of given situations.

3. *Diagnosis*—determining the cause of malfunctions in complex situations based on observable symptoms.

4. *Design*—determining a configuration of system components that meets certain performance goals while satisfying a set of constraints.

5. *Planning*—devising a sequence of actions that will achieve a set of goals given certain starting conditions.

6. *Monitoring*—comparing the observed behavior of a system to its expected behavior.

7. *Debugging and Repair*—prescribing and implementing remedies for malfunctions.

8. *Instruction*—detecting and correcting deficiencies in students' understanding of a subject domain.

9. *Control*—governing the behavior of a complex environment.

8.1 Overview of Expert System Technology

8.1.1 Design of Rule-Based Expert Systems

Figure 8.1 shows the most important modules that make up a rule-based expert system. The user interacts with the expert system through a user interface that makes access more comfortable for the human and hides much of the system complexity (e.g., the

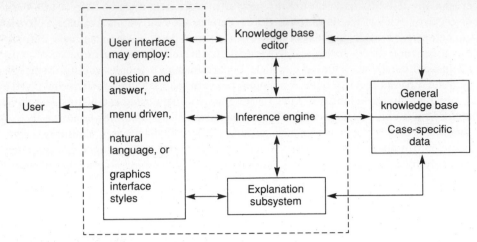

Figure 8.1 Architecture of a typical expert system.

internal structures of the rule base). Expert systems employ a variety of interface styles, including question and answer, menu-driven, natural language, or graphics interfaces.

The program must keep track of *case-specific data*, the facts, conclusions, and other relevant information of the case under consideration. This includes the data given in a problem instance, partial conclusions, confidence measures of conclusions, and dead ends in the search process. This information is separate from the general knowledge base.

The *explanation subsystem* allows the program to explain its reasoning to the user. These explanations include justifications for the system's conclusions (*how queries*, as discussed in Section 8.2.2), explanations of why the system needs a particular piece of data (*why queries*), and, in some experimental systems, tutorial explanations or deeper theoretical justifications of the program's actions.

Many systems also include a *knowledge base editor*. Knowledge base editors can access the explanation subsystem and help the programmer locate bugs in the program's performance. They also may assist in the addition of new knowledge, help maintain correct rule syntax, and perform consistency checks on the updated knowledge base. An example of the Teiresias knowledge base editor is presented in Section 8.4.5.

The heart of the expert system is the general knowledge base, which contains the problem-solving knowledge of the particular application. In a rule-based expert system this knowledge is represented in the form of *if*...*then* rules, as in the auto battery/cable example of Section 8.2. (Other ways of representing this knowledge are discussed in chapters 9 and 14.)

The *inference engine* applies the knowledge to the solution of actual problems. It is the interpreter for the knowledge base. In the production system, the inference engine performs the recognize-act control cycle. The procedures that implement the control cycle are separate from the production rules themselves. It is important to maintain this separation of knowledge base and inference engine for several reasons:

1. The separation of the problem-solving knowledge and the inference engine makes it possible to represent knowledge in a more natural fashion. "If...then" rules, for example, are closer to the way in which human beings describe their own problem-solving techniques than a program that embeds this knowledge in lower-level computer code.

2. Because the knowledge base is separated from the program's lower-level control structures, expert system builders can focus directly on capturing and organizing problem-solving knowledge rather than on the details of its computer implementation.

3. The separation of knowledge and control, along with the modularity of rules and other representational structures used in building knowledge bases, allows changes to be made in one part of the knowledge base without creating side effects in other parts of the program code.

4. The separation of the knowledge and control elements of the program allows the same control and interface software to be used in a variety of systems. The *expert system shell* has all the components of Figure 8.1 except that the knowledge base (and, of course, the case-specific data) contains no information. Programmers can use the "empty shell" and create a new knowledge base appropriate to their application. The broken lines of Figure 8.1 indicate the shell modules.

5. As illustrated in the discussion of production systems (Chapter 4), this modularity allows us to experiment with alternative control regimes for the same rule base.

The use of an expert system shell can reduce the design and implementation time of a program considerably. As may be seen in Figure 8.4, MYCIN was developed in about 20 person-years. EMYCIN (Empty MYCIN) is a general expert system shell that was produced by removing the specific domain knowledge from the MYCIN program. Using EMYCIN, knowledge engineers implemented PUFF, a program to analyze pulmonary problems in patients, in about 5 person-years. This is a remarkable saving and an important aspect of the commercial viability of expert system technology. Expert system shells have become increasingly common, with commercially produced shells available for all classes of computers.

It is important that the programmer choose the proper expert system shell. Different problems often require different reasoning processes: goal-driven rather than data-driven search, for instance. The control strategy provided by the shell must be appropriate to the new application. The medical reasoning in the PUFF application was much like that of the original MYCIN work; this made the use of the EMYCIN shell appropriate. If the shell does not support the appropriate reasoning processes, its use can be a mistake and worse than starting from nothing. As we shall see, part of the responsibility of the expert system builder is to correctly characterize the reasoning processes required for a given problem domain and to either select or construct an inference engine that implements these structures.

Unfortunately, shell programs do not solve all of the problems involved in building expert systems. While the separation of knowledge and control, the modularity of the production system architecture, and the use of an appropriate knowledge representation language all help with the building of an expert system, the acquisition and organization of the knowledge base remain difficult tasks.

8.1.2 Selecting a Problem for Expert System Development

Expert systems tend to involve a considerable investment in money and human effort. Attempts to solve a problem that is too complex, poorly understood, or otherwise unsuited to the available technology can lead to costly and embarrassing failures. Researchers have developed an informal set of guidelines for determining whether a problem is appropriate for expert system solution:

1. *The need for the solution justifies the cost and effort of building an expert system.* For example, Digital Equipment Corporation had experienced considerable financial expense because of errors in configurations of VAX and PDP-11 computers. If a computer is shipped with missing or incompatible components, the company is obliged to correct this situation as quickly as possible, often incurring added shipping expense or absorbing the cost of parts not taken into account when the original price was quoted. Because this expense was considerable, DEC was extremely interested in automating the configuration task; the resulting system, XCON, has paid for itself in both financial savings and customer goodwill. Similarly, many expert systems have been built in domains such as mineral exploration, business, defense, and medicine where there is a large potential for savings in either money, time, or human life. In recent years, the cost of building expert systems has gone down as software tools and expertise in AI have become more available. The range of potentially profitable applications has grown correspondingly.

2. *Human expertise is not available in all situations where it is needed.* Much expert system work has been done in medicine, for example, because the specialization and technical sophistication of modern medicine have made it difficult for doctors to keep up with advances in diagnostics and treatment methods. Specialists with this knowledge are rare and expensive, and expert systems are seen as a way of making their expertise available to a wider range of doctors. In geology, there is a need for expertise at remote mining and drilling sites. Often, geologists and engineers find themselves traveling large distances to visit sites, with resulting expense and wasted time. By placing expert systems at remote sites, many problems may be solved without needing a visit by a human expert. Similarly, loss of valuable expertise through employee turnover or pending retirement may justify building an expert system.

3. *The problem may be solved using symbolic reasoning techniques.* This means that the problem should not require physical dexterity or perceptual skill. Although robots and vision systems are available, they currently lack the sophistication and flexibility of human beings. Expert systems are generally restricted to problems that humans can solve through symbolic reasoning.

4. *The problem domain is well structured and does not require commonsense reasoning.* Although expert systems have been built in a number of areas requiring specialized technical knowledge, more mundane commonsense reasoning is well beyond our current capabilities. Highly technical fields have the advantage of being well studied

and formalized; terms are well defined and domains have clear and specific conceptual models. Most significantly, however, the amount of knowledge required to solve such problems is small in comparison to the amount of knowledge used by human beings in commonsense reasoning.

5. *The problem may not be solved using traditional computing methods.* Expert system technology should not be used to "reinvent the wheel." If a problem can be solved satisfactorily using more traditional techniques such as numerical, statistical, or operations research techniques, then it is not a candidate for an expert system. Because expert systems rely on heuristic approaches, it is unlikely that an expert system will outperform an algorithmic solution if such a solution exists.

6. *Cooperative and articulate experts exist.* The knowledge used by expert systems is often not found in textbooks but comes from the experience and judgment of humans working in the domain. It is important that these experts be both willing and able to share that knowledge. This implies that the experts should be articulate and believe that the project is both practical and beneficial. If, on the other hand, the experts feel threatened by the system, fearing that they may be replaced by it or that the project can't succeed and is therefore a waste of time, it is unlikely that they will give it the necessary time and effort. It is also important that management be supportive of the project and allow the domain experts to take time away from their usual responsibilities to work with the program implementers.

7. *The problem is of proper size and scope.* It is important that the problem not exceed the capabilities of current technology. For example, a program that attempted to capture all of the expertise of a medical doctor would not be feasible; a program that advised MDs on the use of a particular piece of diagnostic equipment would be more appropriate. As a rule of thumb, problems that require days or weeks for human experts to solve are probably too complex for current expert system technology.

Although a large problem may not be amenable to expert system solution, it may be possible to break it into smaller, independent subproblems that are. Or we may be able to start with a simple program that solves a portion of the problem and gradually increase its functionality to handle more of the problem domain. This was done successfully in the creation of XCON: initially the program was designed only to configure VAX 780 computers; later it was expanded to include the full VAX and PDP-11 series (Bachant and McDermott 1984).

8.1.3 Overview of "Knowledge Engineering"

The primary people involved in building an expert system are the *knowledge engineer*, the *domain expert*, and the *end user*.

The knowledge engineer is the AI language and representation expert. His or her main task is to select the software and hardware tools for the project, help extract the necessary knowledge from the domain expert, and implement that knowledge in a correct and efficient knowledge base. The knowledge engineer may initially be ignorant of the application domain.

The domain expert provides the knowledge of the problem area. The domain expert is generally someone who has worked in the domain area and understands its problem-solving techniques, including the use of shortcuts, handling imprecise data, evaluating partial solutions, and all the other skills that mark a person as an expert. The domain expert is primarily responsible for spelling out these skills to the knowledge engineer.

As in most applications, the end user determines the major design constraints. Unless the user is happy, the development effort is by and large wasted. The skills and needs of the user must be considered throughout the design cycle: What level of explanation does the user need? Can the user provide correct information to the system? Is the user interface appropriate? Are there environmental restrictions on the program's use?

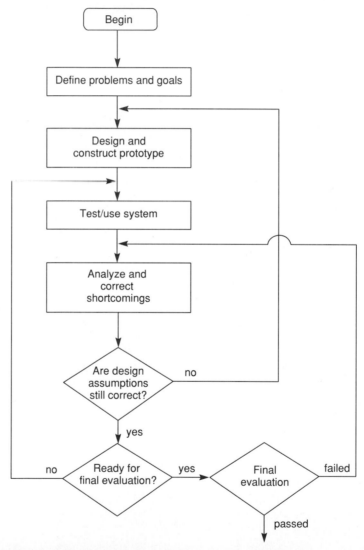

Figure 8.2   Exploratory development cycle for rule-based expert systems.

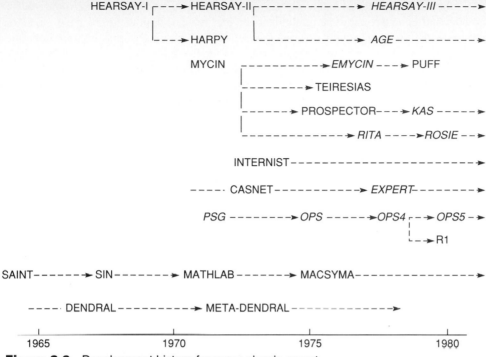

Figure 8.3 Development history for some classic expert
systems (Winston and Prendergast 1984).
Expert system shells in italics.

(An interface that required typing, for example, would not be appropriate for use in the cockpit of a jet fighter.) Will the program make the user's work easier, quicker, more comfortable?

Like most AI programming, expert system development requires a nontraditional development cycle based on early prototyping and incremental revision of the code. This exploratory programming methodology (described in the introduction to Part III) is complicated by the interaction between the knowledge engineer and the domain expert.

Generally, work on the system begins with the knowledge engineer attempting to gain some familiarity with the problem domain. This helps in communicating with the domain expert. This is done in initial interviews with the expert or by reading introductory texts in the domain area. Next, the knowledge engineer and expert begin the process of extracting the expert's problem-solving knowledge. This is often done by giving the domain expert a series of sample problems and having him or her explain the techniques used in their solution.

Here, it is often useful for the knowledge engineer to be a novice in the problem domain. Human experts are notoriously unreliable in explaining exactly what goes on in solving a complex problem. Often they forget to mention steps that have become obvious or even automatic to them after years of work in their field. Knowledge engineers, by virtue of their relative naïveté in the domain, should be able to spot these conceptual jumps and ask for clarification.

Once the knowledge engineer has obtained a general overview of the problem domain and gone through several problem-solving sessions with the domain expert, he or she is ready to begin actual design of the system: selecting a way to represent the knowledge (such as rules or frames), determining the basic search strategy (forward, backward, etc.), and designing the user interface. After making these design commitments, the knowledge engineer builds a prototype.

This prototype should be able to solve problems in a small area of the domain and provides a test bed for preliminary design assumptions. Once the prototype has been implemented, the knowledge engineer and domain expert test and refine its knowledge by giving it problems to solve and correcting its shortcomings. Should the assumptions made in designing the prototype prove correct, it can be built into a complete system.

Expert systems are built by progressive approximations, with the program's mistakes leading to corrections or additions to the knowledge base. In a sense, the knowledge base is "grown" rather than constructed. This approach to programming was proposed by Seymour Papert with his LOGO language (Papert 1980). The LOGO philosophy argues that watching the computer respond to the improperly formulated ideas represented by the code leads to their correction (being debugged) and clarification with more precise code. Other researchers have verified this notion that design proceeds through a process of trying and correcting candidate designs, rather than by such neatly hierarchical processes as top-down design.

It is also understood that the prototype may be thrown away if it becomes too cumbersome or if the designers decide to change their basic approach to the problem. The prototype lets program builders explore the problem and its important relationships by actually constructing a program to solve it. After this progressive clarification is complete, they can often write a cleaner version, usually with fewer actual rules.

The second major feature of expert system programming is that the program need never be considered "finished." A large heuristic knowledge base will always have limitations. The modularity and ease of modification available in the production system model make it natural to add new rules or make up for the shortcomings of the present rule base at any time. DEC, for example, has continued to add new rules to the XCON program to extend its capabilities to the rest of their product line. In 1981, XCON had about 500 rules and could configure the VAX 780; it was progressively refined until, in 1984 with about 4000 rules, it configured most of the DEC product line.

Furthermore, as DEC changed the specifications for its computers, previously correct rules needed updating. One report noted that up to 50% of the XCON rules were changed each year just to keep up with changes in the product line (Soloway et al. 1987). Figure 8.2 presents a schematic overview of the development cycle of expert system software.

Even though expert systems of commercial quality have been available since 1980, research in the development of expert systems has gone on since the middle 1960s. In fact, the emergence of commercially viable expert systems in the present world market has been a direct result of this earlier research. Figure 8.3 shows the history of the programs that are now considered "classic" in this area.

The major development activity for these early programs took place at three universities: Stanford, MIT, and Carnegie Mellon. The main research and development thrust for the rule-based expert system was at Stanford, under the direction of Edward Feigen-

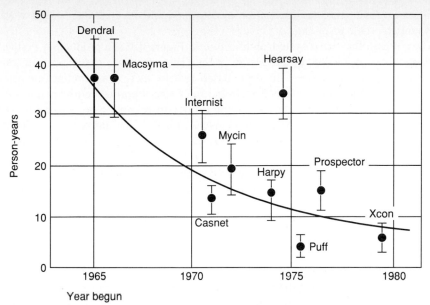

Figure 8.4 Development time for selected expert systems between 1965 and 1985 (Hayes-Roth et al. 1984).

baum, although other work in the area certainly took place at, for instance, Rutgers and the University of Pittsburgh. The early development of the production system model for problem solving, including the development of the OPS languages, took place primarily at Carnegie Mellon University.

Figure 8.4 presents another important aspect of the evolution of expert system programs: the average development time for expert systems has been drastically reduced across the decades of evolution. The emergence of expert system shells was instrumental in reducing the design time. This is perhaps the most important reason for current commercial successes.

8.2 A Framework for Organizing and Applying Human Knowledge

8.2.1 Production Systems, Rules, and the Expert System Architecture

The architecture of rule-based expert systems may be understood in terms of the production system model for problem solving presented in Part II. In fact, the parallel between the two entities is more than a simple analogy: the production system was the intellectual precursor of modern expert system architecture. This is not surprising; when Newell and

Simon began developing the production system model, their goal was to find a way to model human problem solving.

If we regard the expert system architecture in Figure 8.1 as a production system, the knowledge base is the set of production rules. The expertise of the problem area is represented by the productions. In a rule-based system, these condition-action pairs are represented as rules, with the premises of the rules (the if portion) corresponding to the condition and the conclusion (the then portion) corresponding to the action. Case-specific data are kept in the working memory. Finally, the inference engine is the recognize-act cycle of the production system. This control may be either data driven or goal driven.

In a goal-driven expert system, the goal expression is initially placed in working memory. The system matches rule conclusions with the goal, selecting one rule and placing its *premises* in the working memory. This corresponds to a decomposition of the problem into simpler subgoals. The process continues, with these premises becoming the new goals to match against rule conclusions. The system thus works back from the original goal until all the subgoals in working memory are known to be true, indicating that the hypothesis has been verified. Thus, backward search in an expert system corresponds roughly to the process of hypothesis testing in human problem solving.

In an expert system, subgoals are often solved by asking the user for information. Some expert system shells allow the system designer to specify which subgoals may be solved by asking the user. Other inference engines simply ask about all subgoals that fail to match with the conclusion of some rule in the knowledge base; i.e., if the program cannot infer the truth of a subgoal, it asks the user.

Many problem domains seem to lend themselves more naturally to forward search. In an interpretation problem, for example, most of the data for the problem are initially given and it is often difficult to formulate a hypotheses (goal). This suggests a forward reasoning process in which the facts are placed in working memory and the system searches for an interpretation in a forward fashion.

As a more detailed example, let us create a small expert system for diagnosing automotive problems:

Rule 1:

if

the engine is getting gas, and

the engine will turn over,

then

the problem is spark plugs.

Rule 2:

if

the engine does not turn over, and

the lights do not come on

then

the problem is battery or cables.

Rule 3:

if

the engine does not turn over, and

the lights do come on

then

the problem is the starter motor.

Rule 4:

if

there is gas in fuel tank, and

there is gas in carburetor

then

the engine is getting gas.

To run this knowledge base under a goal-directed control regime, place the top-level goal, the problem is X, in working memory as in Figure 8.5. X is a variable that can match with any phrase; it will become bound to the solution when the problem is solved.

There are three rules that match with the expression in working memory, rule 1, rule 2, and rule 3. If we resolve conflicts in favor of the lowest-numbered rule, then rule 1 will fire. This causes X to be bound to the value spark plugs and the premises of rule 1 to be placed in the working memory as in Figure 8.6. The system has thus chosen to explore the possible hypothesis that the spark plugs are bad. Another way to look at this is that the system has selected an or branch in an and/or graph (Chapter 3).

Note that there are two premises to rule 1, both of which must be satisfied to prove the conclusion true. These are and branches of the search graph representing a decomposition of the problem (finding if the spark plugs are bad) into two subproblems (finding

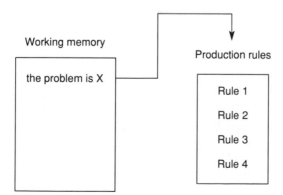

Figure 8.5 Working memory at the start of a consultation in the car diagnostic example.

Figure 8.6 Working memory after Rule 1 has fired.

Figure 8.7 Working memory after Rule 4 has fired.

if the engine is getting gas and if the engine is turning over). We may then fire rule 4, whose conclusion matches with "engine is getting gas," causing its premises to be placed in working memory as in Figure 8.7.

At this point, there are three entries in working memory that do not match with any rule conclusions. Our expert system will query the user directly about these subgoals. If the user confirms all three of these as true, the expert system will have successfully determined that the car will not start because the spark plugs are bad. In finding this solution, the system has searched the **and/or** graph presented in Figure 8.8.

This is, of course, a very simple example. Not only is its automotive knowledge limited at best, but also a number of important aspects of real implementations are

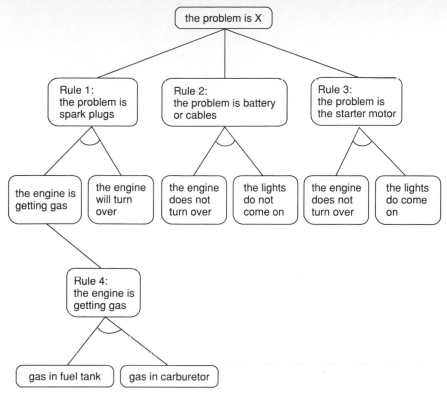

Figure 8.8 And/or graph searched in the car diagnostic example.

ignored. The rules are phrased in English, rather than a formal language. On finding a solution, a real expert system will tell the user its diagnosis (our model simply stops). Also, we should maintain enough of a trace of the reasoning to allow backtracking if necessary; in our example, had we failed to determine that the spark plugs were bad, we would have needed to back up to the top level and try rule 2 instead. Notice that this information is implicit in the ordering of subgoals in working memory of Figure 8.7 and in the graph of Figure 8.8. This example of expert systems underscores their foundation in the production system and **and/or** graph search models of earlier chapters.

At the beginning of this chapter, we emphasized that an expert system needed to be open to inspection, easily modified, and heuristic in nature. The production system architecture is an important factor in each of these requirements. Ease of modification, for example, is made possible by the syntactic independence of production rules: each rule is a chunk of knowledge that can be independently modified. The heuristic nature of these rules is in the knowledge obtained from the domain expert and, as seen in Section 8.3, from use of confidence measures. The next section discusses the way in which this architecture supports explanations and inspection of the reasoning process.

8.2.2 Explanation and Transparency

The production system implements a graph search; the explanation routines of Figure 8.1 keep track of the graph search and use a trace of the search to answer user queries. The production rules themselves document each step of the reasoning process.

In general, the two questions supported by rule-based expert systems are why? and how? In a why query, the user has been asked for information by the program and responds with why, meaning "why did you ask that?" The answer is the current rule that the production system is attempting to fire. The answer to "how did you get that result?" is the sequence of rules that were used to conclude a goal.

Suppose our automotive expert system has an explanation facility and assume that the consultation has reached the stage represented by the working memory configuration in Figure 8.7. The following dialogue begins with the computer asking the user about the goals present in working memory. User responses are in this type.

> gas in fuel tank?
> yes
>
> gas in carburetor?
> yes
>
> engine will turn over?
> why

Here the user enters a why query, i.e., why do you want to know that?

> It has been established that:
>
> 1. engine is getting gas,
>
> therefore if
>
> 2. engine will turn over,
>
> then the problem is spark plugs.

Since the user answered yes to the first two questions, rule 4 was able to fire, verifying the first premise of rule 1. When the why query was made, the system was trying to solve the second premise of rule 1. Note that the explanation is just a restatement of the current rule, but it provides an adequate explanation for why the program wants to know if the engine will turn over. Continuing with the dialogue:

> how engine is getting gas

Here the user asks how the program knew that the engine is getting gas. The response is a trace of the reasoning that led to this conclusion, working back from the goal along the rules that support it to the user responses:

> This follows from Rule 4:
>
> if
>
> gas in fuel tank, and
>
> gas in carburetor
>
> then
>
> engine is getting gas.

gas in fuel tank was given by the user

gas in carburetor was given by the user

This simple example illustrates the explanations that expert systems provide the user. Why queries are answered by showing the current rule that the system is attempting to fire. How queries are answered by giving a trace of the reasoning that led to a goal. Although the mechanisms are conceptually simple, they can exhibit remarkable explanatory power if the knowledge base is organized in a logical fashion.

The production system architecture provides an essential basis for these explanations. Each cycle of the control loop selects and fires another rule. The program may be stopped after each cycle and inspected. Since each rule represents a complete chunk of problem-solving knowledge, the current rule provides a context for the explanation. Contrast this with more traditional program architectures: if we stop a Pascal or FORTRAN program in midexecution, it is doubtful that the current statement will have much meaning.

If explanations are to behave logically, it is important not only that the knowledge base get the correct answer but also that each rule correspond to a single logical step in the problem-solving process. If a knowledge base combines several steps into a single rule or if it breaks up the rules in an arbitrary fashion, it may get correct answers but seem arbitrary and illogical in responding to how and why queries. This not only undermines the user's faith in the system but also makes the program much more difficult for its builders to understand and modify.

8.2.3   Heuristics and Control in Expert Systems

Because of the separation of the knowledge base and the inference engine and the fixed control regimes provided by the inference engine, the only way that a programmer can control the search is through the structure of the rules in the knowledge base. This is an advantage, since the control strategies required for expert level problem solving tend to be domain specific and knowledge intensive. Although a rule of the form if p, q, and r then s resembles a logical expression, it may also be interpreted as a series of procedures for solving a problem: to do s, first do p, then do q, then do r. This dual semantics of rules was already discussed in the introductory PROLOG chapter.

This procedural interpretation allows us to control search through the structure of the rules. For example, we may order the premises of a rule so that the premise that is most likely to fail or is easiest to confirm will be tried first. This gives the opportunity of eliminating a rule (and hence a portion of the search space) as early in the search as possible. Rule 1 in the automotive example tries to determine if the engine is getting gas before it asks if the engine turns over. This is inefficient, in that trying to determine if the engine is getting gas invokes another rule and eventually asks the user two questions. By reversing the order of the premises, a negative response to the query "engine will turn over?" eliminates this rule from consideration before the more involved condition is examined.

Also, from another point of view, it makes more sense to determine whether the engine is turning over before checking to see if it is getting gas; if the engine won't turn over it doesn't matter if it is getting gas. Rule 4 asks the user to check for gas in the fuel tank before asking that the user open up the carburetor and look there. It is performing the easier check first.

In addition to the ordering of a rule's premises, the content of a rule itself may be fundamentally heuristic in nature. In the automotive example, all the rules are heuristic; consequently, the system may obtain erroneous results. For example, if the engine is getting gas and turning over, the problem may be a bad distributor rather than bad spark plugs. In the next section, we examine this problem and some ways of dealing with it.

8.3 Using Uncertainty Measures in Expert Systems

8.3.1 Introduction

Until Section 8.2, our inference procedures followed the model presented with the predicate calculus: from correct premises sound inference rules produce new, guaranteed correct, conclusions. In expert systems, we must often attempt to draw correct conclusions from poorly formed and uncertain evidence using unsound inference rules.

This is not an impossible task; we do it successfully in almost every aspect of our daily survival. We deliver correct medical treatment for ambiguous symptoms; we mine natural resourccs with little or no guarantee of success before we start; we comprehend language statements that are often ambiguous or incomplete, and so on.

The reasons for this ambiguity may be better understood by referring once again to our automotive expert system example. Consider rule 2:

if

the engine does not turn over, and

the lights do not come on

then

the problem is battery or cables.

This rule is heuristic in nature; it is possible (although less likely) that the battery and cables are fine but that the car simply has a bad starter motor and burned-out headlights. This rule seems to resemble a logical implication, but it is not: failure of the engine to turn over and the lights to come on does not necessarily imply that the battery and cables are bad. What is interesting to note, however, is that the *converse* of the rule is a true implication:

if

the problem is battery or cables

then

the engine does not turn over, and

the lights do not come on.

Barring the supernatural, a car with a dead battery will not light its headlamps or turn the starter motor.

This is an example of **abductive** reasoning. Formally, abduction states that from P -> Q and Q it is possible to infer P.

Abduction is an *unsound* rule of inference, meaning that the conclusion is not necessarily true for every interpretation in which the premises are true. For example, if someone says "If it rains then I will not go running at 3:00" and you do not see that person on the track at 3:00, does it necessarily follow that it is raining? It is possible that the individual decided not to go running because of an injury or that he needed to work late, etc.

Although abduction is unsound, it is often essential to solving problems. The "correct" version of the battery rule is not particularly useful in diagnosing car troubles since its premise (bad battery) is our goal and its conclusions are the observable symptoms we must work with. Modus ponens cannot be applied and the rule must be used in an abductive fashion. This is generally true of diagnostic (and other) expert systems. Faults or diseases cause (imply) symptoms, not the other way around, but diagnosis must work from the symptoms back to the cause.

Uncertainty results from the use of abductive inference as well as from attempts to reason with missing or unreliable data. To get around this problem, we can attach some measure of confidence to the conclusions. For example, although battery failure does not always accompany the failure of a car's lights and starters, it almost always does, and confidence in this rule is justifiably high.

Note that there are problems that do not require certainty measures. When configuring a computer, for instance, the components either go together or they do not. The idea that "a particular disk drive and bus go together with certainty 0.75" does not even make sense. Similarly, if MACSYMA is attempting to find the integral of a function, a confidence of "0.6" that a result is correct is not useful. These programs may be either data driven (Digital's XCON) or goal driven (MIT's MACSYMA), but because they do not require abductive rules of inference or do not deal with unreliable data they do not require the use of confidence measures.

In this section we discuss several ways of managing the uncertainty that results from heuristic rules: first, the Bayesian approach (8.3.2), and second, the Stanford certainty theory (8.3.3). Finally, we briefly consider Zadeh's *fuzzy set theory*, the Dempster/Shafer theory of evidential reasoning, and nonmonotonic reasoning.

8.3.2 Bayesian Probability Theory

The Bayesian approach to uncertainty is based in formal probability theory and has shown up in several areas of AI research, including pattern recognition and classification problems. The PROSPECTOR expert system, built at Stanford and SRI International and employed in mineral exploration (copper, molybdenum, and others), also uses a form of the Bayesian statistical model.

Assuming random distribution of events, probability theory allows the calculation of more complex probabilities from previously known results. In simple probability calculations we are able to conclude, for example, how cards might be distributed to a number of players.

Suppose that I am one person of a four-person card game where all the cards are equally distributed. If I do not have the queen of spades I can conclude that each of the others players has it with probability 1/3. Similarly, I can conclude that each player has the ace of hearts with probability 1/3 and that any one player has both cards at 1/3 * 1/3 or 1/9.

In the mathematical theory of probability, individual probability instances are worked out by sampling and combinations of probabilities are worked out as above, using a rule such as:

probability(A and B) = probability(A) * probability(B)

given that A and B are independent events.

One of the most important results of probability theory is Bayes's theorem. Bayes's results provide a way of computing the probability of a hypothesis following from a particular piece of evidence, given only the probabilities with which the evidence follows from actual causes (hypotheses).

Bayes's theorem states:

$$p(H_i \mid E) = \frac{P(E \mid H_i) * P(H_i)}{\sum_{k=1}^{n} (P(E \mid H_k) * P(H_k))}$$

where:

$P(H_i \mid E)$ is the probability that H_i is true given evidence E.

$P(H_i)$ is the probability that H_i is true overall.

$P(E \mid H_i)$ is the probability of observing evidence E when H_i is true.

n is the number of possible hypotheses.

Suppose we desire to examine the geological evidence at some location to see if the location is suited to finding copper. We must know in advance the probability of finding each of a set of minerals and the probability of certain evidence being present when each particular mineral is found. Then we can use Bayes's theorem to determine the likelihood that copper will be present using the evidence we collect at the location. This is the approach taken in the PROSPECTOR program, which has found commercially significant mineral deposits (Duda et al. 1979a) at several sites.

There are two major assumptions for the use of Bayes's theorem: first that all the statistical data on the relationships of the evidence with the various hypotheses are known; second, and more difficult to establish, that all relationships between evidence and hypotheses, or $P(E \mid H_k)$, are independent. Actually, this assumption of independence can be a quite tricky matter, especially when many assumptions of independence are needed to establish the validity of this approach across many rule applications. This represents the entire collected probabilities on the evidence given various hypothesis relationships in the denominator of Bayes's theorem. In general, and especially in areas like medicine, this assumption of independence cannot be justified.

A final problem, which makes keeping the statistics of the "evidence given hypotheses" relationships virtually intractable, is the need to rebuild all probability relationships when any new relationship of hypothesis to evidence is discovered. In many active research areas (again, like medicine) this is happening continuously. Bayesian reasoning requires complete and up-to-date probabilities if its conclusions are to be correct. In many domains, such extensive data collection and verification are not possible.

Where these assumptions are met, Bayesian approaches offer the benefit of a well-founded and statistically correct handling of uncertainty. Most expert system domains do not meet these requirements and must rely on more heuristic approaches. It is also felt that the human expert does not use the Bayesian model in successful problem solving. In the next section we describe certainty theory, a heuristic approach to the management of uncertainty.

8.3.3 A Theory for Certainty

Several early expert system projects (besides PROSPECTOR) attempted to adapt Bayes's theorem to their problem-solving needs. The independence assumptions, continuous updates of statistical data, and other problems mentioned in Section 8.3.2 gradually led these researchers to search for other measures of "confidence." Probably the most important alternative approach was used at Stanford in developing the MYCIN program (Buchanan and Shortliff 1984).

Certainty theory is based on a number of observations. The first is that in traditional probability theory the sum of confidence for a relationship and confidence against the same relationship must add to 1. However, it is often the case that an expert might have confidence 0.7 (say) that some relationship is true and have no feeling about it being not true.

Another assumption that underpins certainty theory is that the knowledge content of the rules is much more important than the algebra of confidences that holds the system together. Confidence measures correspond to the informal evaluations that human experts attach to their conclusions, e.g., "it is probably true" or "it is highly unlikely."

Certainty theory makes some simple assumptions for creating confidence measures and has some equally simple rules for combining these confidences as the program moves toward its conclusion. The first assumption is to split "confidence for" from "confidence against" a relationship:

Call $MB(H|E)$ the measure of belief of a hypothesis H given evidence E.

Call $MD(H|E)$ the measure of disbelief of a hypothesis H given evidence E.

Now either:

$1 > MB(H|E) > 0$ while $MD(H|E) = 0$, or

$1 > MD(H|E) > 0$ while $MB(H|E) = 0$.

The two measures constrain each other in that a given piece of evidence is either for or against a particular hypothesis. This is an important difference between certainty theory and probability theory. Once the link between measures of belief and disbelief has been established, they may be tied together again with the certainty factor calculation:

$CF(H|E) = MB(H|E) - MD(H|E)$.

As the certainty factor (CF) approaches 1 the evidence is stronger for a hypothesis; as

CF approaches −1 the confidence against the hypothesis gets stronger; and a CF around 0 indicates that there is little evidence either for or against the hypothesis.

When experts put together the rule base they must agree on a CF to go with each rule. This CF reflects their confidence in the rule's reliability. Certainty measures may be adjusted to tune the system's performance, although slight variations in this confidence measure tend to have little effect on the overall running of the system (again, "the knowledge gives the power").

The premises for each rule are formed of the and and or of a number of facts. When a production rule is used, the certainty factors that are associated with each condition of the premise are combined to produce a certainty measure for the overall premise in the following manner.

For P1 and P2, premises of the rule,

CF(P1 and P2) = MIN(CF(P1), CF(P2)),   and

CF(P1 or P2) = MAX(CF(P1), CF(P2)).

The combined CF of the premises, using the above combining rules, is then multiplied by the CF of the rule to get the CF for the conclusions of the rule.

For example, consider the rule in a knowledge base:

(P1 and P2) or P3 → R1 (.7) and R2 (.3)

where P1, P2, and P3 are premises and R1 and R2 are the conclusions of the rule having CFs 0.7 and 0.3, respectively. These numbers are added to the rule when it is designed and represent the expert's confidence in the conclusion if all the premises are known with complete certainty. If the running program has produced P1, P2, and P3 with CFs of 0.6, 0.4, and 0.2, respectively, then R1 and R2 may be added to the collected case-specific results with CFs 0.28 and 0.12, respectively.

Here are the calculations for this example:

CF(P1(.6) and P2(.4)) = MIN(.6,.4) = .4.

CF((.4) or P3(.2)) = MAX(.4,.2) = .4.

The CF for R1 is 7 in the rule, so R1 is added to the set of true facts with the associated CF of (7) * (.4) = .28.

The CF for R2 is .3 in the rule, so R2 is added to the set of true facts with the associated CF of (.3) * (.4) = .12.

One further measure is required: how to combine multiple CFs when two or more rules support the same result R. This is the certainty theory analog of the probability theory procedure of multiplying the probability measures to combine independent evidence. By using this rule repeatedly one can combine the results of any number of rules that are used for determining result R. Suppose CFR1 is the present certainty factor associated with result R, and a previously unused rule produces result R (again) with CFR2; then the new CF of R is calculated by:

CF(R1) + CF(R2) − (CF(R1) * CF(R2))   when CF(R1) and CF(R2) are positive

CF(R1) + CF(R2) + (CF(R1) * CF(R2))   when CF(R1) and CF(R2) are negative

$$\frac{CF(R1) + CF(R2)}{1 - MIN(|CF(R1)|, |CF(R2)|)} \quad \text{otherwise}$$

where $|X|$ is the absolute value of X.

Besides being easy to compute, these equations have other desirable properties. First, the CFs that result from applying this rule are always between 1 and −1, as are the other CFs. Second, the result of combining contradictory CFs is that they cancel each other out, as would be desired. Finally, the combined CF measure is a monotonically increasing (decreasing) function in the manner one would expect for combining evidence.

Certainty theory has been criticized as being excessively ad hoc. Although it is defined in a formal algebra, the meaning of the certainty measures is not as rigorously founded as in formal probability theory. However, certainty theory does not attempt to produce an algebra for ''correct'' reasoning. Rather it is the ''lubrication'' that lets the expert system combine confidences as it moves along through the problem at hand. Its measures are ad hoc in the same sense that a human expert's confidence in his or her results is approximate, heuristic, and informal. In Section 8.4, when MYCIN is considered, the CFs will be used in the heuristic search to give a priority for goals to be attempted and a cutoff point when a goal need not be considered further. But even though the CF is used to keep the program running and collecting information, the power of the program is in the content of the rules themselves. This is the justification for the weakness of the certainty algebra.

8.3.4   Other Approaches to Uncertainty

Because of the importance of uncertain reasoning to expert level problem solving and the limitations of certainty theory, work continues in this important area. In concluding this subsection, we mention briefly three other approaches to modeling uncertainty: Zadeh's *fuzzy set theory*, the Dempster/Shafer *theory of evidence*, and *nonmonotonic reasoning*.

Zadeh's main contention (Zadeh 1983) is that, although probability theory is appropriate for measuring randomness of information, it is inappropriate for measuring the *meaning* of information. Indeed, much of the confusion surrounding the use of English words and phrases is related to lack of clarity (vagueness) rather than randomness. This is a crucial point for analyzing language structures and can also be important in creating a measure of confidence in production rules. Zadeh proposes *possibility theory* as a measure of vagueness, just as probability theory measures randomness.

Zadeh's theory expresses lack of precision in a quantitative fashion by introducing a set membership function that can take on real values between 0 and 1. This is the notion of a *fuzzy set* and can be described as follows: let S be a set and s a member of that set. A fuzzy subset F of S is defined by a membership function $mF(s)$ that measures the ''degree'' to which s belongs to F.

A standard example of the fuzzy set is for S to be the set of positive integers and F to be the fuzzy subset of S called ''small integers.'' Now various integer values can have a ''possibility'' distribution defining their ''fuzzy membership'' in the set of small integers: $mF(1) = 1$, $mF(2) = 1$, $mF(3) = 0.9$, $mF(4) = 0.8$, ..., $mF(50) = 0.001$, etc. For the statement that positive integer X is a "small integer," mF creates a possibility distribution across all the positive integers (S).

Fuzzy set theory is not concerned with how these possibility distributions are created, but rather with the rules for computing the combined possibilities over expressions that each contain fuzzy variables. Thus it includes rules for combining possibility measures for expressions containing fuzzy variables. The laws for the or, and, and not of these expressions are similar to those just presented for certainty factors. In fact, the approach at Stanford was modeled on some of the combination rules described by Zadeh (Buchanan and Shortliffe 1984).

Dempster and Schafer approach the problem of measuring certainty by asking us to make a fundamental distinction between uncertainty and ignorance. In probability theory we are *forced* to express the extent of our knowledge about a belief X in a single number P(X). The problem with this (say Dempster and Shafer) is that we simply cannot always know the values of prior probabilities and thus any particular choice of P(X) may not be justified.

The Dempster/Schafer approach recognizes the distinction between uncertainty and ignorance by creating "belief functions." These belief functions satisfy axioms that are weaker than those of probability theory. Thus probability theory is seen as a subclass of belief functions, and the theory of evidence can reduce to probability theory when all the probabilities are obtainable. Belief functions therefore allow us to use our knowledge to bound the assignment of probabilities to events without having to come up with exact probabilities, when these may be unavailable.

Even though the Dempster/Shafer approach gives us methods of computing these various belief parameters, their greater complexity adds to the computational cost as well. Besides, any theory that has probability theory as a special case is plagued by the assumptions that have made probability theory already quite difficult to use. Conclusions using beliefs, even though they avoid commitment to a stronger (and often unjustified) assignment of probability, produce conclusions that are necessarily weaker. But, as the Dempster/Shafer model points out quite correctly, the stronger conclusion may not be justified.

All of the methods we have examined can be criticized for using numeric approaches to the handling of uncertain reasoning. It is unlikely that humans use any of these techniques for reasoning with uncertainty, and many applications seem to require a more qualitative approach to the problem. For example, numeric approaches do not support adequate explanations of the causes of uncertainty. If we ask human experts why their conclusions are uncertain, they can answer in terms of the qualitative relationships between features of the problem instance. In a numeric model of uncertainty, this information is replaced by numeric measures. Similarly, numeric approaches do not address the problem of changing data. What should the system do if a piece of uncertain information is later found to be true or false?

Nonmonotonic reasoning addresses these problems directly. A nonmonotonic reasoning system handles uncertainty by making the most reasonable assumptions in light of uncertain information. It proceeds with its reasoning as if these assumptions were true. At a later time, it may find out that an assumption was erroneous, either through a change in problem data or by discovering that the assumption led to an impossible conclusion. When this occurs, the system must change both the assumption and all of the conclusions that depend on it.

Nonmonotonicity is an important feature of human problem solving and commonsense reasoning. When we drive to work, for example, we make numerous assumptions about the roads and traffic. If we find that one of these assumptions is violated, perhaps by construction or an accident on our usual route, we change our plans and devise an alternative route to work.

Nonmonotonic reasoning contrasts sharply with the inference strategies we have discussed so far in the text. These strategies assume that axioms do not change and the conclusions drawn from them remain true. They are called *monotonic* reasoning systems because knowledge can only be added through the reasoning process. Since information may also be retracted in a nonmonotonic reasoning system when something that was previously thought to be true is later shown to be false, it is important to record the justification for all new knowledge. When an assumed fact is withdrawn, all conclusions that depend on that fact must be reexamined and possibly withdrawn as well. This record keeping is the task of *truth maintenance systems* (Doyle 1979; de Kleer 1986).

8.4   MYCIN: A Case Study

8.4.1   Introduction

Although our small automotive diagnostic example is useful in presenting some of the concepts of expert system design, it is a toy system and ignores much of the complexity encountered in building large knowledge-based programs. For this reason, we end this chapter with a case study of an actual working expert system.

The MYCIN project was a cooperative venture by the Department of Computer Science and the Medical School at Stanford University. The main work on the project was done during the middle and late 1970s, and about 50 person-years were expended in the effort. MYCIN was written in INTERLISP, a dialect of the LISP programming language. One of the earliest expert systems to be proposed and designed, it has become an important classic in the field. Indeed, it is often presented as the archetype for the rule-based program, with many commercial systems (e.g., TI's Personal Consultant) essentially duplicating the MYCIN approach. One of the main reasons for the influence of the MYCIN program is the extensive documentation of the project by the Stanford research teams (Buchanan and Shortliffe 1984).

MYCIN was designed to solve the problem of diagnosing and recommending treatment for meningitis and bacteremia (blood infections). This particular domain was chosen largely because the program architects wanted to explore the way in which human experts reason with missing and incomplete information. Although there are diagnostic tools that can unambiguously determine the identity of the infecting organisms in a case of meningitis, these tools require on the order of 48 hours (chiefly to grow a culture of the infecting organisms) to return a diagnosis. Meningitis patients, however, are very sick, and some treatment must begin immediately. Because of this need, doctors have developed considerable expertise, based on initial symptoms and test results, for forming a diagnosis that *covers* (i.e., includes as a subset) the actual infecting organisms. Treatment begins with this diagnosis and is refined when more conclusive information becomes available. Thus, the domain of meningitis diagnosis provided a natural focus for studying how humans solve problems using incomplete or unreliable information.

Another goal of the MYCIN design team was to pattern the behavior of the program after the way in which human physicians interact in actual consultations. This was seen as an important factor in system acceptability, particularly since medical consultations tend to follow a standard set of protocols.

In the next subsections we examine the composition of the MYCIN rule and fact descriptions, including the syntax of MYCIN rules. Next, we present a trace of a MYCIN consultation, along with explanatory comments and a discussion of the design and structure of the dialogue. We then discuss the problem of evaluating expert systems and, finally, demonstrate the use of an experimental knowledge base editor, *Teiresias*. Editors such as Teiresias assist the domain experts (in this case the doctors) in correcting the MYCIN knowledge base without the need for the computer language expert. Although such tools are still mainly experimental, this is an important area of research and a potential key to increasing the range of applicability of expert system technology.

8.4.2   Representation of Rules and Facts

Facts in MYCIN are represented as *attribute-object-value triples*. The first element of this structure is an attribute of an object in the problem domain. For example, we may wish to describe the identity of a disease organism or its sensitivity to certain drugs. The name of the object and the value of the attribute follow. Since information in this domain may be uncertain, a certainty factor is associated with MYCIN facts. Recall from Section 8.3.3 that this certainty factor will be between 1 and -1, with 1 being certain, -1 indicating certainty that the attribute is not true, and values about 0 indicating that little is known.

For example, MYCIN facts may be represented in English by:

> There is evidence (.25) that the identity of the organism is Klebsiella.

and

> It is known that the organism is not sensitive to penicillin.

These may be translated into the LISP s-expressions:

> (ident organism_1 klebsiella .25)

and

> (sensitive organism_1 penicillin -1.0)

We next present an example MYCIN rule both in English and in its LISP equivalent. This sample rule is a condition-action pair in which the premise (condition) is the conjunction of three facts (attribute-object-value triples) and the action adds a new fact to the set of things known about the patient, the identity of a particular organism that is added to the "cover set" of possible infecting organisms. Because this is an abductive rule of inference (inferring the cause from the evidence), it has an attached certainty factor.

In English:

    if (a) the infection is primary-bacteremia, and
       (b) the site of the culture is one of the sterile sites, and
       (c) the suspected portal of entry is the gastrointestinal tract
    then   there is suggestive evidence (.7) that infection is bacteroid

is rendered for MYCIN:

    IF: (AND (same_context infection primary_bacteremia)
             (membf_context site sterilesite)
             (same_context portal GI))

    THEN: (conclude context_ident bacteroid tally .7).

Syntactically, attribute-object-valve (A-O-V) triples are essentially a restriction of predicate calculus expressions to binary predicates. This restriction is not particularly limiting, since algorithms exist for translating predicates of any arity into a set of binary predicates.

There is a deeper difference between predicate calculus and the A-O-V triples used in MYCIN: predicates may be either true or false. Predicate calculus uses sound rules of inference to determine the truth value of conclusions. In MYCIN, a fact has an attached confidence rather than a truth value. When the system is deriving new facts, it fails to fire any rule whose premise has a certainty value of less than 0.2. This contrasts with logic, which causes a rule to fail if its premise is found to be false.

This comparison of attribute-object-value triples and predicate calculus expressions is included here to emphasize both the similarities and the trade-offs involved in different knowledge representations. At the highest conceptual level, the characteristics that define a rule-based expert system are independent of any commitment to a particular representational format. These characteristics have been discussed in the comparison of rule-based expert systems and the production system model of problem solving. At the level of an implementation, however, the selection of a particular representational formalism does involve a number of important trade-offs. These issues include the clarity of the representation, expressiveness (what knowledge can the formalism effectively capture?), naturalness of expression, and ease of implementing and verifying the system.

The action of a MYCIN rule can perform a number of tasks once the rule is satisfied. It may add new information about a particular patient to the working memory. It may also write information to the terminal (or other output device), change the value of an attribute or its certainty measure, look up information in a table (where this presentation is more efficient), or execute any piece of LISP code.

Although the ability to execute arbitrary LISP code gives unlimited added power, it should be used judiciously, since excessive use of escapes to the underlying language can lose many of the benefits of the production system formalism. (As an absurd example of this, imagine an expert system with only one rule, whose action is to call a large and poorly structured LISP program that attempts to solve the problem!)

MYCIN rule and fact descriptions, like all knowledge representations, are a formal language and have a formal syntactic definition. This formal syntax is essential to the definition of well-behaved inference procedures. Furthermore, the formal syntax of rules can help a knowledge base editor, such as Teiresias, determine when the domain expert has produced an incorrectly formed rule and prevent that rule from entering the knowledge base. Teiresias can detect syntactic errors in a rule and, to an impressive degree, automatically remedy the situation (see Section 8.4.5). This is possible only when the entire program is built on a set of formal specifications.

The syntax of MYCIN rules is given below. It is stated in *BNF* or *Backus-Naur form* (Pratt 1984). BNF is a form of context-free grammar that is widely used to define programming languages. In the notation, keywords in the language are written in uppercase letters. These are terminals in the syntax. Nonterminals are enclosed in angle brackets: <>. The BNF grammar is a collection of rewrite rules; the nonterminal figure to the left of the ::= can be replaced with the expression on the right. If we begin with the <rule> nonterminal, anything that can be produced through a series of legal substitutions is a legal MYCIN rule.

```
<rule> ::= (IF <antecedent> THEN <action> [ELSE <action>])
<antecedent> ::= (AND {<condition>}+)
<condition> ::= (OR {<condition>}+ | <predicate> <associative-triple>)
<associative-triple> ::= (<attribute><object><value>)
<action> ::= {<consequent>}+ | {<procedure>}+
<consequent> ::= (<associative-triple> <certainty-factor>)
<certainty-factor> ranges from -1 (false) to +1 (true).
<predicate> is any LISP predicate.
<procedure> is any piece of LISP code.
```

8.4.3   MYCIN Diagnosing an Illness

MYCIN is a goal-driven expert system. Its main action is to try to determine whether a particular organism may be present in the meningitis infection in the patient. A possible infecting organism forms a goal that is either confirmed or eliminated. It is interesting to note that the decision to make MYCIN a goal-driven system was not based exclusively on the effectiveness of the strategy in pruning the search space. Early in the design of the system, the MYCIN architects considered the use of forward search. This was rejected because the questions the system asked the user seemed random and unconnected. Goal-driven search, because it is attempting to either confirm or eliminate a particular hypothesis, causes the reasoning to seem more focused and logical. This builds the user's understanding and confidence in the system's actions. An expert system needs to do more than obtain a correct answer; it must also do so in an intelligent and understandable fashion. This criterion influences the choice of search strategies as well as the structure and order of rules.

In keeping with this goal of making the program behave like a doctor, MYCIN's designers noted that doctors ask routine questions at the beginning of a consultation (e.g., "how old are you?" and "have you had any childhood diseases?") and ask more specific questions when they are needed. Collecting the general information at the beginning makes the session seem more focused in that it is not continually interrupted by trivial questions such as the name, age, sex, and race of the patient. Certain other questions are asked at other well-defined stages of a consultation (such as when beginning to consider a new hypothesis).

Eventually the questions get more specific (questions 16 and 17 in the trace below) and related to possible meningitis. When positive responses are given to these questions, MYCIN determines that the infection is meningitis, goes into full goal-driven mode, and tries to determine the actual infecting organisms. It does this by considering each infecting organism that it knows about and attempting to eliminate or confirm each hypothesis in turn. Since a patient may have more than one infecting organism, MYCIN searches exhaustively, continuing until all possible hypotheses have been considered.

MYCIN controls its search in a number of ways that have not yet been discussed. The knowledge base includes rules that restrict the hypotheses to be tested. For example, MYCIN concludes that it should test for meningitis when the patient has had headaches and other abnormal neurological signs.

Another feature of MYCIN's inference engine is the order in which it tries the backward chaining rules. After determining the general category of the infection (meningitis, bacteremia, etc.), each candidate diagnosis is examined exhaustively in a depth-first fashion.

To make the search behave more intelligently, MYCIN first examines all the premises of a rule to determine if any of them are already known to be false. This prevents the program from trying to solve several of the premises, only to discover that the rule could have been eliminated immediately by one of the later premises.

MYCIN also attempts to find a *unity path*. In trying to prove a goal, it looks for rules that can conclude that goal with a certainty of 1. If one of these rules succeeds, the system does not have to try other rules; the goal is known to be true. This increases both the efficiency and rationality of the search procedure.

When the confidence measures for a rule premise get below a certain value, the depth-first search is terminated. As mentioned above, the certainty measure for each patient's data is combined with the measures resident in the rules to give the certainty of the new conclusions for the patient. When these get below 0.2, MYCIN abandons the search and goes back up the graph to try another branch of the search space.

When the user wants MYCIN to justify its request for some information, he or she can ask why. Initially, this is answered by the phrase "because I need the information as a necessary attribute of each patient." Once MYCIN begins its backward search for the causes of the patient's problems, however, the why question is answered by printing the rule that MYCIN is currently considering.

As was also mentioned earlier in this chapter, the "Englishlike" interaction that the computer offers the user is not a full English language understanding program. Appropriate forms for English language comments and questions are attached to each rule when it is created so that the proper query can be presented to the user when information is needed for use of the rule or so that a rule can be printed in response to a user query.

The following dialogue is a simulated run of the MYCIN program adapted from transcripts of actual MYCIN consultations. It is not necessary to understand either the medical terminology or the medical reasoning to appreciate MYCIN's problem solving.

Our comments on the MYCIN trace are reproduced in italics throughout the interaction. The MYCIN questions and answers are numbered, with the user's responses in this type.

@ mycin

MYCIN 26-March. . . .

Instructions? (Y or N)

N

26-March 10:42

-----PATIENT-1-----

Mycin has created an object (PATIENT-1) in its dynamic knowledge base or working memory. Certain attributes are immediately requested and are necessary for every patient. These make up the first four questions. . . .

(1) Patient's name:

Λlan Λpt

(2) Age?

34

(3) Sex

Why

MYCIN restates the question before answering. . . .

[i.e., Why is it important to determine the sex of PATIENT-1?]

[1.0] The sex of the patient is one of the four standard parameters that identify a patient. This may be useful later. . . .

[back to question 3 . . .]

Male

(4) Race?

Caucasian

(5) Are there any cultures for Alan Apt that may be related to the present illness, and from which organisms have been grown successfully in the lab?

No

Mycin is a program to analyze and treat infectious diseases, so before it gets into close questioning of the patient's present condition it asks about any present or pending data (cultures) that are available. . . .

(6) Are there any pending cultures for Alan Apt?

Yes

-----CULTURE-1-----

Another object (CULTURE-1) *is created and linked to* PATIENT-1....

> (7) From what site was the specimen for CULTURE-1 taken?
> **CSF**
>
> (8) Please give the date and time when the pending CSF culture was obtained?
> **26-March-7:00**
>
> (9) Was a smear examined at the time the specimen was obtained?
> **Yes**
>
> (10) Were any cultures seen on the smear of the specimen?
> **No**

Indentation indicates that MYCIN's attention has returned from consideration of the new object (CULTURE-1) *back to the original object* (PATIENT-1).

> (11) Are there any other pending cultures?
> **No**
>
> .
>
> .
>
> .
>
> (16) Has Alan Apt recently had symptoms of persistent headache or other abnormal neurologic symptoms (dizziness, lethargy, etc.)?
> **Yes**
>
> (17) Has Alan Apt recently had objective evidence of abnormal neurologic signs (nuchal rigidity, coma, seizures, etc.) documented by a physician?
> **Yes**

With the answers of these last two questions in the affirmative, MYCIN decides to consider meningitis infections and goes into a full back chaining search to try to identify the organisms that might be causing the meningitis.

> The CSF cultures will be considered to be associated with MENINGITIS.
>
> (18) Please give the date on which clinical evidence (symptoms, signs, or laboratory tests) of the meningitis first appeared.
> **25 March 10:00**
>
> .
>
> .
>
> .
>
> (36) Has Alan Apt had neurosurgery?
> **Why**
>
> [i.e., WHY is it important to determine whether PATIENT-1 has had neurosurgery?]

[6.0] This will aid in determining the organisms (other than those seen on cultures or smears) that might be causing the infection.

It has already been established that

[6.1] the culture that requires therapy is meningitis, and

[6.2] organisms were not seen on the stain of the pending csf culture (CULTURE-1), and

[6.3] the type of infection is bacterial

Therefore, if

[6.4] Alan Apt has had neurosurgery, and

[6.5] the time since the neurosurgical operation is less than two months, and

[6.5] the type of neurosurgery is not ventricular-urethral-shunt

then

there is evidence that the organisms that might be causing the infection are staphylococcus-coag-pos (.75), staphylococcus-coag-neg (.5) e.coli (.4), klebsiella. . . . .

Author: Yu

[RULE511]

[back to question 36...]

How [6.3]

The physician is concerned how MYCIN arrived at the conclusion that the infection is bacterial. MYCIN responds, after restating its interpretation of the question the doctor is asking, with the rules it used to determine that the infection was indeed bacterial. The answer to HOW is given as the rules used, as well as their (positive and negative) certainty factors, for determining this result. . . .

[i.e., HOW was it established that the type of infection is bacterial?]

The following rules concluded about: the likelihood that the type of infection is bacterial

Rule		Yes	No
[6.7]	500	(.4)	
[6.8]	501		(.17)
[6.9]	502	(.1)	
[6.10]	524	(.42)	
[6.11]	504	(.28)	

Thus it has been established that the type of infection might be bacterial.

[back to question 36. . .]

No

.

.

.

(42) Is Alan Apt a burn patient?

Yes

I have found evidence (RULE507) that treatment should cover for Diplococcus pneumoniae causing meningitis.

I have found evidence (RULE545) that treatment should cover for e.coli causing meningitis

I have found evidence (RULE545 RULE578) that the treatment should cover for Pseudomonas aeruginosa causing meningitis.

MYCIN now attempts to prescribe appropriate therapies for these infections. First, it must be determined whether the patient has any allergies to antibody therapies. The height and weight of the patient are also requested to determine proper dosages ...

(43) Does Alan Apt have focal neurological signs?

No

[Determining which dosages are desirable for use against the c.coli ...]
[Determining which drugs are desirable for use ...]

INFECTION-1 is MENINGITIS
+ <ITEM-1> DIPLOCOCCUS-PNEUMONIAE (from clinical evidence only)
+ <ITEM-2> E.COLI (from clinical evidence only)
+ <ITEM-3> PSEUD.....

.
.
.

[REC-1] My preferred therapy recommendation is as follows:
   In order to cover for items <1 2 3>:
      Give the following in combination:
      1) AMPICILLIN
      Dose: 3.85g (30.8ml) q4h IV

      2) GENTAMICIN
      Dose: 131mg (3.2ml) q8h IV

      Comments: Monitor serum concentrations
      Since high concentrations of penicillins can inactivate aminoglycosides, do not mix these antibiotics in the same IV bottle.

   Do you wish to see the next choice therapy?

No

If the physician did not like the recommended treatment he or she could have asked for another, eliminating one of the drugs (ampicillin, for instance). MYCIN would then have attempted to find another treatment. ...

8.4.4 Evaluation of Expert Systems

One of the difficult issues faced by expert system design teams is to determine when the program is ready for actual use. This problem is all the more difficult when the program, like MYCIN, deals with life-threatening situations; here, mistakes, such as overlooking an infecting agent, can be catastrophic. Many expert systems, including MYCIN (Buchanan and Shortliffe 1984), have been evaluated by using a form of the Turing test.

Ten randomly selected case histories of meningitis were rediagnosed by MYCIN and eight practitioners at the Stanford Medical School. These included five faculty members, one research fellow in infectious diseases, one resident physician, and one medical student. The actual therapy given by the original doctors on the case was also included, for a total of ten diagnoses.

These ten diagnoses were evaluated by eight infectious-disease experts away from Stanford. The diagnoses were "blind" in that they were uniformly coded so that the experts did not know whether they were looking at the computer's diagnosis or that of the humans. The evaluators rated each diagnosis as acceptable or unacceptable, with a practitioner being given one point for each acceptable rating. Thus, a perfect score would be 80 points. The results of this evaluation are given in Table 8.1:

TABLE 8.1 EXPERTS EVALUATE MYCIN
AND NINE OTHER PRESCRIBERS

PRESCRIBER	SCORE	PERCENT
MYCIN	55	69
Faculty-5	54	68
Fellow	53	66
Faculty-3	51	64
Faculty-2	49	61
Faculty-4	47	59
Actual RX	47	59
Faculty-1	45	56
Resident	39	49
Student	28	35

Table 8.2 presents the results of asking another important question in this "life and death" analysis: In how many cases did the recommended therapy fail to cover for a treatable infection? The results in both tables indicate that MYCIN performed at least as well as the Stanford experts. This is an exciting result, but it should not surprise us as the MYCIN knowledge base represents the combined expertise of some of the best medical minds available. Finally, MYCIN gave fewer drugs than the human experts and thus did not overprescribe for the infections.

Another noteworthy aspect of this evaluation is how little agreement there was among human experts concerning the correctness of diagnoses. Even the best of the diagnosticians failed to receive a unanimous endorsement from the evaluators. This observation underscores the extent to which human expertise is still largely heuristic in nature.

TABLE 8.2 NUMBER OF CASES IN WHICH
THERAPY MISSED A TREATABLE PATHOGEN

PRESCRIBER	NUMBER
MYCIN	0
Faculty-5	1
Fellow	1
Faculty-3	1
Faculty-2	0
Faculty-4	0
Actual RX	0
Faculty-1	0
Resident	1
Student	3

Note: On the average MYCIN gave fewer drugs than the human experts.

These positive evaluation results do not mean that MYCIN is now ready to set up a medical practice and take on patients. In fact, MYCIN is not used for delivering medical care. There are several important reasons. First, and most important, the rules (approximately 600 of them) did not give a speedy response in the doctor-computer interaction. Each session with the computer lasted about one-half hour and required, as can be seen from the trace presented above, a good amount of typing.

Second, the program was "locked into" the particular part of its graph search for response to questions. It was not able to extrapolate to other situations or previous patients, but remained strictly within the nodes and links of the graph it was evaluating.

Third, MYCIN's explanations were limited: when the doctor expected a deep medical justification for some particular result—a physiological or antibacterial justification, say—MYCIN simply returned the "condition action plus certainty factor" relationship contained in its rule base. It is difficult for an expert system to relate its heuristic knowledge to any deeper understanding of the problem domain. MYCIN, for example, does not really understand human physiology; it simply applies rules to case-specific data. Folklore has it that an early version of MYCIN, before recommending a particular drug, asked if the patient was pregnant, in spite of the fact that MYCIN had been told that the patient was male! Whether this actually happened or not, it does indicate the limitations of current expert system technology. Attempting to give expert systems the flexibility and deeper understanding demonstrated by human beings is an important and open area of research.

Finally, unlike humans, who are extremely flexible in the way they apply knowledge, expert systems do not "degrade gracefully" when confronted with situations that do not fit the knowledge in their rule base. That is, while a human can shift to reasoning from first principles or to intelligent guesses when confronted with a new situation, expert systems simply fail to get any answer at all.

All of these issues have meant that MYCIN does not enjoy common use in the medical field. Nonetheless, it does serve as an archetype of this class of expert system and many of its descendants, such as PUFF, are being used in clinical situations.

8.4.5 Knowledge Acquisition and the Teiresias Knowledge Base Editor

Another one of the long-term goals of expert systems research is to design software that will allow the human expert to interact directly with the knowledge base to correct and improve it. This is seen as a potential remedy for what has been called the *knowledge engineering bottleneck*. This bottleneck is caused by the fact that building an expert system generally requires a substantial commitment of time by both the domain expert and the knowledge engineer. This contributes to the expense and complexity of building expert systems. Both of these individuals tend to be highly paid professionals, and the loss in productivity caused by taking the domain expert away from other work during system development can add to the cost of the project. Additional cost and complexity come from the effort needed to communicate the domain expert's knowledge to the knowledge engineer, the logistics of getting these two people together, and the complexity of the programming required for an expert system.

The obvious solution to this problem is to automate as much of the process as possible. This has been done to a great extent through the development of expert system shells and environments that reduce the amount of programming required by the knowledge engineer. However, these shells still require that the programmer understand the methodologies of knowledge representation and search. A more ambitious goal is to eliminate the need for a knowledge engineer entirely. One way to accomplish this is to provide knowledge base editors that allow the domain expert to develop the program, interacting with the knowledge base in terms that come from the problem domain and letting the software handle the details of representation and knowledge organization. This approach has been explored in an experimental program called *Teiresias* (Davis 1982; Davis and Lenat 1982), a knowledge base editor developed at Stanford University as part of the MYCIN project. We discuss the Teiresias project in this section.

Another approach to the problem is to develop programs that can learn on their own by refining their problem-solving efforts in response to feedback from the outside. These approaches have been explored with varying degrees of success by the machine learning community. These issues are introduced in Chapter 15 and continue to be a promising and exciting area of artificial intelligence research.

With the assistance of a knowledge base editor, the domain expert can analyze the performance of a knowledge base, find missing or erroneous rules, and correct the problem in a language appropriate to the expert's way of thinking about the domain. The knowledge base editor designed for MYCIN is called Teiresias after the blind seer of the Greek tragedian Euripides. The name is altogether appropriate, as Teiresias was able to see and describe the relations of the world without the (literal) gift of sight; similarly, this software is able to understand relations in a knowledge base without (literally) understanding the referents of these relations.

Teiresias allows a doctor to step through MYCIN's treatment of a patient and locate problems with its performance. Teiresias also translates the doctor's corrections into the appropriate internal representations for the knowledge base. Thus Teiresias is able to maintain the syntactic consistency of the knowledge base by updating all appropriate program structures when new information is to be integrated into the knowledge base.

For example, MYCIN stores considerable knowledge in the form of tables. Certain rules include LISP code that retrieves information from these tables, such as characteristics of disease organisms. This improves the efficiency of the knowledge base, since a single table can capture information that would require numerous rules to encode. However, if a new object (for example, a disease organism) is added to the knowledge base, then all tables that contain information about disease organisms must be updated to reflect this.

Semantic consistency is a more difficult problem, requiring knowledge of how well the knowledge base actually reflects the problem domain. Although Teiresias cannot be said to truly maintain semantic consistency, it does make an effort to ensure that rules appear consistent with one another. It does this by maintaining *rule models*, or statistical profiles of all the rules. If a new rule is added to the knowledge base, Teiresias compares this new rule with the rule model for all existing rules that draw the same conclusion. The assumption is that rules that draw similar conclusions should examine similar conditions in their premises. This enables Teiresias to detect potential inconsistencies in a new rule and prompt the user for corrections.

To illustrate Teiresias, we analyze its interaction with the doctor after MYCIN has given its recommendations. The doctor disagrees with MYCIN's result, and with Teiresias's help, analyzes MYCIN's solution. The trace is a simulation taken from a session by Stanford researchers, where the analysis is in italics, Teiresias's questions are in regular type, and the doctor's responses are in this type.

When a conclusion is given with which the doctor disagrees, the rule that drew this conclusion is not necessarily wrong. A number of things could have happened, as Teiresias correctly shows: A fact of the rule could have been improperly concluded; the rule might, in fact, be wrong; or another rule might be missing from the knowledge base. Finding the cause of an error is a difficult problem that potentially requires examination of the entire line of reasoning. Teiresias assists the physician in determining the problem by maintaining an and/or graph of the solution process and working systematically through this trace.

All rules are translated into an English language syntax that assists the physician in understanding the trace. Once a problem is located, Teiresias lets the user add the missing rule in the same simplified syntax, translating the rule into an internal representation and checking the new rule for consistency with similar rules in the knowledge base.

MYCIN has reached a set of infections that it feels should be treated (as in the dialogue of Section 8.4.3). These are presented to the physician, who disagrees with MYCIN's analysis:

My therapy recommendation will be based on the following probable
infections and potential causative organisms:

INFECTION-1 is PRIMARY BACTEREMIA
    <item-1> E.COLI
    <item-2> PSEUDOMONAS-AERUGINOSA

Now Teiresias steps in:

Are all these identities correct?

No

Are there any identities missing?

Yes

Which ones?

KLEBSIELLA_PNEUMONIAE, PROTEUS-NON-MIRABILIS

Are there any identities which shouldn't have appeared?

Yes

Which ones?

PSEUDOMONAS-AERUGINOSA

Do you want to
  1) track down the problem yourself, or
  2) allow me to guide the debugging, or
  3) ignore it for now and fix it another time
Type 1, 2 or 3

2

If the doctor had typed 1, he or she could have tried to sort out the problems with the traditional WHY and HOW queries on the preceding solution. Note that Teiresias has already begun to categorize the errors that appeared in the conclusions. It should also be noted that the three problems could well be related (perhaps to one missing rule). Teiresias starts by trying to find out why the wrong organism appeared for treatment. . . .

We'll start with PSEUDOMONAS-AERUGINOSA first:
The following rules were used in deducing that the identity of ORGANISM-1 is PSEUDOMONAS-AERUGINOSA.
RULE 184
  Since
  [1.1] The category of ORGANISM-1 is not known
  [1.2] The gram stain of ORGANISM-1 is gram negative
  [1.3] The morphology of ORGANISM-1 is rod
  [1.4] The aerobicity of ORGANISM-1 is facultative
  There is weakly suggestive evidence (.3) that the identity of
  ORGANISM-1 is PSEUDOMONAS-AERUGINOSA.
Is this rule correct?

Yes

Should its premise have failed in this case?

Yes

Which clause of the premise should have failed?

Clause 1

The expert feels the program should have been able to establish a category and that RULE 184 should not have fired.

Should it have been possible to conclude a category?

Yes

Which one?

ENTEROBACTERIACEAE

There were no rules successfully called in the attempt to deduce this category. The following (potentially applicable) rules were NOT executed because the marked [++] clause failed:

RULE 116

If
1) the identity of ORGANISM-1 is not known
++ 2) the gram stain of ORGANISM-1 is not known
3) the morphology of ORGANISM-1 is not known
4) the site of CULTURE-1 is CSF
5) the infection is meningitis
6) the age of the patient is less than or equal to 2 months
Then there is weakly suggestive evidence (.33) that the category of ORGANISM-1 is ENTEROBACTERIACEAE

RULE 050

If
1) the morphology of ORGANISM-1 is rod
2) the gram stain of ORGANISM-1 is gramneg
3) the aerobicity of ORGANISM-1 is facultative
++ 4) infection ORGANISM-1 was acquired while the patient was hospitalized
Then there is suggestive evidence (.7) that the category of ORGANISM-1 is ENTEROBACTERIACEAE

Are all these rules correct?

Yes

Should any of them have been successfully invoked?

No

Is there a rule missing?

Yes

Would you like to give me such a rule now?

Yes

Good...

If

1 ** THE PATIENT'S INFECTION IS PRIMARY-BACTEREMIA
2 ** THE SITE IS ONE OF THE STERILE SITES
Then:
** THERE IS SUGGESTIVE EVIDENCE (.8) THAT THE CATEGORY IS ENTEROBACTERIACEAE

Teiresias parses this rule into its internal representation and then translates it back into English so the expert can check it. After the expert agrees on the parse, Teiresias attempts to integrate the new rule into the knowledge base....

I hate to criticize, Dr Davis, but did you know that most rules about what the category of an organism might be that mention:
the site of a culture, and
the infection

also mention:

the portal of entry of the organism?

Shall I try to write a clause to account for this?

Yes

How about:

the portal of entry is gastrointestinal. OK?

Yes

Teiresias is itself a knowledge-based program with rules for reasoning about rules and objects in a MYCIN knowledge base. As the above trace illustrates, the program systematically searches back along the trace of the reasoning to find the source of the problem. Once this is done, it helps the user add to or correct the knowledge base. Using the rule models discussed at the beginning of this section, Teiresias is able to check the rule for consistency and correct the missing premise.

To help the user add new information, Teireseas keeps a model of each class of object that appears in the system. The model for a MYCIN object is called a *schema*. Each schema describes how to create new instances of a class of objects such as a new disease organism, drug, or test. The schema for a class of objects also describes how information is to be obtained for rules of that class—for example, to compute it from existing data, look it up, or ask the user.

Schemata record the interrelationships of all classes of objects in the MYCIN rule base. For example, if the addition of a new disease requires that a table of diseases and their sensitivities to various drugs also be updated, this is recorded in the disease schema. Schemata also include pointers to all current instances of each schema. This is very important if it is decided to change the form of the schema throughout the program.

Teiresias organizes its schemata into a hierarchy: A schema for describing bacterial infections may be a specification of a general class schema, which in turn is a specification of a general schema for MYCIN facts. Each schema includes pointers to its parents and children in this hierarchy. (See also the topics of frames, objects, and object-oriented programming in chapters 9 and 14.)

Schemata also contain bookkeeping information. This includes the author and date of creation and addition of each instance to the program. It includes a description of the schema used to create it. Documentation of who created rules when is critical for discussion and analysis of the knowledge base; when rules are primarily condition-action pairs representing important aspects of an application domain and not full explications of these relationships, it is important to be able to trace the rules back to their authors for more complete discussion of the factors underlying their creation.

The top-level structure in the hierarchy of Teiresias's knowledge is the *schema-schema*. This structure is a schema for creating new schemata, when, for instance, the domain expert might wish to create a new category of objects. The schema-schema allows Teiresias to reason about its own knowledge structures, including creating new ones when appropriate. A schema-schema has the same basic structure as a schema itself and provides all the bookkeeping information to reconstitute the entire knowledge base.

Although the development of commercial programs to help with knowledge acquisition is still in the future, Teiresias has shown how and/or graph search and knowledge representation techniques provide a basis for automating knowledge base refinement.

8.5   Epilogue and References

The model for the rule-based expert system is the production system. Whether the final product is data driven or goal driven, the model for the software is production system-generated graph search. This material was presented in chapters 3, 4, and 5.

We implement simple expert system shells in PROLOG and LISP in chapters 12 and 13, respectively. These shells, and some sample rules presented with them, are able to create a goal-driven search much like MYCIN's. The rules can include certainty measures in a limited form for designing a heuristically based search. The student is encouraged to add rules to fill out the knowledge base either along the lines of the analysis of a car that won't start, as in the beginning of this chapter, or to implement some other application.

A number of references complement the material presented in this chapter; especially recommended is a collection of the original MYCIN publications from Stanford entitled *Rule-Based Expert Systems* by Buchanan and Shortliffe (1984).

Other important books on general knowledge engineering include *Building Expert Systems* by Hayes-Roth et al. (1984), *A Guide to Expert Systems* by Waterman (1986), *Expert Systems: Concepts and Examples* by Alty and Coombs (1984), *Expert Systems Technology: A Guide* by Johnson and Keravnou (1985), *Expert Systems: Tools and Applications* by Harmon et al. (1988), and *Expert Systems and Fuzzy Systems* by Negoita (1984).

Because of the domain specificity of expert system solutions, case studies are an important source of knowledge in the area. Books in this category include *Expert Systems: Techniques, Tools and Applications* by Klahr and Waterman (1986), *Competent Expert Systems: A Case Study in Fault Diagnosis* by Keravnou and Johnson (1986), *The CRI Directory of Expert Systems* by Smart and Langeland-Knudsen (1986), and *Developments in Expert Systems* by Coombs (1984).

A pair of more general books that give an overview of commercial uses of AI are *The AI Business* edited by Winston and Prendergast (1984) and *Expert Systems: Artificial Intelligence in Business* by Harmon and King (1985).

8.6   Exercises

1. In Section 8.2 we introduced a set of rules for diagnosing automobile problems. Identify possible knowledge engineers, domain experts, and potential end users for such an application. Discuss the expectations, abilities, and needs of each of these groups.

2. Take Exercise 1 above. Create in English or pseudocode 15 if-then rules (other than those prescribed in Section 8.2) to describe relations within this domain. Create a graph to represent the relationships within these 15 rules.

3. Consider the graph of Exercise 2 above. Do you recommend data- or goal-driven search? breadth- or depth-first search? In what ways could heuristics assist the search? Justify your answers to these questions.

4. Pick another area of interest for designing an expert system. Answer Exercises 1–3 for this application.

5. Implement an expert system using a commercial shell program. These are widely available for personal computers as well as larger machines.

6. Critique the shell you used to do Exercise 5. What are its strengths and weaknesses? What would you do to improve it? Was it appropriate to your problem? What problems are best suited to that tool?

KNOWLEDGE REPRESENTATION

When you notice a cat in profound meditation,
The reason, I tell you, is always the same:
His Mind is engaged in a rapt contemplation of the
Thought, of the thought, of the thought of his name.

—T.S. ELIOT, *Old Possum's Book of Practical Cats*

It is the man determines what is said, not the words.

—HENRY DAVID THOREAU, *Journal*

9.0   Knowledge Representation Languages

In building a knowledge base, a programmer must select the significant objects and relations in the domain and map these into a formal language. The resulting program must contain sufficient knowledge to solve problems in the domain, it must make correct inferences from this knowledge, and it must do so efficiently.

We can think of a knowledge base in terms of a mapping between the objects and relations in a problem domain and the computational objects and relations in a program (Bobrow 1975). The results of inferences on the knowledge base should correspond to the results of actions or observations in the world. The computational objects, relations, and inferences available to programmers are determined by the knowledge representation language they select. The proper language can help the programmer acquire, organize, and debug the knowledge base.

There are general principles of knowledge organization that apply across a variety of domains and can be directly supported by a representation language. For example, class hierarchies are found in both scientific and commonsense classification systems. How may we provide a general mechanism for representing them? How may we represent definitions? What is the relation between a rule and its exceptions? When should a knowledge-based system make default assumptions about missing information and how should it adjust its reasoning if these assumptions prove wrong? How may we best represent time? Causality? Uncertainty? Progress in knowledge-based systems depends on discovering the principles of knowledge organization and supporting them in higher-level representational tools.

It is useful to distinguish between a representational *scheme* and the *medium* of its implementation (Hayes 1974). This is similar to the distinction between data structures and programming languages. Programming languages are the *medium* of implementation; the data structure is the *scheme*. Generally, knowledge representation languages are more constrained than predicate calculus or programming languages like LISP and PROLOG. The constraints take the form of explicit structures for representing categories of knowledge. The medium in which they are implemented might be PROLOG, LISP, or a conventional language like C or ADA.

Over the past 25 years, numerous representational schemes have been proposed and implemented, each of them having its own strengths and weaknesses. Mylopoulos and Levesque (1984) have classified these into four categories:

1. **Logical representation schemes.** This class of representations uses expressions in formal logic to represent a knowledge base. Inference rules and proof procedures apply this knowledge to problem instances. First-order predicate calculus is the most widely used logical representation scheme, but it is only one of a number of logical representations (Turner 1984). PROLOG is an ideal programming language for implementing logical representation schemes.

2. **Procedural representation schemes.** Procedural schemes represent knowledge as a set of instructions for solving a problem. This contrasts with the declarative representations provided by logic and semantic networks. In a rule-based system, for example, an if ... then rule may be interpreted as a procedure for solving a goal in a problem domain: to solve the conclusion, solve the premises in order. Production systems are examples of a procedural representation scheme.

3. **Network representation schemes.** Network representations capture knowledge as a graph in which the nodes represent objects or concepts in the problem domain and the arcs represent relations or associations between them. Examples of network representations include *semantic networks*, *conceptual dependencies*, and *conceptual graphs*.

4. **Structured representation schemes.** Structured representation languages extend networks by allowing each node to be a complex data structure consisting of named slots with attached values. These values may be simple numeric or symbolic data, pointers to other frames, or even procedures for performing a particular task. Examples of structured representations include *scripts*, *frames*, and *objects* (Chapter 14).

Logical representations are discussed in chapters 2 and 11; procedural approaches are discussed throughout the text, particularly in chapters 8 and 14 and in the discussion of production systems in Section 4.3. This chapter introduces network and structured representation schemes.

9.1 Issues in Knowledge Representation

A number of important issues have dominated research in knowledge representation. In this section we introduce a number of these issues and the difficulties they present to designers and users of knowledge representation schemes. Much of this work is motivated by the effort to program a computer to understand human languages such as English. Because of the breadth and complexity of the knowledge required for understanding natural language (Chapter 10), this application has motivated much of the research in representation.

In a pivotal paper, Woods criticized the tendency to base representation languages on intuitive responses to specific domains (Woods 1985). Generally speaking, Woods argued that it was not sufficient to examine the semantics of *natural* language and implement structures that seemed to capture these features, but that more attention should be paid to the semantics of the representation formalism itself. This representation language is the basis for all inferences that will be made by the system and therefore determines what can be known and ultimately expressed. There are a number of questions that must be asked in designing a representation language.

Exactly what "things" can be represented by the objects and relations in the language? For example, if a predicate relates an object to a value, such as hascolor(car, red), how can that predicate be used to represent "John's car is redder than Mary's"? Here, the second argument is not a value at all but a comparison to the color of Mary's car; how should we capture this in our notation?

A related question concerns the granularity of the representation. In predicate calculus and semantic networks we can denote objects in the domain only by using simple symbols. Other representations, such as frames and objects, let us define complex structures by encapsulating multiple features and attributes to indicate a single object in the domain. For example, a person is a single entity that requires many properties for its description. This has the advantage of placing all the information about an object in one place, making it easier to access, update, or delete.

How can representations distinguish between *intensional* and *extensional* knowledge? Briefly, the *extension* of a concept is the set of all things denoted by a given concept; for example, "ball" has as its extension the set of all balls. The *intension* determines what a concept means in the abstract, such as the definition of a ball in terms of its roundness, its ability to roll, bounce, and be thrown, or its use in games. While these two different definitions characterize the same set of objects, their role in understanding is very different. This issue is important if we are linking an expert system and a data base. The data base enumerates objects and relations of a domain (its extension), while the expert system includes the intensional knowledge used to reason about these objects.

How can we best represent *meta-knowledge*, or knowledge about the objects and structures of the representation language itself? This is important if we wish to reason about knowledge, as in describing the sentence "George believes that Tom knows that Mary's car is red." Teiresias (Chapter 8) used meta-knowledge to reason about knowledge and proofs in MYCIN.

Another important feature of knowledge is its organization into class hierarchies. The ability to represent the relationship between an object and its class or between a class and its superclass has proved so useful that many representation languages include mechanisms that define these relationships. *Inheritance* is a relation by which an individual assumes the properties of its class and by which properties of a class are passed on to its subclass.

For example, if chimpanzee is a subclass of primate and Bonzo is a chimpanzee, we may assume that Bonzo has all the properties of chimpanzees and primates. Inheritance provides a natural tool for representing taxonomically structured knowledge bases, as well as an economical means of expressing properties common to a class of objects. It provides benefits such as guaranteeing that all members of a class inherit the appropriate properties, ensuring consistency with the class definition. It reduces the size of the knowledge base, since properties are defined once for the most general type that shares these properties, rather than for all subclasses or individuals. For example, the property of having flexible hands would be defined for primates and inherited by chimps, gorillas, humans, etc. Properties such as being small and highly intelligent, which are not common to all primates, would be specified for the appropriate class, such as chimpanzee. The property of having a spine would be defined at a higher level of abstraction, the type vertebrate, and inherited by all subtypes, including primate and chimpanzee.

Inheritance is also used to implement *default values* and *exceptions*. For example, we may state that all chimpanzees live in the jungle, except Bonzo, who lives in the circus. Default values are simply inherited from the appropriate superclass. We can represent exceptions to these defaults by redefining the property at a lower level in the hierarchy, such as for Bonzo (Section 9.5).

Type hierarchies may assume a number of different forms, including *trees*, *lattices*, or arbitrary graphs. In a tree hierarchy, each type has only one supertype. This is a simple and well-behaved model, but it is not as expressive as hierarchies that allow multiple parent types. Most natural classification systems allow individuals to belong to multiple types and let types have multiple supertypes. For example, Bonzo not only belongs to the type chimpanzee but also belongs to the type circus performer. Although multiple inheritance hierarchies can introduce difficulties in the definition of representation languages, their benefits are great enough to offset these disadvantages. The lattice is a common form for multiple inheritance.

Finally, it is often helpful to attach procedures to object descriptions. These procedures, sometimes referred to as *demons*, are executed when an object is changed or created and provide a vehicle for implementing graphics I/O, consistency checks, and interactions between objects.

This discussion illustrates the subtlety and complexity of the knowledge representation problem. In the next section we show how some of these issues are addressed in the context of a specific network representation scheme.

9.2 A Survey of Network Representations

9.2.1 Associationist Theories of Meaning

Logical representations grew out of the efforts of philosophers and mathematicians to characterize the principles of correct reasoning. The major concern of this work is the development of formal representation languages with sound and complete inference rules. Consequently, the semantics of predicate calculus emphasizes *truth-preserving* operations on well-formed expressions. An alternative line of research has grown out of the efforts of psychologists and linguists to characterize the nature of human understanding. This work is less concerned with establishing a science of correct reasoning than with describing the way in which humans actually acquire and use knowledge of their world. As a result, this work has proved particularly useful to the AI application areas of natural language understanding and commonsense reasoning.

The problems that arise in mapping commonsense reasoning into formal logic can be illustrated through an example. It is common to think of the operators $\vee$ and $\Rightarrow$ as corresponding to the English "or" and "if...then." However, these operators are concerned solely with truth values and ignore the fact that the English "if...then" generally suggests a specific relationship (generally causal) between its premises and its conclusion. For example, the English sentence "If a bird is a cardinal, then it is red" may be written in predicate calculus as

$$\forall\ X\ (cardinal(X) \Rightarrow red(X)).$$

This may be changed, through a series of truth-preserving operations, into the logically equivalent expression

$$\forall\ X\ (\neg\ red(X) \Rightarrow \neg\ cardinal(X)).$$

These two expressions are logically equivalent; that is, the second is true if and only if the first is true. However, truth value equivalence overlooks the more subtle connotations of the original English sentence. If we were to look for physical evidence of the truth of these statements, the fact that this sheet of paper is not red and also not a cardinal is evidence for the truth of the second expression. Since the two expressions are logically equivalent, it follows that it is also evidence for the truth of the first statement. This leads to the conclusion that the whiteness of the sheet of paper is evidence that cardinals are red.

While logically sound, this line of reasoning strikes us as meaningless and rather silly. The reason for this incongruity is that logical implication only expresses a relationship between the truth values of its operands, while the original English sentence implies a causal relationship between membership in a class and the possession of properties of that class. The fact of being a cardinal causes a bird to be red. This relationship is lost in the second version of the expression. While the fact that the paper is not red is consistent with the truth of both sentences, it is simply irrelevant to the color of birds.

To take another example, consider the logical expression

$$(2 + 2 = 5) \Rightarrow color(elephants, green).$$

Since $2 + 2 = 5$ is false and elephants are not green we have an expression that evaluates to $false \Rightarrow false$; this has a value of $true$. On the other hand, our commonsense response to this expression is that it is meaningless. Again, this anomaly is a result of predicate calculus's concern with truth value assignments rather than the semantic relationships between components of a world.

One answer to these problems is to be more careful in establishing conventions for mapping knowledge into predicate calculus or to extend the language with special operators that correspond to specific categories of knowledge.

The limitations of predicate calculus are largely a result of Tarskian semantics: the assignment of a truth value to logical expressions based on an interpretation in some possible world. It is not always enough to know that a statement such as "snow is white" is true; the meaning of the atomic symbols must also be addressed (Woods 1975). The representation should be able to answer questions about these objects such as: "What is snow made of?" "What temperature is Frosty the Snowman?" "If snow is white then what color is a snowman?" This requires that the representation not only preserve truth values when combining expressions but also have some means of making truth assignments based on knowledge of a *particular* world.

Associationist theories define the meaning of an object in terms of a network of associations with other objects in a mind or a knowledge base. Although symbols denote objects in a world, this denotation is mediated by our store of knowledge. When we perceive and reason about an object, that perception is first mapped into a concept in our minds. This concept is part of our entire knowledge of the world and is connected through appropriate relationships to other concepts. These relationships form an understanding of the properties and behavior of objects such as snow. For example, through experience we associate the concept snow with other concepts such as cold, white, snowman, slippery, and ice. Our understanding of snow and the truth of statements like "snow is white" manifests itself out of this network of associations.

There is psychological evidence that in addition to their ability to associate concepts, humans also organize their knowledge hierarchically, with information kept at the highest appropriate levels of the taxonomy. Collins and Quillian (1969) modeled human information storage and management using a semantic network (Fig. 9.1). The structure of this hierarchy was derived from laboratory testing of human subjects. The subjects were asked questions about different properties of birds, for example, "Is a canary a bird?" or "Can a canary sing?" or "Can a canary fly?"

As obvious as the answers to these questions may seem, reaction time studies indicated that it took longer for subjects to answer "Can a canary fly?" than it did to answer "Can a canary sing?" Collins and Quillian explain this difference in response time by arguing that people store information at its most abstract level. Instead of trying to recall that canaries fly, and robins fly, and swallows fly (all stored with the individual bird), humans remember that canaries are birds and that birds have (usually) the property of flying. Even more general properties like eating, breathing, and moving are stored at the "animal" level, and so trying to recall whether a canary can breath should take longer than recalling whether a canary can fly. This is, of course, because the human must travel farther up the hierarchy of memory structures to get the answer.

The fastest recall was for the traits specific to the bird, say, that it can sing or is yellow. Exception handling also seemed to be done at the most specific level. When subjects were asked whether an ostrich could fly, the answer was produced faster than when they were asked whether an ostrich could breathe. Thus the hierarchy ostrich → bird → animal seems not to be traversed to get the exception information: It is stored directly

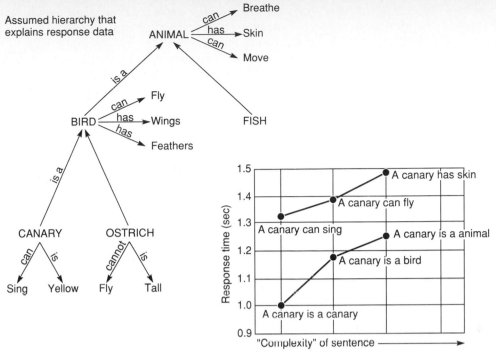

Figure 9.1 Semantic network developed by Collins and Quillian in their research on human information storage and response times (Harmon 1985).

with ostrich. This approach to to knowledge organization has been formalized in inheritance systems.

Several benefits come from inheritance systems. They allow us to store information at the highest level of abstraction, which reduces the size of knowledge bases and helps prevent update inconsistencies. For example, if we are building a knowledge base about birds, we can define the traits common to all birds, such as flying or having feathers, for the general class **bird** and allow particular species of bird to inherit these properties. This reduces the size of the knowledge base by requiring us to define these essential traits only once, rather than requiring their assertion for every individual. Inheritance also helps us to maintain the consistency of the knowledge base when adding new classes and individuals. Assume that we are adding the species **robin** to an existing knowledge base of birds. When we assert that **robin** is a subclass of **songbird**, **robin** automatically inherits all of the common properties of both **songbirds** and **birds**. It is not up to the programmer to remember (or possibly forget) to add this information.

Graphs, by providing a means of explicitly representing relations using arcs and nodes, have proved to be an ideal vehicle for formalizing associationist theories of knowledge. A *semantic network* represents knowledge as a graph, with the nodes

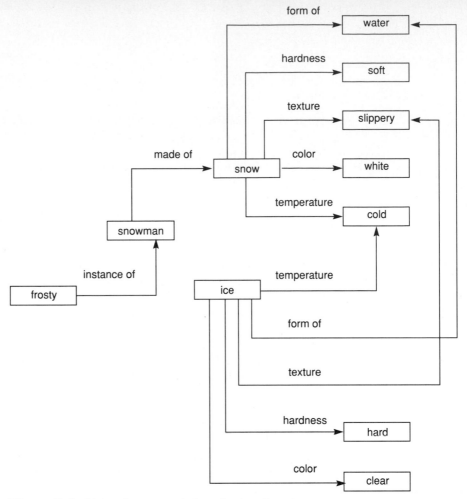

Figure 9.2 Network representation of properties of snow and ice.

corresponding to facts or concepts and the arcs to relations or associations between concepts. Both nodes and links are generally labeled. For example, a semantic network that defines the properties of snow appears in Figure 9.2. This network could be used (with appropriate inference rules) to answer a range of questions about snow, ice, and snowmen. These inferences are made by following the appropriate links to related concepts. Semantic networks also implement inheritance; for example, frosty inherits all the properties of snowmen.

The term *semantic network* encompasses a family of graph-based representations. These representations differ chiefly in the names that are allowed for nodes and links and the inferences that may be performed on these structures. However, a common set of assumptions and concerns is shared by all network representation languages; these are illustrated by a discussion of the history of network representations. In Section 9.4 we examine *conceptual graphs* (Sowa 1984), a modern network representation language that integrates many of these ideas.

9.2.2   Early Work in Semantic Nets

Network representations have almost as long a history as logic; Frege, for example, developed a tree notation for logical expressions. Perhaps the earliest work to have a direct influence on contemporary semantic nets was Charles S. Pierce's system of existential graphs, developed in the nineteenth century (Roberts 1973). Pierce's theory had all the expressive power of first-order predicate calculus, with an axiomatic basis and formal rules of inference.

Graphs have long been used in psychology to represent structures of concepts and associations. Selz (1913, 1922) pioneered this work, using graphs to represent concept hierarchies and the inheritance of properties. He also developed a theory of schematic anticipation that influenced AI work in frames and schemata. Anderson, Norman, Rumelhart, and others have used networks to model human memory and intellectual performance (Anderson and Bower 1973; Norman et al. 1975).

Much of the research in network representations has been done in the arena of natural language understanding. In the general case, natural language understanding requires far more knowledge than the specialized domains of expert systems. It includes an understanding of common sense, the ways in which physical objects behave, the interactions that occur between humans, and the way in which human institutions are organized. A natural language program must understand intentions, beliefs, hypothetical reasoning, plans, and goals. Because it requires such large amounts of broad-based knowledge, natural language understanding has always been a driving force for research in knowledge representation.

The first computer implementations of semantic networks were developed in the early 1960s for use in machine translation. Masterman (1961) defined a set of 100 primitive concept types and used them to define a dictionary of 15,000 concepts. Wilks (1972) continued to build on Masterman's work in semantic network-based natural language systems. Other early AI workers who explored network representations include Ceccato (1961), Raphael (1968), Reitman (1965), and Simmons (1966).

An influential program that illustrates many of the features of early semantic networks was written by Quillian in the late 1960s (Quillian 1967). This program defined English words in much the same way that a dictionary does: a word is defined in terms of other words, and the components of the definition are defined in the same fashion. Rather than formally defining words in terms of basic axioms, each definition simply leads to other definitions in an unstructured, possibly circular, fashion. In looking up a word, we traverse this "network" until we are satisfied that we understand the original word.

Each node in Quillian's network corresponded to a *word concept*, with associative links to other word concepts that formed its definition. The knowledge base was organized into *planes*, where each plane was a graph that defined a single word. Figure 9.3, taken from a paper by Quillian (1967), illustrates three planes that capture three

Plant:1) Living structure that is not an animal, frequently
with leaves, getting its food from air, water, earth.
2) Apparatus used for any process in industry.
3) Put (seed, plant, etc.) in earth for growth.

Figure 9.3   Three planes representing three definitions of
the word "plant" (Quillian 1967).

different definitions of the word ''plant'': a living organism (plant 1), a place where people work (plant 2), and the act of putting a seed in the ground (plant 3).

The program used this knowledge base to find relationships between pairs of
English words. Given two words, it would search the graphs outward from each word in
a breadth-first fashion, searching for a common concept or *intersection node*. The paths
to this node represented a relationship between the two word concepts. For example,
Figure 9.4, from the same paper, shows the *intersection paths* between the words cry and
comfort.

Using this intersection path, the program was able to conclude:

> cry 2 is among other things to make a sad sound. To comfort 3 can be to make 2 something
> less sad (Quillian 1967).

The numbers in the response indicate that the program has selected from among different
meanings of the words.

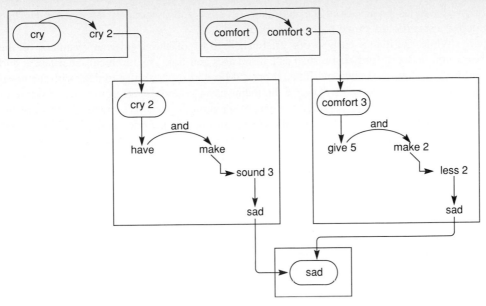

Figure 9.4 Intersection path between "cry" and "comfort" (Quillian 1967).

Quillian suggested that this approach to semantics might provide a natural language understanding system with the ability to:

1. Determine the meaning of a body of English text by building up collections of these intersection nodes.

2. Choose between multiple meanings of words by finding the meanings with the shortest intersection path to other words in the sentence. For example, it could select a meaning for "plant" in "Tom went home to water his new plant" based on the intersection of the word concepts "water" and "plant."

3. Answer a flexible range of queries based on associations between word concepts in the queries and concepts in the system.

Although this and other early work established the power of graphs to model associative meaning, it was limited by the extreme generality of the formalism. Knowledge is generally structured in terms of specific relationships such as object/property, class/subclass, and agent/verb/object. Research in network representations has often focused on the specification of these relationships.

9.2.3   Standardization of Network Relationships

In itself, a graph notation of relationships has little advantage over predicate calculus; it is just another notation for relationships between objects. The power of network representations comes from the definition of links and associated inference rules that define a specific inference such as inheritance.

While Quillian's early work established most of the significant features of the semantic network formalism, such as labeled arcs and links, hierarchical inheritance, and inferences along associational links, it proved limited in its ability to deal with the complexities of many domains. One of the main reasons for this failure was the poverty of relationships (links) that captured the deeper semantic aspects of knowledge. Most of the links represented extremely general associations between nodes and provided no real basis for the structuring of semantic relationships. The same problem is encountered in efforts to use pure predicate calculus to capture semantic meaning: while the formalism is highly expressive and can represent literally any kind of knowledge, it is too unconstrained and places the full burden of constructing appropriate sets of facts and rules on the programmer.

Much of the work in network representations that followed Quillian's focused on defining a richer set of link labels (relationships) that would more fully model the semantics of natural language. By implementing the fundamental semantic relationships of natural language as part of the *formalism*, rather than as part of the *domain knowledge* added by the system builder, knowledge bases require less handcrafting and achieve greater generality and consistency.

Brachman (1979) has stated:

> The key issue here is the isolation of the *primitives* for semantic network languages. The primitives of a network language are those things that the interpreter is programmed in advance to understand, and that are not usually represented in the network language itself.

Simmons (1973) addressed this need for standard relationships by focusing on the *case structure* of English verbs. In this verb-oriented approach, based on work by Fillmore (1968), links define the roles played by nouns and noun phrases in the action of the sentence. Case relationships include *agent*, *object*, *instrument*, *location*, and *time*. A sentence is represented as a verb node, with various case links to nodes representing other participants in the action. This structure is called a *case frame*. In parsing a sentence, the program finds the verb and retrieves the case frame for that verb from its knowledge base. It then binds the values of the agent, object, etc., to the appropriate nodes in the case frame. Using this approach, the sentence "Sarah fixed the chair with glue" might be represented by the network in Figure 9.5.

Thus, the representation language itself captures much of the deep structure of natural language, such as the relationship between a verb and its subject (the agent relation) or that between a verb and its object. Knowledge of the case structure of the English language is part of the network formalism itself. When the individual sentence is parsed, these built-in relationships indicate that Sarah is the person doing the fixing, and that glue is used to put the chair together. Note that *these linguistic relationships are stored in a fashion that is independent of the actual sentence or even the language in which the sentence was expressed.* A similar approach is also taken in network languages proposed by Norman (1972, 1975) and Rumelhart et al. (1972, 1973).

A number of major research endeavors attempted to standardize link names even further (Masterman 1961; Wilks 1972; Schank and Colby 1973; Schank and Nash-Webber 1975). Each effort worked to establish a complete set of primitives that could be

Figure 9.5 Case frame representation of the sentence "Sarah fixed the chair with glue."

used to represent the deep semantic structure of natural language expressions in a uniform fashion. These were intended to assist in reasoning with language constructs and to be independent of the idiosyncrasies of individual languages or phrasing.

Perhaps the most ambitious attempt to model formally the deep semantic structure of natural language is Roger Schank's conceptual dependency theory (Schank and Rieger 1974). Conceptual dependency theory offers a set of four primitive conceptualizations from which the world of meaning is built. These are equal and independent. They are:

ACTs   actions
PPs   objects (picture producers)
AAs   modifiers of actions (action aiders)
PAs   modifiers of objects (picture aiders)

For example, all actions are assumed to reduce to one or more of the primitive ACTs. These primitives, listed below, are taken as the basic components of action, with more specific verbs being formed through their modification and combination.

ATRANS   transfer a relationship (give)
PTRANS   transfer physical location of an object (go)
PROPEL   apply physical force to an object (push)
MOVE   move body part by owner (kick)
GRASP   grab an object by an actor (grasp)
INGEST   ingest an object by an animal (eat)
EXPEL   expel from an animal's body (cry)
MTRANS   transfer mental information (tell)
MBUILD   mentally make new information (decide)
CONC   conceptualize or think about an idea (think)
SPEAK   produce sound (say)
ATTEND   focus sense organ (listen)

These primitives are used to define *conceptual dependency relationships* that describe meaning structures such as case relations or the association of objects and values. Conceptual dependency relationships are *conceptual syntax rules* and constitute a grammar of meaningful semantic relationships. These relationships can be used to construct an internal representation of an English sentence. A list of basic conceptual

PP $\Leftrightarrow$ ACT	indicates that an actor acts.
PP $\Leftrightarrow$ PA	indicates that an object has a certain attribute.
ACT $\overset{O}{\leftarrow}$ PP	indicates the object of an action.
ACT $\overset{R}{\leftarrow}$ $\begin{matrix}\text{PP}\\\text{PP}\end{matrix}$	indicates the recipient and the donor of an object within an action.
ACT $\overset{D}{\leftarrow}$ $\begin{matrix}\text{PP}\\\text{PP}\end{matrix}$	indicates the direction of an object within an action.
ACT $\overset{1}{\leftarrow}$ $\Updownarrow$	indicates the instrumental conceptualization for an action.
$\begin{matrix}X\\\Uparrow\\Y\end{matrix}$	indicates that conceptualization X caused conceptualization Y. When written with a C this form denotes that X COULD cause Y.
PP $\Leftarrow$ $\begin{matrix}\text{PA2}\\\text{PA1}\end{matrix}$	indicates a state change of an object.
PP1 $\leftarrow$ PP2	indicates that PP2 is either PART OF or the POSSESSOR OF PP1.

Figure 9.6   Basic conceptual dependency relations (Schank 1974).

dependencies (Schank and Rieger 1974) appears in Figure 9.6. These capture the fundamental semantic structures of natural language.

For example, the first conceptual dependency in Figure 9.6 describes the relationship between a subject and its verb, and the third describes the verb-object relation. These can be combined to represent a simple transitive sentence such as ''John throws the ball'' (Fig. 9.7).

Finally, tense and mode information must be added to the conceptualizations. Schank supplies a list of attachments or modifiers to the relationships. A partial list of these is:

p	past
f	future
t	transition
k	continuing
t_s	start transition
?	interrogative
t_f	finish transition
c	conditional
/	negative
nil	present
delta?	timeless

Figure 9.7 Conceptual dependency representation of the sentence "John throws the ball."

These relations are the first-level constructs of the theory, the simplest semantic relationships out of which more complex structures can be built. Further examples of how these basic conceptual dependencies can be composed to represent the meaning of simple English sentences appear in Figure 9.8.

Based on these primitives, the English sentence "John ate the egg" is represented as shown in Figure 9.9.

In Figure 9.9 the symbols have the following meanings:

←	indicates the direction of dependency
⇔	indicates the agent-verb relationship
p	indicates past tense
INGEST	is a primitive act of the theory
O	object relation
D	indicates the direction of the object in the action

A more complex example of the structures that can be built with conceptual dependencies is the representation of "John prevented Mary from giving a book to Bill" (Fig. 9.10). This particular example is interesting as a demonstration of how causality may be represented.

Conceptual dependency theory gives a number of important benefits. By providing a formal theory of natural language semantics, it reduces problems of ambiguity. Second, the representation itself directly captures much of natural language semantics.

Conceptual dependency attempts to provide a *canonical form* for the meaning of sentences. That is, all sentences that have the same meaning will be represented internally by *syntactically identical*, not just semantically equivalent, graphs. This is an effort to simplify the inferences required for understanding. For example, we can demonstrate that two sentences mean the same thing with a simple match of conceptual dependency graphs; a representation that did not provide a canonical form might require extensive operations on differently structured graphs.

Unfortunately, it is questionable whether a program may be written to reliably reduce sentences to canonical form. As Woods (1975) and others have pointed out, reduction to a canonical form is provably uncomputable for monoids, a type of algebraic group that is far simpler than natural language. Furthermore, there is no evidence that humans store their knowledge in any sort of canonical form.

Other criticisms of this point of view object to the computational price paid in reducing everything to such low-level primitives. Also, the primitives are not adequate to capture many of the more subtle concepts that are important in natural language. For example, the representation of "tall" in the second sentence of Figure 9.8 does not address the ambiguity of this term as carefully as is done in systems such as fuzzy logic (Zadeh 1983).

Figure 9.8 Some basic conceptual dependencies and their use in representing more complex English sentences (Rich 1983).

Figure 9.9 Conceptual dependency representation of the sentence "John ate the egg" (Schank 1974).

Figure 9.10 Conceptual dependency representation of the sentence "John prevented Mary from giving a book to Bill" (Schank 1974).

However, no one can say that the conceptual dependency model hasn't been fully automated and tested. More than a decade of research guided by Schank has focused on refining and extending the model. One of the most important extensions of conceptual dependencies is the ''scripts'' research, which models continuing action across time and is discussed in Section 9.4.2. Conceptual dependency theory is a fully developed model of natural language semantics with consistency of purpose and wide applicability.

9.3 A Network Representation Language

A number of network languages have been developed to model the semantics of natural language and other domains. In this section, we examine a particular language in detail, to show how the problems of representing meaning have been addressed. J. F. Sowa's *conceptual graphs* (Sowa 1984) are an example of a modern network representation language. We define the rules for forming and manipulating conceptual graphs and the conventions for representing classes, individuals, and relationships. In Chapter 10 we continue developing this formalism and show how it may be used to represent meaning in natural language understanding.

9.3.1 Conceptual Graphs

A conceptual graph is a finite, connected, bipartite graph. The nodes of the graph are either *concepts* or *conceptual relations*. Conceptual graphs do not use labeled arcs; instead the conceptual relation nodes represent relations between concepts. Because conceptual graphs are bipartite, concepts can only have arcs to conceptual relations, and vice versa. In Figure 9.11 **dog** and **brown** are concept nodes and **color** is a conceptual relation. To distinguish these types of nodes, we represent concepts as boxes and conceptual relations as ellipses.

In conceptual graphs, concept nodes represent either concrete or abstract objects in the world of discourse. Concrete concepts, such as a cat, telephone, or restaurant, are characterized by our ability to form an image of them in our minds. Note that concrete concepts include generic concepts such as cat or restaurant along with concepts of

Flies is a 1-ary relation.

Color is a 2-ary relation.

Parents is a 3-ary relation.

Figure 9.11 Conceptual relations of different arities.

Figure 9.12 Conceptual graph of the sentence "Mary gave John the book."

specific cats and restaurants. We can still form an image of a generic cat. Abstract concepts include things like love, beauty, and loyalty that do not correspond to images in our minds.

Conceptual relation nodes indicate a relation involving one or more concepts. One advantage of formulating conceptual graphs as bipartite graphs rather than using labeled arcs is that it simplifies the representation of relations of any arity. A relation of arity n is represented by a conceptual relation node having n arcs. Figure 9.11 illustrates conceptual relations of different arities.

Each conceptual graph represents a single proposition. A typical knowledge base will contain a number of such graphs. Graphs may be arbitrarily complex but must be finite. For example, one graph in Figure 9.11 represents the proposition "A dog has a color of brown." Figure 9.12 is a graph of somewhat greater complexity that represents the sentence "Mary gave John the book." This graph uses conceptual relations to represent the cases of the verb "to give" and indicates the way in which conceptual graphs are used to model the semantics of natural language.

9.3.2 Types, Individuals, and Names

Many early designers of semantic networks were careless in defining class/member and class/subclass relationships, with resulting semantic confusion. For example, the relation between an individual and its class is different from the relation between a class (such as dog) and its superclass (carnivore). Similarly, certain properties belong to individuals, while others belong to the class itself; the representation should provide a vehicle for making this distinction. The properties of having fur and liking bones belong to individual dogs; the class "dog" does not have fur or eat anything. Properties that are appropriate to the class include its name and membership in a zoological taxonomy.

In conceptual graphs, every concept is a unique individual of a particular type. Each concept box is labeled with a *type* label, which indicates the class or type of individual represented by that node. Thus, a node labeled dog represents some individual of that type. Types are organized into a hierarchy. The type dog is a subtype of carnivore, which is a subtype of mammal, etc. Boxes with the same type label represent concepts of the same type; however, these boxes may or may not represent the same individual concept.

Each concept box is labeled with the names of the type and the individual. The type and individual labels are separated by a colon, :. The graph of Figure 9.13 indicates that the dog "Emma" is brown. The graph of Figure 9.11 asserts that some unspecified entity of type dog has a color of brown. If the individual is not indicated, the concept represents an unspecified individual of that type.

Conceptual graphs also let us indicate specific but unnamed individuals. A unique token called a *marker* indicates each individual in the world of discourse. This marker is written as a number preceded by a #. Markers are different from names in that they are unique: individuals may have one name, many names, or no name at all, but they have exactly one marker. Similarly, different individuals may have the same name but may not have the same marker. This distinction gives us a basis for dealing with the semantic ambiguities that arise when we give objects names. The graph of Figure 9.14 asserts that a particular dog, #1352, is brown.

Markers allow us to separate an individual from its name. If dog #1352 is named "Emma," we can use a conceptual relation called name to add this to the graph. The result is the graph of Figure 9.15. The name is enclosed in double quotes to indicate that it is a string. Where there is no danger of ambiguity, we may simplify the graph and refer to the individual directly by name. Under this convention, the graph of Figure 9.15 is equivalent to the graph of Figure 9.13.

Although we frequently ignore it, both in casual conversation and in formal representations, this distinction between an individual and its name is an important one that should be supported by a representation language. For example, if we say that "John" is a common name among males, we are asserting a property of the name itself

Figure 9.13 Conceptual graph indicating that the dog named **emma** is brown.

Figure 9.14 Conceptual graph indicating that a
particular (but unnamed) dog is brown.

Figure 9.15 Conceptual graph indicating that a dog
named **emma** is brown.

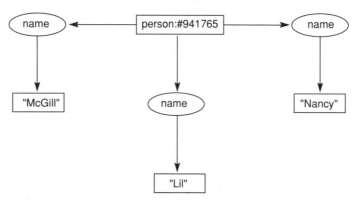

Figure 9.16 Conceptual graph of a person with three
names.

rather than of any individual named "John." This allows us to represent such English
sentences as " 'Chimpanzee' is the name of a species of primates." Similarly, we may
want to represent the fact that an individual has several different names. The graph of
Figure 9.16 represents the situation described in the song lyric: "Her name was McGill
and she called herself Lil, but everyone knew her as Nancy" (Lennon and McCartney
1968).

In addition to indicating an individual by its marker or name, we can use the generic
marker * to indicate an unspecified individual. By convention, this is often omitted from
concept labels; a node given just a type label, **dog**, is equivalent to a node labeled **dog**:*.
In addition to the generic marker, conceptual graphs allow the use of named variables.
These are represented by an asterisk followed by the variable name (e.g., *X or *foo).
This is useful if two separate nodes are to indicate the same, but unspecified, individual.

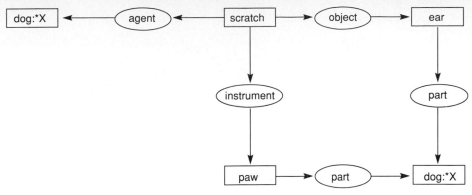

Figure 9.17 Conceptual graph of the sentence "The dog scratches its ear with its paw."

The graph of Figure 9.17 represents the assertion "The dog scratches its ear with its paw." Although we do not know which dog is scratching its ear, the variable *X indicates that the paw and the ear belong to the same dog that is doing the scratching.

To summarize, each concept node indicates an individual of a specified type. This individual is the *referent* of the concept and is indicated by either an individual marker or the generic marker. If it is an individual marker, the concept is an *individual* concept. If the referent is the generic marker, then the concept is a *generic concept*.

9.3.3 The Type Hierarchy

The type hierarchy is a partial ordering on the set of types, indicated by the symbol ≤. If s and t are types and t ≤ s, then t is said to be a *subtype* of s and s is said to be a *supertype* of t. Because it is a partial ordering, a type may have more than one supertype and more than one subtype. If s, t, and u are types, with s ≤ t and s ≤ u, then s is said to be a *common subtype* of t and u. Similarly, if t ≤ s and u ≤ s then s is a *common supertype* of t and u.

The type hierarchy of conceptual graphs is a lattice, a common form of multiple inheritance system. In a lattice, types may have multiple parents and children. However, every pair of types must have a *minimal common supertype* and a *maximal common subtype*. For types s and t, u is a minimal common supertype if s ≤ u, t ≤ u, and for any v, a common supertype of s and t, u ≤ v. Maximal common subtype has a corresponding definition. The minimal common supertype of a collection of types is the appropriate place to define properties common only to those types. Since many types, such as emotion and rock, have no obvious common supertypes or subtypes, it is necessary to add types that fill these roles. In order to make the type hierarchy a true lattice, conceptual graphs include two special types. The *universal type*, indicated by T, is a supertype of all types. The *absurd type*, indicated by ⊥, is a subtype of all types.

9.3.4 Generalization and Specialization of Conceptual Graphs

The theory of conceptual graphs includes a number of operations that allow us to form new graphs from existing graphs. These allow us to create a new graph by either *specializing* or *generalizing* an existing graph. This is done through four operations called *copy*, *restrict*, *join*, and *simplify* (Fig. 9.18). Assume that g_1 and g_2 are conceptual graphs. Then:

The *copy* rule allows us to form a new graph, g, that is the exact copy of g_1.

Restriction allows concept nodes in a graph to be replaced by a node representing their specialization. There are two cases:

1. If a concept is labeled with a generic marker, the generic marker may be replaced by an individual marker.

2. A type label on a concept may be replaced by one of its subtypes, as long as this is consistent with the referent of the concept. In Figure 9.18 we can replace animal with dog because Emma is a dog.

The *join* rule lets us combine two graphs into a single graph. If there is a concept node c_1 in the graph s_1 that is identical to a concept node c_2 in s_2, then we can form a new graph by deleting c_2 and linking all of the relations incident on c_2 to c_1. Join is a restriction rule, since the resulting graph is less general than either of its components.

If a graph contains two duplicate relations, then one of them may be deleted, along with all its arcs. This is the *simplify* rule. Duplicate relations often occur as the result of a join operation, as in graph g_4 of Figure 9.18.

One use of restriction rules is to make two concepts match so that a join can be performed. Together, join and restrict allow the implementation of inheritance. For example, the replacement of a generic marker by an individual implements the inheritance of the properties of a type by an individual. The replacement of a type label by a subtype label defines inheritance between a class and a superclass. By joining one graph to another and restricting certain concept nodes, we can implement inheritance of a variety of properties. Figure 9.19 shows how chimpanzees inherit the property of having a hand from the class primates by replacing a type label with its subtype. It also shows how the individual, Bonzo, inherits this property by instantiating a generic concept.

Similarly, we can use joins and restrictions to implement the plausible assumptions that play a role in common language understanding. If we are told that "Mary and Tom went out for pizza together," we automatically make a number of assumptions: They ate a round Italian bread covered with cheese and tomato sauce. They ate it in a restaurant. Since they are male and female, there is the possibility of a romantic relationship. This reasoning can be done using joins and restrictions (Chapter 10). We form a conceptual graph of the sentence and join it with the conceptual graph (from our knowledge base) for pizzas. The resulting graph lets us assume that they ate tomato sauce.

Join and restrict are specialization rules. They define a partial ordering on the set of derivable graphs. If a graph g_1 is a specialization of g_2, then we may say that g_2 is a *generalization* of g_1. Generalization hierarchies are important in knowledge representation. Besides providing the basis for inheritance and other commonsense reasoning schemes, generalization hierarchies are used in many learning methods, allowing us, for instance, to construct a generalized assertion from a particular training instance.

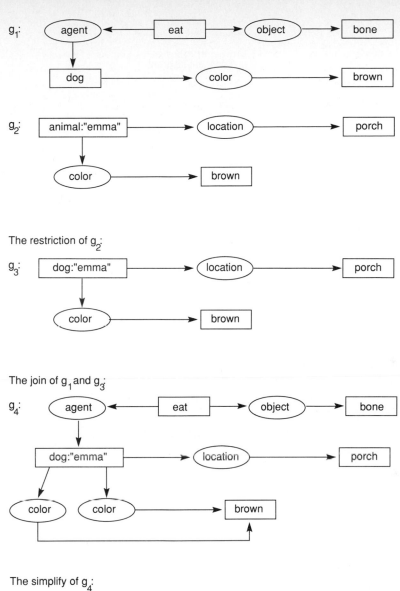

g_1:

g_2:

The restriction of g_2:

g_3:

The join of g_1 and g_3:

g_4:

The simplify of g_4:

g_5:

Figure 9.18 Examples of restrict, join, and simplify operations.

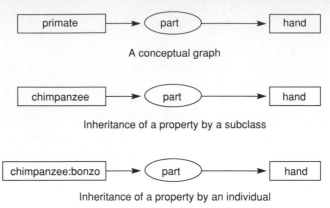

A conceptual graph

Inheritance of a property by a subclass

Inheritance of a property by an individual

Figure 9.19 Inheritance in conceptual graphs.

These rules are not rules of inference. They do not guarantee that true graphs will be derived from true graphs. For example, in the restriction of the graph of Figure 9.18, the result may not be true; Emma may be a white dog. Similarly, the join example of Figure 9.18 is not truth-preserving either: the dog on the porch and the dog that likes bones may be different animals. These operations are *canonical formation rules*, and while they do not preserve truth, they have the subtle but important property of preserving "meaningfulness." This is an important guarantee when we use conceptual graphs to implement natural language understanding. Consider the three sentences:

Albert Einstein formulated the theory of relativity.

Albert Einstein plays center for the Los Angeles Lakers.

Conceptual graphs are yellow flying popsicles.

The first of these sentences is true, while the second is false. The third sentence, however, is meaningless; while grammatically correct, it makes no sense. The second sentence, although false, is meaningful. I can imagine Albert Einstein on a basketball court. The canonical formation rules enforce constraints on meaningfulness; they do not allow us to form nonsensical graphs from meaningful ones. Although they are not sound inference rules, canonical formation rules form a basis for much of the plausible reasoning done in natural language understanding and commonsense reasoning.

9.3.5 Propositional Nodes

In addition to using graphs to define relations between objects in the world, we may also want to define relations between propositions. Consider, for example, the statement "Tom believes that Jane likes pizza." "Believes" is a relation that takes a proposition as its argument.

Conceptual graphs include a concept type, **proposition**, that takes a set of conceptual graphs as its referent and allows us to define relations involving propositions. Pro-

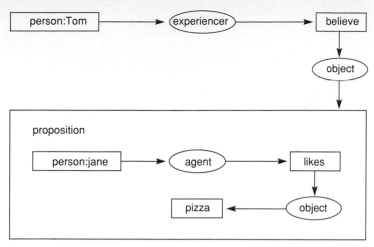

Figure 9.20 Conceptual graph of the statement "Tom thinks that Jane likes pizza," showing the use of a propositional concept.

positional concepts are indicated as a box that contains another conceptual graph. These proposition concepts may be used with appropriate relations to represent knowledge about propositions. Figure 9.20 shows the conceptual graph for the above assertion about Jane, Tom, and pizza. The **experiencer** relation is loosely analogous to the **agent** relation in that it links a subject and the verb. The **experiencer** link is used with belief states based on the notion that they are something one experiences rather than does.

Figure 9.20 shows how conceptual graphs with propositional nodes may be used to express the *modal* concepts of knowledge and belief. *Modal logics* are concerned with the various ways propositions are entertained: believed, asserted as possible, probably or necessarily true, intended as a result of an action, or counterfactual (Turner 1984).

9.3.6 Conceptual Graphs and Logic

Using conceptual graphs, we can easily represent conjunctive concepts such as "The dog is big and hungry," but we have not established any way of representing negation or disjunction. Nor have we addressed the issue of variable quantification.

We may implement negation using propositional concepts and a unary operation called **neg. neg** takes as argument a proposition concept and asserts that concept as false. The graph of Figure 9.21 uses **neg** to represent the statement "There are no pink dogs."

Using negation and conjunction, we may form graphs that represent disjunctive assertions according to the rules of logic. To simplify this, we may also define a relation **or**, which takes two propositions and represents their disjunction.

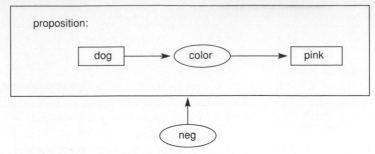

Figure 9.21 Conceptual graph of the proposition "There are no pink dogs."

In conceptual graphs, generic concepts are assumed to be existentially quantified. For example, the generic concept **dog** in the graph of Figure 9.11 actually represents an existentially quantified variable. This graph corresponds to the logical expression:

$$\exists\, X\, \exists\, Y\, (dog(X) \wedge color(X, Y) \wedge brown(Y)).$$

Using negation and existential quantification, we can also represent universal quantification. For example, the graph of Figure 9.21 could be thought of as representing the logical assertion:

$$\forall\, X\, \forall\, Y\, (\neg\, (dog(X) \wedge color(X, Y) \wedge pink(Y))).$$

Conceptual graphs are equivalent to predicate calculus in their expressive power. As these examples suggest, there is a straightforward mapping from conceptual graphs into predicate calculus notation. The algorithm for changing a conceptual graph, g, into a predicate calculus expression is:

1. Assign a unique variable, x_1, x_2, ... ,x_n, to each of the n generic concepts in g.

2. Assign a unique constant to each individual concept in g. This constant may simply be the name or marker used to indicate the referent of the concept.

3. Represent each concept node by a unary predicate whose name is the same as the type of that node and whose argument is the variable or constant assigned to that node.

4. Represent each n-ary conceptual relation in g as an n-ary predicate whose name is the same as the name of the relation. Let each argument of the predicate be the variable or constant assigned to the corresponding concept node linked to that relation.

5. Take the conjunction of all atomic sentences formed under 3 and 4. This is the body of the predicate calculus expression. All the variables in the expression are existentially quantified.

For example, the graph of Figure 9.13 is given by the predicate calculus expression

$\exists\, X_1\, (dog(emma) \wedge color(emma, X_1) \wedge brown(X_1))$

We have presented the basic syntax of conceptual graphs and defined the *restriction* operation as a means of implementing inheritance. We have not yet examined the full range of operations and inferences that may be performed on these graphs, nor have we addressed the problem of defining the concepts and relations needed for domains like natural language. We address these issues in Chapter 10 and use the resulting language to implement a knowledge base for a simple natural language understanding program.

9.4   Structured Representations

9.4.1   Frames

Using network representations, we view knowledge as organized using explicit links or associations between objects in the knowledge base. Alternatively, we can organize knowledge into more complex units that represent complex situations or objects in the domain. These units are called *frames* or *schemas*.

In a 1975 paper, Minsky describes a frame:

> Here is the essence of the frame theory: When one encounters a new situation (or makes a substantial change in one's view of a problem) one selects from memory a structure called a "frame." This is a remembered framework to be adapted to fit reality by changing details as necessary. (Minsky, 1975)

According to Minsky, a frame may be viewed as a static data structure used to represent well-understood, stereotyped situations. Framelike structures seem to organize our own knowledge of the world. We adjust to ever new situations by calling up information structured by past experiences. We then specially fashion or revise the details of these past experiences to represent the individual differences for the new situation.

Anyone who has stayed in one or two hotel rooms has no trouble with entirely new hotels and their rooms. One expects to see a bed, a bathroom, a place to open a suitcase, a telephone, price and emergency evacuation information on the back of the door, and so on. The details of each room can be supplied when needed: color of the curtains, location and use of light switches, etc. There is also default information supplied with the hotel room frame: no sheets: call housekeeping; need ice: look down the hall; and so on. We do not need to build up our understanding for each new hotel room we enter. All of the pieces of a generic hotel room are organized into a conceptual structure that we access when checking into a hotel; the particulars of an individual room are supplied as needed.

We could represent these higher-level structures directly in a semantic network by organizing it as a collection of separate networks, each of which represents some stereotypic situation. Frames, as well as *object-oriented systems*, provide us with a vehicle for this organization, representing knowledge as structured objects consisting of named slots

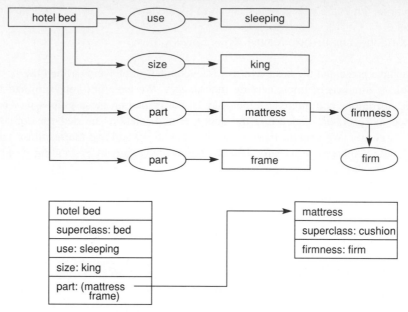

Figure 9.22 Conceptual graph and frame descriptions of a hotel bed.

with attached values. The notion of a frame or schema as a single complex entity is thus reinforced by the notation.

Figure 9.22 shows how a hotel bed may be represented using both conceptual graph and frame approaches. A hotel bed is a specialization of the general bed object. Many of the values in both versions are default assumptions about hotel beds. These include the size and firmness relations. Specific instances of hotel beds may or may not inherit these values. (See Section 9.5 for a more detailed discussion of the inheritance and default knowledge.) The slot names in the frame loosely correspond to the relations in the conceptual graph. The slot values may be values, pointers to other frames (as in the case of the mattress), or even attached procedures for performing some function, such as getting the bed made.

The components of a hotel room can be described by a number of individual frames. In addition to the bed, a frame could represent a chair: expected height is 20 to 40 cm, number of legs is 4 (a default value), has design for sitting. A further frame represents the hotel telephone: This is a specialization of a regular phone except that billing is through the room, there is a special hotel operator (default), and a person can use the hotel phone to get meals served in the room. Figure 9.23 gives a frame representing the hotel room.

Each individual frame may be seen as a data structure, similar in many respects to the traditional "record," that contains information relevant to stereotyped entities. The slots in the frame contain information such as:

1. Frame identification information.

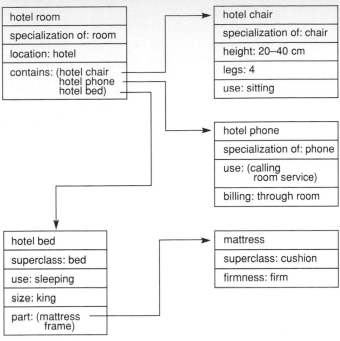

Figure 9.23 Portion of the frame description of a hotel room.

2. Relationship of this frame to other frames. The "hotel phone" might be a special instance of "phone," which in turn might be an instance of a "communication device."

3. Descriptors of requirements for frame match. A chair, for instance, has its seat between 20 and 40 cm from the floor, its back higher than 60 cm, etc. These requirements may be used to determine when new objects fit the stereotype defined by the frame.

4. Procedural information on use of the structure described. An important feature of frames is the ability to attach procedural code to a slot.

5. Frame default information. These are slot values that are taken to be true when no evidence to the contrary has been found. For instance, chairs have four legs, telephones are pushbutton, or hotel beds are made by the staff.

6. New instance information. Many frame slots may be left unspecified until given a value for a particular instance or needed for problem solving. For example, the color of the bedspread may be left unspecified in the definition of bed.

The presence, absence, or amount of detail in the six slots above depends on the particular problem-solving situation addressed.

Frames extend semantic networks in a number of important ways. Although the frame and network descriptions of hotel beds in Figure 9.22 are equivalent, the frame version makes it much clearer that we are describing a bed with its various attributes. In the network version, there is simply a collection of nodes and we depend more on our interpretation of the structure to see the hotel bed as the primary object being described. This ability to organize our knowledge into such structures is an important attribute of a knowledge base.

Frames make it easier to organize our knowledge hierarchically. In a network, every concept is represented by nodes and links at the same level of specification. Very often, however, we may like to think of an object as a single entity for some purposes and only consider details of its internal structure for other purposes. For example, we usually are not aware of the mechanical organization of a car until something breaks down; only then do we pull up our "car engine schema" and try to find the problem.

Procedural attachment is a particularly important feature of frames since certain knowledge does not adapt well to declarative representations. For example, we may want to include the ability to generate graphic images in a knowledge base. A graphics language is more appropriate for this than a network language. We use procedural attachment to create *demons*. A demon is a procedure that is invoked as a side effect of some other action in the knowledge base. For example, we may wish the system to perform type checks or to run consistency tests whenever a certain slot value is changed. We will discuss procedural attachment and demons in greater detail in Chapter 14.

Frame systems support class inheritance. The slots and default values of a class frame are inherited across the class/subclass and class/member hierarchy. For instance, a hotel phone could be a subclass of a regular phone except that (1) all out-of-building dialing goes through the hotel switchboard (for billing) and (2) hotel services may be dialed directly. Default values are assigned to selected slots to be used only if other information is not available: Assume that hotel rooms have beds and are, therefore, appropriate places to go if you want to sleep; if you don't know how to dial the hotel front desk try "zero"; the phone may be assumed (no evidence to the contrary) to be pushbutton.

When an instance of the class frame is created, the system will attempt to fill its slots, either by querying the user, accepting the default value from the class frame, or executing some pre-defined procedure or demon to obtain the instance value. As with semantic nets, slots and default values are inherited across a class/subclass hierarchy. Of course, default information can cause the data description of the problem to be non-monotonic, letting us make assumptions about default values that may not always prove correct.

Minsky's own work on vision provides an example of frames and their use in default reasoning: the problem of recognizing that different views of an object actually represent the same object. For example, the three perspectives of the one cube of Figure 9.24 actually look quite different. Minsky (1975) proposed a frame system that recognizes these as views of a single object by inferring the hidden sides as default assumptions.

The frame system of Figure 9.24 represents four of the faces of a cube. The broken lines indicate that a particular face is out of view from that perspective. The links between the frames indicate the relations between the views represented by the frames. The nodes, of course, could be more complex if there were colors or patterns that the faces contained. Indeed, each slot in one frame could be a pointer to another entire

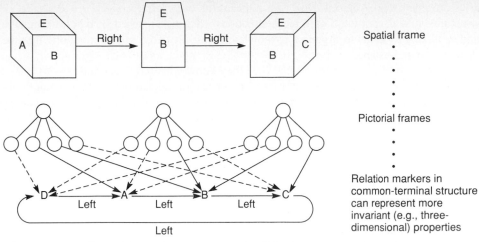

Figure 9.24 Spatial frame for viewing a cube (Minsky 1975).

frame. Also, since given information can fill a number of different slots, face **E** in Figure 9.24, there need be no redundancy in the information that is stored.

Frames add to the power of semantic nets by allowing complex objects to be represented as a single frame, rather than as a large network structure. This also provides a natural way to represent stereotypic entities, classes, inheritance, and default values. Although frames, like logical and network representations, are a powerful tool, many of the problems of acquiring and organizing a complicated knowledge base must still be solved by the programmer's skill and intuition (Section 9.5). Nonetheless, because of their power and generality, frames have emerged as an important representation in AI.

9.4.2 Scripts

A natural language understanding program must use a large amount of background knowledge to understand even the simplest conversation. There is evidence that humans organize this knowledge into structures corresponding to typical situations (Bartlett 1932). If we are reading a story about restaurants, baseball, or politics, we resolve any ambiguities in the text in a way consistent with restaurants, baseball, or politics. If the subject of a story changes abruptly, there is evidence that people pause briefly in their reading, presumably to change knowledge structures. It is hard to understand a poorly organized or structured story, possibly because we cannot easily fit it into any of our existing knowledge structures. There is also a tendency for errors in understanding when the subject of a conversation changes abruptly, presumably because we are confused over which context or schema to use in resolving pronoun references and other ambiguities.

A *script* is a structured representation describing a stereotyped sequence of events in a particular context. The *script* was originally designed by Schank and his research group (Schank and Abelson 1977) as a means of organizing *conceptual dependency* structures into descriptions of typical situations. Scripts are used in natural language understanding systems to organize a knowledge base in terms of the situations that the system is to understand.

Most adults are quite comfortable (i.e., they know what to expect and how to act) in a restaurant. They are met at the entrance (or by a sign indicating that they should continue in) and directed to a seat. Either a menu is available at the table or presented by the waiter, or the customer asks for it. We understand the routines for ordering food, eating, paying, and leaving.

In fact, the restaurant script is quite different from other eating scripts such as the "fast-food" model or the "formal family meal." In the fast-food model the customer enters, gets in line to order, pays for the meal (before eating), waits about for a tray with the food, takes the tray and tries to find a clean table, and so on. These are two different stereotyped sequences of events and each a potential script.

The components of a script are:

Entry conditions or descriptors of the world that must be true for the script to be called. In a restaurant script, these include a restaurant that is open and a customer who is hungry.

Results or facts that are true once the script has terminated; for example, the customer is full and poorer, the restaurant owner has more money.

Props or the "things" that make up the content of the script. These might include tables, waiters, and menus. This allows reasonable default assumptions about the situation: a restaurant is assumed to have tables and chairs unless stated otherwise.

Roles are the actions that the individual participants perform. The waiter takes orders, delivers food, and presents the bill. The customer orders, eats, and pays.

Scenes. Schank breaks the script into a sequence of scenes each of which presents a temporal aspect of the script. In the restaurant there is entering, ordering, eating, etc.

The elements of the script, the basic "pieces" of semantic meaning, are represented using conceptual dependency relationships. Placed together in a framelike structure, they represent a sequence of meanings, or an event sequence. The restaurant script taken from this research is presented in Figure 9.25.

The program reads a small story about restaurants and parses it into an internal conceptual dependency representation. Since the key concepts in this internal description match with the entry conditions of the script, the program binds the people and things mentioned in the story to the roles and props mentioned in the script. The result is an expanded representation of the story contents, using the script to fill in any missing information and default assumptions. The program then answers questions about the story by referring to the script. The script allows the reasonable default assumptions that are essential to natural language understanding. For example:

EXAMPLE 9.4.1

John went to a restaurant last night. He ordered steak. When he paid he noticed he was running out of money. He hurried home since it had started to rain.

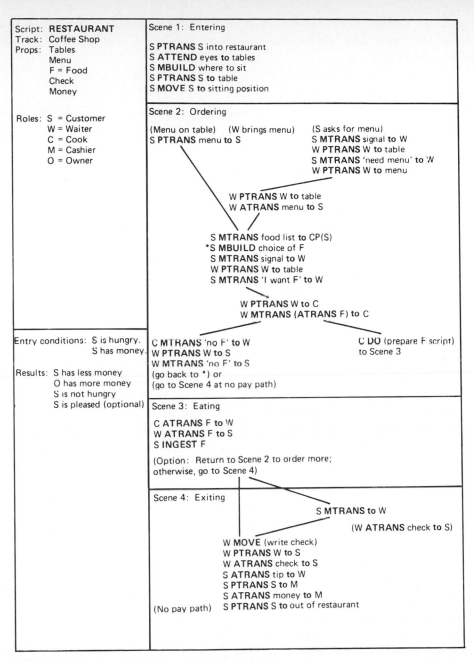

Figure 9.25   A restaurant script (Schank 1977).

Using the script, the system can correctly answer questions like: Did John eat dinner last night? Did John use cash or a credit card? How could John get a menu? What did John buy?

EXAMPLE 9.4.2

Sue went out to lunch. She sat at a table and called a waitress, who brought her a menu. She ordered a sandwich.

Questions that might reasonably be asked of this story include: Why did the waitress bring Sue a menu? Was Sue in a restaurant? Who paid? Who was the "she" that ordered the sandwich? This last question is difficult. The most recently named female is the waitress, an incorrect conclusion. Script *roles* help to resolve pronoun references and other ambiguities.

Scripts can also be used to interpret unexpected results or breaks in the scripted activity. Thus in scene 2 of Figure 9.25 there is the choice point of "food" or "no food" delivered to the customer. This allows the following example to be understood.

EXAMPLE 9.4.3

Kate went to a restaurant. She was shown to a table and ordered steak from the waitress. She sat there and waited for a long time. Finally, she got mad and left.

Questions that can be answered from this story using the restaurant script include: Who is the "she" that sat and waited? Why did she wait? Who was the "she" that got mad and left? Why did she get mad? Note that there are other questions that the script cannot answer, such as why do people get mad when the waiter does not come promptly? Like any knowledge-based system, scripts require the knowledge engineer to correctly anticipate the knowledge required.

Scripts, like frames and other structured representations, are subject to certain problems, including the script *match* problem and the *between-the-lines* problem. Consider Example 9.4.4, which could call either the *restaurant* or *concert* scripts. The choice is critical because "bill" can refer to either the restaurant check or the playbill of the concert:

EXAMPLE 9.4.4

John visited his favorite restaurant on the way to the concert. He was pleased by the bill because he liked Mozart.

It is often difficult to determine which of two or more potential scripts should be used. The script match problem is "deep" in the sense that no algorithm exists for guaranteeing correct choices. It requires heuristic knowledge about the organization of the world, and scripts assist only in the organization of that knowledge.

The between-the-lines problem is equally difficult: It is not possible to know ahead of time the possible occurrences that can break a script. For instance:

EXAMPLE 9.4.5

John was eating dinner at his favorite restaurant when a large piece of plaster fell from the ceiling and landed on his date. . . .

Questions: Was John eating a date salad? What did John do next? Was John's date plastered?

As this example illustrates, structured representations can be inflexible. Reasoning can be locked into a single script, even though this may not be appropriate.

These problems are not unique to script technology but are inherent in the problem of modeling semantic meaning. Eugene Charniak (1972) has illustrated the amount of knowledge required to understand even simple children's stories. Consider a statement about a birthday party: ''Mary was given two kites for her birthday so she took one back to the store.'' We must know about the tradition of giving gifts at a party; we must know what a kite is and why Mary doesn't want two of them; we must know about stores and their exchange policies. In spite of these problems, programs using scripts and other semantic representations can understand natural language in limited domains. An example of this work is a program that interprets messages coming over the news wire services. Using scripts for natural disasters, coups, or other stereotypic stories, programs have shown remarkable success in this limited but realistic domain (Schank and Riesbeck 1981).

9.5 Type Hierarchies, Inheritance, and Exception Handling

Inheritance across class or type hierarchies is an important feature of almost all network and structured representation languages. Inheritance is implemented through relations such as the type hierarchy of conceptual graphs, as well as through various links including ISA, AKO (A Kind Of), and SUPERC (SUPER Class). Figure 9.26 shows a frame-based representation of knowledge about birds with directed arcs indicating the inheritance hierarchy.

A common, although controversial, use of inheritance is to implement default values and exceptions. In the birds example, we have established a class flightless bird, which does not fly. If we assume that the inheritance algorithm searches the hierarchy in order, it would encounter the flightless bird frame before the bird frame and correctly infer that opus cannot fly. Here we have established flying as a default value for birds with the subclass flightless bird overriding that default value.

Several authors (Brachman 1985a; Touretzky 1986) have pointed out a number of anomalies that arise in inheritance, particularly in multiple inheritance hierarchies and in the use of inheritance to implement defaults.

The network of Figure 9.26 illustrates tree inheritance. Each node has only a single parent. Tree hierarchies are well behaved, since an algorithm need only search straight up the hierarchy until it encounters the desired property. If it reaches the top node and still has not found the property, it fails. There is no need for decisions in the inheritance

Figure 9.26 Inheritance system description of birds.

search. The situation is complicated, however, if we allow multiple inheritance, such as in a lattice. Multiple inheritance is supported in many knowledge representation languages since natural entities often belong to more than one class. In the network of Figure 9.27, we have added the class cartoon character and made opus an instance of this class as well as a penguin. Cartoon characters have a habitat of funny papers. It is no longer clear whether opus lives at the south pole or in the funnies.

This problem may be solved in several ways. Most inheritance systems allow the programmer to specify the order with which parent nodes are searched; here we could require that opus inherit the properties of cartoon character before those of penguin. This solution has the undesirable property of violating the declarative semantics of the representation. We must rely on knowledge of the order of search to resolve any ambiguities.

Furthermore, this would not help us if there were two conflicts and we wished to resolve one in favor of penguin and the other in favor of cartoon character. For example, we may state that penguins eat herring and cartoon characters eat hamburgers. How could we represent the fact that opus lives in the funnies and eats fish? We could do this by defining a new class for opus, called cartoon penguin, that would be a subclass of both penguin and cartoon character and resolve these conflicts explicitly (Fig. 9.28). This resolves the problem, although in many cases, introduction of new classes seems

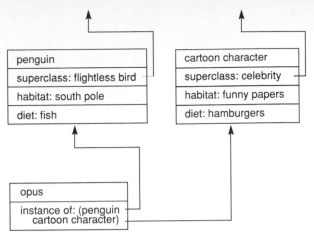

Figure 9.27 An ambiguous multiple inheritance situation.

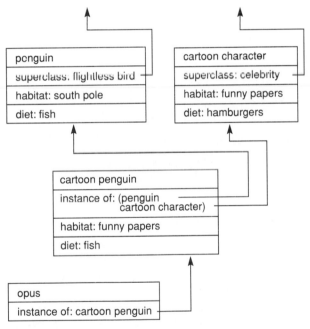

Figure 9.28 Introduction of a new class to resolve ambiguity.

artificial and can lead to further problems and restructuring of the network on later updates.

In addition to the anomalies introduced by multiple inheritance, there are problems that occur when inheritance is used to implement defaults and exceptions. In the network of Figure 9.26, the class flightless bird is introduced to handle exceptions to the

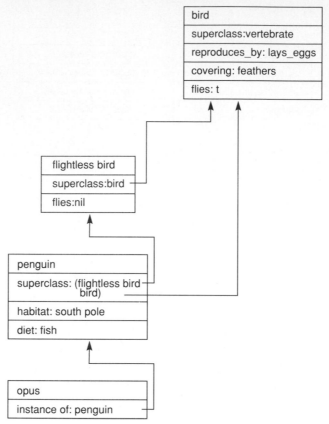

Figure 9.29 Introduction of an anomaly through the transitivity of the subclass relation.

rule that birds fly. It seems reasonable to treat class membership as a transitive relation; from the fact that penguin is a subclass of flightless bird and flightless bird is a subclass of bird, we should be able to infer that penguin is a subclass of bird. Unfortunately, if we allow this intuitively appealing inference and add this link to the graph, we confuse the inheritance of the flies property (Fig. 9.29). We may prohibit these inferences, but that is no more appealing than the other remedies to multiple-inheritance anomalies.

There is a deeper problem in the use of inheritance to handle defaults and exceptions: it compromises the nature of definitions themselves (Brachman 1985a). It seems appropriate to view a frame as a definition of a class. However, if we define a penguin as a bird that doesn't fly, what is to prevent us from asserting that a block of wood is a bird that doesn't fly, doesn't have feathers, and doesn't lay eggs? This careless use of inheritance to implement exception handling illustrates the subtleties that arise in knowledge representation. One solution would be to restrict the representation to a form that does not allow these problems, such as tree inheritance without exception handling. This also eliminates much of the power of inheritance. Another approach is to examine carefully and refine the semantics of the representation. Touretzky (1986) has reformulated inheritance and resolved many of these ambiguities.

Unfortunately, most commercially available inheritance software does not provide a clean enough implementation of inheritance to avoid these problems. This is because many of these problems have not yet been solved or the solutions that are available are either too new or too inefficient to affect the design of current programs. The most effective approach to these problems still requires the programmer to be careful in structuring the knowledge base.

9.6   Further Problems in Knowledge Representation

In this text, we examine the major alternatives for knowledge representation, including the use of logic, rules, semantic networks, and frames. The results of careful study include an increased understanding of the advantages and limitations of each of these representations. Nonetheless, debate continues over the relative naturalness, efficiency, and appropriateness of each approach. Regardless of the representation language selected, a number of important problems remain in the area of knowledge representation.

The first of these is the selection and granularity of atomic symbols for the knowledge base. Objects in the world constitute the domain of the mapping; computational objects in the knowledge base are the range. The nature of the atomic elements in the language largely determines what can be described about the world. For example, if a "car" is the smallest atom of the representation, then the system cannot reason about engines, wheels, or any of the component parts of a car. However, if the atoms correspond to these parts, than a larger structure may be required to represent "car" as a single concept. This introduces a cost in efficiency (in manipulating this larger structure) and expressiveness (the larger structure may obscure the fact that a car is a single conceptual entity).

Another example of the trade-off in the choice of atomic symbols comes from work in natural language understanding. Programs that use single words as elements of meaning may have difficulty in representing complex concepts that do not have a one-word denotation. There is also difficulty in distinguishing between different meanings of the same word or different words with the same meaning. One approach to this problem is to use semantic primitives, language-independent conceptual units, as the basis for representing the meaning of natural language. Conceptual dependency theory takes this approach, and although it avoids the problems of using single words as units of meaning, it involves other trade-offs: many words require complex structures for their definitions; also, by relying on a small set of primitives, many subtle distinctions (e.g., push vs. shove, yell vs. scream) are difficult to express.

Exhaustiveness is a property of a knowledge base that is assisted by an appropriate representation. A mapping is *exhaustive* with respect to a property or class of objects if all occurrences correspond to an explicit element of the representation. Geographic maps are assumed to be exhaustive to some level of detail; a map with a missing city or river would not be well regarded as a navigational tool. Although most knowledge bases are not exhaustive, exhaustiveness with respect to certain properties or objects is a desirable goal. For example, the ability to assume that a representation is exhaustive may allow a planner to ignore possible effects of the *frame* problem.

When we describe problems as a state of the world that is changed by a series of actions or events, these actions or events generally change only a few components of the description; the program must be able to infer side effects and implicit changes in the world description. The problem of representing the side effects of actions is called the *frame problem*. For example, a robot stacking heavy boxes on a truck must compensate for the lowering of the truck bed due to the weight of the boxes. If a representation is exhaustive, there will be no unspecified side effects, and the frame problem effectively disappears. The difficulty of the frame problem results from the fact that it is impossible to build a completely exhaustive knowledge base for most domains. A representation language should assist the programmer in deciding what knowledge may safely be omitted and help deal with the consequences of this omission. (Section 15.1 discusses the frame problem in planning.)

Related to exhaustiveness is the *plasticity* or modifiability of the representation: the addition of knowledge in response to deficiencies is the primary solution to a lack of exhaustiveness. Since most knowledge bases are not exhaustive, it should be easy to modify or update them. In addition to the syntactic ease of adding knowledge, a representation should help to guarantee the consistency of a knowledge base as information is added or deleted. Inheritance, by allowing properties of a class to be inherited by new instances, is an example of how a knowledge representational scheme may help ensure consistency.

Another useful property of representations concerns the extent to which the mapping between the world and the knowledge base is *homomorphic*. Here, homomorphic implies a one-to-one correspondence between objects and actions in the world and the computational objects and operations of the language. In a homomorphic mapping the knowledge base reflects the perceived organization of the domain and can be organized in a more natural and intuitive fashion.

In addition to naturalness, directness, and ease of use, representational schemes may also be evaluated by their *computational efficiency*. Levesque and Brachman (1985) discuss the trade-off between expressiveness and efficiency. Logic, when used as a representational scheme, is highly expressive as a result of its completeness; however, systems based on unconstrained logic pay a considerable price in efficiency. We address this issue again in Chapter 11.

9.7 Epilogue and References

Knowledge representation is a large and difficult field that lies at the heart of modern artificial intelligence. In this chapter we introduce the major problems in representation and offer techniques for their solution.

An important area that we have overlooked involves modifications and extensions to logic that enable it to address the problems of knowledge representation while retaining its well-defined semantics and inference strategies. Important alternatives to first-order predicate calculus include:

1. **Multiple-valued logics**. These extend logic by adding new truth values such as unknown to the standard values of true and false. This can, for example, provide a vehicle for distinguishing between assertions that are known to be false and those that are simply not known to be true.

2. **Modal logics**. Modal logic adds operators that enable it to deal with problems of knowledge and belief, necessity and possibility.

3. **Temporal logics**. Temporal logics enable us to quantify expressions with regard to time, indicating, for example, that an expression is *always* true or *will be true in the future*.

4. **Higher-order logics**. Many categories of knowledge correspond to higher-order logical concepts. Do we really need higher-order logics to deal with this knowledge or can it all be done in first-order logic? If higher-order logics are needed, how may they best be formulated?

5. **Logical formulations of definitions, prototypes, and exceptions**. As we illustrated in the discussion of inheritance, exceptions are a necessary feature of a definitional system. However, careless use of exceptions undermines the semantics of a representation. Another issue is the difference between a definition and a prototype, or representation of a *typical* individual. What is the exact difference between the properties of a class and the properties of a typical member? How should prototypical individuals be represented? When is a prototype more appropriate than a definition?

Logical representation continues to be an important area of research (McCarthy 1968; Hayes 1979; Weyhrauch 1980; Moore 1982). *Logics for Artificial Intelligence* by Turner (1984) is an overview of work done in nonstandard logics.

Associationist theories have been studied as models of both computer and human memory and reasoning (Selz 1913, 1922; Anderson and Bower 1973; Sowa 1984; Collins and Quillian 1969).

Our overview of conceptual graphs owes a considerable debt to John Sowa's book *Conceptual Structures* (1984). The reader is referred to this book for details that we have omitted. In its full treatment, conceptual graphs combine the expressive power of predicate calculus, as well as modal and higher-order logic, with a rich set of built-in concepts and relations derived from epistemology, psychology, and linguistics.

Schema-based reasoning, in many ways similar to frames, was pursued by researchers at the AI Department of the University of Edinburgh (Bundy et al. 1979). Other important work in structured knowledge representation languages includes Bobrow and Winograd's representation language KRL (Bobrow and Winograd 1977) and the development of the LOOPS programming environment (Stefik et al. 1983). Brachman (1979) has developed a representation language called KL-ONE that pays particular attention to the semantic foundations of structured representations.

There are a number of other approaches of interest to the representation problem. For example, Brachman, Fikes, and Levesque have proposed representation that emphasizes *functional* specifications, that is, what can be asked of or told to a knowledge base (Brachman et al. 1985; Levesque 1984).

A number of books can help with an advanced study of these issues. *Readings in Knowledge Representation* by Brachman and Levesque (1985) is a compilation of important articles in this area. Many of the articles referred to in this chapter may be found there, although they were referenced in their original source. *Representation and Understanding* by Bobrow and Collins (1975) is another important collection of articles.

9.8   Exercises

1. Commonsense reasoning employs such notions as causality, analogy, and equivalence, but uses them in a different way from formal languages. For example, if we say that ''Inflation caused Jane to ask for a raise,'' we are suggesting a more complicated causal relationship than is generally found in simple physical laws. If we say ''Use a knife or chisel to trim the wood,'' we are suggesting a different notion of equivalence than is found in most formal languages. Discuss the problems of translating these and other commonsense concepts into a formal language.

2. In Section 9.2.1 we presented some of the arguments against the use of logic for representing commonsense knowledge. Make an argument for the use of logic in representing this knowledge.

3. Translate each of the following sentences into predicate calculus, conceptual dependencies, and conceptual graphs:

   ''Jane gave Tom an ice cream cone.''
   ''Basketball players are tall.''
   ''Paul cut down the tree with an axe.''
   ''Place all the ingredients in a bowl and mix thoroughly.''

4. Read ''What's in a Link'' by Woods (1985). Section IV of this article lists a number of problems in knowledge representation. Suggest a solution to each of these problems using logic, conceptual graphs and frame notations.

5. Translate the conceptual graphs of Figure 9.30 into English sentences.

6. The operations join and restrict define a generalization ordering on conceptual graphs. Show that the generalization relation is transitive.

7. Specialization of conceptual graphs using join and restrict is not a truth-preserving operation. Give an example that demonstrates that the restriction of a true graph is not necessarily true. However, the generalization of a true graph is always true; prove this.

8. Define a specialized representation language to describe the activities of a public library. This language will be a set of concepts and relations using conceptual graphs. Do the same thing for a retail business. What concepts and relations would these two languages have in common? Which would exist in both languages but have a different meaning?

9. Translate the conceptual graphs of Figure 9.30 into predicate calculus.

10. Translate the financial advisor knowledge base (Chapter 2) into conceptual graph form.

11. Give evidence from your own experience that suggests a scriptlike or framelike organization of human memory.

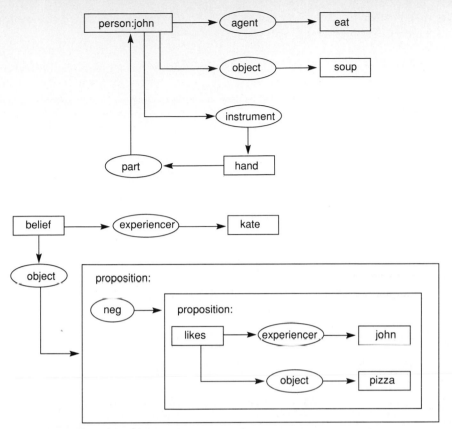

Figure 9.30 Two conceptual graphs to be translated into English.

12. Using conceptual dependencies, define a script for:

    a. A fast-food restaurant.
    b. Interacting with a used-car salesman.
    c. Going to the opera.

13. Construct a hierarchy of subtypes for the concept vehicle; for example, subtypes of vehicle might be land vehicle or ocean vehicle. These would have further subtypes. Is this best represented as a tree, lattice, or general graph? Do the same for the concept move. For the concept angry.

14. Construct a type hierarchy in which some types do not have a common supertype. Add types to make this a lattice. Could this hierarchy be expressed using tree inheritance? What problems would arise in doing so?

15. Each of the following sequences of characters is generated according to some general rule. Describe a representation that could be used to represent the rules for:

    a. 2,4,6,8,...
    b. 1,2,4,8,16,...

c. 1,1,2,3,5,8,...
d. 1,a,2,c,3,f,4,...
e. o,t,t,f,f,s,s,...

Define a representation that could be used to represent any rule for sequences of numbers and letters.

16. Describe a representation that could be used in a program to solve analogy problems like that in Figure 9.31.

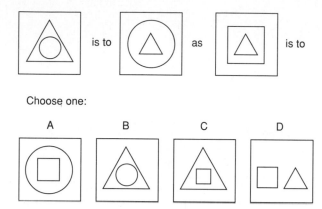

Figure 9.31   Example of an analogy test problem.

This class of problems was addressed by T. G. Evans (1968). The representation must be capable of representing the essential features of size, shape, and relative position.

10

NATURAL LANGUAGE

Quid opus est verbis? (What need is there for words?)

—TERENCE

I understand a fury in your words,
But not the words.

—WILLIAM SHAKESPEARE, *Othello*

They have been to a great feast of languages
And stolen the scraps.

—WILLIAM SHAKESPEARE, *Love's Labours Lost*

I wish someone would tell me what "Ditty wah ditty" means.

—ARTHUR BLAKE

10.0 Role of Knowledge in Language Understanding

Natural language understanding, like expert level problem solving, depends heavily on knowledge of the domain of discourse. Consider, for example, the following conversation about a basketball game.

Tom: "Who do you like tonight, Boston or L.A.?"

(Because there is a basketball game on TV that evening, Mary knows that Tom means the teams, not the cities.)

Mary: "Lakers. You?"

(Tom knows that the Lakers are from Los Angeles. Also, note that Mary is not talking in complete sentences.)

Tom: "Come on, Mary, L.A. can't handle Bird."

(Tom did not directly answer Mary's question; also, Mary knows that "Bird" refers to Larry Bird, a player for the Boston Celtics, not a small winged vertebrate.)

Mary: "I've got a five that says Magic will shut him down."

(Mary's "five" is money and it doesn't literally speak; also, Magic refers to Magic Johnson, not some secret incantation.)

Imagine all the knowledge that is required to understand this short and, by human standards, simple conversation! In addition to an understanding of basketball, the conversation assumes knowledge of geography, slang, gambling, athletic rivalries, and television. Much of the information needed to understand a sentence is assumed to be shared by both speakers and is consequently left out of the conversation. People do not always communicate in grammatically correct sentences; knowledge of the topic lets us interpret these fragments.

These problems and subtleties arise in almost every natural language interaction. Indeed, even parsing a simple sentence may require significant knowledge about nature and human interaction. Consider the sentence "Time flies like an arrow but fruit flies like a banana." Although there are several possible parsings, only one is plausible given our knowledge of the world and the common uses of language.

Because of the knowledge required to understand unconstrained natural language, much progress in the area has come by restricting our focus to *microworlds*, limited domains that require little domain knowledge. This allows researchers to focus more directly on the problems of processing natural language itself. One of the earliest programs to take this approach was Terry Winograd's SHRDLU (Winograd 1972), a program that could converse about a *blocks world* consisting of arrangements of differently shaped and colored blocks and a hand for moving them about (Fig. 10.1).

Figure 10.1 A blocks world.

SHRDLU could respond to English language queries and commands such as "What is sitting on the red block?" "What shape is the blue block on the table?" or "Place the green pyramid on the red brick." It could handle anaphoric references such as "Is there a red block? Pick it up." It could even understand ellipses such as "What color is the block on the blue brick? Shape?" Because of the simplicity of the blocks world, it was possible to provide the system with complete knowledge of the world. Because the blocks world did not involve the more difficult problems of commonsense reasoning such as time, causality, possibilities, and beliefs, the techniques for representing this knowledge were relatively straightforward. However, in spite of its narrow subject matter, SHRDLU did provide a model for the integration of syntax and semantics and demonstrated that a program with sufficient knowledge of the domain of discourse could communicate meaningfully in natural language.

In Section 10.1 we introduce the commonly accepted levels of analysis of natural language. Section 10.2 presents a syntactic analysis; 10.3 combines syntax and semantics using augmented transition network parsing. In 10.4 we consider two applications where natural language understanding programs are useful: question answering and accessing information in data bases.

10.1 The Natural Language Problem

10.1.1 Levels of Analysis

Language is a complicated phenomenon, involving processes as varied as the recognition of sounds or printed letters, syntactic parsing, high-level semantic inferences, and even the communication of emotional content through rhythm and inflection. To manage this complexity, linguists have defined different levels of analysis for natural language:

1. *Prosody* deals with the rhythm and intonation of language. This level of analysis is difficult to formalize and often neglected; however, its importance is evident in the powerful effect of poetry or religious chants, as well as the role played by rhythm in children's wordplay and the babbling of infants.

2. *Phonology* examines the sounds that are combined to form language. This branch of linguistics is important to work in computerized speech recognition and generation.

3. *Morphology* is concerned with the meaningful components (morphemes) that make up words. These include the rules governing the formation of words, such as the effect of prefixes (un-, non-, anti-, etc.) and suffixes (-ing, -ly, etc.) that modify the meaning of root words. Morphological analysis is important in determining the role of a word in a sentence, including its tense, number, and part of speech.

4. *Syntax* studies the rules for combining words into legal phrases and sentences and the use of those rules to parse and generate sentences. This has been the most successfully formalized and consequently the most successfully automated level of linguistic analysis.

5. *Semantics* considers the meaning of words, phrases, and sentences and the way in which it is conveyed in natural language.

6. *Pragmatics* is the study of the way in which language is used and its effects on the listener. For example, pragmatics would address the reasons why "Yes" is *usually* an inappropriate answer to the question "Do you know what time it is?"

7. *World knowledge* includes knowledge of the physical world, the world of human social interaction, and the role of goals and intentions in communication. This general background knowledge is essential to understand the full meaning of a text or conversation.

Although these levels of analysis seem natural and are supported by psychological evidence, they are, to some extent, artificial divisions that have been imposed on language. All of these interact extensively, with even low-level intonations and rhythmic variations having an effect on the meaning of an utterance (e.g., sarcasm). This interaction is evident in the relationship between syntax and semantics, and although some division along these lines seems essential, the exact boundary is difficult to characterize. For example, sentences such as "They are eating apples" have multiple parsings that can be resolved only by attention to meaning and context. Conversely, syntax affects semantics, as will be illustrated by the role of phrase structure in interpreting the meaning of a sentence. Although the exact nature of the distinction between syntax and semantics is often blurred and often debated, both the psychological evidence and its utility in managing the complexity of the problem argue for its retention.

10.1.2 Stages of Natural Language Analysis

While the specific organization of natural language understanding programs varies with different philosophies and applications—e.g., a front end for a data base, an automatic translation system, a story understanding program—all of them must translate the original sentence into an internal representation of its meaning. Generally, natural language understanding follows the stages of Figure 10.2.

The first stage is *parsing*, which analyzes the syntactic structure of sentences. Parsing not only verifies that sentences are syntactically well formed but also determines their linguistic structure. By diagramming the major linguistic relations such as subject-verb, verb-object, and noun-modifier, the parser provides a framework for semantic interpretation. This is often represented as a *parse tree*. The parser employs knowledge of language syntax, morphology, and some semantics.

The second stage is *semantic interpretation*, which produces a representation of the meaning of the text. In Figure 10.2 this is shown as a conceptual graph. Other representations commonly used include conceptual dependencies, frames, and logic-based representations. Semantic interpretation uses knowledge about the meaning of words and linguistic structure, such as case roles of nouns or the transitivity of verbs. In the example of Figure 10.2, the program used knowledge of the meaning of kiss to add the default value of lips for the instrument of kissing. This stage also performs semantic consistency checks; for example, the definition of the verb kiss may include constraints

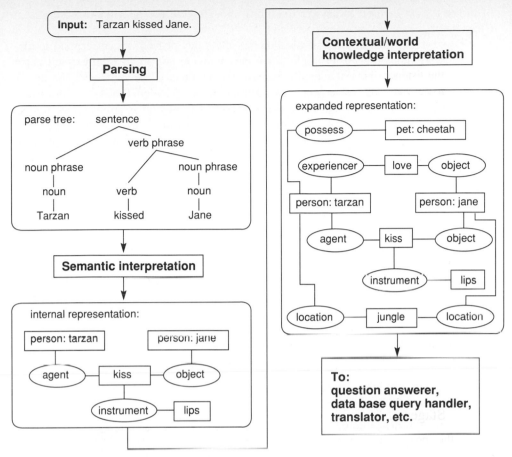

Figure 10.2 Stages in producing an internal representation of a sentence.

that require the object to be a person if the agent is a person, i.e., Tarzan does not (normally) kiss Cheetah.

In the third stage, structures from the knowledge base are added to the internal representation of the sentence to produce an expanded representation of the sentence's meaning. This adds the necessary world knowledge required for complete understanding, such as the facts that Tarzan loves Jane, that Jane and Tarzan live in the jungle, and that Cheetah is Tarzan's pet. This resulting structure represents the meaning of the natural language text and is used by the system for further processing.

In a data base front end, for example, the extended structure would combine the representation of the query's meaning with knowledge about the organization of the data base. This could then be translated into an appropriate query in the data base language. In a story understanding program, this extended structure would represent the meaning of the story and be used to answer questions about it (see the discussion of scripts in Chapter 9).

These stages exist in all systems, although they may or may not correspond to distinct software modules. For example, many programs do not produce an explicit parse tree but generate the internal semantic representation directly. Nevertheless, the tree is implicit in the parse of the sentence. *Incremental parsing* (Allen 1987) is a commonly used technique in which a fragment of the internal representation is produced as soon as a significant part of the sentence is parsed. These fragments are combined into a complete structure as the parse proceeds. They are also used to resolve ambiguities and guide the parser.

10.2 Syntax

10.2.1 Specification and Parsing Using Context-Free Grammars

Chapters 4 and 6 introduced the use of *rewrite rules* to specify a grammar. The rules listed below define a grammar for simple transitive sentences such as ''The man likes the dog.'' The rules are numbered for reference:

1. sentence ← noun_phrase verb_phrase
2. noun_phrase ← noun
3. noun_phrase ← article noun
4. verb_phrase ← verb
5. verb_phrase ← verb noun_phrase
6. article ← a
7. article ← the
8. noun ← man
9. noun ← dog
10. verb ← likes
11. verb ← bites

Rules 6 through 11 have English words on their right-hand side; these rules form a basic dictionary of words that may appear in sentences of the grammar. These words are the *terminals* of the grammar. Terms that describe higher-level linguistic concepts (sentence, noun_phrase, etc.) are called *nonterminals*. Nonterminals appear in this typeface. Note that terminals do not appear in the left-hand side of any rule.

A legal sentence is any string of terminals that can be *derived* using these rules. A derivation begins with the nonterminal symbol sentence and produces a string of terminals through a series of substitutions defined by the rules of the grammar. A legal substitution replaces a symbol that matches the left-hand side of a rule with the symbols on the right-hand side of that rule. At intermediate stages of the derivation, the string may contain both terminals and nonterminals and is called a *sentential form*. A derivation of the sentence "The man bites the dog" is given by:

STRING	APPLY RULE #
sentence	1
noun_phrase verb_phrase	3
article noun verb_phrase	7
The noun verb_phrase	8
The man verb_phrase	5
The man verb noun_phrase	11
The man bites noun_phrase	3
The man bites article noun	7
The man bites the noun	9
The man bites the dog	

This is an example of a *top-down* derivation; it begins with the sentence symbol and works down to a string of terminals. A bottom-up derivation starts with a string of terminals and replaces right-hand-side patterns with those from the left-hand side, terminating when all that remains is the sentence symbol.

A derivation may be represented as a tree structure, known as a *parse tree*, in which each node is a symbol of the grammar. The interior nodes of the tree are nonterminals; each node and its children correspond, respectively, to the left-hand side and right-hand side of a rule in the grammar. The leaf nodes are terminals and the sentence symbol is the root of the tree. The parse tree for "the man bites the dog" appears in Figure 10.3.

Not only does the existence of a derivation or parse tree prove that a sentence is legal in the grammar, it also determines the structure of the sentence. The *phrase structure* of the grammar defines the deeper linguistic organization of the language. For example, the breakdown of a sentence into a noun_phrase and a verb_phrase specifies the relation between an action and its agent. This phrase structure plays an

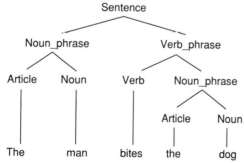

Figure 10.3   Parse tree for the sentence "The man bites the dog."

essential role in semantic interpretation by defining intermediate stages in a derivation at which semantic processing may take place.

Parsing is the problem of constructing a derivation or a parse tree for an input string from a formal definition of a grammar. Parsing algorithms fall into two classes: *top-down parsers*, which begin with the top-level sentence symbol and attempt to build a tree whose leaves match the target sentence, and *bottom-up parsers*, which start with the sentence and attempt to find a series of reductions that yield the sentence symbol.

In parsing, the difficulty is in determining which of several potentially applicable rules should be used at each step of the derivation. If the wrong choice is made, the parser may fail to recognize a legal sentence. For example, in attempting to parse the sentence "The dog bites," in a bottom-up fashion, rules 7, 9, and 11 produce the string "article noun verb." At this point, an erroneous application of rule 2 would produce "article noun_phrase verb"; this could not be reduced to the "sentence" symbol. The parser should use rule 3 instead. Similar problems can occur in a top-down parse.

The problem of selecting the correct rule at any stage of the parse is handled either by allowing the parser to backtrack if an incorrect choice is made (as in *recursive descent parsers*) or by using look-ahead to check the input string for features that will determine the proper rule to apply. With either approach, we must take care to control the complexity of execution while guaranteeing a correct parse.

The inverse problem is that of *generation*, or producing legal sentences from an internal semantic representation. Generation starts with a representation of some meaningful content (such as a semantic network or conceptual dependency graph) and constructs a grammatically correct sentence that communicates this meaning.

Since parsing is particularly important in the processing of programming languages as well as natural language, researchers have developed a number of different parsing algorithms. These include both top-down and bottom-up strategies. While a complete survey of parsing algorithms is beyond the scope of this chapter, we do consider *transition network* parsers in some detail. Although transition network parsers themselves are not sufficiently powerful for natural language, they form the basis for *augmented transition networks*, which have proved to be a powerful tool for natural language work.

10.2.2   Transition Network Parsers

A transition network parser represents a grammar as a set of finite-state machines or *transition networks*. Each network corresponds to a single nonterminal in the grammar. Arcs in the networks are labeled with either terminal or nonterminal symbols. Each path through the network, from the start state to the final state, corresponds to some rule for that nonterminal; the sequence of arc labels on the path is the sequence of symbols on the right-hand side of the rule. The grammar of Section 10.2.1 is represented by the transition networks of Figure 10.4. When there is more than one rule for a nonterminal, the corresponding network has multiple paths from the start to the goal. For example, the rules "noun_phrase ← noun" and "noun_phrase ← article noun" are captured by alternative paths through the noun_phrase network of Figure 10.4.

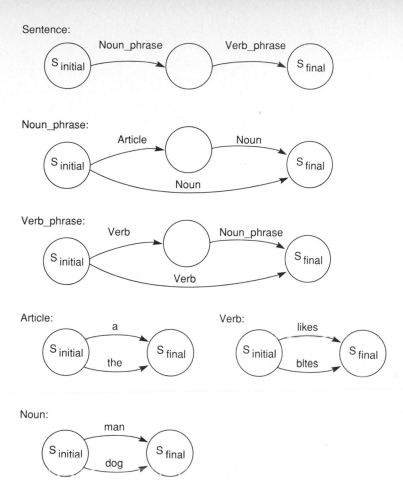

Figure 10.4 Transition network definition of a simple English grammar.

Finding a successful transition through the network for a nonterminal corresponds to the replacement of that nonterminal by the right-hand side of a grammar rule. For example, to parse a sentence, a transition network parser must find a transition through the sentence network. It begins in the start state ($S_{initial}$), and takes the noun_phrase transition and then the verb_phrase transition to reach the final state (S_{final}). This is equivalent to replacing the sentence symbol by the string noun_phrase verb_phrase.

In order to cross an arc, the parser examines its label. If the label is a terminal symbol, the parser checks the input stream to see if the next word matches the arc label. If it does not match, the transition cannot be taken. If the arc is labeled with a nonterminal symbol, the parser retrieves the network for that nonterminal and recursively attempts to find a path through it. If the parser fails to find a path through this network, the top-level

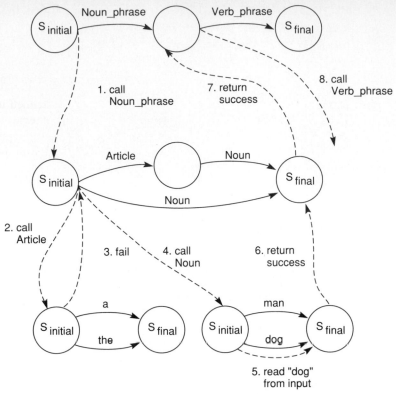

Figure 10.5 Trace of a transition network parse of the sentence "Dog bites."

arc cannot be traversed. This causes the parser to backtrack and attempt another path through the network. Thus, the parser tries to find a path through the **sentence** network; if it succeeds, the input string is a legal sentence in the grammar.

Consider the simple sentence "Dog bites." The first steps in parsing this sentence are illustrated in Figure 10.5:

1. The parser begins with the **sentence** network and tries to move along the arc labeled **noun_phrase**. To do so, it retrieves the network for **noun_phrase**.

2. In the **noun_phrase** network, the parser first tries the transition marked **article**. This causes it to branch to the network for **article**.

3. It fails to find a path to the finish node of the **article** network since the first word of the sentence, "Dog," matches neither of the arc labels. The parser fails and backtracks to the **noun_phrase** network.

4. The parser attempts to follow the arc labeled **noun** in the **noun_phrase** network and branches to the network for **noun**.

5. The parser successfully crosses the arc labeled "dog," since this corresponds to the first word of the input stream.

6. The noun network returns success. This allows the arc labeled noun in the noun_phrase network to be crossed to the final state.

7. The noun_phrase network returns success to the top-level network, allowing the transition of the arc labeled noun_phrase.

8. Similar steps are followed in parsing the verb_phrase portion of the sentence.

Pseudocode for a transition network parser appears below. It is defined using two mutually recursive functions, parse and transition. Parse takes a grammar symbol as argument: If it is a terminal, parse checks it against the next word in the input stream. If it is a nonterminal, parse retrieves the transition network associated with the symbol and calls transition to find a path through the network. Transition takes a state in a transition network as argument and tries to find a path through that network in a depth-first fashion. In order to parse a sentence, call parse(sentence).

```
function parse( grammar_symbol);

begin
 save pointer to current location in input stream;
 case

    grammar_symbol is a terminal:
      if grammar-symbol matches the next word in the input stream
      then return (success)
      else begin
        reset input stream
        return (failure);
      end;

    grammar_symbol is a nonterminal:
      begin
        retrieve the transition network labeled by grammar symbol;
        state := start state of network;
        if transition(state) returns success
        then return (success)
        else begin
          reset input stream
          return (failure);
        end;

    end
end.

function  transition (current_state);

begin
  case

    current_state is a final state:
    return (success)
```

```
current_state is not a final state:
  while there are unexamined transitions out of current_state
   do begin
    grammar_symbol := the label on the next unexamined transition
    if parse(grammar_symbol) returns success
    then begin
     next_state := state at end of the transition;
     if transition(next_state) returns success
     then return (success)
    end;
   end

   return (failure)
 end.
```

Since the parser may make a mistake and have to backtrack, parse retains a pointer to the current location in the input stream. This allows the input stream to be reset to this location in the event the parser backtracks.

This transition network parser determines whether a sentence is grammatically correct, but it does not construct a parse tree. This may be accomplished by having the functions return a subtree of the parse tree instead of the symbol success. Modifications that would accomplish this are:

1. Each time the function parse is called with a terminal symbol as argument and that terminal matches the next symbol of input, it returns a tree consisting of a single leaf node labeled with that symbol.

2. When parse is called with a nonterminal, grammar_symbol, it calls transition. If transition succeeds, it returns an ordered set of subtrees (described below). Parse combines these into a tree whose root is grammar_symbol and whose children are the subtrees returned by transition.

3. In searching for a path through a network, transition calls parse on the label of each arc. On success, parse returns a tree representing a parse of that symbol. Transition saves these subtrees in an ordered set and, on finding a path through the network, returns the ordered set of parse trees corresponding to the sequence of arc labels on the path.

In this fashion, the parser constructs the tree as it exits from the recursive calls.

10.2.3 The Chomsky Hierarchy and Context-Sensitive Grammars

In Section 10.2.1, we defined a small subset of English using a *context-free grammar*. A context-free grammar allows rules to have only a single nonterminal on their left-hand side. Consequently, the rule may be applied to any occurrence of that symbol, regardless of its context. While context-free grammars have proved to be a powerful tool for defining programming languages and other formalisms in computer science, they are not powerful enough, by themselves, to represent the rules of natural language syntax. For example, consider what happens if we add both singular and plural nouns and verbs to the grammar of Section 10.2.1:

noun ← men
noun ← dogs
verb ← bite
verb ← like

While the resulting grammar will parse such sentences as "The dogs like the men," it will also accept ungrammatical sentences such as "A men likes a dogs." The parser will accept the erroneous sentence because the rules cannot use context to determine when the singular or plural forms may be used. For example, the rule defining a sentence as a noun_phrase followed by a verb_phrase cannot require that the subject and verb agree on number; the same problem occurs in trying to enforce article/noun agreement.

Languages defined by context-free grammars are only one in a hierarchy of classes of formal languages. This is the *Chomsky hierarchy* (Hopcroft and Ullman 1979; Chomsky 1965). At the bottom of the hierarchy is the class of *regular languages*. A regular language is one whose grammar may be defined using finite-state machines. Although regular languages have many uses in computer science, they are not powerful enough to represent the syntax of most programming languages.

The *context-free languages* are above the regular languages in the Chomsky hierarchy. Context-free languages are defined using rewrite rules such as in Section 10.2.1; context-free rules may only have one nonterminal symbol on their left-hand side. Transition network parsers are able to parse the class of context-free languages. It is interesting to note that if we *do not* allow recursion in a transition network parser (i.e., arcs may be labeled only with terminal symbols, transitions may not "call" another network), then the class of languages that may be so defined corresponds to regular expressions. Thus, regular languages are a proper subset of the context-free languages.

The *context-sensitive* languages form a proper superset of the context-free languages. These are defined using *context-sensitive grammars*, which allow more than one symbol on the left-hand side of a rule and make it possible to define a context in which that rule can be applied. This is used to ensure satisfaction of global constraints such as number agreement and other semantic checks. The only restriction on context-sensitive grammar rules is that the right-hand side be at least as long as the left-hand side of the rule (Hopcroft and Ullman 1979).

A fourth class, forming a superset of the context-sensitive languages, is the class of *recursively enumerable* languages. Recursively enumerable languages may be defined using unconstrained production rules; since these rules are less constrained than context-sensitive rules, the recursively enumerable languages are a proper superset of the context-sensitive languages. This class is not of interest in defining the syntax of natural language, although it is important in the theory of computer science. The remainder of this section focuses on English as a context-sensitive language.

A context-sensitive grammar for sentences of the form "article noun verb" that enforces number agreement between both article and noun and subject and verb is given by:

sentence ← noun_phrase verb_phrase

noun_phrase ← article number noun

noun_phrase ← number noun

number ← singular

number ← plural

article singular ← a singular

article singular ← the singular

article plural ← some plural

article plural ← the plural

singular noun ← dog singular

singular noun ← man singular

plural noun ← men plural

plural noun ← dogs plural

singular verb phrase ← singular verb

plural verb_phrase ← plural verb

singular verb ← bites

singular verb ← likes

plural verb ← bite

plural verb ← like

In this grammar, the nonterminals singular and plural provide a context to determine when different article, noun, and verb_phrase rules can be applied. This ensures number agreement. A derivation of the sentence "The dogs bite" using this grammar is given by:

The dogs bite.

The dogs plural verb.

The dogs plural verb_phrase.

The plural noun verb_phrase.

article plural noun verb_phrase.

noun_phrase verb_phrase.

sentence.

Similarly, we can use context-sensitive grammars to perform certain checks for semantic agreement. For example, we could disallow sentences such as "Man bites dog" by adding a nonterminal, act_of_biting, to the grammar. This nonterminal could be checked in the rules to prevent any sentence involving "bites" from having "man" as its subject.

While context-sensitive grammars can define language structures that cannot be captured using context-free grammars, they have a number of disadvantages for the design of practical parsers:

1. Context-sensitive grammars increase the number of rules and nonterminals in the grammar drastically. Imagine the complexity of a context-sensitive grammar that would include number, person, and all the other forms of agreement required by English.

2. They also obscure the phrase structure of the language that is so clearly represented in the context-free rules.

3. By attempting to handle more complicated checks for agreement and semantic consistency in the grammar itself, they lose many of the benefits of separating the syntactic and semantic components of language.

4. Context-sensitive grammars do not address the problem of building a semantic representation of the meaning of the text. A parser that simply accepts or rejects sentences is not sufficient; it must return a useful representation of the sentence's semantic meaning.

In the next section we examine *augmented transition networks* (ATNs), an extension of transition networks that can define context-sensitive languages but has several advantages over context-sensitive grammars in the design of parsers.

10.3 Combining Syntax and Semantics in ATN Parsers

An alternative approach to context-sensitive grammars retains the simpler structure of context-free grammar rules but augments these rules with attached procedures that perform the necessary contextual tests. These procedures are executed when a rule is invoked in parsing. Rather than using the grammar to describe such notions as number, tense, and person, we represent these as *features* attached to terminals and nonterminals of the grammar. The procedures attached to the rules of the grammar access these features to assign values and perform the necessary tests. Grammars that use augmentations of context-free grammars to implement context sensitivity include *augmented phrase structure grammars* (Heidorn 1975; Sowa 1984), *augmentations of logic grammars* (Allen 1987), and the *augmented transition network* (ATN).

In this section we present ATN parsing and outline the design of a simple ATN parser for sentences about the "dogs world" introduced in section 10.2.1. We address the first two steps of Figure 10.2: creation of a parse tree and its use to construct a representation of the sentence's meaning. We use conceptual graphs in this example, although ATN parsers can also be used with script, frame, or logic representations.

10.3.1 Augmented Transition Network Parsers

Augmented transition networks extend transition networks by allowing procedures to be attached to the arcs of the networks. An ATN parser executes these attached procedures when it traverses the arcs. The procedures may assign values to grammatical features and perform tests, causing a transition to fail if certain conditions (such as number agreement) are not met. These procedures also construct a parse tree, which is used to generate an internal semantic representation of the sentence's meaning.

We represent both terminals and nonterminals as a basic category (e.g., verb, noun_phrase) with attached features. For example, a word is described using its morphological root, along with features for its part of speech, number, person, etc. Nonterminals in the grammar are similarly described. For example, a noun phrase is described by its article, noun, number, and person. Both terminals and nonterminals can be represented using framelike structures with named slots and values. The values of these slots specify grammatical features or pointers to other structures. For example, the first slot of a sentence frame contains a pointer to a noun phrase definition. Figure 10.6 shows the frames for the sentence, noun_phrase, and verb_phrase nonterminals in our simple grammar.

Individual words are represented using similar structures. Each word in the dictionary is defined by a frame that specifies its part of speech (article, noun, etc.), its morphological root, and its significant grammatical features. In our example, we are only checking for number agreement and only record this feature. More sophisticated grammars indicate person and other features. These dictionary entries may also indicate the conceptual graph definition of the word's meaning for use in semantic interpretation. The complete dictionary for our grammar appears in Figure 10.7.

Figure 10.8 defines an ATN for our grammar, with pseudocode descriptions of the tests performed at each arc. Arcs are labeled with both nonterminals of the grammar (as in Fig. 10.4) and numbers; these numbers are used to indicate the procedure attached to each arc. The procedure is called after the arc is successfully traversed.

When the parser calls a network for a nonterminal, it creates a new frame for that nonterminal. For example, on entering the noun_phrase network it creates a new noun_phrase frame. The slots of the frame are filled by the procedures for that network. These slots may be assigned values of grammatical features or pointers to components of the syntactic structure (e.g., a verb_phrase consists of a verb and a noun phrase). When the final state is reached, the network returns this structure.

When the network traverses arcs labeled noun, article, and verb, it reads the next word from the input stream and retrieves its definition from the dictionary. If the word is not the expected part of speech, the rule fails; otherwise the definition frame is returned.

Figure 10.6   Structures representing the sentence, noun phrase, and verb phrase nonterminals of the grammar.

Word	Definition	Word	Definition

a	PART_OF_SPEECH: article
	ROOT: a
	NUMBER: singular

like	PART_OF_SPEECH: verb
	ROOT: like
	NUMBER: plural

bite	PART_OF_SPEECH: verb
	ROOT: bite
	NUMBER: plural

likes	PART_OF_SPEECH: verb
	ROOT: like
	NUMBER: singular

bites	PART_OF_SPEECH: verb
	ROOT: bite
	NUMBER: singular

man	PART_OF_SPEECH: noun
	ROOT: man
	NUMBER: singular

dog	PART_OF_SPEECH: noun
	ROOT: dog
	NUMBER: singular

men	PART_OF_SPEECH: noun
	ROOT: man
	NUMBER: plural

dogs	PART_OF_SPEECH: noun
	ROOT: dog
	NUMBER: plural

the	PART_OF_SPEECH: article
	ROOT: the
	NUMBER: plural or singular

Figure 10.7   Dictionary entries for a simple ATN.

In Figure 10.8 frames and slots are indicated using a Pascal style record notation; e.g., the number slot of the verb frame is indicated by VERB.NUMBER.

As the parse proceeds, each procedure builds and returns a frame describing the associated syntactic structure. This structure includes pointers to structures returned by lower-level networks. The top-level sentence procedure returns a **sentence** structure representing the parse tree for the input. This structure is passed to the semantic interpreter. Figure 10.9 shows the parse tree that is returned for the sentence ''The dog likes a man.''

While this discussion has been all too brief in its treatment of natural language syntax, it outlines the use of ATNs to parse natural language. The next phase of natural language processing takes the parse tree (such as in Figure 10.9) and builds a semantic representation of the meaning.

sentence:

procedure sentence-1;
```
begin
    NOUN_PHRASE :=structure returned by
        noun_phrase network;

    SENTENCE.SUBJECT :=NOUN_PHRASE;
end.
```

procedure sentence-2;
```
begin
    VERB_PHRASE :=structure returned by
        verb_phrase network;

    if NOUN_PHRASE.NUMBER =
                        VERB_PHRASE.NUMBER
        then begin
            SENTENCE.VERB_PHRASE :=VERB_PHRASE;
            return SENTENCE
        end
        else fail
    end.
```

noun_phrase:

procedure noun_phrase-1;
```
begin
    ARTICLE :=definition frame for next word of input;

    if ARTICLE.PART_OF_SPEECH=article
        then NOUN_PHRASE.DETERMINER :=ARTICLE
        else fail
    end.
```

procedure noun_phrase-2;
```
begin
    NOUN :=definition frame for next word of input;

    if NOUN.PART_OF_SPEECH=noun and
            NOUN.NUMBER agrees with
                NOUN_PHRASE.DETERMINER.NUMBER
        then begin
            NOUN_PHRASE.NOUN :=NOUN;
            NOUN_PHRASE.NUMBER :=NOUN.NUMBER
            return NOUN_PHRASE
        end
        else fail
    end.
```

Figure 10.8 ATN grammar that checks number
agreement and builds a parse tree.

```
procedure noun_phrase-3
  begin
    NOUN :=definition frame for next word of input;

    if NOUN.PART_OF_SPEECH=noun
      then begin
        NOUN_PHRASE.DETERMINER :=unspecified;
        NOUN_PHRASE.NOUN :=NOUN
        NOUN_PHRASE.NUMBER := NOUN.NUMBER
      end
      else fail
  end.
```

verb_phrase:

```
procedure verb_phrase-1
  begin
    VERB :=definition frame for next word of input;

    if VERB.PART_OF_SPEECH=verb
      then begin
        VERB_PHRASE.VERB :=VERB;
        VERB_PHRASE.NUMBER :=VERB.NUMBER;
      end;
  end.
```

```
procedure verb_phrase-2
  begin
    NOUN_PHRASE :=structure returned by
                        noun_phrase network;

    VERB_PHRASE.OBJECT :=NOUN_PHRASE;
    return VERB_PHRASE
  end.
```

```
procedure verb_phrase-3
  begin
    VERB :=definition frame for next word of input;

    if VERB.PART_OF_SPEECH=verb
      then begin
        VERB_PHRASE.VERB :=VERB;
        VERB_PHRASE.NUMBER :=VERB.NUMBER;
        VERB_PHRASE.OBJECT :=unspecified;
        return VERB_PHRASE;
      end;
  end.
```

Figure 10.8 (cont'd.) ATN grammar that checks number
agreement and builds a parse tree.

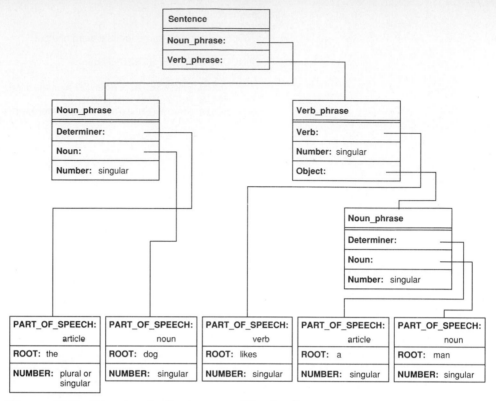

Figure 10.9 Parse tree for the sentence "The dog likes a man" returned by an ATN parser.

10.3.2 Combining Syntax and Semantics

The semantic interpreter constructs a representation of the input string's meaning by beginning at the root, or **sentence** node, and traversing the parse tree. At each node, it recursively interprets the children of that node and combines the results into a single conceptual graph; this graph is passed up the tree. For example, the semantic interpreter builds a representation of the **verb_phrase** by recursively building representations of the node's children, **verb** and **noun_phrase**, and joining these to form an interpretation of the verb phrase. This is passed to the **sentence** node and combined with the representation of the **subject**.

Recursion stops at the terminals of the parse tree. Some of these, such as nouns, verbs, and adjectives, cause concepts to be retrieved from the knowledge base. Others, such as articles, do not directly correspond to concepts in the knowledge base but qualify other concepts in the graph.

The semantic interpreter in our example uses a knowledge base for the "dogs world." Concepts in the knowledge base include the objects **dog** and **man** and the actions **like** and **bite**. These concepts are described by the type hierarchy of Figure 10.10.

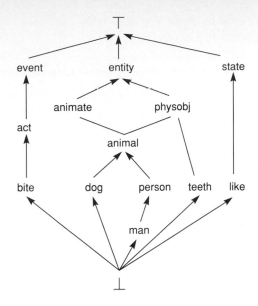

Figure 10.10 Type hierarchy used in "dogs world" example.

In addition to concepts, we must define the relations that will be used in our conceptual graphs. For this example, we use the following concepts:

agent links an **act** with a concept of type **animate**. **agent** defines the relation between an action and the animate object causing the action.

experiencer links a **state** with a concept of type **animate**. It defines the relation between a mental state and its experiencer.

instrument links an **act** with an **entity** and defines the instrument used to perform an action.

object links an **event** or **state** with an **entity** and represents the verb-object relation.

part links two concepts of type **physobj** and defines the relation between a whole and a part.

The verb plays a particularly important role in building an interpretation, as it defines the relationships between the subject, object, and other components of the sentence. We represent each verb using a *case frame* that specifies:

1. The linguistic relationships (agent, object, instrument, etc.) appropriate to that verb. Transitive verbs, for example, will have an object; intransitive verbs will not.
2. Constraints on the values that may be assigned to any component of the case frame. For example, in the case frame for the verb "bites," we have asserted

that the agent must be of the type dog. This will cause "Man bites dog" to be rejected as semantically incorrect.

3. Default values on components of the case frame. In the "bites" frame, we have a default value of teeth for the concept linked to the instrument relation.

The case frames for the verbs like and bite appear in Figure 10.11.

We define the actions that build a semantic representation with rules or procedures for each potential node in the parse tree. Rules for our example are described as pseudocode procedures. In each procedure, if a specified join or other test fails, that interpretation is rejected as semantically incorrect:

```
procedure sentence;
 begin
  call noun_phrase to get a representation of the subject;
  call verb_phrase to get a representation of the verb_phrase;
  using join and restrict, bind the noun concept returned for the subject to
     the agent of the graph for the verb_phrase
  end.

procedure noun_phrase;
  begin
   call noun to get a representation of the noun;
   case
      the article is indefinite and number is singular: the noun concept is generic;
      the article is definite and number is singular: bind an individual marker to the noun
         concept;
      number is plural: indicate that the noun concept is plural
   end
  end.

procedure verb_phrase;
  begin
   call verb to get a representation of the verb;
   if the verb has an object
     then begin
       call noun_phrase to get a representation of the object;
       using join and restrict, bind the concept returned for the object to the object of
          the graph for the verb
     end
  end.

procedure verb;
 begin
  retrieve the case frame for the verb
 end.

procedure noun;
 begin
  retrieve the concept for the noun
 end.
```

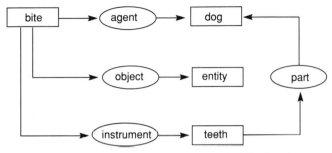

Figure 10.11 Case frames for the verbs "like" and "bite."

Articles do not correspond to concepts in the knowledge base, but determine whether their noun concept is generic or specific. We have not discussed the representation of plural concepts; refer to Sowa (1984) for their treatment in conceptual graphs.

Using these procedures, along with the concept hierarchy of Figure 10.10 and the case frames of Figure 10.11, we trace the actions of the semantic interpreter in building a semantic representation of the sentence "The dog likes a man" from the parse tree of Figure 10.9. This trace appears in Figure 10.12.

The actions taken in the trace are (numbers refer to Figure 10.12):

Beginning at the sentence node, call sentence.

sentence calls noun_phrase.

noun_phrase calls noun. noun returns a concept for the noun dog (1 in Figure 10.12).

Because the article is definite, noun_phrase binds an individual marker to the concept (2) and returns this concept to sentence.

sentence calls verb_phrase.

verb_phrase calls verb, which retrieves the case frame for like (3).

verb_phrase calls noun_phrase, which calls noun to retrieve the concept for man (4).

Since the article is indefinite, noun_phrase leaves this concept generic (5).

The verb_phrase procedure restricts the entity concept in the case frame and joins it with the concept for man (6). This structure is returned to sentence.

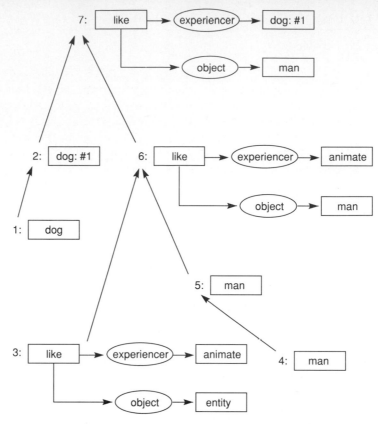

Figure 10.12 Construction of a semantic representation
from the parse tree of Figure 10.9.

sentence joins the concept dog:#1 to the experiencer node of the case frame (7).
This conceptual graph represents the meaning of the sentence.

Section 10.4 shows how a program can build an internal representation of natural
language text. This representation is used by the program in a number of ways, depending on the particular application. Two such applications are discussed in Section 10.4.

Language generation is a related problem addressed by natural language understanding programs. The generation of English sentences requires the construction of a
semantically correct output from an internal representation of meaning. For example,
the agent relation indicates a subject-verb relationship between two concepts. Simple
approaches allow the appropriate words to be plugged into stored sentence *templates*.
These templates are patterns for sentences and fragments, such as noun phrases and
prepositional phrases. The output is constructed by walking the conceptual graph and
combining these fragments. More sophisticated approaches use transformational grammars to map meaning into a range of possible sentences (Winograd 1972; Allen 1987).

10.4 Natural Language Applications

10.4.1 Story Understanding and Question Answering

An interesting test for natural language understanding technology is to write a program that can read a story or other piece of natural language text and answer questions about it. In Chapter 9 we discussed some of the representational issues involved in story understanding, including the importance of combining background knowledge with the explicit content of the text. As illustrated in Figure 10.2, a program can accomplish this by performing network joins between the semantic interpretation of the input and conceptual graph structures in a knowledge base. More sophisticated representations, such as scripts, can help to model more complex situations involving events occurring over time.

Once the program has built an expanded representation of the text, it can intelligently answer questions about what it has read. The program parses the question into an internal representation and matches that query against the expanded representation of the story. Consider the example of Figure 10.2. The program has read the sentence "Tarzan kissed Jane" and built an expanded representation. Assume that we ask the program "Who loves Jane?"

In parsing the question, the interrogative (who, what, why, etc.) indicates the intention of the question. *Who* questions ask for the agent of the action; *what* questions ask for the object of the action; *how* questions ask for the means by which the action was performed, etc. The question, "Who loves Jane?" produces the graph of Figure 10.13. The **agent** node of the graph is marked with a **?** to indicate that it is the goal of the question.

This structure is then joined with the expanded representation of the original text. The concept that becomes bound to the **person:?** concept in the query graph is the answer to the question, i.e., "Tarzan loves Jane."

10.4.2 A Data Base Front End

The major bottleneck in designing natural language understanding programs is the acquisition of sufficient knowledge about the domain of discourse. Current technology is limited to narrow domains with well-defined semantics. An application area that meets these criteria is the development of natural language front ends for data bases. Although data bases store enormous amounts of information, that information is highly regular and

Figure 10.13 Conceptual graph for the question "Who loves Jane?"

narrow in scope; furthermore, data base semantics are well defined. These features, along with the utility of a data base that can accept natural language queries, make data base front ends an important application of natural language understanding technology.

The task of a data base front end is to translate a question in natural language into a well-formed query in the data base language. For example, using the SQL data base language as a target (Ullman 1982), the natural language front end would translate the question ''Who hired John Smith?'' into the query:

```
SELECT MANAGER
FROM MANAGER_OF_HIRE
WHERE EMPLOYEE = 'John Smith'
```

In performing this translation, the program must do more than translate the original query; it must also decide where to look in the data base (the MANAGER_OF_HIRE relation), the name of the field to access (MANAGER), and the constraints on the query (EMPLOYEE = 'John Smith'). None of this information was in the original question; it was found in a knowledge base that knew about the organization of the data base and the meaning of potential questions.

A *relational data base* organizes data in relations across domains of entities. For example, suppose we are constructing a data base of employees and would like to access the salary of each employee and the manager who hired them. This data base would consist of three *domains* or sets of entities: the set of managers, the set of employees, and the set of salaries. We could organize these data into two relations, employee_salary, which relates an employee and her salary, and manager_of_hire, which relates an employee and her manager. In a relational data base, relations are usually displayed as tables that enumerate the instances of the relation. The columns of the tables are often named; these names are called *attributes* of the relation. Figure 10.14 shows the tables for the employee_salary and the manager_of_hire relations. Manager_of_hire has two attributes, the employee and the manager. The values of the relation are the pairs of employees and managers.

If we assume that employees have a unique name, then the employee name is a *key* for both salary and manager. An attribute is a key for another attribute if it uniquely determines the value of elements for the other attribute. A valid query indicates a target attribute and specifies a value or set of constraints on its keys; the data base returns the

manager_of_hire:

employee	manager
John Smith	Jane Martinez
Alex Barrero	Ed Angel
Don Morrison	Jane Martinez
Jan Claus	Ed Angel
Anne Cable	Bob Veroff

employee_salary:

employee	salary
John Smith	$35,000.00
Alex Barrero	$42,000.00
Don Morrison	$50,000.00
Jan Claus	$40,000.00
Anne Cable	$45,000.00

Figure 10.14 Two relations in an employee data base.

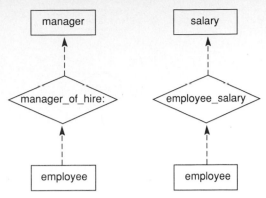

Figure 10.15 Entity-relationship diagrams of the manager_of_hire and employee_salary relations.

specified values of the target attribute. We can indicate the relationship between keys and other attributes graphically in a number of ways, including *entity-relationship diagrams* (Ullman 1982) and *data flow diagrams* (Sowa 1984). Both of these approaches display the mapping of keys onto attributes using directed graphs.

We can extend conceptual graphs to include diagrams of these relationships (Sowa 1984). The data base relation that defines the mapping is indicated by a rhombus, which is labeled with the name of the relation. The attributes of the relation are expressed as concepts in a conceptual graph and the direction of the arrows indicates the mapping of keys onto other attributes. Figure 10.15 shows the entity-relation graphs for the employee_salary and manager_of_hire relations.

In translating from English to a formal query, we must determine the record that contains the answer, the field of that record that must be returned, and the values of the keys that determine that field. Rather than translating directly from English into the data base language, we first translate into a more expressive language such as conceptual graphs. This is necessary since many English queries are ambiguous or require additional interpretation to produce a well-formed data base query. The use of a more expressive representation language helps this process.

The natural language front end parses and interprets the query into a conceptual graph, as described earlier in this chapter. It then combines this graph with information in the knowledge base using join and restrict operations. In this example, we want to handle queries such as "Who hired John Smith?" or "How much does John Smith earn?" For each potential query, we store a graph that defines its verb, the case roles for that verb, and any relevant entity-relationship diagrams for the question. Figure 10.16 shows the knowledge base entry for the verb "hire."

The semantic interpreter produces a graph of the user's query and joins this graph with the appropriate knowledge base entry. If there is an attached entity relation graph that maps keys into the goal of the question, the program can use this entity relation graph to form a data base query. Figure 10.17 shows the query graph for the question "Who hired John Smith?" and the result of joining this with the knowledge base entry

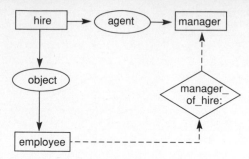

Figure 10.16 Knowledge base entry for "hire" queries.

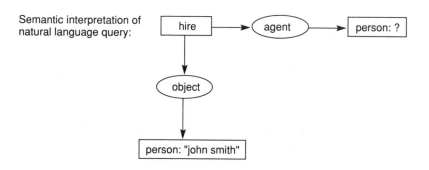

Semantic interpretation of natural language query:

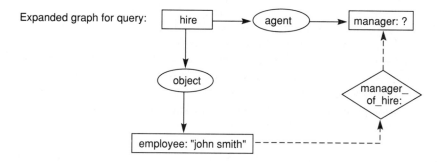

Expanded graph for query:

Query in SQL data base language:

SELECT MANAGER
FROM MANAGER_OF_HIRE
WHERE EMPLOYEE = "john smith"

Figure 10.17 Development of a data base query from the graph of a natural language input.

from Figure 10.16. It also shows the SQL query that is formed from this graph. Note that the name of the appropriate record, the target field, and the key for the query were not specified in the natural language query. These were inferred by the knowledge base.

In Figure 10.17 the agent and object of the original query were known only to be of type person. In order to join these with the knowledge base entry for hire, they were first restricted to types manager and employee, respectively. The type hierarchy could thus be used to perform type checking on the original query. If john smith were not of type employee, the question would be invalid and the program could detect this.

Once the expanded query graph is built, the program examines the target concept, flagged with a ?, and determines that the manager_of_hire relation mapped a key onto this concept. Since the key is bound to a value of john smith, the question was valid and the program could form the proper data base query. Translation of the entity relationship graph into SQL or some other language is straightforward.

Although this example was simplified, it illustrates the use of a knowledge-based approach to building a natural language data base front end. The ideas in our example were expressed in conceptual graphs, but could be mapped into other representations such as frames or logic-based languages.

10.5 Epilogue and References

As this chapter suggests, there are a number of approaches to defining grammars and parsing sentences in natural language. We have presented ATN parsers as a typical example of these approaches, although the serious student should be aware of other possibilities. These include *transformational grammars*, *semantic grammars*, *case grammars* and *feature and function grammars* (Winograd 1983, Allen 1987).

Transformational grammars use context-free rules to represent the *deep structure*, or meaning of the sentence. This deep structure is a parse tree that not only consists of terminals and nonterminals, but also includes a set of symbols called *grammatical markers*. These grammatical markers represent such features as number, tense, and other context-sensitive aspects of linguistic structure. Next, a higher-level set of rules called transformational rules transform between this deep structure and a *surface structure*, which is closer to the actual form the sentence will have. For example, "Tom likes Jane" and "Jane is liked by Tom" will have the same deep structure but different surface structures.

Transformational rules act on parse trees themselves, performing the checks that require global context, and produce a suitable surface structure. For example, a transformational rule may check that the number feature of the node representing the subject of a sentence is the same as the number feature of the verb node. Transformational rules may also map a single deep structure into alternative surface structures, such as changing active to passive voice or forming an assertion into a question. Although transformational grammars are not discussed in this text, they are an important alternative to augmented phrase structure grammars.

The various grammars presented here are not intended as models of the way in which human beings process natural language. This misconception was at the root of many of the criticisms aimed at Chomsky and other early workers in natural language by people who felt that the extreme formality of these approaches was not plausibly implemented in the human mind. Instead, as these linguists have emphasized, these models should be seen as mathematical abstractions that capture the knowledge of syntax that is used by people in the act of producing or understanding language. People may not have ATNs in their heads, but they do use equivalent knowledge of syntax and semantics in their everyday understanding. ATNs are a computationally feasible way of capturing this knowledge.

A comprehensive treatment of grammars and parsing techniques for natural language can be found in Terry Winograd's *Language as a Cognitive Process* (1983). This book offers a particularly thorough treatment of transformational grammars. *Natural Language Understanding* by James Allen (1987) provides an overview of the design and implementation of natural language understanding programs. *Introduction to Natural Language Processing* by Mary Dee Harris (1985) is another general text on natural language that expands on the issues raised in this chapter. Syntax is the most widely explored area of natural language understanding, and there are numerous books that provide further discussion of this topic.

The semantic analysis of natural language involves a number of difficult issues that are addressed in the literature on knowledge representation (Chapter 9). In *Computational Semantics*, Charniak and Wilks have collected articles that address these issues in the context of natural language understanding (Charniak and Wilks 1976).

Because of the difficulty in modeling the knowledge and social context required for natural language interaction, many authors have questioned the possibility of moving this technology beyond constrained domains. *Understanding Computers and Cognition* by Winograd and Flores (1986) and *Minds, Brains, and Programs* by John Searle (1980) address these issues.

Inside Computer Understanding by Schank and Riesbeck (1981) discusses natural language understanding using conceptual dependency technology. *Scripts, Plans, Goals and Understanding* by Schank and Abelson (1977) discusses the role of higher-level knowledge organization structures in natural language programs.

Getting Computers to Talk Like You and Me by Rachel Reichman (1985) and *Speech Acts* by John Searle (1969) discuss the role of pragmatics and contextual knowledge in modeling discourse.

Fass and Wilks (1983) have proposed *semantic preference theory* as a vehicle for modeling natural language semantics. Semantic preference is a generalization of case grammars that allows transformations on case frames. This provides greater flexibility in representing semantics and allows the representation of such concepts as metaphor and analogy.

A full discussion of the Chomsky hierarchy is outside the scope of this chapter; the reader may refer to any text on formal language theory for a full discussion of this subject (Hopcroft and Ullman 1979).

We are indebted to John Sowa's *Conceptual Structures* (1984) for our treatment of conceptual graphs, including the discussion of modeling data base semantics.

10.6 Exercises

1. Classify each of the following sentences as either syntactically incorrect, syntactically correct but meaningless, meaningful but untrue, or true. Where in the understanding process is each of these problems detected?

> Colorless green ideas sleep furiously.
> Fruit flies like a banana.
> Dogs the bite man a.
> George Washington was the fifth president of the USA.
> This exercise is easy.
> I want to be under the sea in an octopus's garden in the shade.

2. Discuss the representational structures and knowledge necessary to understand the following sentences.

> The brown dog ate the bone.
> Attach the large wheel to the axle with the hex nut.
> Mary watered the plants.
> The spirit is willing but the flesh is weak.
> I've got a five that says Magic will shut down the Bird.

3. Parse each of these sentences using the dogs world grammar of Section 10.2.1. Which of these are illegal sentences? Why?

> The dog bites the dog.
> The big dog bites the man.
> Emma likes the boy.
> The man likes.
> Bite the man.

4. Extend the dogs world grammar so that it will include the illegal sentences in Exercise 3. 5. Parse each of these sentences using the context-sensitive grammar of Section 10.2.3.

> The men like the dog.
> The dog bites the man.

6. Produce a parse tree for each of the following sentences. You will have to extend our simple grammars with more complex linguistic constructs such as adverbs, adjectives, and prepositional phrases. If a sentence has more than one parsing, diagram all of them and explain the semantic information that would be used to choose a parsing:

> Time flies like an arrow but fruit flies like a banana.
> Tom gave the big, red book to Mary on Tuesday.
> Reasoning is an art and not a science.
> To err is human, to forgive divine.

7. Extend the dogs world grammar to include adjectives in noun phrases. Be sure to allow an indeterminate number of adjectives. Hint: use a recursive rule, adjective_list, that is either empty or contains an adjective followed by an adjective list. Map this grammar into transition networks.

8. Add the following context-free grammar rules to the dogs world grammar of Section 10.2.1. Map the resulting grammar into transition networks:

```
sentence ← noun_phrase verb_phrase prepositional_phrase
prepositional_phrase ← preposition noun_phrase
preposition ← with
preposition ← to
preposition ← on
```

9. Define an ATN parser for the dogs world grammar with adjectives (Exercise 7) and prepositional phrases (Exercise 8).

10. Define concepts and relations in conceptual graphs needed to represent the meaning of the grammar of Exercise 9. Define the procedures for building a semantic representation from the parse tree.

11. Extend the context-sensitive grammar of Section 10.2.3 to test for semantic agreement between the subject and verb. Specifically, men should not bite dogs, although dogs can either like or bite men. Perform a similar modification to the ATN grammar.

12. Expand the ATN grammar of Section 10.2.4 to include *who* and *what* questions.

13. Extend the data base front end example of Section 10.4.2 so that it will answer questions of the form "How much does Don Morrison earn?" You will need to extend the grammar, the representation language, and the knowledge base.

14. Assume that managers are listed in the employee_salary relation with other employees. Extend the example so that it will handle queries like "Find any employee that earns more than his or her manager."

11

AUTOMATED REASONING

---

*Any rational decision may be viewed as a conclusion reached from certain premises. . . .
The behavior of a rational person can be controlled, therefore, if the value and factual
premises upon which he bases his decisions are specified for him.*

—Simon, *Decision-Making and Administrative Organization*, 1944

Reasoning is an art and not a science. . . .

—Wos et al., *Automated Reasoning*, 1984

11.0 Introduction to Weak Methods in Theorem Proving

Wos et al. describe an *automated reasoning* program as one that "employs an unambiguous and exacting notation for representing information, precise inference rules for drawing conclusions, and carefully delineated strategies to control those inference rules (Wos et al. 1984). They add that applying strategies to inference rules to deduce new information is an art: "A good choice for representation includes a notation that increases the chance for solving a problem and includes information that, though not necessary, is helpful. A good choice of inference rules is one that meshes well with the chosen representation. A good choice for strategies is one that controls the inference rules in a manner that sharply increases the effectiveness of the reasoning program."

Automated reasoning, as just described, uses weak problem-solving methods. It uses a uniform representation such as the first-order predicate calculus (Chapter 2), the Horn clause calculus (chapters 6 and 12), or the clause form used for resolution (Section 11.2). Its inference rules are sound and, whenever possible, complete. It uses general strategies such as breadth-first, depth-first, or best-first search and, as we see in this chapter, *set of support* and *unit preference* to combat the combinatorics of exhaustive search. The design of search strategies is very much an art; we cannot guarantee that they will find a useful solution to a problem using reasonable amounts of time and memory.

Weak method problem solving is an important tool in its own right as well as an essential basis for strong method problem solving. Production systems and rule-based expert system shells are both examples of weak method problem solvers. Even though the rules of the production system or rule-based expert system encode strong problem-solving heuristics, their application is supported by general (weak method) inference strategies.

Techniques for weak method problem solving have been the focus of AI research from its beginning. Quite often these techniques come under the heading of *theorem proving*, although we prefer the more generic title *automated reasoning*. We begin this chapter (Section 11.1) with an early example of automated reasoning, the *General Problem Solver*, and its use of *means-ends analysis* and *difference tables* to control search. In Section 11.2 we present an important product of research in automated reasoning, the *resolution theorem prover*. We discuss the representation language, the resolution inference rule, the search strategies, and the answer extraction process used in resolution theorem proving. We conclude this chapter (Section 11.3) with some brief comments on *natural deduction*, equality handling, and more sophisticated inference rules.

11.1　The General Problem Solver and Difference Tables

The *General Problem Solver (GPS)* (Newell and Simon 1963*b*; Ernst and Newell 1969) came out of research by Allen Newell and Herbert Simon at Carnegie Mellon University, then Carnegie Institute of Technology. Its roots are in an earlier computer program called the *Logic Theorist (LT)* of Newell, Shaw, and Simon (Newell and Simon 1963*a*). The LT program proved many of the theorems in Russell and Whitehead's *Principia Mathematica* (Whitehead and Russell 1950).

As with all weak method problem solvers, the Logic Theorist employed a uniform representation medium and sound inference rules and adopted several strategies or heuristic methods to guide the solution process. The Logic Theorist used the propositional calculus (Section 2.1) as its representation medium. The inference rules were *substitution, replacement,* and *detachment*.

Substitution allows any expression to be substituted for every occurrence of a variable in an axiom or theorem already known to be true. For instance, $(B \lor B) \to B$ may have the expression $\neg A$ substituted for B to produce $(\neg A \lor \neg A) \to \neg A$.

Replacement allows a connective to be replaced by its definition or an equivalent form. For example, the equivalence $\neg A \lor B \Leftrightarrow A \to B$ can lead to the replacement of $(\neg A \lor \neg A)$ with $(A \to \neg A)$.

Detachment is the inference rule we called modus ponens (Chapter 2).

The LT applied these inference rules in a breadth-first, goal-driven fashion to the theorem to be proved, attempting to find a series of operations that led to axioms or theorems known to be true. The strategy of LT consisted of four methods organized in an *executive routine*:

First, the substitution method is directly applied to the current goal, attempting to match it against all known axioms and theorems.

Second, if this fails to lead to a proof, all possible detachments and replacements are applied to the goal and each of these results is tested for success using substitution. If substitution fails to match any of these with the goal, then they are added to a *subproblem list*.

Third, the chaining method, employing the transitivity of implication, is used to find a new subproblem that, if solved, would provide a proof. Thus, if $a \rightarrow c$ is the problem and $b \rightarrow c$ is found, then $a \rightarrow b$ is set up as a new subproblem.

Fourth, if the first three methods fail on the original problem, go to the subproblem list and select the next untried subproblem.

The executive routine continues to apply these four methods until either the solution is found, no more problems remain on the subproblem list, or the memory and time allotted to finding the proof are exhausted. In this fashion, the logic theorist executed a breadth-first search of the problem space.

Part of the executive routine that enables the substitution, replacement, and detachment inference rules is the *matching process*. Suppose we wish to prove $p \rightarrow (q \rightarrow p)$. The matching process first identifies one of the axioms, $p \rightarrow (q \vee p)$, as more appropriate than the others, because the main connective, here $\rightarrow$, is the same in both expressions. Second, the matching process confirms that the expressions to the left of the main connective are identical. Finally, matching identifies the difference between expressions to the right of the main connective. This final difference, between $\rightarrow$ and $\vee$, suggests the obvious replacement for proving the theorem. The matching process helps control the (exhaustive) search that would be necessary for applying all substitutions, replacements, and detachments. In fact, the matching eliminated enough of the trial and error to make the LT into a successful problem solver.

A sample LT proof shows the power of the matching process. Theorem 2.02 of *Principia Mathematica* is $p \rightarrow (q \rightarrow p)$. Matching immediately finds the axiom $p \rightarrow (q \vee p)$ as appropriate for replacement. Substitution of $\neg q$ for q proves the theorem. Matching, controlling substitution and replacement rules, proved this theorem directly without any search through other axioms or theorems.

In another example, suppose we wish LT to prove:

$(p \rightarrow \neg p) \rightarrow \neg p.$

1. $(A \vee A) \rightarrow A$	Matching identifies "best" axiom of five available.
2. $(\neg A \vee \neg A) \rightarrow \neg A$	Substitution of $\neg A$ for A in order to apply
3. $(A \rightarrow \neg A) \rightarrow \neg A$	replacement of $\rightarrow$ for $\vee$, and
4. $(p \rightarrow \neg p) \rightarrow \neg p$	substitution of p for A.

QED

The LT proved this theorem in about 10 seconds using five axioms. The actual proof took two steps and required no search. Matching selected the appropriate axiom for the first step because its form was much like the conclusion it was trying to establish:

(expression) → proposition. Then ¬ A was substituted for A. This allowed the replacement of the second and final step, which was itself motivated by the goal requiring a → rather than a ∨.

The Logic Theorist not only was the first example of an automated reasoning system but also demonstrated the importance of search strategies in a reasoning program. In many instances LT found solutions in a few steps that exhaustive search might never find. Some theorems were not solvable by the LT, and Newell et al. pointed out improvements that might make their solution possible.

At about this time (1957) researchers at Carnegie and others at Yale (Moore 1954) began to examine think-aloud protocols of human subjects solving logic problems. While their primary goal was to identify human processes that could solve this class of problem, researchers began to compare human problem solving with computer programs, such as the Logic Theorist. This was to become the first instance of what is now referred to as *information processing psychology*, where an explanation of the observed behavior of an organism is provided by a program of primitive information processes that generates that behavior (Newell et al. 1958). We address this issue in more detail in Chapter 15.

Closer scrutiny of these first protocols showed many ways that LT's solutions differed from those of the human subjects. The human behavior showed strong evidence of a matching and difference reduction mechanism referred to as *means-ends* analysis. In means-ends analysis the difference reduction methods (the *means*) were strongly linked to the specific differences to be reduced (the *ends*): The operators for difference reduction were indexed by the differences they could reduce.

In a very simple example, if the start statement was p → q and the goal was ¬ p ∨ q, the differences would include the → symbol in the start and ∨ in the goal (as well as the difference of p in the start and ¬ p in the goal). The difference table would contain the different ways that a → could be replaced by a ∨ and that ¬ could be removed. These transformations would be attempted one at a time until the difference was removed.

In most interesting problems the differences between start and goal could not be directly reduced. In this case an operator (from the table) was sought to partially reduce the difference. The entire procedure was applied recursively to these results until no differences existed. This might also require following different search paths, represented by different applications of reductions.

Figure 11.1 presents one of the proofs, from (Newell and Simon 1963a), generated by a human subject. Before the proof, 12 rules are given for "reducing" expressions. The human subject, without experience in formal logic, is asked to change the expression (R ⊃ ¬ P) · (¬ R ⊃ Q) to ¬ (¬ Q · P). In the notation of this text ~ is ¬, · is ∧, and ⊃ is →. The → or ⇔ of Figure 11.1 indicates a legal replacement. The difference reduction table (called the table of connections) for this problem is included as part of Figure 11.2.

Newell and Simon called the algorithm for applying means-ends analysis using difference reduction the *General Problem Solver*. The "methods" for GPS were described by Newell and Simon (1963b) using the flow diagram of Figure 11.2.

In Figure 11.2 the goal is to transform expression A into expression B. The first step is to locate a difference D between A and B. The subgoal, reduce D, is identified in the

Objects are formed by building up expressions from letters (P, Q, R, ...) and connectives • (dot), V (wedge), ⊃ (horseshoe), and ~ (tilde). Examples are P, ~Q, P V Q, ~(R ⊃ S) • ~P; ~~P is equivalent to P throughout.

Twelve rules exist for transforming expressions (where A, B, and C may be any expressions or subexpressions):

R 1. $A \cdot B \rightarrow B \cdot A$
      $A \lor B \rightarrow B \lor A$

R 2. $A \supset B \rightarrow {\sim}B \supset {\sim}A$

R 3. $A \cdot A \leftrightarrow A$
      $A \lor A \leftrightarrow A$

R 4. $A \cdot (B \cdot C) \leftrightarrow (A \cdot B) \cdot C$
      $A \lor (B \lor C) \leftrightarrow (A \lor B) \lor C$

R 5. $A \lor B \leftrightarrow {\sim}({\sim}A \cdot {\sim}B)$

R 6. $A \supset B \leftrightarrow {\sim}A \lor B$

R 7. $A \cdot (B \lor C) \leftrightarrow (A \cdot B) \lor (A \cdot C)$
      $A \lor (B \cdot C) \leftrightarrow (A \lor B) \cdot (A \lor C)$

R 8. $A \cdot B \rightarrow A$
      $A \cdot B \rightarrow B$

Applies to main expression only.

R 9. $A \rightarrow A \lor X$

Applies to main expression only.

R 10. $\left.\begin{array}{l} A \\ B \end{array}\right\} \rightarrow A \cdot B$

A and B are two main expressions.

R 11. $\left.\begin{array}{l} A \\ A \supset B \end{array}\right\} \rightarrow B$

A and A ⊃ B are two main expressions.

R 12. $\left.\begin{array}{l} A \supset B \\ B \supset C \end{array}\right\} \rightarrow A \supset C$

A ⊃ B and B ⊃ C are two main expressions.

1.	$(R \supset {\sim}P) \cdot ({\sim}R \supset Q)$	$\sim({\sim}Q \cdot P)$
2.	$({\sim}R \lor {\sim}P) \cdot (R \lor Q)$	Rule 6 applied to left and right of 1.
3.	$({\sim}R \lor {\sim}P) \cdot ({\sim}R \supset Q)$	Rule 6 applied to left of 1.
4.	$R \supset {\sim}P$	Rule 8 applied to 1.
5.	${\sim}R \lor {\sim}P$	Rule 6 applied to 4.
6.	${\sim}R \supset Q$	Rule 8 applied to 1.
7.	$R \lor Q$	Rule 6 applied to 6.
8.	$({\sim}R \lor {\sim}P) \cdot (R \lor Q)$	Rule 10 applied to 5 and 7.
9.	$P \supset {\sim}R$	Rule 2 applied to 4.
10.	${\sim}Q \supset R$	Rule 2 applied to 6.
11.	$P \supset Q$	Rule 12 applied to 6 and 9.
12.	${\sim}P \lor Q$	Rule 6 applied to 11.
13.	${\sim}(P \cdot {\sim}Q)$	Rule 5 applied to 12.
14.	${\sim}({\sim}Q \cdot P)$	Rule 1 applied to 13. QED.

Figure 11.1 Transformation rules and trace of a GPS proof in the propositional calculus (Newell and Simon 1963a).

second box of the first line and the reduction method is described in the second line of the diagram, where the operator Q is identified for reducing difference D. Actually, a list of potential operators is identified from the table of connections. This list provides ordered alternatives for difference reduction should the chosen operator not be acceptable, for example, by not passing the *feasibility test* (Fig. 11.2). In the third line of Figure 11.2 the operator is applied and D is reduced.

Goal: Transform object A into object B

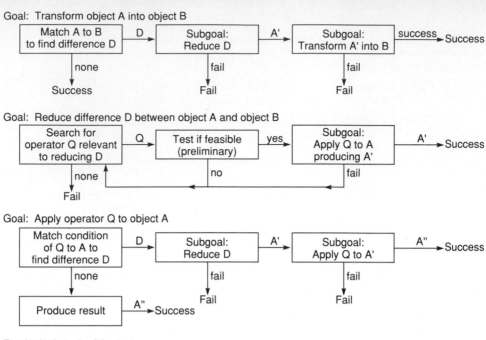

For the logic task of the text.

Feasibility test (preliminary)
    Is the mean connective the same (e.g., A•B → B fails against P∨Q)?
    Is the operator too big (e.g., (A∨B)•(A∨C)→A∨(B•C) fails against P•Q)?
    Is the operator too easy (e.g., A→A•A applies to anything)?
    Are the side conditions satisfied (e.g., R8 applies only to main expressions)?

Table of connections

	R1	R2	R3	R4	R5	R6	R7	R8	R9	R10	R11	R12
Add terms			X				X		X	X	X	X
Delete terms			X				X	X			X	X
Change connective				X	X	X						
Change sign					X							
Change lower sign		X			X	X						
Change grouping				X			X					
Change position	X	X										

X means some variant of the rule is relevant. GPS will pick the appropriate variant.

Figure 11.2 Flowchart and difference reduction table for
the General Problem Solver.

The GPS model of problem solving requires two components. The first is a general procedure for comparing state descriptions and recognizing differences in them. This is similar to the matching process of the LT. The second component of the GPS model is the set of differences or *table of connections* appropriate to a particular application area. One table, like that in Figure 11.2, represents differences in propositional calculus expressions, another could be for reducing differences between algebraic forms, and further tables could list the moves for tasks such as towers of Hanoi or more complex games such as chess. A number of the different application areas of the GPS technique are described by Ernst and Newell (1969).

The structuring of the difference reductions of a problem domain helps organize the search for that domain. A priority order for reduction of different difference classes is implicit in the order of the transformations within the difference reduction table. This priority order might put the more generally applicable transformations before the specialized ones or give whatever order some domain expert might deem most appropriate.

A number of research directions evolved from work in the General Problem Solver. One of these is the use of AI techniques to analyze human problem-solving behavior. In particular, the production system replaced the means-ends methods of GPS as the preferred form for modeling human information processing (Chapter 15). The production rules in modern rule-based expert systems replaced the specific entries in GPS's table of differences.

In another interesting evolution of GPS, the difference table itself evolved in a further fashion, becoming the *operator table* for *planning* research such as STRIPS and ABSTRIPS.

Planning is important in robot problem solving. To accomplish a task, such as to go to the next room and bring back an object, the computer must develop a *plan*. This plan orchestrates the actions of the robot: put down anything it is now holding, go to the door of the present room, go through the door, find the required room, go through the door, go over to the object, and so on. Plan formation for STRIPS (Stanford Research Institute Problem Solver; Fikes and Nilsson 1971, 1972; Sacerdotti 1974) uses an operator table not unlike the GPS table of differences. For each operator (primitive act of the robot) in this table, there is an attached set of *preconditions* that are much like the feasibility tests of Figure 11.2. The operator table also contains *add* and *delete lists*, which update the model of the ''world'' once the operator is applied (Chapter 15).

To summarize, the first models of automated reasoning in AI are found in the Logic Theorist and General Problem Solver developed at Carnegie Institute. Already these programs offered the full prerequisites for weak method problem solving: a uniform representation medium, a set of sound inference rules, and a set of methods or strategies for applying these rules. The same components make up the *resolution proof procedure*, a modern and more powerful basis for automated reasoning.

11.2 Resolution Theorem Proving

11.2.1 Introduction

Resolution is a technique for proving theorems in the predicate calculus that has been a part of AI-problem solving research from the mid-1960s (Bledsoe 1977; Robinson 1965;

Kowalski 1979*b*). Resolution is a sound inference rule that, when used to produce a *refutation* (Section 11.2.3), is also complete. In an important practical application, resolution theorem proving, particularly the resolution refutation system, has made the current generation of PROLOG interpreters possible.

The resolution principle, introduced in an important paper by Robinson (Robinson 1965), describes a way of finding contradictions in a data base of clauses with minimum use of substitution. Resolution refutation proves a theorem by negating the statement to be proved and adding this negated goal to the set of axioms that are known (have been assumed) to be true. It then uses the resolution rule of inference to show that this leads to a contradiction. Once the theorem prover shows that the negated goal is inconsistent with the given set of axioms, it follows that the original goal must be consistent. This proves the theorem.

Resolution refutation proofs involve the following steps:

1. Put the premises or axioms into *clause form* (11.2.2).

2. Add the negation of what is to be proved, in clause form, to the set of axioms.

3. *Resolve* these clauses together, producing new clauses that logically follow from them (11.2.3).

4. Produce a contradiction by generating the empty clause.

5. The substitutions used to produce the empty clause are those under which the opposite of the negated goal is true (11.2.4).

As statement 3 implies, resolution is a sound inference rule in the sense of Chapter 2. Statement 4 implies that resolution refutation is complete; Resolution is *refutation complete*. that is, the empty or null clause can always be generated whenever a contradiction in the set of clauses exists. More is said on this topic when we present strategies for refutation in Section 11.2.4.

Resolution refutation proofs require that the axioms and the negation of the goal be placed in a normal form called *clause form*. Clause form represents the logical data base as a set of disjunctions of *literals*. A literal is an atomic expression or the negation of an atomic expression.

Resolution is applied to two clauses when one contains a literal and the other its negation. If these literals contain variables, they must be unified to make them equivalent. A new clause is then produced consisting of the disjuncts of all the predicates in the two clauses minus the literal and its negative instance (which are said to have been ''resolved away''). The resulting clause receives the unification substitution under which the predicate and its negation are found as ''equivalent.''

Before this is all made more precise in the subsequent subsections, we take a simple example. Resolution will be used to produce a proof similar to one produced already with modus ponens. This is not intended to show that these inference rules are equivalent (resolution is actually more general than modus ponens) but to give the reader a feel for what is going on.

We wish to prove that ''Fido will die'' from the statements that ''Fido is a dog'' and ''all dogs are animals'' and ''all animals will die.'' Changing these three premises to predicates and applying modus ponens gives:

1. All dogs are animals: $\forall(X) (dog(X) \rightarrow animal(X))$.
2. Fido is a dog: dog (fido).
3. Modus ponens and {fido/X} gives: animal (fido).
4. All animals will die: $\forall(Y) (animal(Y) \rightarrow die(Y))$.
5. Modus ponens and {fido/Y} gives: die (fido).

Equivalent reasoning by resolution converts these predicates to clause form:

PREDICATE FORM   CLAUSE FORM
1. $\forall(X) (dog(X) \rightarrow animal(X))$ $\neg\, dog\, (X) \lor animal(X)$
2. dog (fido)   dog (fido)
3. $\forall(Y) (animal(Y) \rightarrow die(Y))$ $\neg\, animal\, (Y) \lor die(Y)$

Negate the conclusion that Fido will die:

4. $\neg$ die (fido) $\neg$ die (fido)

Compare and clash the clauses having opposite literals, producing new clauses by resolution (Fig. 11.3).

The symbol $\square$ in Figure 11.3 indicates that the empty clause is produced and the contradiction found. The $\square$ symbolizes the clashing of a predicate and its negation, that

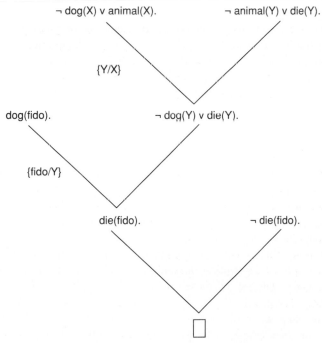

Figure 11.3 Resolution proof for the "dead dog" problem.

is, the situation where two mutually contradictory statements are present in the clause space. These are clashed to produce the empty clause. The sequence of substitutions (unifications) used to make predicates equivalent also gives us the value of variables under which a goal is true. For example, had we asked whether something would die, our negated goal would have been $\neg$ ($\exists$ (Z) die(Z)), rather than $\neg$ die(fido). The substitution {fido/Z} in Figure 11.3 would determine that fido is an instance of an animal that will die. The issues implicit in this example are made clear in the remainder of Section 11.2.

11.2.2. Producing the Clause Form for Resolution Refutations

The resolution proof procedure requires all statements in the data base describing a situation to be converted to a standard form called *clause form*. This is motivated by the fact that resolution is an operator on pairs of disjuncts to produce new disjuncts. The form the data base takes is referred to as a *conjunction of disjuncts*. It is a *conjunction* because all the clauses that make up the data base are assumed to be true at the same time. It is a *disjunction* in that each of the individual clauses is expressed with disjunction (or $\lor$) as the connective. Thus the entire data base of Figure 11.3 may be represented in clause form as:

$$(\neg \, dog(X) \lor animal \, (X)) \land (animal \, (Y) \lor die \, (Y)) \land (dog \, (fido)).$$

To this expression we add (by conjunction) the negation of what we wish to prove: $\neg$ die(fido). Generally, the data base is written as a set of disjunctions and the $\land$ operators are omitted.

We now present an algorithm, consisting of a sequence of transformations, for reducing any set of predicate calculus statements to clause form. It has been shown (Chang and Lee 1973) that these transformations may be used to reduce any predicate calculus expression to an expression in clause form so that no truth value or generality is lost in the process. The clause form will not be strictly equivalent to the original set of predicate calculus expressions in that certain interpretations may be lost. This occurs because skolemization restricts the possible substitutions for existentially quantified variables (Chang and Lee 1973). It will, however, preserve unsatisfiability. That is, if there was a contradiction (a refutation) within the original set of predicate calculus expressions, a contradiction exists in the clause form: the transformations do not sacrifice completeness for refutation proofs.

We demonstrate this process of conjunctive normal form reduction through an example and give a brief description rationalizing each step. These are not intended to be proofs of the equivalence of these transformations across all predicate calculus expressions.

In the following expression, according to the conventions of Chapter 2, uppercase letters indicate variables (W, X, Y, and Z); lowercase letters in the middle of the alphabet indicate constants or bound variables (l, m, and n); and early alphabetic lowercase letters indicate the predicate names (a, b, c, d, and e). To improve readability of the expressions, we have used two types of brackets: ( ) and [ ]. The expression we will reduce to clause form is:

(i)$(\forall X)([a(X) \wedge b(X)] \rightarrow [c(X,I) \wedge (\exists Y)((\exists Z)[c(Y,Z)] \rightarrow d(X,Y))]) \vee (\forall X)(e(X))$

1. First we eliminate the $\rightarrow$ by using the equivalent form (proved in Chapter 2) $a \rightarrow b \equiv \neg a \vee b$. This transformation reduces the expression in (i) above:

(ii)$(\forall X)(\neg [a(X) \wedge b(X)] \vee [c(X,I) \wedge (\exists Y)(\neg (\exists Z)[c(Y,Z)] \vee d(X,Y))]) \vee (\forall X)(e(X))$

2. Next we reduce the scope of negation. This may be accomplished using a number of the transformations of Chapter 2. These include:

$\neg (\neg a) \equiv a$
$\neg (\exists X)\ a(X) \equiv (\forall X) \neg a (X)$
$\neg (\forall X)\ b (X) \equiv (\exists X) \neg b (X)$
$\neg (a \wedge b) \equiv \neg a \vee \neg b$
$\neg (a \vee b) \equiv \neg a \wedge \neg b$

Using the second and fourth equivalences (ii) becomes:

(iii)$(\forall X)([\neg a(X) \vee \neg b(X)] \vee [c(X,I) \wedge (\exists Y)((\forall Z)[\neg c(Y,Z)] \vee d(X,Y))]) \vee (\forall X)(e(X))$

3. Next we standardize all variables so that each quantifier is bound to a unique variable. As indicated in Chapter 2, since variable names are "dummies" or "place holders," the particular name chosen for a variable does not affect either the truth value or generality of the clause. Transformations used at this step are of the form:

$$((\forall X)a(X) \vee (\forall X)b(X)) \equiv (\forall X)a(X) \vee (\forall Y)b(Y)$$

Since (iii) has two instances of the variable X, we rename:

(iv)$(\forall X)([\neg a(X) \vee \neg b(X)] \vee [c(X,I) \wedge (\exists Y)((\forall Z) [\neg c(Y,Z)] \vee d(X,Y))]) \vee (\forall W)(e(W))$

4. Move all quantifiers to the left without changing their order. This is possible since step 3 has removed the possibility of any conflict between variable names. (iv) now becomes:

(v)$(\forall X)(\exists Y)(\forall Z)(\forall W)([\neg a(X) \vee \neg b(X)] \vee [c(X,I) \wedge (\neg c (Y,Z) \vee d(X,Y))]) \vee e(W)$

After step 4 the clause is said to be in *prenex normal* form, because all the quantifiers are in front as a *prefix* and the expression or *matrix* follows after.

5. At this point all existential quantifiers are eliminated by a process called *skolemization*. Expression (v) has an existential quantifier for Y. When an expression contains an existentially quantified variable, for example, $(\exists Z)(foo(\ldots, Z, \ldots))$, it may be concluded that there is an assignment to Z under which foo is true. Skolemization identifies such a value. Skolemization does not necessarily show *how* to produce such a value; it is only a method for giving a name to an assignment that *must* exist. If k represents that

assignment, then we have foo(..., k, ...). Thus if the existentially quantified predicate has only one argument, then Skolemization simply picks a name from the domain of definition of the existentially quantified variable. Thus:

$(\exists X)(dog(X))$ may be replaced by dog(fido)

where the name fido is picked from the domain of definition of X to represent that individual X. fido is called a *skolem constant*. If the predicate has more than one argument and the existentially quantified variable is within the scope of universally quantified variables, the existential variable must be a function of those other variables. This is represented in the skolemization process:

$(\forall X)(\exists Y)(mother(X, Y))$

indicates that every person has a mother. Every person is the X and the existing mother will be a function of the particular person X that is picked. Thus skolemization gives:

$(\forall X)\ mother(X, m(X))$

which indicates that each X has a mother (the m of that X). In another example:

$(\forall X)(\forall Y)(\exists Z)(\forall W)(foo(X, Y, Z, W))$

is skolemized to:

$(\forall X)(\forall Y)(\forall W)(foo(X, Y, f(X, Y), W)).$

We note that the existentially quantified Z was within the scope (to the right of) universally quantified X and Y. Thus the skolem assignment is a function of X and Y but not of W. With skolemization (v) becomes:

$(vi)(\forall X)(\forall Z)(\forall W)([\neg a(X) \lor \neg b(X)] \lor [c(X, l) \land (\neg c(f(X), Z) \lor d(X, f(X)))]) \lor e(W)$

where f is the skolem function of X that replaces the existential Y. Once the skolemization has occurred, step 6 can take place, which simply drops the prefix.

6. Drop all universal quantification. By this point only universally quantified variables exist (step 5) with no variable conflicts (step 3). Thus all quantifiers can be dropped and any proof procedure employed assumes all variables are universally quantified. Formula (vi) now becomes:

$(vii)[\neg a(X) \lor \neg b(X)] \lor [c(X, l) \land (\neg c(f(X), Z) \lor d(X, f(X)))] \lor e(W)$

7. Next we convert the expression to the conjunct of disjuncts form. This requires using the associative and distributive properties of $\land$ and $\lor$. Recall from Chapter 2 that

$$a \lor (b \lor c) = (a \lor b) \lor c$$
$$a \land (b \land c) = (a \land b) \land c$$

which indicates that ∧ or ∨ may be grouped in any desired fashion. The distributive property of Chapter 2 is also used, when necessary, at this point. Since

a ∧ (b ∨ c)

is already in clause form, ∧ is not distributed. However, ∨ must be distributed across ∧ using:

a ∨ (b ∧ c) = (a ∨ b) ∧ (a ∨ c)

The final form of (vii) is:

(viii)[¬ a(X) ∨ ¬ b(X) ∨ c(X,l) ∨ e(W)] ∧
    [¬ a(X) ∨ ¬ b(X) ∨ ¬ c(f(X),Z) ∨ d(X,f(X)) ∨ e(W)]

8. Now call each conjunct a separate clause. In the example (viii) above there are two clauses:

(ixa) ¬ a(X) ∨ ¬ b(X) ∨ c(X,l) ∨ e (W)
(ixb) ¬ a(X) ∨ ¬ b(X) ∨ ¬ c (f(X),Z) ∨ d (X,f(X)) ∨ e (W)

9. The final step is to *standardize the variables apart*. This requires giving the variable in each clause generated by step 8 different names. This procedure arises from the equivalence established in Chapter 2 that

(∀X) (a(X) ∧ b(X)) ≡ (∀X) a (X) ∧ (∀Y) b(Y)

which follows from the nature of variable names as place holders. (ix) now becomes, using new variable names U and V:

(xa) ¬ a(X) ∨ ¬ b(X) ∨ c(X,l) ∨ e (W)
(xb) ¬ a(U) ∨ ¬ b(U) ∨ ¬ c(f(U),Z) ∨ d (U,f(U)) ∨ e (V)

The importance of this final standardization will become apparent only as we present the unification steps of resolution. We find the most general unification to make two predicates within two clauses equivalent, and then this substitution is made across all the variables of the same name within each clause. Thus, if some variables (needlessly) share names with others, these may be renamed by the unification process with a subsequent (possible) loss of generality in the solution.

This nine-step process is used to change any data base of predicate calculus expressions to clause form. The completeness property of resolution refutations is not lost. Next we demonstrate the resolution procedure for generating proofs from these clauses.

11.2.3 The Resolution Proof Procedure

The *resolution refutation* proof procedure answers a query or deduces a new result by reducing the set of clauses to a contradiction, represented by the *null* clause (□). The contradiction is produced by resolving pairs of clauses from the data base. If a resolu-

---

tion does not produce a contradiction directly, then the clause produced by the resolution, the *resolvent*, is added to the data base of clauses and the process continues.

Before we show how the resolution process works in the predicate calculus, we give an example from the propositional or variable-free calculus. For two *parent* clauses p1 and p2 from the propositional calculus:

$$p1: \quad a_1 \lor a_2 \lor \cdots \lor a_n$$
$$p2: \quad b_1 \lor b_2 \lor \cdots \lor b_m$$

having two literals a_i and b_j, where $1 < i \le n$ and $1 \le j \le m$, such that $\neg a_i = b_j$, resolution produces the clause:

$$a_1 \lor \cdots \lor a_{i-1} \lor a_{i+1} \lor \cdots \lor a_n \lor b_1 \lor \cdots \lor b_{j-1} \lor b_{j+1} \lor \cdots \lor b_m.$$

The notation above indicates that the resolvent is made up of the disjunction of all the literals of the two parent clauses except the literals a_i and b_j.

A simple argument can give the intuition behind the resolution principle. Suppose

$$a \lor \neg b \quad \text{and} \quad b \lor c$$

are both true statements. Observe that one of b and $\neg$ b must always be true and one always false ($b \lor \neg b$ is a tautology). Therefore, one of

$$a \lor c$$

must always be true. $a \lor c$ is the resolvent of the two parent clauses $a \lor \neg b$ and $b \lor c$.

Consider now an example from the propositional calculus, where we want to prove a from the following axioms:

$$a \leftarrow b \land c$$
$$b$$
$$c \leftarrow d \land e$$
$$e \lor f$$
$$d \land \neg f$$

We reduce the first axiom to clause form:

$$a \leftarrow b \land c$$
$$a \lor \neg (b \land c) \quad \text{by } l \to m \equiv \neg l \lor m$$
$$a \lor \neg b \lor \neg c \quad \text{by de Morgan's law}$$

The remaining axioms are reduced, and we have the following clauses:

$$a \lor \neg b \lor \neg c$$
$$b$$
$$c \lor \neg d \lor \neg e$$
$$e \lor f$$
$$d$$
$$\neg f$$

The resolution proof is found in Figure 11.4. First the goal to be proved, a, is negated and added to the clause set. The derivation of □ indicates that the data base of clauses is inconsistent.

To use resolution in the predicate calculus, where each literal may contain variables, there must be a process under which two literals with different variable names, or one with a constant value, can be seen as equivalent. Unification was defined in Chapter 2 as the process for determining consistent and most general substitutions for making two predicates equivalent.

The algorithm for resolution on the predicate calculus is very much like that on the propositional calculus except that:

1. A literal and its negation in parent clauses produce a resolvent only if they unify under some substitution σ. σ is then applied to the resolvent before adding it to the clause set.

2. The unification substitutions used to find the contradiction offer variable bindings under which the original query is true.

Answer extraction, the process of finding the substitutions in the original query that make it true, will be explained shortly. First we present an example of a resolution refutation for the predicate calculus.

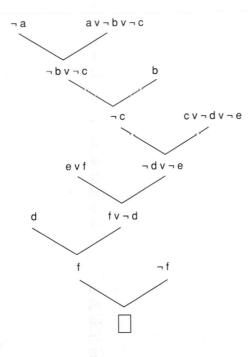

Figure 11.4 Resolution proof for an example from the propositional calculus.

Consider the following story of the "lucky student":

Anyone passing their history exams and winning the lottery is happy. But anyone who studies or is lucky can pass all their exams. John did not study but he is lucky. Anyone who is lucky wins the lottery. Is John happy?

First change the sentences to predicate form:

Anyone passing their history exams and winning the lottery is happy.

$\forall$ X(pass (X,history) $\land$ win (X, lottery) $\to$ happy(X))

Anyone who studies or is lucky can pass all their exams.

$\forall$ X $\forall$ Y (studies (X) $\lor$ lucky (X) $\to$ pass (X,Y))

John did not study but he is lucky.

$\neg$ study (john) $\land$ lucky (john)

Anyone who is lucky wins the lottery.

$\forall$X (lucky(X) $\to$ win (X, lottery))

These four predicate statements are now changed to clause form (Section 11.2.2):

1. $\neg$ pass (X, history) $\lor$ $\neg$ win (X, lottery) $\lor$ happy (X)
2. $\neg$ study (Y) $\lor$ pass (Y, Z)
3. $\neg$ lucky (W) $\lor$ pass (W, V)
4. $\neg$ study (john)
5. lucky (john)
6. $\neg$ lucky (U) $\lor$ win (U, lottery)

Into these clauses is entered, in clause form, the negation of the conclusion:

7. $\neg$ happy (john)

The resolution refutation graph of Figure 11.5 shows the derivation of the contradiction and, consequently, proves that John is happy.

As a final example for this subsection, suppose:

All people that are not poor and are smart are happy. Those people that read are not stupid. John can read and is wealthy. Happy people have exciting lives. Can anyone be found with an exciting life?

We translate the story into the predicate calculus expressions:

$\forall$X (($\neg$ poor (X) $\land$ smart (X)) $\to$ happy (X)
$\forall$Y (read (Y) $\to$ smart (Y))
read (john) $\land$ wealthy (john)
$\forall$Z (happy (Z) $\to$ exciting (Z))

The negation of the conclusion is:

$\neg$ $\exists$ W (exciting (W))

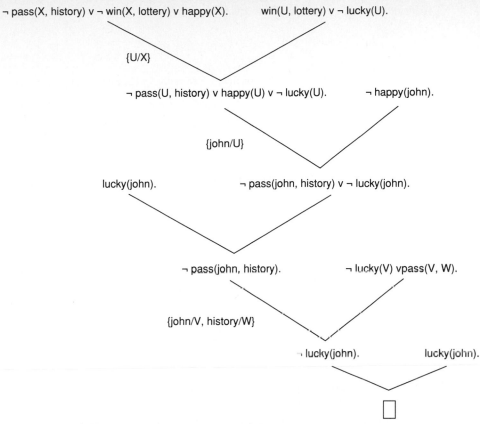

¬ pass(X, history) v ¬ win(X, lottery) v happy(X).   win(U, lottery) v ¬ lucky(U).

{U/X}

¬ pass(U, history) v happy(U) v ¬ lucky(U).   ¬ happy(john).

{john/U}

lucky(john).   ¬ pass(john, history) v ¬ lucky(john).

¬ pass(john, history).   ¬ lucky(V) vpass(V, W).

{john/V, history/W}

¬ lucky(john).   lucky(john).

▢

Figure 11.5 Resolution refutation for the "happy
student" problem.

These predicate calculus expressions are transformed into the following clauses:

poor (X) ∨ ¬ smart (X) ∨ happy (X)
¬ read (Y) ∨ smart (Y)
read (john)
¬ poor (john)
¬ happy (Z) ∨ exciting (Z)
¬ exciting (W)

The resolution refutation for this example is found in Figure 11.6.

11.2.4 Strategies and Simplification Techniques for Resolution

A different proof tree within the search space for the problem of Figure 11.6 appears in
Figure 11.7. There are some similarities in these proofs; for example, they both took five

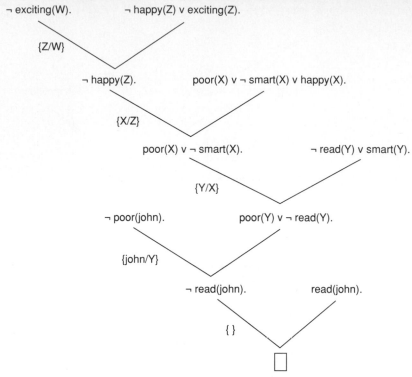

¬ exciting(W).   ¬ happy(Z) v exciting(Z).

{Z/W}

¬ happy(Z).   poor(X) v ¬ smart(X) v happy(X).

{X/Z}

poor(X) v ¬ smart(X).   ¬ read(Y) v smart(Y).

{Y/X}

¬ poor(john).   poor(Y) v ¬ read(Y).

{john/Y}

¬ read(john).   read(john).

{ }

Figure 11.6   Resolution proof for the "exciting life" problem.

resolution steps. Also, the associative application of the unification substitutions found that John was the instance of the person with the exciting life in both proofs.

However, even these two similarities need not have occurred. When the resolution proof system was defined (Section 11.2.3) no order of clause combinations was implied. This is a critical issue: when there are N clauses in the clause space, there are N^2 ways of combining them or checking to see if they can be combined at just the first level! The resulting set of clauses from this comparison is also large; if even 20% of them produce new clauses, the next round of possible resolutions will contain even more combinations than the first round. In a large problem this exponential growth will quickly get out of hand.

For this reason search strategies are very important in resolution proof procedures, as they are in all weak method problem solving. As with the heuristics we considered in Chapter 5, there is no science that can determine the best strategy for any particular problem. Nonetheless, there are some general strategies that can help us survive exponential combinatorics.

Before we describe our strategies, we need to make several clarifications. First, based on the definition of unsatisfiability of an expression in Chapter 2, a *set of clauses is unsatisfiable* if no interpretation exists that establishes the set as satisfiable. Second, an

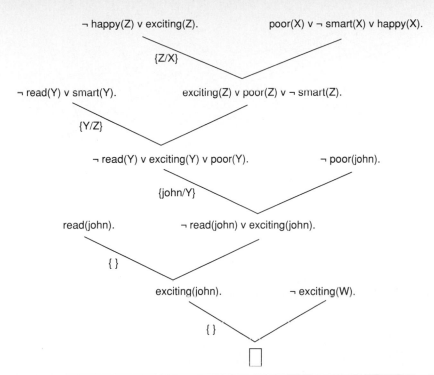

¬ happy(Z) v exciting(Z).　　　　poor(X) v ¬ smart(X) v happy(X).

{Z/X}

¬ read(Y) v smart(Y).　　　exciting(Z) v poor(Z) v ¬ smart(Z).

{Y/Z}

¬ read(Y) v exciting(Y) v poor(Y).　　　¬ poor(john).

{john/Y}

read(john).　　　¬ read(john) v exciting(john).

{ }

exciting(john).　　　¬ exciting(W).

{ }

□

Figure 11.7　Another resolution refutation for the
example of Figure 11.6.

inference rule is *refutation complete* if, given an unsatisfiable set of clauses, the
unsatisfiability can be established by use of this inference rule alone. Resolution has this
property, although it is beyond the scope of this text to prove it (Chang and Lee 1973).
Finally, a *strategy is complete* if by its use with a refutation complete inference rule we
can guarantee finding a refutation whenever a set of clauses is unsatisfiable. *Breadth
first* is an example of a complete strategy.

The *Breadth-First* **Strategy**　The complexity analysis of exhaustive clause comparison
just described was based on breadth-first search. Each clause in the clause space is compared for resolution with every clause in the clause space on the first round. On the
second round, the new clauses produced on the first round plus all clauses of the original
set are compared for resolution. For the nth round all previously generated clauses are
added to the original clause space and all clauses are compared with each other.

This strategy can quickly get out of hand for large problems. It does have an
interesting property, however. Like any breadth-first search, it guarantees finding the
shortest path solution, since it generates every search state for each level before going
any deeper. It also is a complete strategy in that, if it is continued long enough, it is
guaranteed to find a refutation if one exists. Thus when the problem is small, as are the

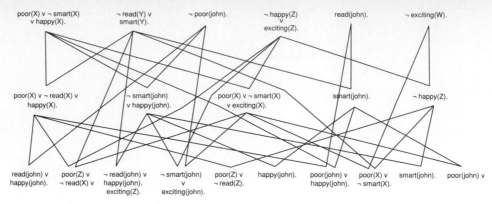

Figure 11.8 Complete state space for the "exciting life" problem generated by breadth-first search (to two levels).

ones we have presented as examples, the breadth-first strategy can be a good one. Figure 11.8 applies the breadth-first strategy to the "exciting life" problem.

The *Set of Support* Strategy   An excellent strategy for large clause spaces is called the set of support (Wos 1968). For a set of input clauses, S, we can specify a subset, T of S, called the set of support. The strategy requires that one of the resolvents in each resolution have an ancestor in the set of support. It can be proved that if S is unsatisfiable and S − T is satisfiable, then the set of support strategy is refutation complete (Wos et al. 1984).

If the original set of clauses is consistent, then any set of support that includes the negation of the original query meets these requirements. This strategy is based on the correct insight that the negation of what we want to prove true is going to be responsible for causing the clause space to be contradictory. The set of support forces resolutions between clauses of which at least one is either the negated goal clause or a clause produced by resolutions on the negated goal.

Figure 11.6 is an example of the set of support strategy applied to the exciting life problem. Since a set of support refutation exists whenever any refutation exists, the set of support can be made the basis of a complete strategy. One way to do this is to perform a breadth-first search for all possible set of support refutations. This, of course, will be much more efficient than breadth-first search of all clauses. One need only be sure that all resolvents of the negated goal clause are examined, along with all their descendants.

The *Unit Preference* Strategy   Observe that in the resolution examples seen so far, the derivation of the contradiction is indicated by the clause with no literals. Thus, every time we produce a resultant clause that has fewer literals than the clauses that are resolved to create it, we are closer to producing the clause of no literals. In particular, resolving with a clause of one literal, called a *unit* clause, will guarantee that the resolvent is smaller than the largest parent clause. The unit preference strategy uses units for resolving whenever they are available.

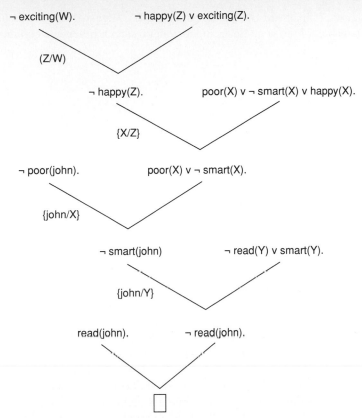

Figure 11.9 Using the unit preference strategy on the "exciting life" problem.

Figure 11.9 uses the unit preference strategy on the exciting life problem. The unit preference strategy along with the set of support can produce a more efficient complete strategy.

Unit resolution is a related strategy that requires that one of the resolvents always be a unit clause. This is a stronger requirement than the unit preference strategy. We can show that unit resolution is not complete using the same example that shows the incompleteness of linear input form.

The *Linear Input Form* Strategy The linear input form strategy is a direct use of the negated goal and the original axioms: Take the negated goal and resolve it with one of the axioms to get a new clause. This result is then resolved with one of the axioms to get another new clause, which is again resolved with one of the axioms. This process continues until the empty clause is produced.

At each stage we resolve the clause most recently obtained with an original axiom. We never use a previously derived clause, nor do we resolve two of the axioms together. Linear input form is not a complete strategy, as can be seen by applying it to the following set of clauses (which are obviously unsatisfiable). Regardless of which clause is taken as the negation of the goal, linear input strategy cannot produce a contradiction:

```
¬ a ∨ ¬ b
a ∨ ¬ b
¬ a ∨ b
a ∨ b
```

Other Strategies and Simplification Techniques   We have not attempted to present an exhaustive set of strategies or even the most sophisticated techniques for proving theorems using resolution inference. These are available in the literature, e.g., in (Wos et al. 1984). Our goal is rather to introduce the basic tools for this research area and to describe how they may be used in problem solving. The resolution proof procedure is but another weak method problem-solving technique.

In this sense, resolution is an inference engine for the predicate calculus, but one that requires much analysis and careful application of strategies before success. Randomly clashing expressions together with resolution is as hopeless as striking random terminal keys and hoping a quality paper will result. The number of combinations is that large!

The examples used in this chapter are trivially small and have all the clauses necessary (and only those necessary) for the solution. This is seldom true of interesting problems. We have given several simple strategies for combating these complexities, and we conclude this subsection by describing a few more important considerations in resolution-based problem solving. Later we show (in Section 12.3) how resolution refutations, with an interesting combination of strategies, define a ''semantics'' for logic programming, especially the design of PROLOG interpreters.

A combination of strategies can be quite effective in controlling search—for instance, the use of set of support plus unit preference. Search heuristics may also be built into the design of rules (by creating a left-to-right ordering of literals for resolving). This order can be most effective for pruning the search space. This implicit use of strategy is important in PROLOG programming (Section 12.3).

The generality of conclusions can be a criterion for designing a solution strategy. On one side it might be important to keep intermediate solutions as general as possible, since this allows them to be used more freely in resolution. Thus the introduction of any resolution with clauses that require specialization by binding variables, for example, {john/X}, should be put off as long as possible. If, on the other side, a solution requires specific variable bindings, such as an analysis of whether John has a staph infection, the {john/Person} and {staph/Infection} substitutions may restrict the search space and increase the probability and speed of finding a solution.

An important issue in selection of a strategy is the notion of completeness. It might be very important in some applications to know that a solution will be found (if one exists). This can be guaranteed by using only complete strategies.

We can also increase efficiency by speeding up the matching process. We can eliminate needless (and costly) unifications between clauses that cannot possibly produce new resolvents by indexing each clause with the literals it contains and whether they are positive or negative. This allows us directly to find potential resolvents for any clause.

Also, we should eliminate certain clauses as soon as they are produced. First, any tautological clause need never be considered; these can never be falsified and so are of no use in a solution attempt.

Another type of clause that gives no new information is one that can be *subsumed*. Subsumption is appropriate when the new clause has a more general instance already in the clause space. For example, if p(john) is deduced for a space that already contains ∀ X(p(X)), then p(john) may be dropped with no loss; in fact, there is a saving because there are fewer clauses in the clause space. Similarly, p(X) subsumes the clause p(X) ∨ q(X). Less general information does not add anything to more general information when both are in the clause space.

Finally, *procedural attachment* evaluates or otherwise processes without further search any clause that can yield new information. It does arithmetic, makes comparisons, or "runs" any other deterministic procedure that can add concrete information to the problem solving or in any manner constrain the solution process. For example, we may use a procedure to compute a binding for a variable when enough information is present to do so. This restricts possible resolutions and prunes the space.

In the next section we show how answers may be extracted from the resolution refutation process.

11.2.5 Answer Extraction from Resolution Refutations

The observant reader has already surmised the role unifications play in a resolution refutation. In fact, the instances under which a hypothesis is true are exactly the substitutions with which the refutation is found. Therefore, retaining information on the unification substitutions gives information for the correct answer. In this subsection we give three examples of this and introduce a bookkeeping method for extracting answers from a resolution refutation.

The answer recording method is simple: retain the original conclusion that was to be proved and, into that conclusion, introduce each unification that is made in the resolution process. Thus the original conclusion is the "bookkeeper" of all unifications that are made as part of the refutation. In the computational search for resolution refutations, this might require extra pointers, for example, when there is more than one possible choice in the search for a refutation. A control mechanism such as backtracking may be necessary to produce alternative solution paths. But still, with a bit of care, this added information may be retained.

Let us see some examples of this process. In Figure 11.6, where a proof was found for the existence of a person with an exciting life, the unifications of Figure 11.10 were made. If we retain the original goal and apply all the substitutions of the refutation to this clause, we find the answer of which person it is who has an exciting life.

Figure 11.10 shows how a resolution refutation not only can show that "no one leads an exciting life" is false but also, in the process of that demonstration, can produce the happy person, John. This is a completely general result, where the unifications that produce the refutation are the same ones that produce the instances under which the original query is true.

A second example is the simple story:

Fido the dog goes wherever John, his master, goes. John is at the library. Where is Fido?

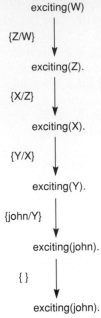

exciting(W)

{Z/W}

exciting(Z).

{X/Z}

exciting(X).

{Y/X}

exciting(Y).

{john/Y}

exciting(john).

{ }

exciting(john).

Figure 11.10   Unification substitutions of Figure 11.6
applied to the original query.

First we represent this story in predicate calculus expressions and then reduce these expressions to clause form. The predicates:

at (john,X) → at (fido,X)
at (john,library).

The clauses:

¬ at (john,Y) ∨ at (fido,Y)
at (john,library)

The conclusion negated:

¬ at (fido,Z)

(Fido is nowhere!)

Figure 11.11 gives the answer extraction process. The literal keeping track of unifications is the original question (where is Fido?):

at (fido,Z).

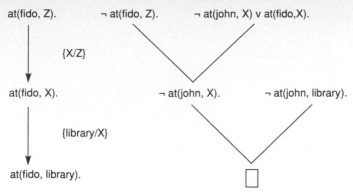

Figure 11.11 Answer extraction process on the "finding fido" problem.

Once again, the unifications under which the contradiction is found tell how the original query is true: Fido is at the library.

The final example shows how the skolemization process can give the instance under which the answer may be extracted. Consider the following situation:

Everyone has a parent. The parent of a parent is a grandparent. Given the person John, prove that John has a grandparent.

The following sentences represent the facts and relationships in the situation above:

Everyone has a parent.

$(\forall X)(\exists Y)\ p(X,Y).$

A parent of a parent is a grandparent.

$(\forall X)(\forall Y)(\forall Z)\ p(X,Y) \wedge p(Y,Z) \rightarrow gp(X,Z).$

The goal is to find a W such that gp(john,W) or $\exists$ (W)(gp(john,W)) The negation of the goal is $\neg \exists$ (W)(gp(john,W)) or:

$\neg$ gp(john,W).

In the process of putting the predicates above in clause form for the resolution refutation, the existential quantifier in the first predicate (everyone has a parent) requires a skolem function. This skolem function would be the obvious function: take the given X and find the parent of X. Let's call this the pa(X) for "find a parental ancestor for X." For John this would be either his father or his mother. The clause form for the predicates of this problem is:

p(X,pa(X))

$\neg$ p(W,Y) $\vee \neg$ p(Y,Z) $\vee$ gp(W,Z)

$\neg$ gp(john,V)

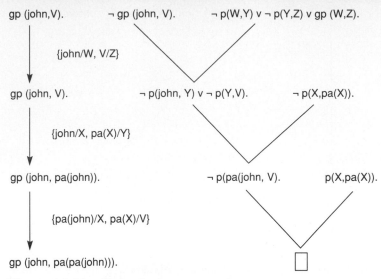

Figure 11.12 Skolemization as part of the answer extraction process.

The resolution refutation and answer extraction process for this problem are presented in Figure 11.12. Note that the unification substitutions in the answer are

gp(john,pa(pa(john))).

The answer to the question of whether John has a grandparent is to "find the parental ancestor of John's parental ancestor." The skolemized function allows us to compute this result.

The general process for answer extraction just described may be used in all resolution refutations, whether they be with the general unifications as in Figures 11.10 and 11.11 or from evaluating the skolem function as in Figure 11.12. The process will yield an answer. The method is really quite simple: The instances (unifications) under which the contradiction is found are exactly those under which the opposite of the negated conclusion (the original query) is true. Although this subsection has not demonstrated how this is true in every instance, it has shown several examples of how the process works; further discussion can be found in the literature (Nilsson 1980; Wos et al. 1984).

11.3 Further Issues in the Design of Automated Reasoning Programs

We described weak method problem solvers as using (a) a *uniform representation medium* for (b) *sound inference rules* that focus on syntactic features of the representation and are guided by (c) *methods or strategies* for combating the combinatorics of exhaustive search. We conclude this chapter with further comments on each of these aspects of the weak method solution process.

11.3.1 Uniform Representations for Weak Method Solutions

The resolution proof procedure requires us to place all our axioms in clause form. This uniform representation then allows us to resolve clauses and simplifies the design of problem-solving heuristics. One major disadvantage of this approach is that much valuable heuristic information can be lost in this uniform encoding.

The if...then format of a rule often conveys more information for use of modus ponens or production system search than one of its syntactic variants. It also offers us an efficient way to use the rule. For instance, If the engine does not turn over and the lights do not come on then the battery may be dead tells us exactly how to check the battery.

The disjunctive form of the same rule obscures this heuristic information about how the rule should be applied. If we express this rule in predicate calculus, $\neg$ turns_over $\land \neg$ lights $\rightarrow$ battery, the clause form of this rule is this: turns_over $\lor$ lights $\lor$ battery. There are a number of equivalent forms that this clause can have, and each of these represents a different implication.

$(\neg$ turns_over $\land \neg$ lights$) \rightarrow$ battery
$(\neg$ turns_over $\rightarrow ($battery $\lor$ lights$))$
$(\neg$ battery $\land \neg$ lights$) \lor$ turns_over
$(\neg$ battery $\rightarrow ($turns_over $\lor$ lights$))$

and so on.

In order to retain heuristic information in the automated reasoning process several researchers, including Nilsson (1980), advocate reasoning methods that encode heuristics by forming rules according to the way in which the human expert might design the rule relationships. We have proposed this approach already in our and/or graph reasoning in Section 3.3. Rule-based expert systems also allow the programmer to control search through the structure of rules. We develop the idea further with the next two examples, one data driven and the second goal driven. Both of these retain the form of implications and use this information to guide search through an and/or graph.

Consider, for data-driven reasoning, the following facts, rules (axioms), and goal:

Fact:
   $(a \lor (b \land c))$
Rules (or axioms):
   $(a \rightarrow (d \land e))$
   $(b \rightarrow f)$
   $(c \rightarrow (g \lor h))$
Goal:
   $e \lor f$

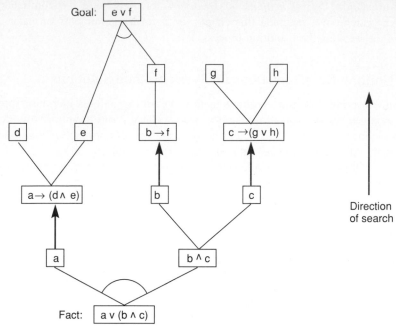

Goal: $e \vee f$

Fact: $a \vee (b \wedge c)$

Figure 11.13 Data-driven reasoning with an and/or graph in the propositional calculus.

The proof of $e \vee f$ is found in the **and/or** graph of Figure 11.13. Note the use of **and** connectors on $\vee$ relations and the **or** connectors on $\wedge$ relations in the data-driven search space. If we are given that either a or $b \wedge c$ is true, then we must reason with both disjuncts to guarantee that our argument is truth preserving; hence these two paths are conjoined. When b and c are true, on the other hand, we can continue to explore either of these conjuncts. Rule matching takes any intermediate state, c for instance, and replaces it with the conclusion of a rule, $(g \vee h)$ for example, whose premise matches that state. The discovery of BOTH states e and f in Figure 11.13 indicates that the goal $(e \vee f)$ is established.

In a similar fashion we use matching of rules on **and/or** graphs for goal-driven reasoning. When a goal description includes a $\vee$, as in the example of Figure 11.14, then either alternative can be explored independently to establish the goal. If the goal is a conjunction, then, of course, both conjuncts must be established.

Goal:

$$(a \vee (b \wedge c))$$

Rules (or axioms):

$$(f \wedge d) \rightarrow a$$
$$(e \rightarrow (b \wedge c))$$
$$(g \rightarrow d)$$

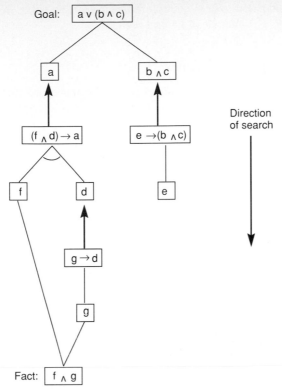

Goal: a v (b ∧ c)

Direction of search

Fact: f ∧ g

Figure 11.14 Goal-driven reasoning with an and/or graph in the propositional calculus.

Fact:

f ∧ g

Although these examples are taken from the propositional calculus, a similar search is generated using predicate calculus facts and rules. Unification makes literals compatible for applying inference rules across different branches of the search space. Of course, unifications must be consistent (that is, unifiable) across different branches of and connectors.

This subsection has suggested a way to preserve heuristic information in the representational medium for weak method problem solving. This is essentially the way the inference engines of expert systems allow the programmer to specify control and heuristic information in a rule. For example, the rule $p \wedge q \wedge r \to s$ tells us that in order to solve s, try p, q, and r in order. Expert systems rely on the rule form for control of search rather than on general weak problem-solving methods. What is lost in this strong method approach is the ability to apply uniform proof procedures, such as resolution, across the representations. As can be noted in the examples of Figures 11.13 and 11.14, modus ponens may still be used. Methods or strategies for inferencing must also be addressed, and a production system control (Chapter 4) using either depth-, breadth-, or best-first search offers one alternative control regime.

11.3.2   Alternative Inference Rules

Resolution is the most general sound inference rule we have presented so far. Several more sophisticated inference rules have been created in an attempt to make resolution more efficient. We will briefly consider two of these: *hyperresolution* and *paramodulation*.

Resolution, as we have presented it, is actually a special variant called *binary resolution*: exactly two parent clauses are clashed. A successful application of hyperresolution replaces a sequence of binary resolutions to produce one clause. Hyperresolution clashes, in a single step, a clause with some negative literals, referred to as the *nucleus*, and a number of clauses with all positive literals, called the *satellites*. These satellites must have one positive literal that will match with a negative literal of the nucleus. There must also be one satellite for each negative literal of the nucleus. Thus the result of an application of hyperresolution is a clause with all positive literals.

An advantage of hyperresolution is that this clause of all positive literals is produced from each hyperresolution inference and the clause space itself is kept smaller because no intermediate results are produced. Unifications across all clauses in the inference step must be consistent.

As an example of an inference using hyperresolution, consider the following clause set:

$\neg$ married(X,Y) $\vee$ $\neg$ mother(X,Z) $\vee$ father(Y,Z)
married(kate,george) $\vee$ likes(george,kate)
mother(kate,sarah)

We draw a conclusion in one step using hyperresolution:

father(george,sarah) $\vee$ likes(george,kate)

The first clause in the example is the nucleus; the second two are satellites. The satellites are all positive, and there is one for each negative literal in the nucleus. Note how the nucleus is just the clause form for the implication:

likes(X,Y) $\wedge$ mother(X,Z) $\rightarrow$ father(Y,Z)

The conclusion of this rule is part of the final result. Note that there are no intermediate results, such as:

$\neg$ mother(kate,Z) $\vee$ father(george,Z) $\vee$ married(george,kate)

which we would find in any binary resolution proof applied to the same clause space.

Hyperresolution is sound and complete when used by itself. When combined with other strategies, such as set of support, completeness may be compromised (Wos et al.

1984). It does require special search strategies to organize the satellite and nucleus clauses, although in most environments where hyperresolution is used, the clauses are often indexed by the name and positive or negative property of each literal. This makes it efficient to prepare the nucleus and satellite clauses for the hyperresolution inference.

Perhaps the most difficult issue in the design of theorem-proving mechanisms is the control of equality. Especially difficult are application areas, such as mathematics, where most facts and relationships have multiple representations, such as can be obtained by applying the associative and commutative properties to expressions. To convince yourself of this with a very simple example, consider the multiple ways the arithmetic fact $3 + (4 + 5)$ can be represented, including $3 + ((4 + 0) + 5)$. This is a difficult issue in that expressions need to be substituted for, unified with, and checked for equality with other expressions within automated mathematical problem solving.

Demodulation is the process of rephrasing or rewriting expressions so that they automatically take on a chosen canonical form. The unit clauses used to produce this canonical form are *demodulators*. Demodulators specify the equality of different expressions, allowing us to replace an expression with its canonical form. With proper use of demodulators all newly produced information is reduced to a specified form before it is placed in the clause space. For example, we might have a demodulator:

equal(father(father(X)),grandfather(X))

and the new clause:

age(father(father(sarah)),78).

Before adding this new clause to the clause space, we apply the demodulator and add instead:

age(grandfather(sarah),78).

The equality problem here is one of naming. Do we wish to classify a person as father(father(X)) or grandfather(X)? Similarly, we can pick out canonical names for all family relations: a brother(father(Y)) is uncle(Y), etc. Once we pick the canonical names to store information under, we then design demodulators such as the equal clause to reduce all new information to this determined form. Note that demodulators are always unit clauses.

Paramodulation is a generalization of equality substitution at the term level. For example, given the expression:

older(mother(Y), Y)

and the equality relationship:

equal(mother(sarah),kate)

we can conclude with paramodulation:

older(kate,sarah)

Note the term-level matching and replacement of {sarah/Y} and mother(sarah) for kate. A vital difference between demodulation and paramodulation is that the latter allows a nontrivial replacement of variables in both the arguments of the equality predicate and the predicate into which the substitution is made. Demodulation does replacement based on the demodulator. Multiple demodulators may be used to get an expression into its final form; paramodulation is usually used only once in any situation.

We have given simple examples of these powerful inference mechanisms. They should be seen as more general techniques for use in a resolution clause space. Like all the other inference rules we have seen, these are tightly linked to the chosen representation and must be controlled by appropriate strategies.

11.3.3 Search Strategies and Their Use

Sometimes the domain of application puts special demands on the inference rules and heuristics for guiding their use. We have already seen the use of demodulators for assistance in equality substitution. Bledsoe, in his *natural deduction system*, identifies two important strategies for preparing theorems for resolution proof. He calls these strategies *split* and *reduce* (Bledsoe 1971).

Bledsoe designed his strategies for use in mathematics and, in particular, for application to *set theory*. The effect of these strategies is to break a theorem into parts to make it easier to prove by conventional methods such as resolution. Split takes various mathematical forms and splits them to appropriate pieces. The proof of $A \wedge B$ is equivalent to the proof of A and the proof of B. Similarly, the proof of $A \leftrightarrow B$ is the proof of $A \rightarrow B$ and the proof of $A \leftarrow B$.

The heuristic reduce also attempts to break down large proofs to their components. For example, the proof of $s \in A \cap B$ may be decomposed into the proofs of $s \in A$ and $s \in B$. Another example might be to prove some property true of $\neg (A \cup B)$ by proving the property for $\neg A$ and $\neg B$. By breaking up larger proofs into smaller pieces, Bledsoe hopes to contain the search space. His heuristics also include a limited use of equality substitution.

As mentioned throughout this book, the appropriate use of heuristics is very much an art that takes into account the application area as well as the representation and inference rules used. We close this chapter by citing some general proverbs, all of which are sometimes false, but which can, with careful use, be very effective. These proverbs sum up thoughts taken from researchers in the area (Bledsoe 1983; Nilsson 1980; Wos et al. 1984; Wos 1988) as well as our own reflections on weak method problem solvers. We state them without further comment.

Use, whenever possible, clauses with fewer literals.

Break the task into subtasks before employing general inferencing.

Use equality predicates whenever this is appropriate.

Use demodulators to create canonical forms.

Use paramodulation when inferencing with equality predicates.

Use strategies that preserve "completeness."

Use set of support strategies, for these contain the potential contradiction.

Use units within resolution, as these shorten the resulting clause.

Perform subsumption checks with new clauses.

Use an ordering mechanism on clauses and literals within the clauses that reflect your intuitions and problem-solving expertise.

11.4 Epilogue and References

Automated reasoning programs and other weak method problem solvers are very important in artificial intelligence. They are used both to design general search strategies in game playing and theorem proving and to support much of our knowledge-based reasoning. Thus we see them in the design of "shells" for expert systems and inference mechanisms for network representations.

Weak method solvers require choosing a representational medium, inference mechanisms, and search strategies. These three choices are intricately interwoven and cannot be made in isolation from each other. The application domain also affects the choice of representation, inference rules, and strategies. The "proverbs" at the end of the previous section should be considered in making these choices.

Resolution is the process of constraining possible interpretations until it is seen that the clause space with the inclusion of the negated goal is inconsistent. This text does not go into the soundness of resolution or the completeness of resolution refutations. The arguments for these important issues are based on Herbrand's theorem (Chang and Lee 1973) and the notion of possible interpretations of the clause set. The interested reader is encouraged to go to the references for these proofs.

A number of other references are appropriate: Chang and Lee (1973) is a very readable introductory text. *Automated Theorem Proving: A Logical Basis* offers a formal approach (Loveland 1978). A number of classic early papers in the field are collected in a series *The Automation of Reasoning: Collected Papers, 1957 to 1970* (Siekmann 1983*a*, 1983*b*). Nilsson (1980), Genesereth (1987), Kowalski (1979*b*), Wos et al. (1984), and Wos (1988) offer valuable summaries of important concepts in automated reasoning. Robinson (1965) and Bledsoe (1977) have made fundamental contributions to the field. An important theorem-proving research contribution is made by Boyer and Moore (1979). The early theorem-proving work by Newell and Simon and their colleagues at Carnegie Institute of Technology is reported in *Computers and Thought* (Feigenbaum and Feldman 1963) and *Human Problem Solving* (Newell and Simon 1972).

11.5 Exercises

1. Take the logic-based financial advisor of Section 2.4, put the predicates describing the problem into clause form, and use resolution refutations to answer queries such as whether a particular investor should make an investment(combination).

2. Use resolution to prove Wirth's statement in Exercise 13, Chapter 2.

3. Use resolution to answer the query in Example 3.3.4.

4. In Section 4.2 we presented a simplified form of the knight's tour. Take the path3 rule, put it in clause form, and use resolution to answer queries such as path3(3,6)? Next, use the recursive path call, in clause form, to answer queries.

5. How might you use resolution to implement a "production system" search?

6. How would you do data-driven reasoning with resolution? Use this to address the search space of Exercise 1. What problems might arise in a large problem space?

7. Use resolution to answer queries in the farmer, wolf, goat, and cabbage problem of Section 6.1.3.

8. Use resolution to solve the following puzzle problem from (Wos et al. 1984). There are four people: Roberta, Thelma, Steve, and Pete. The four hold eight different jobs. Each person has exactly two jobs. The jobs are, without sex bias: chef, guard, nurse, telephonist, police officer, teacher, actor, and boxer. The nurse is a male. The husband of the chef is the telephonist. Roberta is not a boxer. Pete has no education past the ninth grade. Roberta, the chef, and the police officer went golfing together. Who holds which jobs?

9. Work out two examples for hyperresolution where the nucleus has at least four literals.

10. Write a demodulator for sum that would cause clauses of the form equal(ans, sum(5, sum(6, minus(6)))) to be reduced to equal(ans, sum(5, 0)). Write a further demodulator to reduce this last result to equal(ans, 5).

11. Pick a "canonical set" of six family relations. Write demodulators to reduce alternative forms of relations to the set. For example, your "mother's brother" is "uncle."

12. Take the happy student problem of Figure 11.5 and apply three of the refutation strategies of Section 11.2.4 to its solution.

13. Put the following predicate calculus expression in clause form:

$$\forall (X)(p(X) \rightarrow \{\forall(Y)[p(Y) \rightarrow p(f(X,Y))] \land \neg \forall (Y)[q(X,Y) \rightarrow p(Y)]\})$$

14. Create the and/or graph for the following data-driven predicate calculus deduction. Fact: $\neg d(f) \lor [b(f) \land c(f)]$. Rules: $\neg d(X) \rightarrow \neg a(X)$ and $b(Y) \rightarrow e(Y)$ and $g(W) \leftarrow c(W)$. Prove: $\neg a(Z) \lor e(Z)$.

15. Prove the linear input form strategy is not refutation complete.

16. Create the and/or graph for the following problem. Why is it impossible to conclude the goal: $r(Z) \lor s(Z)$? Fact: $p(X) \lor q(X)$. Rules: $p(a) \rightarrow r(a)$ and $q(b) \rightarrow s(b)$.

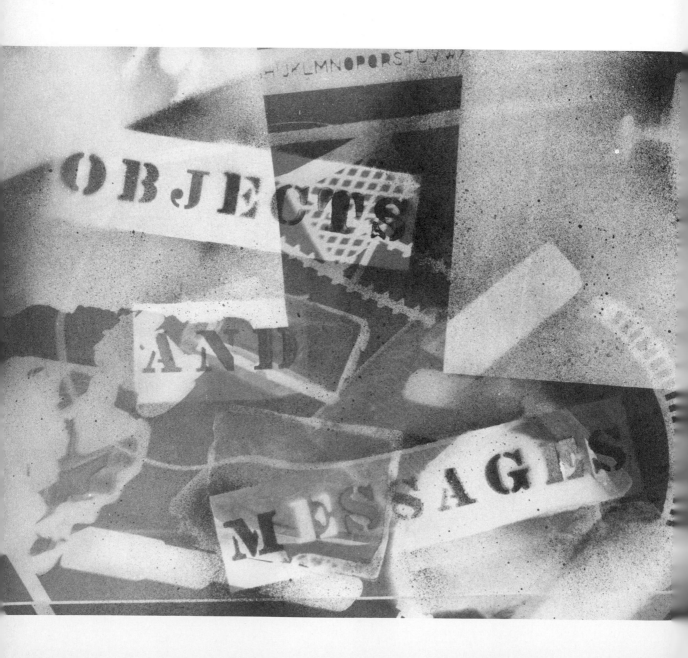

PART V

ADVANCED AI PROGRAMMING TECHNIQUES

"Come, we shall have some fun now!" thought Alice. "I'm glad they've begun asking riddles—I believe I can guess that," she added aloud.

"Do you mean that you think you can find out the answer to it?" said the March Hare.

"Exactly so," said Alice.

"Then you should say what you mean," the March Hare went on.

"I do," Alice hastily replied; "at least—at least I mean what I say—that's the same thing, you know."

"Not the same thing a bit!" said the Hatter. "Why you might just as well say that 'I see what I eat' is the same thing as 'I eat what I see'!"

"You might just as well say," added the March Hare, "that 'I like what I get' is the same thing as 'I get what I like'!"

"You might just as well say," added the Dormouse, who seemed to be talking in his sleep, "that 'I breathe when I sleep' is the same thing as 'I sleep when I breathe'!"

"It is the same thing with you," said the Hatter. . . .

— Lewis Carroll, "A Mad Tea Party," *Alice's Adventures in Wonderland*

AI Languages and Meta-Interpreters

In Part V we implement the representations introduced in the last three chapters. In particular, we build interpreters for production rules and design and build semantic network and frame systems. Chapter 12 presents these programs in PROLOG, Chapter 13 in LISP. Our goals are to give the student an appreciation of the *semantics* or mathematical foundations of each of these programming paradigms and to show the ease with which these languages support the construction of interpreters for AI representations.

Before we continue with the advanced PROLOG and LISP chapters, we introduce a third approach to AI problem solving, *object-oriented programming*. We also discuss an important by-product of object-oriented programming, the *hybrid AI environment*. Chapter 14 presents advanced knowledge representation within the object-oriented paradigm and designs object-oriented interpreters in LISP and PROLOG.

Object-Oriented Programming

Object-oriented programming, unlike LISP and PROLOG, has its roots in software engineering and simulation rather than in abstract mathematics. Smalltalk, the first ''object-oriented'' language, was developed in the early 1970s at Xerox Palo Alto Research Center under the direction of Alan Kay. Xerox engineers began work on the Dynabook, a portable computer the size of a loose-leaf binder, intended to be a general tool for the non–computer scientist. Because of this target user, the operating system and applications software needed to be nontechnical and easily understood. Their solution to this problem was a graphics interface based on the ''desktop metaphor'': multiple process windows (like papers scattered on a desk); use of menus, graphic icons, and pointing devices (a mouse or a touch screen) for selecting options; and a rich set of programs for editing, graphics, and communications. Although the Dynabook was never marketed, its implementation language, Smalltalk, is very important in modern computing. The user interface design of the Dynabook is implemented in computers such as the Apple Macintosh, workstations such as SUN, and the numerous specialized LISP computers available for AI program development.

In a Smalltalk program, everything is represented as an object, an active computational structure of arbitrary complexity. Objects include not only the data types needed to define a computational entity but also the *methods* (executable code) necessary to manipulate the object's values. Objects may be class objects, describing all instances of a type, or instances, representing a single member. When instances of a data type are defined as objects, these instance objects inherit (Chapter 9) both the type definitions and the associated methods from their class. For example, the number 3 is a member of the class integers and inherits the integer operators (+, - , * , MOD) from the class. In order to perform an operation on an object, a message is sent to the object invoking the appropriate method. For example, to add 3 and 4, the message +4 is sent to the object 3; 3 responds with the answer ''7.''

By providing a means for combining data types and the operations on them into a single entity (the object), Smalltalk supports the development of modular code and applies strong typing to both data elements and the code for their manipulation. Since Smalltalk objects are organized into a network of classes, with more specialized objects inheriting part or all of the methods of the more general, it is simple to create new program structures that incorporate the functionality of existing program objects. Thus, any program can readily incorporate the full power of the underlying system, including graphics, editing, and communications. In addition, important software development techniques such as information hiding, operator overloading, on-line documentation, and embedded languages are supported in a natural fashion.

Commercial systems that support the object-oriented approach to knowledge engineering are available for a range of hardware, from personal computers to LISP machines to large timesharing systems. The best known object-oriented environment is *Flavors*, which is supported by most LISP machines. Flavors provides the basis for their windowing and interface, as well as object-oriented knowledge representation. Other such systems include Loops from Xerox; Common Loops, a revised version of Loops for Common LISP; Common Objects, another package developed for the Common LISP dialect; and KEE, a hybrid object-oriented/rule-based knowledge engineering language. ART, NEXPERT, and Knowledge Craft also are in this group.

Most important, Smalltalk defined the methodology of object-oriented programming; packages explicitly supporting object-oriented programming are currently available in most LISP dialects and in a number of commercial expert system development packages. The methodology has emerged as an extremely important AI programming technique (Chapter 14), especially in development of hybrid AI environments.

Hybrid Environments

The demands of knowledge-based programming have led to the development of a number of programming and representation techniques, including production systems, rules, and frame/object-based representations. A hybrid system combines multiple representation paradigms into a single integrated programming environment. Although hybrid environments differ, they generally include the following features:

1. **Frame or object-oriented representations of domain objects**. Such systems support inheritance of class properties and often include a message-passing mechanism for object interactions.

2. **Rules for representing heuristic knowledge**. While frames and objects are the preferred means of describing taxonomies of objects, rules remain the most natural means of describing heuristic problem-solving knowledge. The if...then syntax fits the way human experts describe their decision-making process. Rules are able to access information in objects, either through use of a language that directly reads and writes to slots in an object or by using message passing to query an object indirectly.

3. **Support for a variety of search strategies**. Most systems support both forward and backward search. For example, presentation of a goal query initiates a backward chaining search. Addition of a new fact to working memory may initiate forward reasoning from rules enabled by this new fact.

4. **Definition of demons to implement interactions and side effects**. A *demon* is a procedure that is invoked as a side effect of some other action. A conventional example of the use of demons is a controller in a time-sharing system that is invoked periodically to monitor a printer or other device. They are not called directly, but are invoked by a clock. AI environments extend this idea, allowing the creation of demons that are invoked when an object or slot is created or modified. These are used to update a display in response to a changed slot value, perform consistency checks when the modification of one entity requires a change in a different object, or implement the interactions between objects in a simulation. Such demons are often called *active values*.

5. **Rich graphics-based interfaces**. These include a range of trace facilities that allow both continuous and stepwise monitoring of executions. For example, graphic

displays can describe the rule structure of a knowledge base as a tree structure. An important feature of hybrid environments is the ability to attach (using demons) a graphic display to a slot in an object, allowing a gauge or other graphic to display its value in real time. Similarly, most environments provide high-level support for graphics input devices such as buttons or sliders that may be set using a mouse or other pointing device.

6. **Escapes to an underlying language**. Methods are represented in a special language defined by the environment or, more often, in LISP, PROLOG, or even a conventional language such as C or Pascal. Not only does this allow a natural description of procedural knowledge, it also allows a knowledge-based program to call more conventional languages to perform arithmetic, array manipulation, sensor monitoring, or other actions that are better implemented using conventional algorithmic techniques.

7. **The ability to compile a knowledge base for faster execution or delivery on a smaller machine**. Once a knowledge-based program is completed, the rich interpreted development environment is often an overhead that slows down execution. Most modern AI environments allow applications to be compiled and run under a faster, simpler, often also smaller and cheaper, delivery machine. These environments and their foundations in object-oriented programming are discussed in Chapter 14.

12

ADVANCED REPRESENTATION
IN PROLOG

O body swayed to music, O brightening glance,
How can we know the dancer from the dance?

—W. B. YEATS, "Among School Children"

12.0 Introduction

This chapter addresses three topics. First, in Section 12.1 we introduce a number of *meta-predicates*. These are called *meta* in the sense that the objects they test or manipulate are PROLOG expressions themselves. For example, atom(X) succeeds if X is bound to an atom. This can help us decide how to manipulate X. We also discuss *types* in PROLOG and the use of unification in equality testing and structure creation.

The second topic (Section 12.2) is the design of *meta-interpreters*. We create meta-interpreters for rule-based expert systems (12.2.1) and for inheritance evaluation in semantic nets and frames (12.2.2 and 12.2.3). Along the way, we show how rule, frame, and semantic net representations may be cast in PROLOG.

Third, we emphasize the power that a clean and precise semantics offers AI programmers. In Section 12.3 we use the concept of a resolution refutation with certain strategies as a semantics for PROLOG. We also present Flat Concurrent PROLOG (Shapiro 1987) as an alternative model for logic programming. Flat Concurrent PROLOG will be important for the design of an interpreter for objects, messages, and inheritance in Chapter 14.

This chapter is not intended as a tutorial introduction to programming in PROLOG. Rather we both demonstrate what it is to do AI programming with PROLOG and offer a semantic model for computing with logic. The reader in need of a "PROLOG refresher" should consult the texts suggested in the epilogue to Chapter 6.

12.1 PROLOG Tools: Meta-Predicates, Types, and Unification

12.1.1 Meta-Logical Predicates

Meta-logical constructs offer an important extension to the expressive power of any programming environment. These predicates are outside the scope of first-order predicate calculus as they query the status of the proof as well as create and manipulate predicates within the proof procedure. We refer to these predicates as *meta* because they query and manipulate other predicates rather than the terms or objects these other predicates denote. We need meta-predicates in PROLOG for (at least) five reasons:

1. To determine the "type" of an expression.
2. To add "type" restrictions to logic programming.
3. To build, take apart, and evaluate PROLOG structures.
4. To compare values of expressions.
5. To convert predicates passed as data to executable code.

We have already described how global structures, that is, those that can be accessed by the entire clause set, are entered into a PROLOG program. The command assert(C) adds the clause C to the current set of clauses. We can also add an entire list of clauses to the data base by the command assert([C1,C2,...]). Similarly we can remove clauses using the command retract([C1,C2,...]).

There are many dangers associated with programming with assert and retract. Since they create and remove global structures, these commands introduce side effects and other problems associated with poorly structured programs. We discussed this issue when designing a loop check for graph search in Chapter 6. Yet, it is sometimes necessary to use global structures. We do this when creating *semantic nets* and *frames* in a PROLOG environment. We may also use global structures to describe new results as they are found with our rule-based shell. We want this information to be global so that other predicates (rules) may access it when appropriate (Section 12.2).

Other meta-predicates that are useful for manipulating representations include the following:

var(X) succeeds only when X is an unbound variable.

nonvar(X) succeeds only when X is bound to a nonvariable term.

=.. creates a list from a predicate term.

For example, foo(a,b,c) =.. Y unifies Y with [foo,a,b,c]. The head of the list Y is the function name, and its tail is the function's arguments. =.. can be used "backward," of course. Thus if X =.. [foo,a,b,c] succeeds, then X has the value foo(a,b,c).

functor(A, B, C) succeeds with A a term whose principal functor has name B and arity C.

For example, functor(foo(a,b),X,Y). will succeed with X = foo and Y = 2. functor(A,B,C) can also be used with any of its arguments bound in order to produce the other, for example, all the terms with a certain name and/or arity.

clause(A,B) unifies B with the body of a clause whose head unifies with A.

If p(X) :- q(X) exists in the data base, then clause(p(a),X) will succeed with X = q(a). This is useful for controlling rule chaining in an interpreter.

any_predicate(...,X,...) :- X. executes predicate X, the argument of an arbitrary predicate.

Thus a predicate, here X, may be passed as a parameter and executed at any desired time in the computation.

call(X), where X is a clause, also succeeds with the execution of predicate X.

This short list of meta-logical predicates will be very important in building and interpreting the AI data structures of the preceding three chapters. Because PROLOG can manipulate its own structures in a straightforward fashion, it is easy to implement interpreters that modify the PROLOG semantics. For example, in building a meta-interpreter for production rules (Section 12.2), it is important to be able to determine when data are a rule (clause) or a fact (true) and be able to create new predicates or relationships as needed.

12.1.2   Types in PROLOG

For a number of problem-solving applications the unconstrained use of unification can introduce unintended error. PROLOG is an untyped language; unification simply matches patterns, without restricting them according to type. For example, append (nil,6,6) is deducible from the definition of append (Section 6.3). Strongly typed languages like Pascal have shown how type checking can help the programmer avoid these problems. A number of researchers have proposed the introduction of *types* to PROLOG (Neves et al. 1986; Mycroft 1984).

Typed data are particularly appropriate in the control for a relational date base (Neves 1986; Malpas 1987). The rules of logic can be used as constraints on the data and the data can be typed to enforce consistent and meaningful interpretation of the queries.

Suppose that there is a department store data base of inventory, suppliers, supplier_inventory, and other appropriate relations. We define the data base as relations with named fields; these can be thought of as sets of data tuples. For example, inventory might consist of a set of 4-tuples, where:

< Pname, Pnumber, Supplier, Weight > ∈ inventory

only when Supplier is the supplier name of an inventory item numbered Pnumber that is called Pname and has weight Weight. Suppose also

< Supplier, Snumber, Status, Location > ∈ suppliers

only when Supplier is the name of a supplier numbered Snumber who has status Status and lives in city Location, and

$$< \text{Supplier, Pnumber, Cost, Department} > \in \text{supplier\_inventory}$$

only if Supplier is the name of a supplier of inventory number Pnumber in the amount of Cost to department Department.

We may define PROLOG rules that implement various queries and perform type checking in these relations. For instance, the query "are there suppliers of inventory number 1 that live in London?" is given in PROLOG as:

```
?- getsuppliers (Supplier,1,london).
```

The rule:

```
getsuppliers (Supplier, Pnumber, City) :-
                cktype (City, suppliers, city),
                suppliers (Supplier,_,_,City),
                cktype(Pnumber, inventory, number),
                supplier_inventory (Supplier,Pnumber,_,_),
                cktype (Supplier, inventory, name).
```

implements this query and also enforces the appropriate constraints across the tuples of the data base. First the variables Pnumber and City are bound when the query unifies with the head of the rule; our predicate cktype tests that Supplier is an element of the set of suppliers, that 1 is a legitimate inventory number, and that london is a suppliers city.

We define cktype to take three arguments, a value, a relation name, and a field name, and check that the value is of the appropriate type for that relation. We can implement cktype in any appropriate fashion. For example, we may define lists of legal values for Supplier, Pnumber, and City and enforce data typing by requiring member checks of candidate values across these lists. Alternatively, we may define logical constraints on possible values of a type; for example, we may require that inventory numbers be less than 1000.

We should note the differences in type checking between standard languages like Pascal and PROLOG. We might define a Pascal data type for suppliers as:

```
type supplier = record
                sname: string;
                snumber: integer;
                status: boolean;
                location: string
            end
```

The Pascal programmer defines new types, here supplier, in terms of already defined types, such as boolean or integer. When the programmer uses variables of this type, the compiler automatically performs type checks on their values.

In PROLOG, we could represent the supplier relation as instances of the form:

```
supplier(sname(Supplier),
         snumber(Snumber),
         status(Status),
         location(Location)).
```

We would implement type checking on these instances using rules such as getsuppliers and cktype.

The distinction between Pascal and PROLOG type checking is clear and important: the Pascal type declaration tells the compiler the form for both the entire structure (record) and the individual components (boolean, integer, string) of the data type. In Pascal we declare variables to be of a particular type (record) and then create procedures to access these typed structures.

```
procedure changestatus (X: supplier);
    begin
        if X.status then....
```

Because it is nonprocedural, PROLOG does not separate the declaration from the use of data types. The PROLOG form is an instance of an object and any type checking must be done as the program is executing. Consider the rule:

```
supplier_name(supplier(sname(Supplier),
                       snumber(Snumber),
                       status(true),
                       location (london))) :-
    integer(Snumber), write(Supplier).
```

supplier_name takes as argument an instance of the supplier predicate and writes the name of the supplier. However, this rule will succeed only if the supplier's number is an integer, the status is active (true), and the supplier lives in London. An important part of the type check is handled by the unification algorithm (true, london) and the rest is the built-in system predicate integer. Further constraints could restrict values to be from a particular list; for example, Snumber could be constrained to be from a list of supplier numbers. We define constraints on data base queries using rules such as cktype and supplier_name to implement type checking when the program is executed.

So far, we have seen three ways that data may be typed in PROLOG. First, and most powerful, is the use of unification to constrain variable assignment. Second, PROLOG itself provides predicates to do limited type checking. We saw this with meta-predicates such as var(X), clause(X,Y), and integer(X). The third limited use of typing occurred in the inventory example where rules checked lists of legitimate suppliers, pnumbers, and cities to enforce type constraints.

A fourth, and more radical, approach is the complete predicate and data type check proposed by Mycroft and O'Keefe (Mycroft 1984). Here all predicate names are typed and given a fixed arity. Furthermore, all variable names are themselves typed. A strength of this approach is that the constraints on the constituent predicates and variables of the PROLOG program are themselves enforced by a (meta) PROLOG program. Even though the result may be slower program execution, the security gained through total type enforcement may justify this cost.

Rather than providing built-in type checking as a default, PROLOG allows run time type checking under complete programmer control. This approach offers a number of benefits for AI programmers, including the following:

1. The programmer is not forced to adhere to strong type checking at all times. This allows us to write predicates that work across any type of object. For example, the member predicate performs general member checking, regardless of the type of elements in the list.

2. Flexibility in typing helps exploratory programming. Programmers can relax type checking in the early stages of program development and introduce it to detect errors as they come to better understand the problem.

3. AI representations seldom conform to the built-in data types of languages like Pascal. PROLOG allows types to be defined using the full power of predicate calculus. The data base example showed the advantages of this flexibility.

4. Because type checking is done at run time rather than compile time, the programmer determines when the program should perform a check. This allows programmers to delay type checking until it is necessary or until certain variables have become bound.

5. Programmer control of type checking at run time also lets us write programs that create and enforce new types during execution. This could be of use in a learning program, for example.

12.1.3 Unification, the Engine for Predicate Matching and Evaluation

An important feature of PROLOG programming is the interpreter's behavior as a resolution-based theorem prover, presented in Section 12.3. As a theorem prover PROLOG performs a series of resolutions on data base entries, rather than sequentially evaluating statements and expressions like a traditional language. This has an important result: variables are bound (assigned values, instantiated, . . .) by unification and *not* by evaluation (unless, of course, an evaluation is explicitly requested). There are several important implications of this programming paradigm.

The first and perhaps most important result is the relaxation of the requirement to specify variables as input or output. We already saw (Section 6.3) some of the power of this in the append predicate, which could either join lists together, test whether two lists are correctly appended, or break a list into parts consistent with the definition of append. We also saw unification as a matcher and constraint handler for parsing and generating sentences (Chapter 6).

Unification is a powerful technique for rule-based and frame-based expert systems, where it matches world descriptions to the rules that best meet these specifications. All production systems require a form of this matching, and it is often necessary to write a unification algorithm in languages that don't provide it (see Chapter 7 for a LISP implementation of unification).

An important difference between unification-based computing and the use of more traditional languages is that unification performs syntactic matches (with appropriate parameter substitutions) on structures. It does *not* evaluate expressions. Suppose, for example, we wished to create a successor predicate that succeeds if its second argument is the arithmetic successor of its first. Not understanding unification, one might be tempted to define successor:

successor (X,Y) :- Y = X + 1.

This will fail because the = operator does not evaluate its arguments but only attempts to unify the expressions on either side. This predicate succeeds if Y unifies with the structure X + 1. Since 4 does not unify with 3 + 1, the call successor(3,4) fails! On the other hand, = can test for equivalence, as defined by unification, of *any* two expressions.

To correctly define successor and other arithmetic predicates, we need to evaluate arithmetic expressions. PROLOG provides an operator, is, that performs arithmetic evaluation within the context of an individual predicate. is is essential for doing arithmetic.

is evaluates the expression on its right-hand side and attempts to unify the result with the object on its left. Thus,

X is Y + Z

unifies X with the value of Y added to Z. Since it performs arithmetic evaluation:

1. If Y and Z do not have values (are not bound at execution time) evaluation of the is causes a run-time error. Thus

2. X is Y + Z cannot (as one might think with unification) give a value to Y when X and Z are bound.

3. Programs must use is to evaluate expressions containing arithmetic operators, +, -, *, /, and mod.

Finally, as in the predicate calculus, variables in PROLOG may have one and only one binding. Once given a value, through local assignment or unification, they can never take on a new value, except through a backtrack in the and/or search space of the current interpretation (Section 12.3). Thus, is does not function like a traditional assignment operator; an expression such as X is X + 1 will always fail.

Using is, we can now properly define successor(X, Y) as:

successor (X, Y) :- Y is X + 1.

This will have the correct behavior as long as X is bound to a numeric value. It can be used either to compute Y, given X, or to test values of X and Y:

```
?- successor (3,X).
X = 4
yes
?- successor (3,4).
yes
?- successor (4,2).
no
?- successor (Y,4).
failure, error in arithmetic expression
```

As this discussion illustrates, PROLOG does not evaluate expressions as a default as in traditional languages. The programmer must explicitly indicate evaluation using is. While this feature would be problematic in a language like FORTRAN, which is used chiefly for arithmetic computing, it is extremely useful for symbolic computing. Explicit control of evaluation makes it easy to treat expressions as data, passing them as parameters and creating or modifying them in the program. We do not evaluate the expression until the appropriate time.

This feature, like the ability to manipulate predicate calculus expressions as data and execute them using call, greatly simplifies the development of arbitrary interpreters, such as the expert system shell of the next section.

We close this discussion of the power of unification-based computing with an example that does string catenation through the use of *difference lists*. As an alternative to the standard PROLOG list notation, we can represent a list as the difference of two lists. For example, [a, b] is equivalent to [a,b| []] - [] or [a,b,c] - [c]. This representation has certain expressive advantages over the traditional list syntax. When the list [a,b] is represented as the difference [a, b | Y] - Y, it actually describes the potentially infinite class of all lists that have a and b as their first two elements. Now this representation has an interesting property, namely addition:

$$X - Z = X - Y + Y - Z$$

We can use this property to define the following single-clause logic program:

```
catenate(X - Y, Y - Z, X - Z).
```

This operation joins two lists of any length in constant time by unification on the list structures, rather than by repeated assignment based on the length of the lists (as with append).

To use this approach for string catenation, we make the tail of the first list compatible (unifiable) with the head of the second and Z equal to the empty list. Thus the call:

```
?- catenate ([a,b|Y] - Y, [1,2,3] - [],W).
```

Addition of difference lists:

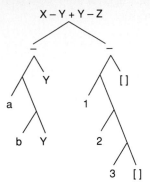

After binding Y to [1, 2, 3], binding Z to [ ], and performing the addition:

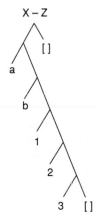

Figure 12.1 Tree diagrams of catenation using difference lists.

gives:

W = [a,b,1,2,3] - []   (Y = [1,2,3])

As noted in Figure 12.1, the (subtree) value of Y in the second parameter is unified with *both* occurrences of Y in the first parameter of **catenate**. This demonstrates the power of unification, not simply for substituting values for variables but for matching general structures: All occurrences of Y take the value of the entire subtree. The example also illustrates the advantages of an appropriate representation. This algorithm is made possible by the ability of difference lists to represent a whole class of lists, including the desired catenation.

In this section we have discussed a number of idiosyncrasies and advantages of PROLOG's unification-based approach to computing. Unification is at the heart of PROLOG's declarative semantics.

12.2 Advanced Representations in PROLOG

The ability to easily design and construct *meta-interpreters* is an important feature of both LISP and PROLOG. A meta-interpreter is an interpreter written in a language for a class of structures also built in that language. For example, a meta-interpreter acting as an expert system shell interprets a knowledge base of rules for reasoning about a particular class of problem. Although the rules are written in the syntax of the underlying language (in our example, PROLOG), the meta-interpreter defines a different semantics for these structures.

As a simple example of a meta-interpreter, we can define the semantics of pure PROLOG using PROLOG itself through the following definition of a solve predicate.

```
solve(true) :-!.
solve(not A) :- not(solve(A)).
solve((A,B)) :- solve(A), solve(B).
solve(A) :- clause(A,B), solve(B).
```

This meta-interpreter defines the semantics of PROLOG using PROLOG; it implements the same left-to-right, depth-first, goal-directed search as the built-in interpreter. In its conciseness and elegance, it illustrates the power of both unification and PROLOG's built-in meta-predicates (clause in this example). It would be much more difficult and require many more lines of code to create a similar definition of Pascal in Pascal.

The ability to easily write meta-interpreters for a language has certain theoretical advantages. For example, McCarthy wrote a simple LISP meta-interpreter as part of a proof that the language is Turing complete (McCarthy 1960). From a more practical standpoint, we can use meta-interpreters to extend or modify the semantics of the underlying language to better fit our application. This is the programming methodology of *metalinguistic abstraction*: the creation of a higher-level language that is more appropriate to solving a given problem.

For example, we may wish to modify the standard PROLOG semantics so that it will ask the user about the truth value of any goal that does not succeed in the knowledge base. We can do so by adding the following rules to the solve definition:

```
solve(A) :- askuser(A).

askuser(A) :- writelist([A, '? Enter true if the goal is true, false otherwise']),
              read(true).
```

We add this definition of solve to the end of the other solve definitions. It is called if all of these fail and invokes askuser to query the user for the truth value of the goal

A. askuser prints the goal and instructions for answering. The read(true) goal attempts to match the user's input with the term true, failing if the user enters false. In this way, we have changed the semantics of solve to extend the basic behavior of PROLOG.

Another extension to the meta-interpreter would allow it to respond to why queries. When the interpreter asks the user a question, the user can respond with why and be given the current rule that the program is trying to solve. We can add this to the meta-interpreter by storing the stack of rules in the current line of reasoning as the second paramenter to solve. Whenever solve calls clause to backward chain on a rule, that rule is placed on the rule stack. Thus, the rule stack records the chain of rules from the top level goal to the current subgoal. The predicate, askuser, is modified to call respond, which either succeeds if the user entered true or prints the top rule on the stack in response to a why query. This meta-interpreter is defined by:

```
solve(true,_) :-!.
solve(not A,Rules) :- not(solve(A),Rules).
solve((A,B),Rules) :- solve(A,Rules), solve(B,Rules).
solve(A,Rules) :- clause(A,B), solve (B,[(A:-B)|Rules]).
solve(A,Rules) :- askuser(A,Rules).

askuser(A,Rules) :- writelist([A,'enter true if goal is true, false otherwise'])
    read(Answer),
    respond(Answer,A,Rules).

respond(true,_,_).
respond(why,A,[Rule|Rules) :- write(Rule), askuser(A,Rules).
respond(why,A,[ ]) :- askuser(A,Rules)
```

Another modification to the basic solve predicate provides the ability to respond to how queries. Explanations of how an inferencing system was able to reach a certain conclusion are generally cast as proof trees; we may modify the pure PROLOG interpreter to build proof trees as it solves a goal. The proof tree is returned in the second parameter of the solve predicate. In solving a conjunction of goals, A and B, we simply conjoin the proof trees for each goal (Proof A,ProofB). In solving a goal A using a rule A :- B, we construct the proof of B and return the structure (A :-ProofB). The definition of a meta-interpreter that constructs proof trees is given by:

```
solve(true, true) :-!.
solve(not A, not ProofA) :- not(solve(A, ProofA)).
solve((A,B),(ProofA,ProofB)) :- solve(A,Proof A), solve(B,ProofB).
solve(A,(A :- ProofB)) :- clause(A,B), solve(B,ProofB).
solve(A,(A:-given)) :- askuser(A).
askuser(A) :- write([A,'t or f']), read(true).
```

In Section 12.2.1 we use this methodology to implement an expert system shell that includes certainty factors, how and why queries, disjunctive goals, working memory to store user responses, and a richer user interface. This program is essentially a combination of the techniques just presented. We urge the reader to implement and study these simple programs as a preparation for understanding the full expert system shell. Although this program, exshell, is much more complex than the PROLOG meta-interpreter, it is really an extension of this basic methodology. Its heart is just a solve predicate that implements a back chaining search of rules and facts.

12.2.1 Shell for a Rule-Based Expert System

In this section we present the key predicates used in the design of an interpreter for a goal-driven rule-based expert system. Although we present only the major components of the definition, the remaining predicates are straightforward. The full code for the meta-interpreter, called exshell, is presented in Appendix 1.1. A trace of an exshell consultation appears at the end of this section (Fig. 12.2 and following). This consultation uses an automotive diagnostic knowledge base that appears in Appendix 1.2. If the reader would prefer to read through this trace before examining exshell's key predicates, we encourage looking ahead.

An exshell knowledge base consists of rules, advice, and specifications of queries that can be made to the user. Rules are represented using a two-parameter rule predicate of the form rule((G :- P), CF). The first parameter is the actual rule. It is written using standard PROLOG syntax. G is the head of the rule and P is the conjunctive or disjunctive pattern under which G is true. CF is the confidence the designer has in the rule's conclusions. An example rule from a knowledge base for diagnosing automotive failures is:

```
rule((bad_component(starter) :-
        bad_system(starter_system), lights(come_on)), 50).
```

This rule states that if the bad system is shown to be the starter system and the lights come on, then conclude that the bad component is the starter, with a certainty of 50.

Because we do not want the interpreter to ask for every unsolved goal, we allow the programmer to specify exactly what information is obtainable from the user. We also give the interpreter request strings that are used when particular information is needed. We do this with the two-argument askable predicate. The first argument is the query string and the second is the goal under consideration. For example:

```
askable(['Does the car start'], car_starts).
```

specifies that the interpreter may ask the user for the truth of the car_starts goal when nothing is known or can be concluded about that goal and gives the string to be used in that query.

In attempting to satisfy a goal G, solve first tries to match G with any facts that it already has obtained from the user. If this fails, solve tries any rules whose head matches G. If this fails, solve then checks if this information is askable of the user; if G is askable, the meta-interpreter generates the appropriate query.

The third component of the knowledge is a set of **advice** specifications. Advice predicates take two arguments, a diagnosis and a string representing the advice to the user. This allows the programmer to specify the program's output in a friendlier form than PROLOG syntax. The knowledge base should include one advice specification for each conclusion. For example, the advice specification for the conclusion **bad_component(starter)** is:

```
advice(fix(starter), ['Replace starter.']).
```

In addition to the programmer-defined knowledge base of rules, askables, and advice, **exshell** maintains its own record of case-specific data. Since the shell asks the user for information, it needs to remember what it has been told. This prevents the program from asking the same question twice during a consultation (decidedly unexpert behavior).

When it encounters a goal that it cannot solve with its knowledge base, **exshell** presents that goal to the user. The user can respond to the query with either **true**, **false**, **unknown**, **yes**, or **no**. exshell assigns the goal a CF of either 100, -100, or 0 for the first three responses. If the response is **yes** or **no**, **exshell** asks the user to specify a confidence, within the range, for their answer.

exshell saves user responses by asserting them into the global data base. We represent facts using the two-parameter **fact(A,CF)** predicate. A represents the fact, e.g., **car_starts** or **gas_in_carb**, and CF represents the user's confidence in this information. CFs range from +100, a fact that is true, to -100, something that is known to be false. If the CF is around 0, the truth value is unknown. **exshell** implements the certainty algebra of MYCIN, presented in Chapter 8.

The heart of the **exshell** meta-interpreter is the set of **solve** predicates. The first of these is the one-argument **solve(Goal)** that takes the top-level goal from the user and calls the full set of **solve** predicates. Before doing this, it calls **retractall(fact(X,C))** to clean up any residual information saved in the previous use of **exshell**. It then calls **setof** to bind a list of all the possible solutions of the top level goal to the variable **Solution**. If **Solution** does not equal the empty list, it prints out the answers, along with their certainty factors. If it finds no solution, it tells the user and quits.

setof(Pattern, Bindings_for_pattern, List_of_pattern) has three arguments. **Pattern** is a template for the entities that are collected, without repetition, in the third argument **List_of_pattern**. The bindings for each new **Pattern** are made from repeated calls to the goals that make up the second parameter of **setof**. We define **solve(Goal)** as:

```
solve(Goal) :-
    retractall(fact(X,C)), nl,
    ((setof((Goal, Advice, C, Proof),
            (solve(Goal,C,[],Proof,1,yes), advice(Goal, Advice)),
            Solution),
    not(Solution==[]),
    print_solution(Solution));
    (nl, write('Sorry, I cannot give advice on the information given.'), nl)).
```

The actual solution of the goal is done by a six-parameter version of solve: solve(Goal, CF, Rulestack, Proof, T, Ask). Goal and CF are the current goal and its attached certainty factor. Rulestack is the stack of rules used in establishing the Goal and is used to respond to why queries. The stack represents the series of rules leading from the top-level goal to the present query. Repeated popping of this stack gives why explanations going back up to the initial goal.

Proof is the full proof tree; it contains every aspect of the proof information produced to the present state in the graph search. Proof is generated by the solve predicate and is passed to printsolution to document the full line of reasoning in a successful solution. These proof trees are also used to answer how queries.

Finally, T and Ask are flags that give important information about the present status of solve. T tells whether we are trying to prove the present Goal true (1) or false (-1). In solving goals of the form not p, we need to prove that p is false rather than true. This requires a different treatment of certainty factors in pruning such goals.

Ask tells whether exshell can go to the user for information (yes) or not (no).

The first solve rule tests whether Goal matches one of the fact relations stored in case-specific data; i.e., it checks to see if the user has already answered the query. It then calls above_threshold to check that the confidence level is above the cutoff. To accept a goal as true, it must have a certainty factor greater than 20. If we are trying to prove the goal false (T = -1), its certainty factor must be less than -20. When the rule succeeds, it records the proof as (A :- given, C); that is, A is known because it was given by the user.

```
solve(A, C, Rules, (A :- given, C), T, Ask) :-
    fact(A,C), !, above_threshold(C,T).
```

The second solve predicate considers the goal not A by changing the T parameter to its opposite value and calling solve for A. If it proves A to be false (with a certainty of less than -20), it computes the certainty of not A and succeeds. solve records the proof of not A as (not Proof) where Proof is the proof of A.

```
solve(not A, C, Rules, (not Proof, C), T, Ask) :- !,
    T1 is -1 * T,
    solve(A, C1, Rules, Proof, T1, Ask),
    C is -1 * C1.
```

The next two solve predicates consider the conjunction of two positive goals (A,B), where B may be bound to a further conjunction of goals.

If we are trying to prove A and B true (the fifth parameter equals 1), we call solve for A. If this succeeds, then we call solve for B. The certainty factor for the conjunction of these goals is the minimum of their certainties. If we wish to prove the conjunction of goals false, the second solve rule (using de Morgan's law) attempts to prove the or of the not of the goals. The final line ensures that at least one of the alternatives succeeds (in being not true). In either case, the proof tree for the c onjunction of goals is the conjunction of the proof trees for the individual goals.

```
solve((A,B), C, Rules, (ProofA, ProofB), 1, Ask) :- !,
    solve(A, C1, Rules, ProofA, 1, Ask), above_threshold(C1,1),
    solve(B, C2, Rules, ProofB, 1, Ask), above_threshold(C2,1),
    minimum(C1,C2,C).

solve((A,B), C, Rules, (ProofA, ProofB), -1, Ask) :- !,
    (solve(not A, C1, Rules, (not ProofA, _), 1, Ask);
    solve(not A, C1, Rules, (not ProofA, _), -1, no);
    (C1 is -100, ProofA = (A :- or_true, 100))         ), !,
    (solve(not B, C2, Rules, (not ProofB, _), 1, Ask);
    solve(not B, C2, Rules, (not ProofB, _), -1, no);
    (C2 is -100, ProofB = (B :- or_true, 100))         ), !,
    maximum(C1,C2,C3), C is -1 * C3, above_threshold(C,-1).
```

The next two **solve** predicates handle the disjunction of two goals, also using de Morgan's relationships.

```
solve((A;B), C, Rules, (ProofA; ProofB), 1, Ask) :- !,
    (solve(A, C1, Rules, ProofA, 1, Ask);
    solve(A, C1, Rules, ProofA, -1, no);
    (C1 is -100, ProofA = (A :- or_fail, C1)) ), !,
    (solve(B, C2, Rules, ProofB, 1, Ask);
    solve(B, C2, Rules, ProofB, -1, no);
    (C2 is -100, ProofB = (B :- or_fail, C2)) ), !,
    maximum(C1,C2,C), above_threshold(C,1).

solve((A;B), C, Rules, (ProofA; ProofB), -1, Ask) :- !,
    solve((not A, not B), C1, Rules, ((not ProofA, _), (not ProofB, _)), 1, Ask),
    C is -1 * C1, above_threshold(C,-1).
```

The previous versions of **solve** handle goals that are already known negations, conjunctions, and disjunctions. If all of these fail, **solve** goes to the knowledge base and attempts to find rules that match the goal. If there is more than one rule that concludes a given goal, we must combine their certainty factors using the MYCIN algebra presented in Chapter 8. This is done by calculate_C using a list of all solutions.

solve calls **solve_rule** to collect (using **bagof**) the list of all the proofs, with their certainty factors, (Proof, C1), for establishing goal **A**. **solve_rule** handles the actual backward chaining of each rule. Note that **solve_rule** recursively calls **solve** to handle the premise for each matching rule. **solve-rule** retrieves the rule from the knowledge base with rule((A :- B), C1). When it does so, it adds the new rule to the rule stack.

```
solve(A, C, Rules, (A :- rules, C, List), T, Ask) :-
    bagof((Proof, C1), solve_rule(A, C1, Rules, (A :- Proof), T, Ask), List),
    not(List==[]), calculate_C(List, C).
```

```
solve_rule(A, C, Rules, (A :- Proof), T, Ask) :-
    rule((A :- B), C1),
    above_threshold(C1,T),
    solve(B, C2, [rule(A,B,C1)|Rules], Proof, 1, Ask),
    C is (C1 * C2) / 100,
    above_threshold(C,T).

solve_rule(A, C, Rules, (A :- true), T, Ask) :-
    rule((A), C),
    above_threshold(C,T).
```

The next solve predicate goes to the user when all previous attempts at solve have failed for goal A, Ask has value yes, and the goal is not already known. known(X) succeeds if there is no fact(X,_) in the data base. solve then calls query to present the goal to the user.

```
solve(A, C, Rules, (A :- given, C), T, yes) :-
    askable(Prompt, A), !,
    not known(A),
    query(Prompt, A, C, Rules, normal),
    above_threshold(C,T).
```

The final solve rule is called to verify that the goal is false if no rules are available to prove it true. This is our attempt to address the *closed world assumption* and is done only with user approval.

```
solve(A, C, Rules, (A :- fail, C), -1, yes) :-
    not (bagof((Proof, C1), solve_rule(A, C1, Rules, (A :- Proof)), _, Ask,List),
    not(List==[])),
    not known(A),
    query(['There are no facts or rules that allow me to solve for:', nl,
        '  ', A, nl, 'May I assume it to be false'], A, C, Rules, assume),
    above_threshold(C,-1).
```

The final two important tasks of exshell are to respond to why and how queries. Note that the second to the last solve predicate, using query, is the only time exshell goes to the user. query prints a prompt, using askable (already described), and receives an answer with the get_answer predicate. Note that query is recursive and can go back to the user again depending on the response.

```
query(Prompt, A, C, Rules, normal) :-
    get_answer(Prompt, Answer),
    respond(Answer, A, C, Rules, Newrules),
    ( member(Answer, [true, false, yes, no, unknown]);
    query(Prompt, A, C, Newrules, normal)  ), !.
```

The user may respond to the query in a number of ways, including a help request. help invokes the print_help predicate, which shows the possible user responses.

```
print_help :-
    nl,
    write('Exshell allows the following responses to queries:'), nl, nl,
    write('   true    --- query is known to be 100% true'), nl,
    write('   false   --- query is known to be 100% false'), nl,
    write('   yes     --- query is known to be partially true'), nl,
    write('              User must input a certainty factor.'), nl,
    write('   no      --- query is known to be partially false'), nl,
    write('              User must input a certainty factor.'), nl,
    write('   unknown --- query is unknown'), nl,
    write('   why     --- displays rule currently under consideration'), nl,
    write('   how(X)  --- if X has been inferred, displays reasoning'), nl,
    write('   help    --- prints this message'), nl,
    write('   All (except help) may be abbreviated to first letter'), nl,nl.
```

respond handles the user's responses. This includes storing the good response with
its attached certainty as a fact in case-specific data. This is done when the user enters
true, false, yes, no, or unknown.

```
respond(true, A, 100, _, _) :-
    assert(fact(A,100) ).

respond(false, A, -100, _, _) :-
    assert(fact(A,-100) ).

respond(yes, A, C, _, _) :-
    get_answer(['What confidence'], C),
    assert(fact(A,C) ).

respond(no, A, C, _, _) :-
    get_answer(['What confidence'], C1),
    C is -1 * C1,
    assert(fact(A,C) ).

respond(unknown, A, 0, _, _) :-
    assert(fact(A,0) ).
```

respond(why,...) presents the top rule in the rule stack as its response to the why
query. This is the current rule that exshell is trying to satisfy. display_rule (defined in
Appendix 1.1) prints the rule in a more readable format. Repeated requests for why go
back up the search path from the current state until the top goal is reached. At this time
the rule stack is empty and no further explanation is possible. (See the trace that follows.)

```
respond(why, A, C, [Rule|Rules], Rules) :-
    display_rule(Rule, unknown).

respond(why, A, C, [], []) :-
    write('Back to goal, no more explanation possible.'), nl, nl.
```

Finally, respond(how(Goal), . . .) uses the respond_how(Goal) predicate to generate the proof tree for Goal. It calls solve with user queries disabled to build the proof tree for Goal and interpret(Proof) to print the proof tree in a readable format. The definition of interpret appears in Appendix 1.1. solve first tries to prove Goal true (1), then false (-1). Note that in this case the final parameter of solve is no, indicating that exshell must already possess all information necessary for a how response. When this is not the case, the final respond_how so indicates.

```
respond_how(Goal) :-
    solve(Goal, C, [], Proof, 1, no),
    interpret(Proof), !.

respond_how(Goal) :-
    solve(Goal, C, [], Proof, -1, no),
    interpret(Proof), !.

respond_how(Goal) :-
    write('Goal does not follow at this stage of consultation.'), nl, nl.
```

We now present a sample run of exshell on a knowledge base cars (Appendix 1.1). cars implements a simple automotive diagnostic expert system. The session is started with the query solve(fix_car(X)). Note the response to why and how queries. The graph searched by exshell in this example is presented in Figure 12.2, with bold lines giving the subgraph that represents the solution.

```
% prolog
C-PROLOG version 1.5
yes
?- [exshell,cars].
exshell consulted 13676 bytes 5.05 sec.
cars consulted 1752 bytes 0.666669 sec.
yes

?- solve(fix(X)).
Does the car start? yes.
What confidence? .75.
Does the car run rough? true.
Is there gas in the carburetor? why.
IF      car_starts    ***Known, Certainty = 75
    AND    runs(rough)    ***Known, Certainty = 100
        AND gas_in_carb
THEN   bad_system(ignition_system)
CF    80
Is there gas in the carburetor? why.
IF      bad_system(ignition_system)
    AND NOT tuned_recently
THEN   bad_component(timing)
CF    80
Is there gas in the carburetor? yes.
What confidence? 75.
```

Does the car run dies? true.
Has the car been tuned recently? false.
Are the spark plugs dirty? yes.
What confidence? 80.

My advice is:
  replace spark plugs
Certainty of this advice is 70.2.

Trace of reasoning to goal? y.
fix(plugs), with CF = 70.2,
was proved using the rule(s):
IF   bad_component(plugs)   ***Known, Certainty = 70.2
THEN fix(plugs)   ***Known, Certainty = 70.2
CF   100
bad_component(plugs), with CF = 70.2,
was proved using the rule(s):
IF   bad_system(ignition_system)   ***Known, Certainty = 78
    AND plugs(dirty)   ***Known, Certainty = 80
THEN bad_component(plugs)   ***Known, Certainty = 70.2
CF   90
bad_system(ignition_system), with CF = 78,
was proved using the rule(s):
IF   car_starts   ***Known, Certainty = 75
    AND   runs(rough)   ***Known, Certainty = 100
        AND gas_in_carb   ***Known, Certainty = 75
THEN bad_system(ignition_system)   ***Known, Certainty = 60
CF   80
car_starts was given with CF = 75.
runs(rough) was given with CF = 100.
gas_in_carb was given with CF = 75.
IF   car_starts   ***Known, Certainty = 75
    AND   runs(dies)   ***Known, Certainty = 100
        AND gas_in_carb   ***Known, Certainty = 75
THEN bad_system(ignition_system)   ***Known, Certainty = 45
CF   60
car_starts was given with CF = 75.
runs(dies) was given with CF = 100.
gas_in_carb was given with CF = 75.
plugs(dirty) was given with CF = 80.

My advice is:
  get the timing adjusted
Certainty of this advice is 62.4.

Trace of reasoning to goal? y.
fix(timing), with CF = 62.4,
was proved using the rule(s):
IF   bad_component(timing)   ***Known, Certainty = 62.4
THEN fix(timing)   ***Known, Certainty = 62.4

```
CF     100
bad_component(timing), with CF = 62.4,
was proved using the rule(s):
IF      bad_system(ignition_system)      ***Known, Certainty = 78
    AND NOT tuned_recently      ***Known, Uncertainty = -100
THEN  bad_component(timing)      ***Known, Certainty = 62.4
CF     80
bad_system(ignition_system), with CF = 78,
was proved using the rule(s):
IF      car_starts      ***Known, Certainty = 75
    AND    runs(rough)      ***Known, Certainty = 100
        AND gas_in_carb      ***Known, Certainty = 75
THEN   bad_system(ignition_system)      ***Known, Certainty = 60
CF     80
car_starts was given with CF = 75.
runs(rough) was given with CF = 100.
gas_in_carb was given with CF = 75.
IF      car_starts      ***Known, Certainty = 75
    AND    runs(dies)      ***Known, Certainty = 100
        AND gas_in_carb      ***Known, Certainty = 75
THEN   bad_system(ignition_system)      ***Known, Certainty = 45
CF     60
car_starts was given with CF = 75.
runs(dies) was given with CF = 100.
gas_in_carb was given with CF = 75.
not (tuned_recently), with CF = 100,
was proved by proving (tuned_recently), with CF = -100.
tuned_recently was given with CF = -100.
```

The full exshell code, plus the rule base for automobile diagnosis, is presented in Appendix 1.1. The student is encouraged to augment this knowledge base and/or build further knowledge bases appropriate for exshell.

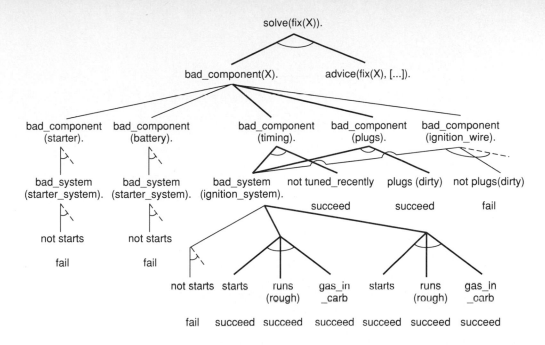

Figure 12.2 Graph searched in automotive diagnostic consultation. Dashed lines indicate branches pruned from consideration; bold lines indicate final solutions.

12.2.2 Semantic Nets in PROLOG

In this section, we discuss the implementation of inheritance for a simple semantic network language (Chapter 9). While our language lacks the full power and generality of a language like conceptual graphs, it allows us to demonstrate the implementation of inheritance in a network representation.

In the semantic net of Figure 12.3, nodes represent individuals such as the canary tweety, classes such as ostrich, crow, or robin, and superclasses such as bird or vertebrate. isa links represent the class hierarchy relationship.

For representational clarity and consistency as well as for ease in building search procedures, we adopt canonical forms for the data relationships within the net. We use

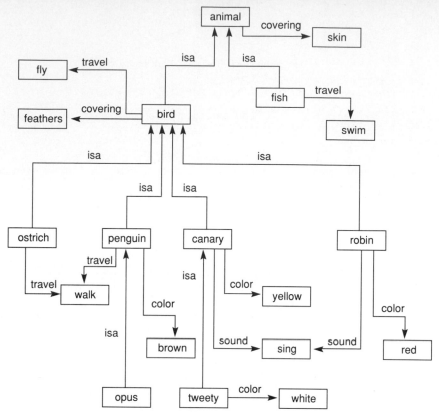

Figure 12.3 Portion of a semantic network describing birds and other animals.

an isa(Type, Supertype) predicate to indicate that Type is a member of Supertype and a hasprop(Entity, Property, Value) predicate to represent each link. hasprop indicates that Entity has Property with Value. Entity and Value are nodes in the network, Property is the name of the link that joins them. A partial list of the predicates necessary to describe the semantic network of Figure 12.3 includes:

isa(canary, bird).   isa(robin, bird).
isa(ostrich, bird).   isa(penguin, bird).
isa(bird, animal).   isa(fish, animal).
isa(opus, penguin).   isa(tweety, canary).
hasprop(tweety, color, white).   hasprop(robin, color, red).
hasprop(canary, color, yellow).   hasprop(penguin, color, brown).
hasprop(bird, travel, fly).   hasprop(fish, travel, swim).
hasprop(ostrich, travel, walk).   hasprop(penguin, travel, walk).
hasprop(robin, sound, sing).   hasprop(canary, sound, sing).
hasprop(bird, cover, feathers).   hasprop(animal, cover, skin).

We create a recursive search algorithm to find whether an entity in our semantic net has a particular property. Properties are located in the net at the most general level at which they are true. Through inheritance, an individual or subclass acquires the properties of its superclasses. Thus the property fly holds for bird and all its subclasses. Exceptions are located at the specific level of the exception. Thus ostrich and penguin travel by walking instead of flying. The hasproperty predicate begins search at a particular object. If the information is not directly attached to that object, hasproperty follows isa links to superclasses. If no more superclasses exist, and hasproperty has not located the property, it fails.

```
hasproperty(Entity, Property, Value) :-
    hasprop(Entity, Property, Value).

hasproperty(Entity, Property, Value) :-
    isa(Entity, Supentity),
    hasproperty(Supentity, Property, Value).
```

hasproperty searches the inheritance hierarchy in a depth-first fashion. Note also that this definition only implements tree inheritance; i.e., each node has only a single parent. In the next section, we show how inheritance can be applied to a frame-based representation and implement both tree and multiple-inheritance relations.

12.2.3 Frames and Schemata in PROLOG

Semantic nets can be partitioned, with additional information added to node descriptions, to give them a frame structure. We redefine the bird example of the previous subsection using frames, where each frame represents a collection of relationships of the semantic net and the isa slots of the frame define the frame hierarchy (Fig. 12.4).

The first slot of each frame names the node, for example, name(tweety) or name(vertebrate). The second slot gives the inheritance links between the node and its parents. Since our example has a tree structure, each node will have only one link, the isa predicate with one argument. The third slot in the node's frame is a list of features that describe that node. In this list we use any PROLOG predicate such as flies, feathers, or color(brown). The final slot in the frame is the list of exceptions and default values for the node, again either a single word or predicate indicating a property.

Each frame organizes its slot names into lists of properties and default values. This allows us to distinguish these different types of knowledge and give them different behaviors in the inheritance hierarchy. Although our implementation allows subclasses to inherit properties from both lists, other representations are possible and may be useful in certain applications. We may wish to specify that only default values are inherited. Or we may wish to build a third list containing the properties of the class itself rather than the members, sometimes called *class values*. For example, we may wish to state that the class canary names a species of songbird. This should not be inherited by subclasses or instances: tweety does not name a species of songbird. Students are asked to define and build different frame representations and inheritance schemes in the exercises.

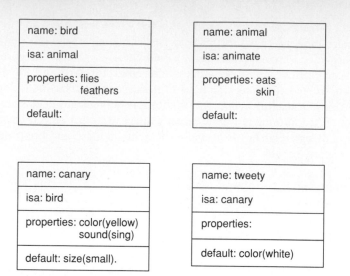

name: bird		name: animal
isa: animal		isa: animate

properties: flies
            feathers
		properties: eats
		            skin

default:		default:

name: canary		name: tweety
isa: bird		isa: canary
properties: color(yellow) sound(sing)		properties:
default: size(small).		default: color(white)

Figure 12.4 Frames from a knowledge base of birds.

We now represent the relationships in Figure 12.4 with the PROLOG fact predicate frame with four arguments. We may use the methods suggested in Section 12.1.2 to check the parameters of the frame predicate for appropriate type, for instance, to ensure that the third frame slot is a list that contains only values from a fixed list of properties.

```
frame(name(bird),
    isa(animal),
    [travel(flies), feathers],
    [color(brown)]).

frame(name(penguin),
    isa(bird),
    [color(brown)],
    [travel(walks)]).

frame(name(canary),
    isa(bird),
    [color(yellow), call(sing)],
    [size(small)]).

frame(name(tweety),
    isa(canary),
    [],
    [color(white)]).
```

Once the full set of descriptions and inheritance relationships are defined for the frame of Figure 12.4, we create procedures to infer properties from this representation:

```
get(Prop, Object) :-
    frame(name(Object), _, List_of_properties, _),
    member(Prop, List_of_properties).

get(Prop, Object) :-
    frame(name(Object), _, _, List_of_defaults),
    member(Prop, List_of_defaults).

get(Prop, Object) :-
    frame(name(Object), isa(Parent), _, _),
    get(Prop, Parent).
```

If the frame structure allows multiple inheritance of properties (Section 9.5), we make this change both in our representation and in our search strategy. First, in the frame representation we make the argument of the isa predicate the list of superclasses of the Object. Thus, each superclass in the list is a parent of the entity named in the first argument of frame. If opus is a penguin and a cartoon_char (Fig. 9.27), we can represent this by:

```
frame(name(opus),
    isa([penguin, cartoon_char]),
    [color(black)],
    []).
```

Now, we test for properties of opus by recurring up the isa hierarchy for both penguin and cartoon_char. We add the additional solve definition between the third and fourth get predicates of the previous example.

```
get(Prop, Object) :-
    frame(name(Object), isa(List), _, _),
    get_multiple(Prop, List).
```

We define get_multiple by:

```
get_multiple(Prop, [Parent|_]):-
    get(Prop, Parent).

get_multiple(Prop, [_|Rest]):-
    get_multiple(Prop, Rest).
```

With this inheritance preference, properties of penguin and its superclasses will be examined before those of cartoon_char.

Finally, any PROLOG procedure may be attached to a frame slot. As we have built the frame representation in our examples, this would entail making a PROLOG rule, or list of PROLOG rules, be a parameter of frame. This is accomplished by enclosing the entire rule in parentheses, as we did for rules in exshell, and making this structure an argument of the frame predicate. For example, we could design a list of response rules for opus, giving him different responses for different questions. This list of rules, each rule in parentheses, would then become a parameter of the frame and, depending on the value of X passed to the opus frame, would define the appropriate response. More complex examples could be rules describing the control of a thermostat or creating a graphic image appropriate to a set of values. These examples are presented in Chapter 14, where attached procedures, often called *methods*, play an important role in object-oriented representations.

12.2.4 Natural Language Understanding in PROLOG

Because of its built-in search and pattern matching, PROLOG easily accommodates natural language processing. We can write natural language grammars directly in PROLOG, as we saw with both the context-free and context-sensitive grammars of Section 6.3. Semantic representations are also easy to create in PROLOG. Semantic relationships can be built either directly using the first-order predicate calculus or by constructing a meta-interpreter for another representation language, as suggested by the frame system of the previous section. Finally, semantic inference (for instance join, restrict, and inheritance in conceptual graphs) can be done directly in PROLOG or with inference procedures built on top of PROLOG.

Conceptual graphs are an example of such an approach. As we saw in Chapter 9, conceptual graphs can be translated directly into predicate calculus and hence into PROLOG. The conceptual relation nodes become the predicate name, and the arity of the relation is the number of arguments of the predicate. Each PROLOG predicate, as with each conceptual graph, represents a single proposition. The conceptual graphs of Figure 9.11 may be rendered in PROLOG as:

```
bird(X), flies(X).

dog(X), color (X,Y), brown(Y).

child(X), parents(X,Y, Z), father(Y), mother(Z).
```

where X, Y, and Z are bound to the appropriate individuals. Type information can be added to parameters as indicated in Section 12.1.2. We can also define the type hierarchy through a variation of isa predicates.

Case frames (Chapter 10) are also easily defined in PROLOG. For instance, we could define an instance of the verb give that requires a subject, object, and indirect object using the case frame:

```
case_frame(give, Subject, Object, Ind_obj):-
            human (Subject),
            agent (Subject, give),
            act_of_giving (give),
            object (Object, give),
            inanimate (Object),
            recipient (Ind_obj, give),
            human (Ind_obj).
```

The right-hand side of this rule defines the constraints on the verb **give**, such as the requirement that the **agent** and **recipient** be human. It may be retrieved using a **clause** predicate as a description of the sentence's meaning. In the English sentence "John gives Mary the book," this structure takes on the obvious assignments.

We could define defaults in a case frame by binding the appropriate values. For example, we could give **bite** a default instrument of **teeth** by

```
case_frame(bite, Subject, Object, teeth):-
                animate (Subject),
                agent (Subject, Action),
                act_of_biting (Action),
                object (Object, Action),
                animate (Object),
                instrument (teeth, Action),
                part_of (teeth, Subject).
```

Again, type constraints (Section 12.1.2) may be used to enforce appropriate variable binding.

Logic programming offers a powerful medium for building grammars as well as representations for semantic meanings. The reader is encouraged to build some of the structures, such as context-sensitive grammars and conceptual graphs, presented in chapters 9 and 10.

12.3 PROLOG and Programming with Logic

12.3.1 Introduction

Only by understanding the implementation of a computer language can we properly guide its use, control its side effects, and have confidence in its results. In this section we describe the semantics of PROLOG. We offer two semantic models for logic programming: the usual PROLOG interpreter (Section 12.3.2) and Flat Concurrent PROLOG (Section 12.3.3).

A serious criticism of the resolution proof procedure (Section 11.2) is that it requires a totally homogeneous data base to represent the problem. When predicate calculus descriptors are reduced or transformed to clause form, important problem-solving information is left out. The omitted information is not the truth or fallacy of any part of the problem but rather the control hints or procedural descriptions on how to *use* the information. For example, a negated goal clause in a resolution format might be of the form:

$$a \vee \neg b \vee c \vee \neg d$$

where a, b, c, and d are the literals. The resolution inference mechanism applies a search strategy to deduce the empty clause. All literals are open to the strategy and the one used depends on the particular strategy selected. The strategies used to guide resolution theorem proving are weak heuristics; they do not incorporate deep knowledge of a specific problem domain.

For example, the negated goal clause in the resolution example above might be a transformation of the predicate calculus statement:

$$a \leftarrow b \wedge \neg c \wedge d$$

This can be understood as "to see if a is true go out and see if b is true and c is false and d is true." The rule was intended as a procedure for solving a and implements heuristic information specific to this use. Indeed, the subgoal b might offer the easiest way to falsify the entire predicate, so the order "try b then see if c is false then test d" could save much problem-solving time. The implicit heuristic says "test the easiest way to falsify the problem first, then if this is passed go ahead and generate the remaining (perhaps much more difficult) part of the solution." Human experts design procedures and relationships that not only are true but also contain information critical for *using* this truth. In most interesting problem-solving situations we cannot afford to ignore these heuristics (Kowalski 1979*b*).

In the next section we present Horn clauses and use their procedural interpretation as an explicit strategy that preserves this heuristic information. We then present the PROLOG interpreter as an instance of the answer extraction process on resolution refutations with Horn clauses. In the final section of this chapter, we show Flat Concurrent PROLOG as an alternative semantic model for logic programming. In Chapter 14 we use Concurrent PROLOG to create objects, methods, and messages in PROLOG.

12.3.2 Logic Programming and PROLOG

To understand the mathematical foundations of PROLOG, we first define *logic programming*. Once we have made this definition, we will add an explicit search strategy to logic programming to approximate the search strategy, sometimes referred to as the *procedural semantics*, of PROLOG. To get full PROLOG, we also discuss the use of not and the *closed world assumption*.

Consider the data base of clauses prepared for resolution refutation (Section 11.2). If we restrict this set to clauses that have at most one positive literal (zero or more negative literals), we have a clause space with some interesting properties. First, problems describable with this set of clauses preserve unsatisfiability for resolution refutations, or are refutation complete (Section 11.2). Second, an important benefit of restricting our representation to this subclass of all clauses is a very efficient search strategy for refutations: a linear input form, unit preference based, left-to-right and depth-first goal reduction (Section 11.2). With well-founded recursion (recursive calls that eventually terminate) and occurs checking, this strategy guarantees finding refutations if the clause space is unsatisfiable (van Emden and Kowalski 1976). A Horn clause contains at most one positive literal; i.e., it is of the form

$$a \vee \neg b_1 \vee \neg b_2 \vee \cdots \vee \neg b_n$$

where a and all the b_is are positive literals. To emphasize the key role of the one positive literal in resolutions, we generally write Horn clauses as implications with the positive literal as the conclusion:

$$a \leftarrow b_1 \wedge b_2 \wedge \cdots \wedge b_n$$

Before we discuss further the search strategy, we formally define this subset of clauses, called *Horn clauses*. These, together with a *nondeterministic* goal reduction strategy, are said to constitute a *logic program*.

DEFINITION

DEFINITION: LOGIC PROGRAM

A *logic program* is a set of universally quantified expressions in first-order predicate calculus of the form:

$$a \leftarrow b_1 \wedge b_2 \wedge b_3 \wedge \cdots \wedge b_n$$

The a and b_i are all positive literals, sometimes referred to as atomic goals. The a is the clause *head*, the conjunction of b_i the *body*.

These expressions are the *Horn clauses* of the first-order predicate calculus. They come in three forms: first, when the original clause has no positive literals; second, when it has no negative literals; and third, when it has one positive and one or more negative literals. These cases are 1, 2, and 3 respectively:

1. $\leftarrow b_1 \wedge b_2 \wedge \ldots \wedge b_n$
   called a *headless* clause or a set of *goals* to be tried: b_1 and b_2 and $\ldots$ and b_n.

2. $a_1 \leftarrow$
   $a_2 \leftarrow$

   .

   .

   $a_n \leftarrow$
   called the *facts*.

3. $a \leftarrow b_1 \wedge \cdots \wedge b_n$
   called a *rule* relation.

Horn clause calculus allows only the forms just presented; there may be only one literal to the left of $\leftarrow$ and this literal must be positive. All literals to the right of $\leftarrow$ are also positive.

The reduction of clauses that have at most one positive literal into Horn form requires three steps. First, select the positive literal in the clause, if there is a positive literal, and move this literal to the very left (using the commutative property of $\vee$). This single positive literal becomes the *head* of the Horn clause, as just defined. Second, change the entire clause to Horn form by the rule:

$$a \vee \neg b_1 \vee \neg b_2 \vee \cdots \vee \neg b_n \equiv a \leftarrow \neg (\neg b_1 \vee \neg b_2 \vee \cdots \vee \neg b_n)$$

Finally, use de Morgan's law to change this specification to:

$$a \leftarrow b_1 \wedge b_2 \wedge \cdots \wedge b_n$$

where the commutative property of $\wedge$ can be used to order the b_i subgoals.

It should be noted that it may not be possible to transform clauses from an arbitrary clause space to Horn form. Some clauses, for instance, $\neg p \vee \neg q$, have no Horn form. To create a Horn clause, there can be at most one positive literal in the original clause. If this criterion is not met it may be necessary to rethink the original predicate calculus specification for the problem. The payoff for Horn form representation is a very efficient refutation strategy, as we see shortly.

The computation algorithm for logic programs proceeds by nondeterministic goal reduction. At each step of the computation where there is a goal of the form:

$$\leftarrow a_1 \wedge a_2 \wedge \cdots \wedge a_n$$

the interpreter *arbitrarily* chooses some a_i for $1 \leq i \leq n$. It then *nondeterministically* chooses a clause:

$$a^1 \leftarrow b_1 \wedge b_2 \wedge \cdots \wedge b_n$$

such that the a^1 unifies with a_i with substitution ς and uses this clause to reduce the goal. The new goal then becomes:

$$(a_1 \wedge \cdots \wedge a_{i-1}, b_1 \wedge b_2 \wedge \cdots \wedge b_n \wedge a_{i+1} \wedge \cdots \wedge a_n)\varsigma$$

This process continues until the computation terminates with the goal set empty.

If we eliminate the nondeterminism by imposing an order on the reduction of subgoals, we do not change the result of the computation. All results that can be found nondeterministically can be found through an exhaustive ordered search. However, by reducing the amount of nondeterminism, we can define strategies that prune unnecessary branches from the space. Thus, a major concern of practical logic programming languages is to provide the programmer with facilities to control and, when possible, reduce the amount of nondeterminism. These facilities allow the programmer to influence both the order in which the goals are reduced and the set of clauses that are used to reduce each goal.

The abstract specification of a logic program has a very clean semantics, that of the resolution refutation system. It can be shown (van Emden 1976) that the smallest interpretation on which a logic program is true is *the* interpretation of the program. The price paid by practical programming languages (such as PROLOG) for control is that programs executed by these interpreters may compute only a subset of their associated interpretations (Shapiro 1987).

Sequential PROLOG is an approximation to an interpreter for the logic programming model, designed for efficient execution on von Neumann computers. This is the interpreter that we have used so far in this text. Sequential PROLOG uses both the order of goals in a clause and the order of clauses in the program to control the search for a proof. When a number of goals are available, PROLOG always pursues them left to right. In the search for a unifiable clause on a goal, the possible clauses are checked in the order they are presented by the programmer. When each selection is made, a backtracking pointer is placed with the recorded unification that allows other clauses to be used (again, in the programmer's order) should the original selection of a unifiable clause fail. If this attempt fails across all possible clauses in the clause space, then the computation fails.

More formally, given a goal:

$$\leftarrow a_1 \wedge a_2 \wedge a_3 \cdots \wedge a_n$$

and a program P, the PROLOG interpreter sequentially searches for the first clause in P whose head unifies with a_1. This clause is then used to reduce the goals. If:

$$a^1 \leftarrow b_1 \wedge b_2 \wedge \cdots \wedge b_n$$

is the reducing clause with ξ the unification, the goal clause then becomes:

$$(b_1 \wedge b_2 \wedge \cdots \wedge b_n \wedge a_2 \wedge a_3 \wedge \cdots \wedge a_n)\xi$$

The PROLOG interpreter then continues by trying to reduce the leftmost goal, b_1 in this example, using the first clause in the program P that unifies with b_1. Suppose it is:

$$b^1 \leftarrow c_1 \wedge c_2 \wedge \cdots \wedge c_p$$

under unification ϕ. The goal then becomes:

$$(c_1 \wedge c_2 \wedge \cdots \wedge c_p \wedge b_2 \wedge \cdots \wedge b_n \wedge a_2 \wedge a_3 \wedge \cdots \wedge a_n)\xi \phi$$

Note that the goal list is treated as a **stack** enforcing depth first search. If the PROLOG interpreter ever fails to find a unification that solves a goal it then backtracks to its most recent unification choice point, restores all bindings made since that choice point, and chooses the next clause that will unify (by the order in P). In this way, PROLOG implements its left-to-right, depth-first search of the clause space.

If the goal is reduced to the null clause ($\square$) then the composition of unifications that made the reductions:

$$(\square)\xi \phi \cdots \omega$$

(here $\xi \phi \cdots \omega$), provides an interpretation under which the original goal clause was true.

Besides backtracking on the order of clauses in a program, sequential PROLOG allows the *cut* or "!." As described in Chapter 6, a cut may be placed in a clause as a goal itself. The interpreter, when encountering the cut, is committed to the current execution path and in particular to that subset of unifications made since the choice of the clause containing the cut. It also commits the interpreter to the choice of that clause itself as the only method for reducing the goal. Should failure be encountered within the clause after the cut, the entire clause fails.

Procedurally, the cut makes it unnecessary to retain backtrack pointers for the reducing clause and all its components *before* the cut. Thus, cut can mean that only some of the possible interpretations of the model are ever computed.

We would like to summarize our discussion of sequential PROLOG by comparing it to the resolution refutation model of Section 11.2.

1. The resolution clause space is a superset of the set of Horn clause expressions in logic programming. Each clause must have at most one positive literal to be in Horn form.

2. The following structures represent the problem in Horn form:

   a. The facts

   $$a_2 \leftarrow$$
   .
   .
   $$a_n \leftarrow$$

   are each separate clauses for resolution.

   b. The goals

   $$\leftarrow a_1 \wedge a_2 \wedge \cdots \wedge a_n$$

   are a list of clause statements that make up the goals to be tested by resolution refutation. Each a_i is in turn negated, unified with, and reduced until the empty clause is found (if this is possible). Finally,

   c. The Horn clause rules or axioms,

   $$a \leftarrow b_1 \wedge b_2 \wedge \cdots \wedge b_n$$

   allow us to reduce matching subgoals.

3. With a *unit preference, linear input form* strategy (always preferring fact clauses and using the negated goal and its descendant resolvents; see Section 11.2), and a left-to-right, depth-first (with backtracking) order for selecting clauses for resolutions, the resolution theorem prover is acting as a PROLOG interpreter. Since this strategy is complete, it guarantees that the solution will be found (provided that part of the interpretation was not pruned away by using cut).

4. Finally, the composition of unifications in the proof provides the answer (interpretation) for which the goal is true. This is exactly equivalent to the answer extraction process of Section 11.2.4. Recording the composition of unifications in the goal literal produces each answer interpretation.

An important issue with current PROLOG interpreters is the *closed world* assumption implicit in their implementation. In predicate calculus, the proof of $\neg\,p(X)$ is exactly the proof that $p(X)$ is logically false. That is, $p(X)$ is false under every interpretation that makes the axiom set true. The PROLOG interpreter, based on the unification algorithm of Chapter 2, offers a more restricted result than the general resolution refutation of Section 11.2. Rather than trying all interpretations, it examines only those explicit in the data base. We now axiomatize these constraints to see exactly the restrictions implicit in PROLOG.

For every predicate p, and every variable X belonging to p, suppose $a_1, a_2, \ldots, a_n$ make up the domain of X. The PROLOG interpreter, using unification, enforces:

1. The *unique name* axiom. For all atoms of the domain $a_i \not\equiv a_j$ unless they are identical. This implies that atoms with distinct names are distinct.

2. The *closed world* axiom.

$$p(X) \rightarrow p(a_1) \vee p(a_2) \vee \cdots \vee p(a_n)$$

This means the only possible instances of a relation are those implied by the clauses present in the problem specification.

3. The *domain closure* axiom.

$$(X = a_1) \vee (X = a_2) \vee \cdots \vee (X = a_n).$$

This guarantees that the atoms occurring in the problem specification constitute all and the only atoms.

These three axioms are implicit in the action of the PROLOG interpreter. They may be seen as added to the set of Horn clauses making up a problem description and thus as constraining the set of possible interpretations to a PROLOG query.

Intuitively, this means that PROLOG assumes as false all goals that it cannot prove to be true. This can introduce anomalies: if a goal's truth value is actually unknown to the current data base, PROLOG will assume it to be false.

There are other limitations implicit in PROLOG, as there seem to be in all computing languages. The most important of these, besides the problem of negation as failure, represent violations of the semantic model for logic programming. In particular, there are the lack of an occurs check (see chapters 2 and 6; this allows a clause to unify with a subset of itself) and the use of cut. The current generation of PROLOG interpreters should be looked at pragmatically. Some problems arise because "no efficient way is currently known" to get around the issue (the occurs check); others arise from attempts to optimize use of the depth-first with backtrack search (the cut).

Many of the anomalies of PROLOG are a result of trying to implement the non-deterministic semantics of pure logic programming on a sequential computer. This includes the problems introduced by the cut. In the next section we present another model for logic programming, Concurrent PROLOG. By defining goal reduction in terms of multiple concurrent processes, the semantics of concurrent PROLOG are closer to the nondeterministic model of pure logic programming.

12.3.3 Semantics of Flat Concurrent PROLOG (E. Shapiro 1987)

The abstract computation model for logic programs (Section 12.3.1) suggests that they are open to parallel execution. A logic program, as we have seen, is the construction of a proof of a goal statement from axioms that describe the problem. The search space for such a program may be described as an and/or graph where the and nodes correspond to the conjunction of a number of goals that may indeed be checked in parallel and the or node corresponds to the different ways to reduce a goal using the axioms (the disjunctive possibilities) of the program, which may also be tested in parallel.

As we have seen, the nondeterministic model of a logic program interpreter is assumed to make the correct and/or selections on the search graph and can thus prune the tree in arbitrary order. The sequential PROLOG interpreter traces and/or trees in depth-first, left-to-right order: the ands of several alternatives are evaluated in program order (depth first) with backtracking. However, other strategies are possible for this search. Concurrent PROLOG assumes that an independent process is assigned to solve each branch of the and/or graph.

Two forms of execution occur in traversing this and/or graph in parallel: *and parallelism*, where the conjunction of goal reductions is done in parallel, and *or parallelism*, where the alternatives for each goal reduction are attempted in parallel. In and parallelism, variables may be shared by several children of an and node; the processes attempting to reduce these goals are not independent and thus may interfere with each other by producing solutions that are not compatible. Noncompatible solutions are two or more solutions (instantiations) of a single variable that are not unifiable. Thus, there is a need to coordinate the computations of and parallel processes. Process synchronization is accomplished through the shared variable with the *read-only* commitment.

Logic programming provides both a declarative and a procedural interpretation of clauses. For the Horn clause

$$a \leftarrow b_1 \wedge b_2 \wedge \cdots \wedge b_m$$

the declarative reading says a is true if b_1 and b_2 and ... and b_m are true. The procedural reading says a can be accomplished by doing b_1 and then b_2 and then ... b_m. The concurrent PROLOG model proposes a third or *behavioral interpretation* of clause reduction: A process a can replace itself by the system of processes that contain b_1 and b_2 and ... b_m. A process terminates by replacing itself with the empty clause. Thus, each of the b_j is an object. State is shown by the variable bindings of each of these predicates (Shapiro 1987).

In the procedural reading of logic clauses, unification provides the mechanism for parameter passing, variable binding, and data access. In the behavioral analysis, unification is the mechanism for sending, receiving, and coordinating the actions of different messages.

To synchronize this process communication, we introduce *read-only* variables. When variables are created as read only, the process suspends until that variable, and every reduction using it, is presented with a bound (nonvariable) value. The variable X is annotated read only in our examples by X?. In the behavioral analysis of the logic clause, as a clause reduces itself to other clauses, variables shared with other clauses (processes) may be instantiated by the unification of that process with the head of the reducing process and thus achieve the effect of process communication.

The second addition of concurrent PROLOG is the *guarded clause* or *commit* operator used to synchronize or parallel execution. A concurrent PROLOG program is made up of a set of guarded clauses or universally quantified axioms of the form:

$$a \leftarrow g_1 \wedge g_2 \wedge \cdots \wedge g_n : b_1 \wedge b_2 \wedge \cdots \wedge b_m \quad m, n \; > = 0$$

The b_i and the g_i are atomic formulas. a is the clause head, the conjunction of the g_i is the guard, and the b_j make up the clause body. The symbol : is the commit operator; when $n = 0$ (for g_n), this operator may be omitted. This model for logic programming is called *flat* because none of the g_i are allowed to be recursive (Shapiro 1987).

The semantics of the : (guard) goal in reducing a process A using clause a above is to unify A with a, reduce the g_i to the empty clause, commit to that clause, and reduce a to the conjunction of the b_j. Each step is taken only if the previous step succeeds; the reduction of clause a may suspend or fail during any of these steps. The unification of the process against the head of the clause suspends if it requires the binding of (unbound) read-only variables in a; it also fails if A and a are not unifiable. The computation of the guard suspends if any of its processes suspend and fails if any of them fail.

Besides allowing the possibility of the or parallel execution of all clauses whose head is a, the guard clause is an attempt to clean up the semantics of the cut. Like the cut, it means that only some of the possible semantic interpretations of the logic programming model are ever computed. Once the guard is satisfied, the unification interpretation is committed to that of the particular clause. The partial results by the first two steps of the reduction, the unification substitution with a and solving the constraints of the guard, are not accessible to the other processes for A's reduction. After the commit, all the other or parallel attempts to reduce A using other clauses are abandoned.

The reduction of all processes in the logic specification is attempted in parallel, as well as the search for clauses to reduce a process. There are still restrictions, however, to complete parallelism. For or parallelism, only the guards are executed in parallel. Once a guard evaluation fails, the computation of other or parallel guards is halted. For and parallelism, read-only restrictions enforce severe constraints on the order and speed of process reduction.

A final construct, the *otherwise* command, is also added to the Concurrent PRO-LOG semantics by Shapiro. Otherwise is described in Chapter 14 to implement default assignments for objects. An otherwise clause is a guard clause that succeeds only when all other parallel or guards fail.

We conclude this section with a simple example of a counter. This example is written in Concurrent PROLOG and taken from a similar example in Shapiro (1987). counter processes streams, implemented in this example as a list of arbitrary length. The stream is made up of four symbols: clear, up, down, and show. The object counter has two arguments; one is an input stream, the other its internal State. When it encounters a clear message in the stream, it resets its State to 0. When it receives an up or down message, it increments or decrements its State by 1. show writes out the current state and the empty message terminates the process. plus(X, Y, Z) suspends until two of its arguments are bound, at which time it returns the third.

counter uses several read-only variables and calls plus, which uses the guard to overcome the variable binding constraint imposed by is. This example implements both and and or parallel processes.

```
counter([clear|S], State) :- counter(S?,0).

counter([up|S], State) :-
    plus(State, 1, Newstate), counter(S?, Newstate?).

counter([down|S], State) :-
    plus(Newstate, 1, State), counter(S?, Newstate?).

counter([show|S], State) :-
    wait_write(State), counter(S?, State).

counter([], State) :- call((write('All done.'), nl)).

plus(X, Y, Z) :- integer(X?), integer(Y?) : Z is X + Y.

plus(X, Y, Z) :- integer(X?), integer(Z?) : Y is Z - X.

plus(X, Y, Z) :- integer(Y?), integer(Z?) : X is Z - Y.
```

If we call counter with the message stream

```
counter([clear,up,up,up,show,down,down,up,show,show,up,show],_).
```

we get the following trace:

```
3 2 2 3 3  All done.
```

This simple example illustrates the behavior of concurrent PROLOG and shows how its concurrent semantics simplify the implementation of streams and objects. In Chapter 14 we refer to the set of procedures counter as an object, because it can be seen as a nonterminating process (taking data from the stream), includes procedures or methods that describe its state at any time, and can communicate with other objects.

Flat Concurrent PROLOG is a model for commitment of multiple coroutining processes to the parallel reduction of a set of logic specifications. An interpreter for Concurrent PROLOG, built as a meta-interpreter in Edinburgh PROLOG by E. Shapiro (1987), is presented in Appendix 1.2.

12.4 Epilogue and References

The comments and references at the end of the first PROLOG chapter (Section 6.4) are also appropriate here. The foundations of PROLOG in theorem-proving research also make the material on resolution theorem-proving presented in Chapter 11 relevant. The semantics of logic programming and declarative specifications is addressed by a number of authors. Especially recommended are Maarten van Emden and Robert Kowalski (van Emden 1976; Kowalski 1979*b*). The closed world axioms and unique naming assumptions are also important in data base research, and discussions may be found in Reiter (1978), Levesque (1984), and Gallaire (1978). The two-volume *Concurrent Prolog: Collected Papers* edited by Ehud Shapiro (1987) offer a valuable introduction and set of example applications in concurrent execution of logic specifications.

Most PROLOG texts (Sterling and Shapiro 1986; Walker et al. 1987) treat the meta-predicates, type constraints, and difference lists as presented in Section 12.1. A more complete discussion of types, as well as suggestions for building a type checker, is presented in *A Polymophic Type System for Prolog* by Alan Mycroft and Richard O'Keefe (1984). The use of rule stacks and proof trees in the design of meta-interpreters for rule-based expert systems was suggested by Leon Sterling and Ehud Shapiro (1986).

Building AI representations such as semantic nets, frames, and objects is discussed in a number of books, especially *Knowledge Systems and Prolog* by Adrian Walker, Michael McCord, John Sowa, and Walter Wilson (1987) and *PROLOG: A Relational Language and Its Applications* by John Malpas (1987).

The PROLOG representation medium is so applicable for natural language understanding that many projects use PROLOG to model language. The first PROLOG interpreter was designed to analyze French using *metamorphosis grammars* (Colmerauer 1975). Fernando Pereira and David Warren (1980) created *definite clause grammars* (1980). Veronica Dahl (1977, 1983), Michael McCord (1982, 1986), and John Sowa (Sowa 1984; Walker et al. 1987) have all contributed to this research.

12.5 Exercises

1. Create a type check that prevents the append(nil,6,6) anomaly.

2. Is the difference list append really a linear time append? Explain.

3. Create the ''inventory supply'' data base of Section 12.1.2. Build type checks for a set of six useful queries on these data tuples.

4. Create and design a type check mechanism for the data base of Section 10.4.

5. Extend the simple definition of PROLOG in PROLOG (Section 12.2) to include or and to include cut.

6. Fill out the rules used with the exshell cars example in Appendix 1.1. You might add new subsystems such as the transmission or brakes.

7. Create a knowledge base in a new domain for exshell.

8. How would you design a data-driven shell in PROLOG? Describe your design and create the top-level solve predicates.

9. Create another example semantic network and design a hasproperty-like inference mechanism to test whether entities in the net have properties.

10. Determine two expert system application areas where tree inheritance is sufficient for simulation and property inheritance. Determine two other application areas where multiple inheritance would seem more appropriate.

11. Take the conceptual graphs used to describe the "dogs world" of Section 9.3. Translate each of the graphs used into PROLOG notation. Design PROLOG rules to the "restrict," "join," and "simplify" operations. Hint: one way to see the problem is to create a list of the propositions whose conjunction make up a graph. Then operations on the graphs become manipulations of the lists.

12. Implement a frame system with inheritance that allows us to define three kinds of slots: properties of a class that may be inherited by subclasses, properties that are inherited by instances of the class but not by subclasses, and properties of the class and its subclasses that are not inherited by instances (class properties in Section 12.2.3). Discuss the benefits, uses, and problems with this distinction.

13. Build in PROLOG the ATN parser of Section 10.2.4. Add who and what questions.

14. Build in PROLOG the relational data base and the English language query mechanisms described in Section 10.4.2.

15. Expand your program for Exercise 14 so that it will answer questions of the form "How much does Don Morrison earn?" and "List all employees that earn more than their managers."

16. Write an object/process specification in Concurrent PROLOG that counts and prints out all odd integers from a stream of integers.

17. Use Concurrent PROLOG to create a stack process. For instance, let stack have two arguments: the first the input stream, the second the stack. pop would be: stack([pop(X)|S], [X|Xs]) :- stack(S?, Xs).

18. Implement counter in sequential PROLOG. Compare the two programs.

13

ADVANCED LISP PROGRAMMING TECHNIQUES FOR ARTIFICIAL INTELLIGENCE

All our knowledge is symbolic.

—GOETHE, *Table Talk*

See simplicity in the complicated.

—LAO TZU

13.0 Introduction: Abstraction and Complexity

In discussing AI programming techniques in LISP, we have emphasized the implementation of AI algorithms using list-based data structures and a functional programming style. A goal of this chapter is to discuss general techniques for managing the complexity of large programs, particularly large AI programs. Abstraction, the organization of a program in terms of increasingly general, higher-level conceptual structures, is the basis of all of these techniques. Abstraction allows the programmer to organize a program in terms appropriate to the problem being solved, rather than at the level of programming language or machine-specific detail.

We continue to use the techniques of procedural and data abstraction introduced in Chapter 7 and introduce two other approaches to program design: *metalinguistic abstraction* and *stream processing*.

Metalinguistic abstraction, the implementation of a higher-level, specialized problem-solving language, is illustrated in programs including a simple logic programming interpreter, an inheritance algorithm for a network representation, and an expert system shell supporting both uncertain reasoning and user queries for missing information.

Many problems may naturally be thought of in terms of the flow of data through a series of operations and filters. We can formalize this data-oriented view of program structure in terms of data structures called *streams*. A stream is a sequence of data elements. The program acts on data streams using maps and filters to produce a stream of solutions. Both the simple logic programming implementation and the more complex expert system shell are based on this stream-oriented view.

While many problems lend themselves to a stream processing point of view, others are naturally thought of as collections of distinct objects and relations. We introduce this approach in the implementation of a semantic network interpreter with inheritance. Chapter 14 further develops this paradigm in the discussion of object-oriented programming. Object-oriented programming is a model for software development that has proved useful as both an implementation tool and a knowledge representation technique.

Finally, the chapter summarizes the ''LISP programming paradigm.'' It provides an overview of the language and its related programming techniques from its origins in purely functional programming to current LISP implementations encompassing the full range of modern programming methods.

13.1 Logic Programming in LISP

As an example of metalinguistic abstraction, we develop a LISP-based logic programming interpreter, using the unification algorithm from Chapter 7. As in PROLOG, our logic programs consist of a data base of facts and rules in the predicate calculus. The interpreter processes queries (or goals) by unifying them against entries in the logical data base. If a goal unifies with a simple fact, it succeeds; the solution is the set of bindings generated in the match. If it matches the head of a rule, the interpreter recursively attempts to satisfy the rule premise in a depth-first fashion, using the bindings generated in matching the head. On success, the interpreter prints the original goal, with variables replaced by the solution bindings.

This interpreter supports only conjunctive goals and implications; or and not are not defined. Features such as arithmetic, I/O, or the usual PROLOG built-in predicates are not supported. Although we do not implement full PROLOG and the exhaustive nature of the search and absence of the *cut* prevent the proper treatment of recursive predicates, the shell captures the behavior of logic programming languages. The addition of such features to the basic interpreter is an interesting and valuable exercise.

13.1.1 A Simple Logic Programming Language

Our logic programming interpreter supports Horn clauses (Section 12.3), a subset of full predicate calculus. Well-formed formulas consist of propositions, conjunctive expressions, and rules written in a LISP-oriented syntax.

A proposition is written as a list in which the first element is a predicate name and the remaining elements are the arguments. Arguments may be either constants, variables, or other propositions. As in the discussion of unify, we represent variables as lists of two elements, the word var followed by the name of the variable. Examples of propositions include:

```
(likes bill music)
(on block (var x))
(friend bill (father robert))
```

A conjunctive expression is a list whose first element is and and whose subsequent arguments are either propositions or conjunctive expressions:

```
(and (smaller david sarah) (smaller peter david))
(and (likes (var x) (var y)) (likes (var z) (var y)))
(and (hand-empty) (and (on block-1 block-2) (on block-2 table)))
```

Implications are expressed in a syntactically sweetened form that simplifies both their writing and recognition. Rules have the form:

```
(rule if <premise> then <conclusion>)
```

where *<premise>* is either a simple or conjunctive proposition and *<conclusion>* is always a simple proposition. Examples of rules include:

```
(rule if (and (likes (var x) (var z))
              (likes (var y) (var z))
          then (friend (var x) (var y))

(rule if (and (size (var x) small)
              (color (var x) red)
              (smell (var x) fragrant))
          then (kind (var x) rose))
```

The logical data base is a list of facts and rules bound to a global variable, *assertions*. We can define an example knowledge base by a call to setq.

```
(setq *assertions* '(
        (likes george beer)
        (likes george kate)
        (likes george kids)
        (likes bill kids)
        (likes bill music)
        (likes bill pizza)
        (likes bill wine)

        (rule
          if (and (likes (var x) (var y))
                  (likes (var y) (var z)))
          then (friend (var x) (var y)))))
```

The top level of the interpreter is a function, logic-shell, that reads in goals and attempts to satisfy them against the logic data base bound to *assertions*. Given the above data base, logic-shell will have the following behavior (comments are added in italics):

```
> (logic-shell)          logic-shell prompts with a ?

?(likes bill (var x))    successful queries are printed with appropriate substitutions
(likes bill kids)
(likes bill music)
(likes bill pizza)
(likes bill wine)

?(likes george kate)
(likes george kate)

?(likes george taxes)    failed query returns nothing

?(friend bill george)
(friend bill george)     from (and(likes bill kids)(likes george kids))

?(friend bill roy)       roy does not exist in knowledge base, query fails

?(friend bill (var x))
(friend bill george)     from (and(likes bill kids)(likes george kids))
(friend bill bill)       from (and(likes bill kids)(likes bill kids))
(friend bill bill)       from (and(likes bill music)(likes bill music))
(friend bill bill)       from (and(likes bill pizza)(likes bill pizza))
(friend bill bill)       from (and(likes bill wine)(likes bill wine))

?quit
bye
>
```

Before discussing the implementation of the logic programming interpreter, we introduce the *stream* data type.

13.1.2   Streams and Stream Processing

As the preceding example suggests, even a small knowledge base can produce complex behaviors. It is necessary not only to determine the truth or falsity of a goal but also to determine the variable substitutions that make that goal true in the knowledge base. A single goal can match with different facts, producing several different substitution sets; conjunctions of goals require not only that all conjuncts succeed but also that the variable bindings be consistent throughout. Similarly, rules require that the substitutions formed in matching a goal with a rule conclusion be made in the rule premise when it is solved. The management of these multiple substitution sets is the major source of complexity in the interpreter. Streams help us to address this complexity by focusing on the movement of sequences of variable substitutions through the constraints defined by the logical data base.

A *stream* is a sequence of data objects. Perhaps the most common example of stream processing is a typical interactive program. The data from the keyboard are viewed as an endless sequence of characters, the program is organized around reading and processing the *next* character from the input stream. Stream processing is a generalization of this idea: streams need not be produced by the user; they may also be generated and modified by functions. A *generator* is a function that produces a stream of data objects. A *map* applies some function to each of the elements of a stream. A *filter* eliminates selected elements of a stream according to some predicate.

The solutions returned by an inference engine may be represented as a stream of different variable substitutions under which a goal follows from a knowledge base. The constraints defined by the knowledge base are used to modify and filter a stream of candidate substitutions, producing this result.

Consider the conjunctive goal

```
(and (likes bill (var z))
     (likes george (var z)))
```

using the logical data base from the preceding section. The stream-oriented view regards each of the conjuncts in the expression as a *filter* for a stream of substitution sets. Each set of variable substitutions in the stream is applied to the conjunct and the result is matched against the knowledge base. If the match fails, that set of substitutions is eliminated from the stream; if it succeeds, the match may create new sets of substitutions by adding new bindings to the original substitution set.

Figure 13.1 illustrates the stream of substitutions passing through this conjunctive goal. It begins with a stream of candidate substitutions containing only the empty substitution set and grows after the first proposition matches against multiple entries in the data base. It then shrinks to a single substitution set as the second conjunct eliminates substitutions that do not allow (likes george (var z)) to succeed. The resulting stream, ((((var z) . kids))), contains the only variable substitution that allows both subgoals in the conjunction to succeed in the knowledge base.

As this example illustrates, a goal and a single set of substitutions may generate several new substitution sets, one for each match in the knowledge base. Alternatively, a goal will eliminate a substitution set from the stream if no match is found. The stream of substitution sets may grow and shrink as it passes through a series of conjuncts.

The basis of stream processing is a set of functions to create, augment, and access the elements of a stream. We can define a simple set of stream functions using lists and variations of the standard list manipulators. The functions that constitute a list-based implementation of the stream data type are:

```
; Cons-stream adds a new first element to a stream
(defun cons-stream (element stream)
   (cons element stream))
```

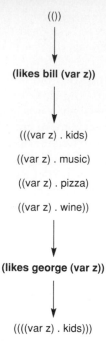

(())

(likes bill (var z))

(((var z) . kids)

((var z) . music)

((var z) . pizza)

((var z) . wine))

(likes george (var z))

((((var z) . kids)))

Figure 13.1   Stream of variable substitutions filtered
through conjunctive subgoals.

```
; head-stream returns the first element of the stream
(defun head-stream (stream) (car stream))
; tail-stream returns the stream with the first element deleted
(defun tail-stream (stream) (cdr stream))
; empty-stream-p is true if the stream is empty
(defun empty-stream-p (stream) (null stream))
; make-empty-stream creates an empty stream
(defun make-empty-stream () nil)
; combine-stream appends two streams
(defun combine-streams (stream1 stream2)
  (cond ((empty-stream-p stream 1) stream 2)
        (t (cons-stream (head-stream stream 1)
              (combine-streams
                    (tail-stream stream1)
                    (stream 2)))))
```

Although the implementation of streams as lists does not allow the full power of
stream-based abstraction, the definition of a stream data type helps us to view the program from a data flow point of view. In Section 13.2 we discuss some limitations of this
list-based implementation of streams and present an alternative approach.

13.1.3 A Stream-Based Logic Programming Interpreter

We invoke the interpreter through a function called logic-shell, a straightforward variation of the read-eval-print loop discussed in Chapter 7. After printing a prompt, "?," it
reads the next s-expression entered by the user and binds it to the symbol goal. If goal
is equal to quit, the function halts; otherwise, it calls solve to generate a stream of substitution sets that satisfy the goal. This stream is passed to print-solutions, which prints
the goal with these different substitutions. The function then recurs. logic-shell is
defined by:

```
(defun logic-shell ()
  (print '? )
  (let ((goal (read)))
    (cond ((equal goal 'quit) 'bye)
          (t (print-solutions goal (solve goal nil))
             (terpri)
             (logic-shell)))))
```

solve is the heart of the interpreter. solve takes a goal and a set of substitutions
and finds all solutions that are consistent with the knowledge base. These solutions are
returned as a stream of substitution sets; if there are no matches, solve returns the empty
stream. From the stream processing point of view, solve is a *source* or *generator* for a
stream of solutions. solve is defined:

```
(defun solve (goal substitutions)
        (cond ((conjunctive-goal-p goal)
                  (filter-through-conj-goals
                        (body goal)
                        (cons-stream substitutions (make-empty-stream))))
              (t (infer goal substitutions *assertions*))))
```

solve first tests if the goal is a conjunction; if it is, solve calls filter-through-conj-
goals to perform the filtering described in Section 13.1.2. If goal is not a conjunction,
solve assumes it is a simple goal and calls infer to solve it against the knowledge base.

solve calls filter-through-conj-goals with the body of the conjunction (i.e., the
sequence of conjuncts with the and operator removed) and a stream that contains only
the initial substitution set. The result is a stream of substitutions representing all of the
solutions for this goal. We define filter-through-conj-goals by:

```
(defun filter-through-conj-goals (goals substitution-stream)
        (cond ((null goals) substitution-stream)
              (t (filter-through-conj-goals (cdr goals)
                        (filter-through-goal (car goals) substitution-stream)))))
```

If the list of goals is empty, the function halts, returning substitution stream
unchanged. Otherwise, it calls filter-through-goal to filter substitution-stream through

the first goal on the list. It passes this result on to a recursive call to filter-through-conj-goals with the remainder of the goal list. Thus, the stream is passed through the goals one at a time, growing or shrinking as it passes through each goal.

filter-through-goal takes a single goal and uses that goal as a filter to the stream of substitutions. This filtering is done by calling solve with the goal and the first set in the substitution stream. The result of this call to solve is a stream of substitutions resulting from matches of the goal against the knowledge base. This stream will be empty if the goal does not succeed under any of the substitutions contained in the stream, or it may contain multiple substitution sets representing alternative bindings. This stream is combined with the result of filtering the tail of the input stream through the same goal:

```
(defun filter-through-goal (goal substitution-stream)
    (cond ((empty-stream-p substitution-stream) (make-empty-stream))
          (t (combine-streams (solve goal (head-stream substitution-stream))
                              (filter-through-goal goal (tail-stream substitution-stream))))))
```

To summarize, filter-through-conj-goals passes the stream through a sequence of goals, and filter-through-goal filters the substitution stream through a single goal. A recursive call to solve solves the goal under each substitution set.

While solve handles conjunctive goals by calling filter-through-conj-goals, simple goals are handled by the function infer, which takes a goal and a substitution set and finds all solutions in the knowledge base. infer's third parameter, kb, is a data base of logical expressions. When solve first calls infer, it passes the knowledge base contained in the global variable *assertions*. infer searches kb sequentially, trying the goal against each fact or rule conclusion. We define infer:

```
(defun infer (goal substitutions kb)
    (cond ((null kb) (make-empty-stream))
          (t (let ((assertion (rename-variables (car kb))))
               (combine-streams
                   (cond ((rulep assertion) (use-rule goal assertion substitutions))
                         (t (use-fact goal assertion substitutions)))
                   (infer goal substitutions (cdr kb)))))))
```

The recursive implementation first checks if kb is empty, returning an empty stream if it is. Otherwise, the first item in kb is bound to the symbol assertion in a let block. If assertion is a rule, it calls use-rule to solve the rule premise recursively. Since a rule may lead to success under more than one possible binding set, the results of use-rule are returned as a stream. If assertion is not a rule, it is treated as a fact; use-fact attempts to unify the goal with the assertion using the bindings in substitutions. Although use-fact can return at most one set of bindings, it returns them in stream form. Combine-stream joins this solution stream to that returned by calling infer on the rest of the knowledge base.

Before the first element of kb is bound to assertion, it is passed to rename-variables to give each variable a unique name. This prevents name conflicts between the variables in the goal and those in the knowledge base entry; e.g., if (var x) appears in a goal, it must be treated as a different variable than a (var x) that appears in the rule or fact. The simplest way to handle this is by renaming all variables in the assertion with unique names. We define rename-variables at the end of this section.

use-rule attempts to infer a goal from a rule if the goal matches the rule conclusion, initiating backward chaining on the rule premise. use-rule first unifies goal with the head of the rule and saves the resulting substitutions in new-substitutions. If this unification fails, use-rule returns the empty stream. Otherwise, it calls solve on the rule premise under the substitutions contained in new-substitutions.

```
(defun use-rule (goal rule substitutions)
  (let ((new-substitutions (unify goal (conclusion rule) substitutions)))
    (cond ((equal new-substitutions 'failed) (make-empty-stream))
          (t (solve (premise rule) new-substitutions)))))
```

use-fact tries to unify a goal with a fact under the given substitutions. If this fails, it returns the empty stream; otherwise it returns a stream containing the new substitution set. Note that unlike use-rule or filter-through-goal, use-fact does not call solve recursively. This function terminates the recursive search of the knowledge base.

```
(defun use-fact (goal fact substitutions)
  (let ((new-substitutions (unify goal fact substitutions)))
    (cond ((equal new-substitutions 'failed) (make-empty-stream))
          (t (cons-stream new-substitutions (make-empty-stream))))))
```

This completes the implementation of the core of the logic programming interpreter. All that remain are a number of straightforward functions for accessing components of knowledge base entries, managing variable substitutions, and printing solutions.

print-solutions takes as arguments a goal and a stream of substitutions. For each set of substitutions in the stream, it prints the goal with variables replaced by their bindings in the substitution set.

```
(defun print-solutions (goal substitution-stream)
  (cond ((empty-stream-p substitution-stream) nil)
        (t (print (apply-substitutions goal (head-stream substitution-stream)))
           (terpri)
           (print-solutions goal (tail-stream substitution-stream)))))
```

The replacement of variables with their values under a substitution set is done by apply-substitutions, which does a car-cdr recursive tree walk on a pattern. If the pattern is a constant, it is returned unchanged. If it is a variable, apply-substitutions tests if it is bound. If it is unbound, the variable is returned; if it is bound, apply-substitutions calls itself recursively on the value of this binding. Thus, the binding value may be either a constant, another variable, or a pattern of arbitrary complexity.

```
(defun apply-substitutions (pattern substitution-list)
  (cond ((is-constant-p pattern) pattern)
        ((varp pattern)
         (let ((binding (get-binding pattern substitution-list)))
           (cond (binding (apply-substitutions (binding-value binding) substitution-list))
                 (t pattern))))
        (t (cons (apply-substitutions (car pattern) substitution-list)
                 (apply-substitutions (cdr pattern) substitution-list)))))
```

infer renamed the variables in each knowledge base entry before matching it with a goal. This is necessary to prevent undesired name collisions in matches. For example, the goal (p a (var x)) should match with the knowledge base entry (p (var x) b), since the scope of each (var x) is restricted to a single expression. As unification is defined, however, this match will not occur. Name collisions are prevented by giving each variable in an expression a unique name. The basis of our renaming scheme is a Common LISP built-in function called gensym that takes no arguments; each time it is called, it returns a unique symbol consisting of a five-digit number preceded by the letter g. For example:

```
> (gensym)
g00004
> (gensym)
g00005
> (gensym)
g00006
>
```

Our renaming scheme replaces each variable name with the result of a call to gensym. rename-variables performs certain initializations (described below) and calls rename-rec to make substitutions recursively in the pattern. When a variable is encountered, the function rename is called to return a new name. Each time a variable is renamed, the new name is placed in an association list bound to the *special* variable *name-list*. The special declaration makes all references to the variable dynamic and shared among these functions. Thus, each access of *name-list* in rename will access the instance of *name-list* declared in rename-variables. Saving names allows multiple occurrences of a variable in a pattern to be given consistent names. rename-variables initializes *name-list* to nil when it is first called. These functions are defined:

```
(defun rename-variables (assertion)
  (declare (special *name-list*))
  (setq *name-list* nil)
  (rename-rec assertion))

(defun rename-rec (exp)
    (declare (special *name-list*))
    (cond ((is-constant-p exp) exp)
          ((varp exp) (rename exp))
          (t (cons (rename-rec (car exp))(rename-rec (cdr exp))))))
```

```
(defun rename (var)
   (declare (special *name-list*))
   (list 'var (or (cdr (assoc var *name-list* :test #'equal))
          (let ((name (gensym)))
            (setq *name-list* (acons var name *name-list*))name))))
```

The remaining functions required for the implementation are concerned with accessing components of rules and goals and are self-explanatory:

```
(defun premise (rule) (nth 2 rule))
```

```
(defun conclusion (rule) (nth 4 rule))
```

```
(defun rulep (pattern)
   (and (listp pattern)
      (equal (nth 0 pattern) 'rule)))
```

```
(defun conjunctive-goal-p (goal)
   (and (listp goal)
      (equal (car goal) 'and)))
```

```
(defun body (goal) (cdr goal))
```

13.2 Streams and Delayed Evaluation

As we demonstrated in the implementation of logic-shell, a stream-oriented view can help with the organization of a complex program. However, our implementation of streams as lists did not provide the full benefit of stream processing. In particular, this implementation suffers from inefficiency and an inability to handle infinitely long data streams.

In the list implementation of streams, all of the elements must be computed before that stream (list) can be passed on to the next function. In logic-shell this leads to an exhaustive search of the knowledge base for each intermediate goal in the solution process. In order to produce the first solution to the top-level goal, the program must produce a list of all solutions. If we want only the first solution on this list, the program must still search the entire space. It would be preferable if the program produced the first solution by searching only that portion of the space needed to produce that goal and delayed finding the rest of the solutions until they were needed.

A second problem is the inability to process infinitely long streams. While this problem does not arise in logic-shell, it occurs naturally in the stream-based solution to many problems. Assume, for example, that we would like to write a function that returns a stream of the first n odd Fibonacci numbers. A straightforward implementation would use a generator to produce a stream of Fibonacci numbers, a filter to eliminate even-valued numbers from the stream, and an accumulator to gather these into a solution list of n elements (Fig. 13.2). Unfortunately, the stream of Fibonacci numbers is infinite in length and we cannot decide in advance how long a list will be needed to produce the first n odd numbers.

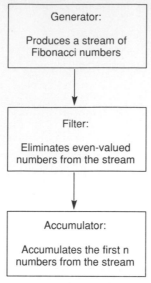

Figure 13.2 Stream implementation of a program to find the first **n** odd Fibonacci numbers.

Instead, we would like the generator to produce the stream of Fibonacci numbers one at a time and pass each number through the filter until the accumulator has gathered n values. This behavior more closely fits our intuitive notion of a stream than does the list-based implementation. We may accomplish this through the use of *delayed evaluation*.

Instead of letting the generator run to completion to produce the entire stream of results, we let the function produce the first element of the stream and then freeze or delay its execution until the next element is needed. When the program needs the next element of the stream, it causes the function to resume execution and produce only that element and again delay evaluation of the rest of the stream. Thus, instead of containing the entire list of numbers, the stream consists of just two components, its first element and the frozen computation of the rest of the stream (Fig. 13.3).

The heart of this implementation of streams is a pair of functions, delay and force. delay takes an expression as argument and does not evaluate it; instead it takes the unevaluated argument and returns a *closure*. A closure consists of a function along with all of its current variable bindings. The "frozen" evaluation described above is a closure. We construct the closure by first making the expression the body of a lambda expression and then using the Common LISP built-in function to construct the closure. force takes a function closure as argument and uses funcall to force its evaluation. These functions are defined:

```
(defmacro delay (exp) '(function (lambda () ,exp)))

(defun force (function-closure) (funcall function-closure))
```

A list-based stream containing an indeterminate number of elements:

$$(e_1 \quad e_2 \quad e_3 \quad e_4 \quad \ldots)$$

A stream with delayed evaluation of its tail containing only two elements but capable of producing any number of elements:

$(e_1$. <delayed evaluation of remainder of stream>)

Figure 13.3 List-based versus delayed evaluation implementations of streams.

delay is an example of a LISP form called a *macro*. We cannot define delay using defun because all functions so defined evaluate their arguments before executing the body. Macros give us complete control over the evaluation of their arguments. We define macros using the defmacro form. When a macro is executed, it does not evaluate its arguments. Instead, it binds the unevaluated s-expressions in the call to the formal parameters and evaluates its body *twice*.

To define the delay macro, we introduce another LISP form, the *backquote*. Backquote prevents evaluation just like a quote, except that it allows us to evaluate selectively elements of the backquoted expression. Any element of a backquoted s-expression preceded by a comma is evaluated and its value inserted into the resulting expression.

For example, assume the call (delay (plus 2 3)). The expression (plus 2 3) is not evaluated; instead it is bound to the formal parameter, exp. When the body of the macro is evaluated the first time, it returns the backquoted expression with the formal parameter, exp, replaced by its value, the unevaluated s-expression (plus 2 3). This produces the expression (function (lambda () (plus 2 3))). This is evaluated again, returning a function closure.

If we later pass this closure to force, it will evaluate the expression (lambda () (plus 2 3)). This is a function that takes no arguments and whose body evaluates to 5. Using force and delay, we can implement streams with delayed evaluation. We rewrite cons-stream as a macro that takes two arguments and conses the value of the first onto the delayed evaluation of the second. Thus, the second argument may be a function that will return a stream of any length; it is not evaluated. We define tail-stream so that it forces the evaluation of the tail of a stream. The other stream functions are not changed. These are defined:

```
(defmacro cons-stream (exp stream) '(cons ,exp (delay ,stream)))

(defun tail-stream (stream) (force (cdr stream)))
```

If we add these definitions to the versions of head-stream, make-empty-stream, empty-stream-p, and combine-streams from Section 13.1.2, we have a complete stream implementation with delayed evaluation. We include the complete set of stream-handling functions in Appendix 2.1.

We can use these functions to solve our problem of producing the first n odd Fibonacci numbers. fibonacci-stream returns a stream of all the Fibonacci numbers; note that fibonacci-stream is a nonterminating recursive function. Delayed evaluation prevents it from looping forever; it produces the next element only when needed. filter-odds takes a stream of integers and eliminates the even elements. accumulate takes a stream and a number n and returns a *list* of the first n elements of the stream.

```
(defun fibonacci-stream (fibonacci-1 fibonacci-2)
  (cons-stream (+ fibonacci-1 fibonacci-2)
               (fibonacci-stream fibonacci-2 (+ fibonacci-1 fibonacci-2))))

(defun filter-odds (stream)
  (cond ((evenp (head-stream stream)) (filter-odds (tail-stream stream)))
        (t (cons-stream (head-stream stream) (filter-odds (tail-stream stream))))))

(defun accumulate-into-list (n stream)
  (cond ((zerop n) nil)
        (t (cons (head-stream stream) (accumulate-into-list (- n 1) (tail-stream stream))))))
```

To obtain a list of the first 25 odd Fibonacci numbers, we simply evaluate:

```
(accumulate-into-list 25 (filter-odds (fibonacci-stream 0 1)))
```

We use these stream functions in the definition of the logic programming interpreter of Section 13.1 to improve program efficiency. In the next section they form the basis of a LISP-based expert system shell. Before presenting the expert system shell, however, we mention two additional stream functions that are used in its implementation: a general map and a general filter function for streams.

In Chapter 7 we presented a general mapping function and a general filter for lists. These functions, map-simple and filter, can be straightforwardly modified to function on streams. We use these functions, filter-stream and map-stream, in the next section. Their implementation is left as an exercise.

13.3 An Expert System Shell in LISP

The expert system shell developed in this section is an extension of the backward chaining engine of Section 13.2. The major modifications include the use of certainty factors to manage uncertain reasoning, the ability to ask the user for unknown facts, and the use of a working memory to save user responses. This expert system shell is called lisp-shell.

13.3.1 Implementing Certainty Factors

In the logic programming shell, a goal was proved to be either true or false under different sets of variable substitutions. A solution is a stream of substitution sets that enabled the goal to succeed against the knowledge base. Bindings that did not allow the goal to be solved against the knowledge base were either filtered from the stream or not generated in the first place. In implementing reasoning with certainty factors, however, simple truth values are replaced by a numeric value between -1 and 1, as described in Chapter 8.

This requires that the solution to a goal (the stream returned by solve) include not only the variable bindings returned by successful matches but also the certainty measure with which the goal is held to be true under those bindings. To implement this, Lisp-shell processes not just streams of substitution sets, but streams of pairs: a substitution set and a certainty factor. The certainty factor is the confidence for the *current* goal under that substitution. One way of thinking about this is to note that truth values in the logic programming shell were represented implicitly: substitutions were eliminated when a goal failed to match under those substitutions. Any substitutions remaining in the stream indicate successful matches.

We implement stream elements as an abstract data type: the functions for manipulating the substitution and certainty factor pairs are subst-record, which constructs a pair from a set of substitutions and a certainty factor; subst-list, which returns the set of bindings from a pair; and subst-cf, which returns the certainty factor. Internally, records are represented as dotted pairs, of the form (*<substitution list>* . *<cf>*). The functions that handle these pairs are:

```
; Returns the list of variable bindings from a substitution/certainty factor pair.
(defun subst-list (substitutions)
   (car substitutions))

; Returns the certainty factor from a substitution/certainty factor pair.
(defun subst-cf (substitutions)
   (cdr substitutions))

; Forms a substitution set/certainty factor pair.
(defun subst-record (substitutions cf)
   (cons substitutions cf))
```

Similarly, rules and facts are stored in the knowledge base with an attached certainty factor. Facts are represented as dotted pairs, (*<assertion>* . *<cf>*), where *<assertion>* is either a simple or conjunctive proposition and *<cf>* is its certainty measure. Rules are in the format (rule if *<premise>* then *<conclusion>* *<cf>*), where *<cf>* is the certainty factor. A sample rule is

```
(rule
   if (and (rose (var x)) (color (var x) red))
   then (kind (var x) american-beauty) 1)
```

The functions for handling rules and facts are:

```
; Returns the premise of a rule.
(defun premise (rule)
   (nth 2 rule))

; Returns the conclusion of a rule.
(defun conclusion (rule)
   (nth 4 rule))

; Returns the cf of a rule.
(defun rule-cf (rule)
   (nth 5 rule))

; Tests whether a given pattern is a rule.
(defun rulep (pattern)
   (and (listp pattern)
      (equal (nth 0 pattern) 'rule)))

; Returns the pattern part of a fact.
(defun fact-pattern (fact)
   (car fact))

; Returns the cf of a fact.
(defun fact-cf (fact)
   (cdr fact))
```

Using these functions, the balance of the rule interpreter is implemented as a modification of the logic programming interpreter (Section 13.2).

13.3.2 Architecture of lisp-shell

solve is the heart of lisp-shell. solve does not return a solution stream directly but first passes it through a filter that eliminates any substitutions whose certainty factor is less than 0.2. This prunes results that lack sufficient confidence.

```
(defun solve (goal substitutions)
   (filter-stream
      (cond ((conjunctive-goal-p goal)
               (filter-conjunctions
                        (cdr (body goal))
                        (solve (car (body goal)) substitutions)))
            (t (solve-simple-goal goal substitutions)))
   #'(lambda (x) (< 0.2 (subst-cf x)))))
```

This has changed only slightly from the definition of solve in logic-shell. It is still a conditional statement that distinguishes between conjunctive goals and simple goals. One difference is the use of the general filter filter-stream to prune all solutions whose certainty factor falls below a certain value (here, 0.2). This test is passed as a lambda expression that checks whether or not the certainty factor of a substitution set /cf pair is less than 0.2. The other major difference is the use of solve-simple-goal in place of infer. The treatment of simple goals is complicated by the ability to ask the user for information. We define solve-simple-goal as:

```
(defun solve-simple-goal (goal substitutions)
  (or (infer goal substitutions *assertions*)
      (told goal substitutions *case-specific-data*)
      (ask-for goal substitutions)))
```

solve-simple-goal uses an or form to try three different solution strategies in order. First it attempts to infer the goal using the rules in *assertions*. If this fails, it calls told to check if the goal has already been solved by the user in response to a previous query. User responses are bound to the global variable *case-specific-data*; told searches this list to try and find a match for the goal. This keeps lisp-shell from asking for the same piece of information twice. Finally, if these fail, it calls ask-for to query the user for the information. These functions are defined below.

The top-level read-solve-print loop has changed little, except for the inclusion of a statement initializing *case-specific-data* to nil before solving a new goal. Note that when solve is called initially, it is not just passed the empty substitution set, but a pair consisting of the empty substitution set and a cf of 0. This certainty value has no real meaning: it is included for syntactic reasons until a meaningful substitution set and certainty factor pair is generated by user input or a fact in the knowledge base.

```
(defun lisp-shell ()
  (setq *case-specific-data* ())
  (print '? )
  (let ((goal (read)))
    (cond ((equal goal 'quit) 'bye)
          (t (print-solutions goal (solve goal (subst-record nil  0)))
             (terpri)
             (lisp-shell)))))
```

filter-conjunctions is not changed, but filter-through-goal-conj must compute the certainty factor for a conjunctive expression as the minimum of the certainties of the conjuncts. To do so, it binds the first element of substitution-stream to the symbol subs in a let block. It then calls solve on the goal and this substitution set; the result is passed through the general mapping function, map-stream, which takes the stream of substitution pairs returned by solve and recomputes their certainty factors as the minimum of the certainty factor of the result and the certainty factor of the initial substitution set, subs. These functions are defined:

```
(defun filter-conjunctions (goals substitution-stream)
  (cond ((null goals) substitution-stream)
        (t (filter-conjunctions
             (cdr goals)
             (filter-through-goal-conj (car goals) substitution-stream)))))
```

```
(defun filter-through-goal-conj (goal substitution-stream)
  (cond ((empty-stream-p substitution-stream) (make-empty-stream))
        (t (let ((subs (head-stream substitution-stream)))
             (combine-streams
               (map-stream (solve goal subs)
                 #'(lambda (x) (subst-record
                                 (subst-list x)
                                 (min (subst-cf x) (subst-cf subs)))))
               (filter-through-goal-conj goal
                 (tail-stream substitution-stream)))))))
```

The definition of infer is unchanged, but both use-rule and use-fact are modified to take certainty factors into account. When use-fact successfully matches a goal against a fact from the knowledge base it adds the certainty factor of the knowledge base entry to the resulting substitution set. On successfully firing a rule, use-rule computes the certainty factors of the result stream as the product of the rule cf and the cf with which the rule premise was solved. These functions are defined:

```
(defun infer (goal substitutions kb)
  (cond ((null kb) (make-empty-stream))
        (t (let ((assertion (rename-variables (car kb))))
             (combine-streams
               (cond ((rulep assertion) (use-rule goal assertion substitutions))
                     (t (use-fact goal assertion substitutions)))
               (infer goal substitutions (cdr kb)))))))

(defun use-rule (goal rule substitutions)
  (let ((match (unify goal (conclusion rule) (subst-list substitutions))))
    (cond ((equal match 'failed) (make-empty-stream))
          (t (map-stream (solve (premise rule)
                           (subst-record match (subst-cf substitutions)))
               #'(lambda (x) (subst-record
                               (subst-list x)
                               (times (subst-cf x) (rule-cf rule)))))))))

(defun use-fact (goal pattern substitutions)
  (let ((match (unify goal (fact-pattern pattern) (subst-list substitutions))))
    (cond ((equal match 'failed) (make-empty-stream))
          (t (cons-stream
               (subst-record match (fact-cf pattern))
               (make-empty-stream))))))
```

Finally, **print-solutions** is modified to take certainty factors into account:

```
(defun print-solutions (goal substitution-stream)
  (cond ((empty-stream-p substitution-stream) nil)
        (t (print (apply-substitutions goal
               (subst-list (head-stream substitution-stream))))
             (write-string " cf = ")
             (print (subst-cf (head-stream substitution-stream)))
             (terpri)
             (print-solutions goal (tail-stream substitution-stream)))))
```

The remaining functions, such as **apply-substitutions** and functions for accessing components of rules and goals, are unchanged from their definition in Section 13.1.

13.3.3 User Queries and Working Memory

The remainder of **lisp-shell** consists of the functions **ask-for** and **told**, which handle user interactions. These are straightforward to implement, although the reader should note that we have made some simplifying assumptions. In particular, the only response allowed to queries is either "y" or "n." This causes the binding set passed to **ask-for** to be returned with a **cf** of either 1 or -1, respectively; the user may not give an uncertain response directly to a query. **ask-rec** prints a query and reads the answer, repeating until the answer is either y or n.

askable verifies whether the user may be asked for a particular goal. Any goal asked of the user must exist as a pattern in the global list ***askables***; the architect of an expert system may in this way determine which goals may be asked and which may only be inferred from the knowledge base. **told** searches through the entries in the global ***case-specific-data*** to find if the user has already answered a query. It is similar to **infer** except it assumes that everything in ***case-specific-data*** is stored as a fact. We define these functions:

```
(defun ask-for (goal substitutions)
  (cond ((askable goal *askables*)
         (let* ((query (apply-substitutions goal (subst-list substitutions)))
                (result (ask-rec query)))
           (setq *case-specific-data* (cons (subst-record query result)
                       *case-specific-data*))
           (cons-stream (subst-record (subst-list substitutions) result)
                 (make-empty-stream))))))
```

```
(defun ask-rec (query)
  (print query)
  (print '>)
  (let ((answer (read)))
    (cond ((equal answer 'y) 1)
          ((equal answer 'n) -1)
          (t (print "answer must be y or n")
             (terpri)
             (ask-rec query)))))

(defun askable (goal askables)
  (cond ((null askables) nil)
        ((nequal (unify goal (car askables) ()) 'failed) t)
        (t (askable goal (cdr askables)))))

(defun told (goal substitutions case-specific-data)
  (cond ((null case-specific-data) (make-empty-stream) )
        (t (combine-streams
             (use-fact goal (car case-specific-data) substitutions)
             (told goal substitutions (cdr case-specific-data))))))
```

This completes the implementation of our LISP-based expert system shell. The complete text appears in Appendix 2.3. In the next section we use lisp-shell to implement a simple classification expert system.

13.3.4 Classification Using lisp-shell

We now present a small expert system for classifying trees and bushes. Although it is far from botanically complete, it illustrates the use and behavior of the tool. The knowledge base resides in two global variables: *assertions*, which contains the rules and facts of the knowledge base, and *askables*, which lists the goals that may be asked of the user. The knowledge base used in this example is constructed by two calls to setq:

```
(setq *assertions* '(

  (rule
    if (and (size (var x) tall ) (woody (var x)))
    then (tree (var x)) .9)

  (rule
    if (and (size (var x) small ) (woody (var x)))
    then (bush (var x)) .9)

  (rule
    if (and (tree (var x)) (evergreen (var x))(color (var x) blue))
    then (kind (var x) spruce) .8)

  (rule
    if (and (tree (var x)) (evergreen (var x))(color (var x) green))
    then (kind (var x) pine) .9)
```

```
(rule
  if (and (tree (var x)) (deciduous (var x)) (bears (var x) fruit))
  then (fruit-tree (var x)) 1)

(rule
  if (and (fruit-tree (var x)) (color fruit red) (taste fruit sweet))
  then (kind (var x) apple-tree) .9)

(rule
  if (and (fruit-tree (var x)) (color fruit yellow) (taste fruit sour))
  then (kind (var x) lemon-tree) .8)

(rule
  if (and (bush (var x)) (flowering (var x)) (thorny (var x)))
  then (rose (var x)) 1)

(rule
  if (and (rose (var x)) (color (var x) red))
  then (kind (var x) american-beauty) 1)))

(setq *askables* '(
  (size (var x) (var y))
  (woody (var x))
  (soft (var x))
  (color (var x) (var y))
  (evergreen (var x))
  (thorny (var x))
  (deciduous (var x))
  (bears (var x) (var y))
  (taste (var x) (var y))
  (flowering (var x))))
```

Although any predicate may be taken as a goal, this knowledge base assumes that the top-level query is of the form (kind individual (var x)). A sample run of the trees knowledge base appears below. The reader is encouraged to trace through the rule base to observe the order in which rules are tried, the propagation of certainty factors, and the way in which possibilities are pruned when found to be false:

```
> (lisp-shell)
:(kind tree-1 (var x))
(size tree-1 tall)>y
(woody tree-1)>y
(evergreen tree-1)>y
(color tree-1 blue)>n
(color tree-1 green)>y
(deciduous tree-1)>n
(size tree-1 small)>n
(kind tree-1 pine)" cf = "0.81
```

```
:(kind bush-2 (var x))
(size bush-2 tall)>n
(size bush-2 small)>y
(woody bush-2)>y
(flowering bush-2)>y
(thorny bush-2)>y
(color bush-2 red)>y
(kind bush-2 american-beauty)" cf = "0.9

:(kind tree-3 (var x))
(size tree-3 tall)>y
(woody tree-3)>y
(evergreen tree-3)>n
(deciduous tree-3)>y
(bears tree-3 fruit)>y
(color fruit red)>n
(color fruit yellow)>y
(taste fruit sour)>y
(size tree-3 small)>n
(kind tree-3 lemon-tree)" cf = "0.72

:quit
```

In this example, several anomalies may be noted. For example, the shell occasion-ally asks if a tree is small even though it was told the tree is tall, or it asks if the tree is deciduous even though it knows the tree is an evergreen. This is typical of the behavior of expert systems. The knowledge base does not know anything about the relationship between tall and small or evergreen and deciduous: they are just patterns to be matched. Since the search is exhaustive, all rules are tried. If a system is to exhibit deeper knowledge than this, the relationships must be coded in the knowledge base. For example, a rule may be written which states that small implies not tall. In this example, lisp-shell is not capable of representing these relationships since we have not imple-mented the not operator. This extension is left as an exercise.

13.4 Network Representations and Inheritance

This section introduces the implementation of semantic networks in LISP. As a family of representations, semantic networks provide a basis for a large variety of inferences, some of which were described in Chapter 9. We do not discuss all of these, but focus on a basic approach to constructing network representations using *property lists*. After these are discussed and used to define a simple semantic network, we define a function for class inheritance.

13.4.1 Representing Semantic Nets in LISP

LISP is a convenient language for representing any graph structure, including semantic nets. Lists provide the ability to create computational objects of arbitrary complexity

Figure 13.4 A simple labeled directed graph.

and these objects may be bound to names, allowing for easy reference and the definition of relationships between objects. Indeed, all LISP data structures are based on an internal implementation as chains of pointers, a natural isomorph to graph structures.

For example, labeled graphs may be represented using association lists: each node is an entry in an association list with all the arcs out of that node stored in the datum of the node as a second association list. Arcs are described by an association list entry that has the arc name as its key and the arc destination as its datum. Using this representation, the built-in association list functions are used to find the destination of a particular arc from a given node. For example, the labeled, directed graph of Figure 13.4 is represented by the association list:

```
((a (1 . b))
 (b (2 . c))
 (c (2 . b) (3 . a)))
```

This approach is the basis of many network implementations. Another way to implement semantic networks is through the use of *property lists*.

Essentially, property lists are a built-in feature of LISP that allow named relationships to be attached to symbols. Rather than using setq to bind an association list to a symbol, property lists allow the direct attachment of named attributes to objects in the global environment. These are bound to the symbol not as a value, but as an additional component called the property list.

Functions for managing property lists are get, setf, remprop, and symbol-plist. get, which has the syntax

```
(get <symbol> <property-name>),
```

retrieves a property from a *<symbol>* by its *<property-name>*. For example, if the atom rose has a color property of red and a smell property of sweet, then get would have the behavior:

```
(get 'rose 'color)
red
(get 'rose 'smell)
sweet
(get 'rose 'party-affiliation)
nil
```

As the last of these calls to get illustrates, if an attempt is made to retrieve a nonexistent property, one that is not on the property list, get returns a value of nil.

Properties are attached to objects using the setf function, which has the syntax:

(setf <*object*> <*value*>)

setf is a generalization of setq; if the first argument to a setf is an atomic symbol, its effect is the same as a setq. If, however, the first argument is a get form, it will have the effect of changing the value of the property to the specified value. For example, the properties of a rose may be attached to the rose atom by:

```
> (setf (get 'rose 'color) 'red)
red
> (setf (get 'rose 'smell) 'sweet)
sweet
```

remprop takes as arguments a symbol and a property name and causes a named property to be deleted. For example:

```
> (get 'rose 'color)
red
> (remprop 'rose 'color)
color
> (get 'rose 'color)
nil
```

symbol-plist takes as argument a symbol and returns its property list. For example:

```
> (setf (get 'rose 'color) 'red)
red
> (setf (get 'rose 'smell) 'sweet)
sweet
> (plist 'rose)
(smell sweet color red)
```

Using property lists, it is straightforward to implement a semantic network. For example, the following calls to setf implement the semantic network description of species of birds from Figure 12.3. The isa relations define inheritance links.

```
(setf (get 'animal 'covering) 'skin)
(setf (get 'bird 'covering) 'feathers)
(setf (get 'bird 'travel) 'flies)
(setf (get 'bird 'isa) animal)
(setf (get 'fish 'isa) animal)
(setf (get 'fish 'travel) 'swim)
(setf (get 'ostrich 'isa) 'bird)
(setf (get 'ostrich 'travel) 'walk)
(setf (get 'penguin 'isa) 'bird)
(setf (get 'penguin 'travel) 'walk)
(setf (get 'penguin 'color) 'brown)
(setf (get 'opus 'isa) 'penguin)
(setf (get 'canary 'isa) 'bird)
(setf (get 'canary 'color) 'yellow)
(setf (get 'canary 'sound) 'sing)
(setf (get 'tweety 'isa) 'canary)
(setf (get 'tweety 'color) 'white)
(setf (get 'robin 'isa) 'bird)
(setf (get 'robin 'sound) 'sings)
(setf (get 'robin 'color) 'red)
```

13.4.2   Implementing Inheritance

Using this representation of semantic nets, we now define hierarchical inheritance. This is simply a search along superclass links until a parent is found with the desired property. The difficult part, as described in Chapter 9, is deciding the type of search to use, the order in which parent links are tried, and the handling of defaults and multiple inheritance. Here we take a simple approach: the parents are searched in a depth-first fashion, and search stops when an instance of the property is found. This is typical of the inheritance algorithms provided by many commercial systems. Variations on this approach include the use of breadth-first search as a search strategy.

inherit-get is a variation of get that first tries to retrieve a property from a symbol; if this fails, inherit-get calls get-from-parents to implement the search. get-from-parents takes as its first argument either a single parent or a list of parents; the second argument is a property name. If the parameter parents is nil, the search halts with failure. If parents is an atom, it calls inherit-get on the parent to either retrieve the property from the parent itself or continue the search. If parents is a list, get-from-parents calls itself recursively on the car and cdr of the list of parents. These functions are defined:

```
(defun inherit-get (object property)
  (or (get object property)
      (get-from-parents (get object 'isa) property)))

(defun get-from-parents (parents property)
  (cond ((null parents) nil)
        ((atom parents) (inherit-get parents property))
        (t (or (get-from-parents (car parents) property)
               (get-from-parents (cdr parents) property)))))
```

In Chapter 14 we introduce a LISP implementation of object-oriented programming that builds on many of the ideas presented in this section. In particular, we use an inheritance algorithm much like the one just defined to let objects inherit properties and methods from superclasses.

13.5 Epilogue and References

In discussing LISP programming techniques for AI, we have followed LISP's historical development. Chapter 7 introduced LISP as a purely functional language. That is, the behavior of a function was determined solely by the values of its input parameters. As the discussion continued, we introduced setq and property lists, both of which allow the definition of functions with side effects.

Both PROLOG and LISP are based on formal mathematical models of computation: PROLOG on logic and theorem proving, LISP on the theory of recursive functions. This sets these languages apart from more traditional languages whose architecture is just a refinement of the architecture of the underlying computing hardware. By deriving their syntax and semantics from mathematical notations, LISP and PROLOG inherit both expressive power and clarity.

However, while PROLOG, the newer of the two languages, has remained close to its theoretical roots, LISP has been extended until it is no longer a purely functional programming language. LISP is, above all, a practical programming language that has grown to support the full range of modern techniques. These include functional programming, data abstraction, stream processing, and object-oriented programming.

For example, in spite of the many advantages of functional programming, some problems are best conceptualized in terms of objects that have a state that changes over time. Simulation problems are typical of this kind of problem. Imagine trying to simulate the behavior of a steam heating system for a large building: the natural way to think of this is as a system of objects (rooms, thermostats, boilers, steam pipes, etc.) that interact to change the temperature and behavior of each other over time. This requires the ability to define objects that have a state that may be modified, a very different idea from functional programming. Chapter 14 discusses object-oriented programming as another programming model and presents a LISP implementation of object-oriented programming.

The strength of LISP, then, is that it has built up a range of modern programming techniques as extensions of its core model of functional programming. This, combined with the power of lists to create a variety of symbolic data structures, forms the basis of modern LISP programming. We hope that these chapters have helped to illustrate that style.

In designing the algorithms of this chapter, we have been influenced by Abelson and Sussman's book, *The Structure and Interpretation of Computer Programs* (1985).

13.6 Exercises

1. Rewrite print-solutions in the logic programming interpreter so that it prints the first solution and waits for a user response (such as a carriage return) before printing the second solution.

2. Modify the logic programming interpreter to handle or and not. Disjunctive expressions should succeed if at least one of the disjuncts succeeds; in processing a disjunctive expression, the interpreter should return the union of all the solutions returned by the disjuncts.

   Negation is more difficult, since a negated goal can succeed only if the goal fails. Thus, it is not possible to return any variable bindings for a negated goal. This is a result of the closed world assumption and the negation as failure rules described in Chapter 12. In adding negation to the interpreter, be aware that it will behave correctly only if given a negated goal that does not contain unbound variables.

3. Implement the general map and filter functions, map-stream and filter-stream, described in Section 13.2.

4. Rewrite the solution to the first n odd Fibonacci numbers problem so that it uses the general stream filter, filter-stream, instead of filter-odds. Modify this to return the first n even Fibonacci numbers and to return the squares of the first n Fibonacci numbers.

5. Expand the logic programming interpreter to include LISP write statements. This will allow rules to print messages directly to the user. Hint: modify solve first to examine if a goal is a write statement. If it is, evaluate the write and return a stream containing the initial substitution set.

6. Expand the logic programming language to include arithmetic comparisons, =, <, and >. Hint: As in Exercise 5, modify solve to detect these comparisons before calling infer. If an expression is a comparison, replace any variables with their values and evaluate it. If it returns nil, solve should return the empty stream; if it returns non-nil, solve should return a stream containing the initial substitution set. Assume that the expressions do not contain unbound variables.

   For a more challenging exercise, define = so that it will function like the PROLOG is operator and assign a value to an unbound variable and simply do an equality test if all elements are bound.

7. Use the logic programming interpreter with arithmetic (Exercise 6) to solve the financial advisor problem of Chapter 2.

8. Select a problem such as automotive diagnosis or classifying different species of animals and solve it using lisp-shell.

9. Expand the expert system shell of Section 13.3 to allow the user responses other than y or n. For example, we may want the user to be able to provide bindings for a goal. This may be done by changing ask-for and the related functions to let the user also enter a pattern, which is matched against the goal. If the match succeeds, ask for a certainty factor.

10. Extend lisp-shell to include not. For an example of how to treat negation using uncertain reasoning, refer to Chapter 8 or the PROLOG-based expert system shell in Chapter 12 and Appendix 1.1.

11. Many expert systems allow the programmer to use rules to define heuristic information and a frame or network representation to define the properties of objects. These are called *hybrid environments* (Chapter 14). Extend lisp-shell so that it may query a semantic network such as that defined in Section 14.4 for properties of objects. Do this by modifying solve-simple-goal to include a query to the semantic network. To simplify the problem, assume that all values in the semantic network are known with a certainty of 1.

Note that this also requires syntactic translation, as a goal of the form (color rose (var x)) must be translated into the query (inherit-get rose color). Predicates with only a single argument may be handled by storing a property of t in the network; thus, we may assert that a tree is woody by executing (setf (get 'tree 'woody) t).

12. Rewrite and expand the botanical classification system of Section 13.3.4 using the hybrid environment of Exercise 10.

13. Write an ATN parser for the subset of English discussed in Chapter 10.

14. Both logic-shell and lisp-shell implemented backward chaining on rules. Implement a forward chaining production system engine using Common LISP. This should be simpler than the interpreters presented in this chapter, since each iteration will simply add a new fact to working memory. Thus the shell will not need to handle rule chaining or backtracking explicitly. In implementing the shell, be sure to include some conflict resolution strategies such as the *recency* rule (Chapter 4) to prevent the production system from looping on the same rule.

14

OBJECTS, MESSAGES, AND HYBRID EXPERT SYSTEM DESIGN

The Medium is the Message . . .

— MARSHALL McLUHAN

14.0 Introduction

Structured representations evolved from simple semantic networks. Their evolution was shaped by the goal of creating data structures that are, in a useful manner, "the same as" or "of the same form as" the world they represent. This is the property of *homomorphism*: the representation is a "direct" image of the world it is intended to describe; it allows programmers to think about the formal representations in the knowledge base in the same terms as they think about objects in the domain.

Structured representation languages provide a tool for building *computational* objects that exhibit the structure and behavior of their *real-world* counterparts. They use multiple slots and values to represent different aspects of a domain object. Values bound to slots describe the state of the object; attached procedures (sometimes referred to as demons) model both the behavior of domain objects and their interactions with each other. Procedural attachment adds considerable expressive power to these formalisms, allowing inherently procedural descriptions to be expressed in an appropriate language and integrated into the framework of a declarative representation.

In an *object-oriented* language, everything is defined as an object or system of interacting objects. Individual objects are implemented as framelike structures whose slots contain either variables or procedural information. Procedures are expressed in an appropriate programming language, such as LISP, PROLOG, or even a rule-based expert system language. This diversity allows the programmer to select the appropriate tool for describing specific properties: a rule base for heuristic or knowledge-oriented descriptions, a procedural language for algorithms.

Relationships between objects, such as causality, and the overall problem specification (what caused X?) are implemented as *messages* between objects. In addition, objects are organized into a hierarchy of classes, allowing the inheritance of properties and procedures.

In Section 14.1 we present objects, messages, and inheritance as a general programming technique and then as a vehicle for knowledge base construction. In Section 14.2 we build a simple object-oriented programming language as a meta-interpreter in LISP and use it to simulate a heater/room/thermostat system. Section 14.3 examines the relationship of the object-oriented model to the logic-based paradigm and discusses PROLOG implementations of objects. Finally, in Section 14.4 we discuss the role of object-oriented programming in knowledge engineering and discuss the architecture of hybrid expert system environments.

14.1 Object-Oriented Knowledge Representation

14.1.1 Using Objects for Inheritance and Abstraction

The basis of object-oriented languages is the ability to define computational objects of arbitrarily complex internal structure, which may be thought of subsequently as a single entity. These computational objects are not passive data structures (such as frames); they encapsulate both state and behavior. Their behaviors are implemented as attached procedures, called *methods*. These are invoked through messages sent to the object by the user or by other objects. On receiving a message, an object executes the designated method and responds accordingly. Objects thus have characteristics of both data and programs in that they retain state variables as well as react procedurally in response to appropriate messages. They are *active* in the sense that the methods are bound to the object itself, rather than existing as separate procedures for the manipulation of a data structure.

It is the active nature of objects that distinguishes them from the structured representations discussed in Chapter 9. Although frames allow the creation of complex objects and the integration of procedural and declarative representations, they are passive data structures that must be acted on by external procedures. The execution of attached procedures requires that the procedure definition be retrieved and evaluated by some external agent. In an object-oriented language, objects execute their methods directly in response to a received message. Object-oriented programming thus provides an alternative to the traditional separation of data and procedure. This departs from traditional ways of organizing programs and further emphasizes the view of computational objects as images of their real-world referents.

The other major feature of object-oriented programming languages is the support of classes and inheritance. In a pure object-oriented system, everything is an object; all objects belong to classes. This allows inheritance of slot names, values, and methods. In addition, each class object defines *instance variables*, which must be instantiated when an individual member of that class is created. Instance objects bind these variables to all the particular information, such as size and location, that distinguishes individuals from each other. The behavior of the members of the class, or the set of all messages to which the class responds, is called the *protocol* of the class.

The remainder of this section illustrates object-oriented programming in an implementation of graphics on a computer screen. The object-oriented approach greatly helped in organizing the complex software required to support this style of interface and remains an important tool for implementing graphics interfaces. This example clearly illustrates the homomorphic relationship between an object-oriented program and the objects it is describing. Although all graphics operations are ultimately operations on pixel arrays, the object-oriented approach lets us organize the program in higher-level graphics objects, such as windows, icons, and pens.

Although the example is reminiscent of Smalltalk, we do not use Smalltalk syntax. Instead, we represent objects in a framelike notation similar to that used in Chapter 9 and describe methods in pseudocode. We have assumed that our pseudocode language is augmented with procedures message, make-object, and make-instance. message sends a message to an object, taking as arguments the name of an object, a message name, and any parameters to the message. make-object and make-instance define new objects and instances, respectively.

Suppose we wish to provide users with the ability to create and manipulate square boxes on the display screen. Figure 14.1 shows the class object, box. Instance variables for this class are location (the box location), tilt, size, color, and scribe. These are the variable names that must be bound in instances of the class. location is bound to the coordinates of the upper left-hand corner, size is the length of each side (it is square), and tilt gives the rotation (from the horizontal) of the box. color is the color of the box, and scribe is an instance of the class pens. pens are objects that allow us to draw lines on the screen. Through these variables, the class object provides a template for defining instances. Instance methods are procedures, attached to the class name, describing the behavior of instances when they receive appropriate messages. The object also includes class methods that we describe shortly.

Suppose we have defined a box, called box1, which is an instance of box with instance variable values location = (200, 200); tilt = 0; size = 20; color = black. scribe is bound to an instance of class pen. box1 inherits methods from the box class. To have this instance of the box object draw itself on the screen, we send the message:

message(box1, draw)

On receiving this message, box1 inherits the draw method from the class object and executes it with the instance variables of box1. For example, all references to location in the method refer to the value of location in the instance box1. draw first sends scribe a message to pick itself up (so no mark will be made), then sends it a message moving it to the location (200, 200). (We assume a screen or drawing surface representing the first quadrant of an X, Y coordinate system, X > 0 and Y > 0.) The pen then turns to 0 degree tilt, puts the drawing pen down to the surface, and repeats the process of going forward 20 units and turning 90 degrees four times. This produces the box1 at the desired location.

Note that everything in the example is executed by messages sent between objects. This view of everything as objects is typical of object-oriented languages. In this exam-

```
┌─────────────────────────────────────────────────┐
│ Class name: box                                 │
├─────────────────────────────────────────────────┤
│ Superclass: display object                      │
├─────────────────────────────────────────────────┤
│ Instance Variables                              │
├─────────────────────────────────────────────────┤
│   location:                                     │
│   tilt:                                         │
│   size:                                         │
│   color:                                        │
│   scribe:                                       │
├─────────────────────────────────────────────────┤
│ Instance Methods                                │
├─────────────────────────────────────────────────┤
│   draw() : begin                                │
│           message(scribe, up);                  │
│           message(scribe, move, location);      │
│           message(scribe, rotate, tilt);        │
│           message(scribe, down);                │
│           for i := 1 to 4 do begin              │
│               message(scribe, forward, size);   │
│               message(scribe, rotate, 90);      │
│             end                                 │
│          end.                                   │
├─────────────────────────────────────────────────┤
│   show(): begin                                 │
│           message(scribe, set-value, ink, color);│
│           message(self, draw);                  │
│          end.                                   │
├─────────────────────────────────────────────────┤
│   erase(): begin                                │
│           message(scribe, set-value, ink, background);│
│           message(self, draw);                  │
│          end.                                   │
├─────────────────────────────────────────────────┤
│   grow(amount): begin                           │
│           message(self, erase);                 │
│           message(self, set-value, size, size*amount);│
│           message(self, show);                  │
│          end.                                   │
├─────────────────────────────────────────────────┤
│ Class Methods                                   │
├─────────────────────────────────────────────────┤
│        . . .                                    │
└─────────────────────────────────────────────────┘
```

Figure 14.1   Definition of a **box** object.

ple, it allows us to understand the code for drawing lines on the screen purely in terms of the functionality of pen. We have assumed that the class pen is already defined, with the methods move, up, down, forward, and rotate. set-value is a method that allows an object to change the value of one of its instance variables. Both pen and box use the set-value method and inherit it from a common ancestor in the inheritance hierarchy (see Figure 14.3).

The show method causes the instance to draw itself using the color bound to the instance variable, color. self is a special local variable that is always bound to the current object; this allows objects to send themselves messages. show sends scribe a message setting the color of its ink to the instance variable, color. It then sends box1 a message to draw itself. Similarly, erase removes box1 by changing the ink color to that of the background and then drawing over itself.

Now consider the method grow. The message

message(box1, grow, 30)

causes box1 to grow by 30 units. Note that the grow method takes a parameter to describe how an existing box should increase its size. In general, messages consist of a destination, a method name, and any required parameters. grow first erases itself, then increases its size, and finally shows itself.

draw, show, erase, and grow are instance methods; they are inherited and used by instances as we have just shown. Classes also include *class methods*. Class methods are not inherited by instances, but rather define the functionality of the class itself. For example, suppose we would like to define a method for creating new instances at a selected location with default values for tilt, size, and color. This method should not be inherited by instances; it properly belongs to the class itself. Therefore, we define it as a class method, which can be passed from a class to a subclass but not to an instance. Figure 14.2 shows this method, new-box-at; the method creates an instance of pen for the new box, and then calls make-instance to create an instance of box with default values for its instance variables. make-instance takes as arguments an instance name, a class, and the values for the instance variables.

Class name: box
Superclass: display object
Instance Variables
. . .
Instance Methods
. . .
Class Methods

new-box-at(name, loc):
  begin
    make-instance(new-pen, pen)
    make-instance(name, box, loc, 0,
                    100,black,new-pen);
  end.

Figure 14.2 box object showing **Class Method**.

For example:

message(box, new-box-at, box2, (300, 300))

causes the box class to construct a new box, box2, at location (300, 300) with a tilt of 0 degrees, a size of 100, and a black border. box2, like box1, will inherit all the functionality of the box class.

The instance/class hierarchy defined above is part of a much larger tree structure that defines the entire software system. Figure 14.3 illustrates a portion of this hierarchy, including the class box, the class window, and the class pen. The box and pen classes are themselves subclasses of the class called displayObject. The figure also shows the classes string and number as branches of the same hierarchy. This portion of the tree has the object object as its root. This is the most general object in the hierarchy and forms the root of the entire inheritance tree. set-value, since it is potentially used by all instances in the system, would be defined at the root of the hierarchy, object.

The superclass of pen and box is displayObject. This class defines the functionality common to all of its subclasses, including the instance variables common to all displayed objects. We could, for example, have defined the location instance variable at this level of the hierarchy rather than in the class box, since it is used to indicate the location of any display item, box, pen, or window. General instance methods could also be attached to this more general class; for example, both show and erase could actually be defined at the displayObject level. These procedures are written in such a fashion that they will function correctly for any subclass of displayObject. Only the definition of draw must be unique to each subclass. This ensures that behaviors that are intuitively seen as common across several classes will indeed have common definitions. Figure 14.4 shows the revised displayObject and box objects.

These definitions also include a general method for moving display objects. The command:

message(box1, move, (400, 200))

tells box1 to move to a new location.

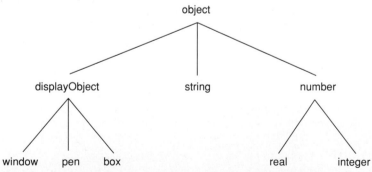

Figure 14.3 Portion of the class hierarchy for the **box** example.

```
┌─────────────────────────────────────┐   ┌─────────────────────────────────────┐
│ Class name: displayObject           │   │ Class name: box                     │
├─────────────────────────────────────┤   ├─────────────────────────────────────┤
│ Superclass: object                  │   │ Superclass: displayObject           │
├─────────────────────────────────────┤   ├─────────────────────────────────────┤
│ Instance Variables                  │   │ Instance Variables                  │
├─────────────────────────────────────┤   ├─────────────────────────────────────┤
│   location:                         │   │   tilt:                             │
│     . . .                           │   │   size:                             │
├─────────────────────────────────────┤   │   color:                            │
│ Instance Methods                    │   │   scribe:                           │
├─────────────────────────────────────┤   ├─────────────────────────────────────┤
│  move(new-location): begin          │   │ Instance Methods                    │
│     message(self, erase);           │   ├─────────────────────────────────────┤
│     message(self, set-value,        │   │  draw() : begin                     │
│       location, new-location);      │   │       message(scribe, up);          │
│     message(self, show, black);     │   │       message(scribe move,          │
│     end.                            │   │         location);                  │
│                                     │   │       message(scribe rotate, tilt); │
│  show(): begin                      │   │       message(scribe down);         │
│       message(scribe, set-value,    │   │       for i := 1 to 4 do begin      │
│         ink, color);                │   │           message(scribe forward,   │
│       message(self, draw);          │   │             size);                  │
│       end.                          │   │           message(scribe rotate,    │
│                                     │   │             90);                    │
│  erase(): begin                     │   │         end                         │
│       message(scribe, set-value,    │   │     end.                            │
│         ink, background);           │   ├─────────────────────────────────────┤
│       message(self, draw);          │   │  grow(amount): begin                │
│       end.                          │   │       message(self, erase);         │
├─────────────────────────────────────┤   │       message(self, set-value,      │
│ Class Methods                       │   │         size, size*amount);         │
├─────────────────────────────────────┤   │       message(self, show);          │
│                                     │   │       end.                          │
│     . . .                           │   ├─────────────────────────────────────┤
│                                     │   │ Class Methods                       │
└─────────────────────────────────────┘   ├─────────────────────────────────────┤
                                           │                                     │
                                           │     . . .                           │
                                           └─────────────────────────────────────┘
```

Figure 14.4 Revised definitions of **box** and **displayObject**.

When box1 receives the message, it attempts to inherit the move method from its class. Since there is no instance method to handle move in the box definition, the message is referred to the superclass, displayObject. displayObject has an instance method called move. move erases the present box1 and assigns the new-location of (400, 200) to the instance variable location. Finally, box1 shows itself at the new location. When the move method is inherited, it is evaluated in the environment defined by the instance. This will provide appropriate bindings for all instance variables and methods used by move. For example, the definition of draw used by the show and erase methods would vary across subclasses of displayObject.

Object-oriented programming is a powerful tool for creating software abstractions. Class objects are defined that organize the world into a hierarchy of classes; functionality is defined at the highest appropriate level of abstraction. In the preceding example, the variable location and the methods for move, erase, and show are part of the superclass displayObject. These instance variables and methods are inherited by *all* of its subclasses unless overridden by a definition lower in the hierarchy. In a very nice way this gives us the ultimate abstraction of instance variables and control mechanisms: Subclasses allow the behavior of classes to be modified for particular instances, where new variables and methods correctly specify the individuating differences. The properties that are common across all subclasses are inherited from the parent.

The entire system is a single inheritance tree, where any two nodes have a common supernode above them. Every pair of nodes in the structure has a *least upper bound* also in the structure. This emphasizes the abstraction principle: Each class is one descendant of a more general class that defines the common properties of all its children. Thus, properties that are shared by several classes are defined *once* in a parent class and inherited by the children, ensuring consistency of the method. The root of the hierarchy is the most general class, called object, which defines the functionality common to the entire structure.

This example illustrates *tree* inheritance: every object is the descendant of a single superclass; Smalltalk is an example of a language with tree inheritance. Many object-oriented languages, including the language implemented in Section 14.2, allow objects to have more than one parent class. The resulting structure is not necessarily a tree but a *directed acyclic graph* or *DAG*. This is also known as the *tangled hierarchy* model. In realistic domains, objects are often thought of as belonging to several classes, inheriting properties from each. A group of people, for instance, can belong to either the male or female class, to the under 30 or 30 or older class, and to other classes based on hometown, religion, income—to any class based on application of the *abstraction* principle. Individuals may belong to many of these superclasses at once, inheriting properties (possibly incompatible; see Section 9.5) from each. While this greatly complicates inheritance, it adds considerable expressive power to the language.

To demonstrate multiple inheritance, we add the label class to the displayObject example. The label class, which might itself be a specialization of a string class, lets us add labels to any of the objects created under displayObject in Figure 14.3. A label includes instance variables for point for character size, font for a particular font, text, and label-location. However, only text and label-location must be directly attached to the label object; point and font are inherited from the string superclass. The ability to draw and erase labels would also be inherited from the string superclass.

New classes can now be created inheriting properties from both the label class and subclasses of displayObject. An example of this class would be the labeledBox of Figure 14.5. An instance of this class would be a box with some label at a particular location. labeledBox inherits its size, shape, and scribe from box and its font, point, text, and label-location from label. A portion of the tangled hierarchy including these classes is presented in Figure 14.5.

There are numerous benefits of this approach to organizing software. By attaching the definition of an operator to an object (a class of operands), operators may be strongly typed without requiring global type checking on the operands. The type of the operand is implicitly defined by the object receiving the message. This implicit typing gives the application both the expressive power and integrity of typed languages while simplifying the addition of new types and operations.

Another consequence of the strong typing and modularity in the object-message model is the *overloading of operators*. For example, suppose we would like to extend the + operator to include strings. Assume that + is defined in the usual fashion for real and integer numbers and a programmer would like to extend its meaning to include string catenation. Since real numbers are an object class (with instances π, e, etc.) and integers are another object class (with instances 1, 2,...), the arithmetic definition of + is attached to those class objects respectively.

To overload the operator + to include strings, the desired definition is attached to

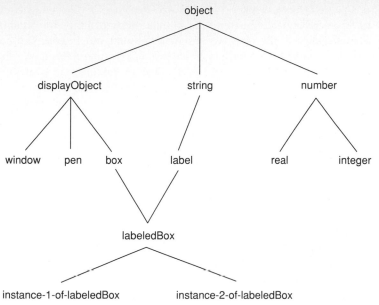

Figure 14.5 The box hierarchy including the **labeledBox** class.

the **string** class and inherited automatically by all string instances. This extends the operator's functionality:

Real number addition:

message(1.3, +, 1.5) returns 2.8.

Integer addition:

message(2, +, 3) returns 5.

String concatenation:

message(COOK, +, BOOK) returns COOKBOOK.

All three messages use + but in each instance + is interpreted differently, according to the method of the object it is sent to. This allows the programmer to use the operator without rewriting centralized global definitions, as would be the case with traditional languages. Overloading allows the creation of *generic operations* such as **erase** that have meaning for any object in the system, even though each class requires its own actual implementation of the method.

Object-oriented programming supports the abstraction of both data and procedures, simplifies the creation of procedures used by many classes of objects, allows the overloading of operators to create generic procedures, and makes it possible to organize code in a way that reflects the natural organization of the problem. In spite of its many benefits, there are limitations to this approach that should be kept in mind in reading this chapter. First, there is no guarantee that different designers would build structures the same way to represent a given situation; the ultimate responsibility for organizing code in a clear fashion lies with the software designer. Second, much work still needs to be done in defining the semantics of object-oriented languages themselves. As discussed in Chapter 9, techniques such as inheritance and its use in defining and overriding default values can introduce severe anomalies into a program or knowledge base.

14.1.2 Object-Oriented Knowledge Base

The properties of object-oriented programming that make it a powerful and natural way to organize large and complex software implementations are equally applicable in the design of knowledge bases. In addition to the benefits of class inheritance for representing taxonomic knowledge, the message-passing aspect of object-oriented systems simplifies the representation of interacting components. As a simple example, consider the task of modeling the behavior of a steam heater for a small office building. This problem is very naturally viewed in terms of interacting components. For example:

> Each office has a thermostat that turns the heat in that office on and off; this functions independently of the thermostats in other offices.

> The boiler for the heating plant turns itself on and off in response to the heat demands made by the offices.

> When the demand on the boiler increases, there may be a time lag while more steam is generated.

> Different offices place different demands on the system; e.g., corner offices with large windows lose heat faster than inner offices. Inner offices may even gain heat from their neighbors.

> The amount of steam that the system may route to a single office is affected by the total demand on the system.

These points are only a few of those that must be taken into account in modeling the behavior of such a system; the possible interactions are extremely complex. An object-oriented representation allows the implementer to focus on describing one object or class of objects at a time. Thermostats, for example, could be described by the temperature at which they call for heat, along with the speed with which they respond to changes in temperature.

The steam plant could be characterized in terms of the maximum amount of heat it can produce, the amount of fuel used as a function of heat produced, the amount of time it takes to respond to increased heat demand, and the rate at which water is consumed.

A room could be described in terms of its volume, the heat loss through its walls and windows, the heat gain from neighboring rooms, and the rate at which the radiator adds heat to the room.

The knowledge base is built up of class objects such as room and thermostat, which define the properties of the class, and instances such as room-322 and thermostat-211, which model individuals. The interactions between components are described by messages between instances. For example, a change in room temperature would cause a message to be sent to a thermostat. If this new temperature was low enough, the thermostat would switch after an appropriate delay. This would cause a message to be sent to the steam plant requesting more heat. This would cause the steam plant to consume more oil or, if the plant was already operating at maximum capacity, to route some heat away from other rooms to respond to the new demand. This could cause other thermostats to trip, and so on.

Using this design, we could test the ability of the system to respond to external changes in temperature, measure the effect of heat loss, or determine if the projected heating is adequate. We could use this simulation in a diagnostic program to verify that a hypothesized fault could indeed produce a particular set of symptoms. For example, if we have reason to believe that a heating problem is caused by a blocked steam pipe, we could introduce such a fault into the simulation and see if it produces the observed symptoms. As we will discuss in Section 14.4, a rule base could send messages to the object-oriented simulation to perform these tests.

The significant thing about this example is the way in which an object-oriented approach allows knowledge engineers to deal with the complexity of the simulation. It enables them to build the model a piece at a time, focusing only on the behaviors of simple classes of objects. The full complexity of the system behavior emerges when the model is executed.

The remaining sections of Chapter 14 discuss ways in which object-oriented programming is implemented in both LISP and PROLOG. In addition, we implement a simplified version of the heating system discussed above using a LISP-based object-oriented language.

14.2 LISP and Object-Oriented Programming

There are a number of similarities between functional and object-oriented programming: function invocations, for example, may be viewed as a form of message passing, with a message (parameters) being passed to an object (function), which replies (returns a result). Both programming models cleanly exploit the *information-hiding* potential found in the ability to create computational entities (functions or objects) that may be treated in terms of their behavior rather than their internal structure. These similarities, along with the ease of writing meta-interpreters and manipulating code as data, make LISP a natural tool for implementing object-oriented programming.

Object-oriented programming differs from pure functional programming, however, in a number of important ways. Perhaps the most fundamental of these differences is that objects, unlike functions, have an internal state that persists and changes across time. Another important feature found in most object-oriented programming languages is the inheritance of variables and methods through class hierarchies.

In this section we build a small object-oriented language in LISP and demonstrate its use in simulating the behavior of a room, thermostat, and heater. We call the language OOPS, for Object-Oriented Programming System. Although much simpler than commercial object languages, OOPS contains mechanisms for object definition, method attachment, message passing, and inheritance. With OOPS we both explore the relationship between object-oriented and functional programming and illustrate some of the practical considerations in implementing an object-oriented language.

14.2.1 OOPS: A Simple Object-Oriented Programming Language

We have defined three functions to do object-oriented programming in OOPS: def-object, def-method, and message. These functions allow the user to create and interact with objects in a class hierarchy. For simplicity, we do not support a distinction between classes and instances. This extension is left as an exercise.

def-object is used to define a new object. It takes three arguments: the name of the new object, the name of its parent or a list of parents, and a list of instance variable/value pairs. For example, the rectangle object in a plane geometry knowledge base might be defined by the call:

```
(def-object 'rectangle 'object
      '((numsides 4) (description "four-sided figure, all angles equal 90°.")))
```

This defines an object, rectangle, that is a child of object. object is the root of the hierarchy and implements much of the functionality of the system in its methods. The third parameter attaches two instance variables, numsides and description, to the rectangle object; the initial values of these variables are defined by the second components of the pairs, 4, and the string that describes rectangles. def-object evaluates these initial values and binds them to their variables.

Other objects in a geometry knowledge base might include the class of squares, as well as instances of this class. Examples of these definitions include:

```
(def-object 'rectangle-1 'rectangle '((length 8) (width 4)))
```

```
(def-object 'square 'rectangle '((description "rectangle whose sides are equal.")))
```

```
(def-object 'square-1 'square '((side 10)))
```

While def-object creates objects in the inheritance hierarchy, def-method is used to bind methods to those objects. def-method takes three arguments: the name of the object, the name of the method, and the definition of the method. Generally, we represent methods as lambda expressions, although the name of a defined function may also be used. For example, a method for computing area is attached to the rectangle object by:

```
(def-method 'rectangle 'area '(lambda () (* length width)))
```

When the area method is evaluated, length and width will be bound to the values of a particular object's instance variables.

Other classes of objects will also require area methods. Although each area method performs the same function, each class of objects requires a different definition of how

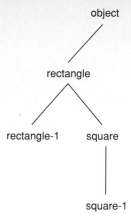

object

rectangle

rectangle-1   square

square-1

Figure 14.6 An OOPS object hierarchy.

area is computed. For example, the class of squares would have an area method defined by:

```
(def-method 'square 'area '(lambda () (expt side 2)))
```

The above definitions create the hierarchy illustrated in Figure 14.6. rectangle-1 is a child of the rectangle object with width and length of 4 and 8 units, respectively; it inherits any variables and methods attached to its ancestors rectangle and object. square is a specialization of rectangle and will inherit any variables attached to rectangle and object, except the method area and the instance variable description, which have been redefined for squares.

This example also illustrates some of the limitations of this simple version of OOPS. Because it does not distinguish between classes and instances, we may not distinguish between class methods and instance methods. Furthermore, lacking this distinction, an instance cannot inherit slot names from its class; this prevents classes from functioning as templates for the creation of instances. These features may be added to the interpreter; this is left as an exercise.

Message passing between objects is effected by the function message. message takes two or more arguments: the first is the name of the object receiving the message; the second is the name of the method. Any arguments required by the method are passed as additional parameters. For example, rectangle-1 may be queried for its area by the call:

```
> (message 'rectangle-1 'area)
32
```

The object rectangle-1 will inherit the area method from its parent object. The method is evaluated in an environment in which the free variables, length and width, are bound to the instance variables of the object rectangle-1. Ensuring that such references to either directly attached or inherited instance variables are handled correctly is an important issue in the implementation of object-oriented languages and is discussed in the next section.

The object square-1 may be asked for its area through a similar call. Note that a different method is applied to the computation of the area:

```
> (message 'square-1 'area)
100
```

Much of the functionality of the system is defined in the methods of the root object, object. These are discussed in the next section and include functions for accessing and changing instance variables. Making object the root of any application is necessary to ensure that these methods are inherited throughout the system. One method defined for all objects is show-value, which takes as argument the name of an instance variable and returns its value. In the following message, square-1 is queried for the value of numsides, a variable inherited from the object rectangle:

```
> (message 'square-1 'show-value 'numsides)
4
```

This small example illustrates the behavior of OOPS, the definition of objects and methods, and the inheritance of both methods and instance variables. The next section discusses the implementation of these and other features.

14.2.2 Implementing OOPS in LISP

OOPS represents objects as symbols in the global LISP environment, using property lists to attach methods and instance variables. Each object is defined by three properties: isa, variables, and methods. The isa property names either a single parent object or a list of parents. The variables property is bound to a list of pairs; the first element is the name of an instance variable and the second is its value. The methods property is an association list of method names and lambda definitions.

def-object, which places an object and instance variables in the hierarchy, is straightforwardly defined as:

```
(defun def-object (obj parent &optional vars)
  (setf (get obj 'isa) parent)
  (setf (get obj 'variables) (evaluate-bindings vars)))
```

evaluate-bindings takes the list of variable-binding pairs provided by the user and evaluates the bindings. This is needed to allow users to specify bindings that are the result of some calculation. It is implemented using mapcar to apply an evaluation function to each element of the variable list. This evaluation is done by a lambda expression that takes as its argument a list of two elements and returns the same list with the second element evaluated:

```
(defun evaluate-bindings (vars)
  (mapcar #'(lambda (x) (list (car x) (eval (cadr x)))) vars))
```

def-method adds a method to an object by updating the association list bound to its methods property. def-method calls replace-method to search the list recursively, replacing any definition of that method that is already present or adding the new method to the end of the list if it was not previously defined. These functions are defined:

```
(defun def-method (obj name definition)
  (setf (get obj 'methods)
    (replace-method name definition (get obj 'methods))))
```

```
(defun replace-method (name definition list-of-methods)
  (cond ((null list-of-methods) (acons name definition nil))
        ((equal name (caar list-of-methods)) (acons name definition (cdr list-of-methods)))
        (t (cons (car list-of-methods)
              (replace-method name definition (cdr list-of-methods))))))
```

message is the function that implements message passing between objects. Its definition is complicated by the need to implement inheritance of both methods and instance variables. Method inheritance is done by inherit-method, which searches the inheritance hierarchy in a depth-first fashion. inherit-method is a slightly modified version of the general inheritance algorithm presented in Chapter 13, using get-method rather than the general get to retrieve a method from an object. Their definitions are:

```
(defun inherit-method (object method)
  (cond ((null object) nil)
        ((atom object)
          (or (get-method object method)
            (inherit-method (get object 'isa) method)))
        (t (or (inherit-method (car object) method)
            (inherit-method (cdr object) method)))))
```

```
(defun get-method (object name)
  (cdr (assoc name (get object 'methods))))
```

Essentially, message calls inherit-method to retrieve the appropriate method definition; if the method is found, it evaluates it using apply. An initial version of this function is:

```
(defun message (object method &rest method-parameters)
  (let ((meth (inherit-method object method)))
    (cond (meth (apply meth method-parameters))
          (t (print "unknown method")
            (print method)))))
```

This version of message uses a cond statement to check whether the method is defined for the object. If it is not, an error message is written; otherwise the method is

---

applied to its arguments. Since the method is examined twice, once by the conditional test for its existence and a second time when it is actually applied to its parameters, a let block is used to bind the definition to the symbol meth. This saves the overhead of multiple searches of the inheritance hierarchy.

There is, however, a serious flaw in this definition. Recall, for example, the definition of the area method for rectangles presented in Section 14.2.

```
(def-method 'rectangle 'area '(lambda () (* length width)))
```

When an area message is sent to rectangle-1 (an instance of rectangle), the body of the method (the lambda expression) is inherited from the rectangle object and evaluated. It is intended that the free variables length and width refer to the so-named instance variables of rectangle-1. If, however, this message is evaluated by the version of message defined above, apply will bind all free variables in the *global LISP environment*, rather than searching the inheritance lattice for their values.

A straightforward way to allow a method to access the instance variables of the recipient object is to define message so that free variables in a method are given bindings as instance variables in the inheritance hierarchy if such bindings exist. Free variables should be given their bindings in the global environment only if they are not inherited as instance variables.

At first glance, an obvious way to do this is to construct a list of all inherited variables and their values by walking the inheritance hierarchy and retrieving all variable-binding pairs inherited by the object. We can use this as the list of variable-value pairs in a let block and evaluate the apply function within this environment. This will not work in Common LISP, however, because the language is *lexically scoped*. That is, references to LISP symbols are determined at compile time based on interpretation of the program text. In order to define local variables in a let block, these variables and the s-expressions that compute their values must be present explicitly in the text of the program. The variable list of a let block may not be computed as the program is run.

Instead, we must dynamically compute such a local environment. The bindings of instance variables cannot in principle be known from the program text (i.e., at compile time) because program execution may result in messages that add, delete, or change these variables. Interestingly, before Common LISP was developed, all LISPs were dynamically scoped; that is, variable bindings were not computed until the program was run. The let block approach to this problem will work in FRANZ LISP and other dynamically scoped dialects of the language.

Fortunately, Common LISP provides a form that solves this problem. progv is a Common LISP function that defines a block containing local variables but, unlike let, allows these variables to be determined at run time. progv takes as arguments a list of symbols, a list of their corresponding values, and a sequence of LISP forms. These forms are evaluated in an environment that binds free variables whose names are in the list of symbols to the corresponding values in the list of values. This provides a means of implementing the needed scoping of free variables in the message function.

We modify the above definition of message so that before evaluating the method, it calls build-env to construct the list of variable-binding pairs. This list is bound to the local variable env. It then computes separate lists of variables and values for the progv block. In addition, it defines a special local variable, self, that refers to the recipient object; this allows a method to specify that the recipient object send itself a message. The final version of message appears below:

```
(defun message (object method &rest method-parameters)
  (let ((meth (inherit-method object method))env)
    (cond (meth
            (setq env (build-env object))
            (progv (cons 'self (mapcar 'car env))
            (cons object (mapcar 'cadr env))
            (apply meth method-parameters) )
          (t (print "unknown method")
            (print method)))))
```

build-env constructs the environment in a fairly straightforward tree walk. The only tricky part is making sure that multiple definitions of an instance variable are treated correctly. If an instance variable is defined in more than one place in the hierarchy, the value inherited should be the first encountered in a left-to-right, depth-first search. build-env does not check for such multiple definitions, as it would be highly inefficient to do so. Instead, it places all variables in the hierarchy in its list in such a fashion that the desired occurrence of the instance variable is the *last* one in the list. progv is defined so that if there are multiple instances of symbol in its list, only the last one will be visible to the enclosed forms. Thus, build-env constructs the list of variable-binding pairs in a way that guarantees that the "leftmost closest" occurrence of an instance variable is the rightmost one in the list. build-env is defined:

```
(defun build-env (obj)
  (cond ((null obj) nil)
        ((listp obj) (append (build-env (cdr obj)) (build-env (car obj))))
        (t (append (build-env (get obj 'isa))
            (get obj 'variables)))))
```

This completes the definition of the interpreter for OOPS. The remaining functionality of the language is defined in OOPS itself, as methods attached to the general root object named (appropriately) object. These are methods that enable an object to return information about itself, such as the values of specific instance variables or the list of its parents. All objects should have object as their farthest ancestor. object has neither parents nor instance variables and is defined:

```
(def-object 'object nil)
```

The method show causes an object to print its internal structure to the screen. This is everything that is *directly* attached to the object: parents, variables, and methods. show is useful for examining and debugging OOPS programs.

```
(def-method 'object 'show
  '(lambda ()
    (terpri)
    (prin1 self) (prin1 "has parents ") (terpri)
    (pprint (get self 'isa))
    (terpri)
    (prin1 self) (prin1 "has attached variables ") (terpri)
    (pprint (get self 'variables))
    (terpri)
    (prin1 self) (prin1 "has attached methods ")
    (pprint (get self 'methods))
    (terpri)))
```

show-parents and show-value return the parents of an object and the value of a named instance variable, respectively. show-parents simply returns the object's isa property. show-value takes the name of an instance variable and evaluates it in the proper environment.

```
(def-method 'object 'show-parents '(lambda () (get self 'isa)))
```

```
(def-method 'object 'show-value '(lambda (name) (eval name)))
```

show-env shows all variables visible to an object, both those directly attached to it and those it inherits. show-env calls build-env to list all instance variables inherited by the object and returns this result.

```
(def-method 'object 'show-env '(lambda () (build-env self)))
```

set-value sets the value of an existing variable or adds a new variable and its binding to an object. This is necessary since objects must be able to change the state of other objects. set-value uses the list function rplacd to modify the association list, variables, in place. That is, rplacd does not return a modified copy of its argument as do most LISP functions; instead, it goes into memory and modifies the original list.

```
(def-method 'object 'set-value
  '(lambda (variable value)
    (let ((pair (assoc variable (get self 'variables))))
      (cond (pair (rplacd pair (list value)))
            (t (setf (get self 'variables) (cons (list variable value) (get self 'variables))))))))
```

These functions define OOPS. The next section demonstrates its use in writing an object-oriented simulation of a simple system.

14.2.3 An Object-Oriented Simulation Using OOPS

A room with a heater and a thermostat provides an interesting domain for object-oriented simulation. In spite of its simplicity, it illustrates the interactions of messages between

Figure 14.7 Inheritance hierarchy for **thermostat** simulation.

objects and the extreme modularity of object-oriented programs. The simulation involves three classes of objects: rooms, heaters, and thermostats. Thermostats have a setting that is defined with a default value of 65 degrees. Rooms are given a default temperature of 65, heaters a default state of off. These classes are defined:

```
(def-object 'thermostat 'object '((setting 65)))

(def-object 'room 'object '((temperature 65)))

(def-object 'heater 'object '((state 'off)))
```

The simulation implemented here focuses on a single room and involves one instance of each of these classes. room-327 has an attached variable naming its thermostat; this allows room-327 to send messages to the thermostat when temperature changes occur. Similarly, thermostat-327 has instance variables that name its location and the heater it controls; heater-327 knows the room it heats.

```
(def-object 'room-327 'room '((thermostat 'thermostat-327)))

(def-object 'thermostat-327 'thermostat '((heater 'heater-327)(location 'room-327)))

(def-object 'heater-327 'heater '((location 'room-327)))
```

These definitions form the hierarchy illustrated in Figure 14.7.

room has a single method, change-temp, that defines what happens if the room's temperature changes. It takes a single parameter, the amount of the change, and computes the new temperature by adding this to the current temperature. It then sends itself a message changing the value of its temperature variable, prints a message to the screen, and sends its thermostat a message to check the temperature.

```
(def-method 'room 'change-temp
  '(lambda (amount-of-change)
     (let ((new-temp (+ amount-of-change temperature)))
       (message self 'set-value 'temperature new-temp)
       (terpri)
       (prin1 "temperature in ")
       (prin1 self)
       (prin1 " changes to ")
       (prin1 new-temp)
       (prin1 " degrees.")
       (terpri)
       (message thermostat 'check-temp))))
```

The thermostat method, check-temp, queries the location for its temperature and compares the reply with its own setting. If the room temperature is less than the setting, it sends the heater a turn-on message, otherwise it sends it a turn-off message.

```
(def-method 'thermostat 'check-temp
  '(lambda ()
     (cond ((< (message location 'show-value 'temperature) setting)
            (message heater 'turn-on))
           (t (message heater 'turn-off)))))
```

The other method defined for thermostats is change-setting, which takes as its argument the new setting. It causes the thermostat object to send itself a message changing the value of its setting and then print a message to the screen. Last, it sends itself a message to check the temperature.

```
(def-method 'thermostat 'change-setting
  '(lambda (temp)
     (message self 'set-value 'setting temp)
     (terpri)
     (prin1 "New setting of ")
     (prin1 self)
     (prin1 " is ")
     (prin1 temp)
     (prin1 "degrees.")
     (terpri)
     (message self 'check-temp)))
```

The heater class has two methods, turn-on and turn-off. These will cause the heater object to send itself a message changing the value of the instance variable, state, if necessary. In addition, the turn-on method sends its location a message to raise its temperature 1 degree.

```
(def-method 'heater 'turn-on
  '(lambda ()
     (cond ((equal state 'off)
             (terpri)
             (prin1 "Heater turns on in ")
             (prin1 location) (terpri)
             (message self 'set-value 'state 'on)))
     (message location 'change-temp 1)))

(def-method 'heater 'turn-off
  '(lambda ()
     (cond ((equal state 'on)
             (terpri)
             (prin1 "Heater turns off in ")
             (prin1 location) (terpri)
             (message self 'set-value 'state 'off)))))
```

After these definitions are evaluated, the simulation is run by sending a message to any object, changing its state. For example, the temperature of the room is changed or the thermostat setting reset. This causes messages to be sent to other objects, reflecting the actual sequence of events that occur in the physical world. We now present a transcript of two sample executions; one is started by changing the temperature of the room, the other by changing the thermostat setting. The reader is urged to trace through the sequence of messages that occurs in each run.

```
> (message 'room-327 'change-temp -5)
Temperature in room-327 changes to 60 degrees.

Heater turns on in room-327

Temperature in room-327 changes to 61 degrees.

Temperature in room-327 changes to 62 degrees.

Temperature in room-327 changes to 63 degrees.

Temperature in room-327 changes to 64 degrees.

Temperature in room-327 changes to 65 degrees.

Heater turns off in room-327
(state off)

> (message 'thermostat-327 'change-setting 70)
New setting of thermostat-327 is 70 degrees.

Heater turns on in room-327

Temperature in room-327 changes to 66 degrees.
```

Temperature in room-327 changes to 67 degrees.

Temperature in room-327 changes to 68 degrees.

Temperature in room-327 changes to 69 degrees.

Temperature in room-327 changes to 70 degrees.

Heater turns off in room-327
(state off)

As this example illustrates, we can use object-oriented representations to perform a *qualitative simulation* of a system of interacting components. We use such models to do hypothetical or "what if" reasoning with a simulation. For example, in the thermostat simulation, we can answer the question, "what happens if the thermostat fails to turn off the heater?" by disabling the turn-off message in the check-temp method and changing the room temperature.

This stands in sharp contrast to the reasoning provided by rule-based diagnostic expert systems. These systems typically have no knowledge of the structure and interactions of what they propose to understand. They are just collections of rules mapping symptoms onto faults. If none of the rules fit the given set of symptoms, then the program simply fails. Object-oriented simulations provide a means for reasoning about the deep structure of the domain.

For example, mechanics could use a deep model of a diesel engine to assist in fault diagnosis. If they suspect that the problem is in the fuel injectors, they may run the simulation with the fuel injectors disabled and see if it produces the same symptoms as the actual engine fault. This may be simpler than replacing the fuel injectors to see if the problem goes away. Similarly, a robot planner may use a deep qualitative model of its domain to verify the effects of planned actions before actually performing them.

Qualitative simulations can also play an important role in training technicians, allowing them to experiment with a model before working on an actual application.

For these reasons, object-oriented programming has emerged as a powerful tool for AI programming. Many hybrid knowledge engineering environments include object-oriented programming as a central part of their architecture. These are discussed in Section 14.4.

14.2.4 Evaluating OOPS

Although OOPS (Appendix 2.4) implements object-oriented programming, it is considerably simpler than commercially available systems. For example, OOPS does not distinguish between classes and instances, supporting only a single kind of object and a simple child-parent relationship; more elaborate software supports this distinction directly, providing a clearer and more robust semantics. OOPS is less efficient than commercial software; since it is a tutorial system, we have chosen simplicity and clarity over speed in defining the interpreter. OOPS has far fewer system-defined options available for defining objects, providing more of a bare-bones architecture for object definition and message passing. OOPS simplifies the definition of objects by using property lists in the global environment; most commercial software accesses memory directly to both increase efficiency and avoid global side effects. However, the advantages of OOPS are precisely in this simplicity. It provides the user with an easily learned tool for exploring both the design and use of object-oriented languages. The reader is encouraged to experiment with extensions to this basic language.

14.3 Object-Oriented Programming and Concurrency in PROLOG

14.3.1 Introduction

The use of declarative representations to describe objects, messages, and inheritance is a new and challenging area of research. In this section, we present one approach (Shapiro 1987) to this problem. We view objects as active processes that receive messages and perform actions on their internal states according to the content of those messages. During computation the object can send messages to other objects; these may thus be thought of as distinct but complete computational entities encapsulating both structure definition and process. To create a computer model that embodies this directly would require a highly parallel asynchronous computational environment, with a processor and memory being assigned to each object. This relationship between object-oriented programming and parallel architectures is a natural one, with object-oriented approaches forming the basis of several languages for parallel computation.

The view of objects as asynchronous parallel computational entities is a useful abstraction, even if their ultimate implementation is sequential. For example, in the room-thermostat-heater example of Section 14.2, no attention was paid to the order of execution of methods; each object was defined independently, with the interactions of messages determining the ultimate sequence of actions. This is a natural way to model physical systems, which are themselves highly parallel. Even when the language is not implemented in a physically parallel architecture, much insight and semantic clarity is gained by viewing it in these terms.

In implementing objects in PROLOG, we adhere to this multi-parallel-process semantics. Like object-oriented programming, PROLOG exhibits strong potential for parallelism. The modularity of predicate definitions and the local scoping of variables suggest a model of evaluation that assigns a processor to each of a set of subgoals.

The standard semantics for PROLOG is based on sequential evaluation using a single processor. The sequential PROLOG interpreter implements *resolution refutation* with *linear input form* and *unit preference* strategies guiding sequential left-to-right and depth-first search of Horn clauses (Section 12.3).

In Section 12.3 we also presented an alternative semantics for PROLOG, designed by Ehud Shapiro, called *Concurrent PROLOG* (Shapiro 1987). This elegant semantics supports a parallel model of PROLOG interpretation and provides a basis for building objects as asynchronous parallel entities. Several new constructs are added to standard

PROLOG, including *read-only* variables and the *commit* operator. These allow the programmer to coordinate parallel interpretation of subgoals.

Concurrent PROLOG itself may be implemented directly on either a parallel or sequential computer architecture, or as a meta-interpreter on top of standard PROLOG. Continuing our philosophy of building a language (interpreter) within an AI language, the following section describes a meta-interpreter that alters the procedural semantics of sequential PROLOG to define Concurrent PROLOG; the parallel constructs of this language are then used to define objects and messages. We present the full code for this meta-interpreter in Appendix 1.2.

14.3.2 Objects in Concurrent PROLOG (E. Shapiro 1987)

From our concurrent point of view, objects correspond to the processes assigned to goals. Concurrent PROLOG realizes objects by creating a perpetual process holding its internal state in unshared arguments. An object acts by reducing itself to other objects. That is, when clause

A:- ..., B,...

is called (A is reduced), then B is created. A perpetual object acts by reducing itself to itself, i.e., by calling itself tail recursively with different arguments. (Most interpreters optimize tail recursion, so this is done in constant space.)

Objects communicate with each other by instantiating shared variables. Parallel processes are created by **and** parallelism. That is, for clauses:

A :- B1, B2, B3.

when A is called, B1 and B2 and B3 are evaluated in parallel. They are activated when all their *read-only* variables are bound and they communicate through shared variables.

Message passing is performed by binding a shared variable to a message. Since a shared variable can be referred to by multiple processes, messages can be sent to multiple objects at once. Successive communication is possible by stream communication, that is, by binding a *channel variable*, also possibly shared, to the binary term <message>.X, where <message> is the message to be sent and X is a new variable to be used in the next communication. In PROLOG this is accomplished by [<message>| X], the PROLOG equivalent of the dotted pair in LISP.

An object becomes active only when it receives a message; otherwise it is suspended. The synchronization mechanism forces a process to suspend (and save state) when it is unable to bind *read-only* variables.

When an object sends a message requiring a response, the response cannot be sent through the same shared variable, since variables in logic are able to have only a single assignment. Two techniques are available for responding to a message. One is to prepare another shared variable for the return communication. The second technique is *incomplete messages*: the sender sends a message that contains an unbound variable and then examines that variable in *read-only* mode. This causes the sender process to suspend until this variable gets bound to the response of the recipient of the message. For example, a sender asks a target object about its internal state with the message show(State), where the variable State is used as the communication channel that carries the response from the target back to the sender. The sender gets this response some time in the future after the message is received and processed. The sender must wait for the response variable to be bound if it needs to refer to the response.

The counter program is a simple example of an object (first presented, with a trace, in Section 12.3):

```
counter ([clear|S], State) :- counter (S?,0).
counter ([up|S], State) :- plus (State, 1, Newstate),
            counter (S?, Newstate?).
counter([down|S], State) :- plus (Newstate, 1, State),
            counter (S?, Newstate?).
counter ([show(State)|S], State) :- counter (S?, State).
counter ([], State).
```

The stream variable, the first argument of counter, is used recursively. At every reduction it is bound to a pair: the message and the new variable to be used in the next communication.

Object-instance creation is accomplished by parallel and. When a new goal is created, the bindings of its variables are the bindings of instance variables. For example, a new instance of the object counter may be created by executing the following code:

```
?- terminal(X), use_counter(X?,C1), counter (C1?,0).
```

terminal is an object that generates the stream of commands produced by a user at a terminal. The use_counter object receives commands from the terminal and passes these commands on to the object counter. When the message is show, use_counter passes it to counter, causes the object use_counter to wait for the response from the object counter, and then writes the response from counter to the screen. Note that the first argument of use_counter and the second argument of the object counter are treated as *read-only* variables, because they are used only when bound to message values received from the terminal.

```
use_counter([show(Val)|Input],[show(Val)|Command]) :-
  use_counter(Input?,Command), wait_write(Val).
use_counter([X|Input],[X|Command]) :-
  dif(X, show(Y)) : use_counter(Input?,Command).
use_counter([],[]).
```

wait_write(X) suspends if X is not instantiated and succeeds otherwise. dif(U, V) is a system predicate that succeeds if and when it can determine that U and V are not variables and are different. Note that the stream variable is used as an object-instance name. Message passing is performed against the stream variable and not against the target object itself, because there are no global names in Concurrent PROLOG, and the only information about an object that is accessible from outside is the communication channels to the object.

A new object-instance is created using a rule in the program. Object-instances created from the same definition are distinguished by the names of their communication channels. The next example demonstrates this. The object use_many_counters is similar to use_counter. It receives a command stream from the terminal. When it receives a create(Name) message, it creates a new object counter and saves its name and a communication channel to it in its internal state. Other messages must be of the form (Name,Command), where Name specifies the name of an object counter to which the message Command should be sent.

```
use_many_counters([create(Name)|Input],List_of_counters)  :-
   counter(Com?,0),
   use_many_counters(Input?,[(Name,Com)|List_of_counters]).
use_many_counters([(Name,show(Val))|Input],List_of_counters)  :-
   send(List_of_counters,Name,show(Val),NewList) :
   use_many_counters(Input?,NewList), wait_write(Val).
use_many_counters([(Name,X)|Input],List_of_counters)  :-
   X \= create(Y),
   X \= show(Y),
   send(List_of_counters,Name,X,NewList) :
   use_many_counters(Input?,NewList).

send([(Name,[Message|Y])|List],Name,Message,[(Name, Y)|List]).
send([C|List],Name,Message,[C|L1])  :- send(List,Name,Message,L1).
```

The object use_many_counters has two arguments. One is an input stream from the terminal and the other is a list of (Name, Channel), where Name is an identifier of the object counter given by the create command and Channel is the communication channel to that object. The object send takes four arguments. The first argument is the same as the second argument of use_many_counters. The second and the third arguments are an identifier of the object counter and a message to be sent, respectively. The fourth argument is the updated list of counters. We now show with a trace of Concurrent PROLOG (Appendix 1.2) using the counter code a situation in which three create commands are processed. Note that since there are no global variables in Concurrent PROLOG, an object must keep channel variables associated with other objects in order to send messages to them.

```
C-Prolog version 1.5
| ?- ['prolog.con',code].
prolog.con consulted 7600 bytes 2.35 sec.
code consulted 3012 bytes 0.95 sec.
```

```
yes
| ?- solve((terminal(In),use_many_counters(In?,[]))).
|: create(c1).
|: create(c2).
|: create(c3).
|: (c1,up).
|: (c2,down).
|: (c3,up).
|: (c3,up).
|: (c1,show(_)).
|: (c2,show(_)).
1
|: (c3,show(_)).
-1
|: end_of_file.
2
```

The next example demonstrates how Concurrent PROLOG can implement default programming, filters, and object hierarchies. The language does not have direct mechanisms to support object hierarchies. However, a programming technique called *filters*, together with a new Concurrent PROLOG construct, otherwise, achieves a similar effect.

Consider the following hierarchy of objects: a rectangular_area; a frame, which is a rectangular_area with four border lines; a window_with_label, which is a frame with a label at the bottom of the window. These can be defined by the class-superclass hierarchy of Figure 14.8.

In a language that supports such hierarchies directly, the functionality of a rectangular_area is inherited by the frame, and the functionality of a frame is inherited by a window with a label. Operationally, an object that receives a message checks whether it knows how to respond to it. If it does not, it defaults to its parent in the

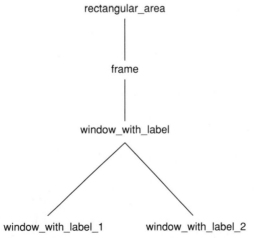

Figure 14.8 Class hierarchy for **window_with_label**

hierarchy for a response. In this sense every object in the hierarchy functions like a filter on a stream of messages.

In Concurrent PROLOG, every object in a hierarchy must have at least one designated input stream and one designated output stream, except the topmost object, which has an input stream only. The hierarchical structure of the objects is reflected by the structure of the communication network that they form. An object A lower in the hierarchy has its output stream connected to the input stream of an object B next above it in the hierarchy. If A receives a message that it cannot respond to, it simply defaults to B by passing it the message.

The following Concurrent PROLOG implementation of the window hierarchy demonstrates this technique. First a rectangular_area is defined.

```
rectangular_area([clear|M], Parameters) :-
   clear_primitive (Parameters), rectangular_area(M?, Parameters).
rectangular_area([ask(Parameters)|M], Parameters) :-
   rectangular_area(M?, Parameters).
```

Parameters is a data structure consisting of four values, in this case the instance variables for rectangular_area: (Xpos, Ypos, Width, Height), where Xpos and Ypos are the coordinates of the upper left corner of the area and Width and Height are the dimensions of the area. clear_primitive is a system-defined predicate that clears the screen area specified in its arguments.

The frame object can be viewed as a filter on the input stream of a rectangular_area. It filters two types of message, for which it knows how to respond: draw and refresh.

```
create_frame(M, Parameters) :-
   rectangular_area(M1?, Parameters), frame(M, M1).
frame([draw|M], [ask(Parameters)|M1]) :-
   draw_lines(Parameters?), frame(M?, M1).
frame([refresh|M], [clear|M1]) :-
   frame([draw|M], M1).
frame([X|M], [X|M1]) :-
   X \= draw, X \= refresh : frame(M?, M1).
```

The first clause specifies the initialization procedure, which creates a rectangular_area object by passing the Parameters and an original frame object with the communication channel to the rectangular_area. The rest of the clauses specify the method for interpreting each message. On receiving a draw message, it asks the rectangular_area about the dimensional Parameters and then draws four border lines. On receiving a refresh message, it sends two messages, clear and draw, to the rectangular_area and self, respectively. On receiving other messages, it passes them to rectangular_area.

The last clause for frame may be replaced by:

```
frame([X|M],[X|M1) :-
   otherwise : frame(M?, M1).
```

An **otherwise** goal that occurs in a guard succeeds if and when all other parallel-or guards fail. If all clauses for an object have empty guards, then **otherwise** can be implemented via a preprocessor that expands it to an appropriate sequence of calls like X \= draw. If the guards are not empty, then **otherwise** may be implemented via a negation-as-failure primitive. In this sense **otherwise** does not increase the expressive power of Concurrent PROLOG more than the addition of negation as failure does. An efficient implementation of **otherwise** requires a modification to the Concurrent PROLOG interpreter.

Now, a window frame with a label is defined.

```
create_window_with_label(M, Label, Parameters) :-
    create_frame(M1?, Parameters),
    window_with_label(M?, Label, M1).
window_with_label([change(Label)|M], OldLabel, M1) :-
    window_with_label(M?, Label, M1).
window_with_label([show|M], Label, [ask(Parameters)|M1]) :-
    show_label_primitive(Label, Parameters?),
    window_with_label(M?,Label,M1).
window_with_label([refresh|M], Label, [refresh|M1]) :-
    window_with_label([show|M], Label, M1).
window_with_label([X|M], Label, [X|M1]) :-
    X \= show, X \= refresh, X \= change,:
    window_with_label(M?, Label, M1).
```

The first clause defines the initialization procedure that creates the object **frame** with the **Parameters** and a **window_with_label** with a communication channel to the object **frame**. The rest of the clauses define the methods for interpreting messages. On receiving a **change** message, it changes the **Label**. On receiving a **show** message, it asks the object **frame** about its **Parameters** and displays the **Label** in the appropriate position in the window, using the predefined predicate **show_label_primitive**. On receiving a **refresh** message, it sends two messages, **refresh** and **show**, to the **frame** and **self**, respectively. On receiving other messages, it passes them on to the **frame**.

In the class-superclass hierarchy, a message that cannot be processed by an object is passed to the superclasses of the object. In Concurrent PROLOG such a hierarchy is simulated by a network of objects connected via communication channels, through which messages are sent. Systems like Flavors and Smalltalk-80 permit objects to access the instance variables of their superclasses. In Concurrent PROLOG, since a superclass of an object is also an object, such direct access to states of other objects is not possible. Instead, an object has to send a message asking about states to the objects that make up its superclasses.

Figure 14.9 shows the relation between objects and acceptable messages. For the object **window_with_label**, there are two types of methods: an *own* method and a *generic* method. Generic methods are invoked by sending messages up the class hierarchy.

In this cooperating object approach, there is no difference between the class-superclass hierarchy and the part-whole relation. In other words, the role of an object in

rectangular_area	
Method	Definition
clear: ask(X):	Clear the area Bind X to parameters

frame	
Method	Definition
draw: refresh: clear and ask(X):	Draw the frame outline clear + draw (Inherited from rectangular_area)

window_with_label	
Method	Definition
change(Label): show: draw, refresh, clear and ask(X):	change label display label (Inherited from frame)

Figure 14.9 Objects and acceptable messages for the
window_with_label example.

a group of cooperating objects is not determined from a structural description (such as superclass or part declarations) but from a behavioral description in the form of a communication network. From this point of view, a rectangular_area can be seen both as a superclass of a frame and as a part of a frame.

We now present a script of the window_with_label code interpreted by Concurrent PROLOG. We do not perform the actual graphics (because of compatibility problems), but we have added trace messages to indicate when messages are sent and received.

```
% This prints text as rectangular_area runs.
show_label_primitive(Label, Parameters) :-
    call(write('window_with_label show_label: Label = '), write(Label),
        write(' Parameters = '), write(Parameters), nl)).

draw_lines(Parameters) :-
    call((write('frame draw_lines: Parameters = '), write(Parameters), n1)).

clear_primitive(Parameters) :-
    call((write('rectangular_area clear'), n1)).

    C-Prolog version 1.5
    | ?- ['prolog.con',code].
    prolog.con consulted 7600 bytes 2.3 sec.
    code consulted 3336 bytes 1.15 sec.
```

```
yes
| ?- solve((terminal(X),create_window_with_label(X?,'Label 1',(0,0,10,20)))).
| : show.
| : draw.
window_with_label show_label: Label = Label 1? Parameters = (0,0,10,20)?
| : refresh.
| : clear.
frame draw_lines: Parameters = (0,0,10,20)?
| : change('Label 2').
window_with_label show_label: Label = Label 1? Parameters = _1741?
rectangular_area clear
frame draw_lines: Parameters = (0,0,10,20)?
| : show.
| : draw.
rectangular_area clear
window_with_label show_label: Label = Label 2? Parameters = (0,0,10,20)?
| : refresh.
| : clear.
frame draw_lines: Parameters = (0,0,10,20)?
| : end_of_file.
window_with_label show_label: Label = Label 2? Parameters = _4865?
rectangular_area clear
frame draw_lines: Parameters = (0,0,10,20)?
rectangular_area clear
```

To summarize: First, the user can never directly access the internal state of an object. All a user can do is send a message that specifies the operation to be performed. Thus, the encapsulation of state is established. Second, component objects of a hierarchy are accessed from the outside, by using incomplete messages. Thus, the encapsulation of abstraction-based hierarchies is also established. With these properties, it is possible to construct complicated simulations of situations from simple objects in a modular fashion.

To conclude: We designed a *meta-interpreter* in PROLOG called Concurrent PROLOG. This interpreter uses (optimized) recursive predicates to describe objects and a form of list-based parameters to encode messages. *Read-only* variables within and parallel goals as well as *guard* operators within or parallel goals allow multiple objects and messages to have a nondeterministic and pseudoparallel interpretation.

14.4 Hybrid Expert System Tools

14.4.1 Hybrid Environments: Integrating Objects, Rules, and Procedures

As mentioned in Chapter 9 and in the introduction to Part V, most single representational formalisms have both advantages and disadvantages for representing domain knowledge. Rules are a natural formalism for representing heuristics and problem-solving knowledge. Inheritance provides the best means of representing taxonomic knowledge.

Object-oriented systems, in addition to supporting inheritance, provide a convenient way of modeling the behavior of interacting objects.

Integration of these elements is surprisingly straightforward. For example, we may allow rules to execute arbitrary pieces of LISP code in their premises, with the premise succeeding if the LISP function returns non-nil. Similarly, rules could send messages to objects and test the responses in their premises.

Assume, for example, a hybrid program for reasoning about actions of a robot arm in a blocks world. We could use an object-oriented knowledge base to represent the properties of differently shaped blocks and a rule base to reason about them. A typical rule might state that it is OK to stack one block on top of another if the top block has a smaller volume than the bottom block. We could write this rule (using the syntax of the LISP shell in Section 13.3) as:

```
(rule
  if (< (message (var x) 'volume) (message (var y) 'volume))
  then (safe-to-stack (var x) (var y)))
```

This rule uses the volume method for the objects bound to (var x) and (var y) to compute their respective volumes and passes these results to the LISP function < to test them. If the test succeeds, then the conclusion that (var x) is safe to stack on (var y) also follows.

We can easily modify lisp-shell from Section 13.3 so that it will handle this type of query. We modify solve-simple-goal so that after it tries to solve a goal using the knowledge base, it tries to solve the goal through evaluation. This requires that it first verify that the goal is an evaluable LISP form and then replace variables with their values under the current substitution set and evaluate the goal using eval. In our safe-to-stack example, the attempt to evaluate the < test would first evaluate the function arguments, causing the messages to be sent to the designated objects. We leave the implementation of this extension as an exercise.

Similarly, an object may access the rule base as part of its methods. This is even easier to add to our lisp-shell/OOPS hybrid environment. Since methods are arbitrary pieces of LISP code, they can access the rule base through a call to the function solve.

This discussion suggests ways in which the OOPS language of this chapter and lisp-shell from Chapter 13 can be combined into a simple hybrid expert systems environment. However, this example does not illustrate a number of other features of commercial hybrid environments. We discuss these in this section.

14.4.2 Facets, Demons, and Graphics in Hybrid Environments

There are a number of commercially available expert system tools that support this hybrid approach to knowledge engineering. These include KEE, ART, Knowledge Craft, NEXPERT, and Goldworks.

In addition to allowing rules and objects to interact as described above, most commercial hybrid environments include such useful features as demons, built-in type checking, and support for a graphics interface. One way in which these are provided is

```
┌─────────────────────────────────────────────────────┐
│  Object: dog                                         │
├─────────────────────────────────────────────────────┤
│  Superclass: (pet, carnivore, mammal)                │
├─────────────────────────────────────────────────────┤
│  Slot: name                                          │
│     value:                                           │
│     minimum cardinality: 1                           │
│     maximum cardinality: 1                           │
│     type: string                                     │
│     default value: fido                              │
│     execute-when-created: ask-user(name.value)       │
│     execute-when-changed:                            │
│        message(owner.value, set-name, name.value)    │
├─────────────────────────────────────────────────────┤
│  Slot: breed                                         │
│     value:                                           │
│     minimum cardinality: 1                           │
│     type: (doberman poodle shorthair shepherd terrier)│
│     active-image: radio buttons                      │
├─────────────────────────────────────────────────────┤
│  Slot: owner                                         │
│     value:                                           │
│     minimum cardinality: 1                           │
│     maximum cardinality: 1                           │
│     type: instance of person                         │
└─────────────────────────────────────────────────────┘
```

Figure 14.10 Typical object showing the slot-facet-value architecture.

through an extension to the slot/value structure to subdivide each slot into multiple *facets*, or named subcomponents. These facets allow the programmer to attach several different components to a single slot, including its value, type specifications, and demons.

Figure 14.10 illustrates an object describing the class dog. dog is a subclass of three classes, pet, carnivore, and mammal, and inherits properties of each. The object shows three slots, name, breed, and owner, with multiple facets. These facets are built into the environment and are bound by the user when an object is created. The value facet of each slot represents the value of the slot.

Other facets include minimum cardinality and maximum cardinality; these allow us to specify the number of values that can be attached to a slot. Both the name and owner slots must have exactly one value. The breed slot must have at least one value but no upper limit is specified; dogs may be mixed breed.

In addition to specifying the cardinality of the slot values, many systems define facets for declaring the type of the slot. In our example, this is the type facet. The name slot is of type string; the owner slot indicates another object, an instance of the class person. In this example, we also allow the programmer to declare enumerated types by attaching a list of allowable values to the type facet; this was done for the breed slot. Another common facet allows the specification of default values, such as a default of fido for the name slot.

Along with type-checking information, most hybrid environments provide facets that allow the attachment of demons to slots. Two common demons illustrated in Figure 14.10 are execute-when-created, which is evaluated when a new instance of the class is defined, and execute-when-changed, which is evaluated every time the slot value of an instance is changed.

In this example, we have used the execute-when-created facet of the name slot to specify how the system should obtain a binding for that slot when a new instance is created. This is a typical application of this type of demon.

name also has an execute-when-changed demon, which sends a message to the instance's owner whenever the dog's name is changed. This implements consistency checking in the knowledge base, making sure that the owner knows the name of her pet. Consistency checking is an important use of execute-when-changed demons; other uses include the implementation of side effects and causal relations for different objects in the knowledge base.

active-images are another kind of demon that many systems provide. They allow graphics images to be selected from a library and attached to a slot to display its value. Typical images include dials, gauges, and button devices. These images may respond to the mouse or other selection device, allowing the user to change the value of the slot by clicking on the image itself. For example, the breed slot of Figure 14.10 has a "radio button" image attached to it. This is a set of selectable labeled "buttons"; the user may select these buttons and change the value of the slot. Figure 14.11 shows the radio button image for the breed slot of an instance of the dog object as it would appear on the screen. In the figure, the user has selected the doberman and shorthair buttons, indicating that the dog is mixed breed.

This section presented a few of the features of hybrid knowledge engineering environments. These tools, which are becoming increasingly available, represent a synthesis of the techniques described in this text, techniques developed through the history of AI to simplify the implementation of intelligent systems.

14.5 Epilogue and References

A number of programming languages support object-oriented programming. The oldest of these is Smalltalk, which is documented by Goldberg and Robson (1983) and MacLennan (1987).

Flavors is a LISP implementation of object-oriented programming that has played an important role in AI implementations and is widely available for LISP implementations. Our implementation of OOPS has been influenced by Flavors. Other LISP-based object-oriented languages include *Common Objects* and *Common Loops*.

doberman   poodle   shorthair   shepherd   terrier

Figure 14.11   Radio button for the breed slot of an
instance of the dog object in Figure 14.10.

A number of commercial expert system packages include object-oriented programming in the context of a hybrid environment. Some of the most notable of these hybrid environments are mentioned in Harmon et al. (1988).

The material for the subsection on implementing objects using Concurrent PROLOG is taken from work by Shapiro and Takeuchi (E. Shapiro 1987). The reader is referred to this resource for further examples and explanations. We include Shapiro's interpreter for Concurrent PROLOG in Appendix 1.2.

14.6 Exercises

1. The implementation of OOPS does not distinguish between class and instance objects. Extend the language so that it makes this distinction and properly handles inheritance for both instance methods and class methods as discussed in Section 14.1.

2. Extend the thermostat example of Section 14.2.3 to include an air conditioner that turns on if the room becomes too hot.

3. Use OOPS to implement a simulation of a steam engine, consisting of a boiler, water tank, fuel tank, engine, and throttle. The components of the engine should interact realistically. For example, increasing the speed of the engine should reflect an increased use of steam and an increased drain on the water and fuel tanks.

4. Use OOPS to implement a simulation of a computer network. Objects would be nodes in the network with certain message-handling capabilities. Classes of objects might include file servers, mainframes, and personal computers. Instances would include variables representing that node's message-handling capability and lists of neighboring nodes. Message queues would also be represented as instance variables. Use this simulation to test the effect of various faults, such as node or line failures, on the system as a whole.

5. OOPS implements objects by using the property lists of symbols in the global LISP environment. Along with always placing objects in the global environment, this does not allow us to create unnamed objects and pass them between functions.

   a. Discuss several reasons why this approach may not be desirable.

   b. Rewrite OOPS so that the function def-object returns unnamed objects that are then bound to global variables using setq or simply passed as parameters. Hint: represent an object as an association list rather than as properties of global symbols.

6. Extend OOPS so that it allows execute-when-changed demons. One way to do this is to add a list called demons to an object definition. This list would pair a variable name with the demon definition. Rewrite set-value so that it inherits and executes any appropriate demon when a variable is changed.

7. Integrate lisp-shell, the LISP expert system shell from Chapter 13, with OOPS as described in Section 14.4.1. Use the resulting hybrid environment to implement an expert system in some appropriate domain.

8. We can use Concurrent PROLOG implementation of a perpetual process to create axiomatic definitions of abstract data types. For example, a *stack* may be defined:

```
stack(S) :- stack(S?, []).
stack([pop(X) | S], [X | Xs]) :- stack(S?, Xs).
stack([push(X) | S], Xs) :- stack(S?, [X | Xs]).
stack([], []).
```

Use Concurrent PROLOG to give an axiomatic definition of a queue (E. Shapiro 1987).

9. Build the rectangle/square hierarchy of Section 14.2.2 in Concurrent PROLOG.

10. Build the room/furnace/thermostat example of Section 14.2.3 in Concurrent PROLOG.

15 ADVANCED TOPICS IN AI PROBLEM SOLVING

"The time has come," the Walrus said,
"To talk of many things:
Of shoes—and ships—and sealing wax—
Of cabbages and kings—
And why the sea is boiling hot—
And whether pigs have wings."

—LEWIS CARROLL, "The Walrus and the Carpenter"

15.0 Introduction

To this point, we have examined techniques for designing intelligent computer programs using explicitly represented problem-solving knowledge. This approach forms the dominant thrust of modern work in artificial intelligence. In Chapter 15 we examine a number of advanced issues in artificial intelligence problem solving.

Planning is the problem of devising a series of actions that will lead to a desired goal. Planning issues arise extensively in robotics applications. In Section 15.1 we introduce planning and present some early work in formulating and storing plans of action. The STRIPS *triangle table* offers a medium for recording operators and mapping their interrelations for generating a plan. We saw the first use of this technique in the *table of connections* used by the General Problem Solver (Section 11.1).

Another important data structure for AI systems is the *blackboard* reasoning architecture, first used in the HEARSAY project at Carnegie Mellon University (Reddy 1976). Blackboards provide a means of coordinating the actions of multiple experts or knowledge sources. We discuss the blackboard architecture in Section 15.2.

Learning is an important and challenging area of research in artificial intelligence. Section 15.3 introduces the problems and major foci of research in machine learning.

In Sections 15.4 and 15.5 we discuss models of human perception and performance. First, in 15.4, we present *cognitive science*, the representation-based science of human problem solving. Cognitive scientists use the techniques of artificial intelligence in an effort to model and understand human cognition.

A number of researchers have questioned the ability of representation-based techniques to achieve intelligence. An important alternative to the traditional AI approach is the development of computational models based on the neural structure of the human brain. In Section 15.5 we present an introduction to *neural networks*, also known as *parallel distributed processing*, a nonrepresentational approach to perception and learning.

15.1 Planning, STRIPS, and Triangle Tables

The task of a planner is to find a sequence of actions that allow a problem solver, often a robot, to accomplish some specific task. In addition to its obvious robotics applications, planning plays a role in expert systems when they must reason about events occurring over time. Planning has many applications in manufacturing, such as automatic process control. It is also important in natural language understanding, where humans frequently discuss plans, goals, and intentions.

In this discussion, we use examples from robotics. The component steps in a plan are the *atomic actions* of a robot. For planning purposes, we do not describe these basic capabilities in hardware or micro-level terms such as ''turn the sixth stepper motor one revolution.'' Instead, planners specify actions at a higher level, in terms of their effect on the world. For example, a planner for a blocks world robot might include such actions as ''pick up object a'' or ''go to location x.'' The micro control of steps to actually make a robot perform the plans is built into these higher-level actions.

Thus a sequence of actions to ''go get block a from room b'' might be:

1. put down what you have
2. go to room b
3. go over to block a
4. pick up block a
5. leave room b
6. return to original location

Plans are created by searching through a space of possible actions until the sequence necessary to accomplish the task is discovered. This space represents states of the world that are changed by applying each of the actions. The search terminates when the goal state (the description of the world) is produced. Thus, many of the issues of heuristic search, including finding A* algorithms, are also appropriate in this domain.

The act of planning does not necessarily depend on the existence of an actual robot to carry out the plans. Especially in the early years of computer planning (1960s), entire plans were formulated before the robot performed its first act. Thus plans were devised without the presence of a robot at all! Only more recently, with the implementation of more sophisticated sensing devices, has research focused on more integrated plan/action sequencing.

In spite of the reliance on basic search techniques, planning problems raise a number of unique issues. For one, the description of the states of the world may be considerably more complex than in previous examples of search. Consider the number of predicates necessary to describe rooms and corridors and objects in the robot's environment. Not only must we represent the robot's world; we must also represent the effect of atomic actions on that world. The full description of each state of the problem space can be quite extensive.

Another difference in planning is the need to characterize what is *not* changed by a particular action. Picking up an object does change (a) the location of the object and (b) the fact that the robot hand is now grasping the object (c) at a new location. It does not change (a) the locations of the doors and the rooms, (b) the locations of other objects, etc. The specification of what is true in one state of the world and exactly what is changed by performing some action in the world has become known as the *frame problem* (McCarthy 1980; McCarthy and Hayes 1969). As the complexity of the problem space increases, the issue of keeping track of the changes that occur with each action and the features of a state description that remain unchanged becomes more important. We present two solutions for coping with the frame problem, but, as will be seen, neither of these is totally satisfactory.

Other important issues include generating plans, saving and generalizing good plans, recovering from unexpected plan failures (part of the world might not be as expected, perhaps by being accidentally moved from its anticipated location), and maintaining consistency between the world and a program's internal model of the world.

In the examples of this section, we limit our robot's world to a set of blocks on a tabletop, and the robot's actions to an arm that can stack, unstack, and otherwise move the blocks about the table. In Figure 15.1 we have five blocks, labeled a, b, c, d, e, sitting on the top of a table. The blocks are all cubes of the same size, and stacks of blocks, as in the figure, have blocks directly on top of each other. The robot arm has a gripper

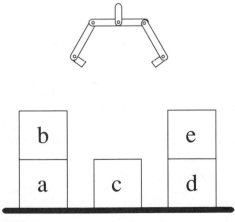

Figure 15.1   The blocks world.

that can grasp any clear block (one with no block on top of it) and move it to any location on the tabletop or place it on top of any other clear block.

We assume the robot arm can perform the following tasks (U, V, W, X, Y, and Z are variables):

goto (X,Y,Z)	Goto location described by coordinates X, Y, and Z. This location might be implicit in the command pickup (W) where block W has location X, Y, Z.
pickup (W)	Pick up block W from its current location and hold it. It is assumed that the block has nothing on top, the gripper is empty at the time of the pickup order, and the computer knows the location of block W.
putdown (W)	Place block W down at some location on the table and record the new location for block W. W must be held by the gripper at the time.
stack (U,V)	Place block U on top of block V. The gripper must be holding U and the top of V must be clear of other blocks.
unstack (U,V)	Remove block U from the top of V. U must be clear of other blocks, V must have block U on top of it, and the hand must be empty before this command can be executed.

We represent the state of the world using a set of predicates and predicate relationships:

location (W,X,Y,Z)	Block W is at coordinates X, Y, Z.
on (X,Y)	Block X is immediately on top of block Y.
clear (X)	Block X has nothing on top of it.
gripping (X)	The robot arm is holding block X.
gripping ( )	The robot gripper is empty.
ontable (W)	Block W is on the table.

ontable (W) is a short form for the predicate location (W,X,Y,Z), where Z is the table level. Similarly, on (X,Y) indicates that block X is located with its bottom coincident with the top of block Y. We can greatly simplify the world descriptions by having the computer record the present location (X,Y,Z) of each block and keep track of its movements to new locations. With this location assumption, the goto command becomes unnecessary; the commands such as pickup(X) or stack(X) implicitly contain the location of X.

A number of truth relations (in the declarative sense) or rules for performance (in the procedural sense) are implicit in the blocks world descriptions seen so far, including specifications for clear (X), ontable(X), and gripping ( ):

1. $(\forall X) (\text{clear}(X) \leftarrow \neg (\exists Y) (\text{on}(Y,X)))$

2. $(\forall Y) (\forall X) \neg (on (Y,X) \leftarrow ontable (Y)))$

3. $(\forall Y) gripping ( ) \leftrightarrow \neg (gripping (Y))$

The first statement says that if block X is clear, there does not exist any block Y such that Y is on top of X. Interpreted procedurally, this can be read "to clear block X go and remove any block Y that might be on top of X.'' The second relationship says that if any block is on the table, it is not on top of any other block.

The blocks world of Figure 15.1 may now be represented by the following predicates. We call this collection of predicates *STATE 1* for our continuing example.

STATE 1

ontable (a).	on (b,a).	clear (b).
ontable (c).	on (e,d).	clear (c).
ontable (d).	gripping ( ).	clear (e).

Because these predicates describing the state of the world for Figure 15.1 are all true at the same time, the full state description is the conjunction ($\wedge$) of these predicates. To produce new states from this description, we now design rules for operating on states. The four operators (pickup, putdown, stack, unstack) are described by predicate calculus rules:

4. $(\forall X) (pickup (X) \rightarrow (gripping (X) \leftarrow (gripping ( ) \wedge clear (X)))$.

5. $(\forall X) (putdown(X) \rightarrow ((gripping ( ) \wedge ontable (X) \wedge clear (X)) \leftarrow$
$gripping (X)))$.

6. $(\forall X) (\forall Y) (stack (X,Y) \rightarrow ((on(X,Y) \wedge gripping ( ) \wedge clear (X)) \leftarrow (clear (Y) \wedge$
$gripping (X))))$.

7. $(\forall X)(\forall Y) (unstack (X,Y) \rightarrow ((clear (Y) \wedge gripping (X)) \leftarrow (on (X,Y) \wedge$
$clear (X) \wedge gripping ( ))))$.

The fourth rule states that for all blocks X, pickup (X) means gripping(X) if the hand is empty and X is clear. Note the form of these rules: $A \rightarrow (B \leftarrow C)$. This says that operator A allows us to produce new predicate(s) B when condition(s) C is true. We use these rules to generate new states in a space. That is, if predicates C are true in a state, then B is true in its child state. In other words, operator A can be used to create a new state described by predicates B when predicates C are true.

But we must first address the *frame problem* before we can use these rule relationships to generate new states of the blocks world. *Frame relations* are rules to tell what predicates describing a state are *not* changed by rule applications and are thus carried over intact to help describe the new state of the world. For example, if we apply the operator pickup block b in Figure 15.1, then all predicates related to the rest of the blocks remain true in the child state. For our world of blocks we can specify several such frame rules:

8. $(\forall X) (\forall Y) (\forall Z) (unstack (Y,Z) \rightarrow (ontable (X) \leftarrow ontable (X)))$.

9. $(\forall X) (\forall Y) (\forall Z) (stack (Y,Z) \rightarrow (ontable (X) \leftarrow ontable (X)))$.

These two rules say that ontable is not affected by the stack and unstack operators. This is true even when X and Z are identical; if Y = Z either 6 or 7 above won't be true.

Other frame axioms say that on and clear are affected by stack and unstack operators only when that particular on relation is unstacked or when a clear relation is stacked. Thus, in our example on (b,a) is not affected by unstack (c,d).

Similarly, frame axioms say that clear (X) relations are unaffected by gripping (Y) even when X = Y or gripping ( ) is true. More axioms say that gripping does not affect on(X,Y) relations but affects only the ontable (X) relation where X is gripped. Thus a number of other frame relations need to be specified for our example.

Together, these operators and frame axioms define a state space, as illustrated by the operator unstack. unstack (X,Y) requires three conditions to be true, namely that on (X,Y) and gripping ( ) and clear (X) are all true. When these conditions are met the new predicates gripping (X) and clear (Y) are produced by unstack. There will be a number of other predicates also true for *STATE 1* that remain true in *STATE 2*. These states are preserved by the frame axioms. We now produce the nine predicates describing *STATE 2* by applying the unstack operator and the frame axioms to the nine predicates of *STATE 1*:

STATE 2

ontable(a).	on(b,a).	clear(b).
ontable(c).	clear(c).	clear(d).
ontable(d).	gripping(e).	clear(e).

To summarize:

1. Planning may be seen as a state space search.
2. New states are produced by general operators such as stack and unstack plus frame rules.
3. The techniques of graph search may be applied to find a path from the start state to the goal state. The operations on this path constitute a plan.

Figure 15.2 shows an example of a state space searched by applying the operators as described above. If a goal description is added to this problem-solving process, then a plan may be seen as a set of operators that produce a path that leads from the present state of this graph to the goal.

This characterization of the planning problem defines its theoretical roots in state space search and predicate calculus representation and inferencing. However, it is important to note how complex this manner of solution can be. In particular, using the frame rules to calculate what remains unchanged between states can add exponentially to the search, as can be seen from the complexity of the very simple blocks problem. In fact, when any new predicate descriptor is introduced (color, shape, size, etc.), new frame rules must be defined to relate it to all appropriate actions!

This discussion also assumes that the subproblems that make up a task are independent and may thus be solved in an arbitrary order. This is certainly very seldom the case in interesting problem areas, where the actions required to achieve one subgoal can conflict with the actions required to achieve another. Next we illustrate these problems and discuss an approach to planning that greatly assists in handling this complexity.

STRIPS, developed at what is now SRI International, stands for Stanford Research Institute Planning System (Fikes and Nilsson 1971, 1972). This controller was used to

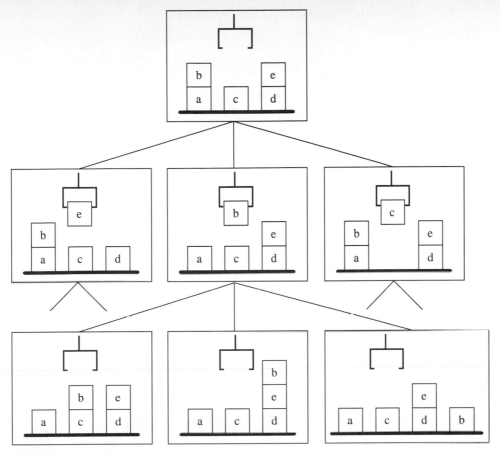

Figure 15.2 Portion of the state space for a portion of the blocks world.

drive the *SHAKEY* robot of the early 1970s. STRIPS addressed the problem of efficiently representing and implementing the operations of a planner. It addressed the problem of conflicting subgoals and provided an early model of learning; succcssful plans were saved and generalized as *macro operators*, which could be used in similar future situations. In the remainder of this section, we present a version of STRIPS-style planning and *triangle tables*, the data structure used to organize and store macro operations.

Using the blocks example, the four operators pickup, putdown, stack, and unstack are represented as triples of descriptions. The first element of the triple is the set of *preconditions* (P), or conditions the world must meet for an operator to be applied. The second element of the triple is the *add* list (A), or the additions to the state description that are a result of applying the operator. Finally, there is the *delete* list (D), or the items that are removed from a state description to create the new state when the operator is applied. These lists eliminate the need for separate frame axioms.

We can represent the four operators in this fashion:

pickup (X)
P: gripping ( ) ∧ clear (X) ∧ ontable (X)
A: gripping (X)
D: ontable (X) ∧ gripping ( )

putdown (X)
P: gripping (X)
A: ontable (X) ∧ gripping ( ) ∧ clear (X)
D: gripping (X)

stack (X,Y)
P: clear (Y) ∧ gripping (X)
A: on (X,Y) ∧ gripping ( ) ∧ clear (X)
D: clear (Y) ∧ gripping (X)

unstack (X,Y)
P: clear (X) ∧ gripping ( ) ∧ on (X,Y)
A: gripping (X) ∧ clear (Y)
D: gripping ( ) ∧ on (X,Y)

The important thing about the add and delete lists is that they specify *everything* that is necessary to satisfy the frame axioms! There is some redundancy in the add and delete list approach. For example, in unstack the *add* of gripping (X) could imply the *delete* of gripping ( ). But the gain of this redundancy is that every descriptor of a state that is not mentioned by the *add* or *delete* remains the same in the new state description.

A related weakness of the precondition-add-delete list approach is that we are no longer using a theorem-proving process to produce (by inference) the new states. This is not a serious problem, however, as proofs of the equivalence of the two approaches can guarantee the correctness of the precondition-add-delete method.

The precondition-add-delete list approach may be used to produce the same results we produced with the inference rules and frame axioms in our earlier example. The state space search, as in Figure 15.2, would be identical for both approaches.

A number of other problems inherent in planning are not solved by either of the two approaches presented so far. In solving a goal we often divide it into subproblems, for instance, unstack (e,d) and unstack (b,a). Attempting to solve these subgoals independently can cause problems if the actions needed to achieve one goal actually undo the other. Incompatible subgoals may result from a false assumption of *linearity* (independence) of subgoals. This can make solution searches unnecessarily difficult or even impossible.

We now show a very simple example of an incompatible subgoal using the start state *STATE 1* of Figure 15.1. Suppose the goal of the plan is *STATE G* as in Figure 15.3, with on (b,a) ∧ on (a,c) and blocks d and e remaining as in *STATE 1*. It may be noted that one of the parts of the conjunctive goal on (b,a) ∧ on (a,c) is true in *STATE 1*, namely on (b,a). This already satisfied part of the goal must be undone before the second subgoal, on (a,c), can be accomplished.

The *triangle table* representation (Fikes and Nilsson 1972; Nilsson 1980) is aimed at alleviating some of these anomalies. A triangle table is a data structure for organizing sequences of actions, including potentially incompatible subgoals, within a plan. It

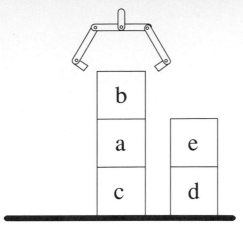

Figure 15.3   Goal state for the blocks world.

addresses the problem of conflicting subgoals by representing the global interaction of sequences of operations. A triangle table relates the preconditions of one action with the postconditions, the combined add and delete lists, of all the actions preceding it.

These are used to determine when that macro operator could be used in building a plan. By saving these macro operators and reusing them, STRIPS increases the efficiency of its planning search. Indeed, we can generalize a macro operator, using variable names to replace the block names in a particular example. Then we can call the new generalized macro to prune search. In Section 15.3, with our presentation of learning, we discuss techniques for generalizing macro operations.

The reuse of macro operators also helps to solve the problem of conflicting subgoals. As the following example illustrates, once the planner has developed a plan for goals of the form stack (X,Y) ∧ stack (Y,Z), it may store and reuse that plan. This eliminates the need to break the goal into subgoals and avoids the complications that may follow.

Figure 15.4 presents a sample triangle table for the macro action stack (X,Y) ∧ stack (Y,Z). This macro action can be applied to states where on(X,Y) ∧ clear(X) ∧ clear(Z). This triangle table is appropriate for starting *STATE 1* with X = b, Y = a, and Z = c.

The atomic acts of the plan are recorded along the diagonal. These are the four actions, pickup, putdown, stack, and unstack, discussed in this section. The preconditions of each of these acts are in the row preceding that act and the postconditions of each act are in the column below the act. For example, row 5 lists the preconditions for pickup(X) and column 6 lists the postconditions (the add and delete lists) of pickup(X). These postconditions are placed in the row of the action that uses them as its preconditions. It organizes these in a manner relevant to succeeding actions. Thus the triangle table's purpose is to properly interleave the preconditions and postconditions of each of the smaller actions that make up the larger goal.

Figure 15.4 Triangle table.

One advantage of triangle tables is the assistance they can offer in attempting to recover from unexpected happenings, such as a block being slightly out of place, or accidents, like dropping a block. Often an accident can require backing up several steps before the plan can be resumed. When something goes wrong with a solution the planner can go back into the rows and columns of the triangle table to check what is still true. Once the planner has figured out what is still true within the rows and columns, it then knows what the next step must be if the larger solution is to be restarted. This is formalized with the notion of a *kernel*.

The *nth kernel* is the intersection of all rows below and including the nth row and all columns to the left of and including the nth column. In Figure 15.4 we have outlined the third kernel in bold. In carrying out a plan represented in a triangle table, the ith operation (that is, the operation in row i) may be performed only if all predicates contained in the ith kernel are true. This offers a straightforward way of verifying that a step can be taken and also allows us to recover systematically from any disruption of a plan. Given a triangle table, we find and execute the highest-numbered action whose kernel is enabled. This not only lets us back up in a plan but also allows for the possibility that an unexpected event might let us jump forward in a plan.

The conditions in the leftmost column are the preconditions for the macro action as a whole. The conditions in the bottom row are the conditions added to the world by the macro operator. A triangle table may be saved as a *macro operator* with its own set of preconditions and add and delete lists.

Of course, the triangle table approach does lose some of the semantic purity of the previous planning models. Notice, for example, that only those postconditions of an act are retained that are also preconditions of later acts. Thus, if guaranteed correctness is a desired result, further verification of the triangle tables, perhaps with additional information that might allow sequences of triangle tables to be composed, might be desirable.

Other problems arise with the use of macro operators in planning. As the number of macro operators increases, the planner has more powerful operations to use, decreasing the size of the state space that must be searched. Unfortunately, at each step of the search, all of these operators must be examined. The pattern matching needed to determine whether an operator may be applied can add considerable overhead to the search process, counteracting the gains made by saving macro operations. The problems of determining when a macro operation should be saved and the best way to determine the next operator to use remain the subject of much research.

Further details of this approach may be found in Fikes and Nilsson (1971), Cohen and Feigenbaum (1982), and Nilsson (1980).

15.2 Blackboard Architecture for Problem Solving

Many problems require the coordination of a number of different types of knowledge. For example, a speech understanding program must first manipulate an utterance represented as a digitized waveform. As the understanding process continues, it must find words in this utterance, form these into sentences, and finally produce a semantic representation of the utterance's meaning.

A related problem occurs when multiple processes must cooperate to solve a single problem. An example of this is the distributed sensing problem (Lesser and Corkill 1983). Assume that we have a network of sensors, each of which is monitored by a separate process. Assume also that the processes can communicate and that proper interpretation of each sensor's data depends on the data received by other sensors in the network. This problem arises in situations as diverse as tracking an airplane across multiple radar sites and combining the readings of multiple sensors in a manufacturing process.

The *blackboard architecture* is a model of control that has been applied to these and other problems requiring the coordination of multiple processes or knowledge sources. A *blackboard* is a central global data base for the communication of independent asynchronous knowledge sources focusing on related aspects of a particular problem. Figure 15.5 gives a schematic of the blackboard design.

In Figure 15.5 each *knowledge source* KS_i gets its data from the blackboard, processes the data, and returns its results to the blackboard to be used by the other knowledge sources. Each KS_i is independent in that it is a separate process operating according to its own specifications and, when a multiprocessing or multiprocessor system is used, it is independent of the other processing in the problem. It is an asynchronous system in that each KS_i begins its operation whenever it finds appropriate input data posted on the blackboard. When it finishes its processing it posts its results and awaits new input data.

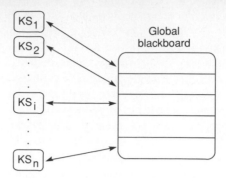

Figure 15.5 Blackboard architecture.

The blackboard approach to organizing a large program was first presented in the HEARSAY-II research (Erman et al. 1980; Reddy 1976). HEARSAY-II was a speech understanding program; it was initially designed as the front end for a library data base of computer science articles. The user of the library would address the computer in spoken English with queries such as "Are any by Feigenbaum and Feldman?" and the computer would answer the question with information from the library data base.

The blackboard architecture allowed HEARSAY to coordinate the several different knowledge sources required for this complex task. The blackboard is usually organized along two dimensions. With HEARSAY these dimensions were the time as the speech act was produced and the level of analysis of the utterance. Each level of analysis was processed by a different class of knowledge sources. The levels of analysis of the utterance were:

KS_1. The waveform of the acoustic signal.

KS_2. The phonemes or possible sound segments of the acoustic signal.

KS_3. The syllables that the phonemes could produce.

KS_4. The possible words as analyzed by one KS.

KS_5. The possible words as analyzed by a second KS (usually considering words from different parts of the data)

KS_6. A KS to try to generate possible word sequences.

KS_7. A KS that puts word sequences into possible phrases.

We can visualize these processes as components of Figure 15.5. In processing spoken speech, the waveform of the spoken signal is entered at the lowest level. Knowledge sources for processing this entry are enabled and post their interpretations to the blackboard, to be picked up by the appropriate process. Because of the ambiguities of spoken language, there may be multiple competing hypotheses at each level of the blackboard. The knowledge sources at the higher levels attempt to disambiguate these competing hypotheses.

The analysis of HEARSAY-II should not be seen as simply one lower level producing data that the higher levels can then analyze. It is much more complex than that. If a

KS at one level cannot process (make sense of) the data sent to it, that KS can request the KS that sent it the data to go back for another try or to make another hypothesis about the data. Furthermore, different KSs can be working on different parts of the utterance at the same time. All the processes, as mentioned previously, are asynchronous and data driven; they act when they have input data, continue acting until they have finished their task, and then post their results and wait for their next task.

One of the KSs, called the *scheduler*, handles the "consume-data post-result" communication between the KSs. This scheduler has ratings on the results of each KS's activity and thus is able to supply some direction in the problem solving. If no KS is active, the scheduler determines that the task is finished and shuts down.

When the HEARSAY program had a data base of about 1000 words it worked quite well, although a bit slowly. When the data base was further extended, the data for the knowledge sources got more complex than they could handle. This has been the only large-scale approach by the AI community to the voiced speech understanding problem until very recently (in the United Kingdom by Plessey and University of Edinburgh). Speech recognition is a very complex problem also addressed with conventional techniques, but no more successfully.

HEARSAY-III (Balzer et al. 1980; Erman et al. 1981) is a generalization of the approach taken by HEARSAY-II. The time dimension of HEARSAY-II is no longer needed, but the multiple KSs for levels of analysis are retained. The blackboard for HEARSAY-III is intended to interact with a general-purpose relational data base system. Indeed, HEARSAY-III is a general shell for the design of expert systems.

An important change in HEARSAY-III has been to split off the scheduler KS (as described above for HEARSAY-II) and to make it a separate blackboard controller for the first (or domain) blackboard. This second blackboard allows the scheduling process to be broken down, just as the domain of the problem is broken down, into separate KSs concerned with different aspects of the solution procedure (for example, when and how to apply the domain knowledge). The second blackboard can thus compare and balance *different* solutions for each problem (Nii and Aiello 1979; Nii 1986a; 1986b).

15.3 Learning

The ability to learn must be part of any system that would exhibit general intelligence. It is also important to continued progress in developing practical knowledge-based programs. Feigenbaum (1983) has called the "knowledge engineering bottleneck" the major obstacle to the widespread use of expert systems. This "bottleneck" refers to the cost and difficulty of building expert systems through the efforts of both knowledge engineers and domain experts. One solution to this problem would be for programs to begin with a minimal amount of knowledge and learn from either their own experience, high-level advice from humans, or planned experiments in the domain.

Simon (1983) defines learning as

> any change in a system that allows it to perform better the second time on repetition of the same task or on another task drawn from the same population.

This definition gives learning a behavioral basis; the effectiveness of a learning algorithm may be measured in terms of the program's efficiency or correctness in some specific task domain. Another important feature of this definition is the implication that learning involves generalizations from experience: that the improved performance is observed on the "repetition of the same task" or on some distinct but related task in the domain. While rote learning is not trivial, the major focus of learning research in the AI community is on programs that infer general principles from their experience in a domain.

Simon's definition is general enough to encompass various approaches to learning, such as adaptive systems and neural networks, as well as programs that acquire explicitly represented domain knowledge. Neural networks are an exciting and promising alternative to mainstream AI and are discussed in Section 15.5. The present section focuses on knowledge-based approaches to learning.

Programs that acquire explicitly represented knowledge may be characterized along several dimensions (Figure 15.6):

1. *The type of training instances, the beginning data for the learning task.*
2. *The language used to represent knowledge.* Specific training instances must be translated into this representation language. In some programs the training instances are in the same language as the internal knowledge base and this step is unnecessary.

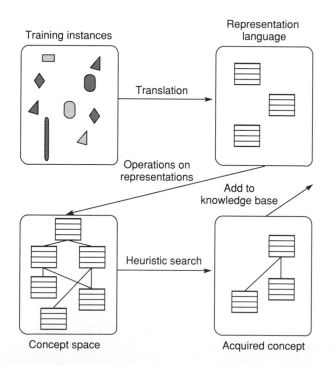

3. *A set of operations on representations.* Typical operations generalize or special-
   ize existing knowledge, combine units of knowledge, or otherwise modify the
   program's existing knowledge or the representation of the training instances.

4. *The concept space.* The operations described in 3 define a space of possible
   knowledge structures that is searched to find the appropriate characterization of
   the training instances and similar problems.

5. *The learning algorithms and heuristics employed to search the concept space.*
   As with all search problems, commitments must be made concerning the order
   of the search and the use of heuristics to guide the search. After the appropriate
   structure is found in the concept space, it is added to the knowledge base.

An example of how these components function in a learning program is found in
Patrick Winston's work on learning structural descriptions from good and bad examples
(Winston 1975*a*). This program constructed a definition of general concepts, such as
''arch,'' in a blocks world, from a series of positive and negative examples of the concept. The training instances consisted of examples of blocks world structures that fit in
the category, along with ''near misses,'' structures that almost fit in the category but
failed on one or two aspects (Figure 15.7). These near misses enabled the program to
single out features that excluded negative instances from the class being learned. Training instances were presented to the program in an order that assisted learning of the
desired concept, much as a teacher structures examples to help a student learn.

The program represents knowledge as semantic networks. It maintains a candidate
description of the concept and refines that description by generalization and specialization. Generalization changes the graph to let it accommodate new examples of the concept. Figure 15.8 shows an arch built of three bricks and a graph that describes it. The

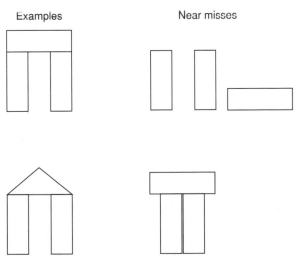

Figure 15.7 Examples and near misses for the concept
"arch."

An example of an arch and its network description:

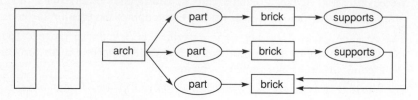

Another example of an arch and its network description:

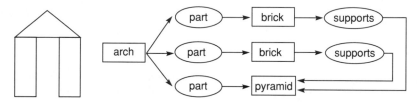

A generalization that includes both examples:

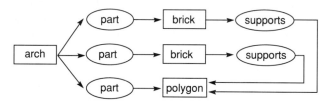

next example is an arch with a pyramid rather than a brick on top. This example does not fit the initial description. The program matches these graphs, associating nodes and links; through this process, it detects differences in the graphs. In Figure 15.8, the graphs fail to match because the top element in the first graph is a brick and the corresponding node of the second example is a pyramid. We may generalize the graph by replacing this node with the least common supertype of brick and pyramid; in this example, it is polygon.

When the program is presented with a near miss, it specializes the candidate description to exclude the example (Figure 15.9). The difference between these graphs is in the touch relations of the near-miss example. The program then specializes the graph by adding links that exclude the near miss. Here it has added must-not-touch links to the graph.

Candidate description of an arch:

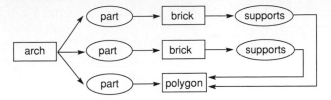

A near miss and its description:

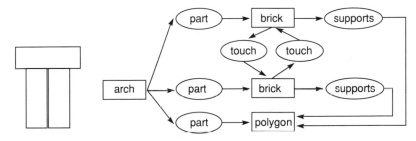

Arch description specialized to exclude the near miss:

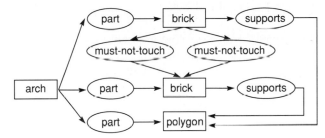

Figure 15.9 Specialization of a description to include a near miss.

These operations define a space of possible structures. Search through this space is controlled by heuristics that try to apply the most appropriate generalization or specialization consistent with the examples.

In the remainder of this section, we examine some of the alternative approaches explored by research in machine learning. Section 15.3.1 characterizes a number of programs in terms of the type of training data used for learning. Section 15.3.2 looks at the effect that choice of a representation can have on the learning problem. In Section 15.3.3 we examine a few of the options for defining and searching a concept space.

15.3.1 Varieties of Training Data and Learning Tasks

There is as yet no unifying theory for machine learning. The following list of common themes, suggested by (Carbonell 1983), will help us present the range of learning research. These are only guidelines for thinking about the problem rather than a strict taxonomy. This list of themes categorizes learning in terms of (a) the specific type of training data and (b) the data structures and operators of the learning program.

There are a number of dimensions along which we characterize the set of training instances. Examples may come from a teacher or the outside environment (1, 2, 3, and 4 below) or they may be generated by the program itself (5 below). The data may be reliable, or contain noise and other errors. They can be presented in a well-structured fashion, as in the structure learning example, or consist of unorganized instances. They may include both positive and negative examples or only positive examples. They may be readily available, or the program may have to construct experiments or use some other form of data acquisition.

1. Rote Learning   This is the simplest type of learning since it involves no modification of input data. Solutions are simply stored and recalled when the same problem instance arises. In spite of this simplicity, rote learning raises a number of interesting issues. If a program saves too many instances, the cost of selecting a stored solution to match new data can lead to an overall degradation of program efficiency. This problem can be attacked through the use of indexing techniques to simplify the selection of stored data. Alternatively, a program may limit the number of stored instances through heuristics or other methods. Samuel (1959) used a form of rote learning to retain interesting checker board situations.

2. Learning from Examples   The induction of general principles from a set of examples is one of the oldest and most important learning problems in computer science. Winston's program for learning structural descriptions is an example of this type of learning. Learning from examples may be either incremental, modifying its concepts in response to each training instance, or single trial, forming concepts once in response to all the data.

3. Learning from Advice   Another important learning task involves improving performance using explicit advice from a teacher. The challenge to learning from advice is the translation of the advice from a high-level language that is convenient to the human teacher into knowledge structures and operations suitable for use by the program. This problem is not trivial; it requires a correct understanding of the advice, a correct translation into the internal representation, and integration of this knowledge into the current knowledge base.

4. Learning from Analogy   This type of learning applies existing knowledge to a new problem instance on the basis of similarities between them. This involves modifications of the existing knowledge to fit the new case. Learning by analogy is common in human learning; for example, we might tell a student that serving a tennis ball is like driving a nail into a point high up on a wall. This area has not been studied as much as learning from examples, although Carbonell (Carbonell 1986; Carbonell et al. 1983) has approached the problem in depth. Other interesting work includes Anderson's investigation of skill acquisition in geometry (Anderson 1983) and Burstein's program for learning the semantics of simple constructs in the BASIC programming language from analogies such as those found in introductory texts (Burstein 1986).

Learning from analogy also plays an important role in *case-based reasoning* (Kolodnor 1987). A knowledge base for case-based reasoning is a set of relevant examples rather than general rules. These cases are applied to new problems by an analogical reasoning process. This is another response to the complexities encountered in trying to handcraft a knowledge base of general rules that will cover all situations. Proponents of case-based reasoning argue that this is closer to human reasoning. Case-based approaches have played an important role in expert programs in law and medicine.

5. Learning by Observation and Discovery   All of the learning programs that we have mentioned so far perform supervised learning. That is, they assume that training instances are presented by a teacher in a generally structured fashion. Programs for learning by discovery address the problem of unsupervised learning. Training data are not organized by a teacher but are either passed to the program in a raw form (such as large amounts of unstructured scientific data) or produced by the program itself through experimentation.

Much work in learning by discovery is done in the areas of scientific and mathematical discovery, since these domains fit well into the formal representations required by AI problem solvers. There also exists an extensive literature on mathematical proof procedures and scientific methodology. Important research in this area includes the BACON research in discovering physical laws (Langley 1981, 1986, 1987) and the Automated Mathematician, AM (Lenat 1977).

In Section 15.3.4 we list more programs from each of these areas, along with references for more detailed study.

15.3.2   Representations and Meta-Operations

Learning programs have been written that use each of the knowledge representations discussed in Chapter 9. Because the approaches discussed in this section learn explicitly represented knowledge, they are sensitive to the compromises associated with the selection of a representation language. For example, the trade-off between expressiveness and efficiency is particularly important in learning, since operations on unconstrained representations can produce enormous spaces.

One common solution to this problem is to restrict the expressiveness of the language for representing learned concepts. For example, a program may reduce the number of features it examines in the data or restrict the representation of learned concepts to conjunctive expressions only, or some other normal form. The ID3 algorithm, discussed in the next section, achieves much of its success by limiting learned concepts to simple decision trees. These restrictions on the expressiveness of representations introduce an *inductive bias* in the program. Allowing the program to learn only concepts that fit into a restricted representation increases the efficiency of the search but may limit the ability of the program to learn the required concepts. Designers must be aware of these trade-offs.

Another source of complexity in a learning program is in the translation of training instances into an internal representation. A program for learning structural examples in the blocks world is complicated by requiring that it translate visual input into semantic network format. The designer should take this problem into account and select a representation that simplifies this translation as well as the learning process itself. This complexity does not occur when the training instances are already represented in the internal language of the program.

The concept space of a learning program is also determined by the meta-operations allowed on representations. The commonest of these are generalization and specialization. There are a number of ways in which a description can be generalized to include a larger set of instances. The most straightforward generalization technique is the replacement of constants with variables in predicate expressions. This was done in the formation of macro operators in the STRIPS research (Section 15.1): before a triangle table was saved, it was generalized by replacing constants with variables. Other forms of generalization include the replacement of a concept or a predicate by a more general concept in a type hierarchy and the elimination of links from a semantic network or predicates from a predicate calculus expression.

Specialization operations are the inverse of generalization operations, such as the addition of constraints (links or predicates) to a description. The join and restrict operations of Section 9.3 were examples of specialization operators for conceptual graphs.

A less common but potentially very exciting approach to modifying representations is the combination of different descriptions. One example of this is the AM discovery program, which includes heuristics for combining different concepts to produce new potential theorems. The SOAR program, discussed in more detail below, learns by forming *chunks*, structures built up of existing knowledge in the program. Genetic algorithms (Section 15.3.4) take this approach, forming new knowledge from the components of two different descriptions.

15.3.3 Search Strategies and Heuristics in Learning Systems

This section looks at a few important machine learning problems and techniques. Our selection is not complete, but it presents a number of the many interesting and important approaches developed by the machine learning community and illustrates the use of operations such as generalization and specialization.

ID3 The ID3 algorithm (Quinlan 1986b) induces a decision tree for classification problems. It derives the tree from examples relating various features of domain objects to their classification. For example, the table in Figure 15.10 lists the relationship between species of animals and the features diet, size, color, and habitat. Given a set of examples such as this, ID3 induces an optimal decision tree for classifying instances.

As Figure 15.10 illustrates, not all of the features presented in the table of examples may be necessary for distinguishing classes. In this example, the size feature is not needed at all for classifying the animals. Similarly, once the brown or gray branches of

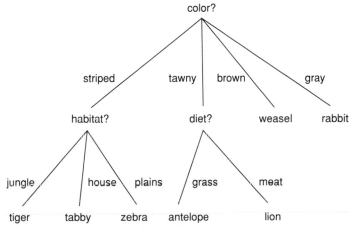

diet	size	color	habitat	species
meat	large	striped	jungle	tiger
meat	large	tawny	jungle	lion
meat	small	striped	house	tabby
meat	small	brown	jungle	weasel
grass	large	striped	plains	zebra
grass	small	gray	plains	rabbit
grass	large	tawny	plains	antelope

Figure 15.10 Table of examples and the optimal decision tree produced by ID3.

the tree are taken, the remaining features can be ignored: color alone is sufficient to distinguish rabbits and weasels from the other animals.

The ID3 algorithm builds a decision tree in which any classification is performed by checking the fewest features. It builds the tree by first ranking all the features in terms of their effectiveness, from an information-theoretic standpoint, in partitioning the set of target classes. It then makes this feature the root of the tree; each branch represents a partition of the set of classifications. The algorithm then recurs on each branch with the remaining features and classes. When all branches lead to single classifications, the algorithm halts.

ID3 is an interesting example of how a restricted representation can simplify the learning process. Because of these constraints, the algorithm is able to construct effective trees in a highly efficient (polynomial time) fashion. In spite of its efficiency, the ID3 algorithm is limited by the expressiveness of the decision tree representation.

Version Space Search   The learning community has developed a number of inductive learning algorithms that overcome the limitations of decision tree approaches. *Version space search* (Mitchell 1978, 1979; Cohen and Feigenbaum 1982) describes an important family of data-driven concept-learning algorithms. Version space search learns gen-

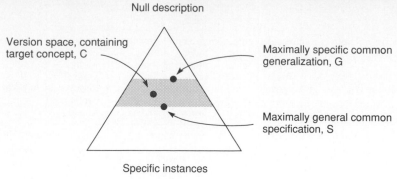

Figure 15.11 Partial ordering of a concept space, showing boundaries on the version space.

eral concepts, given both positive and negative examples. To focus the search, these algorithms capitalize on the partial ordering that generalization operations impose on the set of concepts. Figure 15.11 diagrams this partial ordering of concepts and a type of version space search. The top of the ordering is the null description; this is the most general concept in the space and covers any possible instance. It may be, for example, a predicate with variables for all parameters. At the bottom of the partial ordering are all specific instances, the least general concepts in the space. The search technique illustrated in the figure is Mitchell's *candidate elimination algorithm* (Mitchell 1978, 1979).

The candidate elimination algorithm maintains two sets of candidate concepts, G and S. These sets of concepts define upper and lower bounds on the portion of the space containing the target concept. G is the set of most general descriptions that cover all the positive and none of the negative training instances. S is the set of most specific descriptions that cover only the positive instances.

G is initialized to the null description, that is, the description that could fit any instance. When presented with a negative instance, each concept in G is specialized as little as possible to exclude the negative instance. Since there may be more than one possible specialization of a concept, the number of concepts in G may grow in this step of the search. The algorithm also deletes any candidate concepts in S that include the negative instance.

S is initialized to the first positive example. When presented with subsequent positive examples, concepts in S are minimally generalized to include the new examples. The algorithm also deletes any concepts in G that do not cover the positive examples.

Together, S and G define boundaries on the portion of the space containing the target concept C; that is, $S \leq C \leq G$. The search continues through successive training examples with G growing more specific and S growing more general. Training instances are repeated until G and S converge; that is, both G and S are singletons and $G = S$. This remaining concept covers all positive instances and no negative training instances.

Candidate elimination performs an exhaustive, breadth-first search of the concept space. For this reason, it is slow for very large spaces, although heuristics can be used to prune G and S or guide the selection of generalization operations. Other limitations of this approach include difficulties with noisy data and an inability to learn disjunctive concepts. Alternatives to this algorithm have been explored (Hayes-Roth 1978; Vere 1975, 1978); Dietterich and Michalski (1981) provide a comparison of this and related methods.

Explanation-Based Learning   Version space search and Winston's structural concept learning program are examples of algorithms that perform *similarity-based* learning: they are presented with a set of instances and generalize from the similarities and differences among these instances. The major limitation of similarity-based learning is that it requires multiple training instances to converge on a useful concept. *Explanation-based* learning (Mitchell et al. 1986; DeJong and Mooney 1986; Kedar-Cabelli and McCarty 1987) addresses the problem of learning meaningful generalizations from a single training instance.

Explanation-based learning depends on the program's ability to form an explanation of why a new instance belongs to the target concept. It uses its existing knowledge to form this explanation; the program then generalizes this explanation and saves it as the learned concept.

An instance of explanation-based learning is given by the *EBG*, or *Explanation-Based Generalization*, algorithm (Mitchell et al. 1986). We illustrate this algorithm with an example also taken from Mitchell's paper: learning the safe-to-stack concept in a blocks world.

Explanation-based learning requires a goal concept, a domain theory, which provides the ability to explain this concept in terms of lower-level concepts, and a single training instance. An instance also includes a set of *operationality criteria*; these are restrictions on the form that definitions can take. Our safe-to-stack example is described by:

Goal concept:
The set of pairs of objects X and Y such that safe-to-stack(X, Y),
where $\forall(X, Y)$ safe-to-stack(X, Y) $\leftrightarrow$ lighter(X, Y)

Domain theory:

> lighter(X, Y) $\leftarrow$ weight(X, W1) $\wedge$ weight(Y, W2) $\wedge$ less(W1, W2).
> weight(X, W) $\leftarrow$ density(X, D) $\wedge$ volume(X, V) $\wedge$ equals(W, V * D).
> weight(X, 2) $\leftarrow$ isa(X, brick).

Training Instance:

> on(a, b).   color(a, blue).   color(b, red).
> isa(a, cube).   isa(b, brick).   volume(a, 1).   density(b, 0.5).

Operationality criteria:

> Definitions are built of descriptive concepts such as color, density, volume, and isa.

The task of the learning program is to find a definition of the goal that follows from the domain theory and is consistent with the training example and the operationality criteria. EBG uses theorem proving to show that the goal concept follows from the training instance; it produces a proof tree whose leaves are all in the training instance. Figure

Proof tree for **safe-to-stack(a,b):**

Generalized proof tree for **safe-to-stack(X,Y):**

Figure 15.12 Proof tree and generalized proof tree for **safe-to-stack (a,b).**

15.12 shows the proof tree for this example; the leaves of the tree are aspects of the training instance and meet the operationality criteria. Note the role of the training instance in guiding the theorem prover to a specific proof. The algorithm then generalizes the proof through a form of *goal regression* (Nilsson 1980); this process replaces the constants in the goal with variables and propagates these substitutions through the tree. The resulting generalized tree yields the new concept definition; the conclusion is the goal concept and the premises are the leaves of the generalized tree. In our example, this is:

safe-to-stack(X, Y) ← density(X, D) ∧ volume(X, V) ∧ equals(W, D * V) ∧
    is(Y, brick) ∧ less(W, 2).

This is a general definition that can be used to recognize future instances of the concept. Any instance of **safe-to-stack** that fits this definition can be recognized without requiring the efforts of the theorem prover. In our example, the program has learned that it is safe to stack anything on a brick if it has a weight of less than 2.

EBG is representative of a family of explanation-based learning approaches. These all share the use of domain knowledge to learn from single examples. They take different approaches to the problems of producing an explanation (theorem provers, planners, abductive reasoning), generalizing explanations (goal regression, substitutions from a type hierarchy, modifications of the proof tree), and other aspects of problem representation.

An exciting area of research is the combination of explanation-based and similarity-based methods. While explanation-based learning requires only a single concept for learning, it is constrained by the knowledge in the domain theory. Similarity-based methods do not suffer from this limitation. A combination of the two approaches could exhibit the ability of explanation-based learning to learn from a single instance along with the ability of other approaches to modify the domain theory in response to multiple examples.

15.3.4 Other Approaches

The Meta-DENDRAL program (Buchanan and Mitchell 1978) deduced new rules for interpreting mass spectrographic data for the DENDRAL program. It induced general rules from spectrographic data on compounds with known chemical structure; these rules proved effective in inferring the structure of new compounds. Meta-DENDRAL takes a model-driven approach to learning, beginning with an incomplete theory of the behavior of organic compounds in mass spectrography and refining this theory in response to training instances. Meta-DENDRAL is an important milestone in learning from examples.

The SPARC program (Dietterich and Michalski 1986) induces general rules by observing sequences of playing cards and provides another interesting example of inductive learning. Winston (1986) has also continued work in learning from examples, as has Quinlan (1986a). Rendell (1986) provides a useful summation of this area of learning.

Another interesting and very different approach to learning from examples is found in *genetic algorithms* (Holland et al. 1986). Genetic algorithms induce general descriptions from sets of examples through the unique approach of maintaining a number of competing description hypotheses. As the program receives new training instances, it tests its hypotheses and rates them on their ability to correctly classify the new instances. At each iteration, the algorithm produces new hypotheses through a process that closely resembles genetic reproduction: two hypotheses are combined into a new description that has components of both. Following the model of evolution, successful hypotheses are allowed to produce more offspring. Less successful hypotheses are allowed to reproduce, but with lower frequency; this allows the possibility that such descriptions may contain valuable components. Over a number of trials, successful hypotheses come to proliferate in the population.

Teiresias (Davis 1982), discussed in Chapter 8, is another example of a program that learns from advice. Another early example of learning from advice is Waterman's poker player (Waterman 1968), which improved its performance in the game of poker by taking advice from a teacher. More recent work by Mostow (1983) explored these issues in the context of a program that learned to play the hearts card game.

One of the earliest and most successful programs for learning by discovery is Lenat's AM (Lenat and Brown 1984; Davis 1982). AM, the Automated Mathematician, discovered interesting theories in mathematics. The program began with the axioms of set theory, a set of operations for modifying and combining its knowledge (generalization, specialization), and a set of heuristics for detecting and proposing new instances of "interesting" theorems. AM was successful, beginning with set theory and discovering the natural numbers and several important aspects of number theory including primality.

Sims (1987) developed a mathematical discovery program, IL, that applies a variety of learning techniques to the discovery problem. IL uses analytical methods such as theorem proving and explanation (Section 15.3.2) along with empirical methods in mathematical discovery. IL is being applied to problems in both mathematics and physical sciences.

Another important body of work is the BACON research by Langley, Simon, et al. (1987). This research is aimed at developing a computational model of scientific discovery. BACON has duplicated many of the early discoveries in chemistry, inferring regularities in collections of scientific data.

The SOAR project (Laird 1986a, 1986b; Rosenbloom and Newell 1987) addresses the general learning problem. SOAR's basis is the chunking hypothesis of learning, described by Rosenbloom and Newell (1986):

> A human acquires and organizes knowledge of the environment by forming and storing expressions, called *chunks*, that are structured collections of the chunks existing at the time of learning.

Chunking is based on theories of human intelligence and has been implemented in a search-based problem-solving architecture. SOAR forms chunks from the results of goal-directed problem-solving behavior using rule-based representations. SOAR is unique in that its designers attempted to form a general model that can account for a number of different learning behaviors. It is also unique in the extent to which it is applied to different problem domains and in the extent to which both its performance as a program and its plausibility as a model of human learning have been documented.

In this section we provided a cross section of approaches to the learning problem and examples of techniques proved generally useful in machine learning research. The machine learning literature is rich and includes many techniques not discussed in this introduction. We urge readers to continue their own exploration of the field and provide a number of references in the epilogue to supplement those in this section.

15.4 Cognitive Science

15.4.1 Overview and Application Areas

It is not a coincidence that a major subgroup of the artificial intelligence community has focused on understanding *human* intelligence. Humans provide the best example of intelligent activity, and AI engineers, even though they are usually *not* committed to "making their programs act like humans," seldom ignore the human's solution. Going further, some applications, like delivering medical care (MYCIN), are deliberately modeled on the solution processes of human experts working in the area. Most important, understanding human intelligence is a fascinating and open scientific challenge.

The attempt to understand human intelligence with the assistance of the data structures and other tools from artificial intelligence is referred to as *cognitive science*. The scope of the endeavor is described in a number of important papers (Norman 1981).

Modern cognitive science began with the advent of the digital computer, even though (Chapter 1) there were many intellectual forebears of this discipline, from Aristotle through Descartes to more modern theorists such as Turing, McCullock and Pitts, the founders of the *neural net* model, and John von Neumann. The study became a science, however, with the ability to design and run experiments based on these theoretical notions, that is, with the arrival of the computer. (See the Turing Award quotation at the beginning of Chapter 16.)

The first published research in cognitive science was in the areas of solving logic problems, planning, and verbal and concept learning. At the beginning of Chapter 11 we described the Logic Theorist, a program by Newell, Shaw, and Simon that proved many of the theorems in the first volume of Russell and Whitehead's *Principia Mathematica*. Simple heuristic mechanisms, such as replacing a problem with a series of simpler subproblems, were used to beat the combinatorics involved in exhaustive search.

Coincident with work on the Logic Theorist, the same researchers began to compare their heuristics with those used by human subjects. They took *think-aloud protocols*, in which human subjects were recorded as they thought their way through a logic proof, and compared these protocols with the behavior of the computer program solving the same problem. The researchers found remarkable similarities and interesting differences across both problems and subjects (Feigenbaum 1963; Newell and Simon 1972).

Newell and Simon, in the research that eventually led to the General Problem Solver (GPS), designed a model and then a computer program that expressed these relationships. The difference reduction algorithm that compared two different states of the problem and attempted to recursively reduce the differences between them was called *means-ends analysis*. The link between the differences noted in the states of the problem and their reduction was the *table of connections*, that is, the problem-specific information that linked states of the problem and thus allowed the solution to progress from state to state (see Section 11.1 and Figure 11.2).

The GPS reduction algorithm of Figure 11.1 is an example of a *weak heuristic* method. As AI problem solving evolved toward expert systems, emphasis was placed more on the knowledge implicit in the table of connections for the problem (see Chapter 9) than on the weak method of recursively reducing differences.

Models for memory and concept learning also got attention early in the history of cognitive science. The work of Collins and Quillian on associative models for human memory, Section 9.2, is an important example of this. The semantic network model that resulted from this research has had a far-reaching influence on AI data structures.

During the period 1956 to 1964, Edward Feigenbaum and Herbert A. Simon developed a program called EPAM (Elementary Perceiver And Memorizer). This program modeled human rote learning of nonsense syllables, an area of research called *verbal learning behavior*. The task involves the memorization of nonsense syllables consisting of two constants with a vowel between them, such as JUK, JIR, DAX. These syllables are designed to be free of any (semantic) meaning that might help in their encoding by the human. A data structure called a *discrimination net* was created by Feigenbaum and Simon and modeled the learning behavior of human subjects on this task (Feigenbaum 1963).

These early cognitive science projects offered the research approach that would be taken for the next decade:

1. Based on data from humans solving particular classes of problems, design a data structure and related search strategy for solving a problem.

2. Observe human subjects working on the problem and keep track of important measurable parameters of their solution process, such as think-aloud protocols, eye movements, written partial results, or whatever might aid the researchers in ascertaining what is going on.

3. Run the computer-based model (designed in 1 above) to produce a trace of its problem-solving behavior.

4. Finally, analyze and compare the human and computer solutions and revise the computer model for the next test and comparison.

The most important result of this research paradigm was the *production system* model for human performance (Newell and Simon 1972). This psychological model played an important role in the development (at Carnegie Mellon University) of the OPS family of languages. The OPS (Official Production System) languages also came to express the "software architecture" for the rule-based expert system, as presented in chapters 4 and 8.

In viewing the production system as a model of human problem solving, the production memory took the role of the human's long-term memory or permanent store of problem-solving skills, whether for generating moves in chess or delivering medical treatment. The working memory represented the human's short-term memory or attention. The control mechanism, matching the working memory to the set of production rules, modeled the current focus of attention triggering one of the set of permanent skills. This, in turn, changed the locus of attention.

The production system model also offers an important link between strong and weak heuristic methods for problem solving, as described in chapters 5 and 8. The division between the logic or knowledge and the control mechanism for using the logic allows focus on the general (weak) heuristic methods as used in the control mechanism, or on the number and power of the production rules in the knowledge base (strong methods).

In more recent years, a number of research projects use the production system model to describe human problem-solving performance. Among these are the following.

Intelligent computer-aided instruction. If we conjecture that a person's problem-solving skills can be represented by a set of production rules, then errors in humans' problem-solving efforts can be described by the absence or misuse of one of these rules. Intelligent computer-aided instruction seeks to identify the missing rule and then teach the skill (rule) that is missing. This approach has been used in the areas of:

1. Teaching children subtraction skills (Brown and Burton 1978).

2. Teaching skills in algebra problem solving (Sleeman and Smith 1981; Sleeman 1982).

3. Teaching concepts in debugging electronic circuits (Brown et al. 1982).

4. Teaching computer programming skills (Soloway et al. 1983; Johnson and Keravnou 1985).

5. Teaching medical skills to doctors (Clancey 1983; Clancey and Shortliffe, 1984*a*).

Analysis of game-playing skills. A most thorough analysis of subjects solving cryptarithmetic problems, playing chess, and proving theorems in the propositional calculus is found in Newell and Simon (1972). Simon and his colleagues (Simon 1975) have also studied subjects in the process of acquiring problem-solving skills on the task of solving the four- and five-ring tower of Hanoi problem and its isomorphs (Simon 1975; Luger and Bauer 1978).

Analysis of problem-solving skills in applied mathematics. This problem area includes subjects solving distance-rate-time problems, moment of inertia problems, and energy problems (deKleer 1975; Novak 1977). Research at the University of Edinburgh showed that search strategies responsible for generating systems of simultaneous equations to represent the relationships within these problems could be produced with goal-driven search on a set of production rules, each representing potential relationships within the problem (Bundy et al. 1979; Luger 1981). Other work at Carnegie Mellon University characterized the knowledge that high school students possessed for successfully solving algebra word problems (Hinsley et al. 1977). Genesereth has created a consultation program for MACSYMA users (Genesereth 1982).

Comparisons of novices' and experts' problem-solving skills. These studies describe and compare skills within a particular problem area. For instance, it can be important to understand the differences between the novice and expert problem solver in physics (Larkin et al. 1980; Simon and Simon 1978). Studying these novice/expert differences can lead to better designs for rule bases or object specifications for expert systems, as well as offering suggestions for teaching these skills in the classroom

The principle of separation of knowledge and control and the modularity of the production rules that make this approach a robust model for software development also make it ideally suited for experimentally modeling skilled problem-solving behavior, where altered results can be achieved by removing, adding, or simply changing the priority of the rules (Luger 1981; Neches et al. 1987).

Alternatively, criticisms of this very simplicity (a number of these were mentioned in chapters 9 and 10) have led to more advanced representations for AI problem solving. These have also played an important role in modeling human performance. The clustering of knowledge that seems important in skilled performance—the abstraction principle that allows us to create, orchestrate, and use descriptions of individuals, classes, and the inheritance of properties, as well as the use of attached procedures and default information—suggests the use of network or object-oriented models of performance.

We have already mentioned the Collins and Quillian model of associative memory. Research at Carnegie Mellon (Bhaskar and Simon 1977) used schema-based representation to account for problem solving in applied mathematics. Researchers at the University of Edinburgh examined subjects for schema contents and competency in classes of pulley problems. The result of this research was to produce a running program that simulated much of the experts' problem-solving behavior and offered explicit information content for experts' knowledge schemata (Bundy et al. 1979; Luger 1981).

Research in English language understanding also used AI data structures to model human behavior. Simple tree hierarchies provided models for Linde's (1974) research on apartment descriptions and Grosz's (1977) work on task-based dialogues. Grosz's research is interesting in that she models performance in a complex task: working with an expert to build a pump. This interaction is modeled with a task-subtask hierarchy.

Reichman (1985) makes a contribution to the analysis of pragmatics in discourse, as well as presenting an explicit computational description of the structure of discourse. Reichman uses augmented transition networks to model conversational flow and demonstrates how discourse has both a linear and a hierarchical composition, with the transitions from one position or level to another marked by *cue words*. Reichman's research offers an important balance, with the formal specification (the ATN) supporting the analysis of (actual) human discourse.

15.4.2 Cognitive Science: Open Issues

Even with the help of powerful representation techniques and some impressive early successes, cognitive science is a discipline yet to reach its promise. A number of the deep issues that plague its continued progress are outlined below.

1. Representational indeterminacy. Anderson's representational indeterminacy conjecture (Anderson 1978) states that it may not be possible to determine what representational scheme the human problem solver actually uses. The indeterminacy conjecture says that it may not, in principle, be possible to decide what representations underlie much of human performance. This is an important concern for constructing models but, as we point out in Chapter 16, need not be a limitation to their utility for doing science.

2. The limitations of the physical symbol system hypothesis. Newell and Simon hypothesized that the physical symbol system and its potential for search are necessary and sufficient explanations for intelligence (see Chapter 16). Many researchers in cognitive science take this hypothesis literally. In what sense may it be demonstrated? Or is it, as discussed in Chapter 16, simply a conjecture necessary for doing research in the area?

Even a weak interpretation of this hypothesis—that the physical symbol system and search are a sufficient model for intelligence—has produced many powerful results in the modern field of cognitive psychology. This sufficiency allows creation and testing of symbol-based models for many aspects of human performance (Pylyshyn 1984). But the strong interpretation—that the physical symbol system and search are necessary for explanation of intelligent activity—is open to question (Searle 1980; Weizenbaum 1976; Winograd and Flores 1986).

3. The necessity of designing computational models that are falsifiable. Kuhn (1962), Popper (1959), and others have argued the necessity of using models that are falsifiable as a condition for using them to do science. This means that there must exist circumstances under which the model is not a successful approximation of the phenomenon. The obvious reason for this is that *any* number of confirming experimental instances is not sufficient for confirmation of a model. Much research is done in response to the failure of existing theories. The very general nature of the physical symbol system hypothesis may make it impossible to falsify and therefore useless as a model. (The same criticism can also be made of the conjectures of the phenomenological tradition, as we see in Chapter 16.) Some AI data structures, for example, the semantic network, are so general that they can model almost anything describable. When a cognitive scientist is asked under what conditions his or her model for intelligent activity does *not* work, the answer is as difficult as determining the limitations of any scientific theory.

4. The inadequacy of the scientific method. We discuss this issue, presented by Winograd and Flores (1986), in the summary comments of Chapter 16.

In spite of these limitations, the cognitive science approach currently offers some of our best tools for understanding the mechanisms of human cognition. A number of researchers (e.g., the SOAR group) are attempting to model the full range of human perception, problem solving, and learning. This project offers an opportunity to integrate many of the issues that are too often addressed in a manner isolated from the rest of intellectual activity. This attempt at integrating models into a larger explanatory unit offers important constraints on individual pieces as well as the total model.

In this section we have discussed research on understanding human cognitive processes within assumptions of the physical symbol system hypothesis. A number of workers are exploring other approaches, based on the biological mechanisms of human intelligence. This work focuses on two concepts crucial to a full model of human intelligence: perception and non-symbol based learning. These are addressed in the following section.

15.5   Neural Networks

The techniques discussed in this text have all used explicitly represented knowledge to implement intelligence. A very different approach seeks to build intelligent programs using models that parallel the structure of neurons in the human brain.

A simple schematic of a neuron (Figure 15.13) consists of a cell body that has a number of branched protrusions, called *dendrites*, and a single branch called the *axon*.

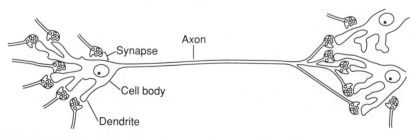

Figure 15.13   Simplified diagram of a neuron (Crick and Asanuma 1986).

Dendrites receive signals from other neurons. When these combined impulses exceed a certain threshold, the neuron fires and an impulse, or ''spike,'' passes down the axon. Branches at the end of the axon form *synapses* with the dendrites of other neurons. The synapse is the point of contact between neurons; synapses may be either *excitatory* or *inhibitory*. An excitatory synapse adds to the total of signals reaching the neuron; an inhibitory synapse subtracts from this total.

This description of a neuron is excessively simple, but it captures those features that are relevant to neural models of computation. In particular, each computational unit is a simple thresholding device that receives signals from other units and passes a signal on to other units when its threshold is exceeded. Instead of using explicit symbols and operations, the knowledge of the system emerges out of the entire network of neural connections and threshold values.

There are a number of reasons why neural architectures are appealing as mechanisms for implementing intelligence. Traditional AI programs tend to be brittle and overly sensitive to noise; rather than degrading gracefully, such programs tend to be either right or fail completely. Human intelligence is much more flexible; we are good at interpreting noisy input, such as recognizing a face in a darkened room from an odd angle or following a single conversation in a noisy party. Even where a human may not be able to solve some problem, we generally can make a reasonable guess as to its solution. Neural architectures, because they capture knowledge in a large number of fine-grained units, seem to have more potential for partially matching noisy and incomplete data.

Neural architectures are also more robust because knowledge is distributed somewhat uniformly around the network. Experience with people who have lost part of their brain from disease or accident has shown that they do not lose specific memories; rather they suffer more general degradations of their mental processes.

Neural architectures also provide a natural model for parallelism, since each neuron is an independent unit. Hillis (1985) has commented on the fact that humans get faster at a task as they acquire more knowledge while computers tend to slow down. This slow-down is due to the cost of sequentially searching a knowledge base; a massively parallel architecture like the human brain would not suffer from this problem.

Finally, there is something intrinsically appealing about approaching the problems of intelligence from a neural point of view. After all, the brain achieves intelligence and it does so using a neural architecture.

15.5.1 Early Work in Neural Computing

The earliest example of a neurally based model of computation was in work done by McCulloch and Pitts in the early 1940s (McCulloch and Pitts 1943). The nets employed an extremely simple model of neurons: each neuron had both inhibitory and excitatory inputs. It fired only if the total number of active excitatory inputs exceeded the number of inhibitory inputs and produced an output value of 1. McCulloch-Pitts neurons did not have any thresholds. In spite of (or perhaps because of) these limitations, McCulloch and Pitts were able to demonstrate that neural networks were equivalent in computational power to Turing machines (and hence, general computers).

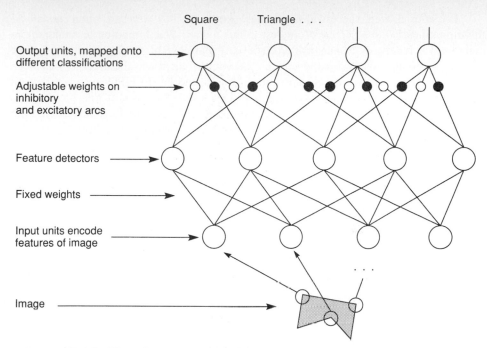

Square   Triangle . . .

Output units, mapped onto
different classifications

Adjustable weights on
inhibitory
and excitatory arcs

Feature detectors

Fixed weights

Input units encode
features of image

Image

Figure 15.14   Three-layer perceptron, after an example
from Hinton and Sejnowski (1987).

Von Neumann also showed that when redundancies were introduced into McCulloch-Pitts networks, they could continue to function reliably in spite of the malfunction of individual elements. This was an important result, as it suggested how the human brain is able to continue functioning in light of the constant loss of brain cells we endure throughout our lives. Redundancy and the consequent robustness is an important feature of neural architectures.

In the 1950s Rosenblatt proposed a neural network architecture that included adjustable thresholds on individual units and developed a procedure under which these networks could learn by systematically adjusting their weights (Rosenblatt 1962). These networks were called *perceptrons* and were capable of learning simple classification problems. Figure 15.14 shows a simple perceptron for classifying patterns. The network consists of three layers. The first is a layer of input units that allow the input of different features of the pattern. These are connected through fixed-weight connections to a layer of feature detectors. These are connected through a set of arcs with adjustable weights to the output units. Each output unit is mapped onto a specific classification. The network was hand coded for the features and categories of a particular problem.

The network learned by a process of adjusting values of weights. If an output is correct, the weights feeding into it are left alone. If an output is 0 and should be 1, the weights on the active input lines are incremented. If the output is 1 and should be 0, the weights on the input lines are decremented. This procedure was shown to converge.

Perceptrons were successful and widely studied. They were a limited model, and the limitations led to a decline of interest in this model. One limitation was the requirement that each network be handcrafted for a particular class of problems, and the number of possible connections was exponential. A deeper problem was the inability of perceptrons to recognize certain types of patterns. Minsky and Papert (1969) showed that this approach could not distinguish patterns like T and C. The basis of this problem was their inability to compute the logical ''exclusive or.'' In spite of their limitations, perceptrons laid much of the foundation for modern work in neural computing.

15.5.2 Current Work in Neural Nets

In the early 1980s researchers began to make progress on the problems of perceptrons and other early models. Their work has led to renewed interest in this idea under the name of *connectionism*. The approaches include Hopfield nets (Hopfield 1982), Boltzmann machines (Hinton and Sejnowski 1986), and multilayer networks with back propagation (Rumelhart et al. 1986).

These approaches have overcome the limitations of the earlier perceptrons by constructing networks with multiple layers of *hidden units*. Where perceptrons mapped input features directly onto outputs through one layer of adjustable weights, these hidden units allow networks to construct more complex patterns of internal weights and learn more complex features. Hidden units also eliminate some of the need for handcrafting the network to a specific problem class.

In addition, multilayered networks use more sophisticated, nonlinear threshold functions and more complex procedures for learning. Multilayer neural nets use a back-propagation algorithm that allows error corrections to be passed through multiple layers of hidden units. Boltzmann machines employ a stochastic process for adjusting weights (Ackley et al. 1985; Hinton and Sejnowski 1986).

Using these techniques, researchers now enjoy success in a number of areas, particularly those involving pattern recognition and learning classifications from noisy data. Sejnowski has developed a program called NETtalk, which learns to pronounce English text by first trying random pronunciations and correcting its performance over a number of trials. It is an interesting experience to hear the program learn correct pronunciations through a process that sounds like a human's progress through babbling into baby talk and finally mature speech (Sejnowski and Rosenberg 1987).

15.5.3 Neural Nets: Problems and Promise

Neural networks are a new and exciting area of research. They show both promise and a number of yet unresolved difficulties. Among the benefits of this approach are the following:

1. They handle noise well. Once trained, neural nets show an ability to recognize patterns even though part of the input data is missing or obscured.

2. They are robust. Because the information is distributed, neural nets can survive the failure of some nodes.

3. They implement parallelism.

4. They are able to learn new concepts.

5. By patterning themselves after the architecture of the brain, they provide a plausible model of intelligent mechanism.

6. They have had success in areas like vision that have frustrated more traditional approaches.

7. They are a promising model of associative memory.

8. They provide a tool for modeling and exploring brain function, much as production systems have helped cognitive scientists study higher-level cognitive processes.

Because of these advantages, research in neural networks is growing rapidly and promises to contribute valuable insights to AI as a whole. However, a number of problems must be addressed if this work is to continue to grow:

1. Neural nets are not brains, in spite of their surface similarity to human neural systems. Brains have a different, more complex structure; they are highly modular, and there is growing evidence that they not only learn by adjusting weights on connections but also are able to grow new connections.

2. Neural nets cannot now model higher-level cognitive mechanisms, like attention, symbols, reference. Whether or not humans prove to be physical symbol systems, they are very good at producing and manipulating symbols; how can this be done in a simulated network? Also, it is not clear how networks can represent mechanisms like focus of attention.

3. Neural nets may be at the wrong level of abstraction; they may be too weak to describe higher-level processes. As an analogy, a body of LISP code is a much more viable description of the function of a program than the associated machine code. Describing higher-level cognitive processes at the level of neural mechanism may be similarly inappropriate and therefore offer an inadequate explanatory mechanism.

4. Higher-level organization and abstractive principles do not disappear. Humans reason from class taxonomies and rules of performance. The brain itself is a highly structured and organized system. It is unlikely that any progress in intelligence will come without an understanding of the principles of this organization.

5. Some human intellectual activity may not be parallel. Much higher-level reasoning and problem-solving behavior seems to be quite serial in nature. In these cases, a production system approach may be much more fruitful.

6. Brains are very large, having trillions of neurons. Although we can certainly achieve useful behavior from smaller systems, the complexity of more highly intelligent programs may require more neurons than we could efficiently implement on a computer. Higher-level symbolic descriptions may ultimately prove more efficient to design and implement.

7. Although neural architectures obviously underlie human intelligence, they may not be the best abstraction for implementing it on a machine.

In spite of these difficulties, neural networks have great promise and will continue to be a major focus of research. We believe that a phenomenon as complex as intelligence will require the efforts of researchers using many different models and approaches for its explanation. Neural networks can provide a lower-level model of intelligent mechanism, and they have already made progress toward modeling perception and associative memory. Higher-level symbolic approaches provide powerful languages for describing related high-level processes. They may also give us clues to the organization and structure of both biological and silicon-based brains. Continued research will constrain these different paradigms to converge on a full and unified understanding of the nature of intelligence in both humans and machines.

15.6 Epilogue and References

The planning section demonstrates some of the data structures and search techniques used for general-purpose planners. Further references include ABSTRIPS or ABstract specification for STRIPS generator relationships (Sacerdotti 1974) and NOAH for nonlinear or hierarchical planning (Sacerdotti 1975, 1977).

Meta-planning is a technique for reasoning not just about the plan but also about the process of planning. This can be important in expert systems solutions. References include Meta-DENDRAL for DENDRAL solutions (Lindsay et al. 1980) and Teiresias for MYCIN solutions (Chapter 8). For plans that interact continuously with the world, that is, model a changing environment, see McDermott (1978).

Further research includes *opportunistic planning* using blackboards and planning based on an object-oriented specification (Smolier 1985). Finally, there are several surveys of planning research in the *Handbook of Artificial Intelligence* (Barr and Feigenbaum 1981; Cohen and Feigenbaum 1981) and the *Encyclopedia of Artificial Intelligence* (Shapiro 1987).

Early work in blackboard models is described in HEARSAY-II research (Reddy 1976; Erman et al. 1980). Later work is described in the HEARSAY-III work (Lesser and Corkill 1983; Nii 1986).

A number of collections provide good references for machine learning: Michalski, Carbonell, and Mitchell have collected a two-volume set of important articles (Michalski et al. 1983, 1986). Klahr, Langley, and Neches have collected papers that focus on the use of production systems to model learning and development. These papers include a strong focus on the psychological aspects of such models (Neches et al. 1987).

More detailed discussions of major research efforts may be found in Laird, Rosenbloom, and Newell's book on the SOAR project (Laird et al. 1986b) and Langley, Simon, Bradshaw, and Zytkow's book on scientific discovery in the BACON project (Langley et al. 1987). Holland et al. (1986) have written a comprehensive study of induction with particular focus on genetic algorithms. Another important source of information on work in learning is the journal *Machine Learning*.

Newell and Simon's *Human Problem Solving* (1972) is a foundation for much of the work in cognitive science. In this book the *physical symbol system* hypothesis was first presented. Norman (1981) has edited an important collection of essays, including presentations by Newell, Simon, Minsky, Lakoff, Searle, and Winograd, justifying aspects of the cognitive science discipline.

Haugeland (1981) and Dennett (1978) describe the philosophical foundations of cognitive science. Anderson's book on cognitive psychology offers valuable examples of information processing models (Anderson 1985). Pylyshyn (1984) and Anderson (1978) give detailed descriptions of many critical issues in cognitive science, including a discussion of representational indeterminacy. We also recommend books on the philosophy of science (Popper 1959; Kuhn 1962).

Rumelhart, McClelland, et al. have produced a comprehensive two-volume collection of essays on parallel distributed processing that covers all the major aspects of neural network research (McClelland et al. 1986). These include biological and psychological models as well as the theory and implementation of neural nets. Churchland (1986) has written a book on the physiology and functioning of the human brain that places these topics in a philosophical framework and addresses many of the issues surrounding the relationship of the brain and the mind. We also recommend articles by Hinton and Sejnowski (1986), Sejnowski and Rosenberg (1987), and Hopfield (1982).

15.7 Exercises

1. Create the remaining *frame axioms* necessary for the four operators pickup, putdown, stack, and unstack described in rules 4 through 7 of Section 15.1.

2. Use the operators and frame axioms of the previous question to generate the search space of Figure 15.2.

3. Use techniques of Chapter 11 for planning that could automatically create a graph search similar to that of Figure 15.2.

4. Describe search heuristics that might be appropriate with the proof techniques of the previous problem. Can you identify an A* heuristic (other than breadth-first search)?

5. Show how the *add* and *delete lists* can be used to replace the frame axioms in the generation of *STATE 2* from *STATE 1* in Section 15.1.

6. Use *add* and *delete lists* to generate the search space of Figure 15.2.

7. Suggest an automated controller that could use *add* and *delete lists* to generate a graph search similar to that of Figure 15.2.

8. Show two more incompatible (precondition) subgoals in the blocks world operators of Figure 15.2.

9. Read the ABSTRIPS research (Sacerdotti 1974) and show how it handles the linearity (or incompatible subgoal) problem in planning.

10. Suggest two applications appropriate for solution using the blackboard architecture. Briefly characterize the organization of the blackboard and knowledge sources for each implementation.

11. Discuss the role of negative examples in an inductive learning algorithm. What makes a negative example a ''near'' miss? What problems arise in inductive learning without negative examples? How may these problems be addressed?

12. A feature vector is a list of values for specific features of an object and provides a simple representation of objects and classes in a world. For example, a feature vector description of objects in a blocks world might be:

[Color, Size, Shape]

where Color may have the values red, blue, green; Size the values small, medium, large; and Shape the values cube, brick, pyramid, etc. Variables in a feature vector indicate that that feature may have any value. For example, the vector

[_, small, _]

represents the class of small objects of any color or shape.

Using feature vectors as a representation, implement the version space algorithm in either LISP or PROLOG.

13. The following prolog predicates, taken from work by Kedar-Cabelli (1987), define the heart of a PROLOG explanation-based learning algorithm. prolog_ebg proves the goal and builds two proof trees. The first is the proof tree for the goal; the second is the proof tree for the goal without any variable bindings that result from unifications with facts (i.e., that it retains any constraints that result from rule chainings (only)).

```
prolog_ebg(A, GenA, A, GenA) :- clause(A, true).

prolog_ebg((A,B), (GenA, GenB), (AProof, BProof), (GenAProof, GenBProof)) :-
    prolog_ebg(A, GenA, AProof, GenAProof).
    prolog_ebg(B, GenB, BProof, GenBProof).

prolog_ebg(A, GenA, (A :- Proof), (GenA :- GenProof)) :-
    clause(GenA, GenB).
    copy((GenA :- GenB), (A :- B)),
    prolog_ebg(B, GenB, Proof, GenProof).
```

Complete this definition with procedures to extract a rule from the generalized proof tree. Use this program to implement the safe-to-stack example (Mitchell 1986) presented in this chapter.

14. Discuss the benefits and limitations of using AI formalisms as models of human intelligence. Take a position on this issue and justify your stand.

15. The Turing test evaluates intelligence in terms of performance, but does not provide an obvious method for determining if a machine or a human employs a particular architecture or structure in problem solving. Propose tests that could be used to verify whether or not an intelligent entity actually uses a specific architecture such as a production system or semantic network. Discuss the limitations of such tests.

This chapter is an introduction to a number of advanced topics in AI. Other appropriate exercises include the continuation of reading on the topics presented.

EPILOGUE

The potential of computer science, if fully explored and developed, will take us to a higher plane of knowledge about the world. Computer science will assist us in gaining a greater understanding of intellectual processes. It will enhance our knowledge of the learning process, the thinking process, and the reasoning process. Computer science will provide models and conceptual tools for the cognitive sciences. Just as the physical sciences have dominated humanity's intellectual endeavors during this century as researchers explored the nature of matter and the beginning of the universe, today we are beginning the exploration of the intellectual universe of ideas, knowledge structures, and language. I foresee significant advances continuing to be made that will greatly alter our lives. The work Tarjan and I started in the 1970s has led to an understanding of data structures and how to manipulate them. Looking ahead, I can foresee an understanding of how to organize and manipulate knowledge.

—J. HOPCROFT, ACM Turing Award Lecture, 1987

What's past is prologue.

—WILLIAM SHAKESPEARE, *The Tempest*

This text has focused on the engineering techniques used to build intelligent computer programs. In concluding, we take a few pages to consider the philosophical foundations of artificial intelligence, reexamine the possibility of a science of intelligence using AI techniques, and speculate on the future of progress in artificial intelligence. As we have noted throughout this text, research on human cognition and problem solving has made many important contributions to the design of AI programs and paradigms. In examining the foundations of AI, we consider several important issues such as the problem of falsifiability of models and the importance of the scientific method. Finally, we argue that AI and epistemology (the science of knowing) offer mutual constraints, the understanding of which adds power and maturity to both disciplines.

16

ARTIFICIAL INTELLIGENCE
AS EMPIRICAL INQUIRY

Computer science is an empirical discipline. We would have called it an experimental science, but like astronomy, economics, and geology, some of its unique forms of observation and experience do not fit a narrow stereotype of the experimental method. None the less, they are experiments. Each new machine that is built is an experiment. Actually constructing the machine poses a question to nature; and we listen for the answer by observing the machine in operation and analyzing it by all analytical and measurement means available. Each new program that is built is an experiment. It poses a question to nature, and its behavior offers clues to an answer. Neither machines nor programs are black boxes; they are artifacts that have been designed, both hardware and software, and we can open them up and look inside. We can relate their structure to their behavior and draw many lessons from a single experiment. . . .

—A. NEWELL AND H. A. SIMON, ACM Turing Award Lecture, 1976

Do I dare to eat a peach?

—T. S. ELIOT, "The Love Song of J. Alfred Prufrock"

16.1 Artificial Intelligence: A Final Definition

A final definition of artificial intelligence:

> *AI is the study of symbol systems for the purpose of understanding and implementing intelligent search.*

Part of the excitement of current work in AI is that its methods are used to engineer successful solutions to many important problems requiring human intelligence: delivering financial advice or medical care, configuring computers, troubleshooting hardware, and controlling processes in factories and spaceflights. The potential applications seem limitless; responsible engineering decisions depend upon an understanding of both the strengths and limitations of this technology.

AI, along with the rest of computer science, is an empirical discipline. Each AI program can be viewed as an experiment; it proposes a question to the natural world, and the results of that program are nature's response. As Newell and Simon indicate, the structure of computers and their programs indicates their potential behavior: they may be examined, and their representations and search algorithms may be understood. Nature's response shapes our understanding of formalism, mechanism, and intelligence.

The guiding principle of the representational AI methodology is the *physical symbol system* hypothesis, as named by Newell and Simon (1976). This hypothesis states that:

> *The necessary and sufficient condition for a physical system to exhibit general intelligent action is that it be a physical symbol system.*
>
> *Necessary* means that any physical system that exhibits general intelligence will be an instance of a physical symbol system.
>
> *Sufficient* means that any physical symbol system can be organized further to exhibit general intelligent action.
>
> *General intelligent action* means the same scope of action seen in human action: that in real situations behavior appropriate to the ends of the system and adaptive to the demands of the environment can occur, within some physical limits.

The major directions of AI and cognitive science (Chapter 15) have explored the territory delineated by the physical symbol system hypothesis; successes in both fields support its validity. Although nonrepresentational approaches, such as neural networks, show promise for answering certain problems, the bulk of progress in AI and cognitive science has come from work in this tradition. Newell and Simon have summarized the arguments for both the *necessity* and *sufficiency* of the hypothesis (Newell and Simon 1976; Newell 1981).

The physical symbol system hypothesis leads us to two significant methodological commitments: (a) the use of symbols and systems of symbols (representations) to describe the world and (b) the empirical view of computer programs as experiments. Tokens in the world, referred to as symbols, can denote or reference something other than themselves. These tokens can stand for or refer to other things in the natural world. Tarski demonstrated the possibility of a science of meaning in this object-referent relationship (Chapter 2). As an empirical science, AI takes a constructive approach: we attempt to understand intelligence by building a working model of it.

AI's use of the physical symbols goes beyond the questions addressed in Tarskian semantics, extending them to represent all forms of knowledge, skill, intention, causality, etc. However, all such efforts rely on the fact that symbols (together with their semantics) can be embedded in formal systems. These define a *representation language*. We studied several representations in detail: the predicate calculus, semantic networks (with either simple or multiple inheritance relations), objects, scripts, conceptual dependencies, and frames. The mathematics of formal systems allows us to argue such important issues as soundness, completeness, and inheritance and to establish more complex (richer) semantic relationships.

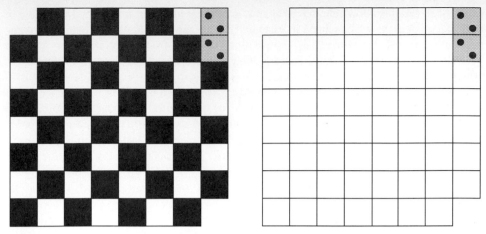

Figure 16.1 Truncated chessboard with two squares covered by a domino.

Closely bound to representational schemata, perhaps inextricably so, is the notion of search. Search is the step-by-step examination of instances within the representational framework, looking for solutions, subproblem goals, problem symmetries, or whatever aspect of the problem is under consideration.

Representation and search are closely linked because the state space searched is determined by a commitment to a particular representation. Indeed, some problems can be made more difficult, or even impossible, solely because of the representational commitment. A dramatic example of the interplay between search and representation and the difficulty of choosing an appropriate representation is the problem of placing dominos on a truncated chessboard. Assume that we have a chessboard and a set of dominos such that each domino will cover exactly two squares of the board (Fig. 16.1). Also, assume that the board has some missing squares; in Figure 16.1 the upper left-hand corner and lower right-hand corner have been truncated. This problem asks if there is a way of placing dominos on the board so that each square is covered and each domino covers two squares.

We can solve the problem by trying all placements of dominos on the board; this is the obvious search-based approach and is suggested by representing the board as a simple matrix of squares, ignoring such seemingly irrelevant features as the color of squares. However, a more sophisticated solution would note that every placement of a domino must cover both a black and a white square. This truncated board has 32 black squares but only 30 white squares; thus, the desired placement is not possible. This solution requires no search. How could we design a representation that allows a problem solver to access knowledge with this degree of flexibility and creativity? This remains a major challenge for artificial intelligence.

Important tools for implementing representation/search-based problem solvers include approaches based on predicate calculus and theorem proving, the production system model, and data- and goal-driven search in rule-based expert systems. The details of these techniques were presented in chapters 2, 3, 4, and 8. A further example of the representation/search approach is information retrieval from the simple or multiple inheritance object-oriented specification. We presented this representation in chapters 9, 10, and 14.

Another issue that arises in search-based approaches to modeling intelligence is the use of heuristics. A heuristic is a mechanism for organizing search across the possible next choices offered by a particular representation. Heuristics are designed to overcome the complexity limitations of exhaustive search, the barrier to useful solutions for most classes of interesting problems. In computers, just as in humans, intelligence is attributed to the informed choice of "what to do next."

For 30 years of AI research, heuristics have taken many forms. The earliest approaches, such as *hill climbing* in Samuel's checker-playing program (Chapter 5), came from the field of operations research and gradually matured into general techniques for AI problem solving. Properties such as *admissibility, monotonicity*, and *informedness* are important results from these early techniques, often referred to as *weak methods*. Weak methods were general search strategies intended to be applicable across entire classes of problem domains (Ernst 1969). We saw these methods and their properties in Chapter 5.

We introduced *strong methods* for AI problem solving with the rule-based expert system (Chapter 8). Strong methods underlie expert systems and other knowledge-intensive approaches to problem solving. There are four aspects of strong methods: the number of rules, the shape of the individual rules, algebras of certainty measures, and, most important, the knowledge content of the rules. Strong methods focus on the information specific to each problem area, such as internal medicine or integral calculus, rather than designing heuristic methods that generalize across problem areas.

The amount of knowledge in a program represents problem-solving power. Human experts in areas such as medicine, mathematics, or configuring computers are expert precisely because they know a lot of things. It has been estimated that a grand master chess player has on the order of 50,000 patterns guiding his or her play. The power of large rule sets is now available in many expert system application programs. The computer configuration expert at Digital Equipment Corporation contains over 6,000 rules (Soloway et al. 1987).

The second source of heuristic power is the shape of individual rules. We saw in Chapter 11 that there are often several equivalent expressions for any predicate calculus relationship. For instance:

$$A \wedge B \rightarrow C \Leftrightarrow A \rightarrow \neg B \vee C \Leftrightarrow \cdots$$

With the equivalence of various forms of the same relationship, which way the rule is presented becomes important for inferencing. Often the human expert's guidance is important in structuring the rules and guiding the inferences. Perhaps the most important of the human expert's skills is the ability to pick the relevant issues from a myriad of possible alternatives and, focusing on important data, use these to draw appropriate conclusions.

The heuristic methods linked through a representation have an important role in modeling intelligent problem solving in an application area. For example, in Chapter 8 the performance of doctors delivering treatment to meningitis patients was closely modeled by MYCIN, a goal-driven rule-based production system operating in depth-first exhaustive search fashion and guided by a certainty factor algebra. We saw not only that MYCIN attempted to duplicate human diagnostic reasoning but also that its performance was equal to or better than that of the human doctor. In this example, the semantics of the computer model is an approximation of the goals, knowledge, and intention of the human doctor delivering treatment to potential meningitis patients.

The third aspect of heuristic search in knowledge-based programs is the management of the uncertainty introduced by heuristic reasoning. As presented in Chapter 8, the certainty or confidence measure was a symbol attached to a production rule so that when it was used abductively it reflected the confidence the expert had in the rule relationship. The use of an algebra for combining and propagating certainty measures is a weak heuristic method (in that it is a general method applicable to a number of problem domains). The assignment of certainty measures to rules in a particular condition-action form is part of a strong method (in that it represents an explicit piece of knowledge).

The development of models of intelligence using representations and heuristic search forms the primary subject matter of artificial intelligence. Our methodology is the use of machine and program to ask questions of nature: to implement and test our models. The structure of machine and program allows for their characterization and manipulation. The results of our empirical queries indicate how well we understand the natural phenomena under scrutiny. In this sense our running programs offer a formal model of intelligent or purposeful human activity.

Table 16.1 presents a taxonomy of formal models of different aspects of intelligent activity. The right column lists particular human intellectual activities. The left column describes a formal model of the activity. We include not only AI models: the first row

Table 16.1 A SELECTION OF FORMAL MODELS AND RELATED HUMAN PROBLEM-SOLVING ACTIVITY

MODEL	HUMAN ACTIVITY
Peano's axioms	Counting, use of integers
Predicate calculus (Fregian semantics)	Simple problem solving such as financial adviser (chapters 2–4), knight's tour (Chapter 4)
Production system	Puzzles, games, other examples (Chapter 15); expert medical care delivery (Chapter 8); see also Newell and Simon (1976)
Semantic networks	Associative memory and simple language as in chapters 9 and 10 (Collins and Quillian 1969)
Hybrid expert systems	Modeling taxonomic knowledge and other complex physical systems (Chapter 14)
Learning models (Chapter 15)	Simple human learning
?????	Sophisticated language use
?????	Sophisticated learning

cites Peano's axiomatic formulation of the integers as a model of counting. In all cases the formal model of the left-hand column is only an approximation of the human activity of the right-hand column. For example, humans do not actually use Peano arithmetic for counting; however, it does describe the knowledge used in that activity. In several areas of human intelligence (learning, language use) we simply do not have very good computational models of the corresponding human intellectual activity; in others, such as problem solving and associative memory, our computational models have demonstrated success and continue to provide a vehicle for fruitful research. As this table indicates, the use of formal symbol systems to model human intelligence is an incomplete task.

In taking this approach, we must be careful to understand exactly what these models explain. MYCIN illustrates the difficulties in devising formal models of human intelligence. While capturing the *performance* of a doctor in a particular problem domain, the MYCIN rule base fails to model deeper aspects of the doctor's intelligence and knowledge of medicine or the architecture of the human mind. For instance, the GUIDON program at Stanford attempted to use the MYCIN knowledge base to teach students to make meningitis diagnoses. GUIDON was limited because the knowledge base, while adequate for performing the task, did not capture the deeper relations of symptoms, diseases, and physiology needed for teaching the medical knowledge to humans. In this case a model for knowing and understanding (*competence*) is quite different from a performance model of medical care delivery in a particular domain. In using symbol systems to model intelligent behavior, we must be careful to specify exactly what we are modeling.

Artificial intelligence techniques may thus be used for two purposes. The first is simply to produce programs that use intelligence to solve practical problems. Expert systems are an example of this approach. The second is to model and *understand* intelligence itself using the physical symbol system metaphor; research with this focus is referred to as *cognitive science* (presented in Chapter 15). In the next section we speculate on future directions and limitations of practical knowledge-based systems. In the final section we address theoretical limits of using formal symbol systems as models for human intelligence.

16.2   Expert Systems and Future Knowledge Media

The effort to produce intelligent problem solvers has led us to the development of knowledge-based systems: programs that use explicitly coded knowledge to solve problems. This approach has proved its viability through a number of successful programs; however, a number of limitations and unfulfilled promises remain. The difficulties in acquiring and organizing sufficient knowledge, along with the likely impossibility of ever proving that such a knowledge base is actually correct, indicate that we must still emphasize the creation of intelligent apprentices rather than autonomous intelligent experts. Other researchers, such as Weizenbaum, have also questioned the morality of letting machines make decisions in such intimately human domains as law, politics, and business (Weizenbaum 1976).

The current generation of intelligent machines may be seen as extending rather than replacing our own intellects. But we have made impressive progress, and this suggests a range of goals that are reachable given today's knowledge. One of the most exciting of these is the continued development and growth of *knowledge media*.

To understand this utility we must remember our distinction between facts and knowledge. Facts are direct statements of relationships such as the predicate likes(george, kate). The tuples that make up a relational data base offer another example of facts. The simplest example of knowledge is the *if-then* rule. Rules, besides being statements of fact relationships, include specifications for their use, for instance: *if you want to establish a conclusion, attempt to verify the conditions that imply that conclusion*. Building information into semantic nets, frames, or objects is a more sophisticated example of knowledge.

Knowledge is organized: a knowledge base captures the functional relations between components of knowledge. Knowledge is dynamic: an expert, either human or machine, can apply the appropriate expertise to a specific problem. Knowledge is flexible: it can be applied freely to a class of problems.

Knowledge-based technologies promise the development of media for storing, replicating, and transmitting knowledge, just as data bases allow us to transmit static information. As knowledge engineering techniques progress and we develop standards for the representation of knowledge, we will see knowledge become a marketable commodity. Rather than handcrafting individual expert systems, as is currently done, people will be able to purchase general knowledge modules and customize them to a particular application. Because knowledge media allow the mass sharing of knowledge, the currently high costs of building expert systems will be reduced.

This could lead to the development of *knowledge utilities* that function like a combination library, university and electric utility. Users could subscribe to a global knowledge base and access the knowledge of the world's premier experts in any subject domain. A knowledge utility consists of:

1. *A collection of knowledge bases about specialized areas of interest*, such as medicine, business, economics, or law.

2. *A query system.* This must handle everything from simple queries to the application of sophisticated learning algorithms to assist researchers in looking for new ideas as well as unsolved problems.

3. *A system for developing customized applications starting with this knowledge.* This would allow a knowledge engineer to build a specialized system based on general knowledge rather than starting from scratch. It would deal with things like helping engineers select the appropriate knowledge bases to include in their application, integrating the new knowledge with the old, ensuring representational consistency and update integrity.

4. *Systems for knowledge base maintenance to help add new knowledge.* Distinct from 3, this would include consistency-checking algorithms, tools for repartitioning the knowledge base when needed, and even natural language tools to assist in encoding new information, such as the contents of journal articles.

Many techniques for building such a knowledge utility are already available. At the time of this writing Lenat is working on such a project (Lenat 1986). CYC, which is short for enCYClopedia, is intended to be a large general base of commonsense knowledge. Builders of expert systems can enlarge on this knowledge base, both simplifying their task and increasing the robustness and correctness of their systems. Knowledge utilities will evolve; they will grow as the technology proves itself and people become aware of the capabilities it provides.

16.3 Representational Models for Intelligence: Current Limitations

like the geometer who strives
    to square the circle and cannot find
    by thinking the principle needed,

was I at that new sight....

—DANTE, *Paradiso*

Although the use of AI techniques to solve practical problems seems well on its way, the use of these techniques to found a general science of intelligence is much more problematic. In Chapter 15 we discussed three limiting aspects of a science of intelligence:

1. *Representational indeterminacy.*
2. *The limitations of the physical symbol system hypothesis.*
3. *The necessity of computational models that are falsifiable.*

A fourth, potentially even more limiting factor of the artificial intelligence enterprise is:

4. *The limitation of the scientific method itself.*

A number of researchers (Winograd and Flores 1986; Weizenbaum 1976) claim that the most important aspects of intelligence are not and, in principle, cannot be modeled, particularly not with a symbolic representation. These areas include learning and understanding and producing speech acts. Many of these issues have deep roots in the philosophical tradition. Winograd and Flores's criticisms, for example, are based on issues raised from the phenomenological viewpoint (Gadamer 1976; Heidegger 1962).

Most of the assumptions of modern AI have their roots in the philosophical tradition going back through Husserl (Husserl 1972), Hume, and Aristotle. This tradition can be summarized by Hume's dictum ''Cognition is computation.'' Husserl carried this view into modern times and argued that all aspects of our understanding of phenomena in the world are in principle understandable.

Heidegger's and Gadamer's writings, however, represent an alternative approach to understanding intelligence. They attempt to show how the fundamentally unrepeatable nature of everyday life and human existence gives reality a significance that cannot be understood in terms of representations. This position, shared by Winograd and Flores, Searle (1980), Dreyfus (1985), and others, argues that a person's understanding of things is rooted in the practical activity of coping with the everyday world. This world is essentially a context of socially organized roles and purposes. This context, and human functioning within it, is not something explained by propositions and understood by theorems. It is rather a flow that shapes and is itself continuously created. In a fundamental sense, human expertise is not knowing *that*, but rather, in a world of evolving social norms and implicit purposes, knowing *how*. We are inherently unable to place our knowledge and most of our intelligent behavior into language, either formal or natural.

Let us consider this point of view. First, as a criticism of the *pure* rationalist tradition, it is correct. Rationalism asserts that all human activity, intelligence, and responsibility can, in principal at least, be represented, formalized, and understood. Most reflective people do not believe this to be the case, reserving important roles for self-affirmation and responsible commitment (at least!). Aristotle himself said, in his *Essay on Rational Action*, ''Why is it that I don't feel compelled to perform that which is entailed?'' There are many activities outside the realms of the scientific method that play an essential role in responsible human interaction; these cannot be reproduced by or abrogated to machines.

This being said, however, the scientific tradition of examining data, constructing models, running experiments, and examining results with model refinement for further experiments has brought an important level of understanding, explanation, and ability to predict to the human community. The scientific method is a powerful tool for increasing human understanding. Nonetheless, there are a number of caveats to this approach that any scientist must understand.

First, scientists must not confuse the model with the phenomenon being modeled. The model allows us to progressively approximate the phenomenon: there will, of necessity, always be a ''residue'' that is not empirically explained. In this sense also representational indeterminacy (Section 15.4) is NOT an issue. A model is used to explore, explain, and predict; and if it allows scientists to accomplish this it is successful (Kuhn 1962). Indeed, different models may successfully explain different aspects of a single phenomenon (for instance, the wave and particle theories of light).

Furthermore, when researchers claim that aspects of intelligent phenomena are outside the scope and methods of the scientific tradition, this statement itself can be verified only by using that very tradition. The scientific method is the only tool we have for explaining in what sense issues may still be outside our current understanding. Every viewpoint, even that from the phenomenological tradition, if it is to have any meaning, must relate to our current notions of explanation—even to give a coherent explanation of the sense in which phenomena cannot be explained.

Perhaps the most exciting aspect of work in AI is that to be coherent and contribute to the endeavor we must address these issues. To understand problem solving, learning, and language we must comprehend the philosophical level of representations and knowledge. In a humbling way we are asked to resolve Aristotle's tension between *theoria* and *praxis*, to fashion a union of understanding and practice, of the theoretical and practical, to live between science and art.

Indeed, we have a tradition of this: Hobbes, Leibniz, Descartes, Babbage, Turing, and others whose contributions we presented in Chapter 1. Engineering and philosophy;

the nature of ideas, knowledge, and skill; the power and limitations of formalism and mechanism: these are the limitations and tensions with which we must live and from which we must continue our explorations.

16.4   References

We refer the reader to the references at the end of Chapter 1 and add *Computation and Cognition* (Pylyshyn 1984) and *Understanding Computers and Cognition* (Winograd and Flores 1986).

We also leave the reader with address information on two important groups:

The American Association for Artificial Intelligence
445 Burgess Drive
Menlo Park, CA 94025

Computer Professionals for Social Responsibility
P.O. Box 717
Palo Alto, CA 94301

APPENDIX 1: PROLOG PROGRAMS

A1.1   exshell and cars

```
% exshell and cars are written by M. McLaughlin and W. A. Stubblefield
% knowledge base for simple automotive diagnostic expert system.
% top level goal, starts search.

rule((fix(X) :-
        bad_component(X)), 100).

% rules to infer bad component:

rule((bad_component(starter) :-
        bad_system(starter_system),lights(come_on) ),50).
rule((bad_component(battery) :-
        bad_system(starter_system),not  lights(come_on)),90).
rule((bad_component(timing) :-
        bad_system(ignition_system),  not tuned_recently),80).
rule((bad_component(plugs) :-
        bad_system(ignition_system),plugs(dirty) ),90).
rule((bad_component(ignition_wires) :-
        bad_system(ignition_system),
        not plugs(dirty), tuned_recently),80).

% rules to infer system that failed.
```

```
rule((bad_system(starter_system) :-
        not car_starts, not turns_over),90).
rule((bad_system(ignition_system) :-
        not car_starts, turns_over,gas_in_carb),80).
rule((bad_system(ignition_system) :-
        car_starts, runs(rough),gas_in_carb),80).
rule((bad_system(ignition_system) :-
        car_starts, runs(dies),gas_in_carb),60).

% rules to make recommendation for repairs.

advice(fix(starter), ['replace starter']).
advice(fix(battery), ['replace or recharge battery']).
advice(fix(timing), ['get the timing adjusted']).
advice(fix(plugs), ['replace spark plugs']).
advice(fix(ignition_wires), ['check ignition wires']).

% askable descriptions

askable(['Does the car start'], car_starts).
askable(['Does the engine turn over'], turns_over).
askable(['Do the lights ', X], lights(X)).
askable(['Does the car run ', X], runs(X)).
askable(['Is there gas in the carburetor'], gas_in_carb).
askable(['Has the car been tuned recently'], tuned_recently).
askable(['Are the spark plugs ', X], plugs(X)).

% exshell solve(Goal) is top level call.  It initializes memory; attempts to
% solve Goal with certainty factor C; prints the results; and asks the user
% if he or she would like a trace of the reasoning used to obtain the solution.

solve(Goal) :-
        retractall(fact(X,C)), nl,
        ( ( setof((Goal, Advice, C, Proof), (solve(Goal,C,[],Proof,1,yes),
                advice(Goal, Advice)), Solution), (not Solution==[]),
          print_solution(Solution) );
          ( nl, write('Sorry, I cannot give any advice based on the
                information received.'), nl, nl ) ).

print_solution([]).
print_solution([(Goal,Advice,C,Proof)|T]) :-
        nl, print('My advice is:'), nl, write('   '), print_list(Advice), nl,
        write('Certainty of this advice is '), write(C), write('.'), nl, nl,
        ask_for_trace(Goal, Proof),
        print_solution(T).
```

```
% solve(Goal, CF, Rulestack, Prooflist, T, Ask)
% Solve predicates attempt to solve Goal by backwards chaining on rules.
% CF is the certainty factor of final conclusion.  Rulestack is the stack
% of rules currently being used (Rulestack is used in why queries).
% Prooflist is a list of the reasoning used to obtain the given
% result (Prooflist is used by how(X) queries).  T is either
% 1 or -1 depending on whether goal is to be proved true or false.  Ask
% is a flag telling whether or not things are askable at the time.

solve(A, C, Rules, (A :- given, C), T, Ask) :-
        fact(A,C), !, above_threshold(C,T).

solve(not A, C, Rules, (not Proof, C), T, Ask) :- !,
        T1 is -1 * T,
        solve(A, C1, Rules, Proof, T1, Ask),
        C is -1 * C1.

solve((A,B), C, Rules, (ProofA, ProofB), 1, Ask) :- !,
        solve(A, C1, Rules, ProofA, 1, Ask), above_threshold(C1,1),
        solve(B, C2, Rules, ProofB, 1, Ask), above_threshold(C2,1),
        minimum(C1,C2,C).

solve((A,B), C, Rules, (ProofA, ProofB), -1, Ask) :- !,
        ( solve(not A, C1, Rules, (not ProofA, _), 1, Ask);
          solve(not A, C1, Rules, (not ProofA, _), -1, no);
          (C1 is -100, ProofA = (A :- or_true, 100))       ), !,
        ( solve(not B, C2, Rules, (not ProofB, _), 1, Ask);
          solve(not B, C2, Rules, (not ProofB, _), -1, no);
          (C2 is -100, ProofB = (B :- or_true, 100))       ), !,
        maximum(C1,C2,C3), C is -1 * C3, above_threshold(C,-1).

solve((A;B), C, Rules, (ProofA; ProofB), 1, Ask) :- !,
        ( solve(A, C1, Rules, ProofA, 1, Ask);
          solve(A, C1, Rules, ProofA, -1, no);
          (C1 is -100, ProofA = (A :- or_fail, C1)) ), !,
        ( solve(B, C2, Rules, ProofB, 1, Ask);
          solve(B, C2, Rules, ProofB, -1, no);
          (C2 is -100, ProofB = (B :- or_fail, C2)) ), !,
        maximum(C1,C2,C), above_threshold(C,1).

solve((A;B), C, Rules, (ProofA; ProofB), -1, Ask) :- !,
        solve((not A, not B), C1, Rules, ((not ProofA, _), (not ProofB, _)), 1, Ask),
        C is -1 * C1, above_threshold(C,-1).

solve(A, C, Rules, (A :- rules, C, List), T, Ask) :-
        bagof((Proof, C1), solve_rule(A, C1, Rules, (A :- Proof), T, Ask), List),
        not(List==[]), calculate_C(List, C).
```

```prolog
solve_rule(A, C, Rules, (A :- Proof), T, Ask) :-
        rule((A :- B), C1),
        above_threshold(C1,T),
        solve(B, C2, [rule(A,B,C1)|Rules], Proof, 1, Ask),
        C is (C1 * C2) / 100,
        above_threshold(C,T).

solve_rule(A, C, Rules, (A :- true), T, Ask) :-
        rule((A), C),
        above_threshold(C,T).

solve(A, C, Rules, (A :- given, C), T, Ask) :-
        askable(Prompt, A), !,
        Ask = yes,
        not known(A),
        query(Prompt, A, C, Rules, normal),
        above_threshold(C,T).
```

% Try to assume goal is false if no rules can be found that imply it is true.

```prolog
solve(A, C, Rules, (A :- fail, C), -1, yes) :-
        not (bagof((Proof, C1), solve_rule(A, C1, Rules, (A :- Proof), _, Ask), List), List==[]),
        not known(A),
        query(['There are no facts or rules that allow me to solve for:', nl,
             '   ', A, nl, 'May I assume it to be false'], A, C, Rules, assume),
        above_threshold(C,-1).
```

% calculate_C(List, CF) is used to obtain a combine certainty factor, CF,
% from a list of certainty factors, List.

```prolog
calculate_C([(_,C)|[]], C):- !.

calculate_C([(_,C1),(_,C2)|[]], C) :-
        combine(C1, C2, C), !.

calculate_C([(_,C1)|T], C) :-
        calculate_C(T, C2), combine(C1, C2, C), !.

combine(C1, C2, C) :-
        C1>=0, C2>=0, C is C1+C2 - ((C1*C2)/100), !.

combine(C1, C2, C) :-
        C1=<0, C2=<0, C is C1+C2 + ((C1*C2)/100), !.

combine(C1, C2, C) :-
        abs(C1, AC1), abs(C2, AC2), minimum(AC1, AC2, MIN),
        C is ((C1+C2)/(100-MIN))*100, !.
```

```
% query(Prompt, A, C, Rules, Type)
% This is used to obtain information from the user about A.  Prompt is a
% string that is printed.  C is the returned certainty factor.
% Rules is the list of rules currently under consideration.  And Type is
% either normal, for a normal query, or assume, for a query about an
% assumption the shell wants to make.  The query is repeated until an
% answer of true, false, yes, no, or unknown is obtained.

query(Prompt, A, C, Rules, normal) :-
        get_answer(Prompt, Answer),
        respond(Answer, A, C, Rules, Newrules),
        ( member(Answer, [true, false, yes, no, unknown]);
          query(Prompt, A, C, Newrules, normal)          ), !.

query(Prompt, A, C, Rules, assume) :-
        get_answer(Prompt, Answer1),
        not member(Answer1, [false, no, unknown]),
        invert(Answer1, Answer),
        respond(Answer, A, C, Rules, Newrules),
        ( member(Answer, [true, false, yes, no, unknown]);
          query(Prompt, A, C, Newrules, assume)          ), !.

% get_answer(Query, Answer)
% Writes Query and reads the Answer.  Abbreviations (t, f, y, n, u, h, w) are
% translated to appropriate commands by filter_abbreviations.

get_answer(Query, Answer) :-
        display_query(Query),
        read(A), nl,
        filter_abbreviations(A, Answer), !.

% filter_abbreviations(Answer, Command)
% filter_abbreviations will expand Answer into Command.  If Answer is not a
% known abbreviation, then Command = Answer.

filter_abbreviations(t, true).
filter_abbreviations(f, false).
filter_abbreviations(y, yes).
filter_abbreviations(n, no).
filter_abbreviations(u, unknown).
filter_abbreviations(w, why).
filter_abbreviations(h(X), how(X)).
filter_abbreviations(X, X).

% invert(Answer, Answer2)
% Changes yes to no and true to false and vice versa.
```

```prolog
invert(yes, no).
invert(true, false).
invert(no, yes).
invert(false, true).
invert(X, X).


% known(Goal)
% Succeeds if Goal is known, i.e., Goal is an asserted fact.

known(Goal) :- fact(Goal, _).

% respond(Answer, Query, CF, Rule_stack, New_Rule_stack).
% "respond" will process Answer, given by the user, (true, false, yes, no,
% unknown, how, why, help).  It asserts to working memory facts about the
% given problem with answers of true, false, yes, no, or unknown.  An answer
% of why will display the current rule from Rulestack, while an answer of
% how(Goal) will show a trace of the reasoning used to obtain Goal. The answer
% help displays help.  Invalid responses are detected and query repeated.

respond(Bad_answer, A, C, Rules, Rules) :-
        not member(Bad_answer, [help,true,false,yes,no,unknown,why,how(_)]),
        write('Answer must be either:'), nl,
        write('  help, (t)rue, (f)alse, (y)es, (n)o, (u)nknown, (h)ow(X), or (w)hy'), nl, nl.

respond(true, A, 100, _, _) :-
        assert(fact(A,100) ).

respond(false, A, -100, _, _) :-
        assert(fact(A,-100) ).

respond(yes, A, C, _, _) :-
        get_answer(['What confidence'], C),
        assert(fact(A,C) ).

respond(no, A, C, _, _) :-
        get_answer(['What confidence'], C1),
        C is -1 * C1,
        assert(fact(A,C) ).

respond(unknown, A, 0, _, _) :-
        assert(fact(A,0) ).

respond(why, A, C, [Rule|Rules], Rules) :-
        display_rule(Rule, unknown).

respond(why, A, C, [], []) :-
        write('Back to goal, no more explanation possible.'), nl, nl.

respond(how(Goal), A, C, Rules, Rules) :-
        respond_how(Goal).
```

```prolog
respond(help, A, C, Rules, Rules) :-
     print_help.

% ask_for_trace(Goal, Proof).
% Invoked at the end of a consultation, ask_for_trace asks the user if
% he or she would like a trace of the reasoning to a goal.

ask_for_trace(Goal, Proof) :-
     write('Trace of reasoning to goal? '),
     read(Answer), nl,
     show_trace(Answer, Goal, Proof), !.

% show_trace(Answer, Goal, Proof)
% If Answer is "yes" or "y," show trace will display a trace of Goal, as
% in a "how" query.  Otherwise, it succeeds in doing nothing.

show_trace(yes, Goal, Proof) :-
     interpret(Proof), nl, !.

show_trace(y, Goal, Proof) :-
     interpret(Proof), nl, !.

show_trace(_, _, _).

% print_help

print_help :-
     nl,
     write('exshell allows the following responses to queries:'), nl, nl,
     write('   true    --- query is known to be 100% true'), nl,
     write('   false   --- query is known to be 100% false'), nl,
     write('   yes     --- query is known to be partially true'), nl,
     write('              User must input a certainty factor.'), nl,
     write('   no      --- query is known to be partially false'), nl,
     write('              User must input a certainty factor.'), nl,
     write('   unknown --- query is unknown'), nl,
     write('   why     --- displays rule currently under consideration'), nl,
     wrlte('   how(X)  --- if X has been inferred, displays trace of reasoning'), nl,
     write('   help    --- prints this message'), nl,
     write('   All commands (except help) may be abbreviated to first letter.'), nl, nl, nl.

% display_query(Query)
% Shows Query to user.  Query is a list of atoms to be displayed.

display_query(Query) :-
     print_list(Query),
     write('? ').

print_list([]).
```

```prolog
print_list([nl|T]) :-
        nl, print_list(T).

print_list([H|T]) :-
        write(H), print_list(T).

% display_rule(rule(Head, Premise, CF), C)
% Prints rule in IF...THEN form.

display_rule(rule(Head,Premise,CF), C) :-
        write('IF    '),
        write_premise(Premise, 7), nl,
        write('THEN   '),
        write(Head),
        ((number(C), write('    ***Known, Certainty = '), write(C), nl); nl),
        write('CF    '), write(CF), nl, nl, !.

% write_premise(A, Spaces)
% write_premise will print the components of a rule premise. If any
% are known to be true, they are so marked. Spaces is used to indent.

write_premise(not A, Spaces) :- !,
        write('NOT '), NSpaces is Spaces+4,
        write_premise(A, NSpaces).

write_premise((A,B), Spaces) :- !,
        write('   '), NSpaces is Spaces+4, write_premise(A, NSpaces), nl,
        tab(Spaces), write('AND '),
        write_premise(B, NSpaces).

write_premise((A;B), Spaces) :- !,
        write('   '), NSpaces is Spaces+3, write_premise(A, NSpaces), nl,
        tab(Spaces), write('OR '),
        write_premise(B, NSpaces).

write_premise(A, Spaces) :- write(A), flag_if_known(A).

% flag_if_known(Goal)
% Called by write_premise, if Goal follows from current state of working
% memory, this will print an indication with CF.

flag_if_known(Goal) :-
        solve(Goal, C, _, _, 1, no),
        write('    ***Known, Certainty = '), write(C), !.

flag_if_known(Goal) :-
        solve(Goal, C, _, _, -1, no),
        write('    ***Known, Uncertainty = '), write(C), !.

flag_if_known(Goal).
```

```
% respond_how(Goal)
% Calls solve to determine if goal follows from current state of working
% memory.  If it does, prints a trace of reasoning, if not, so indicates.

respond_how(Goal) :-
        solve(Goal, C, [], Proof, 1, no),
        interpret(Proof), !.

respond_how(Goal) :-
        solve(Goal, C, [], Proof, -1, no),
        interpret(Proof), !.

respond_how(Goal) :-
        write('Goal does not follow at this stage of consultation.'), nl, nl.

% interpret(Proof).
% Interprets a Proof as constructed by solve, printing a trace for the user.

interpret((Goal :- given, C)) :-
        write(Goal),
        write(' was given with CF = '), write(C), write('.'), nl, nl.

interpret((not Proof, C)) :-
        extract_body(Proof, Goal),
        write('not ('), write(Goal), write(')'),
        write(', with CF = '), write(C), write(','), nl,
        write('was proved by proving ('), write(Goal), write(')'),
        write(', with CF = '), C1 is -1*C, write(C1), write('.'), nl, nl,
        interpret(Proof).

interpret((ProofA, ProofB)) :-
        interpret(ProofA), interpret(ProofB).

interpret((ProofA; ProofB)) :-
        interpret(ProofA), interpret(ProofB).

interpret((Goal :- or_fail, C)) :-
        write(Goal),
        write(' was a term in an OR statement and was also not solvable.'), nl,
        write('It was therefore assumed (by me) to be false with CF = '),
        write(C), write('.'), nl, nl.

interpret((Goal :- or_true, C)) :-
        write(Goal),
        write(' was a term in a negated AND statement and was also not solvable.'), nl,
        write('It was therefore assumed (by me) to be true with CF = '),
        write(C), write('.'), nl, nl.
```

```
interpret((Goal :- rules, C, List)) :-
        nl, write(Goal), write(', with CF = '), write(C), write(','), nl,
        write('was proved using the rule(s):'), nl, nl,
        interpret_rule(Goal, List).

interpret_rule(Goal, []).

interpret_rule(Goal, [(true, C)|T]) :- !,
        rule((Goal), CF),
        write('IF      '),
        write(true),
        write('    ***Known, Certainty = '), write(100), nl,
        write('THEN    '),
        write(Goal),
        write('    ***Known, Certainty = '), write(C), nl,
        write('CF   '), write(CF),
        nl, nl,
        interpret_rule(Goal, T).

interpret_rule(Goal, [(Proof, C)|T]) :-
        extract_body(Proof, Body),
        rule((Goal :- Body), CF),
        display_rule(rule(Goal, Body, CF), C),
        interpret(Proof), nl,
        interpret_rule(Goal, T).

interpret((Goal :- fail, C)) :-
        write(Goal),
        write(' was not solvable and was assumed false with given CF = '),
        write(C), write('.'), nl, nl.

% extract_body(Proof).
% Extracts the body of the top level rule from Proof.

extract_body((Goal :- given, C), Goal).

extract_body((not Proof, C), (not Body)) :-
        extract_body(Proof, Body).

extract_body((ProofA, ProofB), (BodyA, BodyB)) :-
        extract_body(ProofA, BodyA),
        extract_body(ProofB, BodyB).

extract_body((ProofA; ProofB), (BodyA; BodyB)) :-
        extract_body(ProofA, BodyA),
        extract_body(ProofB, BodyB).

extract_body((Goal :- or_fail, C), Goal).

extract_body((Goal :- or_true, C), Goal).
```

```
extract_body((Goal :- rules, C, List), Goal).

extract_body((Goal :- fail, C), Goal).

% Utility Predicates.

retractall(X) :- retract(X), fail.
retractall(X) :- retract((X:-Y)), fail.
retractall(X).

member(X, [X|_]).
member(X, [_|T]) :- member(X,T).

minimum(X,Y,X) :- X =< Y.
minimum(X,Y,Y) :- Y < X.

maximum(X,Y,X) :- X >= Y.
maximum(X,Y,Y) :- Y > X.

abs(X, X) :- X >= 0.
abs(X, Y) :- Y is -1 * X.

above_threshold(X,1) :- X >= 20.
above_threshold(X,-1) :- X =< -20.
```

A1.2   Interpreter for Concurrent PROLOG

```
% An interpreter for a subset of concurrent prolog (Shapiro 1987).
% Modified by Mark McLaughlin, 1988.

:- op(450, xf, '?').
:- op(1150, xfx, ':').

solve(A) :-
        system_predicate(A), !, A.
solve(A) :-
        schedule(A, X, X, Head, [cycle|Tail]),
        solve(Head, Tail, deadlock).
```

```
solve([cycle], [], _) :- !.
solve([cycle|Head], Tail, deadlock) :- !, fail.
solve([cycle|Head], [cycle|Tail], nodeadlock) :- !,
        solve(Head, Tail, deadlock).
solve([A|Head], Tail, DL) :-
        system_predicate(A), !, A,
        solve(Head, Tail, nodeadlock).
solve([A|Head], Tail, DL) :-
        reduce(A, B, DL, DL1),
        schedule(B, Head, Tail, NewHead, NewTail),
        !, solve(NewHead, NewTail, DL1).

reduce(A, B, _, nodeadlock) :-
        guarded_clause(A, G, B),
        solve(G), !.
reduce(A, suspended(A), DL, DL).

guarded_clause(A, G, B) :-
        guarded_clause(A, B1), find_guard(B1, G, B).

guarded_clause(A, B) :-
        functor(A, F, N), functor(A1, F, N),
        clause(A1, B),
        unify(A, A1).

find_guard((A:B), A, B) :- !.
find_guard(A, true, A).

schedule(true, Head, Tail, Head, Tail) :- !.
schedule(suspended(A), Head, [A|Tail], Head, Tail) :- !.
schedule((A,B), Head, Tail, Head2, Tail2) :- !,
        schedule(A, Head, Tail, Head1, Tail1),
        schedule(B, Head1, Tail1, Head2, Tail2).
schedule(A, Head, [A|Tail], Head, Tail).

unify(X, Y) :-
        ( var(X) ; var(Y) ), !, X=Y.

unify(X?, Y) :- !,
        nonvar(X), unify(X, Y).

unify(X, Y?) :- !,
        nonvar(Y), unify(X, Y).

unify([X|Xs], [Y|Ys]) :- !,
        unify(X, Y), unify(Xs, Ys).

unify([], []) :- !.

unify(X, Y) :-
        X=..[F|Xs], Y=..[F|Ys], unify(Xs, Ys).
```

```
% List of system predicates in the form system_predicate(Predicate).

system_predicate(atom(T) ).
system_predicate(bagof(X,P,B)).
system_predicate(call(P) ).
system_predicate(clause(P,Q)).
system_predicate(fail).
system_predicate(functor(T,F,N)).
system_predicate(integer(T) ).
system_predicate(X is Y).
system_predicate(nl).
system_predicate(number(T) ).
system_predicate(print(T) ).
system_predicate(read(T) ).
system_predicate(setof(X,P,B)).
system_predicate(true).
system_predicate(write(T) ).
system_predicate(writeq(T) ).
system_predicate(var(T) ).
system predicate(!).
system_predicate(\+ P).
system_predicate(X<Y).
system_predicate(X=<Y).
system_predicate(X>Y).
system_predicate(X>=Y).
system_predicate(X=Y).
system_predicate(T=..L).
system_predicate(X==Y).
system_predicate(X\==Y).
system_predicate(X@<Y).
system_predicate(X@=<Y).
system_predicate(X@>Y).
system_predicate(X@>=Y).


% C-Prolog does not have the \= operator; this is its definition.
:- op(700, xfx, '\=').
X \= Y :- X=Y, !, fail.
X \= Y.
system_predicate(X\=Y).


% Utilities and "built-in" predicates.

% This is what's referred to as known(X) in chapter 29.
% wait(X, Y) :-
```

```
                      % wait until X is instantiated, "peel-off" extraneous '?'
                      % annotations, and return result in Y. Useful for interfacing
                      % with regular Prolog.
          wait(X) :-
                      wait(X, _).

          wait(X, _) :- var(X), !, fail.
          wait(X?, Y) :- !, wait(X, Y).
          wait(X, X).

          %dif(X, Y) :- X and Y are not unifiable.
          dif(X, Y) :-
                      (var(X) ; var(Y)), !, fail.
          dif(X?, Y) :- !,
                      dif(X, Y).
          dif(X, Y?) :- !,
                      dif(X, Y).
          dif([], []) :- !,
                      fail.
          dif([X|Xs], [Y|Ys]) :- !,
                      dif(X, Y) ; dif(Xs, Ys).
          dif(X, Y) :-
                      X=..[Fx|Xs], Y=..[Fy|Ys],
                      ( Fx\=Fy ; dif(Xs, Ys) ).
          dif(X, Y) :-
                      (var(X) ; var(Y)), !, fail.

          system_predicate(wait(_, _)).
          system_predicate(wait(_)).
          system_predicate(dif(_, _)).

          % Interface to tty
          terminal(Xs) :- % Xs is the current input stream
                      read(X) : terminal(X, Xs).

          terminal(end_of_file, []).
          terminal([], Xs) :-
                      terminal(Y?, Xs), read(Y).
          terminal([X|Xs], [X|Ys]) :-
                      terminal(Xs, Ys).
          terminal(X, [X|Xs]) :-
                      wait(X) : terminal(Y?, Xs), read(Y).

          outstream([X|Xs]) :- % Xs is the current output stream
                      writel(['*** outstream: ', X]), nl : outstream(Xs?).
          outstream([]).

          wait_write(X) :- % wait for X to be instantiated and then output it
                      wait(X, Y) : call((write(Y), nl)).
```

```
% wrap stream elements with an identifying tag
wrap([], _, []).
wrap([X|Xs], W, [WrappedX|Ys]) :-
        WrappedX=..[W, X] : wrap(Xs?, W, Ys).

lt(X, Y) :- wait(X, X1), wait(Y, Y1) : X1 < Y1.
le(X, Y) :- wait(X, X1), wait(Y, Y1) : X1 =< Y1.

% lazy evaluator for arithmetic expressions

':='(X, Y) :- wait(X, Y), integer(Y) : true.
':='(X+Y, Z) :- ':='(X?, X1), ':='(Y?, Y1), plus(X1, Y1, Z).
':='(X-Y, Z) :- ':='(X?, X1), ':='(Y?, Y1), plus(Z, Y1, X1).
':='(X*Y, Z) :- ':='(X?, X1), ':='(Y?, Y1), times(X1, Y1, Z).

plus(X, Y, Z) :- wait(X, X1), wait(Y, Y1) : Z is X1+Y1.
plus(X, Y, Z) :- wait(X, X1), wait(Z, Z1) : Y is Z1-X1.
plus(X, Y, Z) :- wait(Y, Y1), wait(Z, Z1) : X is Z1-Y1.

times(X, Y, Z) :- wait(X, X1), wait(Y, Y1) : Z is X1*Y1.
times(X, Y, Z) :- wait(X, X1), wait(Z, Z1) : Y is Z1/X1.
times(X, Y, Z) :- wait(Y, Y1), wait(Z, Z1) : X is Z1/Y1.
```

APPENDIX 2: LISP PROGRAMS

A2.1 Stream Functions with Delayed Evaluation

```
;;; These functions implement the basic stream handling operations
;;; with delayed evaluation, as used in Chapter 13.

(defmacro delay (exp) '(function (lambda (),exp)))

(defun force (function-closure) (funcall function-closure))

;;; Cons-stream adds a new first element to a stream
(defmacro cons-stream (exp stream)
  '(cons,exp (delay,stream)))

;;; Head-stream returns the first element of the stream
(defun head-stream (stream)
  (car stream))

;;; Tail-stream returns the stream with its first element deleted.
(defun tail-stream (stream)
  (force (cdr stream)))

;;; Empty-stream-p is true if the stream is empty.
(defun empty-stream-p (stream)
  (null stream))

;;; Make-empty-stream creates an  empty stream.
(defun make-empty-stream ()
  nil)
```

```
;;; Combine-streams appends two streams.
(defun combine-streams (stream1 stream2)
  (append stream1 stream2))
```

A2.2   Logic Programming Interpreter

```
;;;; These functions implement the logic programming interpreter described in
;;;; Chapter 13.
;;;; In order to produce the complete code for the logic interpreter, include the
;;;; definition of unify from Chapter 7 and the stream handling functions
;;;; from Appendix 2.

;;;; top level interpreter loop

(defun logic-shell ()
  (print ': )
  (let ((goal (read)))
    (cond ((equal goal 'quit) 'bye)
          (t (print-solutions goal (solve goal nil))
             (terpri)
             (logic-shell)))))

;;;; solve will take a single goal and a set of substitutions and return a
;;;; stream of augmented substitutions that satisfy the goal.

(defun solve (goal substitutions)
  (cond ((conjunctive-goal-p goal) (filter-through-conj-goals (body goal)
                                       (cons-stream substitutions
                                          (make-empty stream))))
        (t (infer goal substitutions *assertions*))))


;;;; filter-through-conj-goals will take a list of goals and a stream of
;;;; substitutions and filter them through the goals one at a time,
;;;; eliminating failures.

(defun filter-through-conj-goals (goals substitution-stream)
  (cond ((null goals) substitution-stream)
        ((filter-through-conj-goals (cdr goals)
            (filter-through-goal (car goals) substitution-stream)))))

;;;; filter-through-goal takes a goal (a pattern) and uses that goal as a filter
;;;; to a stream of substitutions.

(defun filter-through-goal (goal substitution-stream)
  (cond ((empty-stream-p substitution-stream) (make-empty-stream) )
        (t (combine-streams (solve goal (head-stream substitution-stream) )
              (filter-through-goal goal (tail-stream substitution-stream) )))))
```

```
;;; infer will take a goal, a set of substitutions and a knowledge base
;;; and attempt to infer the goal from the kb.

(defun infer (goal substitutions kb)
  (cond ((null kb) (make-empty-stream))
        (t (let ((assertion (rename-variables (car kb))))
             (combine-streams
              (cond ((rulep assertion)
                            (use-rule goal assertion substitutions))
                    (t (use-fact goal assertion substitutions)))
              (infer goal substitutions (cdr kb)))))))

;;; use-rule will attempt to infer a goal from a rule.  This function
;;; performs the backward chaining of a rule.

(defun use-rule (goal rule substitutions)
  (let ((match (unify goal (conclusion rule) substitutions)))
    (cond ((equal match 'failed) (make-empty-stream) )
          (t (solve (premise rule) match )))))

;;; use-fact will attempt to match a goal with a fact, eliminating any
;;; failures.

(defun use-fact (goal pattern substitutions)
  (let ((match (unify goal pattern substitutions)))
    (cond ((equal match 'failed) (make-empty-stream) )
          (t (cons-stream match (make-empty-stream) )))))
;;; apply-substitutions will return the result of applying a
;;; set of substitutions to a pattern.

(defun apply-substitutions (pattern substitution-list)
  (cond ((is-constant-p pattern) pattern)
        ((varp pattern)
         (let ((binding (get-binding pattern substitution list)))
           (cond (binding (apply-substitutions
                           (binding-value binding)
                           substitution-list))
                 (t pattern))))
        (t (cons (apply-substitutions (car pattern) substitution-list)
                 (apply-substitutions (cdr pattern) substitution-list)))))

;;; print solutions will take a goal and a stream of substitutions and
;;; print that goal with each substitution in the stream

(defun print-solutions (goal substitution-stream)
  (cond ((empty-stream-p substitution-stream) nil)
        (t (print (apply-substitutions goal
                                       (head-stream substitution-stream) ))
           (terpri)
           (print-solutions goal (tail-stream substitution-stream) ))))
```

```
;;; rule format is
;;; (rule if <premise> then <conclusion>)

(defun premise (rule) (nth 2 rule))

(defun conclusion (rule) (nth 4 rule))

(defun rulep (pattern)
  (and (listp pattern)
       (equal (nth 0 pattern) 'rule)))

;;; conjunctive goals are goals of the form (and <goal-1> <goal-2> ... <goal-n>)

(defun conjunctive-goal-p (goal)
  (and (listp goal)
       (equal (car goal) 'and)))

(defun body (goal) (cdr goal))

;;; rename variables will take an assertion and rename all its variables
;;; using gensym

(defun rename-variables (assertion)
  (setq *name-list* nil)
  (rename-rec assertion))

(defun rename-rec (exp)
  (cond ((is-constant-p exp) exp)
        ((varp exp) (rename exp))
        (t (cons (rename-rec (car exp))
                 (rename-rec (cdr exp))))))

(defun rename (var)
  (list 'var (or (cdr (assoc var *name-list* :test #'equal))
                 (let ((name (gensym)))
                   (setq *name-list* (acons var name *name-list*))
                   name))))

;;; misc functions

(defun is-constant-p (item)
  (atom item))

(defun varp (item)
  (and (listp item) (equal (car item) 'var)))

(defun get-binding (var substitution-list) (assoc var substitution-list :test #'equal))

(defun binding-value (binding) (cdr binding))
```

A2.3 LISP-Based Expert System Shell

```
;;; These functions implement the LISP based expert systems shell from
;;; Chapter 13.
;;; In order to produce the complete code for the expert system shell, include
;;; the definition of unify from Chapter 7, the stream handling functions
;;; from Appendix 2 and the general filter and mapping functions for streams.

;;;; top level interpreter loop

(defun lisp-shell ()
  (setq *case-specific-data* ())
  (print ': )
  (let ((goal (read)))
    (cond ((equal goal 'quit) 'bye)
          (t (print-solutions goal (solve goal (subst-record nil 0)))
             (terpri)
             (lisp-shell)))))


;;; solve will take a single goal and a set of substitutions and return a
;;; stream of augmented substitutions that satisfy the goal.

(defun solve (goal substitutions)
  (filter-stream
    (cond ((conjunctive-goal-p goal)
           (filter-conjunctions
             (cdr (body goal))
             (solve (car (body goal)) substitutions)))
          (t (solve-simple-goal goal substitutions)))
    #'(lambda (x) (< 0.2 (subst-cf x)))))

(defun solve-simple-goal (goal substitutions)
  (or (infer goal substitutions *assertions*)
      (told goal substitutions *case-specific-data*)
      (ask-for goal substitutions)))

;;; filter-conjunctions will take a list of goals and a stream of
;;; substitutions and filter them through the goals one at a time.

(defun filter-conjunctions (goals substitution-stream)
  (cond ((null goals) substitution-stream)
        ((filter-conjunctions
           (cdr goals)
           (filter-through-goal-conj (car goals) substitution-stream)))))
```

```
(defun filter-through-goal-conj (goal substitution-stream)
  (cond ((empty-stream-p substitution-stream) (make-empty-stream))
        (t (let ((subs (head-stream substitution-stream)))
             (combine-streams
               (map-stream (solve goal subs)
                 #'(lambda (x) (subst-record
                                 (subst-list x)
                                 (min (subst-cf x) (subst-cf subs)))))
               (filter-through-goal-conj goal
                 (tail-stream substitution-stream)))))))
```

;;; infer will take a goal, a set of substitutions and a knowledge base
;;; and attempt to infer the goal from the kb.

```
(defun infer (goal substitutions kb)
  (cond ((null kb) (make-empty-stream))
        (t (let ((assertion (rename-variables (car kb))))
             (combine-streams
               (cond ((rulep assertion)
                      (use-rule goal assertion substitutions))
                     (t (use-fact goal assertion substitutions)))
               (infer goal substitutions (cdr kb)))))))
```

;;; use-rule wlll attempt to infer a goal from a rule. This function
;;; performs the backward chaining of a rule.

```
(defun use-rule (goal rule substitutions)
  (let ((match (unify goal (conclusion rule) (subst-list substitutions))))
    (cond ((equal match 'failed) (make-empty-stream))
          (t (map-stream (solve (premise rule)
                           (subst-record match (subst-cf substitutions)))
               #'(lambda (x) (subst-record
                               (subst-list x)
                               (times x (rule-cf rule))))))))))
```

;;; use-fact will attempt to match a goal with a fact, eliminating any
;;; failures.

```
(defun use-fact (goal pattern substitutions)
  (let ((match (unify goal (fact-pattern pattern) (subst-list substitutions))))
    (cond ((equal match 'failed) (make-empty-stream))
          (t (cons-stream
               (subst-record match (fact-cf pattern))
               (make-empty-stream))))))
```
;;; apply-substitutions will return the result of applying a
;;; set of substitutions to a pattern.

```
(defun apply-substitutions (pattern substitution-list)
  (cond ((is-constant-p pattern) pattern)
        ((varp pattern)
          (let ((binding (get-binding pattern substitution-list)))
            (cond (binding (apply-substitutions
                                  (binding-value binding)
                                  substitution-list))
                  (t pattern))))
        (t (cons (apply-substitutions (car pattern) substitution-list)
                 (apply-substitutions (cdr pattern) substitution-list)))))
```

;;; print solutions will take a goal and a stream of substitutions and
;;; print that goal with each substitution in the stream.

```
(defun print-solutions (goal substitution-stream)
  (cond ((empty-stream-p substitution-stream) nil)
        (t (print (apply-substitutions goal
                          (subst-list (head-stream substitution-stream))))
           (print " cf = ")
           (print (subst-cf (head-stream substitution-stream)))
           (terpri)
           (print-solutions goal (tail-stream substitution-stream)))))
```

```
(defun filter-stream (stream filter)
  (cond ((empty-stream-p stream) (make-empty-stream))
        ((funcall filter (head-stream stream))
          (cons-stream (head-stream stream)
                (filter-stream (tail-stream stream) filter)))
        (t (filter-stream (tail-stream stream) filter))))
```

;;; rule functions
;;; rule format is
;;; (rule if <premise> then <conclusion>)

```
(defun premise (rule) (nth 2 rule))
```

```
(defun conclusion (rule) (nth 4 rule))
```

```
(defun rulep (pattern)
  (and (listp pattern)
       (equal (nth 0 pattern) 'rule)))
```

```
(defun rule-cf (rule) (nth 5 rule))
```

;;; fact functions
;;; fact format is
;;; (<assertion> . CF)

```
(defun fact-pattern (fact) (car fact))
```

```lisp
(defun fact-cf (fact) (cdr fact))

;;; substitutions format is
;;; (<substitution list> . cf)

(defun subst-list (substitutions) (car substitutions))

(defun subst-cf (substitutions) (cdr substitutions))

(defun subst-record (substitutions cf) (cons substitutions cf))


;;; conjunctive goals are goals of the form (and <goal-1> <goal-2> ... <goal-n>)

(defun conjunctive-goal-p (goal)
  (and (listp goal)
       (equal (car goal) 'and)))

(defun body (goal) (cdr goal))

;;; rename variables will take an assertion and rename all its variables
;;; using gensym.

(defun rename-variables (assertion)
  (setq *name-list* nil)
  (rename-rec assertion))

(defun rename-rec (exp)
  (cond ((is-constant-p exp) exp)
        ((varp exp) (rename exp))
        (t (cons (rename-rec (car exp))
                 (rename-rec (cdr exp))))))

(defun rename (var)
  (list 'var (or (cdr (assoc var *name-list* :test #'equal))
                 (let ((name (gensym)))
                   (setq *name-list* (acons var name *name-list*))
                   name))))

;;; misc functions

(defun is-constant-p (item)
  (atom item))

(defun varp (item)
  (and (listp item) (equal (car item) 'var)))

(defun get-binding (var substitution-list) (assoc var substitution-list :test #'equal))

(defun binding-value (binding) (cdr binding))
```

```
;;; ask-for

(defun ask-for (goal substitutions)

  (cond ((askable goal *askables*)
         (let* ((query (apply-substitutions goal
                                            (subst-list substitutions)))
                (result (ask-rec query)))
           (setq *case-specific-data* (cons (subst-record query result)
                                           *case-specific-data*))
           (cons-stream (subst-record (subst-list substitutions) result)
                 (make-empty-stream) )))))

(defun ask-rec (query)
  (print query)
  (print '>)
  (let ((answer (read)))
    (cond ((equal answer 'y) 1)
          ((equal answer 'n) -1)
          (t (print "answer must be y or n")
             (terpri)
             (ask-rec query)))))

(defun askable (goal askables)
  (cond ((null askables) nil)
        ((nequal (unify goal (car askables) ()) 'failed) t)
        (t (askable goal (cdr askables)))))


;;; told
 (defun told (goal substitutions case-specific-data)
  (cond ((null case-specific-data) (make-empty-stream) )
        (t (combine-streams
                (use-fact goal (car case-specific-data) substitutions)
                (told goal substitutions (cdr case-specific-data))))))

;;; stream functions, implementing streams as regular lists.

(defun combine-streams (stream1 stream2) (append stream1 stream2))

(defun cons-stream (element stream)
  (cons element stream))

(defun head-stream (stream) (car stream))

(defun tail-stream (stream) (cdr stream))

(defun empty-stream-p (stream) (null stream))

(defun make-empty-stream () nil)
```

A2.4 OOPS

```
;;;; These functions are the complete definition of the OOPS object-oriented
;;;; programming shell discussed in Chapter 14.
;;;
;;;
;;;; Defines a new object given its parent and optional list of
;;;; instance variables and bindings.

(defun def-object (obj parent &optional vars)
   (setf (get obj 'isa) parent)
   (setf (get obj 'variables) (evaluate-bindings vars)))

;;;; Evaluates the bindings on a list of variables and bindings.

(defun evaluate-bindings (vars)
   (mapcar #'(lambda (x) (list (car x) (eval (cadr x)))) vars))

;;;; Attaches a method to an object.

(defun def-method (obj name definition)
   (setf (get obj 'methods)
         (replace-method name definition (get obj 'methods))))

;;;; Adds a new method to a list of methods if it does
;;;; not already exist; replaces its definition if it does.

(defun replace-method (name definition list-of-methods)
   (cond ((null list-of-methods)
             (acons name definition nil))
         ((equal name (caar list-of-methods))
             (acons name definition (cdr list-of-methods)))
         (t (cons (car list-of-methods)
               (replace-method name definition (cdr list-of-methods))))))

;;;; Searches the inheritance hierarchy for a method.

(defun inherit-method (object method)
   (cond ((null object) nil)
         ((atom object)
             (or (get-method object method)
                      (inherit-method (get object 'isa) method)))
         (t (or (inherit-method (car object) method)
             (inherit-method (cdr object) method)))))

;;;; Retrieves a named method for a given object.

(defun get-method (object name)
   (cdr (assoc name (get object 'methods))))
```

```
;;; Evaluates a message to an object.  The environment for the
;;; evaluation is constructed dynamically from the inheritance hierarchy.

(defun message (object method &rest method-parameters)
  (let ((meth (inherit-method object method)))
        env)
    (cond (meth
            (setq env (build-env object))
            (progv (cons 'self (mapcar 'car env))
                   (cons object (mapcar 'cadr env))
              (apply meth method-parameters) )
          (t (print "unknown method")
             (print method)))))

;;; Walks the inheritance hierarchy in depth first order, constructing a list of
;;; all variable-binding pairs inherited by an object.  Used to construct the
;;; environment for evaluating a method.

(defun build-env (obj)
  (cond ((null obj) nil)
        ((listp obj) (append (build-env (cdr obj))
                             (build-env (car obj))))
        (t (append (build-env (get obj 'isa))
                   (get obj 'varlables)))))

;;; The following definitions of the root object
;;; complete the implementation of OOPS.

(def-object 'object nil)

(def-method 'object 'show
  '(lambda ()
     (terpri)
     (prin1 self) (prin1 "has parents ") (terpri)
     (pprint (get self 'isa))
     (terpri)
     (prin1 self) (prin1 "has attached variables ") (terpri)
     (pprint (get self 'variables))
     (terpri)
     (prin1 self) (prin1 "has attached methods")
     (pprint (get self 'methods))
     (terpri)))

(def-method 'object 'show-parents '(lambda () (get self 'isa)))

(def-method 'object 'show-value
  '(lambda (name)
     (eval name)))
```

```
(def-method 'object 'show-env
  '(lambda ()
     (build-env self)))

(def-method 'object 'set-value
  '(lambda (variable value)
     (let ((pair (assoc variable (get self 'variables))))
       (cond (pair (rplacd pair (list value)))
             (t (setf (get self 'variables)
                      (cons (list variable value)
                            (get self 'variables)))))))))
```

BIBLIOGRAPHY

Abelson, H., and Sussman, G. J. with Sussman, J., 1985. *Structure and Interpretation of Computer Programs*, Cambridge, MA: MIT Press.

Ackley, D. H., Hinton, G. E. and Sejnowski, T. J. 1985. A learning algorithm for Boltzmann machines. *Cognitive Science* 9.

Aho, A. V. and Ullman, J. D. 1977. *Principles of Compiler Design*. Reading, MA: Addison-Wesley.

Allen, J. 1987. *Natural Language Understanding*. Menlo Park, CA: Benjamin/Cummings.

Alty, J. L. and Coombs, M. J. 1984. *Expert Systems: Concepts and Examples*. Manchester: NCC Publications.

Anderson, J. 1983. Acquisition of proof skills in geometry. In Michalski et al. (1983).

Anderson, J. and Bower, G. H. 1973. *Human Associative Memory*. Hillsdale, NJ: Erlbaum.

Anderson, J. R. 1978. Arguments concerning representations for mental imagery. *Psychological Review* 85:249–277.

Anderson, J. R. 1983. *The Architecture of Cognition*. Cambridge, MA: Harvard University Press.

Anderson, J. R., 1985, Cognitive Psychology and Its Implications, New York: W. H. Freeman.

Andrews, P. 1986. *An Introduction to Mathematical Logic and Type Theory: To Truth through Proof*. New York: Academic Press.

Anon. Digitalk. 1986. *Smalltalk/V: Tutorial and Programming Handbook*. Los Angeles: Digitalk.

Appelt, D. 1985. *Planning English Sentences*. London: Cambridge University Press.

Aristotle. 1941. *The Basic Works of Aristotle* (R. P. McKeon, ed.), New York: Random House.

Bach, E. and Harms, R., eds. 1968. *Universals of Linguistic Theory*. New York: Holt, Rinehart & Winston.

Bachant, J. and McDermott, J. 1984. R1 revisited: Four years in the trenches. *AI Magazine* 5(3).

Backus, J., 1978, Can programming be liberated from the von Neumann style? A functional style and its algebra of programs, *Communications of the ACM* 21 (8): 613–641.

Balzer, R., Erman, L. D., London, P. E. and Williams, C. 1980. HEARSAY III: A domain independent framework for systems. *Proceedings AAAI 1980*.

Barr, A. and Feigenbaum, E., eds. 1981. *Handbook of Artificial Intelligence*, Volumes I and II. Los Altos, CA: William Kaufmann.

Bartlett, F. 1932. *Remembering*. London: Cambridge University Press.

Bateson, G., 1979, *Mind and Nature: A Necessary Unity*, New York: Dutton.

Bhaskar, R. and Simon, H. A. 1977. Problem solving in semantically rich domains. *Cognitive Science* 1.

Bledsoe, W. W., 1971, Splitting and reduction heuristics in automatic theorem proving, *Artificial Intelligence* 2:55–77.

Bledsoe, W. W. 1977. Non-resolution theorem proving. *Artificial Intelligence* 9.

Bobrow, D. G. 1975. Dimensions of representation. In Bobrow and Collins (1975).

Bobrow, D. G. and Collins, A., eds. 1975. *Representation and Understanding*. New York: Academic Press.

Bobrow, D. G. and Winograd, T. 1977. An overview of KRL, a knowledge representation language. *Cognitive Science* 1(1).

Boole, G. 1847. *The Mathematical Analysis of Logic*. Cambridge: MacMillan, Barclay & MacMillan.

Boole, G. 1854. *An Investigation of the Laws of Thought*. London: Walton & Maberly.

Boyer, R. S., and Moore, J. S. 1979. *A Computational Logic*. New York: Academic Press.

Brachman, R. J. 1979. On the epistemological status of semantic networks. In Brachman and Levesque (1985).

Brachman, R. J. 1985. I lied about the trees. *AI Magazine* 6(3).

Brachman, R. J., Fikes, R. E., and Levesque, H. J. 1985. KRYPTON: A functional approach to knowledge representation. In Brachman and Levesque (1985).

Brachman, R. J. and Levesque, H. J. 1985. *Readings in Knowledge Representation*. Los Altos, CA: Morgan Kaufmann.

Brodie, M. L., Mylopoulos, J. and Schmidt, J. W. 1984. *On Conceptual Modelling*. New York: Springer-Verlag.

Brown, J. S. and Burton, R. R. 1978. Dianostic models for procedural bugs in basic mathematical skills. *Cognitive Science* 2.

Brown, J. S., Burton, R. R. and deKleer, J. 1982. Pedagogical, natural language and knowledge engineering techniques in SOPHIE. In Sleeman and Brown (1982).

Brownston, L., Farrell, R., Kant, E. and Martin, N. 1985. *Programming Expert Systems in OPS5: An Introduction to Rule-Based Programming*. Reading, MA: Addison-Wesley.

Buchanan, B. G. and Mitchell, T. M. 1978. Model directed learning of production rules. In Waterman and Hayes-Roth (1978).

Buchanan, B. G. and Shortliffe, E. H., eds. 1984. *Rule-Based Expert Systems: The MYCIN Experiments of the Stanford Heuristic Programming Project*. Reading, MA: Addison-Wesley.

Bundy, A. 1983. *Computer Modelling of Mathematical Reasoning*. New York: Academic Press.

Bundy, A., Byrd, L., Luger, G., Mellish, C., Milne, R. and Palmer, M. 1979. Solving mechanics problems using meta-level inference. *Proceedings of IJCAI—1979*, 1017–1027.

Bundy, A. and Welham, R. 1981. Using meta-level inference for selective application of multiple rewrite rules in algebraic manipulation, *Artificial Intelligence* 16:189–212.

Burstall, R. M. and Darlington, J. A. 1977. A transformational system for developing recursive programs. *JACM* 24 (January).

Burstein, M. 1986. Concept formation by incremental analogical reasoning and debugging. In Michalski et al. (1986).

Carbonell, J. G. 1983. Learning by analogy: Formulating and generalizing plans from past experience. In Michalski et al. (1983).

Carbonell, J. G. 1986. Derivational analogy: A theory of reconstructive problem solving and expertise acquisition. In Michalski et al. (1986).

Carbonell, J., Michalski, R. S. and Mitchell, T. M. 1983. An overview of machine learning. In Michalski et al. (1983).

Carpenter, P. A. and Just, M. A. 1977. *Cognitive Processes in Comprehension.* Hillsdale, NJ: Erlbaum.

Ceccato, S. 1961. *Linguistic Analysis and Programming for Mechanical Translation.* New York: Gordon & Breach.

Chang, C. L. and Lee, R. C. T. 1973. *Symbolic Logic and Mechanical Theorem Proving.* New York: Academic Press.

Charniak, E. 1972. Toward a model of children's story comprehension. Report No. TR-266, AI Laboratory, MIT.

Charniak, E. and McDermott, D. 1985. *Introduction to Artificial Intelligence.* Reading, MA: Addison-Wesley.

Charniak, E., Riesbeck, C. K., McDermott, D. V., and Meehan, J. R. 1987, *Artificial Intelligence Programming,* 2nd ed., Hillsdale, NJ: Erlbaum.

Charniak, E. and Wilks, Y. 1976. *Computational Semantics.* Amsterdam: North-Holland.

Chomsky, N. 1965. *Aspects of the Theory of Syntax.* Cambridge, MA: MIT Press.

Church, A. 1941. The calculi of lambda-conversion. *Annals of Mathematical Studies* Vol 6. Princeton: Princeton University Press.

Churchland, P. S., 1986, *Neurophilosophy: Toward a Unified Science of the Mind/Brain,* Cambridge, MA: MIT Press.

Clancey, W. J. 1983. The advantages of abstract control knowledge in expert system design. *AAAI-3.*

Clancey, W. J. and Shortliffe, E. H. 1984*a*. Introduction: Medical artificial intelligence programs. In Clancy and Shortliffe (1984*b*).

Clancey, W. J. and Shortliffe, E. H., eds. 1984*b*. *Readings in Medical Artificial Intelligence: The First Decade.* Reading, MA: Addison-Wesley.

Clocksin, W. F. and Mellish, C. S. 1984. *Programming in PROLOG,* 2nd ed. New York: Springer-Verlag.

Cohen, P. R. and Feigenbaum, E. A. 1982. The *Handbook of Artificial Intelligence,* Volume 3. Los Altos, CA: William Kaufmann.

Collins, A. and Quillian, M. R. 1969. Retrieval time from semantic memory, *Journal of Verbal Learning & Verbal Behavior* 8: 240–247.

Colmerauer, A., 1975, Les Grammaires de Metamorphose, Groupe d'Intelligence Artificielle, Université d'Aix-Marseille II, France.

Colmerauer, A., Kanoui, H., Pasero, R. and Roussel, P. 1973. *Un Système de Communication Homme-machine en Français.* Research Report, Groupe d'Intelligence Artificielle, Université d'Aix-Marseille II, France.

Coombs, M. J., ed. 1984. *Developments in Expert Systems.* New York: Academic Press.

Crick, F. H. and Asanuma, C. 1986. Certain aspects of the anatomy and physiology of the cerebral cortex. In McClelland et al. (1986).

Dahl, V. 1977. Un système déductif d'interrogation de banques de donnes en espagnol, PhD. Thesis, Université d'Aix-Marseille.

Dahl, V. and McCord, M. C., 1983, Treating Coordination in Logic Grammars, *American Journal of Computational Linguistics* 9:69–91.

Davis, R. 1982. Applications of meta level knowledge to the construction, maintenance, and use of large knowledge bases. In Davis and Lenat (1982).

Davis, R. and Lenat, D. B. 1982. *Knowledge-Based Systems in Artificial Intelligence.* New York: McGraw-Hill.

DeJong, G. and Mooney, R. 1986. Explanation based learning: An alternative view. *Machine Learning* 1(2).

deKleer, J. 1975. Qualitative and quantitative knowledge of classical mechanics. Technical Report AI-TR-352, AI Laboratory, MIT.

de Kleer, J. 1986. An assumption based truth maintenance system. *Artificial Intelligence* 28.

Dennett, D. C. 1978. *Brainstorms: Philosophical Essays on Mind and Psychology.* Montgomery, AL: Bradford.

Dennett, D. C. 1984. *Elbow Room: The Varieties of Free Will Worth Wanting.* London: Cambridge University Press.

Dietterich, T. G. and Michalski, R. S. 1981. Inductive learning of structural descriptions: Evaluation criteria and comparative review of selected methods. *Proceedings IJCAI 6.*

Dietterich, T. G. and Michalski, R. S. 1986. Learning to predict sequences. In Michalski et al. (1986).

Doyle, J. 1979. AAAA truth maintenance system. *Artificial Intelligence* 12.

Dreyfus, H. L. and Dreyfus, S. E., 1985, *Mind Over Machine*, New York: Macmillan/The Free Press.

Duda, R. O., Gaschnig, J. and Hart, P. E. 1979*a*. Model design in the PROSPECTOR consultant system for mineral exploration. In Michie (1979).

Duda, R. O., Hart, P. E., Konolige, K. and Reboh, R. 1979*b*. A computer-based consultant for mineral exploration. SRI International.

van Emden, M. and Kowalski, R., 1976, The Semantics of Predicate Logic and a Programming Language, *Journal of the ACM* 23:733–742.

Erman, L., Hayes-Roth, F., Lesser, V. and Reddy, D. 1980. The HEARSAY II speech understanding system: Integrating knowledge to resolve uncertainty. *Computing Surveys* 12(2): 213–253.

Erman, L. D., London, P. E. and Fickas, S. F. 1981. The Design and an Example Use of HEARSAY III. In *Proceedings IJCAI 7.*

Ernst, G. W. and Newell, A., 1969, *GPS: A Case Study in Generality and Problem Solving*, New York: Academic Press.

Etherington, D. W. and Reiter, R. 1983. On inheritance hierarchies with exceptions. *Proceedings AAAI-83,* 104–108.

Euler, L. 1735. The seven bridges of Konigsberg. In Newman (1956).

Evans, T. G. 1968. *A Heuristic Program to Solve Geometric Analogy Problems.* In Minsky (1968).

Fass, D. and Wilks, Y. 1983. Preference semantics with ill-formedness and metaphor. *American Journal of Computational Linguistics* 9:178–187.

Feigenbaum, E. A. 1963. The Simulation of Verbal Learning Behavior. In Feigenbaum and Feldman (1963).

Feigenbaum, E. A. and Feldman, J., eds. 1963. *Computers and Thought*. New York: McGraw-Hill.

Feigenbaum, E. and McCorduck, P., 1983, *The Fifth Generation: Artificial Intelligence and Japan's Computer Challenge to the World*, Reading, MA: Addison-Wesley.

Fikes, R. E. and Nilsson, N. J. 1971. STRIPS: A new approach to the application of theorem proving to artificial intelligence. *Artificial Intelligence* 1(2).

Fikes, R. E. and Nilsson, N. J. 1972. Learning and executing generalized robot plans. *Artificial Intelligence* 3(4): 251–288.

Fillmore, C. J. 1968. The case for case. In Bach and Harms (1968).

Frege, G. 1879. *Begriffsschrift, eine der arithmetischen nachgebildete Formelsprache des reinen Denkens*. Halle: L. Niebert.

Frege, G. 1884. *Die Grundlagen der Arithmetic*. Breslau: W. Koeber.

Gadamer, H. G. 1976. *Philosophical Hermeneutics*. Translated by Linge, D. E. Berkeley: University of California Press.

Gallier, J. H., 1986, *Logic for Computer Science: Foundations of Automatic Theorem Proving*. New York: Harper & Row.

Garey, M. and Johnson, D. 1979. *Computers and Intractability: A Guide to the Theory of NP-Completeness*. San Francisco: Freeman.

Genesereth, M. R. 1982. The role of plans in intelligent teaching systems. In Sleeman and Brown (1982).

Genesereth, M. R. and Nilsson, N. J., 1987, *Logical Foundations of Artificial Intelligence*, Los Altos, CA: Morgan Kaufmann.

Goldberg, A. and Robson, D. 1983. *Smalltalk-80: The Language and Its Implementation*. Reading, MA: Addison-Wesley.

Goldstine, H. H. 1972. *The Computer from Pascal to von Neumann*. Princeton, NJ: Princeton University Press.

Grosz, B. 1977. The representation and use of focus in dialogue understanding. Ph.D. Thesis, University of California, Berkeley.

Harmon, P. and King, D. 1985. *Expert Systems: Artificial Intelligence in Business*. New York: Wiley.

Harmon, P., Maus, R. and Morrissey, W. 1988. *Expert Systems: Tools and Applications*. New York: Wiley.

Harris, M. D. 1985. *Introduction to Natural Language Processing*. Reston, VA: Reston.

Haugeland, J., ed. 1981. *Mind Design: Philosophy, Psychology, Artificial Intelligence*. Cambridge, MA: MIT Press.

Haugeland, J. 1985. *Artificial Intelligence: The Very Idea*. Cambridge/Bradford, MA: MIT Press.

Hayes, P. J. 1974. Some problems and non-problems in representation theory. *Proc. AISB Summer Conference*, 63–69. University of Sussex.

Hayes, P. J. 1977. In defense of Logic. *Proceedings IJCAI-77*, 559–564. Cambridge, MA.

Hayes, P. J. 1979. The logic of frames. In Metzing (1979).

Hayes-Roth, F. and McDermott, J. 1978. An inference matching technique for inducing abstractions. *Communications of the ACM* 26:401–410.

Hayes-Roth, F., Waterman, D. and Lenat, D. 1984. *Building Expert Systems*. Reading, MA: Addison-Wesley.

Heidegger, M. 1962. *Being and Time*. Translated by Masquarrie, J. and Robinson, E. New York: Harper & Row.

Heidorn, G. E. 1975. Augmented phrase structure grammar. In Schank and Nash-Webber (1975).

Helman, P. and Veroff, R. 1986. *Intermediate Problem Solving and Data Structures: Walls and Mirrors*. Menlo Park, CA: Benjamin/Cummings.

Henderson, P. 1980. *Functional Programming: Application and Implementation*. Englewood Cliffs, N.J.: Prentice-Hall.

Hillis, D. W. 1985. *The Connection Machine*. Cambridge, MA: MIT Press.

Hinsley, D., Hayes, J. and Simon, H. 1977. From words to equations: Meaning and representation in algebra word problems. In Carpenter and Just (1977).

Hinton, G. E. and Sejnowski, T. J. 1986. Learning and relearning in Boltzmann machines. In McClelland et al. (1986).

Hinton, G. E. and Sejnowski, T. J. 1987. Neural network architectures for AI. Tutorial, AAAI Conference.

Hodges, A. 1983. *Alan Turing: The Enigma*. New York: Simon & Schuster.

Holland, J. H., Holyoak, K. J., Nisbett, R. E. and Thagard, P. R. 1986. *Induction*. Cambridge, MA: MIT Press.

Hopcroft, J. E. and Ullman, J. D. 1979. *Introduction to Automata Theory, Languages, and Computation*. Reading, MA: Addison-Wesley.

Hopfield, J. J. 1982. Neural networks and physical systems with emergent collective computational abilities. *Proceedings of the National Academy of Sciences 79*.

Horowitz, E. and Sahni, S. 1978. *Fundamentals of Computer Algorithms*. Rockville, MD: Computer Science Press.

Husserl, E., 1972, *Ideas: General Introduction to Pure Phenomenology*, New York: Collier.

Johnson, L. and Keravnou, E. T. 1985. *Expert Systems Technology: A Guide*. Cambridge, MA:Abacus Press.

Johnson, W. L. and Soloway, E. 1985. Proust. *Byte* (April).

Johnson-Laird, P. 1983. *Mental Models*. Cambridge, MA: Harvard University Press.

Kedar-Cabelli, S. T. and McCarty, L. T. 1987. Explanation based generalization as resolution theorem proving. *Proceedings of the Fourth International Workshop on Machine Learning*.

Keravnou, E. T. and Johnson, L. 1985. *Competent Expert Systems: A Case Study in Fault Diagnosis*. London: Kegan Paul.

Klahr, D., Langley, P. and Neches, R. 1987. *Production System Models of Learning and Development*. Cambridge, MA: MIT Press.

Klahr, P. and Waterman, D. A., eds. 1986. *Expert Systems: Techniques, Tools, and Applications*. Reading, MA: Addison-Wesley.

Kolodnor, J. L. 1987. Extending problem solver capabilities through case based inference. *Proceedings of the Fourth International Workshop on Machine Learning*. Los Altos, CA: Morgan Kaufmann.

Korf, R. E. 1987. Search. In Shapiro (1987).

Kowalski, R. 1979*a*. Algorithm = logic + control. *Communications of the ACM* 22:424–436.

Kowalski, R. 1979*b*. *Logic for Problem Solving*. Amsterdam: North-Holland.

Kuhn, T. S. 1962. *The Structure of Scientific Revolutions*. Chicago: University of Chicago Press.

Laird, J., Rosenbloom, P. and Newell, A. 1986*a*. Chunking in SOAR: The anatomy of a general learning mechanism. *Machine Learning* 1(1).

Laird, J., Rosenbloom, P. and Newell, A. 1986b. *Universal Subgoaling and Chunking: The Automatic Generation and Learning of Goal Hierarchies.* Dordrecht: Kluwer.

Langley, P., Bradshaw, G. L., and Simon, H. A., 1981, Bacon 5: The Discovery of Conservation Laws, in *Proceedings of the Seventh International Joint Conference on Artificial Intelligence.*

Langley, P., Simon, H. L., Bradshaw, G. L. and Zytkow, J. M. 1987. *Scientific Discovery: Computational Explorations of the Creative Processes.* Cambridge, MΛ: MIT Press.

Langley, P., Zytkow, J., Simon, H. A., and Bradshaw, G. L., 1986, The Search for Regularity: Four aspects of scientific discovery. In Michalski (1986).

Larkin, J. H., McDermott, J., Simon, D.P. and Simon, H. A. 1980. Models of competence in solving physics problems. *Cognitive Science* 4.

Leibniz, G. W. 1887. *Philosophische Schriften.* Berlin.

Lenat, D. B. 1977. On automated scientific theory formation: A case study using the AM program. *Machine Intelligence* 9:251–256.

Lenat, D. B. 1982. AM: An artificial intelligence approach to discovery in mathematics as heuristic search. In Davis and Lenat (1982).

Lenat, D. B. and Brown, J. S. 1984. Why AM and Eurisko appear to work. *Artificial Intelligence* 23(3).

Lenat, D., Prakash, M., and Shepherd, M. 1986. CYC: Using common sense knowledge to overcome brittleness and knowledge acquisition bottlenecks. *AI Magazine* 6(4).

Lennon, J. and McCartney, P. 1968. Rocky Raccoon. *The White Album.* Apple Records.

Lesser, V. R. and Corkill, D. D. 1983. The distributed vehicle monitoring testbed. *AI Magazine* 4(3).

Levesque, H. 1984. Foundations of a functional approach to knowledge representation. *Artificial Intelligence* 23(2).

Levesque, H. J. and Brachman, R. J. 1985. A fundamental tradeoff in knowledge representation and reasoning (revised version). In Brachman and Levesque (1985).

Linde, C. 1974. Information structures in discourse. Ph.D. Thesis, Columbia University, New York.

Lindsay, R. K., Buchanan, B. G., Feigenbaum, E. A., and Lederberg, J. 1980. *Applications of Artificial Intelligence for Organic Chemistry: The DENDRAL Project.* New York: McGraw-Hill.

Lloyd, J. W. 1984. *Foundations of Logic Programming.* New York: Springer-Verlag.

Lovelace, A. 1961. Notes upon L. F. Menabrea's sketch of the Analytical Engine invented by Charles Babbage. In Morrison and Morrison (1961).

Loveland, D. W. 1978. *Automated Theorem Proving: A Logical Basis.* Amsterdam: North-Holland.

Luger, G. F. 1978. Formal analysis of problem solving behavior. In *Cognitive Psychology: Learning and Problem Solving.* Milton Keynes: Open University Press.

Luger, G. F. 1981. Mathematical model building in the solution of mechanics problems: Human protocols and the MECHO trace. *Cognitive Science* 5:55–77.

Luger, G. F. and Bauer, M. A. 1978. Transfer effects in isomorphic problem solving. *Acta Psychologia* 42.

Machtey, M. and Young, P. 1979. *An Introduction to the General Theory of Algorithms.* Amsterdam: North-Holland.

MacLennan, B. J. 1987. *Principles of Programming Languages: Design, Evaluation, and Implementation,* 2nd ed. New York: Holt, Rinehart & Winston.

Maier, D. and Warren, D. S. 1988. *Computing with Logic: Logic Programming with PROLOG.* Menlo Park, CA: Benjamin/Cummings.

Malpas, J., 1987, *PROLOG: A Relational Language and its Applications*, Englewood Cliffs, N.J.: Prentice-Hall.

Manna, Z. and Waldinger, R. 1985. *The Logical Basis for Computer Programming*, Vol. 1, *Deductive Reasoning*. Reading, MA: Addison-Wesley.

Markov, A. 1954. *A Theory of Algorithms*. National Academy of Sciences, USSR.

Masterman, M. 1961. Semantic message detection for machine translation, using Interlingua. *Proceedings of the 1961 International Conference on Machine Translation*.

McCarthy, J. 1960. Recursive functions of symbolic expressions and their computation by machine. *Communications of the ACM* 3(4).

McCarthy, J. 1968. Programs with common sense. In Minsky (1968), pp. 403–418.

McCarthy, J. 1977. Epistemological problems in artificial intelligence. *Proceedings IJCAI-77*, 1038–1044.

McCarthy, J. 1980. Circumscription—a form of non-monotonic reasoning. *Artificial Intelligence* 13.

McCarthy, J. and Hayes, P. J. 1969. Some philosophical problems from the standpoint of artificial intellience. In Meltzer and Michie (1969).

McClelland, J. L., Rumelhart, D. E. and the PDP Research Group. 1986. *Parallel Distributed Processing*, Volumes 1 and 2. Cambridge, MA: MIT Press.

McCord, M. C. 1982. Using slots and modifiers in logic grammars for natural language, *Artificial Intelligence* 18, 327–367.

McCord, M. C. 1986. Design of a PROLOG based machine translation system, *Proceedings of the Third International Logic Programming Conference*, London.

McCulloch, W. S. and Pitts, W. H. 1943. A logical calculus of the ideas immanent in nervous activity. *Bulletin of Mathematical Biophysics* 5.

McDermott, D. 1978. Planning and acting. *Cognitive Science* 2.

McDermott, J. 1981. R1, the formative years. *AI Magazine* (Summer).

McDermott, J. 1982. R1: A rule based configurer of computer systems. *Artificial Intelligence* 19.

McDermott, J. and Bachant, J. 1984. R1 revisited: Four years in the trenches. *AI Magazine* 5(3).

Meltzer, B. and Michie, D. 1969. *Machine Intelligence 4*. Edinburgh: Edinburgh University Press.

Metzing, D., ed. 1979. *Frame Conceptions and Text Understanding*. Berlin: de Gruyter.

Michalski, R. S., Carbonell, J. G. and Mitchell, T. M., eds. 1983. *Machine Learning: An Artificial Intelligence Approach*. Palo Alto, CA: Tioga.

Michalski, R. S., Carbonell, J. G., and Mitchell, T. M., eds. 1986. *Machine Learning: An Artificial Intelligence Approach*, Volume II. Los Altos, CA: Morgan Kaufmann.

Michie, D., ed. 1979. *Expert Systems in the Micro-Electronic Age*. Edinburgh: Edinburgh University Press.

Minsky, M., ed. 1968. *Semantic Information Processing*. Cambridge, MA: MIT Press.

Minsky, M. 1975. A framework for representing knowledge. In Brachman and Levesque (1985).

Minsky, M. and Papert, S. 1969. *Perceptrons: An Introduction to Computational Geometry*. Cambridge, MA: MIT Press.

Mitchell, T. M. 1978. Version spaces: An approach to concept learning. Report No. STAN-CS-78-711, Computer Science Department, Stanford University.

Mitchell, T. M. 1979. An analysis of generalization as a search problem. *Proceedings IJCAI 6.*

Mitchell, T. M., Keller, R. M. and Kedar-Cabelli, S. T. 1986. Explanation based generalization: A unifying view. *Machine Learning* 1(1).

Moore, O. K. and Anderson, S. B., 1954, Modern logic and tasks for experiments on problem solving behavior, *Journal of Psychology*, 38:151–160.

Moore, R. C. 1982. The role of logic in knowledge representation and commonsense reasoning. *Proceedings AAAI-82.*

Morrison, P. and Morrison, E., eds. 1961. *Charles Babbage and his Calculating Machines.* New York: Dover.

Mostow, D. J. 1983. Machine transformation of advice into a heuristic search procedure. In Michalski et al. (1983).

Mycroft, A. and O'Keefe, R. A., 1984, A Polymorphic Type System for PROLOG, *Artificial Intelligence* 23:295–307.

Mylopoulos, J. and Levesque, H. J. 1984. An overview of knowledge representation. In Brodie et al. (1984).

Nagel, E. and Newman, J. R. 1958. *Godel's Proof.* New York: New York University Press.

Neches, R., Langley, P. and Klahr, D. 1987. Learning, development and production systems. In Klahr et al. (1987).

Negoita, C. V. 1984. *Expert Systems and Fuzzy Systems.* Menlo Park, CA: Benjamin/Cummings.

Neves, J. C. F. M., Luger, G. F. and Carvalho, J. M., 1986, A Formalism for Views in a Logic Data Base, in *Proceedings of the ACM Computer Science Conference, Cincinnati 1986.*

Newell, A. 1981. Physical symbol systems. In Norman (1981).

Newell, A. 1982. The knowledge level. *Artificial Intelligence* 18(1): 87–127.

Newell, A., Shaw, J. C. and Simon, H. A., 1958, Elements of a theory of human problem solving, *Psychological Review*, 65: 151–166.

Newell, A. and Simon, H. 1956. The logic theory machine. *IRE Transactions on Information Theory* 2:61–79.

Newell, A. and Simon, H. 1963a. Empirical explorations with the Logic Theory Machine: A case study in heuristics. In Feigenbaum and Feldman (1963).

Newell, A. and Simon, H. 1963b. GPS: A program that simulates human thought. In Feigenbaum (1963).

Newell, A. and Simon, H. 1972. *Human Problem Solving.* Engelwood Cliffs, NJ: Prentice-Hall.

Newell, A. and Simon, H. 1976. Computer science as empirical inquiry: Symbols and search. *CACM* 19(3):113–126.

Newman, J. R. 1956. *The World of Mathematics.* New York: Simon & Schuster.

Nii, H. P. 1986a. Blackboard systems: The blackboard model of problem solving and the evolution of blackboard architectures. *AI Magazine* 7(2).

Nii, H. P. 1986b. Blackboard systems: Blackboard application systems from a knowledge based perspective. *AI Magazine* 7(3).

Nii, H. P. and Aiello, N. 1979. AGE: A knowledge based program for building knowledge based programs. *Proceedings IJCAI 6.*

Nilsson, N. J. 1980. *Principles of Artificial Intelligence.* Palo Alto. CA: Tioga.

Norman, D. A. 1972. Memory, knowledge and the answering of questions. CHIP Technical Report 25, Center for Human Information Processing, University of California, San Diego.

Norman, D. A. 1981. *Perspectives on Cognitive Science*. Hillsdale, NJ: Erlbaum.

Norman, D. A., Rumelhart, D. E., and the LNR Research Group. 1975. *Explorations in Cognition*. San Francisco: Freeman.

Novak, G. S. 1977. Computer understanding of physics problems stated in natural language. *Proceedings IJCAI 5*.

Papert, S. 1980. *Mindstorms*. New York: Basic Books.

Pearl, J. 1984. *Heuristics: Intelligent Search Strategies for Computer Problem Solving*. Reading, MA: Addison-Wesley.

Pereira, F. and Warren, D. H. D., 1980, Definite Clause Grammars for Language Analysis— A Survey of the Formalism and a Comparison with Augmented Transition Networks, *Artificial Intelligence* 13:231–278.

Polya, G. 1945. *How to Solve It*. Princeton, NJ: Princeton University Press.

Popper, K. R. 1959. *The Logic of Scientific Discovery*. London: Hutchinson.

Post, E., 1943, Formal Reductions of the General Combinatorial Problem, *American Journal of Mathematics*, 65:197–268.

Pratt, T. W. 1984. *Programming Languages: Design and Implementation*. Engelwood Cliffs, NJ: Prentice-Hall.

Pylyshyn, Z. W. 1973. What the mind's eye tells the mind's brain: A critique of mental imagery. *Psychological Bulletin* 80:1–24.

Pylyshyn, Z. W. 1980. The causal power of machines. *Behavioral and Brain Sciences* 3:442–444.

Pylyshyn, Z. W. 1984. *Computation and Cognition: Toward a Foundation for Cognitive Science*. Cambridge, MA: MIT Press.

Quillian, M. R. 1967. Word concepts: A theory and simulation of some basic semantic capabilities. In Brachman and Levesque (1985).

Quinlan, J. R. 1986*a*. Induction of decision trees. *Machine Learning* 1(1).

Quinlan, J. R. 1986*b*. The effect of noise on concept learning. In Michalski et al. (1986).

Raphael, B. 1968. *SIR: A computer program for semantic information retrieval*. In Minsky (1968).

Reddy, D. R. 1976. Speech recognition by machine: A review. *Proceedings of the IEEE* 64 (May).

Reichman, R. 1985. *Getting Computers to Talk Like You and Me*. Cambridge, MA: MIT Press.

Reiter, R. 1978. On closed world databases. In Webber and Nilsson (1981).

Reiter, R. 1985. On reasoning by default. In Brachman and Levesque (1985).

Reitman, W. R. 1965. *Cognition and Thought*. New York: Wiley.

Rendell, L. 1986. A general framework for induction and a study of selective induction. *Machine Learning* 1(2).

Roberts, D. D. 1973. *The Existential Graphs of Charles S. Pierce*. The Hague: Mouton.

Robinson, J. A. 1965. A machine-oriented logic based on the resolution principle. *Journal of the ACM* 12: 23–41.

Rosenblatt, F., 1962, *Principles of Neurodynamics*, New York: Spartan.

Rosenbloom, P. S. and Newell, A. 1986. The chunking of goal hierarchies: A generalized model of practice. In Michalski et al. (1986).

Rosenbloom, P. and Newell, A. 1987. Learning by chunking, a production system model of practice. In Klahr et al. (1987).

Roussel, P. 1975. *PROLOG: Manuel de Référence et d'Utilisation.* Groupe d'Intelligence Artificielle, Université d'Aix-Marseille, Luminy, France.

Rumelhart, D. E., Hinton, G. E. and Williams, R. J. 1986. Learning internal representations by error propogation. In McClelland et al. (1986).

Rumelhart, D. E., Lindsay, P. H. and Norman, D. A. 1972. A process model for long-term memory. In Tulving and Donaldson (1972).

Rumelhart, D. E. and Norman, D. A. 1973. Active semantic networks as a model of human memory. *Proceedings IJCAI3.*

Sacerdotti, E. D. 1974. Planning in a hierarchy of abstraction spaces. *Artificial Intelligence* 5:115–135.

Sacerdotti, E. D. 1975. The nonlinear nature of plans. *Proceedings IIJCAI 4.*

Sacerdotti, E. D. 1977. *A Structure of Plans and Behavior.* New York: Elsevier.

Samuel, A. L., 1959, Some Studies in Machine Learning Using the Game of Checkers, *IBM Journal of R & D* 3:221–229.

Schank, R. and Abelson, R. 1977. *Scripts, Plans, Goals and Understanding.* Hillsdale, NJ: Erlbaum.

Schank, R. C. and Colby, K. M., eds. 1973. *Computer Models of Thought and Language.* San Francisco: Freeman.

Schank, R. C. and Nash-Webber, B. L., eds. 1975. *Theoretical Issues in Natural Language Processing.* Association for Computational Linguistics.

Schank, R. and Rieger, C. J. 1974. Inference and the computer understanding of natural language. *Artificial Intelligence* 5(4):373–412.

Schank, R. C. and Riesbeck, C. K., eds. 1981. *Inside Computer Understanding: Five Programs Plus Miniatures.* Hillsdale, NJ: Erlbaum.

Searle, J. 1969. *Speech Acts.* London: Cambridge University Press.

Searle, J. R. 1980. Minds, brains and programs. *Behavioral and Brain Sciences* 3: 417–424.

Sedgewick, R. 1983. *Algorithms.* Reading, MA: Addison-Wesley.

Sejnowski, T. J. and Rosenberg, C. R. 1987. Parallel networks that learn how to pronounce English text. *Complex Systems* 1.

Selz, O. 1913. *Uber die Gesetze des Geordneten Denkverlaufs.* Stuttgart: Spemann.

Selz, O. 1922. *Zur Psychologie des Produktiven Denkens und des Irrtums.* Bonn: Friedrich Cohen.

Shapiro, E. 1987. *Concurrent PROLOG: Collected Papers*, Volumes 1 and 2. Cambridge, MA: MIT Press.

Shapiro, S. C., ed. 1987. *Encyclopedia of Artificial Intelligence.* New York: Wiley-Interscience.

Siekmann, J. H. and Wrightson, G., eds. 1983*a*. *The Automation of Reasoning: Collected Papers from 1957 to 1970, Vol I*, New York: Springer-Verlag.

Siekmann, J. H. and Wrightson, G., eds. 1983*b*. *The Automation of Reasoning: Collected Papers from 1957 to 1970, Vol II*, New York: Springer-Verlag.

Simmons, R. F. 1966. Storage and retrieval of aspects of meaning in directed graph structures. *Communications of the ACM* 9:211–216.

Simmons, R. F. 1973. Semantic networks: Their computation and use for understanding English sentences. In Schank (1972).

Simon, D. P. and Simon, H. A. 1978. Individual differences in solving physics problems. In Siegler (1978).

Simon, H. A., 1944, Decision making and administrative organization, *Public Administration Review*, 4: 16–31.

Simon, H. A. 1975. The functional equivalence of problem solving skills. *Cognitive Psychology* 7:268–288.

Simon, H. A. 1981. *The Sciences of the Artificial*, 2nd ed. Cambridge, MA: MIT Press.

Simon, H. A. 1983. Why should machines learn? In Michalski et al. (1983).

Sims, M. H. 1987. Empirical and analytic discovery in IL. *Proceedings of the Fourth International Workshop on Machine Learning.* Los Altos, CA: Morgan Kaufmann.

Sleeman, D. 1982. Assessing aspects of competence in basic algebra. In Sleeman and Brown (1982).

Sleeman, D. and Brown, J. S. 1982. *Intelligent Tutoring Systems.* New York: Academic Press.

Sleeman, D. H. and Smith, M. J. 1981. Modelling students' problem solving. *AI Journal* 1981:171–187.

Smart, G. and Langeland-Knudsen, J. 1986. *The CRI Directory of Expert Systems.* Oxford: Learned Information (Europe) Ltd.

Smith, B. 1985. Prologue to reflection and semantics in a procedural language. In Brachman and Levesque (1985).

Smith, R. G. and Baker, J. D. 1983. The Dipmeter Advisor system: A case study in commercial expert system development. *Proc. 8th IJCAI*, 122–129.

Smoliar, S. W., 1985, A View of Goal-oriented Programming, Schlumberger-Doll Research Note.

Soloway, E., Bachant, J. and Jensen, K. 1987. Assessing the maintainability of XCON-in-RIME: Coping with the problems of a very large rule base. *Proceedings AAAI-87.* Los Altos, CA: Morgan Kaufmann.

Soloway, E., Rubin, E., Woolf, B., Bonar, J. and Johnson, W. L. 1983. MENO-II: An AI-based programming tutor. *Journal of Computer Based Instruction* 10(1,2).

Sowa, J. F. 1984. *Conceptual Structures: Information Processing in Mind and Machine.* Reading, MA: Addison-Wesley.

Steele, G. L. 1984, *Common LISP: The Language.* Bedford, MA: Digital Press.

Stefik, M., Bobrow, D., Mittal, S. and Conway, L. 1983. Knowledge programming in LOOPS: Report on an experimental course. *Artificial Intelligence* 4(3).

Sterling, L. and Shapiro, E. 1986. *The Art of PROLOG: Advanced Programming Techniques*, Cambridge, MA: MIT Press.

Sussman, G. J. 1975. *A Computer Model of Skill Acquisition.* Cambridge, MA: MIT Press.

Tarski, A. 1944. The semantic conception of truth and the foundations of semantics. *Philos. and Phenom. Res.* 4:341–376.

Tarski, A. 1956. *Logic, Semantics, Metamathematics.* London: Oxford University Press.

Touretzky, D. S. 1986. *The Mathematics of Inheritance Systems.* Los Altos, CA: Morgan Kaufmann.

Tulving, E. and Donaldson, W. 1972. *Organization of Memory.* New York: Academic Press.

Turing, A. A. 1950. Computing machinery and intelligence. *Mind* 59:433–460.

Turner, R. 1984. *Logics for Artificial Intelligence.* Chichester: Ellis Horwood.

Ullman, J. D. 1982. *Principles of Database Systems.* Rockville, MD: Computer Science Press.

Vere, S. A. 1975. Induction of concepts in the predicate calculus. *Proceedings IJCAI 4.*

Vere, S. A. 1978. Inductive learning of relational productions. In Waterman and Hayes-Roth (1978).

Walker, A., McCord, M., Sowa, J. F. and Wilson, W. G. 1987. *Knowledge Systems and PRO-LOG: A Logical Approach to Expert Systems and Natural Language Processing.* Reading, MA: Addison-Wesley.

Warren, D. H. D. 1976. Generating conditional plans and programs. *Proc. AISB Summer Conference*, Edinburgh, pp. 334–354.

Warren, D. H. D. 1980. Logic programming and compiler writing. *Software-Practice and Experience* 10(2).

Warren, D. H. D., Pereira, F. and Pereira, L. M. 1979. *User's Guide to DEC-System 10 PRO-LOG.* Occasional Paper 15, Department of Artificial Intelligence, University of Edinburgh.

Warren, D. H. D., Pereira, L. M. and Pereira, F. 1977. PROLOG—the language and its implementation compared with LISP. *Proceedings, Symposium on AI and Programming Languages,* SIGPLAN Notices, 12:8.

Waterman, D. A. 1968. Machine learning of heuristics. Report No. STAN-CS-68-118, Computer Science Department, Stanford University.

Waterman, D.A. 1986. *A Guide to Expert Systems.* Reading, MA: Addison-Wesley.

Waterman, D. and Hayes-Roth, F. 1978. *Pattern Directed Inference Systems.* New York: Academic Press.

Webber, B. L. and Nilsson, N. J., 1981, *Readings in Artificial Intelligence*, Los Altos, CA: Tioga Press.

Weizenbaum, J. 1976. *Computer Power and Human Reason.* San Francisco: Freeman.

Welham, R. 1976. *Geometry Problem Solving.* Research Report 14, Department of Artificial Intelligence, University of Edinburgh.

Weyrauch, R. W. 1980. Prolegomena to a theory of mechanized formal reasoning. *Artificial Intelligence* 13(1,2):133–170.

Whitehead, A. N. and Russell, B. 1950. *Principia Mathematica*, 2nd ed. London: Cambridge University Press.

Wilensky, R. 1986. *Common LISPCraft.* New York: Norton Press.

Wilks, Y. A. 1972. *Grammar, Meaning and the Machine Analysis of Language.* London: Routledge & Kegan Paul.

Winograd, T. 1972. *Understanding Natural Language.* New York: Academic Press.

Winograd, T. 1973. A procedural model of language understanding. In Schank and Colby (1973).

Winograd, T. 1983. *Language as a Cognitive Process—Vol. 1: Syntax.* Reading, MA: Addison-Wesley.

Winograd, T. and Flores, F. 1986. *Understanding Computers and Cognition.* Norwood, NJ: Ablex.

Winston, P. H. 1975*a*. Learning structural descriptions from examples. In Winston (1975*b*).

Winston, P. H., ed. 1975*b*. *The Psychology of Computer Vision.* New York: McGraw-Hill.

Winston, P. H. 1984. *Artificial Intelligence*, 2nd ed. Reading, MA: Addison-Wesley.

Winston, P. H. 1986. Learning by augmenting rules and accumulating censors. In Michalski et al. (1986).

Winston, P. H. and Horn, B. K. P., 1984, *LISP*, Reading, MA: Addison-Wesley.

Winston, P. H. and Prendergast, K. A., eds. 1984. *The AI Business*. Cambridge, MA: MIT Press.

Wirth, N. 1976. *Algorithms + Data Structures = Programs*. Engelwood Cliffs, NJ: Prentice-Hall.

Woods, W. 1975. What's in a link: Foundations for semantic networks. In Brachman and Levesque (1985).

Wos, L., 1988, *Automated Reasoning, 33 Basic Research Problems*, Englewood Cliffs, N.J.: Prentice-Hall.

Wos, L., Overbeek, R., Lusk, E. and Boyle, J. 1984. *Automated Reasoning: Introduction and Applications*. Engelwood Cliffs, NJ: Prentice-Hall.

Wos, L. and Robinson, G. A., 1968, Paramodulation and set of support, *Proceedings of the IRIA Symposium on Automatic Demonstration, Versailles, France*, New York: Springer-Verlag, pp. 267–310.

Yuasa, T. and Hagiya, M., 1986, *Introduction to Common LISP*, Boston: Academic Press.

Zadeh, L. A. 1983. Commonsense knowledge representation based on fuzzy logic. *Computer* 16:61–65.

AUTHOR INDEX

Winston, P. H. 21, 116, 280, 331, 565, 575
Wirth, N. 75
Woods, W. 335, 338, 347
Wos, L. 23, 74, 409, 428, 430, 434, 440, 441
Wrightson, G. 441

Yeats, W. B. 449

Young, P. 28
Yuasa, T. 280

Zadeh, L. 313, 347
Zytkow, J. M. 569, 576, 586

SUBJECT INDEX

conceptual graphs *(continued)*
    lattice 353
    marker 351
    modal logics 357
    and predicate calculus 357–359
    quantification 357–359
    referent 353
    restriction 354–355, 398, 403, 474, 570
    simplify 354–355
    specialization 354–356
    subtype 353
    supertype 353
    type hierarchy 351, 353
    types 351
    universal type 353
concurrent PROLOG 449, 475, 482–484, 537–545
concurrent PROLOG functions 482–484, 538–545
    commit operator 538
    counter 483–484, 539
    guard clause 483, 543, 545
    otherwise operator 483, 541, 543
    read-only variables 482, 484, 538–539
condition-action pair 131, 140, 141
conditional evaluation 243, 260
confidence measures 163–168, 309–314,
    316–317, 322, 461, 501–508
    Baysian probability 163, 309–311
    Dempster-Schafer theory of evidence 313–314
    fuzzy set theory 313–314
conflict resolution 131, 140–141, 144, 303
    recency 144
    refraction 144
    specificity 144
conjunctive normal form 418–421
consistent 58
constraint propagation 196–197
contrapositive 46
CYC 599–600

data abstraction 244–246
data bases and natural language 381, 401–405
data-driven parsing 113–114
data-driven search 88–90, 140–142, 163
data flow diagrams 403
decision tree 570–571
default values 336, 360–362, 367–371, 392, 471,
    548
delayed evaluation 497–500
demodulation 439–441
demons 336, 362, 447, 546–548
deMorgan's law 45, 462–478
Dempster-Schafer theory of evidence 313–314
DENDRAL 16–17, 90
dendrite 581–582
depth-first search 92–94, 98–101, 121–123,
    207–213, 264–265, 479, 481, 488, 531, 537
discrimination net 578
distributed sensor problem 561
distributive law 45
domain closure 481
domain expert 297–298

EBG. *See* explanation-based learning
EBL. *See* explanation-based learning
efficiency 28, 372
eight puzzle 84–86, 134–135, 157–163, 167–169
embedded languages 279
empty clause. *See* null clause
EMYCIN 295
environments. *See* programming environments
EPAM 577–578
epistemology 3–13, 591–602
equality substitution 439
exclusive or 74
exhaustive search 37, 150, 488, 508
expert systems 16–19, 285–332, 500–508
    architecture 294–295
    confidence measures 163–168, 311–313,
      316–317, 322, 461, 501–508
    domain expert 297–298
    inference engine 294, 301
    knowledge acquisition 298. *See also* learning
    knowledge engineer 16, 297–298
    performance evaluation 324–325
    problem selection 296–297
expert system shell 295, 460–469, 500–508. *See*
    also hybrid environments
explanation-based learning 573–575
exploratory programming 292
expressiveness 28, 317
extensional knowledge 335

facets 546–548
falsifiability of models 580, 600
farmer, wolf, goat, and cabbage problem 213–218,
    257–262
financial advisor 68–73, 110–111, 139, 169
first-order predicate calculus 9, 31–32, 46–73,
    107–111, 199, 203–232, 317, 334, 357–359,
    409, 415–441, 570
    arity 48–50
    atomic sentence 49–51
    conjunction 51
    consistency 58
    constants 47–49, 53–54
    disjunction 51
    domain 48
    equivalence 51
    functions 47–50, 53–54
    implication 51
    improper symbols 47
    inference 32, 38, 58, 62
    interpretation 53–54
    literal 416, 422–423, 438, 475–481
    logically follows 58–60
    model 59
    negation 51
    predicates 47, 50, 53–54
    proof procedure 60
    quantification 50–51, 54–58
    range 48
    satisfiability 58–60
    scope (of quantifiers) 55

tree 81–82
triangle table 551, 557–561, 570
  add list 557–561
  delete list 557–561
  kernel 560
  macro operators 557, 559–561
  preconditions 557–561
truncated chessboard problem 595
truth maintenance systems 315
truth tables 44–45
Turing test 10–12
type checking 451–454, 472, 546
type hierarchies 336, 351, 353, 362, 367–371,
  396–397, 405, 446, 469–474, 520–522,
  526–527, 533, 541–545, 570

uncertainty 163–168, 308–317, 316–317, 322,
  461, 501–508, 597
undecidability 55
unification 62–68, 124–125, 206–208, 211, 215,

273–277, 423, 430–434, 439–440, 451,
  453–458, 476–484, 488
algorithm for 65–66
binding 63
composition of substitutions 63–64
in LISP 273–277
most general unifier (MGU) 64
occurs check 63, 274, 481
in PROLOG 206–208, 211, 215
unit preference strategy 409, 428–429, 476, 480,
  537
unit resolution 429
unsatisfiability 58–60, 418, 426, 476

verbal learning behavior 577
version space search 571–573

weak methods 286–297, 409–441, 577–578, 596

XCON 17, 134, 293, 296–297, 299

ILLUSTRATION AND TEXT CREDITS

Figure 3.22 from *Problem Solving Methods in Artificial Intelligence* by N. Nilsson. Copyright © 1971 by McGraw-Hill. Reprinted by permission.

Figure 5.22 from *Principles of Artificial Intelligence* by N. Nilsson. Copyright © 1980 by Morgan Kaufmann. Reprinted by permission.

Figure 8.3 from *The AI Business* by P. H. Winston and K. Prendergast. Copyright © 1984 by MIT Press. Reprinted by permission.

Figure 8.4 from *Building Expert Systems* by F. Hayes-Roth, D. A. Waterman, and D. Lenat. Copyright © 1983 by Addison-Wesley, Reading, Mass., Fig 1.1 on p. 8. Reprinted by permission.

Figure 9.1 from *Expert Systems: AI in Business* by P. Harmon and D. King. Copyright © 1985 by John Wiley and Sons. Reprinted by permission.

Figures 9.3 and 9.4 from *Word Concepts: A Theory and Simulation of Some Basic Capabilities* by Ross Quillian. Copyright © 1967 by Society of General Systems Research. Reprinted by permission.

Figures 9.6, 9.9, and 9.10 from "Inference and the Computer Understanding of Natural Language" by R. Schank and C. J. Rieger in *Artificial Intelligence*. Copyright © 1974 by Elsevier Science Publishers. Reprinted by permission.

Figure 9.8 from *Computer Models of Thought and Language* by R. Schank and K. Colby. Copyright © 1973 by W. H. Freeman and Co. Reprinted by permission.

Figure 9.24 from "A Framework for Representing Knowledge" by M. Minsky in *Psychology of Computer Vision* by P. Winston. Copyright © 1975 by McGraw-Hill. Reprinted by permission.

Figure 9.25 from *Scripts, Plans, Goals, and Understanding* by R. Schank and R. Abelson. Copyright © 1977 by Lawrence Erlbaum Assoc. Reprinted by permission.

Figure 11.1 from "GPS: A Program that Simulates Human Thought" by A. Newell and H. A. Simon in *Lernende Automaten*. Copyright © 1961 by R. Oldenbourg. Reprinted by permission.

Figure 11.2 from *Computers and Thought,* edited by E. A. Feigenbaum and J. Feldman. Copyright © 1963 by McGraw-Hill. Reprinted by permission.

Part II, p. 27: A Newell and H. A. Simon, ACM Turing Award Lecture, 1976. Copyright © 1976, Association for Computing Machinery, Inc.

Chapter 5, p. 149: Ibid.

Chapter 8, p. 291: Excerpt from *Knowledge Based Systems in Artificial Intelligence* by Randall Davis. Copyright 1982, p. 330. Reprinted with permission from McGraw-Hill Publishing, Inc.

Chapter 16, p. 593: Ibid.

Part VI, p. 591: J. Hopcroft, ACM Turing Award Lecture, 1987. Copyright © 1987, Association for Computing Machinery, Inc.